The Anatomy of Corporate Insolvency Law

The Anatomy of Corporate Insolvency Law

REINHARD BORK
RENATO MANGANO

Great Clarendon Street, Oxford, OX2 6DP,
United Kingdom

Oxford University Press is a department of the University of Oxford.
It furthers the University's objective of excellence in research, scholarship,
and education by publishing worldwide. Oxford is a registered trade mark of
Oxford University Press in the UK and in certain other countries

© The many contributors 2024

The moral rights of the authors have been asserted

All rights reserved. No part of this publication may be reproduced, stored in
a retrieval system, or transmitted, in any form or by any means, without the
prior permission in writing of Oxford University Press, or as expressly permitted
by law, by licence or under terms agreed with the appropriate reprographics
rights organization. Enquiries concerning reproduction outside the scope of the
above should be sent to the Rights Department, Oxford University Press, at the
address above

You must not circulate this work in any other form
and you must impose this same condition on any acquirer

Public sector information reproduced under Open Government Licence v3.0
(http://www.nationalarchives.gov.uk/doc/open-government-licence/open-government-licence.htm)

Published in the United States of America by Oxford University Press
198 Madison Avenue, New York, NY 10016, United States of America

British Library Cataloguing in Publication Data

Data available

Library of Congress Control Number: 2024931026

ISBN 978–0–19–885209–4 (hbk.)
ISBN 978–0–19–885210–0 (pbk.)

DOI: 10.1093/oso/9780198852094.001.0001

Printed and bound by
CPI Group (UK) Ltd, Croydon, CR0 4YY

Links to third party websites are provided by Oxford in good faith and
for information only. Oxford disclaims any responsibility for the materials
contained in any third party website referenced in this work.

Foreword

Modern insolvency law has nothing in common with the grim reality depicted in certain Victorian novels of debtors subjected not to insolvency proceedings but to imprisonment, even for indefinite periods. Since then, however, insolvency law has become a subject of extraordinary relevance and increasing intellectual fascination.

On the one hand, academics, policymakers, lawmakers, judges, and practitioners have reorientated this field of law in order to facilitate the rescue of distressed companies for as long as possible. On the other hand, this evolution has reshaped some of the most traditional categories of our legal culture. For example, this new deal has introduced into the toolbox of insolvency practitioners a great number of devices that combine the flexibility of contractual workouts with the capability of insolvency proceedings to bind even the most recalcitrant of creditors—as a result, in some cases, the traditional distinction between 'contract' and 'proceedings' has blurred. The same tendency in favour of rescue has persuaded some lawmakers to enable distressed companies to depart from the traditional criteria according to which the debtor's assets must be distributed— traditionally, these criteria were considered as non-negotiable—and even to waive a milestone of every company law according to which a company's shareholders are the company's residual claimants. A further consequence of this new approach is that, in the case of group insolvencies, there has been a tendency to mitigate the traditional single-entity approach according to which there ought to be one set of insolvency proceedings for each distressed company.

This book focuses on corporate insolvency law and aims to explain what corporate insolvency law is and how it works. In order to achieve this aim, corporate insolvency law will be dissected into its main parts and analysed in the light of a comparative and functional approach. This choice of method implies that the following chapters will not be devoted to any specific jurisdiction but will concentrate on problems, in order to ascertain how the same problems may lead to different solutions in different jurisdictions; to what extent two solutions that appear dissimilar really diverge and, vice-versa, to what extent two solutions that appear similar really converge; and, last but not least, which of the solutions adopted in a specific jurisdiction deserve to be exported to another jurisdiction and under what conditions this legal transplant is possible.

The book consists of eleven chapters that cover not only the most relevant topics of corporate insolvency law but also the points where corporate insolvency law intersects with labour law and taxation law. The chapters were written by a team of specialists from three continents and, more specifically, from China, Germany, Italy, Spain, the United Kingdom, and the United States. In alphabetical order, these contributors are: Reinhard

Bork, Laura Carballo Piñeiro, Edward J. Janger, Günter Kahlert, Shuguang Li, Renato Mangano, Jennifer Payne, and Johannes Richter.

We are very grateful for the cooperation of all the distinguished authors who have shared the aim of this project and contributed their valuable expertise to this volume. We also owe a debt of gratitude to Neville Greenup for his effective assistance in the production of this book. We will also be happy to receive from readers observations and questions of any sort regarding its content.

Reinhard Bork
Renato Mangano
Hamburg/Palermo
September 2023

Contents

Table of Cases	xi
Table of Legislation	xxi
List of Abbreviations	xxxiii
List of Contributors	xxxv

1. What Is Insolvency Law? — 1
Renato Mangano

I.	Introduction	1
II.	The Rationale behind IL: A Lack of Cooperation between Competing Claimants	3
III.	The First Task of IL: Either Coercing or Making It Easier for Claimants to Cooperate—The Distinction between Liquidation and Rescue	7
IV.	Liquidation: Concept, Taxonomies, and Devices	14
V.	Rescue: Concept and Taxonomies	15
VI.	Rescue: Devices	19
VII.	The Second Task of IL: Distributing the Debtor's Resources	23
VIII.	Distributing within Reorganization: The US Approach	26
IX.	Distributing within Reorganization: The EU Approach and Its Transposition into German Law	28

2. Distress, Insolvency, and the Likelihood of Insolvency — 32
Shuguang Li

I.	Introduction and Basics	32
II.	Choice of Ways for Debtors to Get Over Distress	34
III.	Conditions for a Distressed Debtor to Enter Insolvency Procedures	35

3. Debt Restructuring Outside Formal Insolvency Proceedings — 52
Jennifer Payne

I.	Introduction	52
II.	Contractual Workouts	54
III.	Restructuring Plans	57
IV.	A Restructuring Moratorium	77
V.	Rescue Finance	83
VI.	Conclusion	86

4. Formal Insolvency Proceedings — 87
Johannes Richter

I.	Introduction and Overview	87
II.	Initiation and Opening of Insolvency Proceedings	89
III.	Consequences of the Commencement	96
IV.	Role and Obligations of the Insolvency Administrator	101
V.	Claims and Involvement of the Creditors	106
VI.	Pending Contracts	114
VII.	Swelling and Liquidation of the Assets	119

viii CONTENTS

VIII. Final Steps of the Liquidation Proceedings	126
IX. Restructuring as an Alternative to Liquidation	128

5. Security Rights and Creditors' Priority and Ranking: Realizable Priority in Rescue — 131

Edward J. Janger

I. Introduction	131
II. Security and Priority Inside and Outside of Bankruptcy	132
III. Security Rights	135
IV. Distinguishing Asset-Based (*in Rem*) and Firm-Based (*in Personam*) Claims of Priority: The Scope of Security	140
V. Asset-Based Claims and Value-Based Claims in Rescue	147
VI. Realizable Priority in Rescue: Asset Value and Firm Value	154
VII. Conclusion	156

6. Transactions Avoidance Rules — 158

Reinhard Bork

I. Introduction	158
II. Basics	159
III. Underlying Principles	161
IV. Effectiveness	162
V. General Prerequisites	163
VI. Avoidance Grounds	169
VII. Legal Consequences	182
VIII. Cross-Border Avoidance	186

7. Directors' Duties in the Vicinity of Insolvency, Disqualification, Piercing the Veil — 189

Renato Mangano

I. The Limits of Limited Liability	189
II. Directors' Liability in the Vicinity of Insolvency	191
III. Directors' Disqualification	208
IV. Piercing the Corporate Veil	213

8. Corporate Groups in Rescue — 220

Edward J. Janger

I. Introduction	220
II. Group Structures	222
III. Corporate Groups in the Vicinity of Insolvency: Fiduciary Duty, Avoidance, and the Liquidation Baseline	223
IV. Administering a Group Case in Liquidation and Rescue	230
V. Allocating Group Value in Rescue	236
VI. Cross-Border Issues: Administering a Global Restructuring	244
VII. Conclusion	247

9. Cross-Border Insolvency Law — 248

Reinhard Bork

I. Introduction	248
II. Details	261

CONTENTS ix

10. **Aspects of Tax Law** 283
Günter Kahlert
  I. Introduction 283
  II. Basic Principles 285
  III. Resolving the Tension in the Relationship between the State and Creditors 287
  IV. Resolving the Tension in the Relationship between the State and the Debtor 296

11. **Aspects of Labour Law** 302
Laura Carballo Piñeiro
  I. Introduction 302
  II. Employment Contracts and Employers' Insolvency 304
  III. Worker Entitlements and Priority of Payment 310
  IV. Worker Entitlements and Guarantee Schemes 315
  V. Comparative Law Approaches to Worker Entitlements Protection 318
  VI. Worker Entitlements and Directors' Liability 322

Bibliography 325
Index 333

Table of Cases

UNITED KINGDOM

Adams v National Bank of Greece [1961] AC 255 .... 9.65
Alderson v Temple (1768) (1746–79) 1 Black W 660, 96 ER 384 .... 6.21
Anglo American Insurance Company Ltd, Re [2001] 1 BCLC 755 .... 3.31
Angove's Pty Ltd v Bailey [2016] UKSC 47 .... 6.03
Arena Corporation Ltd, Re [2003] EWHC 3032 (Ch) 9.03
ARM Asset Backed Securities SA (No. 2), Re [2014] EWHC 1097 (Ch) 9.20
Ayerst v C and K (Construction) Ltd [1976] AC 167 .... 4.28
Blackspur Group plc, Secretary of State for Trade and Industry v Davies, Re [1998]
    1 BCLC 676 .... 7.48
Bluecrest Mercantile BV; FMS Wertmanagement AOR v Vietnam Shipbuilding
    Industry Group [2013] EWHC 1146
(Comm) 3.58
British and Commonwealth Holdings plc (No. 3), Re [1992] 1 WLR 672 .... 3.26
British Aviation Insurance Company Ltd, Re [2005] EWHC 1621 (Ch) 3.33
BTI 2014 LLC v Sequana SA and ors [2019] EWCA Civ 112 .... 6.49, 6.57, 8.14, 8.20
BTI 2014 LLC v Sequana SA and ors [2022] UKSC 25 .... 6.49, 6.57, 7.08
BTR plc, Re [2000] 1 BCLC 740 .... 3.30
Burnden Holdings (UK) Ltd v Fielding [2019] EWHC 1566 (Ch) 6.57
Cambridge Gas Transportation Corporation v Official Committee of Unsecured
    Creditors of Navigator Holdings plc [2006] UKPC 26 .... 9.63, 9.70
ColourOz Investment 2, Re LLC [2020] EWHC 1864 (Ch) 9.64
Cooper, Leite v Amicorp [2020] EWHC 3560 (Ch), (2021), 18 ICR, 137 .... 9.60
Court of Appeal decisions UT/2016/0185, UT/2016/0186 (13 June 2017) 10.09
Crumpler and anor (liquidators of Peak Hotels and Resorts Ltd) v Candey Ltd [2019]
    EWCA Civ 345 .... 6.56
Daisytek–ISA Ltd, Re [2003] BCC 562 .... 9.20
DAP Holding NV, Re [2005] EWHC 2092 (Ch) 9.64
Darty Holdings SAS (as successor to Kesa International Ltd) v Carton–Kelly as Liquidator
    of CGL Realisations Ltd (in
liquidation) [2021] EWHC 1018 (Ch) 6.34
Debtor, Re a [1967] 1 All ER 668 .... 2.15
Deep Ocean 1 UK Ltd, Re The [2021] EWHC 138 (Ch) 3.51
Deposit Guarantee Fund for Individuals, The (as liquidator of National Credit
    Bank PJSC) v Bank Frick and Company AG [2022] EWHC 2221 (Ch) 6.49
Domco SICA Ltd and ors v SBL Carston Ltd and ors [2021] EWHC 3209 (Ch) 6.49
Doyle v Saville [2002] BPIR 947 .... 6.23
Drax Holdings Ltd, Re [2003] EWHC 2743 (Ch) 9.64
DTEK Energy BV and DTEK Finance plc, Re [2021] EWHC 1456 (Ch) 9.64
ED and F Man Holdings Ltd, Re The [2022] EWHC 687 (Ch) 3.24
Express Electrical Contractors Ltd v Beavis [2016] EWCA Civ 765 .... 6.34
Fen v Cosco Shipping (Qidong) Offshore Ltd [2021] CSOH 94 and 95 .... 9.65
Fowlds (a Bankrupt), Bucknall and anor v Wilson, Re [2021] EWHC 2149 (Ch) 6.61
Galbraith v Grimshaw [1910] AC 508 .... 9.53
Gategroup Guarantee Limited, Re [2021] EWHC 304 (Ch) 3.19
Gibbs v La Societe Industrielle et Commercial des Metaux [1890] 25 QBD 399 (CA) 9.65

xii TABLE OF CASES

Global Maritime Investments Cyprus Limited v O.W. Supply and Trading A/S
(under konkurs) [2015] EWHC 2690 (Comm) 9.03
Good Box Company Labs Ltd, Re The [2023] EWHC 274 (Ch) 3.22
Hawk Insurance Company Ltd, Re [2001] EWCA Civ 241 .... 3.33
Haya Holdco 2 plc, Re [2022] EWHC 1079 (Ch) and [2022] EWHC 2732 (Ch) 9.64
HIH Casualty and General Insurance Ltd, Re [2008] UKHL 21 .... 9.08
Hinton (as Trustee in Bankruptcy of John Wotherspoon) v Gillian Wotherspoon [2022]
EWHC 2083 (Ch) 6.49
Holroyd v Marshall [1862] 10 HL Cas. 191 .... 5.41
Houst Limited, Re [2022] EWHC 1941 (Ch) 3.17
Integral Petroleum SA v Petrogat FZE and ors [2023] EWHC 44 (Comm) 6.59
Jagde v Singh Wasu, a Bankrupt, Darren Edwards (TiB of Jagdev Singh Wasu) v Aurora
Leasing Limited and Howard
de Walden Estates Limited, Re [2021] EWHC 96 (Ch) 6.20
Johnson v Unisys Ltd [2001] IRLR 279 .... 11.41
Joint Administrators of Heritable Bank plc v The Winding–Up Board of Landsbanki
Islands hf [2013] UKSC 13 .... 9.65
Ledingham–Smith, Re [1993] BCLC 635 .... 6.34
Lehman Brothers International (Europe) Ltd, Re EWHC 1980 (Ch) 3.40
Lehman Brothers International (Europe) Ltd (in administration), Re The [2022]
EWHC 687 (Ch) 3.24
Leite v Amicorp [2020] EWHC 3560 (Ch) 9.60
Lewis of Leicester Ltd, Re [1995] BCC 514 .... 6.34
Liquidator of West Mercia Safetywear v Dodd (1988) 4 BCC 30 .... 7.08, 7.17
London and Paris Banking Corporation, Re (1874) LR 19 Eq 444 .... 2.15
London Oil and Gas Ltd, Re [2022] EWHC 1672 (Ch) 6.01
MAB Leasing Ltd, Re [2021] EWHC 152 (Ch) and [2021] EWHC 379 (Ch) 3.19, 9.64
Maxwell Communications Corporation plc (No. 2), Re [1994] 1 All ER 737 .... 3.70
McKellar v Griffin and anor [2014] EWHC 2644 (Ch) 9.18
Melars Group Ltd, Re [2022] EWCA Civ 1419 .... 9.36
National Bank of Greece and Athens SA v Metliss [1958] AC 509 (HL) 9.65
New Cap Reinsurance Corporation v Grant [2011] EWCA Civ 971 .... 9.62
Nordic Aviation Capital Designated Activity Company, Re [2020] IEHC 445 .... 3.19
Northsea Base Investment Ltd, Re [2015] EWHC 121 (Ch) 9.18
OJSC Ank Yugraneft, Re [2008] EWHC 2614 (Ch) 9.64
OJSC International Bank of Azerbaijan, Re [2018] EWHC 59 (Ch) 9.65
Oriental Bank Corporation, Re (1886) 32 Ch D 366 .... 4.83
P Macfadyen and Company Ex p Vizianagaram Company Ltd, Re [1908] 1 KB 675 .... 9.69
Paramount Airways Ltd [1993] Ch 223 (CA) 9.53
Powertrain Ltd, Re [2015] EWHC B26 (Ch) 4.47
Rodenstock GmbH, Re [2011] EWHC 1104 (Ch) 9.64
Rubin v Eurofinance SA [2012] UKSC 46 .... 6.23, 6.74, 9.62, 9.70
Safari Holding Verwaltungs GmbH, Re [2022] EWHC 781 (Ch) and [2022]
EWHC 1156 (Ch) 9.64
Savoy Hotel Ltd, Re [1981] Ch 351 .... 3.22
Scottish Lion Insurance Company Ltd v Goodrich Corporation [2010] CSOIH 6 .... 3.18
Sea Assets Ltd v PT Garuda Indonesia [2001] EWCA Civ 1696 .... 3.26
Singularis Holdings Ltd v PricewaterhouseCoopers (Bermuda) [2014] UKPC 36 .... 9.70
Skandinaviska Enskilda Banken AB (Publ) v Conway [2019] UKPC 6.61, 6.63
Smile Telecoms Holdings Ltd, Re [2022] EWHC 387 (Ch) 3.41
Solomons v Ross [1764] 1 H Bl 131n and 126 ER 79 .... 9.70
Sovereign Life Assurance Company v Dodd [1892] 2 QB 573 .... 3.29
Sovereign Marine and General Insurance Company Ltd, Re [2006] EWHC 1335 (Ch) 9.64
Spectrum Plus, Re [2005] UKHL 41, [2005] 2 AC 680 .... 5.41–5.42

TABLE OF CASES xiii

Stein v Blake [1996] AC 243 (HL) 4.70, 9.47
Steinhoff International Holdings NV, Re [2021] EWHC 184 (Ch) 9.64
Sturgeon Central Asia Balanced Fund Ltd (in liquidation) [2019] EWHC 1215 (Ch) 9.33
SwissMarine Corporation Limited v O W Supply and Trading A/S (in bankruptcy)
    [2015] EWHC 1571 (Comm) 9.03
TDG plc, Re [2009] 1 BCLC 445 .... 3.40
Telewest Communications plc, Re [2004] EWCA Civ 728 .... 3.33
Trustees of the Olympic Airlines SA Pension and Life Assurance Scheme v Olympic
    Airlines SA, The [2015] UKSC 27 .... 9.38
Tweeds Garages, Re [1962] Ch 406 .... 2.15
UBS AG New York and ors v Fairfield Sentry Ltd (in liquidation) [2019] UKPC 20 .... 9.53
UDL Holdings Ltd, Re [2002] 1 HKC 172 .... 3.33
Virgin Atlantic Airways Ltd, Re The [2020] EWHC 2376 (Ch) 3.23, 3.51
Wight v Eckardt Marine GmbH [2003] UKPC 37 .... 9.65
Winkworth v Edward Baron Development Company Ltd [1986] 1 WLR 1512 .... 7.06

AUSTRALIA

King v Linkage Access Ltd [2018] FCA 1979 .... 9.53
Kinsela v Russell Kinsela Pty Ltd (1986) 4 ACLC 215 .... 7.08
Nicholson v Permakraft (NZ) Ltd (1985) 3 ACLC 453 .... 7.08, 7.17
Walker v Wimborne (1976) 137 CLR 1 .... 7.08
Wild v Coin Company International plc [2015] FCA 354 .... 9.53

AUSTRIA

VwGH (Supreme Administrative Court), 12 July 1990, 89/16/0054 .... 10.10
OGH (Supreme Court of Justice), August 2011, 3 Ob 103/11 .... 10.17
VwGH (Supreme Administrative Court), 19 February1985, 84/14/0126 .... 10.10
VwGH (Supreme Administrative Court), 24 May 1993, 92/15/0041 .... 10.33
VwGH (Supreme Administrative Court), 4 September 2019, Ro 2017/130009 .... 10.36

BELGIUM

Tribunal de Commerce de Bruxelles, 20 June 1975 = KTS 1978, 247 (German)
    = JCB 1976–IV–629 (French) 9.59

CANADA

Antwerp Bulkcarriers NV v Holt Cargo Systems, Inc [2001] 3 SCR 951 .... 9.71
Essor Steel Algoma Inc, Re, (November 2015) (Ont SCJ) 3.72
Great Basin Gold Ltd, Re, 2012 BCSC 1459 (BC SC) 3.72
Holt Cargo Systems Inc. v ABC Containerline NV (Trustee of) [2001] 3 SCR 907 .... 9.71
Nortel Networks Corporation, Re [2015] ONSC 2987 (Can. Ont. Sup. Ct) 8.34–8.36, 8.41,
                                                                8.54–8.55, 8.58, 8.77, 9.68
Nortel Networks Corporation, Re [2015] ONSC 4170 .... 9.68
Nortel Networks Corporation, Re [2016] ONCA 332 .... 9.68
Nortel Networks Corporation, Re [2016] ONCA 681 .... 9.68
Performance Sports Group Ltd, Re, 2016 ONSC 6800, 2016 CarswellOnt 17492
    (Ont SCJ, Commercial List) 3.71

CZECH REPUBLIC

Vaclav Fischer v D.l. sro, Usneseni Nejvyššiho soudu České republiky sp.zn.
    31 January 2008–R 87/2008, [2008] EIRCR(A) 73 ....9.20

xiv TABLE OF CASES

EUROPEAN FREE TRADE ASSOCIATION (EFTA)

Case E–28/13 LBI hf v Merrill Lynch International Ltd 9.25

EUROPEAN UNION

C–135/83 HBM Abels v The Administrative Board of the Bedrijfsvereniging voor de
Metaalindustrie en de
Electrotechnische Industrie [1985] ECLI:EU:C:1985:55 .... 11.12
C–362/89 D'Urso and Others v Ercole Marelli Eletromeccanica Generale
SpA and Others [1991] ECLI:EU:C:1991:326 .... 11.12
C–10/92 Maurizio Balocchi v Ministero delle Finanze dello Stato [1993]
ECLI:EU:C:1993:846, EuGHE 1993, I–5105 .... 10.21
C–472/93 Spano and Others v Fiat Geotech and Fiat Hitachi [1995] ECLI:EU:C:1995:421 .... 11.12
C–319/94 Jules Dethier Equipement SA v Jules Dassy [1998] ECLI:EU:C:1998:99 .... 11.12
C–399/96 Eurpieces SA (in liquidation) v Wilfried Sanders and Automotive Industries
Holding Company SA [1998] ECLI:EU:C:1998:532 .... 11.12
C–1/04 Susanne Staubitz–Schreiber [2006] ECLI:EU:C:2006:39 .... 9.18, 9.36–9.37
C–341/04 Eurofood IFSC Ltd [2006] ECLI:EU:C:2006:281 .... 9.11, 9.18–9.20, 9.36–9.37, 9.64
C–271/06 Netto Supermarkt GmbH & Co. OHG v Finanzamt Malchin [2008]
ECLI:EU:C:2008:105 / DStR 2008 .... 10.21
C–339/07 Seagon v Deko Martium Belgium NV [2009] ECLI:EU:C:2009:83 .... 9.39
C–444/07 MG Probud Gdynia sp. z o.o. [2010] ECLI:EU:C:2010:24 .... 9.11, 9.20, 9.33
C–396/09 Interedil Srl, in liquidazione contro Fallimento Interedil Srl e Intesa
Gestione Crediti SpA [2011] ECLI:EU:C:2011:67 .... 9.13, 9.36, 9.38
C–477/09 Charles Defossez v Christian Wiart and Others [2011] ECLI:EU:C:2011:134 .... 11.33
C–112/10 Procureur-generaal bij het hof van beroep te Antwerpen v Zaza Retail
BV [2011] ECLI:EU:C:2011:743 .... 9.13, 9.38
C–527/10 ERSTE Bank Hungary Nyrt v Magyar Allam and Others [2012]
ECLI:EU:C:2012:417 .... 9.44–9.45
T–287/11 Heitkamp BauHolding GmbH v European Commission [2016]
ECLI:EU:T:2016:60 .... 10.32
C–328/12 Ralph Schmid v Lilly Hertel [2014] ECLI:EU:C:2014:6 .... 6.70, 9.18, 9.64
C–295/13 H. v H.K. [2014] ECLI:EU:C:2014:2410 .... 9.39
C–327/13 Burgo Group SpA v Illochroma SA and Jérôme Theetten [2014]
ECLI:EU:C:2014:2158 .... 9.13, 9.38
C–557/13 Hermann Lutz v Elke Bäuerle [2015] ECLI:EU:C:2015:227 .... 9.25, 9.44, 9.54
C–649/13 Comité d'entreprise de Nortel Networks SA and Others v Cosme Rogeau
liquidator of Nortel Networks SA and Cosme Rogeau liquidator of Nortel
Networks SA v Alan Robert Bloom and Others [2015] ECLI:EU:C:2015:384 .... 9.14, 9.39
C–292/14 Elliniko Dimosio v Stefanos Stroumpoulis and Others [2016]
ECLI:EU:C:2016:116 .... 11.30
C–310/14 Nike European Operations Netherlands BV v Sportland Oy [2015]
ECLI:EU:C:2015:690 .... 9.16, 9.25, 9.54
C–546/14 Degano Trasporti S.a.s. di Ferrucio Degano & C., in liquidation [2016]
ECLI:EU:C:2016:13, Opinion of Advocate General Sharpston 10.03
C–54/16 Vinyls Italia SpA (in liquidation) v Mediterranea di Navigazione SpA [2017]
ECLI:EU:C:2017:433 .... 9.54
C–126/16 First Steps Federatie Nederlandse Vakvereniging and Others v Smallsteps
BV [2017] ECLI:EU:C:2017:489 .... 11.12–11.13
C–203/16 Dirk Andres v European Commission [2018] ECLI:EU:C:2018:505 ..... 10.03, 10.31–10.32
C–664/16 Lucreţiu Hadrian Vădan contro Agenţia Naţională de Administrare
Fiscală – Direcţia Generală de Soluţionare a Contestaţiilor e Direcţia Generală Regională
a Finanţelor Publice Braşov - Administraţia Judeţeană a Finanţelor Publice Alba [2018]
ECLI:EU:C:2018:933 .... 10.21

TABLE OF CASES   XV

C–509/17 Christa Plessers v PREFACO NV and the Belgian State [2019]
ECLI:EU:C:2019:424 . . . . 11.13
C–47/18 Skarb Panstwa Rzeczpospolitej Polskiej— Generalny Dyrektor Drog
Krajowych i Autostrad v Stephan Riel [2019] ECLI:EU:C:2019:754 . . . . 9.39
C–198/18 CeDe Group AB v KAN sp. z.o.o. (in liquidation), ECLI:EU:C:2019:1001 . . . . 9.39, 9.41
C–394/18 I.G.I. Srl v Maria Grazia Cicenia, Mario Di Pierro, Salvatore de Vito, Antonio
Raffaele [2019] ECLI:EU:C:2020:56 . . . . 6.03
C–493/18 UB v VA, Tiger SCI, WZ and Banque patrimoine et immobilier SA [2019]
ECLI:EU:C:2019:1046 . . . . 9.35, 9.39
C–253/19 MH and NI v OJ and Novo Banco SA [2020] ECLI:EU:C:2020:585 . . . . 9.36
C–73/20 ZM in his capacity as liquidator in the insolvency of Oeltrans
Befrachtungsgesellschaft mbH v E.A. Frerichs [2021] ECLI:EU:C:2021:315 . . . . 9.54
C–182/20 Administraţia Judeţeană a Finanţelor Publice Suceava [2021]
ECLI:EU:C:2021:442 . . . . 10.16
C–237/20 Federatie Nederlandse Vakbeweging v Heiploeg Seafood International BV,
Heitrans International B [2022] ECLI:EU:C:2022:321 . . . . 11.13
C–723/20 Galapagos BidCo. S.a.r.l. v DE and Others [2022] ECLI:EU:C:2022:209 . . . . 9.11, 9.20,
9.36–9.37

FRANCE

Cour de Cassation (chambre commerciale)–3 February 1998–95–20389 = Bull. Civ
1998 IV No. 53 . . . . 6.62
Cour de Cassation (chambre commerciale)–12 October 1999–96–13133 = Bull. Civ
1999 IV No. 166 . . . . 6.17
Cour de Cassation (chambre commerciale)–6 June 2001–98–4355 . . . . 6.21
Cour de Cassation (chambre commerciale)–21 March 2006–04–17869 = Bull. Civ
2006 IV No. 74 . . . . 9.33
Cour de Cassation (chambre commerciale)–11 October 2011–10–11938 = Bull. Civ
2011 IV No. 155 . . . . 6.67
Cour de Cassation (chambre civile 3e)–12 October 2017–21567/2017 . . . . 7.14
Cour d'Appel (Versailles) Klempka v ISA Daisytek SA [2003] BCC 984 . . . . 9.20

GERMANY

BVerfG (Federal Constitutional Court), 27 December 1991–2 BvR 72/90 = BStBl. II
1992, 212 . . . . 10.05
BGH (Federal Court of Justice), 4 February 1960–VII ZR 161/57 = NJW 1960, 774 . . . . 9.59
BGH (Federal Court of Justice), 11 July 1985–IX ZR 178/84 = BGHZ 95, 256 . . . . 9.59
BGH (Federal Court of Justice), 16 September 1985 BGHZ 95, 330 . . . . 7.73
BGH (Federal Court of Justice), 21 March 1988 BGHZ 104, 44 . . . . 7.14
BGH (Federal Court of Justice), 17 September 2001 BGHZ, 149, 10 (Bremer Vulkan) 7.73
BGH (Federal Court of Justice), 18 September 2001–IX ZB 51/00 = NJW 2002, 960 . . . . 9.65
BGH (Federal Court of Justice), 22 January 2004–IX ZR 39/03 = BGHZ 157, 350 . . . . 10.01, 10.21
BGH (Federal Court of Justice), 6 May 2004–IX ZR 47/03 = BGHZ 159, 104 . . . . 4.49
BGH (Federal Court of Justice), 16 July 2007 BGHZ 173, 246 (Trihotel) 7.73, 7.77
BGH (Federal Court of Justice), 28 April 2008 BGHZ 176, 204 (Gamma) 7.80
BGH (Federal Court of Justice), 8 May 2008–IX ZR 229/06 = ZIP 2008, 1127 . . . . 10.21
BGH (Federal Court of Justice), 29 May 2008–IX ZB 102/07 = NZI 2008, 572 . . . . 9.20
BGH (Federal Court of Justice), 9 July 2009–IX ZR 86/08 = ZIP 2009, 1674 . . . . 10.18, 10.21
BGH (Federal Court of Justice), 9 July 2009–IX ZR 86/08 = NZI 2009, 644 . . . . 6.14
BGH (Federal Court of Justice), 14 October 2010–IX ZR 16/10 = NZI 2011, 189 . . . . 6.01
BGH (Federal Court of Justice), 10 February 2011–IX ZR 49/19 = BGHZ 188, 317 . . . . 10.21
BGH (Federal Court of Justice), 22 September 2011–IX ZB 121/11 = NZI 2011, 408 . . . . 10.17

xvi   TABLE OF CASES

BGH (Federal Court of Justice), 26 April 2012–IX ZR 146/11 = NZI 2012, 562 (*Karstadt*) 6.27
BGH (Federal Court of Justice), 14 January 2014–II ZR 192/13 = NZI 2014, 238 .... 9.65
BGH (Federal Court of Justice), 24 June 2014–VI ZR 315/13 = ZIP 2014, 1997 .... 9.60, 9.63
BGH (Federal Court of Justice), 4 February 2016–IX ZR 77/15 = NJW 2016, 2412 .... 6.44
BGH (Federal Court of Justice), 25 February 2016–IX ZB 74/15 = NZI 2016, 365 .... 9.58
BGH (Federal Court of Justice), 18 July 2018–IX ZR 307/16 = NZI 2018, 80 .... 6.40
BGH (Federal Court of Justice), 27 June 2019–IX ZR 167/18 = BGHZ 222,
    283 = NJW 2019, 2923 .... 6.40
BGH (Federal Court of Justice), 12 September 2019–IX ZR 16/18 = NZI 2019, 893 .... 4.52
BGH (Federal Court of Justice), 17 December 2020–IX ZB 72/19 = NZI 2021, 187 .... 9.37
BGH (Federal Court of Justice), 28 January 2021–IX ZR 64/20 = ZRI 2021, 282 .... 6.21
BGH (Federal Court of Justice), 20 April 2021–II ZR 387/18 = NZI 2021, 637 .... 4.45
BGH (Federal Court of Justice), Urt. v 6 May 2021–IX ZR 72/20 = BGHZ 230, 28 .... 6.51
BGH (Federal Court of Justice), 27 October 2022–IX ZR 213/21 = NJW 2023, 603 .... 4.86
BGH (Federal Court of Justice), 8 December 2022–IX ZB 72/19 = NZI 2023, 183 .... 9.37
RFH (Reich Fiscal Court), 22 June 1938– VI 687/37 = RFHE 44, 162 .... 10.07
BFH (Federal Fiscal Court), 10 July 2019–X R 31/16 = BFHE 265, 300 .... 10.17
BFH (Federal Fiscal Court), 18 December 2002–I R 33/01 = BStBl. II 2003, 630 .... 10.10
BFH (Federal Fiscal Court), 16 November 2004–VII R 75/03 = BStBl. II 2006, 193 .... 10.18
BFH (Federal Fiscal Court), 6 March 2008–VI R 6/05 = BStBl. II 2008, 530 .... 10.05
BFH (Federal Fiscal Court), 2 November 2010–VII R 6/10 = BStBl. II 2011, 374 .... 10.18
BFH (Federal Fiscal Court), 2 November 2010–VII R 62/10 = BStBl. II 2011, 439 .... 10.18
BFH (Federal Fiscal Court), 9 December 2010–V R 22/10 = BStBl. II 2011, 996 .... 10.17
BFH (Federal Fiscal Court), 9 February 2011–XI R 35/09 = BStBl. II 2011, 1000 .... 10.17
BFH (Federal Fiscal Court), 24 November 2011–V R 13/11 = BStBl. II 2012, 298 .... 10.18
BFH (Federal Fiscal Court), 23 January 2013–I R 35/12 = BStBl. II 2013, 508 .... 10.35
BFH (Federal Fiscal Court), 16 May 2013–IV R 23/11 = BStBl. II 2013, 759 .... 10.17
BFH (Federal Fiscal Court), 8 August 2013–V R 18/13 = BStBl. II 2017, 543 .... 10.09
BFH (Federal Fiscal Court), 27 February 2014–V R 21/11 = BStBl. II 2014, 501 .... 10.11
BFH (Federal Fiscal Court), 9 December 2014–X R 12/12, BStBl. II 2016, 852 .... 10.17
BFH (Federal Fiscal Court), 29 January 2015–V R 5/14 = BStBl. II 2015, 567 .... 10.05
BFH (Federal Fiscal Court), 1 October 2015–X B 71/15 = BFH/NV 2016 .... 10.07
BFH (Federal Fiscal Court), 21 October 2015–XI R 28/14 = BFH/NV 2016, 873 .... 10.07
BFH (Federal Fiscal Court), 3 August 2016–X R 25/14 = BFH/NV 2017, 317 .... 10.17
BFH (Federal Fiscal Court), 5 April 2017–II R 30/15 = BStBl. II 2017, 971 .... 10.17
BFH (Federal Fiscal Court), 11 April 2018–X R 39/16 = BFH/NV 2018, 1075 .... 10.10
BFH (Federal Fiscal Court), 27 September 2018–V R 45/16 = BFHE 262, 214 .... 10.15
BFH (Federal Fiscal Court), 15 November 2018–XI B 49/18 = BFH/NV 2019, 208 .... 10.28
BFH (Federal Fiscal Court), 15 October 2019–VII R 31/17 = BStBl. II 2023, 262 .... 10.19
BFH (Federal Fiscal Court), 7 July 2020–X R 13/19 = BStBl. II 2021, 174 .... 10.17
BFH (Federal Fiscal Court), 19 August 2020–XI R 32/18 = BFHE 270, 344 .... 10.35
BFH (Federal Fiscal Court), 27 October 2020–VIII R 19/18 = BFHE 271, 15 .... 10.17
BFH (Federal Fiscal Court), 8 March 2022–VI R 33/19 = BStBl. II 2023, 98 .... 10.10
BFH (Federal Fiscal Court), 2 November 2022–I R 29/19 = DStR 2023, 264 .... 10.09

HONG KONG

Industrial Equity (Pacific) Ltd, Re (1991) 2 HKLR 614 .... 3.30

ITALY

Cass., Sez. Un., 9100/2015 .... 7.24
Cass. 24431/2019 .... 7.24
Volare SpA v WLFC, Tribunale di Busto Arsizio–10 July 2012–[2012] EICR(A) 350 .... 9.54

TABLE OF CASES   xvii

SINGAPORE

Pathfinder Strategic Credit LP v Empire Capital Resources Pte Ltd [2019] SGCA 29 . . . . 3.24
Royal Bank of Scotland NV, The v TT International (2012) SGCA 9 . . . . 3.40
Wah Yuen Engineering Pte Ltd v Singapore Cables Manufacturers Pte Ltd [2003] 3 SLR 629 . . . . 3.29

UNITED STATES

Abramson v St Regis Paper Co., 715 F.2d 934 (5th Cir. 1983) 6.23
Alfar Dairy, In re, 458 F.2d 1258 (5th Cir. 1972) 4.71
Awal Bank, In re, 455 BR 73 (Bankr. SDNY 2011). 9.33
Bank of America Strategic Solutions, Inc. v Cooker Rest. Corp., No. 05AP–1126, 2006 WL
    2535734, (Ohio Ct. App. 5 September 2006). 5.35
Bank of America Nat. Trust and Sav Assn v 203 North LaSalle Street Partnership,
    526 US 434 (1999) 5.07
Barclay v Swiss Fin. Corporation Ltd (In re Midland Euro Exch. Inc.), 347 BR 708
    (Bankr. CD Cal. 2006) 6.73
Barclays Bank plc v Kemsley, 992 NYS 2d 602 (NY Sup. Ct. 2014) 9.65
Basis Yield Alpha Fund (Master), In re, 381 BR 37 (Bankr. SDNY 2008) 9.38, 9.60
Bear Stearns High–Grade Structured Credit, In re, 389 BR 325 (SDNY 2008) 9.18, 9.38
Bear Stearns High–Grade Structured Credit Strategies Master Fund, Ltd (Bankr. SDNY
    2007) 122 . . . . 9.60
Berisford, Inc. v Stroock and Stroock and Lavan (In re 1634 Assocs), 157 BR 231
    (Bankr. SDNY 1993) 6.57
Bernard L. Madoff Inv. Sec. LLC, Matter of, 548 BR 13 (Bankr. SDNY 2016) 6.66
Bestwall, In re, (23 January 2022) 8.28
BFP v Resolution Trust Corp., 511 US 531, 114 S. Ct. 1757, 128 L. Ed. 2d 556 (1994) 6.17
Bluxome St Assocs v Fireman's Fund Ins. Co., 254 Cal. Rptr. 198 (Cal. Ct. App. 1988) 5.37
Boberschmidt v Society Nat'l Bank (In re Jones), 226 F.3d 917 (7th Cir. 2000) 6.17
Bovay v HM Byllesby and Co., 38 A.2d 808 (Del. 1944) 7.13
Burtch v Opus LLC (In re Opus East LLC), 698 Fed. Appx. 711 (3d Cir. 2017) 6.45
Cafeteria Operators, LP, In re, 299 BR 400 (Bankr. ND Tex. 2003). 5.40
Canada Southern R. Co. v Gebhard, 109 US 527, 3 S. Ct 363, 27 L. Ed. 1020 (1883). 9.65
Canright v General Finance Corp., 35 F. Supp. 841 (ED Ill. 1940). 6.31
Case v Los Angeles Lumber Products Co., Ltd, 308 US 106 (1939) 5.69
CFTC v Weintraub, 471 US 343 (1985) 4.46
Charter Communications, In re, 419 BR 221 (Bankr SDNY 2009) 3.41
Chrysler LLC, In re, 405 BR 84 (Bankr. SDNY 2009) 2.44
Chrysler LLC, In re, 576 F.3d 108 (2d Cir. 2009) 2.44
CIL Ltd, In re, 582 BR 46 (2018) 9.53
Compania de Alimentos Fargo, SA, In re, 376 BR 427 (Bankr. SDNY 2007) 9.60
Condor Insurance Ltd, In re, 601 F.3d 319 (5th Cir. Miss. 2010) 9.53
Cozumel Caribe, SA de CV, Re, 508 BR 330 (Bankr. SDNY 2014) 9.17
Credit Lyonnais Bank Nederland v Pathe Communications Corp., No. 12150, 1991
    WL 277613 (Del. Ch. 30 December 1991). 7.11, 7.13, 8.20
Czyzewski v Jevic Holding Corporation 137 S. Ct 973, 979 (2017) 3.47
DBSD N. Am., Inc., In re, 419 BR 179 (Bankr. SDNY 2009), aff'd, No. 09 Civ 10156
    (LAK), 2010 WL 1223109 (SDNY 24 March 2010), aff'd in part, rev'd in part,
    627 F.3d 496 (2d Cir. 2010) 5.40
DBSD N. Am., Inc., In re, 634 F.3d 79 (2d Cir. 2011) 5.40
DeGiacomo v Sacred Heart Univ., Inc. (In re Palladino), 942 F.3d 55 (1st Cir. 2019) 6.45
Drabkin v Midland Ross Corporation (In re Auto–Train Corp., Inc.), 810 F.2d 270
    (DC Cir. 1987) 8.37
Eastgroup Properties v Southern Motel Assoc., Ltd, 935 F.3d 245 (11th Cir. 1991) 8.37, 8.76

xviii TABLE OF CASES

ESL Investments, Inc. v Sears Holdings Corporation (In re Sears) (Case 20–3343,
Document 166–1, 14 October 2022) 8.76
Fairfield Sentry, In re, 485 BR 665 (SDNY 2006) 9.53
Federation of Puerto Rico Organizations of Brownsville, Inc., In re, 155 BR 44
(Eastern District of New York 2 June 1993). 10.22
Fogerty v Petroquests Resources Inc. (In re Condor Insurance Co.) (5th Cir. 2010),
601 F.3d 319 . . . . 6.73
French, Re, 440 F.3d 145 (4th Cir. 2006) 6.73, 9.53
General Growth Properties, Inc., In re, 409 BR 43 (Bankr. SDNY 2009) 5.23, 8.09
Global Service Corporation, In re, 316 BR 451 (Bankr. SDNY 2004) 7.41
GMC, In re, 407 BR 463 (Bankr. SDNY 2009) 2.44
Harry P. Begier, In re, 496 US 53 . . . . 10.22
Helms v Certified Packaging Corporation 551 F.3d 675 (7th Cir. 2008) 5.36
Iida, In re, 377 BR 243. (9th Cir. BAP 2007) 9.60
Imagine Fulfillment Services LLC, In re, 489 BR 136 (Bankr. CD Cal. 2013) 6.36
Inman, In re, 95 BR 479 (Bankr. WD Ky. 1988) 5.40
International Banking Corporation Re, BSC, 439 BR 614 (SDNY 2010) 9.53
Irish Bank Resolution Corporation Ltd, In re, Case No. 13–12159 (Bankr. D Del. 2014) 9.60
Jacobs v Altorelli (In re Dewey and LeBoeuf LLP), 518 BR 766 (Bankr. SDNY 2014) 6.57
J.P. Morgan Chase Bank v Altos Hornos de Mexico, SA de CV, 412 F.3d 418 (2d Cir. 2005) 9.60
Kapila v S and G Fin. Servs, LLC (In re S and G Fin. Servs of S. Fla., Inc.), 2011
WL 96741 (Bankr. SD Fla. 2011) 8.38
Kelley v Stone and Baxter, LLP (In re Brownlee), 606 BR 109 (Bankr. MD Ga. 2019) 6.66
Lehman Brothers Special Fin. Inc. v BNY Corporation Tr. Serv Ltd (In re Lehman
Brothers Holdings Inc.), 422 BR 407 (Bankr. SDNY 2010). 8.34, 8.36, 8.56, 8.58, 8.70
Liquidation Trust of Hechinger Inv. Co. of Delaware v Fleet Retail Finance
Group (In re Hechinger Inv. Co. of Delaware), 327 BR 537 (D Del. 2005) 6.52
Loy, In re, 380 BR 154 (Bankr. ED Va. 2007) 9.60
LTL Mgmt LLC, In re, Case No. 21–30589 (MBK) [Docket No. 1572] (Bankr. DNJ 2021) 5.27
LTV Steel Co., In re, 274 BR 278 (Bankr. ND Ohio 2001) 5.23
Maxwell Communication Corporation plc, Re, 186 BR 807 (Bankr. SDNY 1995) 6.73
Maxwell Communications Corp., In re, 93 F.3d 1036 (2d Cir. 1996). 9.53
Mellon Bank, NA v Dick Corp., 351 F.3d 290 (7th Cir. 2003) 6.23
Metcalfe and Mansfield Alternative Investments., Re, 421 BR 685 (Bankr. SDNY 2010) 6.73
MFS/Sun Life Tr.–High Yield Series v Van Dusen Airport Servs Co., 910 F. Supp. 913
(SDNY 1995) 6.45
Millard, In re, 501 BR 644 (Bankr. SDNY) 9.60
Modern Land (China) Co., Ltd, Re, 18 July 2022, Case No. 22–10707 (MG)
(Bankr. SDNY 2022) 9.65
Mottaz v Oswald (In re Frierdich), 294 F.3d 864 (7th Cir. 2002) 6.21
Nat'l Bank of Newport v Nat'l Herkimer County Bank of Little Falls, 225 US 178,
32 S. Ct 633, 56 L. Ed. 1042 (1912) 6.23
Network Solutions, Inc. v Umbro Int'l, Inc., 529 SE 2d 80 (Va 2000) 5.35
New Bank of New England, NA v Tak Commc'ns, Inc. (In re Tax Commc'ns, Inc.),
138 BR 568 (WD Wis. 1992) 5.35
New Jersey v Div of Taxation (In re Chris–Don, Inc.) 367 F. Supp. 2d 696 (DNJ 2005) 5.35
New York Credit Men's Adjustment Bureau Inc. v Weiss (1953) 110 NE.2d 397 . . . . 7.13
Nortel Networks, Inc., In re, 532 BR 494 (Bankr. D Del. 2015) 8.35–8.36, 8.41,
8.54–8.55, 8.58, 9.68
North American Catholic Educational Programming Foundation,
Inc. v Gheewalla–930 A.2d 92 (Del. 2007) 8.14, 8.20
Northshore Mainland Services, Inc., In re, 537 BR 192 (Bankr. D Del. 2015) 9.60
OAS SA, et al., In re, 533 BR 83 (Bankr. SDNY 2015) 9.60
Official Committee v R.F. Lafferty Co., 267 F.3d 340 . . . . 7.39–7.40

Oriental Rug Warehouse Club, Inc., In re, 205 BR 407 (Bankr. D. Minn. 1997) 5.38

Purdue Pharma, In re, Decision and Order on Appeal, <https://por tal.ct.gov/–/
media/AG/Press–Releases/2021/Judge–McMahon–Decision–121621.pdf> 8.21

Quadrant Structured Products Co., Ltd v Vertin, 115 A.3d 535 (Del. Ch. 2015) 8.20

Raiman, In re, 172 BR 933 (9th Cir. 30 September 1994) 10.22

Ran, In re, 390 BR 257 (Bankr. SD Tex. 2008) 9.60

Reade v Livingston, 8 Am. Dec. 520 (NY Ch. 1818) 6.52

Rede Energia SA, In re, 515 BR 69 (Bankr. SDNY 2014) 9.60

Ridgley Commc'ns, Inc., In re, 139 BR 374 (Bankr. D. Md 1992) 5.35

Servicos de Petroleo Constellation SA, Re, 600 BR 237 (Bankr. SDNY 2019) 9.36

Shank, In re 792 F.2d 829 (Ninth Circuit 18 June 1986) 10.22

Sonora Desert Dairy LLC, In re, (2015) WL65301 (US Bankruptcy Appellate Panel 9th Cir.) . . . 3.71

Soundview Elite Ltd, et al., Debtors, Re, 503 BR 571. (Bankr. SDNY 12 December 2014) 9.20

SPhinX, Ltd, In re, 351 BR 103 fn. 17 (Bankr. SDNY 2006) 9.38

Straffi v New Jersey (In re Chris–Don, Inc.), 308 BR 214 (Bankr. DNJ 2004) 5.35–5.36

Tenney Village Co., Re, (1989) 104 BR 562 (Bank Ct D NH) 3.72

Union Savings Bank v Augie/Restivo Baking Co., Ltd (In re Augie/Restivo
Baking Co., Ltd), 820 F.2d 515 (2d Cir. 1988).. . . . . .8.37

United States v Theall, 609 Fed. Appx. 807 (5th Cir. 2015) 6.52

Vitro SAB de CV, In re, 701 F.3d 1031 (5th Cir. 2012) 9.63

Wey, In re, 854 F.2d 196 (7th Cir. 1988) 6.17

Wiersma, In re, 283 BR 294 (Bankr. D. Idaho 2002) 5.36

Table of Legislation

UNITED KINGDOM

Companies Act 2006
Pt 26 . . . . 1.01, 1.21, 1.47
Pt 26A 1.01, 1.21, 1.47
s 170(5) 7.15
s 172 . . . . 7.06
s 172(3) 7.08
s 179(4) 7.08
s 250 . . . . 7.14
s 251(2) 7.15
s 896(1) 3.22
s 899(1) 3.24, 3.28, 3.34
s 899(4) 3.35
s 901A 1.01
s 901A(2) 3.19
s 901A(3)(b) 3.19
s 901C(4) 3.41
s 901F(1) 3.34
s 901G 1.47, 3.41
s 901G(3) to (5) 3.51
s 901G(5) 3.51

**Company Directors Disqualification
Act 1986**
s 6 . . . . 7.57, 7.59
s 6(1) 7.54
s 6(4) 7.55
s 7(1) 7.54
s 8ZA 7.57
s 10 . . . . 7.58–7.59
s 11 . . . . 7.51
s 11(1) 7.52
ss 15A to 15C 7.45
s 76(2) 7.64
s 239 . . . . 7.48
Sch 1 . . . . 7.56

**Corporate Insolvency and Governance
Act 2020** 1.01, 3.01, 3.12, 3.51, 3.70
ss 1 to 6 . . . . 3.57
Schs 1 to 9 . . . . 3.57

**Cross-Border Insolvency Regulations
2006 (CBIR)** 9.05
Sch 1
Art 2(g) 9.36
Art 5 . . . . 9.09, 9.33
Art 15 . . . . 9.60
Art 16(3) 9.36

Art 17(2)(a) 9.36
Art 20 . . . . 9.60
Art 22(1) 9.24
Art. 23 . . . . 6.74, 9.03
Art 23(1) 9.53
Arts 28 et seq 9.33
Art 28 . . . . 9.33, 9.38
Art 32 . . . . 9.21

Employment Rights Act 1996
ss 166 to 169 . . . . 11.32

Enterprise Act 2002
Chapter 40 . . . . 5.43

Finance Act 2020 . . . . 10.15

Insolvency Act 1914
s 33(1)(b) and (c) 11.40

Insolvency Act 1976
Sch 1 Pt 1 . . . . 11.40

Insolvency Act 1986 . . . . 6.23
Pt A1 . . . . 3.57
Pt A1, Ch. 3 . . . . 3.66
Pt A1, Ch. 7 . . . . 3.59
Pt IV 4.02
Pt IV, Chapters II to IV 1.15
Pt IV, Chapter VI 1.15
s A6(1)(d) and (e) 3.66
s A9 . . . . 3.67
s 4(3) 3.25
s 84 . . . . 4.12–4.13
ss 91 et seq 4.12–4.13
s 91 . . . . 6.19
s 100 . . . . 4.14
s 104 . . . . 4.14
s 124(1) 4.14
s 124A(1) 4.17
s 125(1) 4.24
s 127 . . . . 6.20
s 130(2) 4.22
s 135 . . . . 4.20
s 173(1) 4.14
s 175 . . . . 10.15
s 213 . . . . 7.32, 7.58
s 214 . . . . 7.32, 7.36, 7.37, 7.58, 11.42
s 214(4) 7.33–2.34
s 233 . . . . 3.62
s 233A 3.62
s 233B 3.62–3.63
ss 238 to 245 . . . . 6.03

TABLE OF LEGISLATION

s 238(2) 6.17, 6.42, 6.63
s 238(3) 6.59, 6.63
s 238(4) 6.42
s 238(5) 6.42, 6.47
s 239 .... 6.18, 6.34, 6.39
s 239(2) 6.17, 6.63
s 239(3) 6.59, 6.63
s 239(4) 6.30, 6.34
s 239(5) 6.34
s 239(6) 6.34
s 240(1) 6.21
s 240(1)(a) 6.19, 6.34, 6.39, 6.42
s 240(1)(b) 6.34
s 240(2) 6.34, 6.42
s 240(3)(d) and (e) 6.20
s 241 .... 6.63
s 241(2) 6.62, 6.63
s 241(2A) 6.63, 6.67
s 244 .... 6.55
s 244(3) 6.55
s 245 .... 6.56
s 245(2) 6.56
s 245(3)(a) and (b) 6.56
s 245(6) 6.56
s 246ZB 7.32, 7.36
s 246ZD 7.35
s 249 .... 6.30
s. 264(1) 6.01
ss 267 and 268 .... 2.15
s 284 .... 6.20
s 284(3) 6.20
s 338 .... 6.47
ss 339 to 348 .... 6.03
s 339(1) 6.63
s 339(2) 6.59, 6.63
s 339(3) 6.42
s 340(1) 6.63
s 340(2) 6.59, 6.63
s 340(4) 6.34
s 340(5) 6.34
s 341(1) 6.21, 6.42, 6.47
s 341(1)(b) 6.34
s 341(1)(c) 6.34
s 341(2) 6.34
s 341(3)(b) 6.34
s 342 .... 6.63
s 342(2) 6.62, 6.63
s 342(2A) 6.63, 6.67
s 346 ...... 6.17 s 386 .... 10.15
s 387 .... 11.40
ss 423 to 425 .... 6.03
s 423 .... 6.42, 6.49, 6.54
s 423(1) 6.17
s 423(3) 6.49
s 424(1)(a) 6.49
s 424(2) 6.49

s 426 .... 9.05
s 426(4) 9.62
s 432(1) 6.49
s 435 .... 6.30
s 436(1) 6.17, 6.21
Sch 6, para 5 .... 11.40
Sch 6, para 15D 10.15
Sch B1, paras 42 and 43 .... 3.57
Sch ZA1, para. 1 .... 3.60
Small Business, Enterprise and
  Employment Act 2015 .... 7.15
Transfer of Undertakings (Protection of
  Employment) Regulations 2006
  (SI 2006/246) 11.12

AUSTRALIA

Corporations Act 2001
  s 415D 3.62
  s 415D(5) 3.63
  s 434J 3.62
  s 451E 3.62
  s 588FGA 10.24
Treasury Laws Amendment (2017)
  Enterprise Incentives (No. 2)
  Act 2017 .... 3.62–3.63

AUSTRIA

Corporate Income Tax Act
  (*Körperschaftsteuergesetz* KStG)
  s 23a 10.33
Income Tax Act (*Einkommensteuergesetz*
  EStG) 10.33
Insolvency Code (*Insolvenzordnung* IO)
  s 46 .... 10.10
  s 51 .... 10.10
  s 224(2) 9.49

BELGIUM

Law on the Continuity of Businesses
  (*Wet betreffende de continuiteit van de
  ondernemingen* of 31 January 2009)
  Art 61(3) 11.12

CANADA

Business Corporation Act
  s 119 .... 11.42
Companies' Creditors
  Arrangement Act
  s 11.4 .... 3.71
  s 11.52 .... 3.71
Wage Earner Protection Program Act
  2005 .... 11.31

CHILE

Civil Code
Art 2472(5) 11.37
Code of Labour
Art 163bis(2) 11.37
Insolvency Act
Art 148 .... 11.37

CHINA

Civil Code
s 681 .... 2.14
Company Law Act
Art 20 .... 7.76
Enterprise Bankruptcy Law 2.19, 11.35
Chapter VIII 1.21
Chapter X 1.15, 4.02
Art 2 .... 2.03, 2.12, 2.24, 2.36
Art 5 .... 9.60
Art 7 .... 2.03, 2.12
Art 7(2) 4.16
Art 18(1) 4.81
Art 18(1)(2) 4.81
Art 18(2)(1) 4.79
Art 25 .... 4.45
Art 25(1)(8) 4.73
Art 25(5) 4.53
Art 25(9) 4.46
Art 26 .... 4.53
Art 30 .... 4.29
Art 36 .... 4.89
Art 40(1)(1) 4.69
Art 40(2) 4.69, 4.71
Art 45 .... 4.65
Art 46 .... 4.66
Art 61(1) No. 5 et seq 4.73
Art 61(5) 4.53
Art 75(1) 4.22
Art 81 .... 4.113
Art 87 .... 4.114
Art 112(1) and (2) 4.94
Art 120 .... 4.108
Art 121 .... 4.105
Art 125 .... 11.42
Art 130 .... 4.47

EUROPEAN UNION

- Treaties

Charter of Fundamental Rights (CFR)
Art 47 .... 9.19
Treaty on European Union (TEU)
Art 5 .... 9.14
Treaty on the Functioning of the European Union (TFEU)
Art 67 .... 9.11
Art 107(1) 10.31
Art 267 .... 9.37
Art 288 .... 1.71
Art 288(2) 6.70

- Regulations

Regulation (EC) 1346/2000 European Insolvency Regulation
Art 13 .... 9.16
Regulation (EC) 593/2008 Rome I Regulation
Art 12(1)(d) 9.64
Regulation (EU) 2015/848 European Insolvency Regulation (recast) (EIR) 8.81, 9.03, 9.05, 9.13, 11.41
Recital 13 .... 9.18, 11.41
Recital 24 .... 9.25
Recital 41 .... 9.38
Recital 48 .... 9.22
Recital 49 .... 9.69
Recital 65 .... 9.11, 9.19
Recital 67 .... 9.25
Recital 83 .... 9.19
Recital 86 .... 9.13–9.14
Recital 88 .... 6.69, 9.03
Art 1(1) 9.65
Art 2 No. 7(ii) 9.37
Art 2(1) 9.38
Art 3 .... 6.70, 9.18, 9.37
Art 3(1) 9.35, 9.37
Art 3(1)(1) 9.36
Art 3(1)(4) 9.36
Art 3(2) 9.33, 9.38
Art 3(4)(a) 9.34
Art 3(4)(b)(ii) 11.33
Art 4(1) 9.18
Art 6 .... 9.39
Art 6(1) 9.39
Art 7 .... 6.70, 9.42, 9.63
Art. 7(2) lit. m, 16 .... 6.22, 6.69, 6.71
Art 7(2)(d) 9.47
Art 7(2)(e) 9.49, 9.51, 11.15
Art 7(2)(m) 9.54
Arts 8 to 18 .... 9.43
Art 8 .... 9.45–9.48
Art 8(1) 9.44, 9.46
Art 9 .... 9.47
Art 9(1) 9.47
Art 9(2) 9.47
Art 10 .... 9.48
Art 10(1) 9.48
Art 10(2) 9.49
Art 11 .... 9.50
Art 13 .... 9.51, 11.15
Art 13(2) 11.16, 11.33

TABLE OF LEGISLATION

Art 16 . . . . 6.69–6.71, 9.16,
9.19, 9.25, 9.54–9.55
Arts 19 et seq 9.59
Art 19(1) 9.19, 9.27, 9.37, 9.64
Art 20(1) 9.33, 9.61
Art 21(1) 9.63
Art 23 (2) 9.21
Art 32 . . . . 9.59, 9.61
Art 32(1) 9.63–9.65
Art 33 . . . . 9.59
Art 34 . . . . 9.27, 9.38
Arts 34 et seq 9.33
Art 34, sentence 3 . . . . 9.33
Arts 41 et seq 9.12, 9.67
Arts 56 et seq 9.12
Art 56(1) 9.65
Art 56(2) 9.28, 9.65
Art 60(1)(b) 9.28
Regulation (EU) 1215/2012 Brussels
I Regulation (recast)
Recital 26 . . . . 9.11

- Directives

Directive (EC) 1998/59 Collective
Redundancies Directive 11.07
Recital 2 . . . . 11.09
Directive (EC) 2001/23 Employees'
Rights in the Event of Business Transfer
Directive 11.07, 11.09, 11.11–11.14
Recital 60 . . . . 11.09
Recital 62 . . . . 11.09
Art 3 . . . . 11.11
Art 3(3) 11.11
Art 5 . . . . 11.11
Art 6(1) 11.11
Art 13 . . . . 11.09
Directive (EC) 2008/94 Employees'
Protection in the Event of Employer's
Insolvency Directive 11.07, 11.28
Arts 1 and 2 . . . . 11.33
Art 1(2) 11.28
Art 1(3) 11.28
Art 2(2) and (3) 11.28
Art 3 . . . . 11.29
Art 4 . . . . 11.29
Art 4(3) 11.29
Art 9(1) 11.33
Art 9(2) and (3) 11.33
Art 9(4) 11.09
Directive (EEC) 77/91 Capital Directive
Art 17 . . . . 7.26
Directive (EU) 2012/30 Second Capital
Directive 7.26

Directive (EU) 2017/1132 Company Law
Codification Directive
Art 58 . . . . 7.26
Art 58(1) 7.26
Directive (EU) 2019/1023 Restructuring
Directive 1.25, 1.71–1.74,
3.01–3.02, 3.19–3.24, 3.64,
5.58–5.59, 5.68,
7.26–7.29, 8.14, 11.07
Recital 17 . . . . 3.73
Recital 24 . . . . 3.19
Recital 52 . . . . 1.72
Recital 55 . . . . 1.72
Recital 62 . . . . 11.09
Art 2(1) 3.24
Art 2(2) 7.17, 7.28
Art 4(1) 3.19
Art 4(8) 3.22
Art 6 . . . . 4.22
Art 6(4) 3.61
Art 6(6) 3.67
Art 6(8) 3.67
Art 6(9)(c) 3.68
Art 7(1) 3.60
Art 7(4) and (5) 3.62
Art 9(4) 1.49
Art 9(6) 3.34
Art 10(2) 1.72
Art 11 . . . . 1.71–1.73
Art 11(1) 1.72
Art 11(1)(a) 1.72
Art 11(1)(b)(i) and (ii) 1.72
Art 11(1)(c) 1.71–1.72, 3.50
Art 11(1)(d) 1.72
Art 11(2) 1.72
Art 11(2)(a) 3.50
Art 16 . . . . 3.54
Arts 17 and 18 . . . . 1.42, 3.71
Art 19 . . . . 7.17, 7.28, 7.37
Art 32 . . . . 7.26
Art 1129(b) 1.50

FRANCE

Civil Code (*Code Civil*)
Art 632(1) 6.50
Art 1833 . . . . 6.50
Art 2327 . . . . 10.23
Art 2331 . . . . 11.39
Art 2375 . . . . 11.39
Art 632(1) 6.50
Arts 2011 et seq 10.23
Commercial Code (*Code de
Commerce*) 2.18, 6.21

Art L526-6(1)	7.01	Art L1233-91	11.09
Art L600-1	9.36	Art L1243-10	11.39
Art L600-1(1)	4.50	Art L3253-2	11.39
Art L611-11(1)	4.98	Art L3253-6	11.39

Regulation on reorganization and judicial
liquidation of enterprises (*Liquidation
judiciaire*) 1.15

Art 3	2.18

Tax Code (*Code General des Impots*)

Arts 1920 et seq	10.23
Art 1929 ter	10.23

Arts L620-1 to L628-3	1.21
Art L621-2	7.71–7.72
Art L621-4(5)	4.17
Art L621-43(1)	4.34
Art L622-7(1)	4.36, 4.71
Art L622-13(2)(1)	4.86
Art L622-13(3) No. 1	4.81
Art L622-17	4.61
Art L622-17(2)	4.98
Art L622-21	4.36
Art L622-24(1)(3)	4.64
Art L624-1	4.67
Art L625-9	4.61
Art L626-10	4.113
Art L626-29	3.14
Arts L631-1 to L632-4	1.21
Art L631-4	4.13
Art L631-8	6.37
Art L631-17	4.83
Art L632	6.64
Arts L632-1 to L632-4	6.03
Art L632-1	6.17, 6.19, 6.50, 6.69
Art L632-1(1)	6.37, 6.60, 6.64, 6.67
Art L632-1(1) Nos 1 and 2	6.43
Art L632-1(1)(1)	6.37
Art L632-1(2)	6.43, 6.59, 6.60, 6.64
Art L632-2	6.17, 6.18, 6.37, 6.39, 6.54, 6.59, 6.60, 9.55
Art L632-2(2)	6.17
Art L632-3	6.55, 6.69
Art L632-4	6.60, 6.64
Art L632-4(2)	6.23
Art L633-21(1)	4.64
Arts L640-1 to L643-13	1.15, 4.02
Art L641-1(3)	4.74
Art L641-3(1)	4.71
Art L641-3(4)	4.64
Art L641-9(1)	4.28–4.29
Art L641-10(3)	4.83
Art L641-11-1(1)(2)	4.79
Art L641-11-1(2)(1)	4.78, 4.81, 4.86
Art L641-11-1(6)(1)	4.83
Art L643-6	4.59
Art L643-7	4.59
Art L643-9(2)	4.108
Art L651-2	4.13, 7.24
Art L651-4(2)	4.16
Arts L654-1 et seq	4.13

Labour Code (*Code du Travail*)

Art L1233-1	11.09

GERMANY

Act on Limited Liability Companies
(*Gesetz betreffend die Gesellschaften mit
beschränkter Haftung* GmbHG)

s 6(2) No. 3	7.51
s 43(1)	7.12, 7.21–7.23
s 64	7.44
s 90	7.05

Act on Proceedings in Family Matters
and in Matters of Non-Contentious
Jurisdiction (*Gesetz über das
Verfahren in Familiensachen und in
den Angelegenheiten der freiwilligen
Gerichtsbarkeit* FamFG)

s 394	10.35

Act on the Development of Restructuring
and Insolvency Law (*Gesetz zur
Fortentwicklung des Sanierungs- und
Insolvenzrechts* SanInsFoG) 1.74–1.77

s 1 para. 9	1.49
s 1 para. 28(2)(1)	1.74, 1.76–1.77
s 1 para. 28(2)(2)	1.74–1.75
s 1, Pt 2, Chapter 1	1.21
s 5(9)	7.30
s 17(2), sentence 1	2.18
s 18	2.21
s 18 para. 2	2.22
s 19 para. 2	2.28
s 42	7.29
s 43	7.29

Act on the Framework for Stabilisation and
Restructuring of Enterprises (*Gesetz über
den Stabilisierungs- und
Restrukturierungsrahmen fur Unternehmen*
StaRUG)

ss 2 to 100	10.27
s 2(4)	3.24
s 8	3.26
s 9	3.29
s 9(1)	3.30
s 14	3.23

TABLE OF LEGISLATION

s 25(1) 3.34
s 28 .... 3.49
s 29(1) 3.19, 3.66
s 29(2) 3.64
s 42(1) 3.60
ss 49 et seq 3.07, 3.57
s 49(2)(sentence 2) 3.61
s 51 .... 3.66
s 53 .... 3.67
s 63 .... 3.36
s 66 .... 3.54
s 67(1) 3.54
s 89 .... 3.71
s 90 .... 6.35
s 901A(2) 6.35

Bankruptcy Act (*Konkursordnung* KO)
s 59(1) No. 3-a 11.38
s 60(1) 11.38
s 61(1) 11.38
s 61(1) No. 2 .... 10.15–10.16

Civil Code (*Bürgerliches Gesetzbuch* BGB)
s 15a(1) 4.89
s 121(1)(1) 4.81
s 823(1) 7.43
s 823(2) 4.89, 7.43
s 826 .... 4.89, 7.77, 7.80

Civil Procedure Code
(*Zivilprozessordnung* ZPO)
s 240 .... 10.11

Commercial Code (*Handelsgesetzbuch* HGB)
s 128 .... 7.73

Corporate Income Tax Act
(*Körperschaftsteuergesetz* KStG)
s 8(1) 10.29, 10.32, 10.35
s 8c(1) 10.32
s 8c(1a) 10.03, 10.32
s 11(1) to (7) 10.35

Criminal Code (*Strafgesetzbuch* StGB)
s 70(1) 7.60
ss 283 to 283d 7.51
s 283 .... 4.13

Employment Promotion Act
(*Arbeitsförderungsgesetz* AFG)
s 141a 11.38

Fiscal Code (*Abgabenordnung*, AO)
s 34 .... 10.08
s 69 .... 10.08

Income Tax Act (*Einkommensteuergesetz* EStG)
s 3a 10.27, 10.31, 10.32
s 3a(1) 10.29
s 3a(3) 10.30
s 3c(4) 10.27, 10.30–10.31
s 5(1) 10.35
s 10d 10.32

Insolvency Code (*Insolvenzordnung*
InsO) 11.38
Chapter 15 .... 6.72
Pt 6 .... 1.21
ss 1 to 216 .... 1.15, 4.02
s 1(1) 4.04, 4.103, 10.15
s 3 .... 9.36, 9.64
s 3(1) 4.50
s 9 .... 9.47
s 14(1)(1) 4.16
s 14(2) 4.16
s 15a(1) 4.12, 7.27, 7.42
s 15a(4) 4.13
s 15b(1) 4.89
s 15b(4) 4.89
s 15b(8) 10.24
s 17 .... 10.08, 10.24
s 17(2)2 .... 4.16
s 19 .... 10.08, 10.24
s 19(2)(2) 4.63
s 21(2) (1), No 1, 22 .... 4.20
s 22(1) (1), No 1, 2 .... 4.21
s 22(1)(2) No. 2 .... 4.53
s 22(2) (2), No 1, 3 .... 4.22
s 23(1) 4.25
s 26(1) 4.24
s 28(1) 4.65
s 29(1) No. 1 .... 4.73
s 36(1) 4.29
s 38 .... 4.34, 10.10, 10.17, 10.28
s 39(1), No. 5 .... 1.59
s 39(1)(1) No 5 .... 4.63, 7.83
s 39(1)(4) 4.63
s 39(1)(5) 4.63
s 39(2) 4.63
s 41 .... 4.66
s 45(1) 4.66
s 45(2) 4.66
s 47 .... 4.37, 10.21
s 51(1) No. 4 .... 10.21
s 52 .... 4.59
s 53 .... 4.75, 4.98, 10.17
s 54 No. 2 .... 4.75
s 54(1) 4.79
s 55(1) 4.98
s 55(1) No. 1 .... 10.17, 10.25
s 55(4) 10.10, 10.15
s 56(1) 4.41
s 56a(2) 4.44
s 57 .... 4.44
s 57(1) 4.73
s 57(2) 4.44
s 60(1) 4.47
s 61 .... 4.49

s 61(1) No. 2	4.79	s 158(1)	4.53, 4.74
s 67(2)	4.75	ss 159 et seq	4.94
s 73(1)	4.75	s 160	4.94
s 74	4.73	s 160(1)	4.53, 4.73–4.74
s 76(2)	4.44, 4.73	s 160(2)	4.73
s 80(1)	4.28	s 162	4.73, 4.96
s 87	4.36	s 166	4.59
s 89	4.36, 10.10	s 166(1)	4.100
ss 94 to 96	6.18	s 170(1)	4.59
s 94	4.69	s 172(1)	4.32
s 96(1) Nos 1 and 2	4.71	s 173(1)	4.100
s 96(1) No 3	10.18–10.19	ss 174 et seq	10.04
s 97	4.35	s 176(2)	4.67
s 98(3)	4.35	s 177	4.65
s 101(1)	4.35	s 179(1)	4.67
s 101(31)	6.30	s 190(1)	4.59
s 101(32)	6.36	s 199(2)	4.63
s 101(54)	6.13, 6.17	s 200(1)	4.108
s 103(1)	4.78, 4.81	s 201(1)	10.35
s 103(2)(1)	4.81	ss 208 et seq	10.20, 10.25
s 103(2)(3)	4.81	ss 217 et seq	10.26, 10.28–10.29
s 108(1) and (2)	4.88	s 217	4.113
s 108(1)(1)	4.83–4.84	s 220 et seq	4.113
s 109(1)	4.84	s 248(1)	4.114
s 111	4.88	ss 250 et seq	4.114
s 112	4.79	ss 270 et seq	4.39
s 113(1) and (2)	4.83	s 270b(2) No. 1	10.12
s 115	4.76	s 276a(3)	10.09
s 116	4.76	s 287(2)	4.107
s 119	4.86	s 287b	4.107
s 129	10.21	ss 335 et seq	9.05
ss 129 et seq	10.18, 10.21	s 335	9.42, 9.59–9.60
ss 129 to 147	6.03	s 336	9.50
s 129(1)	6.19–6.20, 6.23	s 337	9.51
s 129(2)	6.17	s 338	9.47
ss 130 to 146	6.19	s 343	9.33, 9.59, 9.60
s 130	6.18, 6.30, 6.35, 6.39	s 343(1)	9.64
s 130(1)	4.92, 6.35	s 343(2)	9.61, 9.63–9.64
s 130(3)	6.35	s 351(1)	9.44
s 131	6.18, 6.35	ss 354 et seq	9.33
s 131(1)	6.35	s 523(a)	6.73
s 133	6.35, 6.51, 6.54	s 538(a)(1)(A)	6.52, 6.54
s 133(4)	6.51	s 541(a)(3)	6.66
s 134	6.44	s 544(a)	6.56
s 134(2)	6.44	s 544(b)	6.52
s 135	6.57, 9.55	s 545(2)	6.56
s 137	6.55	s 545(3)	6.56
s 140	6.21	s 545(4)	6.56
s 142	6.35, 6.39	s 546	6.56
ss 143 et seq	6.59	s 546(a)	6.66
s 143(1)	6.65	s 547	6.36
s 143(2)	6.61, 6.65	s 547(a)(2)	6.36
s 145	6.62, 6.65	s 547(b)	6.17
s 147	4.73	s 547(b)(1)	6.36

xxviii TABLE OF LEGISLATION

s 547(b)(2) 6.36
s 547(b)(4) 6.36
s 547(b)(4)(A) 6.19
s 547(b)(5) 6.23, 6.36
s 547(c) 6.36
s 547(c)(1) 6.36
s 547(c)(2) 6.36, 6.39
s 547(c)(4) 6.36
s 547(c)(8) 6.36
s 547(c)(9) 6.36
s 547(e) 6.21, 6.56
s 547(f) 6.36
s 548 .... 6.52
s 548(a)(1) 6.17, 6.45
s 548(a)(1)(B) 6.45, 6.52
s 548(a)(1)(B)(i) 6.45
s 548(a)(1)(B)(ii) 6.45
s 548(a)(2) 6.45
s 548(a)(2)(c) 6.52
s 548(b) 6.57
s 548(d) 6.56
s 548(d)(1) 6.21
s 549 .... 6.20
s 549(b) 6.36
s 550 .... 6.66
s 550(a) 6.23, 6.61
s 550(a)(2) 6.62, 6.67
s 550(b) 6.62, 6.67
s 550(c) 6.36, 6.56
s 551(a)(3) 6.66
s 552(b) 6.20
s 553 .... 6.18
Introductory Act to the Insolvency Code
(*Einführungsgesetz zur
Insolvenzordnung* EGInsO) 9.20
Real Estate Tax Act (*Grundsteuergesetz
GrStG*)
s 12 .... 10.21
Social Code (*Sozialgesetzbuch* SGB)
s 165 .... 11.38
s 167 .... 11.38
Stock Corporation Act (*Aktiengesetz*) 7.05
s 58(4) 7.11
s 76 et seq 7.05
s 76(3) 7.51
s 92 .... 7.26
s 93(1) 7.11, 7.19
s 93(3) 7.11
s 93(5) 7.11, 7.18, 7.21
s 95 et seq 7.05
s 291 .... 7.73
s 311 .... 7.73
Trade Tax Act (*Gewerbesteuergesetz
GewStG*)
s 7b 10.27, 10.29

ITALY

Act to Reform the Mercantile Law of Tuscany
1713 (*Riforma degli Statuti di Mercanzia
della Toscana*) 11.24
Business Crisis and Insolvency Code (*Codice
della crisi d'impresa e dell'insolvenza*)
Arts 84 to 120 .... 1.21
Arts 121 to 139 .... 1.15
Art 255 .... 7.21
Art 324 .... 1.42
Civil Code (*Codice Civile*) 7.05
Art 2394 .... 7.10, 7.18, 7.21, 7.24
Art 2394-*bis* 7.21
Art 2446(6) 7.26
Art 2467 .... 7.83
Art 2476(6) 7.10, 7.18, 7.21, 7.24
Art 2476(8) 7.80
Art 2482-*bis* 7.26
Art 2497-*quinquies* 7.83
Art 2639 .... 7.15

JAPAN

Act on Recognition of, and Assistance
for, Foreign Insolvency Proceedings
(ARAFIP); Act No. 129 of 29 November
2000 .... 9.09
Bankruptcy Act
Arts 15 and 16 .... 2.29
Art. 15(2) 2.29
Company Reconstruction Law and Civil
Rehabilitation Act 2.36
Insolvency Statute
Art 3 .... 9.09

KOREA

Wage Claim Guarantee Act
Art 17 .... 11.32

MEXICO

Constitution
Art 123 .... 11.37
Federal Labour Law
Art 113 .... 11.37
Art 114 .... 11.37

NETHERLANDS

Act on the Confirmation of Extrajudicial
Restructuring Plans (*Wet Homologatie
Onderhands Akkoord*) .. 3.13, 3.19, 3.22–3.23
Art 381(7) and (8) 3.34
Art 384(4)((b) 3.49

Art 385 . . . . 3.54
Bankruptcy Act
Arts 203 et seq. 9.05
Civil Code
Art 7:666 . . . . 11.12
Law on the Continuity of Businesses (*Wet*
*Continuiteit Ondernemingen***)**
Pt 1, *Kamerstukken II* 2014/15,
34 218, 2. . . . . 11.12

POLAND

Bankruptcy And Rehabilitation Act 2003
Art 463(2) 9.49

ROMANIA

Insolvency Law (KO)
Art 123 . . . . 10.16

SINGAPORE

Companies Act
s 210(3AB)(a) and (b) 3.34
Insolvency, Restructuring and Dissolution
Act 2018 (IRDA)
ss 64 to 66 . . . . 3.57
s 67 . . . . 3.71
s 70.3 . . . . 1.51, 3.01, 3.48
s 239 . . . . 7.37
s 440(4) 3.62

SPAIN

Law 4859/2020 of 5 May 2020 (Insolvency
Law *Ley Concursal***)**
Arts 721 et seq. 9.05
Order 20 August 1985 supplementing Art.
32 of the Royal Decree 505/1985, 6 March
on the Conclusion of Restructuring
Agreements on Debts Owed to the Wage
Guarantee Fund 11.27

UNITED STATES

Bankruptcy Abuse Prevention and
Consumer Protection Act 2005 . . . . 10.19
Bankruptcy Code (*Title 11 of the US*
*Code***)** 1.01, 5.51
Chapter 7 . . . . 1.15, 2.36, 9.53,
10.07, 10.22
Chapter 11 . . . . 1.18–1.21,
1.47, 1.67–1.68, 2.36–2.37, 3.02,
3.12, 3.22–3.23, 3.41, 3.45–3.46,
3.50, 3.52, 3.62, 3.64,

3.67, 5.03, 5.10, 5.13, 5.16, 5.26, 5.37–5.38,
5.60, 5.66, 5.69, 8.51, 8.72,
9.53, 9.63, 10.07, 10.34, 11.10
Chapter 12 . . . . 10.07
Chapter 13 . . . . 10.07
Chapter 15 . . . . 9.05, 9.17–9.18
§§ 9-102(28) 5.15
§ 101(32) 7.39
§ 101(10)(A) 4.34
§ 101(a)(5) 5.16
§ 301 . . . . 1.02, 2.35
§ 301(a) and (b) 4.18
§ 303 . . . . 1.02, 2.35
§ 303(b) 4.16, 4.24
§ 303(d) 4.16
§ 303(g) 4.20
§ 303(h) 2.17
§ 321 . . . . 4.43
§ 323(a) 4.28
§ 341(a) 4.73
§ 346 . . . . 10.07
§ 350(a) 4.108
§ 361 . . . . 5.11
§ 362 . . . . 10.10, 10.19
§ 362(a) 3.64, 4.37
§ 362(a)(7) 5.26
§ 362(b)(26) 10.19
§ 362(d) 5.11
§ 362(d)(1) 5.61
§ 363 . . . . 4.94
§ 363(b) 5.47, 5.50
§ 363(b)(1) 4.53
§ 363(c)(1) 4.53
§ 363(f) 4.95, 5.31
§ 364 . . . . 5.10
§ 364(c)(1) 4.98
§ 364(d) 3.71, 5.11
§ 365 . . . . 4.81
§ 365(e) 3.62–3.63, 4.86
§ 365(h) 4.88
§ 502 . . . . 5.16, 5.61
§ 502(b)(9) 4.65, 5.16
§ 503 . . . . 11.24
§ 503(b)(1)(A) 11.24
§ 506 . . . . 5.16, 5.26
§ 506(a) 5.61
§ 506(a)(1) 4.70
§ 506(c) 5.11
§ 507 . . . . 5.10, 10.22, 11.40
§ 507(a)(2) and (3) 5.03
§ 507(b) 5.11
§ 510(c) 7.84
§ 521(a)(4) 4.35, 4.37
§ 523 . . . . 10.34
§ 541 . . . . 5.61

§ 541(1) 4.29
§ 541(a) 10.07
§ 541(c) 3.62
§§ 544 to 553 . . . . 6.03
§ 544(a)(1) 10.22
§ 545(2) 10.22
§ 547 . . . . 8.22, 8.30, 10.22
§ 547(b) 8.18, 8.76
§ 548(1)(A) 8.22
§ 548(1)(B) 8.22
§ 552 . . . . 5.40
§ 552(a) 5.39
§ 552(b) 5.39–5.40, 5.61
§ 553 . . . . 4.71, 5.26
§ 553(a) 4.69
§ 553(a)(1) 4.70
§ 554 . . . . 4.93
§ 555 . . . . 5.26
§ 556 . . . . 5.26
§§ 559 to 562 . . . . 5.26
§ 586 . . . . 4.43
§§ 701 to 784 . . . . 4.02
§ 701 . . . . 4.20
§ 701(a) 4.43
§ 701(c) 4.20
§ 702 . . . . 4.43, 4.73
§ 702(d) 4.20, 4.43
§ 704 . . . . 4.45
§ 723(2) and (3) 4.65
§ 724(b) 10.22
§ 1110 . . . . 5.21
§ 1121 et seq 9.63
§ 1121 . . . . 3.67
§ 1121(c) 3.22
§ 1122 . . . . 3.29, 5.49
§ 1122(b) 10.16
§ 1123 . . . . 4.113
§ 1125 . . . . 5.49
§ 1125(b) 3.23
§ 1126 . . . . 3.34, 5.49
§ 1129 . . . . 3.47
§ 1129(a) 5.49, 8.72, 9.63
§ 1129(a)(7) 3.47, 8.14
§ 1129(a)(7)(A)(ii) 4.01
§ 1129(a)(10) 1.67, 3.47
§ 1129(a)(11) 3.47
§ 1129(b) 1.18, 3.47, 5.60
§ 1129(b)(1) 1.51, 1.67
§ 1129(b)(2)(A) 5.61–5.62
§ 1129(b)(2)(B) 3.47
§ 1129(b)(A) 3.47
§§ 1181 to 1195 . . . . 1.69
§ 1191 . . . . 1.69, 5.69
§ 1408 . . . . 8.33
§ 1501(a)(2) 9.18
§ 1501(a)(3) 9.19, 9.24
§ 1501(a)(4) 9.22
§ 1502(2) 9.38
§ 1502(4) 9.36
§ 1504 . . . . 9.60
§ 1505 . . . . 9.09, 9.33, 9.60
§ 1509 . . . . 9.60
§ 1515 . . . . 9.60
§ 1516(c) 9.36
§ 1517(b) 9.36
§ 1520 . . . . 9.60
§ 1522(a) 9.24
§ 1523(a) 9.53
§§ 1528 et seq 9.33
§ 1528 . . . . 9.33, 9.38
§ 1532 . . . . 9.21
§ 1930 . . . . 4.24
Bankruptcy Reform Act 1898 . . . . 1.01
s 3 . . . . 2.17
Federal Rules of Bankruptcy Procedure
r 2003(b)(3) 4.73
r 3002 . . . . 4.65
r 5009(a) 4.108
r 6004 . . . . 4.94
Internal Revenue Code (IRC)
s 108(a)(1)(A) 10.34
s 108(b)(2) 10.34
s 547(c)(6) 10.22
ss 3401 et seq 10.22
s 6321 . . . . 10.22
s 6323(a) 10.22
s 7501(a) 10.22
New York Civil Practice and Legal Rules
s 5234 . . . . 5.07
New York Real Property Law (2020)
s 291 . . . . 5.19
New York Vehicle and Traffic Law
Title X (Uniform Vehicle Certificate of Title Act)
ss 2118 and 2119 . . . . 5.19
Restatement of the Law (3rd) of Property: Mortgages (2022) 5.07, 5.32
Sarbanes-Oxley Act 2002
s 1105 . . . . 7.63
Securities and Exchange Act 1934
s 21C 7.63
Small Business Reorganization Act of 2019
s 2 . . . . 5.69
Uniform Commercial Code (UCC)
Art 9: Secured Transactions (2010) 5.07, 5.15, 5.31, 5.33–5.34, 5.36–5.38

TABLE OF LEGISLATION xxxi

§ 1-201(35) 5.08–5.09
§ 1-201(b)(35) 5.34
§ 1-203 .... 5.08–5.09
§ 9-102(a)(64)(A) and (C) 5.38
§ 9-109 .... 5.31, 5.34
§ 9-109(d) 5.34
§ 9-203(a) and (b) 5.33
§ 9-203(f) 5.38
§ 9-204(a) 5.38
§ 9-204(a)(42) 5.38
§ 9-308 .... 5.33, 5.37
§§ 9-310 to 9-316 .... 5.33
§§ 9-310 to 9-317 .... 5.37
§ 9-315(a)(2) 5.38
§ 9-315(b)(2) 5.38
§ 9-315(c) 5.38, 5.39
§ 9-315(d) 5.38
§ 9-320 .... 5.37
§§ 9-322 to 9-324 .... 5.37
§ 9-406 .... 5.36
§ 9-408 .... 5.36
§ 9-501 .... 5.19
§ 9-506 .... 5.36
§ 9-544 .... 5.37–5.38
§ 9-615 .... 5.07
Uniform Voidable Transactions Act 1998
   s 4 .... 8.22, 8.30
   s 4(b)(9) 6.52
   s 5 .... 8.22, 8.30, 8.50
Worker Adjustment and Retraining
   Notification Act (WARN) 11.08–11.09

OTHER INSTRUMENTS

Council of Europe European Social
   Charter (ESC)
   Art 25 .... 11.27
European Convention on Human
   Rights (ECHR)
   Art 6 .... 9.19
Havana Convention of 20 February 1928
   ('Code Bustamante') Title IX Art. 414 ... 9.03
ILO Protection of Wages Convention, 1949
   (No. 95) 11.41
   Art 5 .... 11.25
   Art 6 .... 11.26
   Art 8 .... 11.25
   Art 11 .... 11.25
   Art 11(1) 11.24
   Art 11(3) 11.24
ILO Protection of Workers' Claims
   (Employer's Insolvency) Convention,
   1992 (No. 173) 11.25

Part II 11.36–11.37
Part III 11.28, 11.36
ILO Protection of Workers'
   Claims (Employer's Insolvency)
   Recommendation, 1992 (No. 180) 11.25
ILO Termination of Employment
   Convention, 1982 (No. 158)
   Arts 4 to 6 .... 11.08
   Art 11 .... 11.08
   Art 13 .... 11.08
Montevideo Treaty on Commercial
   International Law 1889
   Title X Arts 35 et seq 9.03
Montevideo Treaty on International
   Commercial Terrestrial Law 1940
   Arts 40 et seq 9.03
Montevideo Treaty of International
   Procedural Law 1940
   Arts 16 et seq 9.03
Nordic Bankruptcy Convention 1933
   ('Copenhagen Convention')
   Annex 38 .... 8.84–8.85
UNCITRAL Model Law on Cross-border
   Insolvency (MLCBI) 6.72–6.74, 8.06,
      8.81, 9.04–9.05, 9.35, 9.39, 9.42, 9.61
   Preamble 9.18–9.19, 9.22, 9.24
   Art 2 .... 9.33
   Art 2(b) 9.36
   Art 2(f) 9.38
   Art 5 .... 9.09, 9.60
   Art 7 .... 9.63
   Art 10 .... 9.63
   Art 15 .... 9.60
   Art 16(3) 9.36
   Art 17(2)(a) 9.36
   Art 20 .... 9.60
   Art 21(1) 9.63
   Art 22 .... 9.24
   Art. 23 .... 6.74
   Art 23(1) 9.53
   Arts 25 et seq 9.12, 9.67
   Arts 28 et seq 9.33
   Art 28 .... 9.33, 9.38
   Art 32 .... 9.21
UNCITRAL Model Law on Enterprise
   Group Insolvency (MLEGI) 8.81, 9.61
   Art 2(g) 8.83
   Art 19 .... 8.83
   Art 21 .... 8.84
   Art 23 .... 8.84
   Art 24 .... 8.84
   Art 26 .... 8.84–8.85
   Art 27 .... 8.85–8.86

Art 28 . . . . 8.85
Art 29 . . . . 8.85
UNCITRAL Model Law on Recognition
and Enforcement of Insolvency-Related
Judgments (MLIRJ)
Art 2(d) 9.39
UNIDROIT Convention on International
Interests in Mobile Equipment (2001) and
Protocol to the Convention on Matters

Specific to Aircraft Equipment
(2001) 5.21
United Nations, Charter of
Art 2(1) 9.10
OHADA Uniform Act Organising
Collective Proceedings for
Wiping off Debts of 10
April 1998
Art 247 . . . . 9.03

List of Abbreviations

ABI	American Bankruptcy Institute
AFG	*Arbeitsförderungsgesetz* (German Employment Promotion Act)
ALI	American Law Institute
AO	*Abgabenordnung* (German Fiscal Code)
APR	absolute priority rule
ARAFIP	Act on Recognition of and Assistance for Foreign Insolvency Proceedings
BEIS	Department for Business, Energy & Industrial Strategy
BGB	*Bürgerliches Gesetzbuch* (German Civil Code)
BJR	business judgment rule
CBIR	Cross-Border Insolvency Regulations 2006
CERIL	The Conference on European Restructuring and Insolvency Law
CJEU	Court of Justice of the European Union
COMI	centre of main interests
CRAR	capital-to-risk (weighted) assets ratio
CRO	Chief Reorganization Officer
DIP	debtor in possession
ECGI	European Corporate Governance Institute
EEC	European Economic Community
EFTA	European Free Trade Association
EGInsO	*Einführungsgesetz zur Insolvenzordnung*
EIR	European Insolvency Regulation
EStG	*Einkommensteuergesetz* (German or Austrian Income Tax Act)
EU	European Union
FamFG	*Gesetz über das Verfahren in Familiensachen und in den Angelegenheiten der freiwilligen Gerichtsbarkeit* (German Act on Proceedings in Family Matters and in Matters of Non-Contentious Jurisdiction)
FCC	Federal Communications Commission
FDIC	Federal Deposit Insurance Corporation
FOGASA	*Fondo de Garantía Salarial* (Spanish Wage Guarantee Fund)
G-SIBs	global systematically important banking groups
GewStG	*Gewerbesteuergesetz* (German Municipal Trade Tax Act)
GFC	global financial crisis
GrStG	*Grundsteuergesetz*
HMRC	His Majesty's Revenue & Customs
IIR	Individual Insolvency Register
IL	insolvency law
ILO	International Labour Organization
IMF	International Monetary Fund
InO	*Insolvenzordnung* (Austrian Insolvency Code)
InsO	*Insolvenzordnung* (German Insolvency Code)
IP	insolvency practitioner

IRDA	Insolvency, Restructuring and Dissolution Act 2018
IRS	Internal Revenue Service
KO	*Konkursordnung (*German Insolvency Code in force until 31 December 1998)
KStG	*Körperschaftsseuergesetz* (German or Austrian Corporate Income Tax Act)
M&A	mergers and acquisitions
MERS	Mortgage Electronic Registration System
MLEG	Modal Law on Enterprise Group Insolvency
NAFTA	North American Free Trade Agreement
OHADA	Organisation for the Harmonisation of Business Law in Africa
PAYE	pay-as-you-earn
PEIL	Principles of European Insolvency Law
PRC	People's Republic of China
RPR	relative priority rule
SDG	Sustainable Development Goal (UN)
SEC	Securities and Exchange Commission (USA)
SME	small and medium-sized enterprise
SanInsFoG	*Sanierungsrechtsfortentwicklungssetz* (German Act on the Further Development of Restructuring and Insolvency Law)
StaRUG	*Gesetz über den Stabilisierungs- und Restrukturierungsrahmen für Unternehmen* (German Corporate Stabilization and Restructuring Act)
TFEU	Treaty on the Functioning of the European Union
UCC	Uniform Commercial Code (USA)
UNCITRAL	United Nations Commission on International Trade Law
USC	US Code
UStG	*Umsatzsteuergesetz* (German VAT Act)
WARN Act	Worker Adjustment and Retraining Notification Act
WEPP	Wage Earner Protection Program (Canada)
ZPO	*Zivilprozessordnung* (German Civil Procedure Code)

List of Contributors

Reinhard Bork
Dr iur.; Professor at University of Hamburg; Visiting Professor, Radboud University Nijmegen, The Netherlands; Senior Research Fellow, Commercial Law Centre, Harris Manchester College, Oxford, UK

Laura Carballo Piñeiro
Dr iur.; Full Professor of Private International Law, University of Vigo

Edward J. Janger
David M. Barse Professor, Brooklyn Law School

Günter Kahlert
Dr iur.; Lawyer and Certified Tax Advisor, Associated Partner, Flick Gocke Schaumburg, Hamburg

Shuguang Li
Dr iur.; Professor of Law, China University of Political Science and Law (CUPL); Chair of Bankruptcy Law and Restructuring Research Centre of CUPL

Renato Mangano
Dr iur.; Professor of Law, Chair of Commercial Law and Insolvency Law, University of Palermo

Jennifer Payne
Professor of Corporate Finance Law and Warden, Merton College, Oxford

Johannes Richter
Dr iur.; lecturer at the Institute for German and International Civil Procedural Law, Chair of Civil Law and Insolvency Law, University of Bonn

1

What Is Insolvency Law?

Renato Mangano

I. Introduction

Over the past forty years, insolvency law—which, in this Introduction, includes both corporate insolvency law and personal insolvency law[1]—has made considerable progress and become a vibrant field of both research and practice.[2] However, during this time, insolvency law has also come to enlarge its toolbox and is now more sophisticated so that, nowadays, there is no definition of insolvency law that exhaustively lists the elements that this field of law consists of. In addition, the very term 'insolvency law' might even sound deceptive, since increasingly more jurisdictions regulate insolvency law procedures and proceedings that do not strictly require a situation of insolvency.[3]

1.01

Nevertheless, everyone who is familiar with the subject would agree about what insolvency law is for. In fact (from a functional point of view), scholars, judges, and practitioners are inclined to state that

1.02

- when a distressed debtor is indebted to more than one creditor, these competing claimants do not cooperate with each other, tend to act opportunistically, and prefer to grab the debtor's assets on a first-come, first-served basis;

---

[1] In this field, language varies, even within English-speaking countries. Therefore, for the sake of clarity, it is appropriate to stipulate that, here, the British English term 'insolvency law'—which, in England and Wales, refers to corporate insolvency law only—is to be understood as having the same extension as the American English term 'bankruptcy law' and, consequently, as including both corporate insolvency law and personal insolvency law.

[2] At a global level, it is difficult to determine any exact point in time for this cultural shift. But it seems reasonable to maintain that, at global level, this change in pace has coincided with the worldwide dissemination of the culture of rescuing distressed companies. In the United States, this culture was endorsed by the Bankruptcy Reform Act of 1978, which replaced the former Bankruptcy Act of 1898 with the current Bankruptcy Code.

[3] Traditionally, insolvency law has required a situation of the debtor's insolvency. However, the more the narratives of discharge and rescue prevail over the culture of mere liquidation, the more jurisdictions tend to anticipate the point in time for insolvency law measures to be put into operation. For example, this happens in the United States where 11 U.S.C. §§301 and 303, which (also) regulate applications for voluntary and involuntary liquidation proceedings (Chapter 7) and reorganization proceedings (Chapter 11), do not require a situation of debtor distress. This also happens in China, where Art. 2 of the Enterprise Bankruptcy Law of the People's Republic of China has relaxed the prerequisite that is required for reorganization proceedings; in the European Union (EU), where Art. 4 of the EU Directive 2019/1023 on preventive restructuring frameworks lays down that the national law prerequisite for restructuring should be a situation of mere 'likelihood of insolvency'; and in the UK, where the Corporate Insolvency and Governance Act 2020 has introduced into Part 26A of the Companies Act 2006 a new procedure which (only) requires that the company has 'encountered, or is likely to encounter, financial difficulties that are affecting, or will or may affect, its ability to carry on business as a going concern' (Art. 901A of Companies Act 2006). Moreover, it should be borne in mind that, in the UK, the regulation on schemes of arrangement, laid down by Part 26 of the Companies Act 2006 and still in force, has never required a situation of debtor distress. Historically, these schemes, which date back to 1870, were conceived as multifunction company law procedures.

Renato Mangano, *What Is Insolvency Law?* In: *The Anatomy of Corporate Insolvency Law.* Edited by: Reinhard Bork and Renato Mangano, Oxford University Press. © Renato Mangano 2024. DOI: 10.1093/oso/9780198852094.003.0001

2 WHAT IS INSOLVENCY LAW?

- this lack of cooperation (even though advantageous to some creditors, when taken individually) dramatically decreases the debtor's resources and makes all the claimants, when considered as a group, worse off;
- insolvency law aims to cure this failure, to preserve the aggregate value of the debtor's resources, to maximize the aggregate satisfaction of the debtor's claimants, and, when possible, to salvage the debtor's firm;
- for such purposes, insolvency law performs two essential tasks and, very often, many additional optional tasks;
- the first essential task consists either in coercing claimants' behaviours or in facilitating cooperation between competing claimants and, when appropriate, in incentivizing the debtor and his or her creditors to negotiate. If negotiations occur, the debtor and his or her creditors are asked to reach an agreement about the fate of the debtor's firm and, very often, about the distribution of the debtor's resources;
- the second essential task consists in distributing the debtor's resources among competing claimants in accordance with the relevant law or, if the claimants have also negotiated about distribution, in accordance with the outcome of their negotiation;
- very often, insolvency law also aims to make it easier for individual overindebted debtors to be discharged from their debts and make a 'fresh start', regardless of the fact that the debtors' creditors either have not been paid in full or have not been paid at all—from the moment they are discharged, these debtors can achieve new incomes and purchase new assets without the concern that their unsatisfied creditors will foreclose on the new resources.

1.03   This chapter focuses on the essential tasks of insolvency law in order to provide a brief overview of what insolvency law is for. By contrast, no reference will be made to its additional tasks—even though these may be crucial for the success of procedures and proceedings.[4] In this context, sections II–IX refer only to business insolvency law, including both corporate insolvency law and non-consumer individual insolvency law. Therefore, even though these sections refer to 'he' or 'she', in principle, no distinction will be made here between individuals, companies, and other non-corporate entities unless otherwise specified. By contrast, this chapter will not deal either with consumer insolvency law, or insolvency law regarding banks and other financial institutions, or with these regulations regarding the default of states and other sovereign entities. These regulations are rooted in different principles.

---

[4] There are many and various additional tasks. Just to list a few, they may consist in: regulating the so-called executory contracts (i.e. those contracts that were concluded between the debtor and a third party before the date of the opening of insolvency proceedings and that, on this date, are still pending); setting aside the transactions performed before the date of the opening of insolvency proceedings that prove to be detrimental to the general body of creditors; ensuring that the company directors who, before the date of the opening of insolvency proceedings, negligently, or even intentionally, injured the company's creditors will give them adequate compensation; and so on. These tasks will be dealt with in the following chapters. For example, the regulations on executory contracts will be dealt with in Chapter 4 (4.76–4.84); the avoidance of debtors' detrimental acts will be dealt with in Chapter 6, while the liability of company directors will be dealt with in Chapter 7 (7.06–7.46).

This chapter illustrates the machinery of insolvency law by employing basic no- **1.04**
tions of descriptive law and economics and basic notions of game theory. Therefore,
throughout the text, the reader will come across the term 'efficiency' and the adjective
'efficient'. Both words must be understood in a broad sense as referring to a concept of
efficiency that has been developed in organization theory, where a method or a solution
is understood to be efficient if it demands a lesser amount of resources than do competing methods or solutions.[5]

Last but not least, when a reference is made to UK law, the analysis will cover the law **1.05**
of England and Wales only. Indeed, throughout this chapter, 'England' is used to signify 'England and Wales' and 'English law' to signify 'the law of England and Wales'.
Moreover, hereafter the abbreviation 'IL' is used to signify 'insolvency law'.

II. The Rationale behind IL: A Lack of Cooperation between Competing Claimants

Originally, IL had a punitive connotation and dealt with the punishment inflicted by **1.06**
medieval Italian guilds on those merchants who had cheated their creditors and left
them unpaid. The guild to which the cheating merchant belonged broke the bench that
the cheating merchant had in the market place and, as a result, the punished merchant
was called 'bankrupt' (*bancarotta*), that is one whose bench (*banca*) was broken (*rotta*).[6]
Moreover, these fraudulent merchants were subjected to additional penalties and their
assets were liquidated. In the mid-sixteenth century, statutes dealing with the liquidation of fraudulent debtors' property, modelled on the statutes of the medieval Italian
cities, spread throughout Europe. Here, IL dealt with the punishment inflicted on insolvent merchants and, subsequently, on ordinary overindebted people. Depending on
their behaviours, both insolvent merchants and ordinary indebted people might even
be sentenced to death.[7] Fortunately, those gloomy times have disappeared and IL has
gradually lost its punitive purpose.

By contrast, modern IL is primarily—but not exclusively—a debt-collection device **1.07**
based on the assumption that when a distressed debtor is indebted to more than one
creditor, there is a flaw in cooperation. On this point, Thomas Jackson, in *The Logic and
Limits of Bankruptcy Law*, a book as highly acclaimed as it was severely criticized, wrote:

> [a] solvent debtor is like a show for which sufficient tickets are available to accommo-
> date all prospective patrons and all seats are considered equally good. In that event

---

[5] Rizwaan J. Mokal, *Corporate Insolvency Law. Theory and Application* (OUP 2005) 20 ss at 25–6, who labels this concept of efficiency as 'transaction cost efficiency'.

[6] Douglas G. Baird, *Elements of Bankruptcy* (6th edn, Foundation Press 2014) 4.

[7] Walter Pakter, 'The Origins of Bankruptcy in Medieval Canon and Roman Law' in Peter Linehan (ed.), *Proceedings of the Seventh International Congress of Medieval Canon Law* (Biblioteca Apostolica Vaticana 1988) 485 ss.

4 WHAT IS INSOLVENCY LAW?

one's place in line is largely a matter of indifference. But when there is not enough to go around to satisfy all claimants in full, this method of ordering will define winners and losers based principally on the time when one gets in line.[8]

Indeed, in this respect Jackson specified:

> [c]reditor remedies outside of bankruptcy [...] can be accurately described as a species of 'grab law', represented by the key characteristic of first-come, first-served. The creditor first staking a claim to particular assets of the debtor generally is entitled to be paid first out of those assets. It is like buying tickets for a popular rock event or opera: the people first in line get the best seats; those at the end of the line may get nothing at all.[9]

1.08 This pitfall in cooperation is very common in everyday life, even outside IL cases, and can be well illustrated by the dynamics of the 'prisoner's dilemma game', where two completely rational individuals, who cannot communicate with each other and who have the dilemma of deciding whether to cooperate or not, intentionally decide not to cooperate even if it is in their best interests to do so.[10] Consider the following example, which assumes that there is a distressed debtor and two creditors, namely Creditor A and Creditor B. Both Creditor A and Creditor B have two choices: either to cooperate or not to cooperate, that is either to mutually share the debtor's resources or foreclose individually on the debtor's assets. Each creditor must make a choice depending on the other creditor's possible choice but without knowing what the other creditor will really do. This is the dilemma, which is illustrated by Table 1.1 below. Creditor A chooses a row in order to decide whether to cooperate or not. Creditor B chooses a column in order to decide whether to cooperate or not. The outcomes of the game are expressed in terms of pay-offs. These range from one to five points. The points conventionally quantify to what extent creditor behaviours are individually efficient. The sum of the pay-offs referred to in a single cell expresses how efficient creditor behaviours are for the case as a whole. Suppose that Creditor A thinks that Creditor B will cooperate. Creditor A has two choices: namely, either to cooperate or not to cooperate. Here, the first column of Table 1.1 shows the two possible outcomes. If Creditor A cooperates, he or she will receive a pay-off of three points; here, Creditor B will receive three points

---

[8] Thomas H. Jackson, *The Logic and Limits of Bankruptcy Law* (Harvard University Press 1986) 9–10. Certainly, this book and its language constitute a watershed in the literature on IL, and in particular, the expression and concept of 'creditors' bargain' have strongly influenced US (but not just US) law and economics research on this subject. However, while almost every scholar accepts Jackson's idea that IL aims to solve a problem of cooperation (but, for a few of those who reject this idea, see section III.C), practically no one accepts Jackson's statement that IL should not have redistributive effects. In this respect, see section VII. Put differently, while almost every scholar accepts Jackson's position regarding what we will call the first task of IL, practically no one accepts Jackson's position regarding what we will call the second task of IL. This point, which will be discussed in greater detail in section VII, explains why, in the text to which this footnote refers, we stated '[b]y contrast, modern insolvency law is *primarily—but not exclusively—*a debt collection device based on the assumption that when a distressed debtor is indebted to more than one creditor, there is a flaw in cooperation' (emphasis added).

[9] Jackson, *The Logic* (n 8) 8–9.

[10] The prisoner's dilemma game is the game that reproduces the strategic interaction of two or more decision makers who face a situation of conflict that harms both or all concerned. On this point, see Eric Rasmusen, *Games and Information. An Introduction to Game Theory* (4th edn, Blackwell Publishing 2007) 19.

Table 1.1 The prisoner's dilemma game of the debtor's creditors

		Creditor B	
		To cooperate	Not to cooperate
Creditor A	To cooperate	Creditor A = 3 Creditor B = 3	Creditor A = 0 Creditor B = 5
	Not to cooperate	Creditor A = 5 Creditor B = 0	Creditor A = 1 Creditor B = 1

Source: author.

too. By contrast, if Creditor A does not cooperate, he or she will receive a pay-off of five points, while Creditor B will receive no points. Now, let us suppose that Creditor A thinks that Creditor B will not cooperate. Again, Creditor A has two choices: namely, either to cooperate or not to cooperate. Here, the second column of the matrix shows the two possible outcomes. If Creditor A cooperates, he or she receives a pay-off of no points, while Creditor B will receive five points. By contrast, if Creditor A does not cooperate, he or she will receive a pay-off of one point—here, Creditor B will receive one point too. This means that no matter what Creditor B does, Creditor A will receive higher pay-offs by not cooperating than by cooperating: five points are more than three points and even more than one or no points. But this also means that if neither Creditor A nor Creditor B cooperates, both do worse than if both had cooperated (one point is less than three points). Similarly, this logic holds for Creditor B.[11]

1.09 This model is an oversimplification of a real-world setting, not only because debtors are usually indebted to more than two creditors but also because the tension between individual interests and collective interests may have further dimensions. Consider,

---

[11] Situations of distress that are less severe than formal insolvency may give rise to common pool problems too. In this respect, see Nicolaes Tollenaar, *Pre-Insolvency Proceedings. A Normative Foundation and Framework* (OUP 2019) para. 1.22, who states: ' "Pre-insolvency" can also be confusing. Pre-insolvency proceedings are typically not used unless there is a financial reason to do so—that is, the company is in financial difficulties. To this extent, pre-insolvency proceedings can be regarded as insolvency proceedings.' In the same vein, Irit Mevorach and Adrian Walters, 'The Characterization of Pre-Insolvency Proceedings in Private International Law', European Business Organization Law Review, 21(4) (2020) 855 et seq. These authors affirm that 'attempts to sever restructuring law (which responds to likelihood of insolvency) and insolvency law (which responds to factual insolvency) might do more harm than good [...] Insolvency and restructuring law are on a continuum' (878–9); and again,

> Insolvency and restructuring law is, therefore, a unified body of law that maps onto the continuum, rather than two discrete bodies of law. One thing bleeds into the other. A debtor that has a likelihood of insolvency risks breaching loan covenants or triggering events of default and moving swiftly from 'pre-insolvency' to full-blown crisis. Rigid framings that distinguish pre-insolvency (restructuring) proceedings from insolvency proceedings lose sight of this fluidity. (879–80)

But, for a different view, according to which pre-insolvency proceedings would be outside the realm of IL since these would not aim to solve common pool problems, see Stephan Madaus, 'Leaving the Shadows of US Bankruptcy Law: A Proposal to Divide the Realms of Insolvency and Restructuring Law', European Business Organization Law Review, 19(3) (2018) 615 et seq.; and again, Stephan Madaus, 'Restrukturierungsverfahren mit Insolvenzprinzipien und Insolvenzverfahren mit Restrukturierungsziel? Eine Betrachtung der Grundannahmen des Insolvenz- und Restrukturierungsrechts' in Cristoph Paulus and Angelika Wimmer-Amend (eds), *Festschrift für Dr. K. Wimmer* (Nomos 2017) 446 et seq. In the same vein, see Jennifer Payne in this book, at 3.03 et seq.

6 WHAT IS INSOLVENCY LAW?

for example, a case involving Debtor Z and Creditor Y.[12] This hypothetical is slightly more complicated than the case that has just been described, since here, the position of the two players is qualitatively different: one player is a debtor while the other player is a creditor so that their moves may not be totally identical. Nevertheless, this case, too, may give rise to a dilemma which induces the players to look for an equilibrium that, eventually, will prove to be collectively inefficient. Debtor Z runs a firm that is distressed but potentially profitable, while Creditor Y has a claim which has a face value that is higher than the total amount of Debtor Z's assets. Suppose that Debtor Z thinks that Creditor Y will cooperate, which here means that he or she will be willing to accept the debtor's rescue plan or at least agree not to foreclose on the debtor's assets. Here, Debtor Z has two choices: namely, either to cooperate or not to cooperate, that is either to propose a plan of rescue and give the creditor some concessions, in the hope that the firm will be rescued, or to remain in full control of his or her firm and see whether the situation will improve without any intervention. Now, suppose that Debtor Z thinks that Creditor Y will not cooperate and will reject any rescue proposal. In this case, Debtor Z has two choices: namely, either to cooperate or not to cooperate, that is either to satisfy the creditor's request for payment or to conceal his or her assets so that Creditor Y will have difficulty in foreclosing on them and these assets will no longer be available for the business. This implies that (at least in the short run), no matter what Creditor Y does, Debtor A will gain more advantage from not cooperating than from cooperating. Debtor Z will keep full control of his or her firm and, if Creditor Y does not cooperate, Debtor Z's assets will be protected from foreclosure. But this also means that if neither Debtor Z nor Creditor Y cooperates, both are worse off than if both had cooperated. If there is no cooperation on either side, the firm will no longer have any chance of recovering its profitability—there will be no rescue plan and the assets will no longer be available for the business. This dilemma is depicted in Table 1.2, where conventional pay-offs are assigned to the players' outcomes.

1.10 Finally, the framework of the prisoner's dilemma game may be extended from a context where there is a tension between individual interests and collective interests to a context where there is a tension between two types of collective interests—which is the standard scenario in reorganization law. Consider, for example, the case of Company X, which has a complex financial structure, belongs to a group of companies the parent of which is also distressed, owns three branches in three foreign countries, and intends to propose a rescue plan to its creditors. In this case, there might be a lack of cooperation not only between the company, considered as a legal entity, and its creditors, considered as a group, but also

---

[12] In this respect, see Thomas H. Jackson, 'A Retrospective Look at Bankruptcy's New Frontiers', University of Pennsylvania Law Review, 66(7) (2018) 1872, where he states:

> [i]n a move I came to regret—somewhat—I labeled it a "creditors' bargain" to signify its locus in a hypothetical contract among the likely recipients of a distribution of the bankruptcy estate; that phrase, unfortunately, came to suggest to some that I had a bias in favor of creditors over debtors. In retrospect, I might have better labeled it a "claimants' bargain" or something broader.

Table 1.2 The prisoner's dilemma game of the debtor and his or her creditors

		Debtor Z	
		To cooperate	Not to cooperate
Creditor Y	To cooperate	Creditor Y = 3 Debtor Z = 3	Creditor Y = 0 Debtor Z = 5
	Not to cooperate	Creditor Y = 5 Debtor Z = 0	Creditor Y = 1 Debtor Z = 1

Source: author.

- within the group of Company X's shareholders, because these may have heterogeneous expectations depending on both the type of their shares and the type of their interest in the company's business;
- within the group of Company X's creditors, because some of them are secured, some are unsecured, and some are mezzanine lenders;
- between the group of the creditors of Company X's parent company and the group of Company X's creditors, because the former would prefer that the court that has opened the proceedings concerning the parent company should have full control also over Company X's proceedings, or even that only one set of proceedings should be opened (if this is allowed by the relevant law), while the latter would desire the two cases to be treated separately; and
- between Company X's local creditors and Company X's foreign creditors, because the former would prefer that only one set of main proceedings should be opened, while the latter would prefer that—in addition—the courts of the places where Company X has its three branches should also open three sets of ancillary (secondary) proceedings.[13]

III. The First Task of IL: Either Coercing or Making It Easier for Claimants to Cooperate—The Distinction between Liquidation and Rescue

If the setting described above is the usual location for distress management, the first **1.11** task of IL consists in ensuring that those who are involved in the debtor's distress, including the distressed debtor, cooperate with each other. To express this concept,

---

[13] For this expansion of the scope of the prisoner's dilemma game from a tension between individual interests and collective interests to a tension between two types of collective interests, see Renato Mangano, 'From "Prisoner's Dilemma" to Reluctance to Use Judicial Discretion: The Enemies of Cooperation in European Cross-Border Cases', International Insolvency Review, 26(3) (2017) 319 s. However, for the sake of simplicity, this chapter focuses on the conflicts arising in a standing-alone company with no foreign creditors. The issues related to group and cross-border insolvencies will be treated in Chapters 8 and 9, respectively.

8   WHAT IS INSOLVENCY LAW?

scholars usually rely on metaphors. In particular, they say that a debtor's distress gives rise to a situation which is similar to any case where there is a natural resource that is openly accessible (such as a lake, a park, water, and so on) and where the people who use this common resource tend to misuse their prerogatives, overuse the common resource, and, by so doing, jeopardize its very existence. Therefore, these scholars continue, the first task of IL consists in solving a common pool problem.[14]

1.12 For such a purpose, each jurisdiction follows its own path. Nevertheless, from a functional point of view, it seems that nearly all legal frameworks follow the same paradigms. These are (a) authority, (b), regulated self-governance, and (c) privatization.

A. Authority

1.13 Traditionally, IL solves the problem of cooperation that arises among competing claimants by adopting a command-and-control strategy and, more specifically, by coercing the claimants' behaviours and reducing their plurality to unity. Usually, the insolvency practitioner (IP) will represent both the debtor and the debtor's creditors. In particular, insolvency laws attain this result, on the one hand, by prohibiting debtors from managing and transferring their assets—these rights will be vested in the IP—and, on the other hand, by prohibiting the debtors' creditors from foreclosing on the debtors' assets—the debtors' creditors will have to lodge their claims in insolvency proceedings so that, from then on, the creditors' rights will be looked after by the IP.

1.14 These insolvency laws are grounded in the public-interest approach to regulation. This approach claims that, as a general rule, the State must not interfere with market forces except when these are not able to generate outcomes that are consistent with the expected economic welfare. Here, in particular, IL intervention is based on the idea that both distressed debtors and their creditors are not able to coordinate their behaviours.[15]

1.15 The authority paradigm permeates the regulation of many proceedings around the world. Prominent examples of these are the regulation on liquidation proceedings laid down by Chapter 7 of the US Bankruptcy Code, the regulation on liquidation proceedings laid down by Chapter X of the Enterprise Bankruptcy Law of the People's Republic of China, the regulations on company liquidation proceedings laid down by the UK Insolvency Act 1986 (Chapters II–IV on 'Voluntary winding up' and Chapter VI on 'Winding up by the court'), the French regulation on judiciary liquidation (*liquidation*

---

[14] For example, in this respect Jackson (*The Logic* (n 8) 11) wrote that when a debtor is insolvent and there is a lack of cooperation between competing claimants, this situation resembles what happens when many fishermen fish in the same lake, which gives rise to a problem of overfishing. Arguably, the metaphors of a common resource and a common pool problem are still appropriate in modern IL when, to use an EU law definition, the expression 'collective proceedings' may 'include all or *a significant part of a debtor's creditors*, provided that, in the latter case, the proceedings do not affect the claims of creditors which are not involved in them' (Art. 2.1 of EU Regulation 2015/848; emphasis added). In fact, 'the significant part of a debtor's creditors' encounters the same problems of coordination that have previously been described.

[15] Anthony I. Ogus, *Regulation. Legal Form and Economic Theory* (OUP 1994) 29 and 41–2.

judiciaire) laid down by Arts L640-1–L643-13 of the French *Code de Commerce*, the regulation on judiciary liquidation (*liquidazione giudiziaria*) laid down by Arts 121–39 of the Italian *Codice della crisi d'impresa e dell'insolvenza*, and the regulation on insolvency proceedings (*Insolvenzverfahren*) laid down by paras 1–216 of the German *Insolvenzordnung*. In this last case, since proceedings are structured as double-track proceedings that, depending on the debtor's situation, may be employed either to liquidate or rescue, many of the cited prescriptions refer to rescue as well.

B. Regulated Self-Governance

Alternatively, insolvency laws adopt a regulatory design strategy that consists in creating a legal framework where a debtor and his or her creditors can organize themselves in a way that allows them to tackle the debtor's distress in a self-governed way.[16] Here, in principle, insolvency laws do not aim to prohibit, impose, or control; rather, they aim mainly to stimulate those actions that lawmakers regard as efficient for the debtor and his or her creditors, considered as a group.

1.16

The regulations that are based on the paradigm of regulated self-governance cannot be explained through the public-interest approach only, since here, lawmakers do not restrict their remits to solving a problem of cooperation but employ a great deal of discretion in designing an architecture that, in its turn, facilitates free choices. This explains why, especially in the United States, these regulations are analysed through the lenses of social choice theory or, sometimes, through the less benevolent lenses of interest group theory.[17] Moreover, if a regulation that is based on the regulated self-governance paradigm fails to achieve the regulatory goals, it is debatable whether the lawmaker responsible for this regulation has thoroughly considered every factor that may have influenced the effectiveness of the legal framework and its capacity to trigger the expected reactions. This observation is particularly appropriate when a regulation that endorses the regulated self-governance paradigm has been exported from one country to another.[18] The fact that a regulation has proved successful in one country does not ensure

1.17

---

[16] The expression 'regulated self-governance', which is employed in other fields of law, highlights the fact that this paradigm is a combination of the authority of law and the self-governance of agreement. In its turn, the concept of regulatory design strategy may be structured in different ways, depending on its goals. Regulatory design strategy may be employed to stimulate the choice of a single norm addressee or the choice of a group of people and their strategic interactions. This is the case of the insolvency laws that adopt the regulated self-governance paradigm. For the regulatory design strategy, even though outside the field of IL, see Richard H. Thaler, Cass R. Sunstein, and John P. Balz, 'Choice Architecture' (2010) <https://ssrn.com/abstract=1583509> accessed 4 May 2021. In this respect, see also Ian Ayres and Robert Gertner, 'Filling Gaps in Incomplete Contracts: An Economic Theory of Default Rules', Yale Law Journal, 99(1) (1989) 97 ss, where the authors refer to the so-called penalty default rules, which, 'by definition, give at least one party to the contract an incentive to contract around the default'.

[17] David A. Skeel, Jr, *Debt's Dominion. A History of Bankruptcy Law in America* (Princeton University Press 2004) 14–15.

[18] Of course, this observation goes far beyond the general criticisms expressed against the idea, put forward by Alan Watson, *Legal Transplants* (2nd edn, University of Georgia Press 1993) 21, according to which the reception of foreign law might be considered a legal transplant. For these criticisms, see Pierre Legrand, 'The Impossibility of "Legal Transplants"', Maastricht Journal of European & Comparative Law, 4(2) (1997) 111 ss.

10   WHAT IS INSOLVENCY LAW?

that—as such—it will also prove successful in another country. In effect, especially in the case of legal frameworks based on the regulated self-governance paradigm, cultural diversities between the two countries (and between the behaviours of the relevant debtors, creditors, courts, and IPs) might be of decisive importance. For example, this was understood by those countries that decided to import into their jurisdictions the successful English schemes of arrangement laid down by Part 26 of the UK Companies Act 2006. These countries felt the need to modify the structure of the English schemes in order to accommodate them to their own jurisdictions.[19]

1.18 Jurisdictions that adopt the regulated self-governance paradigm encourage the claimants to communicate, cooperate, and negotiate under the threat that, if they fail to reach an agreement, they will be worse off. For example, this happens in the United States, where 11 U.S.C. §1129(b) lays down that a restructuring plan under Chapter 11 that has not been approved consensually by claimants may, under certain conditions, be confirmed by the court, which—this is a crucial point—might treat such claimants much worse than they had hoped during the negotiation of the plan.

1.19 The dynamic of Chapter 11 will be dealt with in section VIII. Nevertheless, from a game theory point of view, the strategy endorsed by the regulated self-governance paradigm consists in transforming a game where the players cannot communicate with each other, such as the 'prisoner's dilemma game', into a game where the players can communicate with each other, such as the 'bargaining game'.[20] Adapted to an IL setting, this game may be described as follows. Firm Alpha has an estimated value of 200 and two claimants (namely Claimant A and Claimant B), who must share this sum between them under the following conditions. Each claimant must express his or her demand. If the total amount of their demands equals 200 (or if this is even lower than 200), they will receive what they have demanded; by contrast, if the total amount of their demands is more than 200, they will not reach an agreement and will be worse off. Of course, each player would like to have a greater portion of the stake, but each of them is also concerned about a worse-off scenario. Therefore, since they can communicate with each other, they prefer to communicate, cooperate, negotiate, and reach an agreement that satisfies the rules of the game. For example, they can agree that Claimant A will have 150 and Claimant B will have 50 or that Claimant A will have 50 and Claimant B will have 150. Table 1.3 depicts, with conventional pay-offs, the outcomes of this game. These, clockwise, are the (theoretical) case where they reach a deal that is unsatisfactory for both, since the sum of their demands is lower than the stake to be divided; the case where they reach a deal that is more advantageous for Claimant A; the case where they reach no deal because their requests are higher than the stake to be divided; and the case where they reach a deal that is more advantageous for Claimant B.

---

[19] In this respect, see Jennifer Payne (ed.), 'The Continuing Importance of the Scheme of Arrangement as a Debt Restructuring Tool', European Company and Financial Law Review 15(3) (2018) and especially the contributions by Ignatio Tirado, Wee Meng Seng, Umakanth Varottil, and Renato Mangano.

[20] Martin Peterson, *An Introduction to Decision Theory* (CUP 2009) 247–8.

Table 1.3 An insolvency case and the bargaining game

	Claimant A: 50	Claimant A: 150
Claimant B: 50	Claimant A = 0 Claimant B = 0	Claimant A = 4 Claimant B = 1
Claimant B: 150	Claimant A = 1 Claimant B = 4	Claimant A = 0 Claimant B = 0

Source: author.

The idea of addressing the problem of non-cooperation existing between competing claimants by employing the regulated self-governance paradigm is particularly useful, since these solutions are flexible and tend to fit into every situation, even the most peculiar ones. However, regulated self-governance is much more problematic than authority. First, facilitating cooperation by employing the regulated self-governance paradigm may give rise to other forms of opportunistic behaviour. When there are more than two claimants, as usually happens, a claimant might refrain from cooperating because of concerns that he or she may give the other parties increased bargaining power and thereby reduce his or her own advantages. (This is the so-called holding-up problem.) This problem will be dealt with in this section, section III.C, and section VI. Second, in the 'bargaining game', players have many possibilities of cooperating so that they can potentially reach various agreements.[21] For example, they may concur with each other that Claimant A will receive 1 and Claimant B 199, or that Claimant A will receive 2 and Claimant B 198, and so on, and all these pairs of outcomes will satisfy the rules of the game. However, when a jurisdiction adopts the regulated self-governance paradigm, it is debatable whether the claimants are completely free to negotiate around the rules according to which the debtor's resources should be distributed or whether, in this respect, they will encounter some limits. This point will be dealt with in section VII.B.

1.20

The regulated self-governance paradigm permeates the regulation of both out-of-court procedures and (in-court) proceedings. Prominent examples of the former are the two types of English schemes regulated by Part 26 and Part 26A of the UK Companies Act 2006. By contrast, well-known examples of the latter are the reorganization proceedings regulated by Chapter 11 of the US Bankruptcy Code, the reorganization proceedings regulated by Chapter VIII of the Enterprise Bankruptcy Law of the People's Republic of China, the plan proceedings (*Planverfahren*) regulated by Part 6 of the German *Insolvenzordnung*, the restructuration plan proceedings (*Restrukturierungsplan*) regulated by Art. 1, Part 2, Chapter 1 of the recent German *Gesetz zur Fortentwicklung des Sanierungs- und Insolvenzrechts*,[22] the protection proceedings (*sauvegarde*) and the

1.21

---

[21] In this respect, scholars say that the players of the bargain game have more than one equilibrium: see ibid 248.
[22] These proceedings will be dealt with in section IX.

12   WHAT IS INSOLVENCY LAW?

judicial recovery proceedings (*redressement judiciaire*) regulated by Arts L. 620-1–628-3 and by Arts L. 631-1–632-4 of the French *Code de Commerce*, and the preventative settlement proceedings (*concordato preventivo*) regulated by Arts 84–120 of the Italian *Codice della crisi d'impresa e dell'insolvenza*.

C. Privatization

1.22 A few distinguished US scholars deny that a debtor's distress triggers a problem of co-operation. In particular, these scholars maintain that the only task of IL should consist in distributing the debtor's resources. They even go on to state that the distributional task might be performed by contract law more appropriately than by IL so that the latter would become superfluous, or, if a more moderate position were adopted, it should be laid down as an opt-out regulation only.[23]

1.23 This position introduces a third way of dealing with debtors' distress. However, this statement is true not because there would be no common pool problem—in fact, it has been thoroughly demonstrated that these scholars do not necessarily rule out the need for distressed debtors to impose a general stay on their creditors[24]—but because these authors suggest that a lawmaker should approach the (denied) common pool problem not by either authority or regulated self-governance but by using a third paradigm, which, in accordance with the studies carried out on openly accessible resources, could be labelled 'privatization of the common pool problem', or 'privatization of insolvency law', or simply 'privatization'.[25]

1.24 This group of scholars is variegated, and each position would deserve a specific commentary, which, here, is neither possible nor appropriate. Nevertheless, when these scholars say that debtors' distress does not give rise to a common pool problem, in actual fact, they want to suggest that the claimants, including the debtor, on the one hand, should exploit the common pool situation (including the surplus that this produces) by playing an anti-coordination game and that, on the other hand, they should

---

[23] In particular, reference is here made to Barry E. Adler, 'Finance's Theoretical Divide and the Proper Role of Insolvency Rules', California Law Review, 72(67) (1994) 1107 ss; Michael Bradley and Michael Rosenzweig, 'The Untenable Case for Chapter 11', Yale Law Journal, 101(5) (1992) 1043 ss; Robert K. Rasmussen, 'Debtor's Choice: A Menu Approach to Corporate Bankruptcy', Texas Law Review, 71(1) (1992) 51 ss; Alan Schwartz, 'A Contract Theory Approach to Business Bankruptcy', Yale Law Journal, 107(6) (1998) 1807 ss. In Europe, for a more recent version of this approach, see Madaus, 'Leaving the Shadows' (n 11) 615 ss.

[24] Susan Block-Lieb, 'The Logic and Limits of Contract Bankruptcy', Illinois Law Review, 2001(2) (2001) 5023 ss, who, moreover, states that

> despite assertions to the contrary, many of the proposed private-law bankruptcy substitutes would create immense decision-making costs, and all of the bankruptcy contract proposals would impose enforcement costs of a magnitude both substantial and comparable to the legislative rules these contracts are meant to replace. In short, there are simple contractual solutions for complex business bankruptcies.

[25] As regards the terminology employed in the text to which this footnote refers, see Elinor Ostrom, *Governing the Commons. The Evolution of Institutions for Collective Actions* (CUP 2015) 12–13. Moreover, this terminology corresponds to the slogan employed by the supporters of the contractual approach to insolvency: 'privatize bankruptcy'.

Table 1.4 An insolvency case and the chicken game

	Claimant A: is willing to have less	Claimant A insists on having more
Claimant B is willing to have less	Claimant A = 2 Claimant B = 2	Claimant A = 4 Claimant B = 1
Claimant B insists on having more	Claimant A = 1 Claimant B = 4	Claimant A = 0 Claimant B = 0

Source: author.

not have any restrictions in the distribution. From a game theory point of view, this situation may be illustrated by the 'chicken game', where two drivers race towards each other, each driver hoping the other will swerve first.[26] Here, the rules of the game require that the only way to win the game consists in inducing the other party to swerve first, while there are three ways to lose. These, ranked in decreasing order of desirability, may be described as follows: (a) swerve at the same time as the other party, (b) swerve first, and (c) crash into the other party. If adapted to an IL scenario, the 'chicken game' may be described as follows. Claimant A and Claimant B are engaged in negotiation in order to rescue a firm and distribute between themselves the firm's value. A deal that will produce surplus is worth making regardless of exactly how that surplus is divided up, but each party would prefer to receive a larger portion. Here, 'driving straight ahead' means insisting on having more, 'swerving first' means being willing to have less in order to facilitate the bargain, and 'crashing' means that the deal will fall apart for both the players. This situation, with the use of conventional pay-offs, is depicted in Table 1.4.

To our knowledge, this position has not been endorsed by any jurisdictions, at least in these radical terms. Even though every jurisdiction allows a debtor and his or her creditors to tackle a firm's distress by means of a contract, this possibility is always regarded as feasible as long as there is no risk of anti-coordination initiatives. For example, the use of contractual workouts was possible in England at the time of the so-called

1.25

---

[26] Lee Anne Fennell, 'Commons, Anticommons, Semicommons' in Kenneth Ayotte and Henry E. Smith (eds), *Research Handbook on the Economics of Property Law* (Edward Elgar 2011) 43. Moreover, at 44, this author highlights the fact that there is a continuity between the so-called tragedy of the commons and tragedy of the anticommons and between the bargaining game and the chicken game. In particular, on this point, Fennell writes:

> Returning to the earlier interaction between Rowena [who corresponds to Claimant B in Tables 1.3 and 1.4] and Columbo [who corresponds to Claimant A in Tables 1.3 and 1.4] illustrates not only how the game of chicken works, but also how the tragedy of the anticommons connects to the tragedy of the commons. When we last saw them, our protagonists were locked in a Prisoner's Dilemma, each tempted to add more cattle than would be efficient. If they could agree among themselves to refrain from adding the extra ungulates, the tragedy of the commons could be averted, and a surplus […] could be enjoyed between them. Each would be better off with even a little of this surplus but each would prefer to get more of it rather than less. Their attempts to assemble the acts of forbearance that will produce the surplus, and their struggle over how that surplus will be divided, makes up the Chicken game.

14 WHAT IS INSOLVENCY LAW?

'London approach', when the Bank of England employed its powers of moral suasion to facilitate cooperation between English banks and a debtor intending to restructure his or her debts owed to these banks;[27] and, again, this possibility still occurs when a debtor is indebted to a very restricted number of creditors within a cooperative environment where there is no risk that a bargaining game may result in a chicken game.[28] However, the idea that a legal framework might even allow debtors to exploit reorganizations and force creditors to accept a distribution that—with only a minimum sacrifice on the part of the debtors—massively undermines the position of some creditors has influenced the recent EU Directive 2019/1023. This point will be examined in section IX.

1.26 Theoretically, all three paradigms may be employed to both liquidate and rescue a firm; indeed, in the law in the book, there are even examples which demonstrate that, sometimes, the above-mentioned paradigms may be employed interchangeably to pursue the same goals. However, in practice, the cases where authority may be employed to sell the debtor's assets in their entirety in order to keep the firm's organization intact are quite rare—very often, the rescue of a firm by a firm sale requires a more flexible tool.[29] By contrast, the cases where the regulated self-governance and privatization paradigms may be employed to liquidate a distressed firm are theoretically possible but practically unrealistic, since the use of these approaches would involve more (financial and transactional) costs than would the use of authority.[30]

1.27 This statement implies that, in this chapter, it is to be understood that the aim of the authority paradigm is to liquidate firms, while the aim of the regulated self-governance and privatization paradigms is to rescue firms.

IV. Liquidation: Concept, Taxonomies, and Devices

1.28 Traditionally, insolvency laws have aimed to liquidate distressed firms so that all insolvency laws provide liquidation proceedings. Usually, these have a straightforward

---

[27] Vanessa Finch, *Corporate Insolvency Law. Perspectives and Principles* (2nd edn, CUP 2009) 307–8. However, at 312–13, this author highlights that, nowadays, the situation has changed because 'large UK companies are resorting less to bank loans and making more use of intermediated debt finance'; this change 'produces new levels of opacity concerning the nature and extent of different parties' interests' and '[t]he markets in credit products are now global in nature'.

[28] There is evidence that the smaller a group is, the more willing its members are to cooperate. In this respect, see Mancur Olson, *The Logic of Collective Action. Public Goods and the Theory of Groups* (Harvard University Press 1971) 58.

[29] E.g. as regards US law, Baird, *Elements* (n 6) 19, states:

> [l]iquidation under Chapter 7 does not require that all the assets be broken up and sold piecemeal. To the contrary, the trustee is obliged to sell the assets for as much as possible, and sometimes this means selling the assets together as a going concern. In practice, however, operating businesses rarely file Chapters 7 petitions.

[30] The situation is quite different in Germany. Here, when there is need for more flexibility, the regulated self-governance paradigm endorsed by the proceedings laid down by paras 217 ss of the *Insolvenzordnung* is also employed to liquidate the debtor's assets. So see Reinhard Bork, *Einführung in das Insolvenzrecht* (10th edn, Mohr Siebeck 2021) 212, para 367.

structure, which aims to delineate the debtor's assets, to collect the creditors' claims, to arrange for the debtor's assets to be sold, and to distribute the sale proceeds between the creditors who have lodged their claims in the proceedings.

In principle, insolvency laws only regulate the procedural aspects of liquidation proceedings. By contrast, the substantive law aspects of these proceedings are regulated by other branches of law to which insolvency laws, explicitly or (more often) implicitly, refer.[31] For example, the IP who intends to delineate the debtor's assets must refer to property law and contract law; the IP who intends to collect the claims lodged by the debtor's creditors must verify them in accordance with contract law and, when these claims are secured, also with the relevant security right law. However, sometimes, insolvency laws regulate both the procedural and substantive aspects of the issues. For example, this happens in connection with the so-called executory contracts, that is those contracts concluded by the debtor before the date of the opening of insolvency proceedings which, after this date, are still pending. **1.29**

As a general rule, legal frameworks lay down that IPs must liquidate the debtor's assets in a way that best satisfies the creditors' interests. Therefore, jurisdictions usually lay down that the realization of the debtor's assets may be performed either by piecemeal sales or by one or more sales that tend to keep the value of the organization intact. **1.30**

Liquidation insolvency laws may be structured in various ways. Nevertheless, they always lay down a prohibition forbidding debtors to manage and dispose of their assets and a prohibition forbidding the debtors' creditors to foreclose on the debtors' assets. Moreover, these prohibitions may contain exceptions that vary from jurisdiction to jurisdiction. **1.31**

V. Rescue: Concept and Taxonomies

Scholars, courts, and practitioners have demonstrated that, to tackle a firm's distress, liquidation is not always the best solution. Indeed, they have proved that when a firm is potentially profitable, or (to express the same concept in a different way) when it has a going-concern value higher than its liquidation value, the best solution consists in rescue. This is because, when this situation occurs, rescue will make all the claimants, considered as a group, better off. **1.32**

This statement explains why rescue culture is increasingly more popular and why insolvency laws increasingly more often regulate restructuring rescue procedures or proceedings. Of course, systems vary to a great extent. Nevertheless, most jurisdictions tend to regulate two ways of rescue, which may be classified as (a) rescue by a firm sale and (b) rescue by firm reorganization. **1.33**

---

[31] Baird, *Elements* (n 6) 4, who states: '[b]ankruptcy law is built on nonbankrutpcy law'.

A. Rescue by a Firm Sale

1.34 The first rescue method consists in selling the firm as a going concern and paying the debtor's creditors through the sale proceeds. It goes without saying that this form of rescue salvages the firm but not the person or the company who/that owns it. This person, or this company will definitively lose the firm.

1.35 Theoretically, this sale operation could be performed either by opening liquidation proceedings and selling the firm as a going concern or by concluding a regular contract of sale outside an IL framework. However, both possibilities happen only rarely. The former is rare because liquidation proceedings destroy the firm's reputation; the latter is rare because selling a firm as a going concern may involve various parties who may behave in a non-cooperative manner. Indeed, sometimes the use of an IL framework is necessary even to 'persuade' debtors to sell their firms. This point will be expanded in the section devoted to the second task of IL, which deals with the possibility that debtors will propose plans which would ensure that they received more than expected under pre-insolvency priorities.

1.36 Many jurisdictions facilitate the rescue by a firm sale, thus regulating the so-called 'pre-packaged plans', which, in the United States, are better known as 'pre-packs'. For example, this is the case in US law, where 11 U.S.C. §1126(b) lays down that, under certain conditions, 'a holder of a claim or interest that has accepted or rejected the plan before the commencement of the case [...] is deemed to have accepted or rejected such plan'. Here, the sequence 'first, opening proceedings—then, looking for a potential buyer' is reversed in the sense that the debtor first looks for a potential buyer of the firm and then files for the opening of proceedings. These proceedings aim to impose the sale on a small group of dissenting, recalcitrant claimants.[32]

---

[32] Jeffrey Ferriel and Edward J. Janger, *Understanding Bankruptcy* (4th edn, Carolina Academic Press 2019) 748–9. Usually, English law literature uses the term 'pre-packs' as a shorthand for 'pre-packaged sales' (or 'pre-packaged administration', also known as 'business transfer scheme'), which, in the United States, are better known as 'sales under § 363 of the *Bankruptcy Code*'. For the English law expression, see Kristin van Zwieten, *Goode on Principles of Corporate Insolvency Law* (5th edn, Sweet & Maxwell 2019) 493 ss. However, these two forms of 'pre-pack' are operations of different kinds, even though both aim to quickly sell the firm as a going concern. In effect, while 'pre-packaged plans' aim to facilitate the confirmation of the plan for a sale that had already been arranged before the commencement of insolvency proceedings, 'pre-packaged sales' aim to skip IL measures by using the narrative that the value of the debtor's firm is declining. This explains why, on both sides of the Atlantic, 'pre-packaged sales' give rise to many concerns both about transparency and whether they are always in the best interest of creditors. For a better understanding of US and English law on 'pre-packaged sales', see, for US law, 11 U.S.C. §363; Ferriel and Janger, *Understanding Bankruptcy*, 775 ss, and Melissa B. Jacoby and Edward J. Janger, 'Ice Cube Bonds: Allocating the Price of Process in Chapter 11 Bankruptcy', Yale Law Journal, 123(4) (2014) 865 ss; for English law, The Administration (Restrictions on Disposal etc. to Connected Persons) Regulations 2021, SI 2021/427, <https://www.legislation.gov.uk/ukdsi/2021/9780348220421/contents> accessed 4 May 2021. These regulations, which were enacted on 29 March 2021 and entered into force on 30 April 2021, place restrictions on the disposal of a company's business or assets to a connected person during the first eight weeks of administration procedure and, especially, require an independent evaluator to estimate the operation. Moreover, as regards the general concerns that pre-packaged sales give rise to in England, see van Zwieten, *Principles* 493 ss, paras 11–38 ss.

B. Rescue by Firm Reorganization

The second method of rescue consists in reorganizing the firm. This is the most sophis-   **1.37**
ticated rescue method in that it salvages both the position of the debtor, as the firm's
owner, and the firm.

Rescue by means of a firm sale is not always feasible. Very often, people are unwilling   **1.38**
to buy a distressed firm, even though this is potentially profitable. Sometimes, this happens because no one trusts the firm's potentiality, especially when the potential buyer
is not someone involved in the firm's management. If this situation occurs, the potential buyer does not know the firm in depth and must only rely on the usual methods
for determining the firm's going-concern value. Though these methods are becoming
increasingly sophisticated, they are still mere speculations about the future. At other
times, the difficulty in selling a distressed firm that is potentially profitable depends on
the fact that it is not only distressed but also too big to be sold. For example, this happened in the United States in the nineteenth century when courts and practitioners
experienced difficulty in rescuing the US railways by firm sale and laid the basis for
modern reorganization law.[33]

The second method of rescue therefore consists in 'simulating' a sale where the   **1.39**
going-concern value of the firm is redistributed among the claimants through
a change in the company's financial structure.[34] The financial structure of the old
company will be changed and, usually, its name will be changed as well. By definition, the aggregate of the nominal values of the shares issued by the restructured
company will equal the going-concern value of the old company. By contrast, the
creditors of the old company will be paid either with the old company's cash; or by
the sale proceeds of some of the old company's assets; or by receiving bonds of the
new company; or by being transformed into shareholders of the new company (this
is the outcome of the so-called debt-equity swap) and, therefore, by receiving shares
of the new company; or—which happens more frequently—by a combination of two
or more of these methods.

Consider the following example, where, for the sake of simplicity, one assumes that   **1.40**
each share of the old company is worth one unit, each bond of the old company is worth
one unit, one share of the new company has the same value as one share of the old
company, and one bond of the new company has the same value as one bond of the old
company—they differ in the maturity date only. Company A (the *Oldco*) is distressed
but still potentially profitable. Company A has a financial structure that is arranged as
follows: creditors are entitled to 100, bondholders have bonds to the amount of 100,

---

[33] Skeel, *Debt's Dominion* (n 17) 48 ss.

[34] For this image, and more generally, for the conceptual shift from rescue by a firm sale to rescue by firm reorganization, see Walter J. Blum, 'The Law and Language of Corporate Reorganization' University of Chicago Law
Review, 17(4) (1949) 565 ss.

18   WHAT IS INSOLVENCY LAW?

shareholders have shares to the amount of 100. Nobody is willing to buy this company. However, since the going-concern value of Company A is 150, it starts restructuring, and the parties involved in the negotiation agree to change the financial structure of this Company A, which, from now on, will be called Company B (the *Newco*). In particular, they agree that the creditors will be paid 50% in cash, by using half of Company A's cash, and 50% by receiving 50 shares of Company B; bondholders of Company A will be paid 50% by receiving 50 shares of Company B and 50% by receiving bonds of Company B. Unlike the Company A bonds, which had a maturity date on 31 December 2024, the Company B bonds have a maturity date on 31 December 2029. The shareholders of Company A will still remain in the new financial structure, but they will have 50 shares only of Company B. This process of restructuration is depicted in Table 1.5, which compares and contrasts the financial structure of the same firm before and after reorganization (Company A v. Company B).

1.41   Sometimes, the distinction between the two methods of rescue is clear-cut. If a third party takes money out of his or her pockets to buy a firm, this is a case of rescue by a firm sale. By contrast, if there is no sale, and the claimants receive shares or bonds of the new company, this is a case of rescue by firm reorganization. However, sometimes, the distinction is blurred. For example, consider a case where a third party takes money out of his or her pocket to buy the bonds of a distressed company and then employs his or her position as claimant to negotiate with the debtor and the other creditors in order to arrange for the firm to be reorganized. This operation may be classified either as a complex firm sale or a firm reorganization that includes a sale. This classification will depend on the relevant legal framework; on the policy choices that this endorses in tax law and labour law; and, last but not least, on the preference of the parties, who, having considered all these elements, will opt for the arrangement that proves to be the most convenient for them.

Table 1.5 A reorganization through a change in the company's name and financial structure

Values and entitlements	Company A (*Oldco*)	Company B (*Newco*)
Company value/capital	100	150
Cash	100	50
Creditors	100	0
Bondholders	100 (maturity date: 31 December 2024)	50 (maturity date: 31 December 2029)
Shareholders	100	150

Source: author.

VI. Rescue: Devices

Sometimes, debtors who want to rescue their firms employ plain contracts. **1.42** Traditionally, these contracts are called 'contractual workouts' or simply 'workouts'. Usually, insolvency laws do not contain specific regulations on these contracts so that the claimants who want to rescue a firm by means of a contract must rely on the whole toolbox of contract law. Sometimes, however, insolvency laws do regulate specific aspects of workouts. For example, this happens when regulations lay down that if a debtor has tried to rescue his or her firm by means of a contract and when, later on, this attempt has proved to be unsuccessful and liquidation proceedings have been opened, the appointed IP cannot regard the workout concluded by the debtor and his creditor as a fraudulent device and, therefore, cannot challenge the transactions that have been performed in the execution of that workout.[35] Moreover, the same protection may be extended to financial contracts aiming to inject new resources into those firms in workouts.[36] Depending on the relevant jurisdiction, these regulations may also prevent these debtors from being charged with criminal offences because they have intentionally delayed the opening of liquidation proceedings or have engaged in similar behaviours.[37]

These regulations on specific aspects of workouts play a crucial role in rescuing busi- **1.43** nesses, because not only do they ensure that IL does not *ex post* disappoint the expectations of the people involved but also they *ex ante* encourage the debtors and the other parties potentially involved in a firm rescue to conclude workouts without the concern that if their attempt proves unsuccessful and liquidation proceedings are opened, their behaviours will be frustrated or even punished.

Contracts are champions of flexibility and are particularly appropriate in arranging be- **1.44** spoke solutions. Moreover, in the field of IL, the use of contracts has the advantage of allowing the distressed debtor to keep the firm secrets hidden from those who are not participating in the agreement—there is no need to involve either courts or those entities, such as small creditors, who will not be affected by the renegotiation. This explains the attractiveness of the 'London approach'. However, these contracts also have their limits, for which see para. 1.25 and the accompanying footnotes.

Lawmakers are aware of the fact that the use of contracts may produce holding- **1.45** up problems. This explains why, alternatively, jurisdictions include the regulated self-governance paradigm in other devices that combine the flexibility of contract with the authority of law and—this is the crucial point—lay down that, for decision-making, the principle of unanimous consent (which is typical of contracts) can be replaced by the principle of the consent of a majority of the parties involved in the operation. Consequently, more advanced rescue laws lay down that—under certain

---

[35] See, e.g. Art. 18 of the EU Directive 2019/1023.
[36] See, e.g. ibid Art. 17.
[37] See, e.g. Art. 324 of the Italian *Codice della crisi d'impresa e dell'insolvenza*.

20   WHAT IS INSOLVENCY LAW?

conditions—the decision taken by the majority in value of the claimants is binding for those claimants who, deliberately or not deliberately, have not participated in the negotiations and even for those who have voted against the rescue proposal. Of course, the exact way in which the majority principle is adopted may vary from one jurisdiction to another. For example, a lawmaker may require that this majority in value should be greater than the threshold of 50% plus one or that the majority in value of 50% plus one should be supplemented by a majority in number. For example, in England, s. 899 of the UK Companies Act 2006 lays down that a scheme of arrangement under Part 26 must be approved by 'a majority in number representing 75% in value of the creditors'.

1.46   This shift from the principle of unanimous consent to the majority principle must be legally justified.[38] In other fields of the law, the adoption of the majority principle is grounded on the fact that, before the process of decision-making begins, the parties have already unanimously agreed upon the fact that the will of the majority is binding on the minority. For example, this happens in company law, where those who participate in the formation of a company and, later on, those who become new shareholders in a company that has already been formed must individually agree that the general meeting will observe the majority principle. Of course, in IL, jurisdictions cannot require that the claimants who are involved in rescue procedures or proceedings should have previously accepted the majority principle. Therefore, in this case, jurisdictions justify the use of the majority principle by requiring a court to check the legitimacy and accountability of the process. Of course, the criteria adopted for this check vary from jurisdiction to jurisdiction; but, on the whole, one has the impression that the attention paid to procedural justice prevails over any concern about substantial justice and distributional fairness.[39]

1.47   The worldwide panorama is extremely variegated and, across the world, the names and contents of these instruments vary to a great extent. Nevertheless, scholars tend to group these instruments into two broad categories depending on the role that is played by the court applied to. In particular, scholars use expressions such as 'insolvency out-of-court procedures', 'insolvency plan procedures', or simply 'insolvency procedures' to denote those arrangements that are entirely negotiated and concluded out of court but that are subsequently submitted to a court for its approval—here, the court's approval is necessary for these arrangements to become binding also on dissenting claimants. The most popular examples of these arrangements are the English schemes of arrangement laid down by Parts 26 and 26A of the UK Companies Act 2006. By contrast, scholars use the phrases 'insolvency plan proceedings' or simply 'plan proceedings' to denote

---

[38] E.g. in political philosophy, this point is highlighted by Ernst Barker, *Reflections on Governments* (OUP 1948) 65, who states that the majority principle must be grounded on the unanimous prior acceptance of 'the decision of the greater number as the decision of all'.

[39] On this point, see also what will be said as regards the second task of IL. Moreover, as regards English law, see the analysis carried out by Sarah Paterson, 'Debt Restructuring and Notions of Fairness', Modern Law Review, 80(4) (2017) 600 ss. Here, the author demonstrates that, in English rescue law, the concerns about distributional fairness are very often based on vague or imprecise notions of fairness.

those arrangements made entirely before a court that has full control of the case and, within this process, impose them on dissenting creditors. The most prominent examples of these instruments are the proceedings laid down by Chapter 11 of the US Bankruptcy Code.

Very often, the adoption of the majority principle is combined with the possibility that those who drew up a plan may divide creditors into classes and put those with similar claims into the same class. In principle, the division into classes is based on a concept of equality of influence according to which, if claimants have heterogeneous interests, they ought to have a greater share in the control over decisions in which they are more interested than in the control over decisions in which they are less interested. This concept of majority-of-the-minority means that if a debtor is indebted to ten creditors, three of whom are the debtor's employees claiming for the payment of the salaries that have accrued in the last few months of work, the plan will better protect their interests by putting the three employee creditors in a separate class. For the practice of division into classes and the possible unintended consequences of this device, see paras 1.52–1.53. **1.48**

Depending on jurisdictions, the division into classes may be either optional or mandatory. If the division into classes is optional only, its adoption may also be the object of the negotiations. However, in most jurisdictions, the division into classes is mandatory. For example, Art. 9.4 of the recent EU Directive 2019/1023 lays down that '[a]s a minimum, creditors of secured and unsecured claims shall be treated in separate classes for the purposes of adopting a restructuring plan', while Art. 1 para. 9, of the German *Gesetz zur Fortentwicklung des Sanierungs- und Insolvenzrechts*, in transposing this point of the directive, lays down that the plan must treat as separate classes four categories of claimants: namely, secured creditors, unsecured creditors, creditors whose claims have been subordinated by law, and shareholders. **1.49**

Usually, plans must be approved consensually, in the sense that all the classes must approve them unanimously (it does not matter if, within each class, claimants have approved the treatment reserved to their own class by a majority decision). However, in its turn, a division into classes can give rise to another holding-up problem, since a single class may strategically delay or block the approval of the plan in order to obtain better treatment. For this reason, jurisdictions that provide for division into classes may equip their toolbox with another device, which is traditionally called 'cross-class cramdown' or simply 'cramdown'.[40] **1.50**

The term 'cramdown' expresses the idea that when this device is deployed, the plan is crammed down the claimants' throats. From a technical point of view, the introduction **1.51**

---

[40] In the past, a cramdown was always a cross-class cramdown. However, nowadays, the application of the majority principle within each class tends to be called 'cramdown' too so that one tends to distinguish between an 'intra-class cramdown' and a 'cross-class cramdown'. For example, Art. 11 of the EU Directive 2019/1023 is entitled 'Cross-class cram-down'. Nevertheless, for the purposes of this chapter, 'cramdown', without any other specification, will always mean 'cross-class cramdown'.

22   WHAT IS INSOLVENCY LAW?

of this device consists in a further shift from the principle of unanimous consent to the majority principle, which—this time—refers to classes instead of to individual claimants. Of course, this shift must, again, be justified through the intervention of a court, which must supervise the procedure and its 'fairness'. The most prominent example of cramdown is provided by 11 U.S.C. §1129(b)(1), which lays down that—under certain conditions—a plan may be confirmed despite the rejection of the plan by one or more classes and may be imposed on them coercively. The US example has influenced many rescue proceedings in both Asia and Europe. Moreover, the US cramdown has recently been inserted into the architecture of some out-of-court procedures, such as the reformed Singaporean schemes (s. 70.3 of the Singaporean Insolvency, Restructuring and Dissolution Act 2018) and the newly introduced English schemes regulated by Part 26A of the UK Companies Act 2006 (s. 901G of the UK Companies Act 2006).[41]

1.52   To complete this analysis of the first task of IL, something more should be said about the division of claimants into classes. As already mentioned, in principle, the division into classes is a device to give better protection to creditors. However, in practice, this is not always true, since a division into classes may be the object of manoeuvres aiming to facilitate a plan to be approved consensually or to be crammed down. In fact, even though insolvency laws usually specify under what conditions two claims must be regarded as similar, a division into classes may be manipulated: first, because the prescriptions that specify under what conditions two claims must be regarded as similar may be open-textured so that there might be room for creative interpretations; second, because, usually, these prescriptions do not prohibit the separation of similar claims into different classes in accordance with the old strategy of 'dividing and conquering' (*divide et impera*).

1.53   Regarding the division into classes, every jurisdiction has its own prescriptions and case law.[42] Nevertheless, from a functional point of view, it is worth noting that, as a general rule, differences in these manoeuvres depend on whether they are performed in procedures or proceedings that are not equipped with cramdown or in procedures or proceedings that are equipped with cramdown. In the former cases, these manoeuvres

---

[41] An analysis of law in action (instead of law in the book) demonstrates that a jurisdiction that does not adopt a cramdown may sometimes obtain a similar result by different routes. For instance, this is the case in England where lawyers have achieved a Chapter 11-style reorganization by means of a combination between the scheme of arrangements laid down by Part 26 of the Companies Act 2006 and a pre-packaged administration. On this point, see Sarah Paterson, 'Rethinking Corporate Bankruptcy Theory in the Twenty-First Century', Oxford Journal for Legal Studies, 36(4) (2015) 1 ss, at 13, and, more recently, Sarah Paterson, *Corporate Reorganization Law and Forces of Change* (OUP 2020) 232 ss. Here, she states: 'England has a range of tools which can be adapted to assist with a reorganization case: the scheme of arrangement; a company voluntary arrangement; administration; fixed charge receivership; and, where a relevant exception applies in the Enterprise Act 2002, administrative receivership.'

[42] E.g. as regards US Chapter 11 proceedings and UK Part 26 schemes of arrangements, see: Ferriel and Janger, *Understanding Bankruptcy* (n 32) 726–31 and Jennifer Payne, *Schemes of Arrangements. Theory, Structure and Operation* (2nd edn, CUP 2021) para. 2.3.2, respectively. On this point, Payne states:

> The general test to determine whether members or creditors should meet as a whole or as separate classes is relatively easily stated, although it has proved difficult to apply in practice. It is notable that this test does not appear in the statutory provisions regarding schemes, and has therefore been developed by the courts.

On this point, see also Payne in this volume, 3.27–3.33.

aim to make it easier for each class to approve the plan with the required majorities, while in the latter cases, manoeuvres may aim either to make it easier for each class to approve the plan with the required majorities or to make it possible for the court to which application has been made to cram down dissenting creditors.

VII. The Second Task of IL: Distributing the Debtor's Resources

The second task of IL consists in distributing the debtor's assets. In principle, in order to **1.54** perform this task, jurisdictions tend to rely on the priorities that they lay down outside insolvency proceedings (the so-called pre-insolvency priorities). In fact, if insolvency laws introduced an entirely new regime of distribution that could be more favourable for either the debtor or some categories of the debtor's creditors, or for both, these parties would have an incentive to ensure that insolvency procedures or proceedings were opened, even though these were not necessary.

However, the real world is neither black nor white but a shade of grey so that the ap- **1.55** plication of the above-mentioned assumption is no easy matter, especially in rescue proceedings. Indeed, the author who emphasized this assumption and elevated it to an uncontested axiom by stating that IL must never have redistributive effects produced a theory of IL that was regarded as ideological. This theory, its critics objected, aimed to disguise the inequality of society and legitimize the gap in power and affluence that existed between some better-positioned categories of creditors, such as banks, and other less fortunate categories of claimants, such as the workers in a firm.[43]

This statement explains why, to unveil the intricacies of distribution, it might be appro- **1.56** priate to proceed step by step and, especially, to distinguish between (a) liquidation and (b) rescue.

A. Liquidation

Liquidation proceedings are the most respectful of the assumption that IL should rely **1.57** on pre-insolvency entitlements and must observe the priorities that are in force outside insolvency proceedings. Of course, the ranking of priorities varies from jurisdiction to jurisdiction. These points will be dealt with in Chapter 5 'Security Rights and Creditors'

---

[43] The author who emphasized that IL must not modify pre-insolvency entitlements and priorities is Jackson. On this point, see Jackson, *The Logic* (n 8) chs 1 and 2 and at 16–17. Jackson's theory (which was better specified in many papers written by Jackson alone, or by Jackson and Douglas Baird, or by Jackson and Robert Scott) is labelled 'Creditors' bargain theory'. The term 'Creditors' bargain theory' is still present in US literature, even though this refers to different approaches to IL that do not have Jackson's implications. Jackson's and Baird's positions were especially criticized by Elisabeth Warren, 'Bankruptcy Policy', University of Chicago Law Review, 54(3) (1987) 775 ss and Elisabeth Warren, 'Bankruptcy Policymaking in an Imperfect World', Michigan Law Review, 92(2) (1993) 336 ss.

24 WHAT IS INSOLVENCY LAW?

Priority and Ranking: Realizable Priority in Rescue', Chapter 10 'Aspects of Tax Law', and Chapter 11 'Aspects of Labour Law', respectively.

1.58 Nevertheless, most insolvency laws tend to converge in many respects, and a tentative list of priorities that may hold true for many countries could be arranged as follows:

- preferential creditors,
- secured creditors,
- unsecured creditors,
- subordinated creditors,
- debtor/shareholders.

1.59 Basically, preferential creditors are those creditors who have a claim against the insolvency assets because they have provided a service or an item in favour of the administration of insolvency proceedings. The most important cases of preferential creditors are IPs, whose fees must be paid, and the parties to contracts concluded by IPs in favour of the insolvency administration—it does not matter if these contracts were originally signed by the debtor and, after the commencement of insolvency proceedings, were suspended by law and subsequently resumed by the IPs or if these contracts were first signed by the IPs.[44] Secured creditors are those creditors who have secured their claims by means of a security right *in rem* or a similar device.[45] Unsecured creditors are creditors who have trusted the debtor's integrity only and, therefore, cannot rely on a specific security right or interest encumbering the assets of the debtor or of a third party. Subordinated creditors are those creditors who, by law or because of a specific agreement concluded with the debtor, are ranked after the unsecured creditors.[46]

1.60 Finally, at the bottom of the list, there is the debtor, who is entitled to have what remains after all the other claimants have been paid in full. This situation, however, rarely happens in the real world, since the value of an insolvent debtor's assets is usually less than the value of his or her liabilities. Of course, when a debtor is a corporate entity, the company's shareholders have the position of residual claimants.

---

[44] In order to incentivize rescue, most jurisdictions lay down that when a rescue attempt has been unsuccessful and liquidation proceedings have been opened, those people who had financed the rescue plan must be treated in liquidation proceedings as preferential creditors. Indeed, US law even gives them the position of super-preferential creditors by ranking them above preferential creditors. This point will be dealt with in Chapter 5 'Security Rights and Creditors' Priority and Ranking: Realizable Priority in Rescue'.

[45] When a creditor is secured by a security right *in rem* or a similar device, this creditor is entitled to have 100% of the proceeds of the sale concerning that asset. However, at least in liquidation proceedings, this statement does not also imply that this creditor could have 100% of the face value of his or her claim. In fact, if the sale proceeds do not cover the face value of the claim, the creditor will retain 100% of the proceeds, while for that part of the claim which is not covered by the proceeds of the encumbered asset, they will be treated as an unsecured creditor and compete with the other unsecured creditors.

[46] Some jurisdictions, such as Germany, have mechanisms aiming to postpone by law the treatment of those shareholders who, when the fate of the company was uncertain, preferred to lend money to the company instead of making contributions to its share capital. When the company is subject to insolvency proceedings, these creditors are treated as subordinated claimants and are ranked after unsecured creditors. See para. 39(1), No. 5 *Insolvenzordnung*.

In liquidation proceedings, this list of priorities is always arranged as an 'absolute pri- **1.61**
ority rule' (APR) in the sense that, for a lower-ranked class of claimants to receive anything, the higher-ranked classes must first have been paid in full. Finally, every IL lays
down that when there are creditors who are equally ranked, these compete on a pro rata
basis, in accordance with the *pari passu* principle. This implies that if the sale proceeds
amount to 200 and there are only two ranks of creditors (namely, preferential creditors
who are owed 100 and unsecured creditors who are owed 400), the APR implies that
the proceeds will be allocated as follows: 100 to preferential creditors and 100 to unsecured creditors on a *pari passu* basis.

B. Rescue

The situation is quite different as regards rescue, whether performed by a firm sale or by **1.62**
firm reorganization. Here, insolvency laws struggle to achieve a difficult compromise
between the need to rely on pre-insolvency priorities and the need to change these in
order to incentivize the debtor and the debtor's creditors to negotiate and manage the
reorganization of the firm.

To understand this point, consider the following example, where, for the sake of sim- **1.63**
plicity, one assumes that Company A has a capital divided into 100 shares, the value
of each equalling one unit, and this company owes 100 to a secured creditor, whose
claim is covered by the value of the encumbered asset and 100 to an unsecured creditor.
Company A runs a potentially profitable business but is managed in an unsatisfactory
way. Therefore, while its liquidation value amounts to 100 (which equals the value of
the encumbered asset), its going-concern value amounts to 200—here, the difference
between liquidation value and going-concern value depends on the fact that if management is improved, the company is expected to become profitable again. In this case, it is
self-evident that rescue would be more appropriate than liquidation, since here, rescue
is expected to provide all the claimants, considered as a group, with more resources.
Moreover, since rescue keeps the firm productive, this operation will save jobs. This
situation is illustrated by a comparison between Table 1.6 and Table 1.7.

Table 1.6 A liquidation under an APR distribution

Liquidation		
Value of the firm	Claimants	APR distribution of the liquidation value
Liquidation value 100	Secured creditor 100	Secured creditor 100
	Unsecured creditor 100	Unsecured creditor 0
	Shareholders 100	Shareholders 0

Source: author.

26 WHAT IS INSOLVENCY LAW?

Table 1.7 A reorganization under an APR distribution

	Restructuring	
Value of the firm	Claimants	APR distribution of the going-concern value
Going-concern value 200	Secured creditor 100	Secured creditor 100
	Unsecured creditor 100	Unsecured creditor 100
	Shareholders 100	Shareholders 0

Source: author.

1.64 However, if it is expected that the APR will be applied thoroughly, there is the risk that neither the shareholders nor the secured creditor will have any incentive to negotiate. In fact, whether the company is liquidated or reorganized, the shareholders will receive nothing, while the secured creditor will receive 100; consequently, the debtor will remain apathetic, the secured creditor will prefer to individually foreclose on the debtor's assets, and the unsecured creditor might perhaps apply for liquidation proceedings in the hope that the application of transactions avoidance rules or similar devices may swell the insolvency assets.[47]

1.65 The existence of a lack of motivation is a crucial issue in rescue insolvency laws around the world. To solve this, jurisdictions tend either to incentivize claimants to negotiate around the APR or to replace the APR with a more relaxed rule of distribution. These policies work in very different ways, and both of them have their pros and cons. This point will be examined in sections VIII and IX, which compare and contrast the US approach, which incentivizes claimants to negotiate around the APR, with the recent EU approach, which lays down two alternative regimes of distribution, one of which replaces the APR with a more relaxed distributional rule.

VIII. Distributing within Reorganization: The US Approach

1.66 Basically, the US law in the book lays down the APR. Nevertheless, the US law in action demonstrates that cases where the APR is applied thoroughly are rare.[48]

---

[47] But a similarly unsuccessful scenario will occur if the relevant IL also allows creditors to propose the plan. This is because if an unsecured creditor proposes a plan, neither the debtor nor the secured creditor will agree to negotiate. The debtor will be reluctant to waste his or her time just to favour the unsecured creditors. By contrast, the secured creditor will prefer to foreclose on the encumbered assets or, if liquidation proceedings have been opened, to lodge his or her secured claim in these proceedings.

[48] Jonathan M. Seymour and Steven Schwarcz, 'Corporate Restructuring under Relative and Absolute Priority Default Rules: A Comparative Assessment', Illinois Law Review, 21(1) (2021) 3. On this point, see also Douglas B. Baird, *The Unwritten Law of Corporate Reorganizations* (CUP 2022) 108 ss and Stephen J. Lubben, *American Business Bankruptcy: A Primer* (Edward Elgar 2021) 139 ss.

The regulation laid down by Chapter 11 of the US Bankruptcy Code will be dealt with **1.67** in great detail in Chapter 4 'Formal Insolvency Proceedings'. Nevertheless, for a better understanding of the second task of IL, it can be anticipated concisely that this regulation allows a distressed debtor to propose a rescue plan; that this plan may divide claimants, including the debtor, into classes; that this plan must be approved by all the classes of claimants; and—this is the crucial point—that if the plan is rejected by one or more classes, a court can impose the plan on the dissenting classes, provided that

- the plan has been accepted by at least one class of claimants who have been impaired by the plan and do not belong to the category of shareholders or other insiders;[49]
- the plan is complaint with the APR;[50]
- the plan must satisfy the 'best-interest-of-creditors' test in the sense that the creditors impaired by this plan must receive at least as much as they would receive through liquidation proceedings;
- the plan does not unfairly discriminate between creditors, either by putting non-similar creditors into the same class or by treating creditors of the same class differently.[51]

This is the law in the book. However, in practice, the parties involved regard confirm- **1.68** ation through cramdown as a threat: first, because the application of the APR reduces the advantages for lower ranked claimants; second, because the process of confirmation through cramdown is lengthy, expensive, and uncertain—no one can be sure that the court will approve the going-concern value of the company that was at the basis of the plan.[52] Therefore, the parties prefer to avoid this scenario and search for an equilibrium where all the classes vote in favour of the plan. From a game theory point of view, the Chapter 11 policy may be described as a strategy that forces the debtor and its creditors to play a 'bargaining game'. Consider the example that was described in section VII. Here, the parties will prefer to reach an agreement that satisfies the rules of the game and avoids a cramdown scenario. For example, they might agree that the secured creditor will have 100, the unsecured creditor will have 50, and the shareholders will have 50. This game is depicted in Table 1.8.

Moreover, US law lays down two important exceptions to the APR. These are the new **1.69** value exception, according to which the plan may allow distributions to shareholders as long as they provide the company with new resources of (at least) the same amount;[53] and the small business reorganization exception, according to which the plan may allow distributions to shareholders of a small company on condition that the debtor

---

[49] See 11 U.S.C. §1129(a)(10).
[50] See ibid §1129(b)(1). For such a purpose, this uses the expression 'fair and equitable'.
[51] See ibid §1129(b)(1).
[52] Kenneth Ayotte and Edward R. Morrison, 'Valuation Disputes in Corporate Bankruptcy', Pennsylvania Law Review, 166(7) (2018) 1819 ss.
[53] For this case-law exception, see Ferriel and Janger, *Understanding Bankruptcy* (n 32) 770 ss.

28   WHAT IS INSOLVENCY LAW?

Table 1.8 A reorganization under US law

US reorganization law			
Value of the firm	Claimants	Threat	Outcome
		If there is no agreement, the court will cram down the plan and shareholders will have nothing	Negotiations to avoid cramdown and distribute the firm's going-concern value equitably
Going-concern value 200	Secured creditor 100		Secured creditor 100
	Unsecured creditor 100		Unsecured creditor 50
	Shareholders 100		Shareholder 50

Source: author.

company will distribute all of its projected disposable income over at least three years and no more than five from the date when the first payment is due under the plan.[54]

1.70   The US approach has been criticized in many respects, and in 2014, a proposal for a better regulation was put forward by the American Bankruptcy Institute (ABI). This is still pending.[55] Nevertheless, in practice, this system works quite smoothly.[56] This explains why the US approach has influenced most jurisdictions. For example, China has adopted it,[57] as well as many European States, such as Germany, Italy, Spain, etc. However, the situation in Europe is changing. This statement will be expanded in section IX.

IX. Distributing within Reorganization: The EU Approach and Its Transposition into German Law

1.71   On 20 June 2020, the European Union enacted EU Directive 2019/1023 on early restructuring, which must be transposed by Member States by 17 July 2021. This instrument is a directive; therefore, it 'shall be binding, as to the result to be achieved, upon each Member State to which it is addressed, but shall leave to the national authorities the choice of form and methods' (Art. 288 of the Treaty on the Functioning of the European Union (TFEU)). In particular, as regards distribution, Art. 11 of the EU

---

[54] See 11 U.S.C. §1191. This exception was introduced by the US Small Business Reorganization Act 2019, which added to 11 U.S.C. §§1181–95 in order to facilitate small and medium-sized business reorganization.

[55] See American Bankruptcy Institute, 'Commission to Study the Reform of Chapter 11: 2012–2014 Final Report and Recommendations' (2014) <https://abiworld.app.box.com/s/vvircv5xv83aavl4dp4h> accessed 4 May 2021. This also included some proposals to facilitate the reorganization of small businesses (ch. VII).

[56] Seymour and Schwarcz, 'Corporate Restructuring' (n 48) 8 ss.

[57] Zinian Zhang, *Corporate Reorganisations in China. An Empirical Analysis* (CUP 2018) 12 ss.

Directive 2019/1023 obliges Member States to adopt either an US-style APR regime; or a totally new (not just for European countries) regime, which is based on a relative priority rule (RPR); or a regime which combines the APR with the RPR. The RPR implies that, for a lower-ranked class of claimants to receive anything, the more highly ranked classes must be paid more favourably, but—this is the difference from the APR—not necessarily in full (Art. 11(1)(c) of the EU Directive 2019/1023).[58]

The introduction of the RPR is a watershed for reorganization law in Europe. Moreover, **1.72** even though each Member State has a free choice in choosing the regime that it considers most suitable for its jurisdiction, the arrangement of Art. 11 makes it clear that the RPR regime must be regarded as the regime preferred by the European Union (EU).[59] EU Directive 2019/1023 is examined in Chapter 4 'Formal Insolvency Proceedings', where the European RPR regime is analysed in depth. Nevertheless, for a better understanding of the second task of IL, it can be stated concisely that if a Member State adopts the RPR, a distressed debtor may propose a rescue plan; that this plan may, and in some cases must, divide claimants, including the debtor, into classes; and that this plan must be approved by all the classes of claimants, but, if the plan is rejected by one or more classes, a court can impose the plan on the dissenting classes, provided that

- the plan is accepted by 'a majority of the voting classes of affected parties, provided that at least one of those classes is a secured creditors class or is senior to the ordinary unsecured creditors class';[60]
- the plan must satisfy the 'best-interest-of-creditors' test in the sense that the creditors impaired by this plan must receive at least what they would receive through liquidation proceedings or other available alternatives;[61]
- the plan is complaint with the RPR, and no class will receive or keep under this plan more than the full amount of its claims or interests;[62]
- the plan does not unfairly discriminate between creditors, either by putting non-similar creditors into the same class or by treating creditors of the same class differently.[63]

---

[58] The term 'relative priority rule' (RPR) is also employed in the United States but with different meanings. For one of these, see, e.g. Douglas G. Baird, 'Priority Matters: Absolute Priority, Relative Priority, and the Costs of Bankruptcy', Pennsylvania Law Review (2017) 785 ss. By contrast, for the meaning in the EU Directive 2019/1023, see Lorenzo Stanghellini, Rizwaan J. Mokal, Christoph Paulus, and Ignatio Tirado, *Best Practices in European Restructuring* (Wolters Kluwer 2018).

[59] Compare Art. 11(1) with Art. 11(2) of the EU Directive 2019/1023, and see its Recital 55.

[60] See Art. 11(1)(b)(i) of the EU Directive 2019/1023. Moreover, this article states that when this prerequisite fails, the plan must be approved by

at least one of the voting classes of affected parties or where so provided under national law, impaired parties, other than an equity-holders class or any other class which, upon a valuation of the debtor as a going concern, would not receive any payment or keep any interest, or, where so provided under national law, which could be reasonably presumed not to receive any payment or keep any interest, if the normal ranking of liquidation priorities were applied under national law.

(Art. 11(1)(b)(ii) of the EU Directive 2019/1023)

[61] See Art. 11(1)(a), which refers to Art. 10(2) of the EU Directive 2019/1023. See also Recital 52.

[62] See ibid Art. 11(1)(c) and (d).

[63] See ibid Art. 11(1)(a), which refers to Art. 10(2) of the EU Directive 2019/1023.

30 WHAT IS INSOLVENCY LAW?

1.73 Unlike the US law in the book, the RPR European regime facilitates rescues, since distressed debtors and other claimants may have more incentives to reorganize distressed firms. However, since the RPR European regime gives the debtor much discretionary power, this regime may also induce the debtor to act opportunistically and transform a bargaining game into a chicken game. For example, consider again the above-mentioned hypothetical. Here, the debtor might even propose a plan according to which the debtor does not make any sacrifice in reorganizing its firm since the firm's whole going-concern value is divided between the shareholders and the secured creditor, while the unsecured creditor is squeezed out. Presumably, in this case, the unsecured creditor will vote against the plan. However, since the plan is compliant with cramdown rules, and the unsecured creditor would receive nothing under liquidation proceedings or other feasible alternatives, the debtor will be able to have the plan imposed on the unsecured creditor in accordance with Art. 11 of the EU Directive 2019/1023. The final outcome of the process is depicted in Table 1.9.

1.74 On 22 December 2020, Germany transposed the EU Directive 2019/1023 by a new law instrument, which, with some exceptions that are irrelevant to the topic at issue, entered into force on 1 January 2021. This law is called 'Act for further development of both restructuring law and insolvency law' (*Gesetz zur Fortentwicklung des Sanierungs- und Insolvenzrechts*) and is officially abbreviated to '*Sanierungs- und Insolvenzrechtsfor tentwicklungsgesetz*' or simply '*SanInsFoG*'. The central part of the '*SanInsFoG*' contains the 'Act on the Stabilisation and Restructuring Framework for Businesses' (*Gesetz über den Stabilisierungs- und Restrukturierungsrahmen für Unternehmen*', which is officially abbreviated to '*Unternehmensstabilisierungs- und Restrukturierungsgesetz*' or simply 'StaRUG'. The StaRUG introduced a new type of proceedings that is called 'Plan proceedings of restructuration' (*Restrukturierungsplan—Verfahren*), which aim to achieve

Table 1.9 A reorganization under EU law

EU reorganization law			
Value of the firm	Claimants	Incentive	Outcome
		Since the EU Directive allows the debtor to adopt the RPR, the debtor could try to have a greater slice of the pie	Privatization of the distress and transformation of the bargaining game into a chicken game
Going-concern value 200	Secured creditor 100		Secured creditor 100
	Unsecured creditor 100		Unsecured creditor 0
	Shareholders 100		Shareholders 100

Source: author.

the EU Directive goals. In this chapter, it is not possible or appropriate to examine in depth the new German instrument. However, to further develop this examination of the second task of IL, it can be stated briefly that, as a general rule, the new German regulation adopts the APR but that this instrument exceptionally allows a debtor to deviate from it in two alternative cases, which are regulated by § 28(2)(2) and 28(2)(1) StaRUG.

In particular, § 28(2.2) StaRUG lays down that a plan may deviate from the APR if **1.75**

- the plan affects the creditors' claims only to a limited extent, which, for example, may occur when the plan does not establish 'haircuts' or when the date on which the claims fall due is delayed for a period of time, which must be no longer than 18 months.

On the other hand, § 28(2.1) StaRUG lays down that a plan may deviate from the APR if **1.76**

- the debtor, or the people connected with the debtor, play an essential role in the firm's reorganization and
- the plan lays down that the debtor, or the people connected with the debtor, will offer the firm their cooperation in the reorganization and/or new values during a period of time that must not be longer than five years.[64]

The German StaRUG contains a compromise between the US-style regulation and the **1.77** EU-style RPR, including an expanded new-value exception. However, it is too early to evaluate this choice of policy. In particular, as regards the exception laid down by § 28(2.1) StaRUG, one may wonder whether a contribution, whatever type and size it is, to the reorganization allows the debtor to deviate from the APR or whether there should be a proportion between the debtor's contribution (or the contribution of the people connected with the debtor) and the sacrifice imposed on some of the creditors. Certainly, the difference between the two options may change the dynamic of the proceedings considerably. From a game theory point of view, if the first alternative is adopted, this regulation will be able to trigger a chicken game where debtors try to exploit the situation, while if the second alternative prevails, the debtors and their creditors will be forced to negotiate about the extent of their respective contributions or sacrifices in order to find an equilibrium that would prove to be satisfactory for both sides in the negotiation.

---

[64] In addition, § 28(1) StaRUG lays down that a plan may establish that a creditor who should be treated like other creditors of the same class may be treated better, provided that this different treatment is appropriate for the success of the reorganization. However, § 28(1) regards this better treatment as inappropriate by definition when the relevant class possesses more than half of the voting rights.

2

Distress, Insolvency, and the Likelihood of Insolvency

Shuguang Li

I. Introduction and Basics

2.01 Enterprises may be in distress during their operations. There are many reasons for the distress, such as uncompetitive products or services, high costs, poor management, improper decision-making, marketing failure, poor asset quality, debts provided by external guarantees, external environment deterioration, the impact of the economic cycle, etc. The distress can be divided into financial distress and business distress. Some companies are in financial distress and do not have enough cash flow to fulfil their debts. In severe cases, they are even overindebted. Some companies are facing business distress, whose income is not enough to cover costs, with operating losses and poor economic efficiency. And financial distress may also exist at the same time. However, some companies have the ability to repay their debts even though they are caught in business distress, without financial distress, causing no harm to creditors, and their problems are confined to the enterprise and not directly involved in legal issues. Business distress tends to lead to financial distress. But financial distress is not always caused by business distress. The distinction between them is of great significance in determining the solution. Financial distress leads to the loss of creditors' interests, and its impact affects the outside of the company, which will trigger a series of legal issues that threaten the survival of the company. Measures must be taken to solve it as a priority problem, otherwise the enterprise may withdraw from the market. Therefore, the need for legal intervention in financial distress is even stronger.

2.02 Consumers may also fall into personal financial difficulties for various reasons. For individuals, financial distress is not always caused by excessive debt. Even if someone does not have any debt, they can fall into financial distress just because of poverty. From a subjective point of view, two people with the same assets and debts may experience different levels of distress.[1] Therefore, consumers and enterprises in difficult situations face multiple solutions and legal methods, and it is not always necessary to go into insolvency procedure. And the criteria about whether they can start the insolvency

---

[1] Stephen J. Ware, 'Debt, Poverty, and Personal Financial Distress', American Bankruptcy Law Journal, 89 (2015) 495–507.

Shuguang Li, *Distress, Insolvency, and the Likelihood of Insolvency* In: *The Anatomy of Corporate Insolvency Law.*
Edited by: Reinhard Bork and Renato Mangano, Oxford University Press. © Shuguang Li 2024.
DOI: 10.1093/oso/9780198852094.003.0002

procedure are relatively strict. Because of the complexity of the insolvency procedure of enterprises, this chapter is mainly devoted to business insolvency law.

The typical manifestation of financial distress is the inability to pay off debts. For **2.03** an enterprise, if it is unable to pay off its debts due to pure lack of liquidity, without overindebtedness, it can be called technical inability to pay. However, when the liquidity is seriously inadequate, it may reach the bankruptcy standard. When the enterprise is overindebted, it is called inability to pay in the sense of insolvency. This distinction does not necessarily conform to the provisions of the insolvency laws of various countries on the cause of insolvency.[2] However, it still has a certain explanatory effect in reality because, judging from the insolvency cases, most of the enterprises in insolvency proceedings have reached the state of overindebtedness. Technical inability to pay only indicates that the company is unable to fully meet the repayment requirement of the due debt. This is an obvious signal of liquidity problems. It may be temporary, but it does not rule out the possibility of insolvency. Overindebtedness is closely related to insolvency, leading to a higher insolvency risk. In the modern economy, more causes for bankruptcy are based on liquidity. Some enterprises have more assets than liabilities, but they cannot be realized or sold off immediately, leading to a situation of insufficient cash flow. As a result, they fall into bankruptcy. For financial companies, there is also a capital adequacy ratio standard. And they will fall into bankruptcy when the ratio is insufficient. In addition, if an enterprise provides guarantees to others without restraint, and the guaranteed person gets into trouble, the company is likely to fall into distress, even into bankruptcy, because of the guarantee responsibility.

The relationship between a creditor's rights and debts is based on enterprise credit, **2.04** which is uncertain. The security right can only improve the possibility of debt performance to a certain extent without complete guarantee. The debt performance still mainly depends on the debtor's credit. When the debtor loses its ability to pay due to overindebtedness or lack of liquidity, it is of great importance to the society to decide how to deal with the relationship between creditor's rights and debts and how to distribute the debtor's limited assets. The insolvency law is emerging to solve this problem. When the debtor is unable to pay off the due debts, there is a cause for insolvency. The debtor who meets certain conditions can enter the insolvency procedure and can solve the problem of abnormal creditor's rights and debts with inability to pay through a strict, scientific, efficient, and standardized procedure. A debtor in a less bad situation can choose to negotiate a settlement or out-of-court reorganization with the creditor to get out of the distress. Eligible debtors can apply for insolvency for protection and exemption, and creditors can also apply for insolvency of the debtor to fairly distribute the debtor's property or promote its recover. In addition, the debtor can also choose

---

[2] For instance, according to §§ 2 and 7 of the Enterprise Bankruptcy Law of the People's Republic of China (PRC), where an enterprise fails to clear off its debt as due, and if its assets are not enough to pay off all the debts or if it is obviously incapable of clearing off its debts, it may file an application for insolvency. German's insolvency law provides inability to pay, likely inability to pay, and overindebtedness as the causes of insolvency. In Japan, when an enterprise fails to pay due debts or is overindebted, it can enter the insolvency proceedings.

34 DISTRESS, INSOLVENCY, AND THE LIKELIHOOD OF INSOLVENCY

pre-packaged reorganization, combining the advantages of both out-of-court and in-court procedures.[3] It involves the issue of the cause of insolvency when referring to the conditions the debtor has to meet to start the insolvency procedure and the evidences needed to be provided before applying for insolvency of the debtor. The cause of insolvency is the threshold for the debtor to enter the insolvency liquidation process. The main condition is that the debtor's inability to pay and the likely inability to pay, overindebtedness, and cessation of payments are auxiliary conditions. As for the reorganization procedure, because of its different goals from the liquidation procedure, corresponding entry thresholds should be set separately.[4] The above issues will be discussed in detail in this chapter.

II. Choice of Ways for Debtors to Get Over Distress

2.05 When the debtor is in distress, it is difficult to get rid of this through conventional means. So, the use of extraordinary measures is unavoidable, and its options are limited. The debtor may choose out-of-court reorganization, insolvency procedure, or the pre-packaged reorganization, etc. Out-of-court reorganization is characterized by no direct participation of the court, a high level of freedom, and usually one-to-many contracts (one debtor to many creditors). There are also other ways. Out-of-court reorganization has advantages such as high efficiency, low cost, flexible procedures, strong confidentiality, preservation of business operations, and benefit to stakeholders, making it the preferred self-rescue method for distressed companies when there are no other obstacles. The disadvantages include problems such as information asymmetry between creditors and the internal management of the enterprise, conflicts of interest between different creditors, clampdown by creditors, overcomplicated creditor's rights and debt relations, and insufficient binding force. Therefore, it may be difficult to achieve the expected goals.

2.06 Because of the inherent costs to society of the failure of business enterprises, laws and procedures have been established (a) to protect the contractual rights of interested parties, (b) to orderly liquidate unproductive assets, and (c) when deemed desirable, to provide for a moratorium on certain claims to give the debtor time to become rehabilitated

---

[3] See Daniel J. Bussel and David A. Skeel, Jr, *Bankruptcy* (10th edn, Foundation Press 2015) 575–6: ' "Prepackaged bankruptcies" or "pre-packs" are Chapter 11 cases that are filed solely to implement an already fully negotiated restructuring contingent on confirmation of a reorganization plan.' See also 11 U.S.C. §§1126(b), 1125(g). In China, the Supreme People's Court issued the Minutes of the Countrywide Court Trial Work Conference in 2018, which raised the point that the establishment of a cohesive mechanism for out-of-court mergers and reorganizations and in-court bankruptcy procedures should be actively promoted, and the exploration and research on the pre-packaged reorganization system shall be strengthened. China is already establishing, and gradually exploring, the pre-packaged reorganization system.

[4] For instance, China's insolvency law provides special provisions for the cause of reorganization. Except for the inability to pay and overindebtedness or apparent inability to pay, if an enterprise is obviously likely to lose its ability to pay, it can go into the reorganization proceeding as well.

and to emerge from the process as a continuing entity.[5] A major goal of insolvency is to preserve value. It preserves economic value, even in liquidation. The collective approach to orderly liquidation of assets is more value-preserving than the often chaotic process of seizure and sale by a host of competing creditors. Besides, in some instances, the firm, although unable to meet current financial obligations, is still worthwhile as a continuing enterprise. Or at least, that prospect of profitable continuance is a question for exploration and litigation.[6] So the reorganization procedure is needed to preserve the 'going-concern' value of a continuing business, reflecting the simple economic fact that businesses, like people, are often worth more alive than dead. The insolvency system preserves social values as well. Insolvency liquidation is an orderly and efficient way to bury a failed business, while insolvency reorganization offers the hope of saving jobs and the communities that depend on them, as well as ameliorating the inevitable social pain of business failure.[7] The insolvency procedure provides a unified system for solving the problem of creditors' rights and debts in the market economy, but it is more than that. It is the constitution of the market economy.[8] Insolvency law and its system play an important role in the economy and society.

And the enterprises are not limited to the choice of in-court or out-of-court settlements when faced with difficulties. They can also choose the pre-packaged reorganization, which is an effective linkage mechanism between out-of-court reorganization and in-court insolvency procedures.[9] It combines the advantages of the two to save costs, improve reorganization efficiency and effectiveness, increase information disclosure, and combine corporate interests with social interests, etc. **2.07**

III. Conditions for a Distressed Debtor to Enter Insolvency Procedures

Once the insolvency process begins, it will have a significant impact on creditors, debtors, and debtor's employees, suppliers, consumers, and other stakeholders. Therefore, sufficient legitimate conditions must be met for the initiation of this process **2.08**

---

[5] Edward I. Altman, Edith Hotchkiss, and Wei Wang, *Corporate Financial Distress, Restructuring, and Bankruptcy: Analyze Leveraged Finance, Distressed Debt, and Bankruptcy* (4th edn, John Wiley & Sons 2019) 11.

[6] Mark J. Roe and Frederick Tung, *Bankruptcy and Corporate Reorganization: Legal and Financial Materials* (4th edn, Foundation Express 2016) 18.

[7] Elizabeth Warren, Jay Lawrence Westbrook, Katherine Porter, and John A.E. Pottow, *The Law of Debtors and Creditors: Text, Cases, and Problems* (7th edn, Wolters Kluwer Law & Business 2014) 7–8.

[8] See Shuguang Li, 'The Constitutional Value and the Market-Based Economic Value of the Bankruptcy Law', Journal of Peking University (Philosophy and Social Sciences), 56(01) (2019) 149–50. See Art. 1, s. 8 of the US Constitution. See also Charles A. Beard, *An Economic Interpretation of the Constitution of the United States* (The Free Press 1986).

[9] Pre-packaged reorganization was first established and developed in the United States. Many negotiating parties come to a deal before a bankruptcy petition is filed. The debtors arrive in bankruptcy with their plan already drafted, filing their disclosure statements the same day as their petitions, nonchalantly mentioning that the creditors already support the plan. These 'pre-packs' often sail quickly through the bankruptcy process (see Warren et al., *The Law of Debtors and Creditors* (n 7) 58–9).

36 DISTRESS, INSOLVENCY, AND THE LIKELIHOOD OF INSOLVENCY

in many countries. A few countries, such as the United States, do not provide the conditions for entering insolvency proceedings but block the abuse of insolvency during the subsequent proceedings. In the insolvency laws of most countries, the conditions for entering the insolvency proceedings refer to the legal facts with which the distressed debtor or qualified creditors can apply for insolvency, and the judges can allow them to do so. In a broad sense, insolvency conditions also include procedural requirements— the number of creditors. Here, they only refer to substantial insolvency conditions, that is the cause of insolvency. And it should be distinguished from the reason leading to insolvency. If the main cause of insolvency is the inability to pay, the reasons for the failure to pay off may include poor management, serious losses, guarantee responsibility, poverty, natural disasters and man-made disasters, etc. These specific facts will not be discussed in this chapter. Regardless of the specific reasons for the insolvency, nothing affects the judgement of whether the debtor can start insolvency proceedings. The conditions for a distressed debtor to enter the insolvency procedure are related to the interest relationship between the creditor and the debtor, the frequency of the bankruptcy procedure, and the choice of the way it exits the market. So, the conditions should be neither too strict nor too loose. Excessively strict conditions will discourage applicants and make it difficult to initiate insolvency procedures or maybe lead to delays, while unduly loose conditions may easily cause the insolvency procedures to be abused and harm the interests of creditors or debtors. The main purpose of setting such conditions is to promptly initiate the insolvency procedure when the debtor is in financial trouble, to avoid debt accumulation and asset idleness, and to reduce the debtor's moral hazard and creditor's losses in difficult situations. The conditions should be clear and definite and should have a certain degree of flexibility so that the courts and relevant parties can make accurate judgements and initiate insolvency proceedings conveniently and quickly. In view of the difference between the liquidation and reorganization procedure, the requirements for entering those two procedures are also different and should be discussed separately.[10] The causes of reorganization procedure tend to be more complicated than for the liquidation procedure.

A. General Conditions for a Distressed Debtor to Enter the Insolvency Liquidation Process

2.09   Generally speaking, compared with the reorganization procedure aimed at debtor saving and rebirth, the liquidation procedure, as the last hurdle for the debtor's enterprise to withdraw from the market, and as an important step for the debtor's personal exemption, often has a higher barrier to entry. Insolvency liquidation is a special method to solve the relationship between creditor's rights and debts, whose starting conditions are concentrated on the debtor's solvency. In general, when the debtor loses

---

[10] Some countries have no criterion of causes, while some have various criteria.

the ability to pay off the debt, it is necessary to initiate the insolvency proceedings. Whether the debtor has the ability to pay needs to be judged by the property status or the facts regarding debt performance. Various countries have different regulations on the access requirements for insolvency liquidation. Most countries adopt multiple standards. On the whole, the criteria for the debtor to start the liquidation process can be divided into four categories: inability to pay, likely inability to pay, overindebtedness, and cessation of payments. Among them, the overindebtedness is the core criterion for deciding whether the debtor can enter the insolvency liquidation and is the fundamental basis for the debtor to settle the creditor's rights and debts by liquidation. If a country adopts a single standard, the standard should simply be inability to pay. It is often difficult to judge whether a company or a person can repay the debt, and more specific and feasible judgement standards need to be introduced. The other three standards are used to specifically determine whether the insolvency conditions are met and play an auxiliary role. Generally, they are not regarded as independent standards. Countries adopting multiple standards will introduce one or more of the other three standards as a supplement in addition to the inability to pay. The debtor has a significantly better grasp of its own solvency than the creditor. So, when the creditor applies for the debtor's bankruptcy, he or she should approve it mainly through presumable facts. Different countries have different attitudes towards the conditions for debtors to file for insolvency. Some countries believe that debt repayment through insolvency procedures is not substantially different from individual repayment, so there is almost no requirement for the debtor to apply for insolvency, and there is no need to judge the debtor's solvency. This procedure is regarded as a debt settlement procedure that the debtor can choose, like in the United States. In other countries, in considerations of saving judicial resources and improving the efficiency of repayment, debtors who have not lost the ability to pay are not allowed to apply for insolvency, and they are even required to prove their inability to pay more adequately.

1. Core criterion: Inability to pay

Inability to pay means that the debtor is incapable of paying off its due debts. Property, **2.10** credit, capacity, or any other means cannot be used to pay off the debts. The inability to pay is roughly equivalent to the aforementioned financial distress. It is a continuous objective state of fact rather than a temporary capital turnover problem. And it is a generally accepted bankruptcy condition applicable to any debtor in various countries. There are three elements constituting the inability to pay: (a) the debtor has not paid off the debt. The debtor does not, and cannot, discharge the debt by any means, such as property, credit, services, etc. It is objectively unable to discharge the debt rather than the debtor's subjectively not wanting to pay off, mistakenly believing that it cannot be repaid or maliciously evading the debt; (b) What the debtor cannot pay off is the debt that is due, with the request by the creditor to settle and without reasonable dispute. The expected insolvency of unexpired debts will be discussed in section III.A.5 'Likely inability to pay'; (c) the debtor is in a continuous state of inability to pay. If the debtor is unable to pay off the debt on time just because of temporary cash-flow difficulties or

38   DISTRESS, INSOLVENCY, AND THE LIKELIHOOD OF INSOLVENCY

other reasons but can pay off the debt in instalments or postponed in the short term, it should not be judged with inability to pay leading to insolvency. However, if the debt cannot be paid off continuously for a long time, it will constitute the inability to pay. The length of time depends on the law or practice. For example, some countries provide that if the debtor fails to settle the debt within three months after the expiration of the debt performance period and the creditor calls, the debtor is deemed unable to pay.

2.11   From the perspective of economics, there are mainly three ways to determine the ability to pay of an enterprise and infer whether the enterprise will fall into insolvency.

a. Balance-sheet test

2.12   This test is based on the fact that if the debtor's balance sheet shows obvious insolvency, it indicates that it has fallen into the financial distress of inability to pay. It mainly focuses on the ratio of the assets to the liabilities of an enterprise, which is used to judge whether the enterprise is overindebted and thereby helps to judge the solvency of the enterprise and whether the enterprise may enter insolvency proceedings.[11] This test will be discussed in detail in the standard of overindebtedness below.

b. Cash-flow test

2.13   The cash-flow test focuses on whether the enterprise's own cash can pay off due debts. If not, then the enterprise is insolvent or the enterprise has cash-flow problems or liquidity problems. This test has increasingly become an important criterion for modern market economy to judge whether a debtor is solvent. For example, an enterprise has 10 million assets and 8 million liabilities. The assets are greater than the liabilities, but its liabilities are cash liabilities. The assets include plant, equipment, and warehouse inventory. Although the asset value is 10 million, its cash is 0 or only 3 million. At this time, even if its assets are greater than its liabilities, it may be insolvent. The cash-flow standard has increasingly become an important standard for judging whether a debtor has solvency, and it is also a standard increasingly adopted by modern society.[12]

c. Contingent liability test

2.14   The contingent liability test takes security as its core. It inspects whether an enterprise provides security for others or acts as a guarantor for other debtors. Such security may

---

[11]   According to §§ 2 and 7 of the Enterprise Bankruptcy Law of PRC, where an enterprise fails to clear off its debt as due, and if its assets are not enough to pay off all the debts or if it is obviously incapable of clearing off its debts, it may file an application for insolvency.

[12]   See ibid. Actually, there is another method to determine the solvency of enterprises, especially whenever these are banks, that is the Capital Adequacy Ratio, also known as capital-to-risk (weighted) assets ratio (CRAR). It measures the ratio of a bank's total capital to its risk-weighted assets. The capital adequacy ratio test focuses on whether the amount of capital held by an enterprise is too low compared to the business in which it is engaged. If the capital does not match the business in which the enterprise operates or if the capital is unsustainable, the enterprise is overindebted. Especially for banks and other financial institutions, capital adequacy ratio is the capital ratio that is necessary for normal operation and development. If the amount of capital held by a bank is too low compared to the business engaged in by the commercial bank (including the business that the management states has been engaged in and the business being engaged in), the capital would not match the business operated by the bank, and the solvency of the bank would be in question.

affect the future solvency of enterprises and cause them to be insolvent. Especially in China, unlike the mortgages and pledges that are popular in Europe and the United States, the guarantee is more common in China. Some listed companies have become guarantors for some enterprises with distressed debts.[13] In 2017, the International Monetary Fund (IMF) went to assess Chinese companies and invited some experts to exchange views. The experts were particularly concerned about the guaranteeing situation of Chinese companies. A company may have a good balance sheet and a good cash flow, but the solvency of the company may still be in question. The reason is that by guaranteeing companies that are about to go insolvent, their credit is tainted and affected. Now a lot of guarantees rely on the letter of guarantee issued by the bank. In fact, the guarantor does not have the ability to pay off the debt. Once the debt cannot be repaid, it will cause a chain reaction, especially affecting the paying ability of the guarantor.[14] So, the contingent liability can be the basis to judge whether the debtor has the ability to pay and whether it will be insolvent. Therefore, while examining a company's balance sheet and cash-flow statement, it is also necessary to investigate whether there is a problem with the guarantees provided by the company.

Inability to pay off the due debt is the basic condition of the debtor's insolvency, and it **2.15** is the most common cause of insolvency in the bankruptcy law of various countries. The World Bank guidelines in its *Principles for Effective Insolvency and Creditor/Debtor Regimes* states that the preferred condition for commencement of insolvency proceedings is that the debtor is unable to discharge its debts as they fall due.[15] For example, the 1986 UK Insolvency Act provides that a petition for insolvency can be accepted if the debtor appears to be unable to pay a debt, and it sets out the conditions for insolvency.[16] The first of these conditions is that a creditor has served a statutory demand on the company and the company is indebted to that creditor for more than £750 and has not paid the debt, provided security, or reached a reasonably satisfactory settlement with the creditor within three weeks thereafter. In contrast, it appears unlikely that several creditors with claims against the company of less than £750 would have joined together to serve a statutory debt collection letter. The specific criteria can be seen in two cases. *Re London and Paris Banking Corporation*[17] shows that failure to repay a debt means

---

[13] According to § 681 of the Civil Code of the PRC, 'Contract of suretyship' means a contract by which a surety performs the obligation or assumes the responsibility under an agreement between the surety and the creditor in order to protect the realization of the obligation, in case the debtor fails to perform the obligation due or the circumstances agreed upon by the parties occur. And even if the suretyship is only in credit without any collateral, when the guarantee goes bankrupt, the surety will be influenced and also go bankrupt.

[14] For instance, Sichuan Topsoft Investment Co., Ltd fell into reorganization because of excessive guarantees. Founded in 1987, the company is mainly engaged in the computer software business. It was originally a listed company. However, in the few years after its listing, it made guarantee transactions aggressively and provided more than 100 guarantees within 4 years. As of 2003, the ratio of debt guarantees to the company's net assets has reached a record 78.79%. Solvency problems have been caused by a large number of high-frequency, huge-amount, and serious illegal guarantees. In 2017, because of the ceased operations for many years and its insufficient assets for paying off all its debts, TopSoft filed for reorganization to the Intermediate Court of Zigong, Sichuan Province. In 2019, the court approved the reorganization plan.

[15] The World Bank, *Principles for Effective Insolvency and Creditor/Debtor Regimes* (World Bank 2021).

[16] See ss 267 and 268 of the UK Insolvency Act 1986.

[17] (1874) LR 19 Eq 444.

40   DISTRESS, INSOLVENCY, AND THE LIKELIHOOD OF INSOLVENCY

refusal to repay without good reason. Therefore, refusal to repay with reason of substantive disputes over the debt shall not be grounds for issuing the liquidation order. *Re Tweeds Garages*[18] shows that where the fact of indebtedness is not in dispute but only the amount of the debt, if the amount of the undisputed debt exceeds £750, a statutory debt collection letter can be served in that amount. When there is real dispute over the issue of whether a company has a duty to pay its creditors, the court will usually reject the application, and the creditors will have to sue the company to discharge its debts and have established rights to apply for liquidation. In addition, s 123(1)(e) of the UK Insolvency Act provides that a company is found to be unable to pay if the court is satisfied that it cannot pay its debts as they fall due. This also provides an alternative to the statutory debt collection letter, but it does not apply to personal insolvency.[19] However, the *Re a Debtor* (No. 17 of 1966)[20] shows that the inability to pay is specifically applied to the debt currently due[21] (i.e. the inability to pay is only valid for the debt that has matured), and it cannot be used as a cause of insolvency for undue debts or for future contingent debts.

2.16   The US bankruptcy law is very lenient in voluntary filings, with almost no requirements. The debtor is not required to prove his or her incapacity to pay his or her debts or to take an oath to prove his or her financial condition, distress, or inherent need for relief. The debtor filing voluntarily need not be insolvent in either the bankruptcy or equity sense; the essential requirement is that the petitioner has debts. Petitions are often filed when a debtor is finally fed up with being hounded by creditors ranging from the anxious to the belligerent. When a corporation is insolvent, shareholder approval or authorization to the filing of a petition is, in some situations, unnecessary; the board of directors may have the power to initiate proceedings.[22] The petition is the basic request for bankruptcy relief and is signed by the debtor, on penalty of perjury, as certification that all the information contained in the filing is true. The completed petition and required fee are filed with the clerk of court and date-stamped with the minute, hour, and day of filing. In a voluntary case, this is the instant at which the bankruptcy estate is created and the automatic stay on all collection actions arises.[23]

2.17   The relatively minimal screening in voluntary cases comes not at the point of commencement but rather through the process of dismissal,[24] while the petitions for commencement are more closely scrutinized in involuntary cases, which are applied by creditors rather than debtors. § 3 of the American Bankruptcy Act of 1898 used to require creditors to prove that the debtor had an 'act of bankruptcy' within the previous four months in order to compel insolvency.[25] Act of bankruptcy includes fraudulent

---

[18]   [1962] Ch 406.

[19]   Fiona Tolmie, *Corporate and Personal Insolvency Law* (2nd edn, Cavendish Publishing 2003).

[20]   [1967] 1 All ER 668.

[21]   Tolmie, *Corporate and Personal Insolvency Law* (n 19).

[22]   Grant W. Newton, *Bankruptcy and Insolvency Accounting: Practice and Procedure (Volume One)* (7th edn, John Wiley & Sons 2010) 264.

[23]   Warren et al., *The Law of Debtors and Creditors* (n 7) 58–9.

[24]   Charles Jordan Tabb, *Law of Bankruptcy* (4th edn, West Academic Publishing 2016) 119.

[25]   See § 3 of the US Bankruptcy Act of 1898.

transfers, preferences, and self-liquidations for the benefit of specific creditors. In practice, however, it is very difficult for creditors to discover and prove that a debtor has engaged in 'act of bankruptcy'. So in 1978, when the US Code was reformed, Congress abolished this system and, instead, established two new conditions for involuntary bankruptcy commencement in §303(h) (either one of which is sufficient): (a) the debtor's generally not paying its debts as they become due and (b) a custodian being appointed to take charge of all (or most) of the property of the debtor within 120 days before the date of filing of the petition. Theoretically, the overall unliquidated matured debt marks the emergence of this comprehensive financial distress, and the second condition (the appointment of a custodian) is actually a specific instance indicating that the first condition is likely to be satisfied. At one time, the 'equity insolvency' standard of the US bankruptcy law emphasized the debtor's paying ability, while the current code only requires an examination of whether the debtor has discharged the debt in fact. It can be seen that the US bankruptcy law also favours the short-term objective insolvency standard over the overindebtedness standard with uncertainty. Moreover, in the application of inability to pay, debts with 'real disputes' are excluded from maturity claims.

According to the definition in § 17(2), sentence 1 of the German Insolvency Statute, **2.18** a debtor is unable to pay if it is unable to meet its obligations for which payment is due.[26] The recognition of inability to pay is usually determined at the time of the ruling on the bankruptcy petition. According to Art. 3 of the 'Reorganization and Judicial Liquidation of Enterprises' of the French Commercial Code, the reason for the insolvency of an enterprise is the inability to pay its debts as they fall due with the assets at its disposal.[27] The essence of this provision is still 'inability to pay its debts as they fall due', except that it does not emphasize 'overindebtedness' but only 'inability to pay', even if the total assets of the enterprise are greater than the total liabilities but the available assets are unable to pay the debts as they fall due. In this case, the insolvency proceedings can still be initiated.

In addition, China's insolvency law also sets inability to pay as the primary and neces- **2.19** sary condition for liquidation proceedings. According to § 2 of Provisions (I) of the Supreme People's Court on Several Issues concerning the Application of the Enterprise Bankruptcy Law of the People's Republic of China (2011), when all of the following conditions are met, it should be determined that a debtor is unable to repay a due debt: (a) the debt relationship has been legally established, (b) the period for repayment of the debt has expired; and (c) the debtor has not fully repaid the debt.[28] The standard of inability to pay in China also requires that the creditor–debtor relationship is undisputed and the period of satisfaction has expired.

---

[26] See § 17(2) of the German Insolvency Statute (1994).
[27] See s. 3 of the French Commercial Code.
[28] Provisions (I) of the Supreme People's Court on Several Issues concerning the Application of the Enterprise Bankruptcy Law of PRC (2011) s 2, <https://www.pkulaw.com/en_law/c6775597d0864b2cbdfb.html> accessed 8 January 2024.

42 DISTRESS, INSOLVENCY, AND THE LIKELIHOOD OF INSOLVENCY

2. Likely inability to pay

2.20 In addition to inability to pay, likely inability to pay is also used in some countries as an auxiliary criterion to determine whether an enterprise can enter into insolvency liquidation proceedings. Among the inability-to-pay standards, the ones that cannot be repaid are the claims that have expired, while the likely-inability-to-pay standards include future claims. An enterprise may also be allowed to open insolvency proceedings if it is clear that it is insolvent with respect to claims that will become due in the future.

2.21 This standard is particularly widely applied in German insolvency law. German insolvency law treats inability to pay as a general cause for commencement of insolvency, which applies to all types of debtors. § 18 of the German Insolvency Statute also allows the debtor to file for insolvency on the basis of a failure to pay that may have to occur but has not yet occurred.[29] Its purpose is to provide the tool of insolvency law in advance, when insolvency itself has become clearly apparent. However, this criterion only applies in cases where the debtor, not the creditor, files for insolvency, in order to prevent creditors from abusing the insolvency application to pressurize the debtor in the pre-insolvency period.

2.22 According to § 18 (2) of the German Insolvency Act, the debtor shall be deemed to be faced with imminent insolvency if he or she is likely to be unable to meet his or her existing obligations to pay on the date of their maturity.[30] Accordingly, this includes not only debts that are not currently due but also debts that have not yet been established but whose emergence is foreseeable, for example wages. When making projections, the overall development of the debtor's financial situation is considered, and the available liquidity and expected income are compared with the debt expected to become due in an appropriate period of time, and it is examined whether the emergence of insolvency is more likely than its prevention.[31]

2.23 Because likely inability to pay is a judgement of whether a claim can be satisfied in the future, its judging standard is vague, uncertain, and difficult to prove. And this standard is often applied to voluntary filings. Inability to pay allows the debtor to file for insolvency earlier, when future financial distress is expected to be unavoidable, without further decaying an already unstable company or reducing the consortium.[32]

2.24 According to Art. 2 of China's Enterprise Bankruptcy Law, where an enterprise legal person fails to clear off its debt as due, and if its assets are not enough to pay off all the debts or if it is obviously incapable of clearing off its debts, its liquidation procedures may be initiated. In combination with the Provisions (I) of the Supreme People's Court on Several Issues concerning the Application of the Enterprise Bankruptcy Law of the

---

[29] See § 18 of the German Insolvency Statute (1994).

[30] ibid § 18(2).

[31] See Reinhard Bork, *Introduction to German Insolvency Law (6th ed.)*, trans. Wang Yanke (1st edn, Peking University Press 2014) 44–7.

[32] See Ulrich Foerste, *Insolvency Law of Germany*, trans. Zhang Yuhui (1st edn, China Legal Publishing House 2020) 71.

People's Republic of China, an enterprise is deemed to be eligible for liquidation under the following two circumstances: (a) it fails to clear off its debt as due, and its assets are not enough to pay off all the debts and (b) it fails to clear off its debt as due, and it is obviously incapable of clearing off its debts. China's insolvency law regards inability to pay as a necessary condition for entering liquidation, while insolvency and obvious lack of solvency (equivalent to likely inability to pay) are auxiliary criteria. One of the two is required to enter insolvency proceedings.

3. Auxiliary criterion: Overindebtedness

Overindebtedness, also known as debt overhang, means that the debtor's assets are insufficient to pay back the full amount of all its debts. According to this criterion, only property considerations are generally taken into account, while other aspects of the business such as credit and capacity are not, and outstanding debts are viewed as the liability. This may be a symptom of a cash-flow or liquidity shortfall, which may be viewed as a temporary, rather than a chronic, condition.[33] When a debtor is overindebted, it will not necessarily be in liquidation if it is able to repay its debts by borrowing or other means. On the contrary, even if the debtor's assets exceed its liabilities, it may be difficult to turn around most of its assets into cash, and then it may fall into inability to pay off due debts due to a lack of liquidity. It can be seen that overindebtedness is not the same as inability to pay, and there is no necessary causal relationship between them. But the two are intertwined and closely related. In reality, it is common for overindebted debtors to be unable to pay off their debts. As a result, overindebtedness is generally not considered as an independent cause of insolvency but rather as an auxiliary criterion to determine whether a debtor may be subject to insolvency proceedings. And, generally speaking, an overindebted debtor may face inability to pay. Overindebtedness is generally used in the context of a capital joint venture rather than a human joint venture or a natural person because of the limited liability of a capital joint venture, which may jeopardize the interests of creditors in the event of overindebtedness. **2.25**

The balance-sheet test is commonly used in economics to determine whether an enterprise is overindebted. If the estimated assets of an enterprise exceed its estimated liabilities, it can be concluded that the enterprise is overindebted. This assumes that both the asset and liability values in the balance sheet are reasonably accurately estimated. For example, if an enterprise has assets of $100 million and liabilities of $50 million, then the gearing ratio is 50%, and the assets are greater than the liabilities, so it can be said that the leverage ratio is 50%, and the company is healthy and positive. Internationally, it is considered that when the leverage ratio is 60%, the enterprise has no problem. When an enterprise has assets of $100 million and liabilities of $120 million, the gearing ratio is 120%, and the enterprise is overindebted. **2.26**

---

[33] Altman, Hotchkiss, and Wang, *Corporate Financial Distress* (n 5) 7.

44 DISTRESS, INSOLVENCY, AND THE LIKELIHOOD OF INSOLVENCY

2.27 However, there is a difficulty with the application of the balance-sheet test. Some insolvency cases are obvious, others not. The key lies in how to value the assets, which depends on how the evaluation agency and the court confirm the valuation. The valuation methods are different when the company is in a healthy operating state and when it is on the verge of insolvency; namely, the way to valuate is different when the business continues to operate or is about to go into liquidation. The typical approach is to determine whether the debtor is, in fact, a going concern or 'dying' at the relevant date, and then to value the assets accordingly.[34] If the business has lost the possibility of continuing to operate and can only sell its assets to pay off its debts, the property should be valued at liquidation value, which may be lower than the value recorded on the balance sheet. And it will qualify for insolvency if it is overindebted at that valuation. If the business can continue to operate, it should be valued at going-concern value, which is often higher than the liquidation value. In practice, it would be unfair to drive a viable business out of the market.

2.28 German insolvency law applies the overindebtedness criterion to legal persons and to human joint ventures where no natural person is personally liable, for example limited liability companies and limited partnership. And insolvency proceedings of these entities may be commenced on the basis of overindebtedness. According to the definition of § 19(2) of the German Insolvency Statute, first sentence, 'Overindebtedness exists if the debtor's assets no longer cover existing obligations to pay, unless it is highly likely, considering the circumstances, that the enterprise will continue to exist.'[35] However, this cause of insolvency does not apply to natural persons and, in principle, to human joint ventures in general. This is because such enterprises benefit, to a considerable extent, from the personal capacity of the operator, which is almost impossible to value. The real 'capital' in this case is the operator's business capacity, which cannot be included in the property settlement. And it would be unfair to use liquidated overindebtedness as a cause of commencement of insolvency proceedings. An investigation into overindebtedness requires an overindebtedness settlement, that is a comparison of assets and liabilities. To do this, the subject matter of the asset property that should be included needs to be valued at the liquidation value, that is the value obtained by separately realizing the individual subject matter in the process of breaking down the enterprise. If an estimated overindebtedness is concluded on this basis, a further projection of going concern is made in accordance with § 19(2) of the German insolvency law, first sentence.[36] This projection involves an investigation into whether the going concern is more likely, which entails ascertaining the debtor's willingness to continue and the viability of the business in the medium-to-long term. If the investigation shows that it is difficult to continue the business, overindebtedness is confirmed; if to the contrary, the enterprise is not overindebted. However, for the majority of

---

[34] See J.B. Heaton, 'Debt and Insolvency', Review of Banking & Financial Law, 38 (2018) 373.
[35] See § 19(2) of the German Insolvency Statute (1994).
[36] See ibid s. 19(2).

enterprises in Germany, insolvency is usually filed on the grounds of inability to pay rather than overindebtedness. Inability to pay and overindebtedness often, but not necessarily, occur together. It is perfectly possible for a debtor who is not overindebted to be unable to pay. For example, when valuable assets become trapped, they cannot be used as proof of credit or sold. It is also perfectly possible for a debtor who has the ability to pay to be overindebted. For example, an overindebted limited liability company can still obtain a loan. The latter example demonstrates precisely that overindebtedness, a cause of insolvency, often brings forward the moment of insolvency.[37]

According to Art. 16 of the Japan Bankruptcy Act, overindebtedness is recognized as **2.29** a cause of insolvency in addition to inability to pay. Overindebtedness in Japanese insolvency law refers to the condition in which a debtor is unable to pay its debts in full with its property.[38] In this case, assets do not include credit, labour, and skills, and debts includes outstanding debts, which is different from the maturity criterion for debts due to inability to pay. The overindebtedness criterion also applies only to capital joint ventures and not to human joint ventures, because the credit of a capital joint venture to its creditors is based solely on the company's property, and the the realization of debt payment is based solely on the company's property.[39]

In the early days, countries looked primarily at the assets and liabilities of a debtor to **2.30** determine whether it was able to pay the debts. In modern times, however, it is not sufficient to look at assets and liabilities alone. This is because many debtors, such as commercial banks, now have fewer assets than liabilities, but it is still not possible to conclude that the business has no solvency based on that fact alone. Especially in the early stage of the emergence of some new industries, some enterprises may be willing to accept a lower profit or even operate at a loss in order to gain a higher market share in the fierce market competition, resulting in a high debt ratio, such as some bicycle-sharing enterprises in China, which have a high debt ratio but have a good cash flow, and thus there is no problem for their solvency.

It is not necessary for an overindebted debtor to commence insolvency proceedings, **2.31** nor is it necessary for a debtor to commence insolvency proceedings on the grounds of overindebtedness. In particular, a creditor filing for the insolvency of a debtor generally does not have to prove that the debtor is overindebted because creditors do not have control over the financial condition of the assets of the enterprise, while a debtor filing for insolvency may need to prove that it is overindebted. However, the fact that the solvency of an overindebted debtor is often in doubt can be used as an auxiliary criterion to determine the debtor's inability to pay. Some countries provide for overindebtedness as a cause of insolvency applicable to specific subjects or special circumstances. In addition, in order to protect the interests of creditors and prevent moral hazard such as

---

[37] See (German) Bork, *Introduction to German Insolvency Law* (n 31) 47–9.
[38] See s. 16 of the Japan Bankruptcy Act (2004).
[39] See ibid ss 15, 16.

46 DISTRESS, INSOLVENCY, AND THE LIKELIHOOD OF INSOLVENCY

concealment of property and preferences after the debtor has been overindebted, some countries and regions require that certain subjects (such as directors, supervisors, controlling shareholders, and beneficial owners of a company) have the obligation to file for insolvency in a timely manner when they are aware of the existence of overindebtedness and will bear the corresponding legal responsibility if they violate this obligation.

4. Auxiliary criterion: Cessation of payments

2.32 A cessation of payments is an act of representation by the debtor to the creditor that he or she cannot pay the debt in accordance with his or her subjective intention. First, a cessation of payments is an external act of non-payment of the debt by the debtor in accordance with his or her subjective intention and not necessarily an objective inability to pay the debt, which is the main difference between it and inability to pay. Second, the intention to cease making payments includes both explicit and implied forms. A debtor who explicitly states in writing or verbally that he or she will not pay his or her debts is certainly a cessation of payments, while avoidance, flight and hiding, closure of the enterprise, concealment of assets, etc. can also be considered as a cessation of payments. Third, the same as inability to pay, the object of a cessation of payments should also be due debts without legal disputes. The UNCITRAL *Legislative Guide on Insolvency Law* states that indicators of a debtor's general cessation of payments may include its failure to pay rent, taxes, salaries, employee benefits, trade accounts payable, and other essential business costs.[40] Finally, a cessation of payments should be of a continuing nature, not a temporary act, and should continue at least until the time of the court's verdict to allow entry into insolvency proceedings. This is because the cessation of payments may be a temporary problem with the debtor's solvency; the debtor may otherwise be sound, and it would be unreasonable to take such a debtor off the market. A cessation of payments occurs where there is the inability to pay, but the cessation may also not be due to inability to pay. Generally speaking, a cessation of payments, per se, cannot be an independent cause of insolvency, and whether there is a genuine inability to pay on the part of the debtor should also be examined. However, the inability to pay is often accompanied by a cessation of payments, which, in some countries, is presumed to be the inability to pay. Generally, the combination of a cessation of payments and overindebtedness to determine whether the debtor is unable to pay is highly persuasive. The determination that a debtor is in a state of inability to pay requires an extremely high degree of judgement, and in order to make this determination easy, Japan's insolvency law has designed presumption provisions. A cessation of payments is used as a condition for presumption of inability to pay, thus allowing insolvency. According to Art. 15(2) of the Japan Bankruptcy Act, when a debtor has suspended payments, the debtor shall be presumed to be unable to pay debts.[41] The explicit indication of the cessation of payments includes notice to creditors of inability to pay and a statement posted

---

[40] United Nations Commission on International Trade Law (UNCITRAL), *Legislative Guide on Insolvency Law* (UNCITRAL 2005) 46.

[41] See s. 15(2) of the Japan Bankruptcy Act.

on the shop front, etc., and the implied indication includes non-payment of bills due to insufficient funds in the bank account, closure of the shop, night flight, etc. It is generally difficult to prove inability to pay, so inability to pay is generally presumed from the cessation of payments, which is easier to be proved, based on the rule of thumb that if there is a cessation of payment, there is usually an inability to pay. The debtor, in turn, can rebut the presumption of inability to pay by adducing evidence to the contrary.

German insolvency law also provides for a presumption of overindebtedness from a **2.33** cessation of payments, which requires not only non-payment but also a condition of inability to pay that is already externally visible to the circle of persons and parties with whom the debtor interacts. At this point, the debtor itself has made it clear that it can no longer receive any help, and therefore inability to pay can be presumed from the cessation of payments.[42]

B. Conditions for the Debtor to Enter the Reorganization Process

Large enterprises are more willing to choose reorganization systems and procedures **2.34** in their insolvency for three reasons. First, large enterprises have many intangible assets that are difficult to value. It takes many years for the brand of a large company to be established, and the simple death of a company is devastating to the brand. Take the United Airlines' insolvency as an example: the aviation company has many operational values, including its flight safety, the speed of aircraft take-off and landing, its global customer network, marketing team, operation management team, trade secrets, and the provision of taxation and jobs. These are all difficult to value, so it is not possible to judge whether the company should go bankrupt and liquidate purely from the value of the company's assets or its liabilities. Second, if some operating elements, production elements, and service elements in an enterprise can be replaced with low-price elements, new value will be generated. The key is to decide whether the enterprise has operational value, that is to say, discover factors that may not have been noticed by the original operators and the original market conditions. At this time, it is generally necessary to bring in reorganization experts, such as the 'Chief Reorganization Officer' (CRO) system in the United States. He or she can quickly find out whether the company has reorganization value, mainly depending on whether there is operational value, and then change its management structure and the way of operation, reducing the cost of business operations. 'Lean management' is now very popular in Japan, which is actually reducing various costs of the enterprise. Through such methods, enterprises can obtain reorganization value. Third, large enterprises have huge social welfare, and their death (liquidation) will bring about market confidence problems, a large number of unemployment problems, etc., which will cause certain detriment to the public interest.

---

[42] See Bork, *Introduction to German Insolvency Law* (n 31) 44–7.

48 DISTRESS, INSOLVENCY, AND THE LIKELIHOOD OF INSOLVENCY

However, the objectives and procedures for reorganization is different from liquidation, and their access conditions are also different.

2.35 The US bankruptcy law has no substantial restrictions on the application conditions for reorganization, and the threshold is relatively low. As long as the debtor voluntarily makes an application, or the creditors who meet the requirements for the number and amount of claims apply, the reorganization procedure can start.[43] In order to prevent possible abuses of reorganization, the US bankruptcy law gives some control to the reorganization procedures by the principle of absolute priority and the principle of the best interests of creditors to achieve better reorganization results. Japan's bankruptcy law provides that the causes for the initiation of the civil rehabilitation procedure are (a) there is a fact constituting the grounds to commence bankruptcy proceedings or (b) the debtor is unable to pay debts that are due without causing significant hindrance to business continuation. Among them, (a) refers to the fact that there is a risk of inability to pay or insolvency and (b) refers to the fact that, with the bad turnover of capital if the debt is left to be paid off, it will lead to the inability to continue the operation.[44] In China, an enterprise can go into reorganization if it fails to clear off its debt as due and if its assets are not enough to pay off all the debts, or if it is obviously incapable of clearing off its debts, or there is a possibility of loosing the ability to pay. On the whole, reorganization has relatively low requirements for the inability to pay, but it has other requirements, such as the need for the enterprise to have reorganization value. In addition, China's bankruptcy law also provides the bankruptcy reconciliation procedure. Reconciliation can only be applied voluntarily by the debtor, and the conditions for entering the reconciliation procedure are the same as those of liquidation.

1. Basic conditions: On the verge of, or already in, financial distress

2.36 In principle, enterprises with cause of insolvency also meet the basic conditions for reorganization. The goal of reorganization is to restore the company's ability to repay debt, which is different from the goal of liquidation. In order to save the debtor in a timely and effective manner and make the reorganization more likely to be successful, it is not required that the enterprise has reached a full level of inability to pay, but it should be on the verge of, or have fallen into, financial distress to prevent the application for reorganization when the company is able to operate normally, harming the interests of creditors and wasting judicial resources. For instance, Japan's Company Reconstruction Law and Civil Rehabilitation Act provide consistent provisions on the reasons for reorganization; that is, the debtor may have cause of insolvency, or if the debtor pays off the debts that have expired, it may seriously affect the continuity of business. These two conditions are obviously looser than the conditions for applying for liquidation. And China's Enterprise Insolvency Law provides that, in addition to meeting the conditions of liquidation (unable to pay off due debts and assets are not

---

[43] See 11 U.S.C. §§301, 303.
[44] Kazuhiko Yamamoto, *Introduction to Insolvency Law*, trans. Chun Jin (4 edn, Law Press China 2016) 122.

sufficient to pay off all of the debts or obviously lack the ability to pay), if the company has the obvious possibility of inability to pay, it can also apply for the reorganization of the enterprise.[45] The reorganization conditions are also more relaxed than liquidation. The US insolvency law is more relaxed about the opening of reorganization proceedings. Insolvency is not a condition precedent to a voluntary Chapter 11 petition. If the Chapter 11 petition has been filed by an eligible debtor, no formal adjudication is necessary. And the requirements for an involuntary (i.e. creditor-initiated) Chapter 11 case are the same as the requirements for an involuntary Chapter 7 case in which the debtor should generally not be paying debts as they come due or the debtor's property is taken possession by a general receiver, etc.[46] Both the debtor and the creditor can apply for reorganization, but the specific criteria for applying for reorganization shall be different. If the debtor applies for reorganization, it shall be on the verge of, or have fallen into, financial distress; if the creditor applies for reorganization, it shall adopt the cessation of payments.

2. Additional condition: The reorganization value

The main purpose of filing Chapter 11 is to maximize the value of assets by utilizing the special powers of bankruptcy. This has generally been done through reorganization whereby the debtor's assets remain relatively intact and functioning following the bankruptcy, often under new ownership, but minus certain debt and other obligations.[47] In order to achieve the objectives of reorganization, additional conditions are required, primarily that the business should have reorganization value. The premise is that the firm may be worth more as a going concern than liquidated.[48] An enterprise is suitable for reorganization proceedings if it has the potential to be rescued and has reorganization value. And the reorganization value can be measured by the following three dimensions.

a. Whether there is an operating value

Operating value is the most common scenario where an enterprise has reorganization value. If the operating value of a troubled enterprise exceeds its liquidation value, and it has future profitability, then reorganization may be considered as a means of resolving financial distress. Whether an enterprise can continue to operate and whether it is worth saving is a matter of judgement based on a combination of internal and external circumstances. There are four specific criteria for determining whether an enterprise's reorganization value exceeds its liquidation value.

The first is the prospect of the industry in which the enterprise is located and the status of the enterprise in the industry. The 'Opinions on Several Issues Concerning the Correct Trial of Enterprise Insolvency Cases to Provide Judicial Guarantees for the Maintenance

2.37

2.38

2.39

---

[45] See s. 2 of the Enterprise Insolvency Law of the PRC.
[46] David G. Epstein, *Bankruptcy and Related Law in a Nutshell* (8th edn, West 2013) 287.
[47] Daniel A. Austin and Stephen P. Parsons, *Business Bankruptcy Law in Focus* (Wolters Kluwer 2017) 194.
[48] Kenneth Ayotte and Edward R. Morrison, 'Valuation Disputes in Corporate Bankruptcy', University of Pennsylvania Law Review, 166 (2018) 1820.

of Market Economic Order' issued by the Supreme People's Court of China in 2009 states that, for enterprises that, although they have developed the cause of insolvency or have a clear possibility of losing their solvency, are in line with the national policy of industrial restructuring and still have prospects for development, the people's courts should give full play to the role of reorganization and reconciliation proceedings to actively and effectively rescue them. It is a basic judgement whether the industry to which an enterprise belongs is in line with the needs of the state and the direction of social development is a strategic factor for the survival of the enterprise. When an enterprise has a good brand effect and brand image, consumers are more likely to expect its continued existence, which is an important factor to support the continued operation of the enterprise.

2.40 The second criterion is the shareholding structure of the enterprise and the strength of its shareholders. A clear shareholding structure and the absence of excessive historical problems will enable the enterprise to minimize its own attrition caused by internal games and to get out of trouble and onto the right track more quickly. The strength of the shareholders will influence the difficulty of restructuring. For companies that are worthy of reorganization, shareholders have certain expectations for the success of the reorganization, and powerful shareholders can help reorganize the company through their financial strength and influence.

2.41 The third criterion is the enterprise's own governance and internal culture. The commencement of insolvency proceedings for capital-troubled enterprises is mostly caused by temporary financial problems. And there are no major flaws in the business team or sales network. It is possible for the original management team familiar with the business to continue to govern the enterprise and improve the efficiency of the restructuring. For enterprises with a better internal culture, a sense of responsibility, survival, and unity among the members of the enterprise can be stimulated in distress. The fact that an enterprise remains cohesive in difficult times, rather than having its last hope of survival consumed by factional rivalry, is an important factor in whether a company is worth reorganizing.

2.42 The fourth criterion is the creditworthiness and level of indebtedness of the enterprise. The level of indebtedness of an enterprise is an important reflection of its existing financial position, especially for traditional enterprises. It is more advantageous for an enterprise to get out of trouble when it has few liabilities, few guarantees, lighter due debts and interest, or the possibility of debt-for-equity conversion. Of course, for emerging enterprises, the asset-and-liability profile does not allow for an accurate judgement of the operability of the enterprise. Its commencement of insolvency proceedings mainly results from cash-flow problems, and its creditworthiness needs to be examined. If it still has some credit capacity to raise funds from banks or the market, the enterprise may achieve financial relief more quickly.

b. Whether there is a qualification value

2.43 Some industries need to be approved by the government to operate in certain countries, such as finance, construction, post and telecommunications, etc. For those franchised industries, an enterprise's government licence qualification is a scarce and important asset in itself. If it can be reorganized to get out of financial difficulties and retain that qualification, it is also a reflection of the reorganization value. For example, the 'shell' resources of public companies in the current environment in China are also important assets that can be realized and are attractive to strategic investors.[49]

c. Whether there is a public-interest value

For enterprises that have a significant impact on people's livelihood and have a public-interest purpose, involving military security, medical care, education, pension, financial infrastructure, etc., they are not suitable for liquidation due to their public attributes, which determine their reorganization value.[50] **2.44**

In addition, it is more important for strategic investors to have an exit route after a successful restructuring. It is important for them to be able to resell or go public after reorganization and to have the possibility to exit after a successful reorganization to achieve their investment objectives. **2.45**

It follows that whether a business has reorganization value is not only a legal judgement but also, more importantly, a commercial and market judgement. However, there may be lots of valuation disputes between experts. And judges could announce that they will apply a 'final-offer arbitration' approach to valuation disputes. Under this approach, judges would select the valuation report that is most persuasive and adopt it in its entirety. Judges would not average valuations across experts; nor would they adopt a valuation that combines pieces of each expert's report. The virtue of this 'final-offer arbitration' approach is that it might induce experts to be less extreme or biased in their reports. The more extreme or biased a report is, the less likely the judge will choose the report, and the more likely the judge will select the other expert's report.[51] Also, it is an important test of the administrator's ability to make a judgement based on the circumstances and to propose a reasonable reorganization plan. The reorganization of a particular business is carried out within the framework of judicial proceedings and is underpinned by legal compulsion, as distinct from out-of-court mergers and acquisitions (M&A) restructuring. The judge plays an important role in an in-court restructuring. The judge is the final barrier to determining whether the business is worthy of restructuring, and whether reorganization proceedings can be commenced, and plays an important role in the approval process. The judge should be careful to base the outcome of the reorganization proceedings on the various criteria mentioned above. **2.46**

---

[49] Under the approval system, it was difficult for Chinese companies to go public. Also, there are some industries requiring special licences to operate in China, such as medicine, the construction industry, etc. When applying for these licences requires a high cost, many companies hope to purchase 'shell' resources to gain the corresponding qualifications.

[50] See *In re Chrysler LLC*, 405 BR 84 (Bankr. SDNY 2009); *In re Chrysler LLC*, 576 F.3d 108 (2d Cir. 2009); *In re GMC*, 407 BR 463 (Bankr. SDNY 2009), in which the US and Canadian governments got involved to help the companies' reorganization and avoid their liquidation.

[51] Ayotte and Morrison, 'Valuation Disputes' (n 48) 1846.

3

Debt Restructuring Outside Formal Insolvency Proceedings

Jennifer Payne

I. Introduction

3.01 Where a company is in financial difficulties, the options available to it will depend on whether the business model is fundamentally flawed (referred to as economic distress) or the company is merely financially distressed and there is a business that is capable of being saved.[1] Where a company is financially distressed, the trading out of its difficulties or a disposal of the assets or the business is likely to be preferable to liquidation. One option for a financially distressed company is the sale of the business on a going-concern basis to a third party as part of an auction process, which may not require any restructuring of liabilities. However, a sale of the business to a new owner will not always be possible or desirable, especially in times of financial crisis where markets are illiquid leading to a loss of value if assets are sold at 'fire sale' prices or if a sale can only occur on a break-up basis.[2] Debt restructuring can be a means of enabling a financially distressed but viable company to avoid liquidation. It provides for a change in the capital structure rather than a sale to a third party. The new debt and equity can be distributed to the existing investors in return for their old stakes in the debtor. Such a reorganization can be beneficial not only for the company and its managers, if the restructuring allows a business to flourish rather than to fail, but also for creditors and other stakeholders. It is no coincidence that in the aftermath of the 2008 global financial crisis (GFC), jurisdictions across the world sought to introduce effective debt restructuring regimes,[3]

---

[1] For a discussion of the distinction between financial and economic distress, see D.G. Baird, 'Bankruptcy's Uncontested Axioms', Yale Law Journal, 108 (1998) 573.

[2] See, e.g. A. Shleifer and R. Vishny, 'Liquidation Values and Debt Capacity: A Market Equilibrium Approach', Journal of Finance, 42 (1992) 1343. There may be other reasons why a sale will not be possible, such as where the transfer of crucial assets to a new entity is not feasible. Outside these scenarios, sales can have some advantages over restructurings as they avoid the need for potentially costly bargaining between the company and its stakeholders.

[3] See, e.g. Directive (EU) 2019/1023 of the European Parliament and of the Council of 20 June 2019 on preventive restructuring frameworks, on discharge of debt and disqualifications, and on measures to increase the efficiency of procedures concerning restructuring, insolvency and discharge of debt, and amending Directive (EU) 2017/1132 (hereafter, EU Restructuring Directive); Singapore Insolvency, Restructuring and Dissolution Act 2018. See M.S. Wee, 'The Singapore Story of Injecting US Chapter 11 into the Commonwealth Scheme', European Company and Financial Law Review, 15 (2018) 553; W.Y. Wan, C. Watters, and G. McCormack, 'Schemes of Arrangement in Singapore: Empirical and Comparative Analyses', American Bankruptcy Law Journal 94 (2020) 463.

Jennifer Payne, *Debt Restructuring Outside Formal Insolvency Proceedings* In: *The Anatomy of Corporate Insolvency Law*. Edited by: Reinhard Bork and Renato Mangano, Oxford University Press. © Jennifer Payne 2024. DOI: 10.1093/oso/9780198852094.003.0003

an aim that was intensified by the financial distress created by the COVID-19 pandemic.[4]

There has been an element of regulatory competition to the development of these debt restructuring mechanisms too, since some jurisdictions appeared to be ahead in the race to create such a mechanism, perhaps most notably the United States (with the Chapter 11 regime) and the United Kingdom (with its scheme of arrangement). So, for example, it has been very common in the post-GFC period for financially distressed companies elsewhere in the world to make use of the UK scheme of arrangement to restructure their debts.[5] This has incentivized other regimes to develop their own debt restructuring mechanisms. The EU Restructuring Directive,[6] for example, may be regarded as a response in part to the use of the UK scheme of arrangement by EU companies. Similarly, the Singaporean debt restructuring reforms of 2017 were designed to turn Singapore into a debt restructuring centre.[7] Another element of regulatory competition has been the World Bank Doing Business figures. This project, which began in 2004, has been influential, and some debt restructuring reforms have been driven by a desire on the part of jurisdictions to boost their position in these rankings, although some concerns around these reports have since been raised.[8]

3.02

This chapter considers the debt restructuring options available to a financially distressed company outside formal insolvency. The debt restructuring mechanisms discussed in this chapter may be compared with the insolvency regimes discussed in Chapter 4 'Formal Insolvency Proceedings'. Insolvency law may be regarded as a means of reallocating the capital of a financially distressed company once the financial creditors have decided that they no longer wish to be invested in it. It is a debt-enforcement mechanism that imposes a collective procedure in order to minimize the incentive for individual enforcement and maximize the value of the business and thus the returns to creditors as a whole.[9] By contrast, the mechanisms described in this chapter are a means of facilitating a new bargain between the existing creditors of a financially distressed company as to their future relationship. The majority of the creditors want to

3.03

---

[4] See, e.g. the UK Corporate Insolvency and Governance Act 2020, which introduced changes to the UK debt restructuring regime specifically to address the financial distress created by the COVID-19 pandemic; J. Payne, 'Debt Restructuring in Transition', Law Quarterly Review, 139 (2023) 101.

[5] See, e.g. J. Payne 'Cross-Border Schemes of Arrangement and Forum Shopping', European Business Organization Law Review, 14 (2013) 563; J. Payne, *Schemes of Arrangement: Theory, Structure and Operation* (2nd edn, CUP 2021) ch. 7.

[6] See EU Restructuring Directive (n 3).

[7] W.M. Seng and H. Tijo, 'Singapore as International Debt Restructuring Center: Aspiration and Challenges', Texas International Law Journal, 57 (2021–22) 1.

[8] See World Bank, 'Business Ready (B-READY): The World Banks's Flagship Report on Business Environment Worldwide', <http://www.doingbusiness.org/en/rankings and www.doingbusiness.org/en/doingbusiness> accessed 8 January 2024. There have been difficulties with the World Bank Doing Business project. After data irregularities on Doing Business 2018 and 2020 were reported, in June 2020, World Bank management paused the next Doing Business report and initiated a series of reviews and audits of the report and its methodology.

[9] See, e.g. S. Paterson, 'Rethinking Corporate Bankruptcy in the Twenty-First Century', Oxford Journal of Legal Studies, 36 (2016) 697.

continue to be invested in the company or business[10] but must agree a new bargain, because the change in the company's financial circumstances means that the existing bargain no longer reflects the risks of the business. As compared to a liquidation in which the assets of the debtor are sold as a going concern or on a piecemeal basis and the creditors receive a cash payment in accordance with their priority ranking, in a restructuring the creditors agree to receive debt or equity in the debtor for their unpaid claim. Instead of a sale to a third party, a restructuring involves a reorganization of the capital of the company or business in the hands of the existing creditors/shareholders. The debt restructuring mechanisms in this chapter can have some advantages over the insolvency mechanisms discussed in Chapter 4; in particular, they can avoid the stigma of insolvency and can operate at an earlier point in time.

3.04 The debt restructuring mechanisms discussed in this chapter are fundamentally a matter of contract law,[11] although there is an important difference between contractual workouts discussed in section II and debt restructuring mechanisms discussed in section III (referred to in this chapter collectively as 'restructuring plans' despite the different terms sometimes given to these mechanisms in different jurisdictions). In a workout the parties unanimously consent to the restructuring, whereas in a restructuring plan some form of coercion or interference with creditor rights is involved, with different restructuring plans involving different levels of interference, as discussed in section III. While a contractual workout represents the use of contract alone to reorganize the relationships between the parties, in a restructuring plan, that contractual agreement is court-assisted, and its binding force (in particular on dissenting creditors) flows from that involvement. This raises the issue of minority protection and the role of the law in ensuring that minority abuse does not occur.

3.05 The structure of this chapter is as follows: in section II, contractual workouts are discussed including their operation, their advantages, and their shortcomings; in section III, restructuring plans are analysed; and in sections IV and V, two common ancillary mechanisms that complement the operation of restructuring plans are considered, namely restructuring moratoria (section IV) and rescue finance (section V).

II. Contractual Workouts

3.06 Financial restructuring is, at its heart, a private matter between parties who need to renegotiate an agreement that no longer reflects the risks against which they agreed

---

[10] The distinction between business and corporate rescue is regarded as important in some jurisdictions. However, there is some benefit in thinking more holistically about this situation since 'society has no interest in the preservation or rehabilitation of the company as such': Insolvency Law and Practice: Report of the Review Committee (Cmnd 8558, 1982) (Cork Report) para. 193.

[11] See S. Madaus, 'Leaving the Shadows of US Bankruptcy Law: A Proposal to Divide the Realms of Insolvency and Restructuring Law', European Business Organization Law Review, 19 (2018) 615.

terms. Additional statutory intervention, or the involvement of the courts, is not strictly necessary. Instead, stakeholders can bargain for the reorganization they want via a contractual workout. For large companies with multi-bank lending facilities in place, guidelines have emerged to facilitate this process, most notably the London Approach[12] and the INSOL Principles.[13] These principles recognize that the 'interests of relevant creditors are best served by coordinating their response to a debtor in financial difficulty'.[14]

There are typically a number of different stages to a contractual workout.[15] The first step is often to agree a standstill period or informal moratorium to buy the debtor some breathing space to gather information and formulate and consider restructuring proposals.[16] Without such an agreement, it will be open to the creditors to assert their contractual claims against the debtor and perhaps petition for liquidation.[17] These actions can undermine the possibility of a successful restructuring. It will therefore be important to include in the standstill arrangement all the significant creditors and those whose claims are likely to be restructured. The second stage relates to information gathering. Detailed information will be needed about the company's financial position and a report made to creditors.[18] It is common for the lenders and the company to appoint a steering committee to represent the main classes of creditors in order to manage the restructuring on behalf of all creditors.[19] The next stage is to formulate the restructuring itself, which can take a variety of forms including debt-to-equity swaps, the adjustment of secured creditors' rights, the extension of the terms of debts, and compromises whereby creditors waive part of their claims. New companies may be set up and corporate groups may be restructured. There may also be new money injected at this stage to keep the company trading, and this may lead to negotiations over the priority that any claim by a new lender will have as compared to existing lenders.[20]

3.07

There are a number of benefits to contractual workouts. There is no need for the intervention of a court or an insolvency practitioner, and therefore they can be quicker and cheaper than some of the alternative mechanisms on offer. The directors stay in control during the restructuring process, in contrast to the position in many formal insolvency

3.08

---

[12] See J. Armour and S. Deakin, 'Norms in Private Insolvency Procedures: The "London Approach" to the Resolution of Financial Distress', Journal of Corporate Law Studies, 1 (2001) 21.

[13] INSOL International, *Statement of Principles for a Global Approach to Multi-Creditor Workouts* (2nd edn, INSOL International April 2017).

[14] ibid principle 4.

[15] See R. Olivares-Caminal, R. Guynn, A. Kornberg et al., *Debt Restructuring* (3rd edn, OUP 2022).

[16] In some jurisdictions (e.g. Germany, §§ 49 et seq. of the Act on the Stabilisation and Restructuring Framework for Businesses of 22 December 2020 (BGBl. I, 3256) (hereafter StaRUG)), statutory moratoria may be available alongside informal contractual mechanisms, although even so, there may be reasons why the parties may need to, or prefer to, make use of a contractual standstill arrangement. See, in the context of the UK restructuring moratorium introduced in 2020, which is prima facie available for use alongside a workout, J. Payne, 'An Assessment of the UK Restructuring Moratorium', Lloyd's Maritime and Commercial Law Quarterly (2021) 454.

[17] See principles 1 and 2 of INSOL International, *Multi-Creditor Workouts* (n 13).

[18] ibid principle 7.

[19] ibid principle 4.

[20] ibid principle 8.

56 DEBT RESTRUCTURING OUTSIDE FORMAL INSOLVENCY

proceedings.[21] The merits of a debtor-in-possession process have been debated at length.[22] Broadly, studies suggest that having the directors remain in control of the company during the restructuring process can be valuable where the shareholder base is broad and the company's financial distress is not a result of the directors' incompetence or wrongdoing. The directors' knowledge of the company and its creditors make them well placed to negotiate the changes in contractual arrangements. Furthermore, a fear of being sidelined by an external manager might dissuade directors from seeking a rescue option; leaving them in control can therefore operate as an incentive for them to tackle the company's difficulties via a restructuring.

3.09 Another benefit is that contractual workouts can be utilized at any point in time; there is no need for the company to be insolvent. Difficulties can therefore be tackled at an early stage, and any stigma of insolvency can be avoided. In addition, a contractual workout can involve all the creditors or a subset, unlike formal insolvency proceedings which are generally collective in the sense that they involve all the creditors of the company.[23] This provides flexibility for workouts. Plus, reducing the number of participants and involving only the sophisticated creditors who are repeat players can simplify negotiations and increase the likelihood of agreement. It is not uncommon for workouts to include all bank and financial institution creditors but leave out small trade creditors on the basis that they will be paid in full in any case. Contractual workouts also have the benefit of keeping the terms of the agreement private to the parties involved.

3.10 A major downside of contractual workouts, however, is the need for all relevant creditors to consent to be bound. Of course, creditors can agree *ex ante* on a procedure to enable a prescribed majority of creditors to bind others to any reorganization of a company's debt, but if no such procedure is in place, any change in the terms of the debtor's liabilities will require the consent of all creditors whose claims are to be affected. It is therefore open to minority creditors to hold out for better terms or repayment in full.[24] By refusing to agree to the workout or (in the absence of a standstill agreement or moratorium) threatening to enforce their debt or put the debtor into liquidation, minority creditors can seek to use their hold-up rights to extract value for themselves. Thus, individual creditors can delay, or even prevent, the successful agreement of a contractual workout. This may well be value destructive for the company concerned and may influence the availability and cost of capital for a company *ex ante*.

---

[21] For further discussion, see para 4.03 et seq.

[22] See, e.g. D. Hahn, 'Concentrated Ownership and Control of Corporate Reorganizations', Journal of Corporate Law Studies, 4 (2004) 117; S. Franken, 'Creditor- and Debtor-Oriented Corporate Bankruptcy Regimes Revisited', European Business Organization Law Review, 5 (2004) 645. G. McCormack, 'Control and Corporate Rescue: An Anglo-American Evaluation', International and Comparative Law Quarterly, 56 (2007) 515; N. Martin, 'Common Law Bankruptcy Systems: Similarities and Differences', American Bankruptcy Institute Law Review, 11 (2003) 367.

[23] For discussion, see H. Eidenmüller, 'What Is an Insolvency Proceeding?', American Bankruptcy Law Journal, 92 (2018) 53.

[24] For a discussion, see M.J. Roe, 'The Voting Prohibition in Bond Workouts', Yale Law Journal, 97 (1987) 232; R. Gertner and D. Scharfstein, 'A Theory of Workouts and the Effects of Reorganization Law', Journal of Finance, 46 (1991) 1189.

Furthermore, a process of prolonged informal negotiation while the debtor seeks to satisfy the requirements of all creditors can be disadvantageous and may be impractical if the debtor is facing an acute liquidity crisis.

Given this inherent limitation of contractual workouts, they operate best when the lenders comprise a small group of like-minded individuals or organizations. Changes in the debt structures of large corporates, including the introduction of new credit-providers such as hedge funds, and the increasing fragmentation of debt puts pressure on the use of contractual workouts.[25] As a result, reaching a purely contractual solution, while not impossible, will not always be straightforward, and the use of one of the mechanisms discussed in section III may well be valuable as a means of restructuring a company's debt. These mechanisms seek to constrain the ability of individual creditors to exercise their hold-up rights by interfering with creditors' contractual rights in various ways. In addition, the law may seek to assist debtors further by putting in place a statutory stay that can operate alongside a debt restructuring mechanism to prevent individual creditors from enforcing their claims or putting the debtor into liquidation. These are discussed further in section IV.

III. Restructuring Plans

Many jurisdictions have in place one or more mechanisms that are designed to facilitate debt restructuring of financially distressed but viable companies outside formal insolvency procedures. Some of these mechanisms have been in existence for some time, such as the UK scheme of arrangement,[26] whereas others are of much more recent origin.[27]

In common with contractual workouts, restructuring plans can avoid some of the potential disadvantages of formal insolvency procedures. They tend to be debtor-in-possession[28] and to operate at an earlier stage than formal insolvency

---

[25] See, e.g. Paterson, 'Rethinking Corporate Bankruptcy' (n 9).

[26] See Payne, *Schemes of Arrangement* (n 5) 1.2. Although Chapter 11 has been the inspiration behind many of the recent debt restructuring mechanisms introduced around the world, Chapter 11 itself does not completely fit the model described in this chapter. Chapter 11 sits within the US Bankruptcy Code. Although the debtor may voluntarily use reorganization proceedings anytime and without any insolvency test as long as it acts in good faith, all restructuring proceedings (regardless of the actual insolvency of the debtor) are bankruptcy proceedings under the Code. Further, the arrangement is made entirely before the court, and the court has full control of the case. The insolvency underpinnings of Chapter 11 are visible in the fact that the moratorium is automatic rather than optional (see section IV) and the process is collective without the option of dealing with a subset of creditors.

[27] See, e.g. the debt restructuring regime contained in the EU Restructuring Directive (n 3), and the restructuring plan introduced in the UK Corporate Insolvency and Governance Act 2020.

[28] See, e.g. UK schemes of arrangement, UK restructuring plans, UK Company Voluntary Arrangements, Singaporean schemes of arrangement, and the Dutch scheme of arrangement (see Dutch Act on the Confirmation of Extrajudicial Restructuring Plans or Wet Homologatie Onderhands Akkoord (hereafter WHOA)). In some circumstances an insolvency practitioner may be appointed alongside the directors for a specific purpose, such as to monitor a restructuring moratorium (see section IV).

58 DEBT RESTRUCTURING OUTSIDE FORMAL INSOLVENCY

procedures.[29] Given the aim of encouraging the existing creditors of the company to determine how best to reorganize the capital of the company and renegotiate their bargain, there is no need to wait until the company is insolvent before utilizing a restructuring plan and there is some benefit in tackling these issues early. There is no need to remove incumbent management while the debtor negotiates with its creditors to put in place the new capital structure, and it may be beneficial to leave the directors in charge thereby reducing disruption to the company's operations. Given the coercive effect of restructuring plans (in contrast to contractual workouts) they have the potential to be used opportunistically by management and senior creditors to obtain an unfair advantage, and although the directors are left in charge an independent arbiter will be needed to oversee the process. This could be an insolvency practitioner[30] but it is more commonly the court. This raises issues about the potential cost of the restructuring proceedings, which can be particularly relevant to the accessibility of these procedures for small and medium-sized enterprises (SMEs). For this reason, although court oversight is central to the process[31] some regimes provide for a slightly lighter role for the court than others. While the English scheme of arrangement, for example, has a minimum of two court hearings (a convening hearing and a sanctioning hearing), the Dutch and the German schemes of arrangement focus the court's role on the sanctioning stage.

3.14 Restructuring plans can have significant advantages compared to contractual workouts. As discussed in section II, one of the downsides of contractual workouts is that they provide creditors with the ability to disrupt the restructuring by refusing to consent to it. This has been referred to as the tragedy of the anticommons.[32] This is an issue that arises in restructuring but not in insolvency. Restructuring plans address these concerns by moving away from the position in which unanimous agreement of all creditors is required for the restructuring to go ahead. Effectively, restructuring plans provide a mechanism for resolving the deadlock that otherwise faces the creditors seeking to negotiate a new bargain between themselves as to their future involvement in the company. Instead, jurisdictions implement some form of majority approval mechanism whereby the restructuring can be imposed on dissenting creditors (with the approval levels varying from jurisdiction to jurisdiction), which is then confirmed

---

[29] See section III.A.

[30] See, e.g. S. Paterson, 'Bargaining in Financial Restructuring: Market Norms, Legal Rights and Regulatory Standards', Journal of Corporate Law Studies, 14 (2014) 333.

[31] Although the court has a key part to play in restructuring plans, a distinction can be drawn between this role and that of the court in the insolvency proceedings (see Chapter 4), which generally involve the court having full control of the case.

[32] See, e.g. R. De Weijs, 'Too Big to Fail as a Game of Chicken with the State: What Insolvency Law Theory Has to Say about TBTF and Vice Versa', European Business Organization Law Review, 14 (2013) 210; M. Schillig, 'Corporate Insolvency Law for the Twenty-First Century: State Imposed or Market Based?', Journal of Corporate Law Studies, 14 (2014) 1.

by the court.[33] A second way in which creditors can disrupt a contractual workout is by asserting their contractual rights against the company. This is familiar as a problem in insolvency law and is generally referred to as the common pool problem. In order to preserve the assets of the debtor for the benefit of all creditors insolvency law generally responds to this with some form of statutory stay or moratorium. The same tool is sometimes made available to restructuring mechanisms as an adjunct, in order to constrain the ability of creditors to assess their contractual rights during the period of the restructuring. This is discussed further in section IV.

Restructuring plans therefore inevitably involve an interference with creditors' rights **3.15** to a greater or lesser extent, and this interference requires justification.[34] Various explanations have been put forward. One explanation is that creditors agree to having their rights altered in accordance with the law that governs their contracts. So, where a creditor's agreement with a debtor is governed by the law of Utopia, for example, that creditor agrees to the restructuring of that debt by way of a Utopian restructuring plan which has a majority approval requirement in place of less than 100%, so that the creditor can be bound without its consent if the appropriate approvals are obtained. This explanation is not entirely satisfactory, however, and fails to account for involuntary creditors and other non-adjusting creditors that may be bound by the plan. Another explanation is that these constraints are justified on the basis of the greater economic good of a particular economy: 'the general interest of saving companies and jobs'.[35] This sits uncomfortably with traditional notions in insolvency law, however, which justify the interference with creditors' rights by reference to the creditors' bargain theory.[36] This theory suggests that the inability of a debtor to satisfy its debts is likely to lead to uncoordinated creditor enforcement actions which will lead to an unnecessary destruction in value. An insolvency process therefore takes away creditors' enforcement rights and replaces them with a collective procedure which aims to realize the available value in a coordinated way that leads to the maximization of proceeds for the creditors as a group. A similar analysis can justify the interference with creditor rights at the slightly earlier stage when the debtor is financially distressed but not yet insolvent. This would mean that the interference with creditor rights *ex ante* can be justified on the basis of a social contract in circumstances where the outcome for creditors as a whole

---

[33] Another option would be to give the restructuring decision to the court even where it does not have creditor support. See, e.g. the French *procédure de sauvegarde* for smaller businesses, which requires the confirmation of the court but no creditor (committee) support: Art. L626-29 of the *Code de Commerce*.

[34] See, e.g. R. Bork, 'Preventive Restructuring Frameworks: A "Comedy of Errors" or "All's Well That Ends Well"?', International Corporate Rescue, 14 (2017) 417.

[35] See, e.g. European Commission, 'Impact Assessment Study on Policy Options for a New Initiative on Minimum Standards in Insolvency and Restructuring Law' (November 2016) 59.

[36] T.H. Jackson, 'Bankruptcy, Non-Bankruptcy Entitlements, and the Creditors' Bargain', Yale Law Journal, 91 (1982) 857; D.G. Baird and T.H. Jackson, 'Corporate Reorganizations and the Treatment of Diverse Ownership Interests: A Comment on Adequate Protection of Secured Creditors in Bankruptcy', University of Chicago Law Review, 51 (1984) 97; T.H. Jackson, *The Logic and Limits of Bankruptcy Law* (Harvard University Press 1986). This theory has spawned a huge literature of comment, analysis, and alternative bankruptcy theories: see Kristin van Zwieten, *Goode on Principles of Corporate Insolvency Law* (5th edn, Sweet & Maxwell 2019) (ch. 2). Cf. R. Bork, *Corporate Insolvency Law* (Intersentia 2020) para. 1.13 et seq.

60   DEBT RESTRUCTURING OUTSIDE FORMAL INSOLVENCY

will be improved compared to the position in which creditors are free to utilize their rights in an unconstrained way. On this analysis, the permissibility of the constraints on the rights of individual creditors that accompany debt restructuring mechanisms, including the imposition of the restructuring on creditors without their consent and restructuring moratoria, is based on those measures being in the interests of the creditors as a whole.

3.16   While the constraints on creditors' rights involved in restructuring plans can be justified on this basis, they nevertheless raise the potential for abuse of individual creditors. There may be circumstances in which the interference with creditors' rights leads to a better outcome for the creditors collectively but involves an unjustified transfer of value from one group of creditors to another or one individual to another. The possibility of wealth transfers at the expense of the minority needs to be addressed by the legal regime. This is important not just for the creditors concerned; if a regime facilitates or allows expropriation it risks damaging the market for capital for healthy companies since creditors will be wary of the risk of expropriation *ex post* when deciding to advance credit *ex ante*. A balance is needed; capital must be allocated to the companies best able to use it, but this should not occur by expropriating value from those with an ongoing interest in the company, who ought to be protected. This issue of who has an ongoing interest in the company is not straightforward, however, and much will depend on the valuation mechanism adopted, as discussed at paras 3.43–3.53.

3.17   Different jurisdictions and different restructuring plans address these concerns in different ways, depending on the nature of the constraints involved. The more significant the potential for abuse, the more significant the protection that is required. Examples of forms of minority protection include rules regarding the information that must be provided to creditors and protections around the approval process, the division of creditors into classes, and the role of the court in deciding whether to confirm the plan. Restructuring plans are effectively contractual workouts with court involvement, that involvement being necessary to address the hold-out problem and the interference with creditor rights which flow from that. The involvement of the court and the other protections put in place to mitigate the coercive effect of restructuring plans inevitably raise their cost as compared to contractual workouts, where the minority do not require the same level of protection since their contractual rights are left intact. This can raise issues around the suitability and availability of restructuring plans for SMEs.[37]

---

[37]   In the United Kingdom, for example, while SMEs do occasionally make use of restructuring plans (see, e.g. *Re Houst Limited* [2022] EWHC 1941 (Ch)), this is relatively uncommon.

A. Commencement of the Restructuring Plan

1. Timing

3.18 Given that restructuring involves those committed to remaining in the company having the opportunity to renegotiate their bargain and decide how best to allocate their capital, there is a value to this occurring at an early stage. This can help to avoid the problem of zombie companies, which have so much debt that they must use all their cash resources to service interest payments. Early access to the procedure can help to head off the chances of the company becoming economically distressed, at which point liquidation on a break-up basis may be the most suitable option. Unlike insolvency procedures, therefore, there is no reason in principle why restructuring plans should not take place at any point in time. So, for example, UK schemes of arrangement impose no financial conditions on the ability of a company to access the procedure.[38]

3.19 However, given that restructuring plans involve the curtailment of creditor rights, there is the potential for them to be used by unscrupulous debtors and senior creditors as a way of ridding the company of junior creditors (or shareholders) who still have some economic value in the company. This danger is most apparent when the company is wholly solvent, at which point the company can meet its debts as they fall due. For this reason, restructuring plans often do impose financial conditions, although these do not generally require the insolvency of the company. For example, in order to be eligible to use a UK restructuring plan, the company must satisfy two hurdles. First, it must have encountered, or be likely to encounter, financial difficulties that are affecting, or will or may affect, its ability to carry on business as a going concern.[39] Second, the purpose of the compromise or arrangement proposed must be to prevent or mitigate the effects of the company's financial difficulties.[40] The European Union (EU) Restructuring Directive provides that debtors should have access to a restructuring plan 'where there is a likelihood of insolvency'.[41] To be eligible to use the Dutch scheme it must be 'reasonably likely' that the debtor cannot continue to pay its debts as they fall due',[42] and in Germany a 'likelihood of insolvency' is required.[43]

3.20 These financial conditions recognize a concern that restructuring procedures should not be misused. The extent of the constraint on creditor rights has a part to play here. One way to understand the lack of conditions in the UK scheme of arrangement is to recognize that the extent to which dissenting creditor rights can be overridden

---

[38] See, e.g. *Scottish Lion Insurance Co Ltd v Goodrich Corp.* [2010] CSOIH 6.

[39] See s. 901A(2) of the Companies Act 2006. This has raised difficult issues as to whether the UK restructuring plan should be regarded as an 'insolvency proceeding' for the purposes of the bankruptcy exclusion to the Lugano Convention. See, e.g. *Re Gategroup Guarantee Limited* [2021] EWHC 304 (Ch). The issue of whether a scheme of arrangement should be regarded as an 'insolvency proceeding' for other purposes has also been discussed, e.g. *Re MAB Leasing Ltd* [2021] EWHC 152 (Ch) and [2021] EWHC 379 (Ch); *Re Nordic Aviation Capital Designated Activity Company* [2020] IEHC 445.

[40] See s. 901A(3)(b) of the Companies Act 2006.

[41] See Art. 4(1) and Recital 24 of the EU Restructuring Directive (n 3).

[42] See Art. 370(1) of the WHOA (n 28).

[43] See § 29(1) StaRUG.

62 DEBT RESTRUCTURING OUTSIDE FORMAL INSOLVENCY

is less than that in the UK restructuring plan, the restructuring plan within the EU Restructuring Directive, or in the Dutch and German arrangements: in a UK scheme there can only be cramdown within a class, whereas in the other mechanisms cross-class cramdown is possible. In addition, in the UK scheme there is a significant element of court oversight which can adjust the level of minority protection according to the financial condition of the company. For example, the determination of the appropriate number and composition of the classes in which creditors should vote on the scheme reflects the financial position of the company and takes account of the alternative outcome should the restructuring fail. Ultimately, each jurisdiction will want to balance the incentive for debtors and creditors to act early to allocate the company's resources as efficiently as possible, while avoiding the danger of the restructuring mechanism being used by the unscrupulous to gain an unfair advantage at the expense of others within the company.

2. Who may commence the plan?

3.21 Restructuring plans are effectively court-assisted contractual agreements between the debtor and its creditors. In general, it is the debtor who will propose a restructuring plan. Jurisdictions vary somewhat on the question of whether individual creditors can propose a plan.

3.22 Some restructuring plans allow for the possibility of a plan being proposed by an individual creditor but require the creditor to have the consent of the debtor.[44] By contrast, in US Chapter 11, after an initial period within which the debtor has the exclusive right to propose a plan, 'any party of interest' may propose a plan including a creditor, trustee, or shareholder. Under the Dutch scheme of arrangement there is no exclusivity period and any creditor, shareholder, employee works council or other employee representative may request the court to appoint a 'restructuring expert' who is then entitled to propose a plan to the exclusion of the debtor.[45] It has been suggested that the lack of a specific creditor right to propose a plan may be problematic.[46] This is on the basis that a mechanism that grants the exclusive right to propose the plan to the debtor in effect gives controlling shareholders a hold-out position and could, therefore, lead to a struggle between the shareholders and creditors over the value of the business. Whether this is a real concern will depend on a number of factors including the balance of power between the shareholders and creditors at the point in time when the plan is being proposed. The nature of the senior creditors will also be relevant and whether there is a controlling shareholder or a more dispersed shareholding structure. The legal provisions within the jurisdiction will also be important, in particular the extent to which the focus of directors' duties shifts from the shareholders to the creditors as the company becomes financially distressed. This issue does not seem to have caused

---

[44] See Art. 4(8) of the EU Restructuring Directive (n 3).
[45] See Art. 371 of the WHOA (n 28).
[46] N. Tollenaar, 'The European Commission's Proposal for A Directive on Preventive Restructuring Proceedings', Insolvency Intelligence, 30 (2017) 65, 73.

a problem in jurisdictions such as the United Kingdom in which debt restructuring schemes of arrangement have operated successfully for decades despite being proposed by debtors on all occasions as a matter of practice.[47] The potential conflict between these stakeholder groups can then be dealt with by the court at the convening hearing, by way of the number and constitution of the class meetings that are held, and at the sanctioning hearing.

Another question that arises is whether the court needs to be involved at all at this pre-liminary stage and, in particular, whether there is a role for the court in approving the disclosure statement. Information disclosure to the creditors is one form of minority protection as it gives the creditors information on the basis of which they can determine how the plan will affect them, how to vote on it, and how active they need to be in defending their position. Therefore, there can be value in the court having oversight of this issue. In some restructuring processes the court is involved at this early stage,[48] but this is not universal. Concerns around the costs involved in restructuring plans some-times mean that this stage is not supervised by the court. Under the EU Restructuring Directive, for example, the debtor can directly propose a plan to its creditors without any application to the court being required and without prior court approval of the disclosure statement.[49] The Dutch scheme of arrangement is an example of a regime in which court involvement at this early stage is kept to a minimum: there is no convening hearing and there is no prior approval of the disclosure statement.[50]

3.23

B. Content of the Plan

In general, there is a wide variety of options that might be utilized by a financially dis-tressed company in order to secure its rescue. Many of these relate to dealing with the debt overhang.[51] Commonly, therefore, plans seek to make use of a range of measures including the postponement of imminent liabilities into the more distant future, the conversion of fixed liabilities into more fluid ones (debt-for-equity swaps), and debt write-downs whereby all creditors of a particular type agree a pro rata reduction in the value of their claims. There are other means by which financial difficulties can be ad-dressed, however, including a sale of part, or even the entirety, of the business. Although it is possible to restrict the permitted content of restructuring plans, it is preferable for

3.24

---

[47] In a UK scheme of arrangement, while the legislative provisions (s. 896(1) of the Companies Act 2006) recog-nize that a creditor can make an application to court for scheme meetings to be summoned even without the con-sent of the debtor, hostile creditor schemes face a number of practical challenges (see *Re Savoy Hotel Ltd* [1981] Ch 351). UK restructuring plans face similar constraints but can occur; see, e.g. *Re The Good Box Co Labs Ltd* [2023] EWHC 274 (Ch).

[48] In US Chapter 11, for example, see 11 U.S.C. §1125(b). In the UK, the court will have regard to the adequacy of disclosure at the first court hearing of a scheme or a restructuring plan (see, e.g. *Re Indah Kiat International Finance Company BV* [2016] EWHC 246 (Ch); *Re Virgin Atlantic Airways Ltd* [2020] EWHC 2376 (Ch)).

[49] The same holds true for Germany: see § 14 StaRUG.

[50] See the WHOA (n 28).

[51] Some restructuring plans can be used to amend equity documents as well as debt. See, e.g. the UK restruc-turing plan: *Re ED & F Man Holdings Ltd* [2022] EWHC 687 (Ch).

64   DEBT RESTRUCTURING OUTSIDE FORMAL INSOLVENCY

the ambit to be as extensive as possible. Article 2(1) of the EU Restructuring Directive therefore provides that 'restructuring' means measures aimed at restructuring the debtor's business that include changing the composition, conditions, or structure of a debtor's assets and liabilities or any other part of the debtor's capital structure, such as sales of assets or parts of the business and, where so provided under national law, the sale of the business as a going concern, as well as any necessary operational changes or a combination of these elements. The approach adopted in relation to the UK scheme of arrangement is similarly broad.[52] Indeed, the UK approach is such that a scheme can be used to effect releases by creditors of claims against third parties, such as guarantees, where the relevant third-party claims are 'closely connected with their rights against the company as creditors'.[53] This flexibility can enhance the effectiveness of the restructuring procedure.

3.25 Restructuring plans may be capable of binding all types of capital providers or a subset of them. The UK Company Voluntary Arrangement, for example, can only bind secured creditors with their consent, and this mechanism therefore cannot be used to impose a restructuring on dissenting secured creditors.[54] More commonly, restructuring plans are formulated to include secured creditors, preferential creditors, unsecured creditors, and possibly even shareholders. The extent to which shareholders are involved in a restructuring plan will often depend on the depth of the company's financial distress. For example, where the company is solvent and shareholders thus have an economic interest in the company, if their rights are to be compromised by the plan then they will generally need to be included in it and given the right to vote on it. Whether the plan can then go ahead without their consent will depend on the operation of any cross-class cramdown. Where the company is severely financially distressed such that the shareholders have no remaining economic interest in the company there may be no need to include them.

3.26 One of the benefits noted in relation to contractual workouts is the ability to include a subset of the creditors, which can simplify negotiations and increase the chances of success, particularly if the creditors involved in the restructuring are sophisticated creditors who are repeat players. It is a common feature of restructuring plans that they can similarly involve a subset of creditors.[55] For example, in UK schemes of arrangement a company is free to decide with whom it proposes any compromise or arrangement, although any creditors whose rights are to be affected by the scheme must be brought

---

[52] For discussion of the concept of a 'compromise or arrangement' between the parties, which is at the core of the scheme provisions (s. 899(1) of the Companies Act 2006), see, e.g. *Re Lehman Brothers International (Europe) (in administration)* [2009] EWCA Civ 1161.

[53] ibid [83] *per* Longmore LJ. A similar approach is followed in Singapore. See, e.g. *Pathfinder Strategic Credit LP v Empire Capital Resources Pte Ltd* [2019] SGCA 29. Dutch schemes of arrangement also allow for such releases, and the same holds true for Germany: see § 2(4) StaRUG for inter-group security rights.

[54] See s. 4(3) of the UK Insolvency Act 1986.

[55] For discussion, see S. Paterson and A. Walters, 'Selective Corporate Restructuring Strategy', Modern Law Review, 86 (2023) 436.

within its scope.[56] The same approach has been adopted elsewhere, for example in the German restructuring mechanism.[57] This is an example of a difference between the restructuring mechanisms discussed in this chapter and the insolvency processes discussed in Chapter 4. Insolvency always has a collective effect in order to overcome the common pool problem.[58]

C. Approval of the Plan by Creditors

1. Vote by the creditors: Constituting class meetings

3.27 One of the valuable aspects of a restructuring plan as compared to a contractual workout is the ability for the majority to bind the minority rather than creditors only being bound if they consent to the restructuring. Interfering with creditors' rights in this way requires protection to ensure that the minority are not unfairly treated. One of the ways in which minority protection is commonly provided in restructuring plans is to separate into classes the creditors (and shareholders where relevant) that are within the scope of the plan being proposed, with each class then meeting separately to vote on the plan.

3.28 The separation of creditors into classes to vote on a restructuring plan can operate as a valuable source of minority creditor protection. This is particularly the case in those restructuring mechanisms, such as the UK scheme of arrangement, where the imposition of the plan on dissenting creditors can only operate within classes and not between classes. In a UK scheme of arrangement the court is only able to confirm a plan if all the classes have voted in favour of it.[59] One of the concerns regarding the imposition of a plan on dissenting creditors is the possibility of wealth transfers between the creditors. However, where creditors meet and vote with like-minded creditors then the opportunity for wealth transfers diminishes, since the minority creditors in a class ought to be able to rely on the self-interest of the rest of the class (whose interests are aligned with those of the minority creditors) not to consent to such a transfer. Where cross-class cramdown becomes possible the protection against wealth transfers provided by the requirement for class meetings is reduced but not eliminated. In either case, the level of minority protection provided by this mechanism will depend on how the classes are constituted.

3.29 In constituting classes, the aim is to form them in such a way that the class is 'confined to those persons whose rights are not so dissimilar as to make it impossible for them to consult together with a view to their common interest',[60] or, to put it another way, the

---

[56] *Re British & Commonwealth Holdings plc (No. 3)* [1992] 1 WLR 672; *Sea Assets Ltd v PT Garuda Indonesia* [2001] EWCA Civ 1696. The same approach has been adopted in relation to UK restructuring plans: *Re Virgin Atlantic Airways Ltd* (n 49).

[57] See § 8 StaRUG.

[58] See Eidenmüller, 'What Is an Insolvency Proceeding?' (n 23) 53.

[59] See s. 899(1) of the UK Companies Act 2006.

[60] *Sovereign Life Assurance Co. v Dodd* [1892] 2 QB 573 at 583 *per* Bowen LJ. The same test is applied elsewhere; see, e.g. in Singapore: *Wah Yuen Engineering Pte Ltd v Singapore Cables Manufacturers Pte Ltd* [2003] 3 SLR 629 at [11]. See Art. 9(4) of the EU Restructuring Directive (n 3), and in Germany see § 9 StaRUG.

66 DEBT RESTRUCTURING OUTSIDE FORMAL INSOLVENCY

separation into classes is based on the premise that claims or interests may be placed in the same class only if they are 'substantially similar' to the rest of the class.[61]

3.30 What is relevant here is the rights of the parties rather than their interests as such. So, for example, if several creditors all have the same capital rights (regarding repayment, security, interest payments, and so on) but one has a potentially different interest in the outcome of the plan from the other creditors with those rights (perhaps it is part of the same group as the debtor company, or it has investments in more than one class, or it has hedged its risk and bought credit derivatives in relation to the debtor), generally these issues will not to be taken into account in determining the appropriate classes.[62] There are a number of practical advantages to focusing on rights rather than interests. The rights of the members or creditors will generally be easier for the company to identify and apply. It will often be difficult for the company to assess their different interests without requiring a considerable amount of personal information from them. In addition, unless a practical approach of this kind is adopted, there is a danger that a very large number of classes will be created. This is not to say that these interests, to the extent that they are known, are irrelevant. These issues can and should be taken into account by the court in determining whether to confirm a plan (discussed at section III.D). This approach does have the overall effect of reducing the number of classes and of increasing the potential importance of the court confirmation stage as a mechanism for minority protection.

3.31 The question whether creditors should be placed in different classes turns both on the nature of their existing rights and whether their rights are being altered in the same way under the plan. Small differences (e.g. as to the interest rate being charged) may not of themselves require creditors to be separated into different classes; the question should be whether those rights are sufficiently different that the creditors can no longer consult together with a view to their common interest. A balancing act is required. A class with genuinely different rights requires the protection of a separate meeting, but if too many artificial distinctions are drawn then this will lead to a proliferation of classes: '[i]f one gets too picky about potential different classes, one could end up with virtually as many classes as there are members of a particular group'.[63] Depending on the extent of the cramdown in a restructuring plan, this could impact the likelihood of the plan being approved.

3.32 In determining the similarity or dissimilarity of creditors' rights, the courts will often have regard to the correct comparator, that is what would be the outcome if the plan were not to go ahead. This is for two reasons. First, part of the determination of classes depends on a fair comparison between creditors' rights if there is no plan and its rights

---

[61] See 11 U.S.C. §1122.

[62] See, e.g. the approach of the English courts to this issue: *Re BTR plc* [2000] 1 BCLC 740. The same approach is adopted elsewhere: see, e.g. Hong Kong (*Re Industrial Equity (Pacific) Ltd* (1991) 2 HKLR 614) and Germany (see § 9(1) StaRUG).

[63] *Re Anglo American Insurance Co. Ltd* [2001] 1 BCLC 755 at 764 *per* Nourse J.

under the proposed plan, which depends on ascertaining the nature and quality of the rights in the 'non-plan world', and the latter depends on the appropriate comparator. Second, only by identifying this comparator can the likely practical effect of what is proposed be assessed and the likelihood of sensible discussion between the holders of various rights be weighed fairly.

An example illustrates the importance of this issue. In a UK scheme of arrangement case, *Re Hawk Insurance Co. Ltd*,[64] the question arose whether different types of unsecured creditors, some with vested claims and some with contingent claims, should be treated as being part of the same class for the purposes of voting on a proposed scheme of arrangement. It was suggested that these creditors should be treated as comprising different classes: those with vested claims should be treated as being in the same class as other unsecured creditors, since they all had an accrued claim against the company on which they had an immediate right to sue, but those with contingent claims had no such immediate right. The structure of the scheme was such that those whose claims had not yet accrued would have those claims scaled down to proportions less than 100%. Although these creditors would rank equally on insolvency (as they were all unsecured creditors), it was suggested that these differences meant that they should not be treated as comprising one class for scheme purposes. The Court of Appeal did not agree that separate classes were needed. The correct comparator in this instance was regarded as being a winding up of the company and on that basis the court held that all of the unsecured creditors, including those with contingent rights and those with vested rights, could meet as a single class.[65] As a result, where the correct comparator is winding up, it is likely that there will be little or no differentiation between unsecured creditors for this purpose, though higher-ranking creditors may require differentiation. If a different comparator is applied then a different outcome in terms of division into classes is likely. For example, if the comparator were instead a solvent run-off of the company it is very likely that the differences in the rights of the unsecured creditors in *Re Hawk Insurance* would be sufficient to place them in different classes.[66]

3.33

2. Vote by the creditors: Approval levels

Once the classes are formed, different restructuring plans take different approaches as to the majority approval level required. In general, bare '50 per cent plus one' majorities are not utilized in this context, and this is understandable. Debt restructuring plans depend on agreement of the creditors and have a contractual basis. Even though they have moved away from the unanimity required for contractual workouts, a substantial level of approval is needed for any plan to be successful, given that restructuring plans do not involve a sale to a third party but envisage the creditors staying in the company or business and continuing to cooperate. A reasonably high level of agreement as to the

3.34

---

[64] [2001] EWCA Civ 241.
[65] This broad approach to the analysis of classes for scheme purposes has subsequently been followed. See, e.g. *Re Telewest Communications plc* [2004] EWCA Civ 728; *Re UDL Holdings Ltd* [2002] 1 HKC 172.
[66] See, e.g. *Re British Aviation Insurance Co. Ltd* [2005] EWHC 1621 (Ch).

68 DEBT RESTRUCTURING OUTSIDE FORMAL INSOLVENCY

future direction is needed amongst the creditors, albeit avoiding the hold-up potential of unanimity. Thus, a supermajority of creditors is generally required. It is common for a two-thirds[67] or 75% majority to be set.[68] The EU Restructuring Directive leaves this to Member States, although it provides that the majority should not be higher than 75% of the claims or interests in the relevant class.[69] The UK scheme of arrangement provides that approval be by a majority in number representing 75% by value of the class of creditors present and voting,[70] in other words both a majority in value test and a headcount test. This headcount test is problematic and is subject to potential abuse.[71] It is preferable if a straightforward majority-in-value test is utilized as seen, for example, in the UK restructuring plan[72] or the Dutch scheme of arrangement.[73] It is typical (and preferable) for this test to be determined according to those creditors that participated in the vote rather than a percentage of the amount of claims or interests in each class,[74] in order to avoid the problem of absenteeism.

D. Confirmation by the Court

1. Introduction

3.35 In order to be effective, restructuring plans generally need to be confirmed by the court. Some jurisdictions also require an additional procedural step. For example, in a UK scheme of arrangement, the court order sanctioning the scheme takes effect once a copy is delivered to the Registrar of Companies.[75]

3.36 It is usual for the court to have a role in ensuring that all of the requisite statutory provisions have been complied with, such as the fact that the correct approval levels have been met in class meetings and any specified financial conditions for the availability of the plan have been met.[76] The court will also generally want to ensure that it has jurisdiction to approve the plan, something that may be relevant in plans involving foreign companies. In a UK scheme of arrangement, for example, the court will want to assure itself that there is a 'sufficient connection' between the scheme and England.[77]

---

[67] See, e.g. 11 U.S.C. §1126; Art. 381(7)(8) of the WHOA (n 28). In Canada, the statutory provisions do not specify the approval threshold for scheme meetings, and this is left to the courts to determine; the usual practice is for the approval threshold to be 66⅔% by value.

[68] See, e.g. UK scheme of arrangement (s. 899(1) of the UK Companies Act 2006); the UK restructuring plan (s. 901F(1) of the UK Companies Act 2006); the Singaporean scheme of arrangement (s. 210(3AB)(a),(b) of the Singapore Companies Act).

[69] See Art. 9(6) of the EU Restructuring Directive (n 3).

[70] See s. 899(1) of the UK Companies Act 2006.

[71] See Payne, *Schemes of Arrangement* (n 5) 2.3.3.2.

[72] See s. 901F(1) of the UK Companies Act 2006.

[73] See Art. 381(7)(8) of the WHOA (n 28).

[74] Cf. German law where the requirement is 75% of the *affected* creditors, not of those present and voting: see § 25(1) StaRUG.

[75] See s. 899(4) of the UK Companies Act 2006.

[76] For example, in Germany if a plan confirmation is applied for the court has to check whether the debtor is in the state of likely inability to pay its debts, whether the rules on content and procedural treatment of the plan have been met, and whether the satisfaction of the claims (as regulated in the plan) is evidently impossible (see § 63 StaRUG).

[77] See, e.g. Payne, *Schemes of Arrangement* (n 5) ch. 7.

Generally, the court will also want to ensure that there are no technical or legal defects associated with the plan which will mean that it does not work on its own terms or would otherwise infringe some mandatory provision of law in the relevant jurisdiction, for example where the plan involves some manipulation of the company's capital that has not been carried out in accordance with the relevant company law provisions.

Crucially, the court's role is discretionary and not a rubber-stamping exercise. Even if all the creditors have approved it, the court retains the ability to refuse to sanction the plan. There are certain key functions that the court will undertake before it confirms the plan, not only of the technical nature just described but also—crucially—to ensure that the minority have been properly protected. This role varies from jurisdiction to jurisdiction. Some jurisdictions specify the court's role in detail in the legislation, whereas in others the legislative provisions are relatively sparse and it is left to the courts themselves to develop the relevant legal principles. Different plans may create different roles for the court. This may depend on the extent to which the plan allows creditors' rights to be compromised without their consent; in general, the greater the interference with creditor rights, the more significant the role for the court at this stage. This varies not only between jurisdictions but also between different mechanisms in the same jurisdiction.[78] Other differences are observable too. For example, in some jurisdictions, minority protection is only granted where applied for by a dissenting creditor, whereas in others the court can consider these issues whether or not requested to do so by such a creditor. **3.37**

One of the key issues in the court's role in protecting minorities at this stage is the extent of the cramdown that the mechanism allows. The potential for abuse of the minority is greater in a mechanism that allows for a cross-class cramdown (i.e. for the restructuring to go ahead despite the dissent of one or more classes of creditors) than one in which only a cramdown within classes is possible. It is therefore unsurprising that the role of the court is different, and more significant, in the former situation. **3.38**

2. The court's role where there is cramdown within a class

Where a plan can only be sanctioned where all classes have approved it, so that it can only be imposed on dissenting creditors within a class, there are generally two forms of protection for the minority.[79] First, they meet in classes comprised of those with the same rights who are being treated in the same way within the plan. However, the focus **3.39**

---

[78] In the United Kingdom, for example, the scheme of arrangement involves the potential for the restructuring to be imposed only on dissenting creditors within a class (cramdown within a class), whereas the UK restructuring plan allows for a plan to be imposed on one or more dissenting classes of creditors (cross-class cramdown). For discussion of the different role of the court in sanctioning these different mechanisms see *Strategic Value Capital Solutions Master Fund LP v AGPS Bondco plc* [2024] EWCA Civ 24.

[79] While UK schemes of arrangement only allow for cramdown within classes, practitioners have developed a way in which a *de facto* cross-class cramdown can be achieved by twinning a scheme with administration (generally a pre-pack administration), in which case the same sorts of minority protection issues arise as discussed in section II.D(3) below. For discussion, see J. Payne, 'Debt Restructuring in English Law: Lessons from the US and the Need for Reform', Law Quarterly Review, 130 (2014) 282.

70 DEBT RESTRUCTURING OUTSIDE FORMAL INSOLVENCY

on creditor rights rather than creditor interests in separating creditors into classes creates a danger that the creditors may not be sufficiently like-minded to provide this protection. Where, for example, the debtor has provided financial incentives to a subset of the group to vote in favour of the plan, this might undermine the protection of the minority that the division into classes ought otherwise to provide.

3.40 The second form of protection for the minority is therefore the court's oversight of the plan at the sanctioning hearing. In deciding whether to confirm the plan the court will want to assure itself that the class was fairly represented by those attending and voting at the class meeting. So, for example, if there is a special interest of some creditors not shared by the class as a whole, and the approval level has only been reached as a result of those with special interests voting in favour, this can be taken into account by the court in determining whether to approve the plan.[80] Broadly, the question is whether those voting in the class meeting are doing so bona fide in the interests of the class as a whole. The court might also take account of the level of voting and voting outcomes to determine the extent to which the decision at the class meeting should be regarded as determinative of the views of the class.[81] These two forms of protection taken together can operate as an effective form of protection for minority creditors against intra-creditor wealth transfers where cramdown can only occur within classes.

3. The court's role in a cross-class cramdown

3.41 A number of restructuring mechanisms allow for the restructuring to be imposed not only on the dissenting creditors within a class but also on whole classes of dissenting creditors.[82] Examples include the UK restructuring plan, the Dutch scheme of arrangement, the German scheme, and the Singaporean scheme of arrangement. These follow a model that exists in Chapter 11 proceedings whereby the plan can be approved by the court despite one or more classes of creditors voting against it.[83]

3.42 In these circumstances, the measures of minority protection discussed above in relation to cramdown within classes will be insufficient to protect the minority. Even if like-minded creditors gather to vote on the plan, the fact that the dissent of a whole group can be ignored raises potential concerns about wealth transfers. For example, senior creditors could act with the directors to reorganize the debtor in a way that cuts out

---

[80] This approach is adopted by the UK courts in relation to schemes of arrangement: *Re Lehman Bros International (Europe) Ltd* [2018] EWHC 1980 (Ch). A similar approach is adopted by the Singaporean courts: *The Royal Bank of Scotland NV v TT International* (2012) SGCA 9.

[81] See, e.g. *Re TDG plc* [2009] 1 BCLC 445. A low turnout at the meeting is unlikely of itself be a valid reason for the court to refuse to sanction, since there can be a variety of reasons for non-attendance, but it might be relevant in considering whether the result could have been affected by collateral factors.

[82] Typically, this involves a cramdown (i.e. the imposition of the restructuring on a junior class), but the possibility of a cram up exists in some restructuring plans whereby junior creditors impose the plan on a dissenting class of senior creditors. This is possible under US Chapter 11 (see, e.g. *In re Charter Communications*, 419 BR 221 (Bankr SDNY 2009)). There is also the potential for this to occur in the UK restructuring plan: see s. 901G of the UK Companies Act 2006 and *Re Houst Ltd* (n 37), albeit that this involved a cram across rather than a cram up.

[83] Another way to exclude out-of-the-money shareholders/creditors is at the convening stage such that they do not vote on the restructuring plan at all, as can occur in the UK restructuring plan: see s. 901C(4) of the Companies Act 2006 and *Re Smile Telecoms Holdings Ltd* [2022] EWHC 387 (Ch).

the claims of the junior creditors, providing the senior creditors with all (or the lion's share) of equity and debt in the debtor company and leaving the subordinated classes with little or nothing after the restructuring. Faced with such a situation, the court will need to determine whether to approve a plan that excludes the junior creditors in this way. It may, after all, be a reasonable way forward where the financial distress of the debtor is such that there are only sufficient assets available to pay the senior creditors. Fundamentally, courts will want to assess what value each class of creditors had before the restructuring and what they have afterwards to see if an inappropriate wealth transfer has taken place. This analysis will have to balance the protection of the minority creditors with a need to prevent the minority exercising hold-up rights in a manner that inappropriately extracts value and threatens the successful outcome of the plan.

At the heart of this issue is the difficult question of who should retain a continuing stake **3.43** in the company or business. This then turns on how to value the company or business in a restructuring context. In an insolvency scenario this is relatively straightforward. The role of insolvency law is to impose a collective process so as to minimize individual enforcement so that the business can be kept together and sold for a higher price. The value of the business is determined by a sale of the business or its assets to a third party, usually in some form of auction process. Insolvency law may include safeguards against the sale being at too cheap a price, but the value can readily be determined in this way. In a going-concern sale or auction process the question of valuation is removed from the ambit of the creditors and from the court and is a matter for the market to determine. The division of the assets obtained in the sale amongst the creditors is also straightforward: the firm's value is distributed according to the priorities of the parties. By contrast, in a reorganization there is no sale to third parties. The existing creditors have committed to remaining within the company and continuing to fund it. Without a sale to a third party, some other form of valuation is required.

In the context of a cross-class cramdown, a central concern is for the courts to determine whether the value of the business if it continues will be greater than the value of **3.44** the business if it is sold at the time of the reorganization (whether this is a sale as a going concern or a sale on a break-up basis). However, this proposition is not as straightforward as it seems. The issue of valuation is fraught with difficulties. Should the debtor always be valued on a break-up basis or on a going concern basis or should this vary from case to case, and if so who determines which is relevant? If a going-concern basis is utilized, how should this be assessed in the absence of a sale to a third party? Should the valuation collapse all future values of the debtor into the immediate value at the date of reorganization or should those future possibilities be taken into consideration in some way? The choices made by different jurisdictions on these issues are tightly interwoven with the issue of minority protection in cross-class cramdowns. Furthermore, the purpose of a restructuring will generally be to preserve and add value to the debtor, and therefore the mere fact that the junior creditors receive the same value in the restructuring as they would in a sale on a break-up basis does not guarantee that there has been no wealth transfer to the senior creditors. There will often be a surplus generated by

72   DEBT RESTRUCTURING OUTSIDE FORMAL INSOLVENCY

the restructuring over and above the value arising if no restructuring takes place. This is sometimes referred to as the 'restructuring surplus' and the court will also want to consider the distribution of this sum amongst the relevant creditor classes as part of the decision whether to approve the plan.

3.45   In this context, there is often a focus on the question of priorities. The issue of priorities is a core consideration in the context of insolvency. Insolvency law seeks to coordinate debt enforcement to increase the total realizations available to the creditors as a group. Those realizations must be distributed in accordance with the priority rules. Perhaps because of the origins of many of the rules in this area in US Chapter 11, which is a bankruptcy process rather than a restructuring process per se, the issue of priority rules has also crept into this area, and discussions of various priority rules are commonplace. These discussions can sometimes obscure the question that the court is being asked to determine in this context, namely whether the dissenting creditors are being treated fairly both by reference to the position if the restructuring were not to occur, and in the proposed successful restructuring. The relative rank of the parties will be one important factor in this analysis, but there may be others, such as the extent to which the parties are prepared to put new value into the business.

3.46   Different jurisdictions have adopted different mechanisms to try to ensure that the minority are protected in this scenario. Perhaps the best known is that found in US Chapter 11, which has at its heart the absolute priority rule. This rule has been replicated (with some amendments) in other jurisdictions that have introduced cross-class cramdowns.

3.47   In Chapter 11 it is possible for the court to approve a plan even where one or more classes have dissented, as long as at least one class of impaired creditors votes in favour of the plan[84] and a number of other safeguards set out in 11 U.S.C. §1129 are met. Specifically, the court will want to ensure that the plan (a) is feasible and that it is not likely to be followed by liquidation or further financial reorganization unless that is part of the plan;[85] (b) meets the 'best interests of the creditors' test i.e. the plan cannot give impaired classes less than they would receive in a liquidation;[86] (c) treats each member of each class fairly;[87] and (d) is fair and equitable.[88] The feasibility test is part of the bigger question that courts need to ask about whether to confirm the plan, but the other tests focus on the question of fairness and whether a plan can be imposed on dissenting creditors. A part of the fair and equitable test is the absolute priority rule,[89] which has been described as 'bankruptcy's most important and famous rule' and 'the cornerstone

---

[84]   See 11 U.S.C. §1129(a)(10).

[85]   The court will want to see that the debtor will be able to meet the obligations that the plan imposes on it and that it will not leave Chapter 11 only to fail again: see ibid §1129(a)(11).

[86]   ibid §1129(a)(7).

[87]   ibid §1129(b).

[88]   ibid.

[89]   The 'fair and equitable' rule also contains other elements; in particular it includes specific rules for cramming down dissenting classes of secured creditors: see ibid §1129(b)(A).

of reorganization practice and theory',[90] although it has faced a growing level of scepticism from commentators in recent years.[91] The plan of reorganization must pay any non-consenting class in full before any junior class receives anything under the plan on account of its interest. Furthermore, a senior class may not receive more than 100% of its claim where a dissenting junior class will receive less than 100%. The general principle of the US system is therefore that a dissenting class can only be crammed down if it receives its share of the reorganization value of the debtor (i.e. the value realized through the plan) in accordance with its rank on liquidation. Each creditor class retains its own expert to value the business and the assets of the company using standard valuation methodology, of which the discounted cash-flow method is one of the most commonly used.[92] If the parties do not agree, there may be a valuation hearing before a judge. This is referred to as the bargaining and litigation approach.[93]

The absolute priority rule that appears in Chapter 11 has been influential in the design of other debt restructuring mechanisms around the world. For example, a version of the absolute priority rule was introduced in the Singapore regime in 2017 alongside cross-class cramdowns in order to provide minority protection.[94] Proponents of the rule emphasize, in particular, its value in providing certainty to the parties about the value of their entitlements in the event that negotiations fail, which can promote successful negotiations. The absolute priority rule has its critics, however. Some argue that it subjects approval of the plan to a condition that may lack reality, specifically, that the debtor's business may no longer retain sufficient value to return 100 cents on the dollar to members of the dissenting class.[95] The valuation process can be long and costly[96] and the valuations unpredictable given the level of subjectivity in the approach. Further, the out-of-the-money creditors may fear the valuation fight less than the senior creditors as they have less to lose. This may incentivize the senior creditors to give something to the junior classes to effectively buy out their ability to hold up the restructuring by forcing the matter into a contentious court hearing. The out-of-the-money creditors may thus capture returns to which they are not strictly entitled. Of necessity, the process of valuation is an inexact **3.48**

---

[90] ibid §1129(b)(2)(B) and see *Czyzewski v Jevic Holding Corp.* 137 S. Ct 973, 979 (2017).

[91] See, e.g. D.G. Baird, 'Priority Matters: Absolute Priority, Relative Priority, and the Costs of Bankruptcy', University of Pennsylvania Law Review, 165 (2017) 765; E.J. Janger, 'The Logic and Limits of Liens', University of Illinois Law Review (2015) 589; S.J. Lubben, 'The Overstated Absolute Priority Rule', Fordham Journal of Corporate & Financial Law, 21 (2016) 581. See also American Bankruptcy Institute, *Commission to Study the Reform of Chapter 11, 2012–2014: Final Report and Recommendations* (American Bankruptcy Institute 2014).

[92] For discussion, see K. O'Rourke, 'Valuation Uncertainty in Chapter 11 Reorganizations', Columbia Law Review (2005) 403; M. Simkovic, 'The Evolution of Valuation in Bankruptcy', American Bankruptcy Law Journal, 91 (2017) 299.

[93] D.G. Baird and D.S. Bernstein, 'Absolute Priority, Valuation Uncertainty, and the Reorganization Bargain', Yale Law Journal, 115(8) (2006) 1930.

[94] See s. 70 of the Singapore Insolvency, Restructuring and Dissolution Act 2018. There are some differences between Chapter 11 and the Singapore regime, however. For discussion, see Wan, Watters, and McCormack, 'Schemes of Arrangement in Singapore' (n 3) 463; Wee, 'The Singapore Story of Injecting US Chapter 11 into the Commonwealth Scheme' 553.

[95] L. Stanghellini, R. Mokal, C. Paulus, and I. Tirado, *Best Practices in European Restructuring* (Wolters Kluwer 2018).

[96] See Baird, 'Priority Matters' (n 92) 807.

74   DEBT RESTRUCTURING OUTSIDE FORMAL INSOLVENCY

science, fraught with uncertainties, particularly where it seeks to assess the future value of the company following reorganization, and this valuation uncertainty is often cited as a cause of the noted deviations from the absolute priority rule in Chapter 11 cases.[97] The results may also be less than ideal: 'The fog and uncertainty of financial distress allows some creditors to manipulate the process to capture value from others.'[98]

3.49   The difficulties created by the rigidity of the Chapter 11 absolute priority rule have led the US courts to accept deviations from the rule in some circumstances.[99] Indeed, Professor Lubben has stated that 'there is no absolute priority rule of the kind described in the literature under current law'.[100] Unsurprisingly, given these concerns when other regimes have introduced such a rule it has often been with modifications. In the Dutch scheme of arrangement, for example, the Act provides for the absolute priority rule to apply 'unless there are reasonable grounds for [...] deviation [from the priority regime] and the interests of [the dissentients] are not prejudiced by it'.[101] Similarly, the German StaRUG scheme requires compliance with the absolute priority rule unless 'an arrangement deviating from [the absolute priority rule] is appropriate in view of the type of the economic difficulties to be overcome and the circumstances'.[102]

3.50   Concerns over the operation of the absolute priority rule in some circumstances have led to alternatives being developed. One of these is the relative priority rule. When the EU Restructuring Directive introduced the possibility of cross-class cramdown, it included a version of the absolute priority rule found in Chapter 11, alongside other safeguards,[103] but as an alternative, the Directive allows Member States to adopt a 'relative priority rule' whereby dissenting voting classes of affected creditors must simply be treated at least as favourably as any other class of the same rank and more favourably than any junior class.[104] Proponents of the relative priority rule within the Directive state that it provides optionality for Member States and counters the disadvantages of the absolute priority rule. However, a number of concerns have been raised regarding this priority rule,[105] including that it creates legal uncertainty for both investors and

---

[97] L. LoPucki and W. Whitford, 'Bargaining over Equity's Share in the Bankruptcy Reorganization of Large, Publicly Held Companies', University of Pennsylvania Law Review, 139 (1990) 125; Baird and Bernstein, 'Absolute Priority' (n 94) 130; J.L. Westbrook, 'A Comparison of Bankruptcy Reorganization in the US, with Administration Procedure in the UK', Insolvency Law & Practice (1990) 86.

[98] Baird, 'Priority Matters' (n 92) 821.

[99] See, e.g. *Czyzewski v Jevic Corp.* (n 91)

[100] Lubben, 'The Overstated Absolute Priority Rule' (n 92) 581, 584.

[101] See Art. 384(4((b) of the WHOA (n 28).

[102] See § 28 StaRUG.

[103] These include (a) a best-interests-of-the-creditors test whereby a creditor would be better off in the plan than in a liquidation (Art. 10(2)(d) and Recital 52); (b) a requirement that no class of affected parties can, under the restructuring plan, receive or keep more than the full amount of its claims or interests (Art. 11(1)(d)); and (c) the 'no unfair discrimination principle' that dissenting voting classes of affected creditors shall be treated at least as favourably as any other class of the same rank (Art. 11(1)(c)).

[104] Of these two alternatives, the default position appears to be the relative priority rule: Art. 11(1)(c), with the absolute priority rule in Art. 11(2)(a) being a derogation from this position. The relative priority rule within the Directive is not identical to the relative priority rule that has been proposed by US academics as an alternative to the absolute priority rule found in US Chapter 11: see, e.g. Baird, 'Priority Matters' (n 92).

[105] For discussion of the advantages and disadvantages of the rule, see T. Richter and A. Thery, *INSOL Europe: Guidance Note on the Implementation of Preventive Restructuring Frameworks under EU Directive 2019/*

judges over the exact amount of incremental value that will constitute better treatment of the senior class over the junior class in order to satisfy the 'more favourably' requirement. Legal uncertainty may also be generated by the fact that this rule is generally less well understood than the tried-and-tested absolute priority rule.

Another approach to minority protection was adopted in the UK restructuring plan. **3.51** Two conditions are provided for a cross-class cramdown to occur: (a) the compromise or arrangement has been accepted at a class meeting of at least one class of creditors/ members who would receive a payment, or have a genuine economic interest in the company, in the event of the relevant alternative[106] and (b) the court must be satisfied that, if the compromise or arrangement were to be sanctioned, none of the members of the dissenting class would be any worse off than they would be in the event of the relevant alternative.[107] The 'relevant alternative' for these purposes is whatever the court considers would be most likely to occur in relation to the company if the plan is not confirmed.[108] The benefit of this provision compared to the absolute priority rule within Chapter 11 is that the 'floor' below which dissentients' entitlements may not be allowed to fall is their return in the relevant alternative (which may therefore be zero if the alternative is liquidation and value breaks in the senior debt) as compared with the 'floor' in Chapter 11 which is the face value of the dissentients' claims. In a restructuring where the debtor is sufficiently financially distressed that it cannot pay its debts in full (and the dissenting creditors will not receive full value for their claims), there is value in this more flexible approach. This does not deal with the issue of how a restructuring surplus above the level of any relevant alternative should be distributed. For this the UK courts will need to exercise their discretion. No statutory guidance is provided for this purpose.[109] One possible downside of this approach is a lack of certainty compared to other jurisdictions in which the test is set out more clearly. The case law on these issues is in the process of being developed by the English courts.[110]

The approach of the English courts to valuation is to have regard to the price that the **3.52** business would fetch in the market if sold on the date of the reorganization, effectively

---

1023: *Claims, Classes, Voting, Confirmation and the Cross-Class Cram-Down* (INSOL Europe April 2020) 35–6; R. de Weijs, A. Jonkers, and M. Malakotipour, 'The Imminent Distortion of European Insolvency Law: How the European Union Erodes the Basic Fabric of Private Law by Allowing "Relative Priority"', Amsterdam Law School Research Paper No. 2019-10; Madaus, 'Leaving the Shadows of US Bankruptcy Law' (n 11); R. Mokal and I. Tirado, 'Has Newton Had His Day? Relativity and Realism in European Restructuring', European Restructuring (2018) 20; J.M. Seymour and S.L. Schwarcz, 'Corporate Restructuring under Relative and Absolute Priority Default Rules: A Comparative Assessment', University of Illinois Law Review (2021) 1.

[106] See s. 901G(5) of the UK Companies Act 2006. This raises the danger that artificial classes may be created in order to satisfy this condition, something for which the courts must be alert. For discussion, see, e.g. *Re Virgin Atlantic Airways Ltd* (n 49); *Re Deep Ocean 1 UK Ltd* [2021] EWHC 138 (Ch).

[107] See s. 901G(3) of the UK Companies Act 2006.

[108] ibid s. 901G(4).

[109] The Explanatory notes accompanying the 2020 Act state that the court has discretion to decline to sanction a plan if it is not 'just and equitable', although this is not a test that has been applied previously in the context of UK schemes of arrangement or restructuring more generally, and no statutory guidance is provided as to how courts should apply this provision: Department for Business, Energy & Industrial Strategy (BEIS), 'Explanatory Notes Accompanying the Corporate Insolvency and Governance Act 2020', para. 190.

[110] See, e.g. *Re Virgin Active Holdings Ltd* [2021] EWHC 1246 (Ch); *Re Deep Ocean 1 UK Ltd* (n 107); *Re Houst Ltd* (n 37 *Strategic Value Capital Solutions Master Fund LP v AGPS Bondco Plc* (n 79).

76   DEBT RESTRUCTURING OUTSIDE FORMAL INSOLVENCY

treating the business as being sold to the existing creditors. This has the benefit of flexibility, allowing the valuation to be on a going-concern basis or break-up basis as relevant in the circumstances and it has the advantage of providing an objective measure (avoiding the bargaining and litigation approach of the US Chapter 11 regime), but it also includes some potential pitfalls. It relies on expertise by the judge to determine the relevant alternative and to reach a decision on the appropriate valuation. Determining a going-concern valuation can be particularly tricky. As there is no actual sale, this figure can be determined in a number of ways. It may be assessed on the basis of market-valuation opinions provided by expert valuers (which can lead to costly and lengthy valuation fights between the parties that can be difficult for the court to mediate) or market price valuation of the business, which is sometimes said to be preferable[111] but is open to misuse by the senior creditors if they utilize a temporary dip in the market to cut out the junior creditors.

3.53   This counterfactual approach has sometimes been described as 'too blunt an instrument' for the balancing act that the court needs to engage in during this process, namely balancing the desire to allocate capital to the companies best able to make use of it and support the views of existing creditors who wish to remain invested in a company with the need to ensure that the reorganization put in place does not expropriate value from creditors who still have an interest.[112] An alternative approach is to provide the junior creditors with an option with a strike price equal to the full amount of the senior claims to enable them to participate in the upside should the reorganization allow the company to flourish in the future.[113] This approach has its critics too[114] and has not been adopted to date.

4. Effect of confirmation of a plan

3.54   Although restructuring plans resemble a contract between the debtor and its creditors, the plan has binding force as a result of the statutory process underpinning it. Once the court confirmation (and any additional steps, such as registration of the court's decision) have taken place then the restructuring is binding on the company and on all the relevant creditors including any dissenting creditors.[115] One issue that arises is the ability of the restructuring plan to be challenged at this point. The EU Restructuring Directive does not require the confirmation decision to be subject to appeal but recognizes this as an option for Member States.[116] Any appeal process will, however,

---

[111]   Baird, 'Bankruptcy's Uncontested Axioms' (n 1).

[112]   Paterson, 'Rethinking Corporate Bankruptcy' (n 9).

[113]   See, e.g. L. Bebchuk, 'A New Approach to Corporate Reorganizations', Harvard Law Review, 101 (1988) 775; Baird, 'Priority Matters' (n 92).

[114]   See, e.g. M. Roe, 'Bankruptcy and Debt: A New Model for Corporate Reorganization', Columbia Law Review, 83 (1983) 527.

[115]   See, e.g. Art. 385 of the WHOA (n 28) and § 67(1) StaRUG.

[116]   See Art. 16 of the EU Restructuring Directive (n 3). The Dutch scheme of arrangement, for example, does not include an option for appeal. By comparison, the German regime (§ 66 StaRUG) makes the confirmation subject to immediate appeal by dissenting creditors, but the appellate court may dismiss the appeal if it appears to be preferable that the restructuring plan take effect as soon as possible.

extend the period before the plan can be fully implemented, adding to the uncertainty of the situation and potentially undermining the ability to resolve the company's difficulties satisfactorily, and it is preferable for the possibility of any appeal to be subject to a high bar.

IV. A Restructuring Moratorium

During the period of a debt restructuring, absent any legal intervention there is the potential for one or more creditors to disrupt the restructuring, either by exercising their contractual rights (to demand repayment, for example) or by seeking to put the company into insolvency. One way to address the former concern is to reduce the creditors' ability to exercise hold-up rights by removing the unanimity requirement for the arrangement to go ahead, as discussed in section III. Another way to address these concerns is the imposition of a statutory stay or moratorium to provide the company with a breathing space to negotiate the restructuring, as discussed in this section. This could involve a stay on creditors asserting their ability to enforce a debt claim against the company or preventing the initiation of insolvency proceedings and other legal processes, or both. Another restriction that can be allied to the statutory stay is a constraint on the ability of creditors to make use of *ipso facto* clauses. *Ipso facto* clauses allow a creditor to terminate a contract on the basis of insolvency alone. Constraining the creditor's right to utilize such a clause means that the assets or services remain within the company or business during this period.

3.55

Whereas the constraints on creditors' contractual rights described in section III respond to the anticommons problem whereby individual creditors can seek to frustrate the wishes of the majority, the constraints described in this section respond both to this concern and to the 'common pool' problem.[117] If there is no stay, then creditors may seize assets that are useful or even essential for the carrying on of the debtor's business and this could therefore jeopardize the prospects of a successful restructuring. This is not identical to the situation in insolvency, where the aim is to provide a collective process and minimize the incentive for individual enforcement so that a statutory stay is crucial to the procedure. A restructuring is not a collective debt enforcement procedure. It involves the situation where the creditors wish to remain invested in the company but renegotiate their bargain. It may involve only a subset of the creditors. The common pool problem does not necessarily arise. However, in some circumstances individual incentives to enforce will exist. There may be a minority of creditors who have their own idiosyncratic reasons for preferring to enforce and in these circumstances restructuring law might usefully borrow the idea of a statutory stay from insolvency law,

3.56

---

[117] See Jackson, *The Logic and Limits of Bankruptcy Law* (n 36).

78   DEBT RESTRUCTURING OUTSIDE FORMAL INSOLVENCY

with appropriate adjustments to take account of the differences between restructuring and insolvency, as discussed below.

3.57   The benefits of a moratorium in the context of insolvency are well understood as a means of keeping the business and assets together so that they can be sold for the highest possible price.[118] Until relatively recently moratoria were less often seen in a restructuring context, although this is changing. In the United Kingdom, for example, while a statutory stay has attached to administration since its introduction in the 1985–6 insolvency law reforms,[119] a restructuring moratorium was only introduced in 2020.[120] Other recent examples include the debt restructuring reforms introduced in Singapore[121] and Germany,[122] both of which include a restructuring moratorium as part of the reform package.

3.58   The benefits of a moratorium will depend on various factors within a jurisdiction and how the debt restructuring mechanisms are structured. For example, a debt restructuring involving a small number of sophisticated and homogenous creditors whose interests are aligned and who understand the benefits of maximizing the value of the company as a going concern, may not require the intervention of the law to prevent them exercising their rights. A contractual standstill arrangement between them may be sufficient. Debt restructuring mechanisms that can involve a subset of the creditors, specifically the financial creditors, can facilitate this situation.[123] The existence of an effective market for distressed debt can also be beneficial since creditors unhappy with the restructuring are able to sell their debt rather than having to challenge the proposed restructuring or enforce their claim.[124] However, where such options are not available and where the restructuring involves large numbers of heterogeneous creditors,[125] there may be a need for intervention by the law. This can be facilitated by the courts,[126] but more commonly, statutory intervention is involved.

3.59   While a statutory stay can clearly provide benefits for the company and for creditors as a whole, these benefits occur at the expense of party autonomy since creditors are

---

[118] See, e.g. Jackson, 'Bankruptcy, Non-Bankruptcy Entitlements, and the Creditors' Bargain' (n 36) 857; T.H. Jackson and R.E. Scott, 'On the Nature of bankruptcy: An Essay on Bankruptcy Sharing and the Creditors' Bargain', Virginia Law Review, 75 (1989) 155.

[119] See Sch. B1, paras 42–3 of the UK Insolvency Act 1986.

[120] See ss 1–6 and Schs 1–9 of the UK Corporate Insolvency and Governance Act 2020, introducing a new Part A1 to the UK Insolvency Act 1986. For discussion, see Payne, 'An Assessment of the UK Restructuring Moratorium' (n 16) 454.

[121] See ss 64–6 of the Singapore Insolvency, Restructuring and Dissolution Act 2018.

[122] See §§ 49 et seq. StaRUG.

[123] This helps to explain why the UK scheme of arrangement has operated successfully for many years without having access to a restructuring moratorium. See Payne, 'An Assessment of the UK Restructuring Moratorium' (n 16) 454.

[124] See Paterson, 'Rethinking Corporate Bankruptcy' (n 9).

[125] Debt markets are evolving, and it is becoming more common for companies to be financed by large numbers of heterogeneous creditors, driving a need for a statutory stay even in markets that have not traditionally needed such a device during restructuring. See, e.g. S. Paterson, *Corporate Reorganization Law and Forces of Change* (OUP 2021).

[126] For example, the English court has been prepared to grant a temporary stay to facilitate a scheme of arrangement in some circumstances, e.g. *Bluecrest Mercantile BV; FMS Wertmanagement AÖR v Vietnam Shipbuilding Industry Group* [2013] EWHC 1146 (Comm).

prevented from exercising their contractual and other rights. A balance is therefore required between the benefits to the company and the creditors as a whole on the one hand, and the rights of the individual creditors on the other. As with the constraints discussed in section III, this raises the need for a third party, such as a court, to ensure that the balance between the parties is maintained. Typically, courts are involved in a statutory stay, whether that is at specific points in the process (for instance, to approve the commencement of the moratorium) or in a more general oversight role. However, it is also usual for an insolvency practitioner or other third party to be appointed to perform specific tasks. Given that the restructuring process is debtor-in-possession, the directors are left in control during the restructuring moratorium and subject to their usual directors' duties, although additional obligations and offences may also be created as part of the moratorium process.[127]

A. The Scope of the Statutory Stay

There are a number of different ways that a statutory stay can be structured in terms **3.60** of its scope. The stay might just prevent enforcement by creditors, but it will be much more useful to the debtor if creditors are also prevented from commencing insolvency proceedings.[128] Beyond this, a stay can be formulated so that creditors are prevented from asserting all contractual rights or enforcing all claims against the company or only some; it might be formulated such that creditors will be prevented from commencing all legal processes against the company or only some. A statutory stay might encompass all companies or exclude certain types, such as those that have already utilized a moratorium in the recent past.[129]

Another question is whether a debtor has a choice between a moratorium that affects **3.61** all creditors[130] and one that is targeted towards specific creditors.[131] A restructuring moratorium where the only option is to affect all creditors would seem to reflect the insolvency origins of this concept, where the proceedings are necessarily collective. A preferable, and more flexible, approach is to allow a moratorium to be targeted at a subset of creditors. This approach provides companies with the option of excluding certain creditors, for example smaller creditors or those in financial difficulties themselves, on whom the burden of the moratorium might fall disproportionately.

---

[127] See, e.g. in the UK restructuring moratorium, the offence of fraud during or in anticipation of a moratorium: Part A1, Ch. 7 of the Insolvency Act 1986.

[128] In jurisdictions in which companies are obliged to commence insolvency proceedings in certain circumstances, the moratorium may also need to remove this requirement: see Art. 7(1) of the EU Restructuring Directive (n 3) and § 42(1) StaRUG.

[129] The UK restructuring moratorium excludes companies that have entered into a moratorium within the previous 12 months without an order of the court: Sch. ZA1, para. 1 of the Insolvency Act 1986.

[130] This is the approach adopted in the UK restructuring moratorium, for example.

[131] See, e.g. Art. 6(4) of the EU Restructuring Directive (n 3) and § 49(2)(sentence 2) StaRUG. Other jurisdictions also adopt a more flexible approach: see, e.g. the Canadian approach described in J. Sarra, *Rescue! The Companies' Creditors Arrangement Act* (2nd edn, Thomson Reuters Canada Ltd 2013).

80 DEBT RESTRUCTURING OUTSIDE FORMAL INSOLVENCY

3.62 As an adjunct to the moratorium, jurisdictions may impose constraints on the ability of creditors to terminate their contracts on the basis of insolvency alone (*ipso facto* clauses).[132] *Ipso facto* clauses can be beneficial for creditors, offering an automatic remedy for a creditor without the time and expense of judicial enforcement proceedings since the creditor can demand accelerated payments or terminate the contract, thus saving the transaction costs associated with default. Again, the potential benefit that can arise for debtors and creditors as a whole in constraining their use and keeping the company or business together during the period of the restructuring needs to be balanced with the interference with individual creditor rights, and this balancing process is often performed by a court. Examples of the protection that may be built in for individual creditors where the ability to utilize *ipso facto* clauses is constrained include personal guarantees from the insolvency practitioner[133] and the ability of creditors to terminate their contracts in some circumstances despite the constraints, such as where the court approves the termination.[134]

3.63 Where jurisdictions impose constraints on *ipso facto* clauses, they often make different policy choices about the scope and ambit of such constraints. Some jurisdictions include all executory contracts within the scope of the constraints (subject to carve-outs),[135] whereas others have a narrower scope. The UK regime, for example, covers only contracts for the supply of goods or services.[136] Different choices are made regarding the trigger for these provisions. For example, UK schemes of arrangement are excluded from the ambit of these provisions (despite having access to the restructuring moratorium), whereas the Australian *ipso facto* provisions do include schemes of arrangement, although the legislation restricts the provisions to circumstances in which the scheme is being used 'for the purpose of the body avoiding being wound up in insolvency'.[137] There can also be variation regarding what the constraint includes: is it simply termination by the creditor or is the prohibition broader? Most jurisdictions seem to include exceptions for financial creditors. There is some sense to this exclusion. In the absence of this carve-out, financial creditors may be prompted to incorporate earlier triggers into financial documentation to enable them to withdraw from the company the working capital necessary for the company's ongoing operation at a point

---

[132] Some of these have been around for some time, such as the provisions within the US Chapter 11 regime (§§365(e) and 541(c)). Other provisions are more recent, such as the constraints on *ipso facto* introduced in Singapore (s. 440 of the Singapore Insolvency Restructuring and Dissolution Act 2018), Australia (ss 415D, 434J, and 451E of the Australian Corporations Act 2001, inserted by Treasury Laws Amendment (2017) Enterprise Incentives (No. 2) Act 2017), and Art. 7(4) and (5) of the EU Restructuring Directive (n 3). For discussion, see J. Sarra, J. Payne, and S. Madaus, 'The Promise and Perils of Regulating Ipso Facto Clauses', International Insolvency Review, 31 (2022) 45.

[133] See, e.g. ss 233 and 233A of the UK Insolvency Act 1986 (but cf. s. 233B).

[134] ibid s. 233B(5)(c). A similar provision exists in s. 440(4) of the Singapore Insolvency, Restructuring and Dissolution Act 2018.

[135] See 11 U.S.C. §365(e).

[136] See s. 233B of the UK Insolvency Act 1986, as amended.

[137] See s. 415D(5) of the Australian Corporations Act 2001, inserted by the Treasury Laws Amendment (2017 Enterprise Incentives No. 2) Act 2017.

when insolvency is reasonably likely in order to avoid the effects of the *ipso facto* constraint, an outcome that is likely to be detrimental to a distressed company.

B. Automatic or Voluntary?

The statutory stay may attach automatically, once a restructuring mechanism is commenced, or it may be left for the company to determine whether to opt for it. Given the benefits of a statutory stay for the company, discussed above, it might seem advantageous for the stay to arise automatically, without the company having to do any more. In US Chapter 11, for example, the statutory stay arises automatically upon the filing of the bankruptcy petition and then stays all litigation and prevents the enforcement of judgments and of security without leave of the court.[138] While an automatic statutory stay exists in relation to insolvency proceedings and makes sense in that context, more optionality is beneficial in the restructuring context since some distressed companies may be wary of announcing moratorium protection because of the unwanted publicity this may draw to their financial position.[139] Furthermore, because restructuring (in contrast to insolvency proceedings) deals with the situation in which creditors wish to remain invested in the firm, the imposition of a statutory stay may not be needed. To the extent that creditors need to agree not to exercise their contractual rights in this context, it may be preferable to do so by other means, such as via a contractual standstill agreement.

3.64

C. Timing

A question arises as to the financial condition of a company that may access the statutory stay and the time at which a statutory stay will arise. This links to the more general question regarding the availability of the debt restructuring mechanism to which the moratorium is linked, discussed above in section III.A(1). Given that the curtailment of creditor rights is justified in order to overcome the anticommons problems and (potentially) the common pool problem, the use of the moratorium cannot be justified at all points in time. The need to balance the benefit of the moratorium to the company and creditors as a whole with the interference of individual creditors' rights is relevant here.

3.65

Creditors may be concerned about directors making use of the moratorium to shake off liabilities that the company is capable of meeting. At the same time, creditors may worry that directors will use a moratorium to prop up a company that is not economically

3.66

---

[138] See 11 U.S.C. §362(a).

[139] For examples of restructuring moratoria that are not automatic, see the UK restructuring moratorium, the Singaporean restructuring moratorium, the German restructuring moratorium (§§ 29(2) No. 3, 49 et seq. StaRUG), and the moratorium included in the EU Restructuring Directive (n 3).

82 DEBT RESTRUCTURING OUTSIDE FORMAL INSOLVENCY

viable such that the moratorium simply prolongs the moment when the company's difficulties are dealt with, with the company continuing to lose money in the meantime. Jurisdictions therefore tend to impose conditions regarding the financial state of the company that may utilize a moratorium, although pinpointing this issue is not always straightforward. While the use of a moratorium, and the resulting interference with creditor rights, is hard to justify when a company is wholly solvent and capable of paying its debts as they fall due, leaving its use until the company is insolvent is also potentially problematic. Even before the company is insolvent, creditors may be concerned about a possible future insolvency and may be inclined to pre-emptively enforce their claims in order to avoid being bound by a procedure alongside other creditors and denied their individual rights. Sophisticated creditors may use this knowledge to threaten action in order to extract gains in this period at the expense of less sophisticated creditors.[140] Jurisdictions generally seek to position the moratorium as being available in the period when the company is financially distressed but still viable and capable of rescue.[141] So, for example, a condition of obtaining the UK restructuring moratorium is that directors have to state their view that the company is, or is likely to become, unable to pay its debts[142] as a way of tackling the concern about directors of viable companies shaking off liabilities that the company is capable of meeting. There is also a requirement that the insolvency practitioner appointed to oversee the moratorium should be prepared to state that the moratorium is likely to result in the rescue of the company as a going concern[143] as a way of dealing with the concern that directors may seek to prop up an unviable company.

D. Duration

3.67 Another issue is the length of the moratorium. Clearly, there is a benefit to the company and creditors as a whole in having a lengthy period within which to negotiate and implement the restructuring, but individual creditors will want the moratorium and the infringement of their rights to be kept as short as possible. Jurisdictions take a range of approaches to this issue. In US Chapter 11 debtors are given the exclusive right to formulate a plan of reorganization for 120 days from the date of filing. This period can be extended if sufficient reasons are established up to a maximum of 18 months from the filing date.[144] The EU Restructuring Directive includes a moratorium with an initial 4-month period, extendable up to 12 months.[145] By contrast, the UK

---

[140] H. Eidenmüller, 'Trading in Times of Crisis: Formal Insolvency Proceedings, Workouts, and the Incentives for Shareholders/Managers', European Business Organization Law Review, 15 (2006) 239.

[141] See, e.g. Germany, where §§ 29(1), 51 StaRUG requires the likely inability to pay debts and that the restructuring endeavour must not be unpromising ('no prospects of success').

[142] See Part A1, Chapter 3, ss A6(1)(d) of the UK Insolvency Act 1986.

[143] ibid Part A1, Chapter 3, ss A6(1)(e).

[144] See 11 U.S.C. §1121.

[145] See Art. 6(6) and 6(8) of the EU Restructuring Directive (n 3). In Germany, the initial duration is three months, extendable under strict conditions to a maximum of eight months (§ 53 StaRUG).

restructuring moratorium automatically ends 20 business days from the day after the moratorium comes into force,[146] although this can be extended by a further 20 business days without creditor consent and can be extended for up to 12 months with the consent of creditors and/or a court order.[147] While there is clearly a concern to protect creditors by not having an overly long moratorium, this needs to be weighed against the value of the mechanism as a breathing space for companies within which to negotiate the restructuring. It may be questioned whether the period available in the UK restructuring moratorium is sufficiently valuable for companies, particularly those contemplating complex restructurings.[148]

E. The Opportunity to Challenge the Moratorium

3.68 A way of seeking to protect individual creditors is to allow them to challenge a moratorium.[149] This may involve challenging the actions of directors and any insolvency practitioner or third party appointed to have oversight of the process. The challenge may be on the basis that the eligibility requirements or qualifying conditions for the moratorium were not satisfied such that the moratorium should not have been imposed at all, so that the moratorium should not apply to any creditors. Alternatively, it may be that the creditors wish to assert that although the moratorium is *per se* valid it should not apply to a subset of creditors, on the basis that one or more creditors have been unfairly prejudiced[150] or unfairly harmed. In general, this will require the court to balance the interests of the individual creditor with those of the creditors/stakeholders as a whole, against the backdrop of the company's financial distress and the aims of the restructuring.

V. Rescue Finance

3.69 A further component of an effective restructuring regime is the existence of rescue finance, that is finance designed to both keep the 'lights on' for a period in order to enable the debtor to negotiate with its creditors and to enable the restructuring agreed between the parties to be implemented. The availability of both these forms of financing can be seen as a key aspect of effective corporate restructuring, since the injection of financing by new or existing lenders can enable the continued operation of the business of the debtor or the preservation of the value of the assets of the estate.[151] There can also

---

[146] See Part A1, Chapter 3, s. A9 of the UK Insolvency Act 1986.

[147] ibid Part A1, Chapter 3, ss A10–A13.

[148] See Payne, 'An Assessment of the UK Restructuring Moratorium' (n 16) 454.

[149] In some jurisdictions, the moratorium order is not challengeable, e.g. in Germany, where creditors can only apply for removal.

[150] This is the language utilized by Art. 6(9)(c) of the EU Restructuring Directive (n 3).

[151] See the UNCITRAL *Legislative Guide on Insolvency Law* (UNCITRAL 2004), recommendation 63; J. Payne and J. Sarra, 'Tripping the Light Fantastic: A Comparative Analysis of the European Commission's Proposals for New and Interim Financing of Insolvent Businesses', International Insolvency Review, 27 (2018) 178.

84 DEBT RESTRUCTURING OUTSIDE FORMAL INSOLVENCY

be a signalling effect, since the injection of additional financing can send a message to the market and/or the debtor company's creditors that there is confidence in the future prospects of the business.

3.70 This is something that can be developed by the market, without the need for specific legal intervention, and indeed it may be possible for lenders to agree these matters amongst themselves, particularly where existing lenders can contractually subordinate their claims to those new lenders if they choose to do so.[152] Existing lenders may be regarded as well placed to determine whether a distressed company is capable of rescue and therefore whether a further injection of funding is worthwhile. Where market-based solutions operate successfully, there may be no need for specific legal intervention on this issue.[153] However, in jurisdictions without such solutions legislative intervention can be beneficial and some jurisdictions have developed mechanisms to encourage rescue financing.

3.71 There are various ways in which this can be achieved. For instance, there could be a special priority charge for critical suppliers;[154] the costs of the rescue finance may be given priority as administrative expenses;[155] or the new lender might be given protection from the financing being declared void, voidable, or unenforceable subsequently.[156] Perhaps the most common, however, is the use of provisions whereby lenders who provide funds to the company during the restructuring process can obtain priority over existing creditors in certain circumstances.[157] The issue of how the new financing will rank compared to existing lenders is likely to be a concern for rescue financiers. Given the financial distress of the company, the rescue financier is taking on a more significant risk than a lender to a solvent company and will want to extract a premium for this risk, such as priority in payment. Of course, if there are assets that are unencumbered this will be straightforward but commonly, given the company's financial distress, there will be limited or no unencumbered assets available. Therefore, priority can only be given to new creditors where existing secured creditors consent to the new creditor having priority over their claims or a legislative regime enables the rights of existing creditors to

---

[152] See, e.g. in the United Kingdom, *Re Maxwell Communications Corporation plc (No. 2)* [1994] 1 All ER 737.

[153] In the United Kingdom, for example, although there was some discussion of the introduction of legislative reforms specifically designed to facilitate rescue finance in the United Kingdom (see Insolvency Service, *A Review of the Corporate Insolvency Framework: A Consultation on Options for Reform* (Insolvency Service May 2016)), this was not supported by the market (See Insolvency Service, *Summary of Responses—A Review of the Corporate Insolvency Framework* (Insolvency Service September 2016) and BEIS, *Insolvency and Corporate Governance: Government Response* (BEIS 26 August 2018)) and these reforms did not find their way into the UK Corporate Insolvency and Governance Act 2020.

[154] In Canada, for example, if the court makes an order designating the supplier a critical supplier, the court must, in the order, declare that all or part of the property of the company is subject to a security or charge in favour of the person declared to be a critical supplier in an amount equal to the value of the goods or services supplied under the terms of the order: s. 11.4 of the Canadian Companies' Creditors Arrangement Act.

[155] UNCITRAL *Legislative Guide* (n 152) 116. For an example see s. 11.52 of the Canadian Companies' Creditors Arrangement Act, discussed in *Re Performance Sports Group Ltd*, 2016 ONSC 6800, 2016 CarswellOnt 17492 (Ont SCJ, Commercial List).

[156] See, e.g. Arts 17 and 18 of the EU Restructuring Directive (n 3) and, for Germany, §§ 89 and 90 StaRUG.

[157] See, e.g. 11 U.S.C. §364(d).

be overridden.[158] Given the effect on existing creditors, this often involves a role for the court. 11 U.S.C. §364(d), for example, allows the debtor to seek approval from the court for rescue financing that is secured on a priority basis that is by a lien equal or senior to an existing lien if the applicant can establish that it was unable to obtain credit otherwise and there is 'adequate protection' for existing creditors.[159]

Rescue financing is often regarded as a vital aspect of the debt restructuring regime **3.72** in those jurisdictions in which it has been introduced. It can have a positive effect for the company in question,[160] with empirical studies in the US finding that firms that received rescue finance were likely to spend less time in bankruptcy proceedings than those that did not have access to such financing and were more likely to ultimately exit the process as a going-concern business.[161] There are also some significant risks, however. The request for rescue financing will generally be brought on an urgent basis and this raises issues of time pressures and potential information asymmetry. There may be high costs associated with such financing, given the limited pool of distressed debt financiers globally,[162] and this can make it more difficult for SMEs in particular to access this form of financing. The provision of rescue financing is linked to fundamental changes in governance and capital structures and this raises a risk that the terms and conditions may be overly onerous for the debtor company, leading to potential prejudice for the creditors being subordinated.[163] There is also the risk that the rescue finance will involve an unnecessary or inappropriate disruption in the priority of claims. Some disruption of creditor priority of claims is inevitable, of course, if priority is granted to the rescue financier. The court needs to operate as an effective gatekeeper to ensure that any such priority awarded is justified in the circumstances, balancing the rights of the individual creditors to their contractual entitlements against the benefits to creditors as a whole if the rescue finance enables the company (or business) to be restructured and rescued. Ultimately, the court needs to balance the interference with creditor rights often involved in the provisions promoting rescue finance with the goal of benefiting

---

[158] This could involve the rights of all existing creditors being overridden or could subordinate only certain groups, e.g. unsecured creditors.

[159] Unsurprisingly, determining the question of 'adequate protection' is not straightforward. For discussion, see *In re Sonora Desert Dairy LLC* (2015) WL65301 (US Bankruptcy Appellate Panel 9th Cir.). Other jurisdictions adopt different thresholds; for example, under s. 67 of the Singapore Insolvency, Restructuring and Dissolution Act 2018, it must be demonstrated that the rescue finance would not have been obtained but for the granting of the relevant order of priority. For discussion, see A. Chia, M.P. Sandrasegara, and S. Menon, 'Super Priority in Rescue Financing: Lifeline or Lasso?', Journal of International Banking and Financial Law, 5 (2017) 286.

[160] See, e.g. S. Chatterjee, U. Dhillon, and G. Ramirez, 'Debtor-in-Possession Financing', Journal of Banking and Finance, 16 (2005) 1.

[161] S. Dahiya, K. John, M. Puri, and G. Ramirez, 'Debtor-in-Possession Financing and Bankruptcy Resolution: Empirical Evidence', Journal of Financial Economics, 69 (2003) 259. See also F.A. Elayan and T.O. Meyer, 'The Impact of Receiving Debtor-in-Possession Financing on the Probability of Successful Emergence and Time Spent under Chapter 11 Bankruptcy', Journal of Business Finance and Accounting, 28 (2001) 905.

[162] See, e.g. W. Rostrom and C. Fell, 'Recent Trends in Interim Financing', International Review of Intellectual Property and Competition Law, 47 (2016) 1.

[163] One possibility is that the rescue financier appoints one or more directors to the board and may even gain control over incumbent management. The courts in some jurisdictions have specifically recognized the risk of rescue financiers seeking control provisions that are overreaching. See, for instance, the approach in Canada: *Re Great Basin Gold Ltd*, 2012 BCSC 1459 (BC SC); *Essor Steel Algoma Inc.* (November 2015) (Ont SCJ). In the United States, see *In re Tenney Village Co.* (1989) 104 BR 562 (Bank Ct D NH).

VI. Conclusion

3.73   In recent years, jurisdictions have increasingly recognized the value of including an effective debt restructuring mechanism outside insolvency as one of the options available to financially distressed companies. The number of such mechanisms has proliferated in recent years. To work effectively, however, these mechanisms must be designed well. The goal is to create a regime that will enable the creditors to renegotiate their bargain in order to remain invested in a distressed company. Restructuring plans need to find a way to solve the potential deadlock situation whereby one or more creditors refuse their consent as a way of exercising their hold-up rights in a way that does not facilitate expropriation of the dissenting creditors. Failure to do so will have ramifications not only for the particular creditors but also for the market for capital, because this risk of expropriation *ex post* will be factored in by creditors lending money to companies *ex ante*. This is a delicate balance and one which requires the oversight of an independent arbiter. The court's role in overseeing the operation of these mechanisms is central, as discussed in this chapter. This does have implications, however, particularly regarding the costs involved. It is notable that often the stated ambition of these restructuring mechanisms is that they should be available to companies of all sizes.[164] Of course, companies of all sizes can experience financial distress and need effective tools to manage that distress. The reality, however, is that the restructuring mechanisms discussed in this chapter are generally used by large companies, and different solutions may therefore be required to manage the financial distress of micro, small, and medium-sized enterprises.[165]

---

[164] See Recital 17 of the EU Restructuring Directive (n 3).
[165] See, e.g. UNCITRAL, *Legislative Recommendations on Insolvency of Micro- and Small Enterprises* (UNCITRAL 2021).

4

Formal Insolvency Proceedings

Johannes Richter

I. Introduction and Overview

When a company faces financial difficulties or may even have become insolvent, **4.01** most legal systems provide for several different types of insolvency-related proceedings: debtors may be given the opportunity to restructure their debts, to work out a 'rescue plan', and to attempt an economic restart through contractual agreements with their creditors. Thus, in many systems, formal insolvency proceedings can be used not only to distribute the debtor's 'leftovers' but also to overcome the debtor's financial difficulties.[1] Insolvency law usually provides for the possibility of reorganization if the creditors do not receive less by saving the debtor than they would in a winding-up scenario and if the benefits can be maximized for the creditors (and possibly also for society) by continuing the debtor's business.[2]

More often than not, however, there is no viable prospect of the debtor being success- **4.02** fully restructured and saved, the company may have already ceased operations, the liquidity gap is too large, the burden of debt too high for a new investor to be found—the debtor company no longer has a realistic chance of success. In these cases, *liquidation* is the only reasonable option in response to insolvency.[3] In formal, collective proceedings, the debtor's assets must be liquidated so that the proceeds can be used to repay the creditors in the most efficient way. This chapter focuses particularly on these 'traditional' *formal insolvency proceedings* leading to liquidation. Such proceedings present themselves as a process of collective enforcement of debt akin to individual execution but on a *pari passu* basis.[4] Important regulatory examples of such procedures are 11 U.S.C. §§701–84, the French regulation on judiciary liquidation (Arts L640-1–L643-13 of the *Code de Commerce*), the German provisions on 'regular' insolvency proceedings (§§ 1–216 of the *Insolvenzordnung*), the winding-up procedures of English law (Part IV

---

[1] K. van Zwieten, *Principles of Corporate Insolvency Law* (Thomson Reuters 2018) para. 2.02; R. Bork, *Corporate Insolvency Law* (Intersentia 2020) paras 8.3 et seq. For details on debt restructuring outside formal insolvency proceedings. see Chapter 3 'Debt Restructuring Outside Formal Insolvency Proceedings'.

[2] United Nations Commission on International Trade Law (UNCITRAL), *Legislative Guide on Insolvency Law* (UNCITRAL 2005)11 para. 6; cf. 11 U.S.C. §1129(a)(7)(A)(ii). See on this 'best-interest test', G. McCormack, A. Keay, and S. Brown, *European Insolvency Law* (Edward Elgar 2017) para. 6.9.

[3] H. Anderson, *The Framework of Corporate Insolvency Law* (OUP 2017) para. 7.01; Bork, *Corporate Insolvency Law* (n 1) para. 8.2.

[4] *See* Brightman LJ in *Re Lines Bros Ltd* [1983] Ch 1 (CA) 20E; van Zwieten, *Principles of Corporate Insolvency Law* (n 1) paras 8.02 et seq.; on this principle, see below, para. 4.56.

Johannes Richter, *Formal Insolvency Proceedings* In: *The Anatomy of Corporate Insolvency Law*. Edited by: Reinhard Bork and Renato Mangano, Oxford University Press. © Johannes Richter 2024. DOI: 10.1093/oso/9780198852094.003.0004

88 FORMAL INSOLVENCY PROCEEDINGS

of the UK Insolvency Act 1986) and Chapter X of the Enterprise Bankruptcy Law of the People's Republic of China (PRC).

4.03 Such proceedings are usually determined by the paradigm of authority: although some jurisdictions also provide a legal framework aiming to tackle insolvency through a self-governed procedure, typical insolvency proceedings (aimed at liquidation) are based on the intervention of state authority,[5] which coordinates the relationship between the debtor and its creditors and, even more importantly, between the creditors themselves. The alternatives to a winding-up procedure, namely the reorganization or restructuring of the debtor, are addressed briefly in section IX.

4.04 While the fundamental issues and questions associated with a person's insolvency are largely the same in different jurisdictions, and the solutions provided by the respective law may be very similar in the end, the legal systems differ considerably when it comes to the specific details of the formal procedures. In the following, the most important stages of a typical insolvency procedure will be presented, highlighting similarities and differences between the legal systems. Here, there will be a focus particularly on the law of the United States, England and Wales, France, Germany, and China. The way in which proceedings are structured in these jurisdictions is strongly influenced by the different insolvency philosophies: certain legal systems consider insolvency proceedings primarily as a vehicle for the collection and redemption of debts. At their core, such proceedings primarily aim to satisfy the creditors as completely and equally as possible.[6] Other jurisdictions also assign other objectives to insolvency proceedings and serve the interests of other stakeholders, for example the debtor who may be given a fresh start, the employees, or the society.[7]

4.05 This chapter follows the typical course of insolvency proceedings: the first question that arises is how, and by whom, such proceedings can be initiated, that is whether an application must be submitted to a court; whether, and when, the creditors can force the debtor to enter into the proceedings; and what requirements need to be demonstrated in order to do so (section II). Once the proceedings have been opened (or started in some other way), some crucial consequences arise, particularly regarding the debtor, his assets, and the insolvency estate, as well as the creditors and their rights (section III). Typically, an insolvency administrator will be appointed to take the central role in the proceedings (section IV) and is responsible, among other things, for collecting the creditors' claims, observing priority and subordination, and communicating with the creditors and their representatives (section V). The administrator may often have to decide how to deal with pending contracts (section VI), augment the estate, and collect and realize the debtor's assets (section VII). After the final distribution of the proceeds

---

[5] See in detail above, paras 1.13 et seq.
[6] See, e.g. § 1(1) of the *Insolvenzordnung*; cf. L. Häsemeyer, *Insolvenzrecht* (Carl Heymanns 2007) para. 1.12.
[7] H. Eidenmüller, 'Comparative Corporate Insolvency Law', European Corporate Governance Institute (ECGI) Law Working Paper No. 319 (2016) 9 et seq.

II. Initiation and Opening of Insolvency Proceedings

Formal insolvency proceedings result in extensive constraints on both the rights of the debtor and of the creditors. While previously, each individual creditor had the right, but also the burden, of ensuring that he or she obtained everything the debtor owed him or her, in insolvency proceedings, the state intervenes in the realization of claims and overrides the otherwise largely dominant private autonomy to a great extent. At what point formal proceedings over a debtor company are necessary and justified—at what point the law should possibly even impose such a step—is one of the most crucial questions of insolvency law and policy.[8]

4.06

A. Insolvency as the Starting Point of the Proceedings

The key requirement of formal insolvency proceedings (aimed at liquidation) is that the debtor is *substantively insolvent*. Proceedings aimed at restructuring can often be commenced without the need for the debtor to show that he or she is unable to pay his or her debts.[9] Winding-up proceedings, on the other hand, may only be carried out in most jurisdictions if there is a justifying reason: insolvency. This factor acts as a *gateway* to protect the debtor but also the creditors or minority shareholders. The extraordinary measures available in insolvency proceedings could be used in one way or another to encroach on the rights of others in a manner that would not be possible under general private law. Therefore, in most laws, a debtor's eligibility for insolvency proceedings is determined by a showing of substantive insolvency.[10]

4.07

However, there are many different ways of assessing when such a situation justifying insolvency proceedings has arisen. The main approaches for defining insolvency are 'overindebtedness', which is determined on the basis of a balance sheet test, and the 'inability to pay', which is determined on the basis of a liquidity (or cash-flow) test.[11] In the latter case, the factor that debts due are not paid on time plays a crucial role. In most jurisdictions, the main concern is the liquidity test, not least because the

4.08

---

[8] ibid 12 et seq.; D.G. Baird, 'The Initiation Problem in Bankruptcy', International Review of Law and Economics, 11 (1991) 223.

[9] This is certainly true in cases of *voluntary* proceedings; cf. J. Kilborn, in D. Faber, N. Vermunt, J. Kilborn, and T. Richter, *Commencement of Insolvency Proceedings* (OUP 2012) National Report for the United States, para. 20.5; Bork, *Corporate Insolvency Law* (n 1) para. 3.19.

[10] J.L. Westbrook, C.D. Booth, C.G. Paulus, and H. Rajak, *A Global View of Business Insolvency Systems* (Martinus Nijhoff 2010) para. 3.4.2; McCormack, Keay, and Brown, *European Insolvency Law* (n 2) para. 5.2.1; cf. above, Chapter 2 'Distress, Insolvency, and the Likelihood of Insolvency'.

[11] Bork, *Corporate Insolvency Law* (n 1) paras 1.15 et seq.; cf. above, paras 2.09 et seq.

90 FORMAL INSOLVENCY PROCEEDINGS

determination of the inability to pay is much clearer and simpler than the determination of overindebtedness—especially for the creditors.

4.09 Insolvency, in itself, is not enough to trigger (most of) the decisive legal consequences of insolvency proceedings. Rather, formal proceedings must be initiated by a person competent to do so; many jurisdictions also require the official commencement of such proceedings.[12] These two most important steps at the beginning of the insolvency proceedings will be discussed in the following sections: the initiation or filing of the petition (section II.B) and the formal opening of the proceedings (section II.D). Although some proceedings start immediately with the corresponding decision of the debtor or are opened shortly after a petition has been filed, there may also be an interim phase between the request and the start of the formal proceedings during which special rules apply (section II.C).

B. Filing for Insolvency Proceedings

4.10 The right to initiate formal insolvency proceedings is generally vested in both the debtor and the creditors; furthermore, a right to file for insolvency may be granted to public authorities in the public interest. However, there are usually significant differences concerning the question of whether the debtor enters into the proceedings voluntarily or is forced to do so: depending on who initiates the proceedings, different grounds and procedural requirements may have to be presented. Also, the question of which incentives lead to the initiation of proceedings must be answered differently.

1. Initiation by the debtor

4.11 Proceedings initiated by the debtor company itself (or better, by its directors) are less problematic in that the imminent liquidation and winding up is not triggered against the resistance of the debtor. But why should a debtor make such a move? What motivates him or her to take the (economically inevitable) step of entering into insolvency proceedings? Many jurisdictions seek to provide *positive incentives* to encourage the timely commencement of proceedings. Such incentives may include, for example, the debtor retaining control during the proceedings ('debtor in possession', DIP) and the chance that the company (and not just the business) can be saved and that the shareholders may (at least in principle) retain their investments. These beneficial features are usually associated with reorganization procedures and can be seen as 'carrots'[13] for the directors and shareholders.

---

[12] van Zwieten, *Principles of Corporate Insolvency Law* (n 1) para. 4.01. The moment of insolvency (prior to the proceedings) may have important consequences, in particular regarding liability for failure to initiate proceedings (cf. below, para. 7.27) or for the question of transactions avoidance (cf. below, para. 6.51).

[13] Eidenmüller, 'Comparative Corporate Insolvency Law' (n 7) 13 et seq.; cf. Baird, 'The Initiation Problem in Bankruptcy' (n 8) 223, 227 et seq.

Such incentives, however, will fail where liquidation is foreseeable: a procedure that in-   **4.12**
evitably leads to a winding up is (in case of insolvency)[14] practically never initiated by
the debtor voluntarily but based only on a corresponding legal obligation. Herein lies
the second reason why the debtor would initiate insolvency proceedings: the (directors
of the) debtor might be forced to do so by law.[15] While many jurisdictions adopt such
an approach, there is no widely agreed consensus on this.[16] Such *involuntary proceedings* and the obligations to initiate proceedings that can lead to liability or punishment
usually do not apply to all debtors. They are relevant especially for corporate debtors
where the limited liability threatens the creditors' satisfaction.

Failure to comply with a legal obligation may result in liability or criminal prosecution.   **4.13**
French law, for example, states that the (former) directors of the debtor company may
have to provide compensation payments if a management error is found to have led
to overindebtedness.[17] Similarly, English law imposes potential liability on directors
if they delay the initiation of insolvency proceedings, resulting in *wrongful trading*.[18]
Provisions of criminal law also aim to ensure that the debtor or the company's management initiates insolvency proceedings in due time so that the creditors do not suffer
any greater damage than is already the case. For instance, German law imposes criminal sentences for those who do not comply with their obligation to file for insolvency.[19] Such threats of legal consequences are essential, especially if the proceedings
are not likely to be triggered by other parties, in particular by the creditors or public
institutions.[20]

In some jurisdictions, a further distinction can be made as to whether the proceedings   **4.14**
are conducted with or without the involvement of the court. For example, English law
provides two options for directors who have realized that the company is insolvent: they
can not only (as the creditors) initiate winding-up proceedings by order of the court[21]
but also arrange for the shareholders to initiate proceedings which, in principle,[22] do
not involve the courts and which are largely controlled by the creditors.[23]

---

[14] Proceedings in which a *solvent* company shall be terminated and wound up for reasons other than insolvency differ significantly from this but are nevertheless addressed by insolvency law in some jurisdictions, e.g. ss 84, 91 et seq. of the UK Insolvency Act 1986 ('Members' Voluntary Winding Up').

[15] See, e.g. § 15a(1) of the *Insolvenzordnung*.

[16] Cf. UNCITRAL, *Legislative Guide on Insolvency Law* (n 2) 49 para. 35; such an approach is not adopted, for instance, by US and Chinese law; cf. Bork, *Corporate Insolvency Law* (n 1) para. 3.4.

[17] See Art. L 651-2 of the *Code de Commerce*; Art. L 631-4 states that the application must be filed within 45 days of the occurrence of insolvency.

[18] See ss 84 and 91 et seq. of the UK Insolvency Act 1986.

[19] See § 15a(4) of the *Insolvenzordnung*. See also § 283 of the *Strafgesetzbuch*; cf. Arts 654-1 et seq. of the *Code de Commerce*.

[20] Cf. UNCITRAL, *Legislative Guide on Insolvency Law* (n 2) 50 para. 35.

[21] See s. 124(1) of the UK Insolvency Act 1986.

[22] Judicial confirmation of the proceedings is necessary in particular if the result of the proceedings shall be recognized in other states.

[23] For example, the creditors can nominate a person to be liquidator (ss 100 and 104 of the UK Insolvency Act 1986) and can decide on the relief of the liquidator (ibid s. 173).

92 FORMAL INSOLVENCY PROCEEDINGS

2. Initiation by creditors or state authorities

4.15 In many, though not all,[24] jurisdictions, insolvency proceedings initiated by creditors are often more important than proceedings initiated voluntarily or compulsorily by the debtor. The creditors may, and will have to, consider whether it is more beneficial for them to enforce their claims through individual enforcement procedures or whether they expect to have better prospects of obtaining satisfaction in insolvency proceedings.[25] If it becomes apparent, even from an outside perspective, that the debtor will not be able to pay his debts in full, it may be reasonable for an affected creditor to initiate the process of collective enforcement of debt. For this reason, practically all legal systems provide for the insolvent debtor to be forced into insolvency proceedings by his or her creditors. However, there are considerable differences regarding the question of who can initiate the procedure, under which conditions this should be possible, and who carries the burden of proof.

4.16 In most jurisdictions, every creditor has the right to initiate proceedings, regardless of the nature of the claim,[26] but often it is required that a *substantial part* of the claim is undisputed and free of offset.[27] Some states (e.g. the United States) even demand a certain number of creditors to support the insolvency petition and/or require a certain amount of claims.[28] Typically, the creditor must show that he or she has a claim against the debtor that has not been paid even though it is due and that it is likely that the debtor is insolvent;[29] for this purpose, it is often necessary to resort to circumstantial evidence, such as the debtor's cessation of payments.[30] The application usually has to be submitted to a court, which then examines whether the (more or less strict) requirements for proceedings are met.[31] In this procedural step, the debtor is given the opportunity to respond to the application.[32] The debtor may, in turn, demonstrate that there is no insolvency or that the petition cannot be approved for other reasons. However, he or she may also join the petition or seek to have another type of proceeding take place and avoid liquidation.[33]

4.17 Some jurisdictions provide for *state authorities* to initiate the insolvency proceedings as well, not only in cases where the state itself is a creditor but also more generally in the public interest. The rationale behind such regulations is that it is in the interest of

---

[24] Especially in the United States, involuntary proceedings initiated by creditors are rare; cf. Kilborn (n 9) National Report for the United States, para. 20.5.

[25] See G. McCormack in Faber et al., *Commencement of Insolvency Proceedings* (n 9) National Report for England, para. 8.5.

[26] Cf. Art. L 651-4(2) of the *Code de Commerce* ('*quelle que soit la nature de sa creance*').

[27] UNCITRAL, *Legislative Guide on Insolvency Law* (n 2) 50 para. 37.

[28] See 11 U.S.C. §303(b); cf. McCormack, Keay, and Brown, *European Insolvency Law* (n 2) para. 5.3.1.

[29] See Art. 7(2) of the Enterprise Bankruptcy Law of the PRC; § 14(1)(1) of the *Insolvenzordnung*. Often, statutory presumptions are necessary in order for the creditor to be able to show *general* cessation of payments: see UNCITRAL, *Legislative Guide on Insolvency Law* (n 2) 50 et seq. para. 37.

[30] See, e.g. § 17(2)2 of the *Insolvenzordnung*.

[31] UNCITRAL, *Legislative Guide on Insolvency Law* (n 2) 56 et seq. paras 54 et seq.; cf. on German law, Häsemeyer, *Insolvenzrecht* (n 6) paras 7.11 et seq.

[32] See 11 U.S.C. §303(d); § 14(2) of the *Insolvenzordnung*; UNCITRAL, *Legislative Guide on Insolvency Law* (n 2) 60 para. 67.

[33] See Kilborn (n 9) National Report for the United States, para. 20.5.

commercial traffic and the economy in general that insolvent companies should disappear from the market as quickly as possible so that they do not cause further damage to creditors.[34] In France, the ex officio opening of proceedings has been abolished, but insolvency proceedings can still be initiated by a state authority, namely by the public prosecutor (*ministère public*).[35] In a similar way, English law states that the Secretary of State may present a petition for a company to be wound up where it is expedient in the public interest.[36]

C. Preliminary Proceedings and Interim Protection

In some jurisdictions, the debtor can start insolvency proceedings merely by making **4.18** a formal declaration,[37] allowing some crucial effects of formal proceedings to take effect immediately. Usually, however, winding-up proceedings are initiated through an application but only start once a court has adjudicated on that application and opened the proceedings. In these cases, a gap occurs: *de facto*, the debtor is already insolvent, but *de jure* insolvency has not yet been declared. This phase of uncertainty, in which insolvency is very likely but has not yet been determined with certainty, is particularly acute when the court must carry out extensive assessments; the time span between the initiation of insolvency proceedings and their actual, formal commencement varies substantially.

This gap creates the need for *interim protection*—both from the debtor's and the **4.19** creditor's point of view:[38] under normal circumstances, the debtor's assets and business cannot and should not (yet) be 'taken out of his hands' as long as it has not been determined whether he or she is insolvent at all. On the other hand, the creditors have a legitimate interest, especially in this phase, in ensuring that the value of the debtor's assets—which are already insufficient to cover all debts—is preserved; transactions that are detrimental to the satisfaction of creditors are to be prevented. At the same time, any existing business should remain in operation to preserve the going-concern value. For all these reasons, various interim measures may be taken between the filing of the application and the opening of the proceedings.[39] Such measures are permissible only if the need for interim protection is urgent and outweighs the potential harm resulting from it.[40]

---

[34] UNCITRAL, *Legislative Guide on Insolvency Law* (n 2) 52 para. 43.
[35] See Art. L 631-5(1) of the *Code de Commerce*; the *ministère public* also has further competences, e.g. he or she can propose who should become administrator (ibid Art. L 621-4(5)).
[36] See s. 124A(1) of the UK Insolvency Act 1986.
[37] UNCITRAL, *Legislative Guide on Insolvency Law* (n 2) 49 para. 33; O. Radley-Gardner, H. Beale, and R. Zimmermann, *Fundamental Texts on European Private Law* (Hart 2016) § 2.1(2) of the Principles of European Insolvency Law; 11 U.S.C. §301(a), (b).
[38] Westbrook et al., *A Global View of Business Insolvency Systems* (n 10) para. 3.6.1.1.
[39] See Radley-Gardner et al., *Fundamental Texts on European Private Law* (n 37) § 3.5 of the Principles of European Insolvency Law; Bork, *Corporate Insolvency Law* (n 1) paras 3.6 et seq.
[40] UNCITRAL, *Legislative Guide on Insolvency Law* (n 2) 90 para. 47.

94 FORMAL INSOLVENCY PROCEEDINGS

1. Interim administrator

4.20 Prior to the formal opening of insolvency proceedings, a provisional administrator may be appointed to ensure the protection of the assets in the interim phase;[41] often, this person will ultimately be appointed as the 'permanent' insolvency administrator.[42] If a preliminary administrator is appointed, he or she will generally not have as extensive authority as the insolvency administrator subsequently appointed at the opening of proceedings.[43] In particular, he or she may neither have the duty nor the right to liquidate the debtor's assets; an exception may be made if the immediate sale of individual (e.g. perishable) goods is necessary to prevent larger losses.[44]

4.21 If the debtor is still running an active business, it should (temporarily) be kept going during the preliminary proceedings: Should insolvency proceedings ultimately be opened and the debtor wound up, it is often considerably more profitable (and thus in the creditor's interest) to sell the company as a whole and as a functioning entity instead of breaking it up and selling the assets individually.[45] In order to keep this option open, an important task of the provisional administrator may be to ensure (or to supervise) the continuity of the debtor's business.[46]

2. Provisional moratorium

4.22 A typical problem of insolvency is the collision of individual and collective interests: once the proceedings have been opened, the creditors can no longer enforce their claims individually but only through submission and admission under the conditions of the proceedings.[47] The purpose of collective enforcement—providing the best possible, pro rata satisfaction of all creditors[48]—would be jeopardized if creditors were able to enforce their claims during the application process or to exercise security interests without restriction. Therefore, a *provisional moratorium* might be imposed to prevent individual creditors from obtaining last-minute advantages.[49] However, the same term is also used to describe measures taken to protect the debtor so that he or she can

---

[41] See s. 135 of the UK Insolvency Act 1986; 11 U.S.C. §§303(g) and 701; §§ 21(2)(1) No. 1, 22 of the *Insolvenzordnung*.

[42] See, e.g.11 U.S.C. §702(d).

[43] UNCITRAL, *Legislative Guide on Insolvency Law* (n 2) 91 para. 50; Westbrook et al., *A Global View of Business Insolvency Systems* (n 10) para. 3.6.1.1.

[44] UNCITRAL, *Legislative Guide on Insolvency Law* (n 2) 91 para. 50. In contrast, under US law, the provisional trustee has very far-reaching powers (11 U.S.C. §701(c); cf. Bork, *Corporate Insolvency Law* (n 1) para. 3.12).

[45] See in detail below, paras 4.97 et seq.

[46] See, e.g. § 22(1) No. 2 of the *Insolvenzordnung*; UNCITRAL, *Legislative Guide on Insolvency Law* (n 2) 91 para. 49.

[47] See Radley-Gardner et al., *Fundamental Texts on European Private Law* (n 37) § 3.3 of the Principles of European Insolvency Law; Bork, *Corporate Insolvency Law* (n 1) paras 1.3, 3.7, 5.6.

[48] UNCITRAL, *Legislative Guide on Insolvency Law* (n 2) 10 para. 5; D. Faber and N. Vermunt, in Faber et al., *Commencement of Insolvency Proceedings* (n 9) National Report for the Netherlands, para. 13.2.1; C. G. Paulus and M. Berberich in Faber et al., *Commencement of Insolvency Proceedings* (n 9) National Report for Germany, para. 10.2.

[49] See s. 130(2) of the UK Insolvency Act 1986; § 21(2)(2) No. 3 of the *Insolvenzordnung*; Bork, *Corporate Insolvency Law* (n 1) para. 3.7.

temporarily continue his or her business without disruption, for example to restructure it and prevent insolvency.[50]

D. Opening of Insolvency Proceedings

The provisional measures usually end with the formal opening decision being issued **4.23** and the actual commencement of the insolvency proceedings. In order for the momentous opening decision to be made, various conditions must be met to the satisfaction of the court. Determining substantive insolvency is certainly the central aspect; due to its crucial importance, this topic is dealt with in detail in Chapter 2 'Distress, Insolvency, and the Likelihood of Insolvency'.

In addition, several formal questions must be answered, such as whether the applica- **4.24** tion is supported by a sufficient number of creditors[51] or whether application fees have been paid.[52] Some legal systems also stipulate that insolvency proceedings may only be opened if the *costs of the proceedings* will (probably) be covered. While there is a broad consensus that the costs of the proceedings (e.g. the payment of the insolvency administrator) will have to be paid out of the insolvency estate and that they take priority over other claims,[53] it is usually not assessed in advance whether there are sufficient assets to do so.[54] In order to ensure that the necessary winding-up proceedings take place, most jurisdictions address the question of costs only after commencement. English law, for example, stipulates, that the court shall not refuse to make a winding-up order on the ground only that the company has no assets.[55] By contrast, under German law, the court has to dismiss the petition for insolvency if the debtor's estate is found to be insufficient to cover the costs of the proceedings,[56] which may lead to the undesirable consequence of unresolved insolvency. For this reason, the time between petition and decision may have to be used to evaluate possible (liability) claims in order to enable the commencement of proceedings.

When the proceedings are finally opened, this fact needs to be disclosed to the creditors **4.25** and the general public; it is typically mentioned in an official gazette, in newspapers

---

[50] See Bork, *Corporate Insolvency Law* (n 1) para. 3.7; Art. 6 of the Directive (EU) 2019/1023; Art. 75(1) the Enterprise Bankruptcy Law of the PRC.

[51] See 11 U.S.C. §303(b); Kilborn (n 9) National Report for the United States, para. 20.5.

[52] See, e.g. Chapter 28 § 1930 of the US Code on Judiciary and Judicial Procedure; Bork, *Corporate Insolvency Law* (n 1) para. 3.22 fn. 63.

[53] See Radley-Gardner et al., *Fundamental Texts on European Private Law* (n 37) § 5.1(1) of the Principles of European Insolvency Law; Eidenmüller, 'Comparative Corporate Insolvency Law' (n 7) 18; Westbrook et al., *A Global View of Business Insolvency Systems* (n 10) para. 3.7.3.

[54] Bork, *Corporate Insolvency Law* (n 1) para. 3.22.

[55] See s. 125(1) of the UK Insolvency Act 1986; not having enough assets to cover costs may be one reason why compulsory liquidation is initiated, where the 'Official Receiver' serves as liquidator and is paid through public funds: see McCormack (n 25) National Report for England, para. 8.8.1.

[56] See § 26(1) of the *Insolvenzordnung*; these costs include the expenses of the court, the insolvency administrator, and the creditors' committee (ibid § 54).

96 FORMAL INSOLVENCY PROCEEDINGS

and/or recorded in (trade) registers.[57] The filing of the petition is usually not yet made public; this is particularly important for the solvent debtor because even an unjustified insolvency petition can damage his or her reputation. However, if provisional measures are taken to safeguard the assets, these might have to be published.[58]

III. Consequences of the Commencement

4.26 Even though the application and the provisional measures may have quite incisive effects, the most significant and consequential moment is the commencement of proceedings. The debtor loses the power to freely manage (and sell) his or her assets, to run his or her business, to create new (insolvency) claims, etc. His or her property is seized; it is no longer to be utilized in his or her interest, but rather must be used (as the *'insolvency estate'*) to satisfy the creditors. With the commencement of insolvency proceedings, the administrator is appointed; he or she assumes the central role in the proceedings. In the interest of, and in cooperation with, the creditors, he or she is responsible for ensuring the most profitable liquidation of the debtor.

4.27 The commencement of proceedings is also the separating moment (the 'cut-off date')[59] regarding the treatment of existing and newly arising claims: while claims that arose prior to the commencement (as a result of the debtor's actions) are paid only on a pro rata basis under the proceedings, new claims that arise as a result of the insolvency proceedings enjoy priority,[60] which is particularly important in respect of the administrator's activities. Pending contracts (i.e. those that have not yet been fulfilled in full) are not immediately invalid or automatically terminated due to the opening of insolvency proceedings; generally, the insolvency administrator determines how these contracts are to be dealt with.[61]

A. Constitution of the Insolvency Estate

1. Seizure of the debtor's assets

4.28 With the opening of proceedings, the debtor does generally not yet lose his or her rights to the remaining assets[62] but the power to administer and to dispose of them. This

---

[57] UNCITRAL, *Legislative Guide on Insolvency Law* (n 2) 332 para. 107; C. Dupoux and C. Nerguararian in Faber et al., *Commencement of Insolvency Proceedings* (n 9) National Report for France, para. 9.9; McCormack (n 25) National Report for England, para. 8.9.

[58] See, e.g. § 23(1) of the *Insolvenzordnung*.

[59] Anderson, *The Framework of Corporate Insolvency Law* (n 3) paras 7.18 et seq.

[60] van Zwieten, *Principles of Corporate Insolvency Law* (n 1) paras 8.17, 8.35 et seq; cf. below, para. 4.60.

[61] See Radley-Gardner et al., *Fundamental Texts on European Private Law* (n 37) § 6.1 of the Principles of European Insolvency Law; cf. in detail below at section VI.

[62] Only in a few legal systems is legal title over the assets transferred to the insolvency administrator; usually, only the right of administration and the right of disposal are transferred: see Bork, *Corporate Insolvency Law* (n 1) para. 5.4; UNCITRAL, *Legislative Guide on Insolvency Law* (n 2) 2 para. 2.

seizure[63] reveals the fundamental shift brought about by the insolvency proceedings: until now, the debtor was free to manage his or her affairs autonomously, to satisfy creditors at his or her discretion and to do business in his or her own interest. Now, in the public interest, but more importantly in the interest of the creditors, a kind of trust is established, for it is now clear that the creditors are entitled to claim the value of the assets, that economically the assets are 'theirs'. This fact is reflected in the concept and the term of the *insolvency estate*.[64] All the debtor's assets (including the business) are to be managed by the insolvency administrator, who acts as a trustee on behalf of the creditors.[65] The defining characteristic of this trust-like estate is that it must 'not be used or disposed of by the legal owner for his own benefit, but must be used or disposed of for the benefit of other persons'.[66]

2. Assets of the insolvency estate

A key element of insolvency proceedings and insolvency law is the question of what the estate consists of, that is which assets can be used to satisfy the creditors. To begin with, the insolvency estate includes all of the debtor's assets—tangible assets (e.g. cash, business equipment, real estate, etc.) as well as intangible assets (e.g. intellectual property, stocks and bonds, contractual rights, etc.). This includes not only assets acquired by the debtor prior to but also assets acquiredwithin the proceedings, for example by the insolvency administrator.[67] Excluded are those assets of the debtor that could not be seized in individual enforcement proceedings either[68] and rights that are not transferable or not commercialized.[69]   **4.29**

Objects belonging to the debtor but not in his or her current possession are also part of the insolvency estate. In this case, the insolvency administrator has the right and the duty to demand the return of these assets.[70] The estate also includes all assets or their value that have been recovered through *avoidance proceedings*.[71] Important are,   **4.30**

---

[63] See Art. L 641-9(1) of the *Code de Commerce* ('*dessaisissement*'); § 80(1) of the *Insolvenzordnung*.

[64] Cf. on this term and concept, UNCITRAL, *Legislative Guide on Insolvency Law* (n 2) 75 paras 1 et seq.; Bork, *Corporate Insolvency Law* (n 1) ch. 4; Anderson, *The Framework of Corporate Insolvency Law* (n 3) ch. 14.

[65] See Radley-Gardner et al., *Fundamental Texts on European Private Law* (n 37) § 3.2 of the Principles of European Insolvency Law; US law even uses the term 'trustee' (e.g. 11 U.S.C. §323(a)).

[66] Lord Diplock in *Ayerst v C & K (Construction) Ltd* [1976] AC 167. See also McCormack (n 25) National Report for England, para. 8.20; Anderson, *The Framework of Corporate Insolvency Law* (n 3) paras 7.14 et seq.

[67] UNCITRAL, *Legislative Guide on Insolvency Law* (n 2) 76 paras 4 et seq., 81 para. 23; Radley-Gardner et al., *Fundamental Texts on European Private Law* (n 37) § 3.2(1) of the Principles of European Insolvency Law; Art. L 641-9(1) of the *Code de Commerce*; Art. 30 of the Enterprise Bankruptcy Law of the PRC; 11 U.S.C. §541(1).

[68] See, e.g. § 36(1) of the *Insolvenzordnung*; Bork, *Corporate Insolvency Law* (n 1) paras 4.2 and 4.14; this usually only becomes important where the debtor is a natural person: see UNCITRAL, *Legislative Guide on Insolvency Law* (n 2) 80 paras 18 et seq.; Radley-Gardner et al., *Fundamental Texts on European Private Law* (n 37) § 3.1(2) of the Principles of European Insolvency Law.

[69] Bork, *Corporate Insolvency Law* (n 1) paras 4.12 and 4.15; Anderson, *The Framework of Corporate Insolvency Law* (n 3) paras 14.12 et seq.

[70] See ss 144(1) and 234 (2) of the UK Insolvency Act. See Anderson, *The Framework of Corporate Insolvency Law* (n 3) paras 14.03, 14.18 et seq.

[71] UNCITRAL, *Legislative Guide on Insolvency Law* (n 2) 79 para. 15; Dupoux and Nerguararian (n 57) National Report for France, para. 9.19; Kilborn (n 9) National Report for the United States, para. 20.19; cf. below, paras 4.90 et seq.

98 FORMAL INSOLVENCY PROCEEDINGS

for example, cases where the debtor transferred assets or rights prior to the insolvency proceedings in a way that is voidable under insolvency law. Due to its major significance, this topic will be dealt with in detail in Chapter 6 'Transactions Avoidance Rules'.

4.31 In contrast, objects belonging to a third party are generally not part of the insolvency estate, even if the debtor has them in his or her possession. The owners of such assets have the right to 'separation' such that they can demand the return of the object without being bound by the insolvency proceedings.[72] This applies, for example, to assets that are subject to an agreement that provides for a right to use but does not transfer legal title, for example an (expired) lease.[73] Such assets must ultimately be returned, but they may be used temporarily, under certain conditions, to enable a continuation of the debtor's business.[74] Also not included in the insolvency estate are assets bought by the debtor and delivered under retention of title. Such property cannot be realized for the benefit of all creditors if the pending purchase contract is not fulfilled.[75] The same applies if the debtor holds the title, but only as trustee; in this case, the beneficial owner can claim restitution of the asset.[76]

4.32 A complex issue is the treatment of encumbered assets, that is those belonging to the debtor but encumbered with a security right for the benefit of a creditor. Some legal systems include these assets in the insolvency estate, but they provide for the secured party to be satisfied with priority out of the proceeds of this asset.[77] This approach has the benefit that the secured creditors cannot immediately claim the asset, thus enabling the insolvency administrator to continue to use the asset in the company for the time being or to sell the asset as part of a bundle, for example when selling the company in an asset deal.[78] Other jurisdictions exclude encumbered assets from the insolvency estate so that creditors may have greater confidence in the collateral and thus enhance the availability of credit in general.[79]

---

[72] Bork, *Corporate Insolvency Law* (n 1) paras 4.3 and 7.22; van Zwieten, *Principles of Corporate Insolvency Law* (n 1) paras 6.40 and 8.17.

[73] UNCITRAL, *Legislative Guide on Insolvency Law* (n 2) 80 para. 17; the handling of such cases (e.g. lease) is often subject to special provisions concerning the treatment of pending contracts (ibid 78 para. 10; see also below, section VI).

[74] UNCITRAL, *Legislative Guide on Insolvency Law* (n 2) 78 para. 10, 110 paras 90 et seq.

[75] Anderson, *The Framework of Corporate Insolvency Law* (n 3) paras 14.26 et seq. Many legal systems stipulate that, in this case, the administrator can choose whether the contract should still be performed in full: see Bork, *Corporate Insolvency Law* (n 1) paras 5.33 and 7.22.

[76] McCormack (n 25) National Report for England, para. 8.19; van Zwieten, *Principles of Corporate Insolvency Law* (n 1) paras 6.41 et seq.

[77] See Radley-Gardner et al., *Fundamental Texts on European Private Law* (n 37) § 9.2(2) of the Principles of European Insolvency Law; UNCITRAL, *Legislative Guide on Insolvency Law* (n 2) 77 para. 7; Bork, *Corporate Insolvency Law* (n 1) para. 4.3. See also below, para. 4.59.

[78] For instance, German law provides for a right to use (§ 172(1) of the *Insolvenzordnung*) and a right to realize/sell (ibid §§ 165 et seq.); cf. below, para. 4.100.

[79] UNCITRAL, *Legislative Guide on Insolvency Law* (n 2) 77 para. 9; an example is English law. The asset is not part of the estate but just the equity of redemption; cf. *Buchler v Talbot* [2004] UKHL 9; Anderson, *The Framework of Corporate Insolvency Law* (n 3) para. 14.29.

B. Rights and Obligations of the Debtor

For the debtor, the main consequence of the commencement of proceedings results **4.33** from the seizure of the estate: while proceedings aiming to restructure commonly leave the debtor in possession,[80] in liquidation proceedings, the power to dispose of and to manage the assets is taken away from the debtor (or the directors) and transferred to the administrator. This shift in power relates to the insolvency estate and its assets: the transfer of such objects made by the debtor after the opening are invalid or voidable by law so that the asset must be returned to the administrator.[81] In the same way, the debtor is not entitled to collect receivables that belong to the insolvency estate or to terminate pending contracts.[82]

Generally, however, the debtor is only 'disenfranchised' to the extent that the seizure **4.34** takes effect. The debtor retains the right to dispose of assets that are outside the estate. He or she may also still create new liabilities, although these have no effect on the estate and the insolvency proceedings.[83] Such new creditors, who have entered into a contract with the debtor deprived of substantial rights, may only pursue their claims once the proceedings have been terminated against the debtor's remaining or new assets—if there are any. This illustrates that the commencement of proceedings is a key moment of separation: the proceedings and the estate serve to satisfy such claims that already existed before the opening.[84]

From the moment of the commencement, the debtor is under a duty to support the **4.35** proceedings and to cooperate with the court and the administrator.[85] It is often essential for the proceedings that the debtor (or its directors)[86] surrenders control of assets, business records, and books and provide other vital information so that the insolvency administrator is able to take effective control of the estate.[87] If the debtor is a natural person, their cooperation will often be ensured as otherwise, discharge of debt could be denied.[88] However, if the proceedings are aimed at the liquidation of a corporate entity, the directors will have no intrinsic incentive to take further measures in favour of the insolvent company.[89] For this reason, different instruments—'a combination of sticks

---

[80] McCormack, Keay, and Brown, *European Insolvency Law* (n 2) para. 6.4; cf. also below, para. 4.113.
[81] Westbrook et al., *A Global View of Business Insolvency Systems* (n 10) para. 3.11.
[82] Bork, *Corporate Insolvency Law* (n 1) para. 5.4.
[83] ibid paras 2.17, 5.4, 5.9.
[84] See Radley-Gardner et al., *Fundamental Texts on European Private Law* (n 37) § 3.3 of the Principles of European Insolvency Law; § 38 of the *Insolvenzordnung*; 11 U.S.C. §101(A); Art. L. 621-43(1) of the *Code de Commerce*.
[85] UNCITRAL, *Legislative Guide on Insolvency Law* (n 2) 168 para. 23; Radley-Gardner et al., *Fundamental Texts on European Private Law* (n 37) § 2.3(1) of the Principles of European Insolvency Law; 11 U.S.C. §521(a)(4); § 97 of the *Insolvenzordnung*; cf. Anderson, *The Framework of Corporate Insolvency Law* (n 3) paras 16.06 et seq.
[86] See Radley-Gardner et al., *Fundamental Texts on European Private Law* (n 37) § 2.3(2) of the Principles of European Insolvency Law: 'If the debtor is a partnership, a company or other legal entity, this duty applies to its managing partners or directors.' See also s. 235 of the UK Insolvency Act.
[87] UNCITRAL, *Legislative Guide on Insolvency Law* (n 2) 168 paras 23 et seq.; Bork, *Corporate Insolvency Law* (n 1) para. 5.56.
[88] McCormack, Keay, and Brown, *European Insolvency Law* (n 2) para. 7.4; cf. below, paras 4.106 et seq.
[89] Cf. Kilborn (n 9) National Report for the United States, para. 20.11.

100 FORMAL INSOLVENCY PROCEEDINGS

and carrots'[90]—may be provided to enforce the duty to cooperate, such as the threat of a fine.[91]

C. Automatic Stay (Moratorium)

4.36 Insolvency proceedings are characterized by their collective nature, thus the interests of the whole group of creditors must be protected against the disruptive action of a single creditor. Therefore, an *automatic stay* (also known as a 'moratorium')[92] takes effect when proceedings are commenced,[93] meaning that (ordinary) creditors can no longer pursue their claims individually and are prevented from commencing actions to enforce their rights by resorting to official enforcement bodies.[94] Their 'insolvency claims' can only be pursued within the framework and under the rules of the proceedings; individual enforcement is prohibited.[95]

4.37 However, various exceptions are made to this stay. For example, creditors who have a right to separation can typically claim—without being restricted by the moratorium—that their asset is in the possession of the administrator, that it does not belong to the insolvency estate and must be surrendered.[96] Some jurisdictions also grant such an advantage to secured creditors, meaning that they are not affected by the stay and can therefore proceed to enforce their legal and contractual rights.[97]

4.38 An important exception concerns the enforcement of claims through *set-off* (i.e. the netting[98] of one's claims against the other party with the debt owed to it): if the creditor not only has a claim against the debtor but also has to fulfil a counterclaim, the possibility of set-off is preserved in many legal systems in insolvency proceedings. Although the claim would be subject to the moratorium, it is possible to obtain full satisfaction in this way.[99]

---

[90] Westbrook et al., *A Global View of Business Insolvency Systems* (n 10) para. 3.7.

[91] See s. 235(5) of the UK Insolvency Act. German law even provides (for extreme cases) that the directors can be brought before the court by force and possibly even taken into custody: see §§ 98(3) and 101(1) of the *Insolvenzordnung*.

[92] Cf. on different terminology, Bork, *Corporate Insolvency Law* (n 1) para. 5.17.

[93] A provisional moratorium may apply even before the commencement: see above, para. 4.22.

[94] UNCITRAL, *Legislative Guide on Insolvency Law* (n 2) 83 para. 26; Bork, *Corporate Insolvency Law* (n 1) paras 5.16 and 5.59.

[95] See Radley-Gardner et al., *Fundamental Texts on European Private Law* (n 37) § 3.3 of the Principles of European Insolvency Law; §§ 87 and 89 of the *Insolvenzordnung*; Arts 622-21, 622-7(1), 622-21 of the *Code de Commerce*; 11 U.S.C. §362(a).

[96] See, e.g. § 47 of the *Insolvenzordnung* pointing to the law as it applies outside of insolvency proceedings; cf. Bork, *Corporate Insolvency Law* (n 1) paras 5.62 and 7.22.

[97] UNCITRAL, *Legislative Guide on Insolvency Law* (n 2) 77 para. 9, 87 paras 36 et seq.; on English law, see McCormack (n 25) National Report for England, para. 8.18.

[98] The term 'netting' is often used synonymously with 'set-off', but it also denotes (especially in the financial sector) the offsetting of multiple claims between several parties: cf. van Zwieten, *Principles of Corporate Insolvency Law* (n 1) para. 9.09.

[99] See below, paras 4.69 et seq.

IV. Role and Obligations of the Insolvency Administrator

In most jurisdictions and most cases, insolvency proceedings aimed at liquidation are **4.39** managed by an insolvency administrator. He or she is the 'key player' within the proceedings,[100] has the right to administer and liquidate the estate, to decide on the fate of pending contracts and the debtor's business, to enforce the debtor's claims, to assert liability claims, and to ultimately determine who will participate in the proceeds and to what extent. Since he or she plays such a significant role, it is crucial that he or she is *independent* and acts *impartially*.[101] He or she will have to respect and adequately consider the rights and interests of both the debtor and the various creditors.[102] The factor of personal independence may be limited if the debtor has voluntarily entered into liquidation proceedings, allowing the debtor or a person of the debtor's volition to manage the proceedings;[103] yet here, too, the administration must be conducted in a fair and unbiased manner.

Furthermore, the administrator's *qualifications* are usually subject to high standards: al- **4.40** though the requirements may vary depending on the nature, scope, and difficulties of the procedure, the factors of (legal) knowledge and (economic) experience are practically always of importance.[104] This expertise is ensured by the jurisdictions in very different ways so that the complex task of (company) liquidation is managed successfully and leads to the highest possible proceeds. In France, for example, administrators must have completed a three-year internship and passed a final examination before they can be appointed.[105] English law ensures qualification through authorization by a professional body;[106] acting without this necessary qualification is even considered an offence.[107]

A. Appointment

In many jurisdictions, the insolvency administrator is selected and appointed by a **4.41** court. Often, the court selects a qualified person at its discretion, for example according to a rotation system; it may, however, be preferable to choose the person who is most qualified to conduct the particular case.[108] German law provides, for example, that the

---

[100] Bork, *Corporate Insolvency Law* (n 1) para. 2.40.
[101] See Radley-Gardner et al., *Fundamental Texts on European Private Law* (n 37) § 2.2 of the Principles of European Insolvency Law; McCormack, Keay, and Brown, *European Insolvency Law* (n 2) para. 2.8.
[102] W. Weiguo in Faber et al., *Commencement of Insolvency Proceedings* (n 9) National Report for the People's Republic of China, para. 6.12.5; UNCITRAL, *Legislative Guide on Insolvency Law* (n 2) 176 paras 42 et seq.
[103] See s. 100(1) of the UK Insolvency Act.; §§ 270 et seq. of the *Insolvenzordnung*.
[104] UNCITRAL, *Legislative Guide on Insolvency Law* (n 2) 175 paras 39 et seq.; Bork, *Corporate Insolvency Law* (n 1) para. 2.41.
[105] On this 'tough selection process', see Dupoux and Nerguararian (n 57) National Report for France, para. 9.12.
[106] See ss 390(2), 390A(2), 391 of the UK Insolvency Act.
[107] ibid 389(1).
[108] UNCITRAL, *Legislative Guide on Insolvency Law* (n 2) 177 para. 45.

102 FORMAL INSOLVENCY PROCEEDINGS

court shall select and appoint the person who is suited *to the case at hand*, who is particularly experienced in business affairs and independent of the creditors and of the debtor.[109]

4.42 It may also be provided that the debtor or the creditors have the right to propose, or even appoint, a person. In English law, the liquidator is an officer of the court in the case of compulsory winding up;[110] once the creditors have nominated another person, that person should, and usually will be, appointed.[111] In the case of a (creditors') voluntary liquidation, the liquidator appointed by the members holds office with limited powers until the creditors have appointed another person to act as liquidator.[112]

4.43 The US system, on the other hand, provides for a government authority (the 'US Trustee') to determine who shall administer the specific (Chapter 7) proceedings as 'trustee', first provisionally and later permanently.[113] Here too, the creditors have the power to choose and appoint a different (qualified) person to administer the proceedings;[114] however, in practice, the provisional trustee (appointed by the US Trustee) usually continues to carry out this role.[115]

4.44 In Germany, creditors can also influence the decision on who should act as insolvency administrator. The decision initially rests with the court, which is generally only bound by a unanimous proposal from the preliminary creditors' committee.[116] After the opening, however, the creditors can elect another person as administrator by majority vote.[117]

B. Duties and Responsibilities

4.45 The overall duty of the administrator is to collect and take over the debtor's assets, to realize them at the best possible price, and to distribute the proceeds among the creditors.[118] But what follows from this in detail depends on the specific situation and the individual proceedings. The insolvency administrator generally has very wide-ranging

---

[109] See § 56(1) of the *Insolvenzordnung*.

[110] van Zwieten, *Principles of Corporate Insolvency Law* (n 1) para. 5.02.

[111] See s. 139(2)(3) of the UK Insolvency Act; cf. McCormack (n 25) National Report for England, para. 8.12.

[112] Anderson, *The Framework of Corporate Insolvency Law* (n 3) para. 7.07.

[113] See 11 U.S.C. §§701(a), 702(d), §321; Chapter 39 § 586 of the US Code on Judiciary and Judicial Procedure. See also UNCITRAL, *Legislative Guide on Insolvency Law* (n 2) 177 para. 46.

[114] See 11. U.S.C. §702.

[115] This is because the required majorities are rarely achieved at the creditors' meeting; cf. Kilborn (n 9) National Report for the United States, para. 20.12.

[116] See § 56a(2) of the *Insolvenzordnung*.

[117] ibid §§ 57, 76(2); the appointment of the elected person may only be refused by the court if the person is not qualified to serve in the office: ibid § 57(2).

[118] See Radley-Gardner et al., *Fundamental Texts on European Private Law* (n 37) §§ 2.2(1) and 4.1 of the Principles of European Insolvency Law; *Ayerst v C & K (Construction) Ltd* (n 66); Anderson, *The Framework of Corporate Insolvency Law* (n 3) paras 7.05 et seq.

powers and independence to a large extent.[119] Typical responsibilities of the administrator include, among other things,[120]

- taking immediate control of the insolvency estate and the debtor's business records to prevent any losses;
- investigating the debtor's financial situation and issuing a report on the matter;
- protecting the assets and preserving the value of the estate, in particular—if possible—by (temporarily) continuing the debtor's business so that it may be sold as a going concern;
- initiating a creditors' meeting, providing the creditors with information, and consulting with them;
- examining pending contracts and deciding to continue or reject performance;
- enforcing liability and other claims and exercising avoidance powers;
- participation in lawsuits, arbitration, or other legal proceedings for the benefit of the estate;
- managing and realizing the assets of the estate;
- verifying and admitting (insolvency) claims;
- distributing the proceeds of the realization of the insolvency estate to the creditors in accordance with their (preferential or subordinate) claims.

4.46 The law often defines responsibilities only in general terms orientated towards the basic purposes of the proceedings, which typically includes an obligation to protect the estate, maximize its value for the benefit of the creditors, and to realize the best price reasonably obtainable on the sale.[121] In some jurisdictions, the court (or the creditors) can issue binding orders to the administrator and thus define his or her duties.[122]

C. Liability

4.47 Due to the extensive powers and freedoms granted to the insolvency administrator, the question arises as to whether, and how, he or she is personally liable for his or her activities. There is a broad consensus that the administrator is personally liable for damages resulting from his or her misconduct or misfeasance, although differences remain regarding the standard to be applied (negligence, gross negligence, intent).[123] In

---

[119] BGH, 20 April 2021–II ZR 387/18 = NZI 2021, 637 para. 23; McCormack (n 25) National Report for England, para. 8.12; this extensive power has to be counterbalanced by adequate control and liability regulations: see Bork, *Corporate Insolvency Law* (n 1) para. 2.43.

[120] An overview regarding these typical duties can be found in Art. 25 of the Enterprise Bankruptcy Law of the PRC as well as UNCITRAL, *Legislative Guide on Insolvency Law* (n 2) 179 para. 49. See also 11 U.S.C. §704; E. Bailey and H. Groves, *Corporate Insolvency Law* (LexisNexis 2007) paras 15.26, 15.32 et seq.

[121] UNCITRAL, *Legislative Guide on Insolvency Law* (n 2) 179 para. 50. See also the US Supreme Court in *CFTC v Weintraub*, 471 US 343 (1985); Häsemeyer, *Insolvenzrecht* (n 6) para. 6.31; van Zwieten, *Principles of Corporate Insolvency Law* (n 1) para. 2.04.

[122] See Art. 25(9) of the Enterprise Bankruptcy Law of the PRC; UNCITRAL, *Legislative Guide on Insolvency Law* (n 2) 180 para. 49(t).

[123] Westbrook et al., *A Global View of Business Insolvency Systems* (n 10) para. 3.6.1.3; UNCITRAL, *Legislative Guide on Insolvency Law* (n 2) 183 para. 61.

104 FORMAL INSOLVENCY PROCEEDINGS

Germany, for example, the insolvency administrator is liable for damages if he or she culpably violates the duties under insolvency law; his or her actions must be as diligent as those of a prudent and conscientious administrator.[124] Chinese law stipulates that an administrator who fails to perform his or her duties diligently and faithfully may not only be fined but also be liable for compensation if the debtor, creditors, or third parties suffer damages as a result of his or her actions.[125] Under English law, the court may grant a discharge to the liquidator where he or she acted honestly and reasonably and ought fairly to be excused.[126]

4.48 Considerably more difficult (and answered quite differently) is the question of liability for obligations that arose in the course and interest of the proceedings but could not be fulfilled using the debtors' assets.[127] This may become particularly important if the administrator enters into new contracts and relies on further services in order to enable the debtor's business to continue. If the business cannot ultimately be sold at the expected price, these obligations may (partly) remain unpaid, although they have priority. If the administrator is liable for these obligations, this has the advantage that new suppliers can be more certain that they will be paid, so they will be more willing to provide their services despite the insolvency. In addition, the administrator is encouraged to only create liabilities that can be paid out of the estate.[128] This risk of liability, however, can also operate as a disincentive; the administrator could act too cautiously and thus refrain from taking economically viable measures. He or she might, for example, close the debtor's business too hastily, thus destroying the chances of selling it as a going concern. This is especially true if the risks are not matched by the expected earnings of the administrator.[129]

4.49 In order to balance these interests, German law stipulates that the administrator is liable for such obligations, but only if he or she could, and should, have recognized that the estate would probably not be sufficient to meet them.[130] As the burden of proof lies with the insolvency administrator, he or she is encouraged to monitor and document the financial situation throughout the proceedings.[131] US law also provides for such personal liability of the trustee, though this only arises in the rarest of cases, for example for breach of fiduciary duty, which is extremely difficult to establish.[132]

---

[124] See § 60(1) of the *Insolvenzordnung*; Häsemeyer, *Insolvenzrecht* (n 6) paras 6.39 et seq.

[125] See Art. 130 of the Enterprise Bankruptcy Law of the PRC. See also Weiguo (n 102) National Report for the People's Republic of China, para. 6.12.8.

[126] Cf. *Re Powertrain Ltd* [2015] EWHC B26 (Ch); van Zwieten, *Principles of Corporate Insolvency Law* (n 1) para. 5.03 (liability under s. 212 of the UK Insolvency Act is limited by s. 1157 of the Companies Act).

[127] UNCITRAL, *Legislative Guide on Insolvency Law* (n 2) 184 para. 63; Westbrook et al., *A Global View of Business Insolvency Systems* (n 10) para. 3.6.1.3.

[128] Westbrook et al., *A Global View of Business Insolvency Systems* (n 10) para. 3.6.1.3.

[129] UNCITRAL, *Legislative Guide on Insolvency Law* (n 2) 184 para. 63; Westbrook et al., *A Global View of Business Insolvency Systems* (n 10) para. 3.6.1.3.

[130] See § 61 of the *Insolvenzordnung*. See also Paulus and Berberich (n 48) National Report for Germany, para. 10.12.5.

[131] Cf. BGH, 6 May 2004–IX ZR 47/03 = BGHZ 159, 104.

[132] Kilborn (n 9) National Report for the United States, para. 20.12 fn. 86.

D. Supervision

Practically all legal systems provide that the insolvency administrator is under a cer- **4.50**
tain degree of supervision by the court and/or by the creditors. Typically, the courts
supervise the administrator and rule if his or her actions are challenged by an affected
person.[133] Often, there is a particular court that is responsible for all relevant judgments
concerning the proceedings, which is usually the court at the debtor's registered office
or the centre of main interest.[134] However, in some countries (e.g. England), different
courts may be involved in the proceedings at certain points if one of the parties submits
an application to them; the proceedings are not overseen by the same judge from beginning to end.[135]

The insolvency administrator may be obliged to report to the court on a regular basis **4.51**
or concerning specific actions.[136] Usually, the court will only intervene in exceptional
situations, two of which shall now be highlighted: when it is called upon by a person
involved and when the administrator seeks to make a particularly important decision.

The first issue concerns challenging the decisions made by the administrator; in prin- **4.52**
ciple, unlike judicial decisions, these cannot be challenged in a technical sense.[137]
However, the affected parties—typically, the creditors—can obtain judicial protection
where the administrator can be shown to have committed misconduct, which might
include negligence in the performance of duties, significant procedural errors, or mis-
appropriation of funds.[138] The law may also provide for judicial protection if a decision
or act is (obviously) contrary to the interests of creditors.[139] The consequences of such
breaches of duty vary: there is often a provision for financial compensation, which
the creditors can claim (at court).[140] Another approach is stated explicitly in English
law: any person aggrieved by an act or decision of the liquidator may apply to the court.
In this case, the court may confirm, reverse, or modify the act or decision and issue any
order of its own as it thinks just.[141] Finally, in exceptional cases, the *ultra vires* doctrine
may apply: if the administrator's act evidently exceeds his or her power and clearly and
unambiguously contravenes the purpose of the insolvency proceedings, the 'abusive
act' may be invalid.[142]

---

[133] Eidenmüller, 'Comparative Corporate Insolvency Law' (n 7) 15; Bork, *Corporate Insolvency Law* (n 1) para.
2.38; cf. UNCITRAL, *Legislative Guide on Insolvency Law* (n 2) 178 para. 48.

[134] See, e.g. § 3(1) of the *Insolvenzordnung*; Art. R. 600-1(1) of the *Code de Commerce*; the centre of main interests (COMI) is particularly relevant regarding international jurisdiction; cf. Art. 3(1) of the European Insolvency
Regulation. See also UNCITRAL, *Legislative Guide on Insolvency Law* (n 2) 4 para. 12(f), 41 paras 12 et seq.

[135] McCormack (n 25) National Report for England, para. 8.13.

[136] UNCITRAL, *Legislative Guide on Insolvency Law* (n 2) 178 para. 48.

[137] Bork, *Corporate Insolvency Law* (n 1) para. 2.44.

[138] UNCITRAL, *Legislative Guide on Insolvency Law* (n 2) 186 para. 70.

[139] ibid.

[140] See above at fn. 123 et seq.

[141] See s. 168(5) of the UK Insolvency Act (regarding compulsory liquidation proceedings); Bailey and Groves,
Corporate Insolvency Law (n 120) para. 7.15; Anderson, *The Framework of Corporate Insolvency Law* (n 3) paras
12.30 et seq.

[142] BGH, 12 September 2019–IX ZR 16/18 = NZI 2019, 893 para. 11. See also Bork, *Corporate Insolvency Law* (n
1) paras 5.6 et seq.

106 FORMAL INSOLVENCY PROCEEDINGS

4.53 The second aspect mentioned concerns the administrator's duty to consult and to get approval. In principle, the administrator is largely free in his or her decision-making, particularly when acting in the ordinary course of business.[143] However, very important, pivotal decisions may require the involvement and approval of some other institution.[144] This includes, for example, the decision on whether the debtor's business should be continued or whether it should be shut down. In a number of jurisdictions, the creditors are supposed to decide on this kind of particularly significant measure;[145] if the administrator seeks to take action before the first creditors' meeting, this decision might need to be approved by the court.[146]

4.54 For some laws, the authority and autonomy of creditors is at the heart of liquidation proceedings. Here, the creditors—typically organized in the *creditors' meeting* and the *creditors' committee*—can set the course of the proceedings and give instructions to the administrator.[147] In other jurisdictions, however, creditors are not involved to the same extent; their participation may be limited to the right to be heard and to appear in the proceedings, leaving the insolvency administrator to make all important decisions and the creditors with little influence.[148]

V. Claims and Involvement of the Creditors

4.55 This last point already addresses another central issue of insolvency proceedings: the question of what position the creditors take in a procedure that is primarily intended to serve them. First of all, the creditors (i.e. those who have a claim against the debtor from the time before the proceedings) are the *substantial beneficiaries*.[149] Regarding their satisfaction, it is particularly important whether, and how, their claims are taken into account and whether they are subject to the general principle of equal treatment. Furthermore, this substantive entitlement of the creditors usually results in a procedural involvement as well, typically ensured via a plenary meeting of creditors or via representation.

---

[143] See, e.g. 11 U.S.C. §363(b)(1), (c)(1); similarly, UNCITRAL, *Legislative Guide on Insolvency Law* (n 2) 191 para. 80.

[144] See Radley-Gardner et al., *Fundamental Texts on European Private Law* (n 37) § 4.2 of the Principles of European Insolvency Law; cf. the distinction between Pts I, II, and III in Sch. 4 of the UK Insolvency Act. See also on this, Bailey and Groves, *Corporate Insolvency Law* (n 120) para. 15.21.

[145] See Art. 61(5) of the Enterprise Bankruptcy Law of the PRC; §§ 158(1) and 160(1) of the *Insolvenzordnung*; cf. UNCITRAL, *Legislative Guide on Insolvency Law* (n 2) 196 para. 96.

[146] See Arts 25(5) and 26 of the Enterprise Bankruptcy Law of the PRC; similarly, German law stipulates that the *provisional* administrator may only shut down the debtor's business with the court's consent: § 22(1)(2) No. 2 of the *Insolvenzordnung*; for the period between the commencement and the first creditors' meeting, cf. ibid § 158.

[147] For instance, German and Chinese law: see above at fn. 145; UNCITRAL, *Legislative Guide on Insolvency Law* (n 2) 191 paras 79 et seq.

[148] UNCITRAL, *Legislative Guide on Insolvency Law* (n 2) 190 paras 76 and 78; cf. on US and French law, Bork, *Corporate Insolvency Law* (n 1) para. 2.35.

[149] Cf. Bork, *Corporate Insolvency Law* (n 1) para. 2.11; UNCITRAL, *Legislative Guide on Insolvency Law* (n 2) 4 para. 12(j).

A. Ranking of Creditors and the *Pari Passu* Principle

A fundamental tenet of insolvency proceedings is the *pari passu* principle: since the **4.56** debtor's assets are not sufficient to satisfy all creditors in full, collective enforcement proceedings take place to realize the remaining assets and distribute the value among all creditors at the same rate. Insolvency proceedings put an end to the race of creditors, the previous principle of 'first come, first served' gives way for an orderly liquidation for the benefit of all.[150] Now it is acknowledged by the law that all creditors are in the same position (*par conditio creditorum*)[151] so that all (unsecured) insolvency claims rank on the same level and are to be treated equally.[152] Each creditor should receive—on a per-centage basis—as much (or as little) of the total proceeds as all the others. The *pari passu* principle also helps to explain, at least in part,[153] the mechanism of transactions avoidance in insolvency, which (partially) aims to ensure equal treatment between the creditors satisfied before and those satisfied through the proceedings.[154]

However, there are exceptions to this generally accepted principle in all legal systems, **4.57** which lead to different creditors being ranked unequally. The question of who should be given priority in the situation of insolvency and who should bear the resulting burden is one of the most important questions of insolvency law, which is answered quite differently by the various jurisdictions.[155] The hierarchy of creditors is the result of 'difficult political decisions about how to allocate losses between equally innocent parties'.[156] This central topic is only outlined here and will be dealt with in detail in Chapter 5 'Security Rights and Creditors' Priority and Ranking: Realizable Priority in Rescue'. In essence, it is about how the 'waterfall' of the distribution of the proceeds is structured: only when all prior creditors have been fully satisfied—so when the top basin is completely filled—does something flow downstream.

1. Exceptions and priorities

Entirely unaffected by the *pari passu* principle are those creditors who can claim that **4.58** they are entitled to an asset that does not belong to the insolvency estate at all. The 'pri-ority' that such creditors enjoy is not, in fact, an exception to the basic rule; rather, the rule does not even go that far; their right to separation doesn't fall within the scope of the insolvency proceedings as such.[157]

---

[150] van Zwieten, *Principles of Corporate Insolvency Law* (n 1) para. 8.02.

[151] This expression is used to refer to the principle of equal treatment, e.g. in Germany, Italy, and Austria; see in detail on this principle, Häsemeyer, *Insolvenzrecht* (n 6) paras 2.17 et seq.

[152] The principle has been expressly incorporated in English law in s. 107 of the UK Insolvency Act (regarding voluntary winding up); cf. van Zwieten, *Principles of Corporate Insolvency Law* (n 1) para. 8.02 et seq.

[153] Cf. on the different grounds for avoidance from a comparative law perspective, R. Bork, 'Anfechtung als Kernstück der Gläubigergleichbehandlung', Zeitschrift für Wirtschaftsrecht, 17 (2014) 797.

[154] For more details, see Chapter 6 'Transactions Avoidance Rules'.

[155] Eidenmüller, 'Comparative Corporate Insolvency Law' (n 7) 6 et seq.

[156] UK Law Commission, Consumer Prepayments on Retailer Insolvency (Law Com. No. 368) para. 8.4; cf. Anderson, *The Framework of Corporate Insolvency Law* (n 3) paras 21.01 et seq.

[157] van Zwieten, *Principles of Corporate Insolvency Law* (n 1) para. 8.17; Bork, *Corporate Insolvency Law* (n 1) para. 2.23. See above, para. 4.31.

108 FORMAL INSOLVENCY PROCEEDINGS

4.59 Something similar, or even the same, may be true for secured creditors, especially in the case of a right *in rem*. For instance, the person who delivered goods to the debtor under retention of title can typically reclaim them without having to share the value of the assets with the other creditors.[158] In some legal systems, encumbered assets are not part of the insolvency estate in any case and are therefore not subject to the *pari passu* distribution.[159] Others include such assets in the insolvency estate so that they can be realized by the administrator; but here, too, the priority of the secured creditors is recognized: the proceeds resulting from the realization of the object shall primarily be distributed in their favour. Only the value exceeding the secured claim is distributed among the other (unsecured) creditors.[160] If the proceeds are not sufficient to satisfy the secured creditor in full, he or she is treated as an ordinary insolvency creditor in respect of the exceeding part;[161] to that extent, the *pari passu* principle applies.

4.60 Preferential treatment is also granted to those creditors who carry out, finance, or support the proceedings: Before the ordinary insolvency creditors can access the value of the estate, the administrator (and his or her employees) will have to be paid, as well as debts arising from his actions, from continuing contractual obligations, etc.[162] This is necessary in order to allow for orderly proceedings (and especially business continuation), as no one would provide goods or services during the proceedings if they were not certain that they would be paid in full.[163] However, this is not an exception to *pari passu*, as the principle only covers insolvency claims, that is only those that existed prior to the commencement, which led to insolvency.[164]

4.61 In contrast, some other privileges established for social or political reasons are in direct conflict with the principle of equal treatment. For reasons that do not necessarily have anything to do with the system of insolvency law, special claims are given priority. A typical, practically very important example are *claims of employees* that are still unpaid when proceedings are opened.[165] For social and political reasons, there is a strong aversion to allowing these ('vital') claims of this special group of creditors to remain unpaid, so they are often given (super-)priority.[166] However, the consequence of any priority is a reduction in the insolvency estate; that is, less can be handed out to the

---

[158] Anderson, *The Framework of Corporate Insolvency Law* (n 3) paras 14.26 et seq.

[159] UNCITRAL, *Legislative Guide on Insolvency Law* (n 2) 77 para. 9; Anderson, *The Framework of Corporate Insolvency Law* (n 3) paras 14.29 and 21.04; Bork, *Corporate Insolvency Law* (n 1) para. 7.17.

[160] See, e.g. §§ 166 and 170(1) of the *Insolvenzordnung*; Radley-Gardner et al., *Fundamental Texts on European Private Law* (n 37) § 9.2(2) of the Principles of European Insolvency Law.

[161] See Arts L643-6, L-643-7 of the *Code de Commerce*; §§ 52 and 190(1) of the *Insolvenzordnung*.

[162] UNCITRAL, *Legislative Guide on Insolvency Law* (n 2) 270 para. 66; Radley-Gardner et al., *Fundamental Texts on European Private Law* (n 37) §§ 5.1(1) and 6.3(1) of the Principles of European Insolvency Law; Bork, *Corporate Insolvency Law* (n 1) para. 7.23.

[163] Therefore, in some systems, these expenses outrank secured creditors; cf. Westbrook et al., *A Global View of Business Insolvency Systems* (n 10) para. 3.7.3.

[164] van Zwieten, *Principles of Corporate Insolvency Law* (n 1) para. 8.17.

[165] UNCITRAL, *Legislative Guide on Insolvency Law* (n 2) 272 paras 72 et seq.; Westbrook et al., *A Global View of Business Insolvency Systems* (n 10) paras 6.2.1 et seq.

[166] A particularly striking example is French law; here, workers' claims enjoy priority even over secured claims: Arts L-622-17 and L-625-9 of the *Code de Commerce*; Art. L3253-2 et seq. of the *Code de Travail*; cf. M. Bayle in O.E.F. Lobo, *World Insolvency Systems* (Thomson Reuters 2009) Insolvency Law in France, 267 et seq.; as a comparative, Bork, *Corporate Insolvency Law* (n 1) paras 7.26 et seq.

remaining (non-preferred) creditors. Every advantage is 'paid for' by the ordinary insolvency creditors.[167]

2. Ordinary and subordinated claims

Only when the preferential creditors have been satisfied in full will the ordinary, unsecured insolvency creditors have a prospect of being satisfied. These make up the largest group of creditors; their satisfaction is the primary purpose of the proceedings, which is why they enjoy important procedural rights.[168] Such creditors, as already seen, cannot independently enforce their claims during the proceedings;[169] they normally have to file their claims with the insolvency administrator and, if necessary, prove them in order to receive a share in the distribution. The principle of equal treatment particularly takes effect within this group. However, certain creditors may enjoy a special economic advantage if they have the possibility to set off their claim and thus obtain full satisfaction.[170]

4.62

Finally, most jurisdictions provide for *subordinated creditors* to receive payment only when all other creditors have been paid in full. Since the debtor's financial difficulties are so severe that they have led to insolvency proceedings, this case is quite rare; subordinated creditors will rarely receive any distribution.[171] Such a subordination may result, for example, from a contractual agreement by which the creditor voluntarily moves to the end of the queue.[172] Another important example is certain claims of the shareholders: if they have provided a loan to the debtor company instead of granting equity, their claim is often settled only on a subordinated basis. German law, for example, classifies the claim for loan repayment as subordinate if the creditor is a shareholder of a limited liability company.[173] Even greater consensus between the legal systems is found regarding the subordination of claims arising from equity interests; such claims are generally at the bottom of the distribution waterfall.[174]

4.63

B. Submission and Admission of Insolvency Claims

Not only must the debtor's assets (the distributable estate) be identified in the insolvency proceedings but also his or her debts. To eventually distribute the proceeds, it is

4.64

---

[167] Similar, in a critical tone, UNCITRAL, *Legislative Guide on Insolvency Law* (n 2) 270 para. 67; Häsemeyer, *Insolvenzrecht* (n 6) paras 1.13, 2.20, 17.11 et seq.

[168] Bork, *Corporate Insolvency Law* (n 1) paras 7.5 et seq. See below, paras 4.72 et seq.

[169] See above, para. 4.36.

[170] Cf. the excursus below, paras 4.69 et seq.

[171] UNCITRAL, *Legislative Guide on Insolvency Law* (n 2) 273 para. 76.

[172] See, e.g. § 510(a) of the US Bankrupty Code; § 39(2) of the *Insolvenzordnung*. The reason for such a contractual arrangement may be that insolvency may be prevented in this way, such as overindebtedness in German law (§ 19(2)(2) of the *Insolvenzordnung*).

[173] See § 39(1)(1) No. 5, (4), (5) of the *Insolvenzordnung*; cf. Paulus and Berberich (n 48) National Report for Germany, paras 10.15.1 and 10.16.2.

[174] UNCITRAL, *Legislative Guide on Insolvency Law* (n 2) 273 para. 76; see, e.g. § 199(2) of the *Insolvenzordnung*. On English and US law, see van Zwieten, *Principles of Corporate Insolvency Law* (n 1) para. 8.30.

110 FORMAL INSOLVENCY PROCEEDINGS

necessary to assess which debts exist and are actually provable, that is which creditors are entitled to a part of the proceeds (and in which order). These issues generally do not need to be actively dealt with by the insolvency administrator; rather, the onus is on the creditors. Even if the debtor's business records disclose 'valid claims', the administrator is neither obliged nor allowed to simply accept them.[175] Instead, creditors have to be informed that, and how, they can and must submit their claims, including the time, place, procedure, and form for the submission; the consequences of failure to submit a claim are also usually pointed out.[176] Often, the administrator is responsible, in addition to a possible public announcement, for contacting and informing some or all known creditors.[177] Since this information may be particularly problematic in cross-border cases, there are often special regulations in this regard.[178]

4.65 To ensure that claims are filed promptly and that the insolvency proceedings are not unnecessarily prolonged, there is often a deadline for submission. The time within which claims must be filed may be fixed (e.g. based on the date of commencement) or may be set flexibly by the court or the administrator.[179] Chinese law, for example, stipulates that the time limit is set by the court and that it should be a minimum of 30 days and a maximum of 3 months.[180] A claim filed after the deadline is usually not taken into account in the distribution of the proceeds if the creditor was sufficiently informed.[181]

4.66 If a creditor has a claim that would only have become due in the future, he or she will be treated as if it were already due, but the claim may be admitted for its discounted value.[182] Non-monetary claims, such as a right to performance of an obligation, are converted into monetary claims, typically based on the value at the time of the opening of proceedings.[183] The same applies to claims in foreign currencies; these are converted into the currency of the country in which the proceedings take place, based on the exchange rates at a fixed point in time (often the commencement).[184]

---

[175] Anderson, *The Framework of Corporate Insolvency Law* (n 3) paras 19.10 et seq.; UNCITRAL, *Legislative Guide on Insolvency Law* (n 2) 253 paras 17 et seq.

[176] UNCITRAL, *Legislative Guide on Insolvency Law* (n 2) 66 Recital 25, 250 para. 5; Radley-Gardner et al., *Fundamental Texts on European Private Law* (n 37) § 10.1 of the Principles of European Insolvency Law.

[177] *Pulsford v Devenish* [1903] 2 Ch 625; cf. Anderson, *The Framework of Corporate Insolvency Law* (n 3) para. 19.11. See also the special provision of French law in Arts L 633-21(1), 622-24(1)(3), and 641-3(4) of the *Code de Commerce*.

[178] See Art. 54 of the European Insolvency Regulation (EU) 2015/848; Art. 14 of the UNCITRAL Model Law on Cross-Border Insolvency. See also UNCITRAL, *Legislative Guide on Insolvency Law* (n 2) 253 para. 15.

[179] UNCITRAL, *Legislative Guide on Insolvency Law* (n 2) 252 para. 13.

[180] See Art. 45 of the Enterprise Bankruptcy Law of the PRC; the German law is quite similar in this regard; cf. § 28(1) of the *Insolvenzordnung*.

[181] See, e.g. 11 U.S.C. §§502(b)(9) and 723(2)(3); US Bankruptcy Rule 3002; cf. *In re North Carolina New Schools Inc.* (Case No. 16-80411, Bankr. MDNC Oct. 26, 2020)—less strict is the German law; cf. § 177 of the *Insolvenzordnung*).

[182] See Radley-Gardner et al., *Fundamental Texts on European Private Law* (n 37) § 10.4(1) of the Principles of European Insolvency Law; UK Insolvency Rule 14.44; § 41 of the *Insolvenzordnung*; Art. 46 of the Enterprise Bankruptcy Law of the PRC.

[183] See Radley-Gardner et al., *Fundamental Texts on European Private Law* (n 37) § 10.4(4) of the Principles of European Insolvency Law; § 45(1) of the *Insolvenzordnung*.

[184] UNCITRAL, *Legislative Guide on Insolvency Law* (n 2) 255 para. 22; UK Insolvency Rule 14.21; § 45(2) of the *Insolvenzordnung*.

An important task of the insolvency administrator (or the court)[185] is to examine and **4.67** accept or challenge the claims that have been submitted. In some systems, the claim must be positively acknowledged in order to entitle to pay out; other jurisdictions provide for automatic admission of claims combined with the administrator's right to challenge the claim.[186] Because every (unjustified) claim is at the expense of the insolvency creditors, they usually also have the right to object to the claims of others.[187] The aim is to ensure that no one receives money out of the (already insufficient) insolvency estate if they would not be able to enforce the asserted claim in ordinary civil proceedings either. The following dispute concerns the existence or the quantum of the submitted claim; the burden of proof usually lies with the creditor concerned—he or she will generally be required to produce evidence as to the basis of the debt and the amount of the claim.[188]

Certain types of claims may be excluded from this system in different jurisdictions. **4.68** A simpler procedural route may be available, for example, for small claims[189] or to claims of employees.[190] In addition, claims that arise in, and as a result of, the insolvency proceedings—such as those established by the administrator for the continuation of the business—do not have to be submitted and proven in the manner described above. Those are simply paid (with priority) out of the estate.[191]

C. Excuses: Set-Off in Insolvency

An important option for creditors to break out of the *pari passu* treatment and obtain **4.69** more than just pro rata satisfaction lies in the possibility of set-off. The general right to set off debts against claims that are reciprocally owed to and by the debtor is commonly recognized (possibly under special conditions) in insolvency proceedings;[192] it may even become compulsory and self-executing.[193] If this were not possible, the creditor would have to pay his or her obligation in full towards the insolvency estate; however, in the final distribution, he or she would only receive a small share of the proceeds on

---

[185] In France, the claims are assessed by the administrator; his or her proposal on the claims to be recognized must then be confirmed or rejected by the court (Art. L 624-1 of the *Code de Commerce*); cf. Bork, *Corporate Insolvency Law* (n 1) para. 7.9.

[186] Westbrook et al., *A Global View of Business Insolvency Systems*, para. 3.7.4; UNCITRAL, *Legislative Guide on Insolvency Law* (n 2) 257 paras 31 et seq., 259 para. 36.

[187] See §§ 176(2) and 179(1) of the *Insolvenzordnung*; cf. Westbrook et al., *A Global View of Business Insolvency Systems* (n 10) para. 3.7.4.

[188] UNCITRAL, *Legislative Guide on Insolvency Law* (n 2) 253 para. 17.

[189] UK Insolvency Rules 14.3(3) and 14.31; cf. Anderson, *The Framework of Corporate Insolvency Law* (n 3) para. 19.14.

[190] See, on such features of French law, Bayle (n 166) Insolvency Law in France, 248, 267 et seq.

[191] van Zwieten, *Principles of Corporate Insolvency Law* (n 1) paras 8.17, 8.35, 8.37.

[192] UNCITRAL, *Legislative Guide on Insolvency Law* (n 2) 155 paras 204 et seq.; Radley-Gardner et al., *Fundamental Texts on European Private Law* (n 37) § 9.3 of the Principles of European Insolvency Law; 11 U.S.C. §553(a); § 94 of the *Insolvenzordnung*; Art. 40(1)(1) of the Enterprise Bankruptcy Law of the PRC.

[193] Westbrook et al., *A Global View of Business Insolvency Systems* (n 10) para. 3.9.9. See, e.g. on English law, *National Westminster Bank Ltd v Halesowen Presswork & Assemblies Ltd* [1972] AC 785 (HL); on French law, Bork, *Corporate Insolvency Law* (n 1) para. 5.51.

112 FORMAL INSOLVENCY PROCEEDINGS

the basis of his or her own claim. The debt would be satisfied at 100%, the claim only at a fraction. However, if set-off is possible and exercised, debts and claims are extinguished in the same amount; economically, the debtor can obtain full satisfaction of his or her claim in a form of self-help.[194]

4.70 Not withdrawing the right of set-off in insolvency proceedings is important, first, to prevent strategic abuse of the proceedings.[195] Second, in this way, it is also acknowledged that the creditor with the right of set-off has a form of security;[196] in fact, US law explicitly recognizes this.[197] A person providing a service or goods to the debtor without being paid immediately in return is granting credit and accepting a risk since it is not certain whether the other person will be able to fulfil his or her part of the deal later on. If, however, the creditor owes something to the debtor in turn, he or she can be sure that, instead of having to rely on actual payment, he or she can simply set it off—there is no need for the debtor to worry about satisfaction (insofar as the debt owed is at least as high as his or her claim).[198]

4.71 Considering this, many legal systems provide for special conditions or restrictions for offsetting in insolvency proceedings. Under French law, for example, claims that were (both) certain, due, and enforceable before the commencement of proceedings are automatically cleared;[199] for other set-off situations, a special provision of insolvency law applies: the set-off of *connected claims* (*créances connexes*) is excluded from the automatic stay,[200] and the claims must be registered but are not subject to the principle of equal treatment. The key requirement of connection is fulfilled, for example, when the claims arise from a single contract or from the same contractual relationship or when the obligations are carried out under separate contracts that constitute a single global contractual arrangement.[201] German law, on the other hand, emphasizes that only 'safe' set-off situations are protected: if the creditor obtained his or her debt or his or her claim against the debtor *after* the opening of proceedings, he or she never had the 'security' (prior to the insolvency) of being able to set off. Therefore, offsetting might not be possible within proceedings.[202] Similar rules are laid down in Chinese law[203] as well as in US law.[204]

---

[194] van Zwieten, *Principles of Corporate Insolvency Law* (n 1) para. 8.19.

[195] UNCITRAL, *Legislative Guide on Insolvency Law* (n 2) 155 para. 204 (the protection of such rights is 'highly desirable').

[196] Cf. *Stein v Blake* [1996] AC 243 (HL) (insolvency set-off enables the 'creditor to use his indebtedness to the bankrupt as a form of security').

[197] See 11 U.S.C. §§506(a)(1) and 553(a)(1); cf. Bork, *Corporate Insolvency Law* (n 1) para. 5.53.

[198] Bork, *Corporate Insolvency Law* (n 1) para. 5.49; the right to set-off is described as an *equivalent to fulfilment* by Häsemeyer, *Insolvenzrecht* (n 6) para. 19.02.

[199] Bork, *Corporate Insolvency Law* (n 1) para. 5.51.

[200] See Arts L 622-7(1) and L 641-3(1) of the *Code de Commerce*.

[201] Dupoux and Nerguararian (n 57) National Report for France, para. 9.18 fn. 54; Bork, *Corporate Insolvency Law* (n 1) para. 5.51.

[202] See § 96(1) Nos 1 and 2 of the *Insolvenzordnung*; a possibility of set-off that was given at *the time of opening* remains unaffected (ibid § 94).

[203] See Art. 40(2) No. 1 of the Enterprise Bankruptcy Law of the PRC.

[204] See 11 U.S.C. §553; here, the time limit is even brought forward by 90 days. The offset of post-petition claims against post-petition debt is not mentioned in the Code but also accepted; cf. *In re Alfar Dairy*, 458 F.2d 1258 (5th Cir. 1972).

D. Meeting and Representation of the Creditors

Given that the insolvency proceedings are, in essence, intended to serve the interests of **4.72** the insolvency creditors and that the estate no longer 'belongs' to the debtor—at least in terms of its value—but to the creditors, they generally have a right to participate in the conduct of the proceedings in one way or another. They form the party with the primary economic stake in the outcome of the proceedings and therefore may have the right to be informed, to be heard, and to have a say in (important) issues of the proceedings. The legal systems, however, differ widely in the nature and extent of these rights.[205]

Many legal systems provide for the participation of creditors via a *general meeting*: all **4.73** the creditors are invited (usually by the insolvency administrator)[206] to the meeting and are given the opportunity to inform themselves about the situation and the planned proceedings.[207] They may also be given the chance to influence, confirm, or reject the planned measures.[208] An important decision the creditors' meeting might be called to take is whether to replace the designated administrator.[209] However, because the procedure would not be manageable in a meaningful way if all creditors were able to continuously participate in the decision-making process, the concrete decisions on the liquidation are typically left to the administrator. If at all, only major decisions may require the consent of the creditors' meeting.[210] Of course, such decisions do not have to be unanimous, but they do require a majority vote, which is usually based on the value of the (non-subordinated) claims.[211]

Involving all creditors, and possibly even arranging an actual assembly, is very time- **4.74** consuming, costly, and cumbersome; while this may be possible for a few creditors, it becomes extremely difficult in practice if many thousands have to be involved.[212] Therefore, indirect involvement of creditors through representatives is crucial. In some jurisdictions, a single person is appointed to represent all creditors (or a specific group of creditors).[213] Much more important, however, is indirect participation via *creditors' committees*. These committees are seen as a key tool to efficiently ensuring the protection of

---

[205] UNCITRAL, *Legislative Guide on Insolvency Law* (n 2) 190 paras 75 et seq.; Bork, *Corporate Insolvency Law* (n 1) para. 2.30.

[206] See, e.g. Art. 25(1)(8) of the Enterprise Bankruptcy Law of the PRC; 11 U.S.C. §341(a); under German law, the court carries out this task (§§ 29(1) No. 1, 74 of the *Insolvenzordnung*).

[207] Westbrook et al., *A Global View of Business Insolvency Systems* (n 10) para. 3.6.2.3.

[208] Bork, *Corporate Insolvency Law* (n 1) paras 2.31 et seq.

[209] See 11 U.S.C. §§341(a) and 702; § 57(1) of the *Insolvenzordnung*; cf. above, paras 4.42 et seq.

[210] See §§ 147, 160(1)(2), 162 of the *Insolvenzordnung*; Art. 61(1) No. 5 et seq. of the Enterprise Bankruptcy Law of the PRC; see UNCITRAL, *Legislative Guide on Insolvency Law* (n 2) 196 para. 96 ('Where actions [...] will have a significant impact on the creditor body, it is desirable that all creditors be entitled [...] to vote on, those actions').

[211] See § 76(2) of the *Insolvenzordnung*; US Bankruptcy Rule 2003(b)(3); UNCITRAL, *Legislative Guide on Insolvency Law* (n 2) 197 para. 98; cf. Bork, *Corporate Insolvency Law* (n 1) paras 2.33 et seq.

[212] Bork, *Corporate Insolvency Law* (n 1) para. 2.31.

[213] Westbrook et al., *A Global View of Business Insolvency Systems* (n 10) para. 3.6.2.1. The French *mandataire judiciaire* represents the creditors in *sauvegarde* or *redressement judiciaire* proceedings (cf. Dupoux and Nerguararian (n 57) National Report for France, para. 9.12.1); in the event of liquidation, he or she is appointed as liquidator: Art. L 641-1(3) of the *Code de Commerce*.

114 FORMAL INSOLVENCY PROCEEDINGS

creditors' interests and the involvement of individual creditors who would otherwise be inhibited from being involved individually.[214] Although creditors' committees are more important in rehabilitation than in liquidation proceedings,[215] they nevertheless play a decisive role in many countries: First, they have an advisory function, both towards the administrator and towards the creditors as a whole.[216] Second, they may supervise the administrator, hence they typically need to be provided with up-to-date information on the financial affairs of the debtors' business, etc.[217] Third, the creditors' committee has, albeit rather rarely, the power to make decisions on certain important matters of the proceedings, replacing the participation of the creditors' meeting.[218]

4.75 The committee is typically (and, in some jurisdictions, mandatorily) composed of creditors, although it is often envisaged that external experts may also be appointed to act as professional representatives or proxies.[219] Some jurisdictions stipulate that certain creditor groups must be represented on the committee, typically major creditors (such as banks) and employees.[220] One issue that is not free of problems concerns the remuneration of committee members: in some jurisdictions, members are not paid, so serving in the committee is often rather unattractive.[221] Due to the complex and laborious nature of this job, other legal systems provide for remuneration, which is usually paid (with priority) out of the insolvency estate.[222] For this reason, the ratio of costs and benefits has to be considered in order to decide in which cases it is worthwhile to set up such a representative body.[223]

VI. Pending Contracts

4.76 Another important issue that arises with the commencement of insolvency proceedings concerns the treatment of pending and ongoing contracts.[224] The debtor may

---

[214] See the European Commission's explanatory statement on its proposal to make such committees mandatory throughout the EU (Proposal for a directive harmonising certain aspects of insolvency law, COM(2022) 702 final, 19 et seq., Recitals 47 et seq., Arts 58 et seq.).

[215] Westbrook et al., *A Global View of Business Insolvency Systems* (n 10) para. 3.6.2.2; on the limited significance within Chapter 7 proceedings in the United States, see Kilborn (n 9) National Report for the United States, para. 20.15.2.

[216] UNCITRAL, *Legislative Guide on Insolvency Law* (n 2) 200 paras 110 et seq.; Bailey and Groves, *Corporate Insolvency Law* (n 120) paras 16.5 et seq.

[217] Bork, *Corporate Insolvency Law* (n 1) para. 2.35; UNCITRAL, *Legislative Guide on Insolvency Law* (n 2) 201 para. 112.

[218] See, e.g. §§ 158(1) and 160(1) of the *Insolvenzordnung*; cf. Bork, *Corporate Insolvency Law* (n 1) para. 2.35. On the different categories of Sch. 4 of the UK Insolvency Act, see McCormack (n 25) National Report for England, para. 8.15.2.

[219] Bork, *Corporate Insolvency Law* (n 1) para. 2.34; in detail on potential committee members, see UNCITRAL, *Legislative Guide on Insolvency Law* (n 2) 197 et seq. paras 101 et seq.

[220] See § 67(2) of the *Insolvenzordnung*; cf. Bork, *Corporate Insolvency Law* (n 1) para. 2.34.

[221] For instance, in English law, therefore, the service may seem like throwing good money after bad: see McCormack (n 25) National Report for England, para. 8.15.2.

[222] See, e.g. in German law, §§ 53, 73(1), 54 No. 2 of the *Insolvenzordnung*.

[223] UNCITRAL, *Legislative Guide on Insolvency Law* (n 2) 197 paras 99 et seq.

[224] See on this and the following, Bork, *Corporate Insolvency Law* (n 1) paras 5.25 et seq.; Thomas H. Jackson, *The Logic and Limits of Bankruptcy Law* (Harvard University Press 1986), ch. 5, 105 et seq.; Westbrook et al., *A Global View of Business Insolvency Systems* (n 10) para. 3.9.1; UNCITRAL, *Legislative Guide on Insolvency Law* (n 2) 119 et seq. paras 108 et seq.

have ordered goods not yet delivered or commissioned future services. Furthermore, there will be many ongoing contractual relationships, for example employment contracts, tenancy agreements, contracts with energy suppliers, with communication providers, with licensors, with banks, etc. In most cases and most jurisdictions, these contracts are not automatically terminated because the proceedings have been opened.[225]

Mostly unproblematic are contracts that have already been completely fulfilled by the debtor or the creditor, that is where only one side remains to perform: if the debtor has already performed, the other party must fulfil its debt for the benefit of the estate so that the value can be distributed among all creditors. If, on the other hand, the debtor still has to perform, the counterparty is a typical insolvency creditor, who must file its claim and assert it in the insolvency proceedings.[226] More problems (and more need for regulation), however, exist with regard to contracts underperformed on both sides. The way in which such *executory contracts*[227] are to be dealt with is handled differently by the legal systems, usually depending on the nature of the contract.[228] An important principle in this regard is that claims and debts are, and remain, tied to each other.[229] The creditor has not provided any goods or services to the debtor prior to the insolvency— he or she has not given any (unsecured) credit. Therefore, he or she does not have to be treated in the same way as the insolvency creditors: in principle (but not without exception), he or she only has to fulfil his or her obligations if, in return, he or she is paid in full and with priority from the estate.[230] **4.77**

A. Acceptance or Rejection of Contractual Performance

Often, the right to decide on the fate of these pending contracts lies with the insolvency administrator,[231] who has to identify all pending contracts, determine their terms, and then decide on the fulfilment based on a cost–benefit analysis. Some contracts **4.78**

---

[225] See Radley-Gardner et al., *Fundamental Texts on European Private Law* (n 37) § 6.1 of the Principles of European Insolvency Law. Usually, only certain types of contracts are automatically terminated, e.g. agency agreements; cf. §§ 115 and 116 of the *Insolvenzordnung*.

[226] Bork, *Corporate Insolvency Law* (n 1) para. 5.25.

[227] This term is particularly used in US law to describe contracts under which the obligations of both parties are so far unperformed that the failure of either to complete performance would constitute a material breach excusing the performance of the other: see V. Countryman, 'Executory Contracts in Bankruptcy: Part I', Minnesota Law Review, 57 (1973) 439, 460; Jackson, *The Logic and Limits of Bankruptcy Law* (n 224) 105 et seq.; van Zwieten, *Principles of Corporate Insolvency Law* (n 1) para. 6.22.

[228] UNCITRAL, *Legislative Guide on Insolvency Law* (n 2) 123 et seq. paras 120 et seq.

[229] Cf. Jackson, *The Logic and Limits of Bankruptcy Law* (n 224) 106: 'executory contracts [...] are nothing more than mixed assets and liabilities arising out of the same transaction'.

[230] See Radley-Gardner et al., *Fundamental Texts on European Private Law* (n 37) § 6.3(1) of the Principles of European Insolvency Law; This is, for example, the basis of the *Lundy Granit* principle of English law; cf. van Zwieten, *Principles of Corporate Insolvency Law* (n 1) paras 6.23 and 8.36. Jurisdictions that do not provide for a decision by the insolvency administrator on the continuation of the contract may stipulate that the claims do not have priority and rank *pari passu* with other unsecured claims; cf. UNCITRAL, *Legislative Guide on Insolvency Law* (n 2) 127 para. 132.

[231] Westbrook et al., *A Global View of Business Insolvency Systems* (n 10) para. 3.9.1; see, e.g. German law (§ 103(1) of the *Insolvenzordnung*) or French law (Art. L 641-11-1(2)(1) of the *Code de Commerce*).

116 FORMAL INSOLVENCY PROCEEDINGS

will be of little or no use to the debtor (respectively, the insolvency estate); because the counterparty's claims would have to be paid with priority out of the estate, it might not be worthwhile to enforce the debtor's claim. Such burdensome and 'onerous'[232] agreements, where the ongoing costs of performance exceed the benefits, should be rejected.[233] The rejection is generally treated as a breach of contract that occurred before the proceedings; thus, only insolvency claims can be filed. In this case, the other party cannot enforce performance by the administrator but can only expect satisfaction of the outstanding claim on a *pro rata* basis.[234]

4.79 Other contracts, by contrast, can be very beneficial for the estate and the creditors if they are fulfilled by both parties. This includes, for example, the 'good deal' that the debtor has made because he or she bought a good for below its (current) value. In this case, the other party—even if paid with priority—has an interest in getting out of the contract but will generally not have the opportunity to do so in the insolvency proceedings.[235] Even if the debtor was in breach of his or her obligations prior to the opening, the other party may have to perform.[236] The resulting risk of non-payment is minimised in some jurisdictions by requiring the administrator to provide some form of guarantee or by making him or her personally liable.[237]

4.80 The administrator and the estate will also be interested in the fulfilment of contracts that are crucial for the continuation of the debtor's business. Because realizing all (or many) assets as a business unit promises particularly high revenues, it is often helpful to keep the operation going, to continue purchasing electricity, receiving goods, paying employees, etc. Compared to the case of the (obvious) 'good deal' presented above, the decision as to whether such contracts offer more advantages than disadvantages is much more difficult.

4.81 Typically, the decision as to which contracts are beneficial, and therefore to be accepted, and which are detrimental, and therefore to be rejected, lies with the insolvency administrator.[238] The other party usually only has the possibility to create certainty by demanding the administrator to make a decision. Typically, from this point on, he or

---

[232] This term is used in English law for contracts that are subject to a disclaimer (see s. 178(3)(a) of the UK Insolvency Act); cf. van Zwieten, *Principles of Corporate Insolvency Law* (n 1) paras 6.26 et seq.

[233] UNCITRAL, *Legislative Guide on Insolvency Law* (n 2) 120 et seq. paras 108 and 112; Jackson, *The Logic and Limits of Bankruptcy Law* (n 224) 108 et seq.

[234] See Radley-Gardner et al., *Fundamental Texts on European Private Law* (n 37) §§ 6.2 and 6.3(2) of the Principles of European Insolvency Law; UNCITRAL, *Legislative Guide on Insolvency Law* (n 2) 128 et seq. paras 134 et seq.; Kilborn (n 9) National Report for the United States, para. 20.23.

[235] See UNCITRAL, *Legislative Guide on Insolvency Law* (n 2) 120 et seq. para. 109; Westbrook et al., *A Global View of Business Insolvency Systems* (n 10) para. 3.9.3.

[236] Explicitly stated in Art. L 641-11-1(1)(2) of the *Code de Commerce*. Similar provisions may apply to rental and leasing contracts (§ 112 of the *Insolvenzordnung*) or to supplies of gas, water, electricity, etc. (s. 233(2)(b) of the UK Insolvency Act); cf. UNCITRAL, *Legislative Guide on Insolvency Law* (n 2) 126 para. 130.

[237] Westbrook et al., *A Global View of Business Insolvency Systems* (n 10) para. 3.9.4. See, e.g. Art. 18(2)(1) of the Enterprise Bankruptcy Law of the PRC (demanding a guarantee); §§ 54(1) and 61(1) No. 2 of the *Insolvenzordnung* (establishing a liability).

[238] See 11 U.S.C. §365; § 103(1) of the *Insolvenzordnung*; Arts L 622-13(2)(1) and L 641-11-1(2)(1) of the *Code de Commerce*; Art. 18(1) of the Enterprise Bankruptcy Law of the PRC; s. 178(2), (3) of the UK Insolvency Act.

PENDING CONTRACTS **117**

she has only a limited period of time to decide.[239] Often, the law provides that the contract will be terminated or become ineffective if the administrator does not make his or her decision in time; quite often this poses a problem, as the process of assessing every pending contract may be excessively costly and cumbersome.[240]

B. General and Specific Provisions

When dealing with pending contracts, the various laws often provide for a general rule, **4.82** which may be overridden by special provisions for certain types of contracts. In general, the administrator may decide on the performance as described above, but in specific cases, he or she may only have the 'regular' contractual termination rights as the debtor had prior to the commencement. Other contracts might—in deviation from the basic principle—be terminated by law so that the administrator has no possibility to preserve them.[241] Since certain contracts are associated with particular social and economic difficulties, special treatment of such contracts is unavoidable. Because the (often political) decision as to which situations are to be treated in a special way is taken very differently, national rules vary significantly in this regard.[242] Two examples may be highlighted in the following.

Employment contracts are an important case in point.[243] In many legal systems, the **4.83** debtor's employees are given special protection. Under German law, for example, employment contracts are exempt from the administrator's general right to decide on continuation. They remain in force despite the opening of proceedings and cannot simply be rejected but can only be terminated if notice periods are observed.[244] A similar approach is taken by French law; here, too, the administrator cannot simply reject the employment contracts. Termination is only possible under certain substantive and procedural restrictions.[245] Chinese law allows the administrator to terminate employment contracts only in accordance with general labour laws, regulations, and the contract itself.[246] Employment contracts are also given special treatment under English law but in an inverse manner: the (compulsory) winding-up order operates as notice of

---

[239] See Radley-Gardner et al., *Fundamental Texts on European Private Law* (n 37) § 6.3(3) of the Principles of European Insolvency Law; § 103(2)(1) of the *Insolvenzordnung*; Art. L 622-13(3) No. 1 of the *Code de Commerce*; Art. 18(1)(2) of the Enterprise Bankruptcy Law of the PRC; cf. Westbrook et al., *A Global View of Business Insolvency Systems* (n 10) para. 3.9.1.

[240] UNCITRAL, *Legislative Guide on Insolvency Law* (n 2) 124 para. 121; on German law, which prescribes a decision without culpable hesitation, see § 103(2)(3) of the *Insolvenzordnung*; § 121(1)(1) of the *Bürgerliches Gesetzbuch* (BGB); Häsemeyer, *Insolvenzrecht* (n 6) para. 20.17.

[241] Bork, *Corporate Insolvency Law* (n 1) para. 5.27.

[242] Westbrook et al., *A Global View of Business Insolvency Systems* (n 10) para. 3.9.7; Bork, *Corporate Insolvency Law* (n 1) para. 5.31.

[243] Cf. Bork, *Corporate Insolvency Law* (n 1) paras 5.40 et seq.; UNCITRAL, *Legislative Guide on Insolvency Law* (n 2) 130 et seq. para. 145.

[244] See §§ 108(1)(1) and 113(1), (2) of the *Insolvenzordnung*.

[245] See Arts L 631-17, L 641-10(3), L 641-11-1(6)(1) of the *Code de Commerce*; Bork, *Corporate Insolvency Law* (n 1) para. 5.44.

[246] Weiguo (n 102) National Report for the People's Republic of China, para. 6.16.1.

118 FORMAL INSOLVENCY PROCEEDINGS

dismissal to all the employees of the debtor; employment contracts will only continue if the administrator takes action and calls on the employees (who are important to him or her) to continue working, and they agree.[247] US law, on the other hand, does not have any special provisions in this regard, so the trustee may accept or reject in the usual way.

4.84 Some jurisdictions also have special regulations for the *lease of land and premises*, often distinguishing between residential and commercial leases.[248] The focus is often on the protection of the debtor (as the lessee). If the debtor is a natural person, insolvency shall not lead to immediate homelessness; if the debtor is a company, the lease of the premises is often an essential part of the business and shall therefore be preserved. Because this goal can often be achieved through the administrator's right of decision, it is not uncommon that the general principle remains in force, though certain modifications may be made.[249] German law, on the other hand, excludes the lease of immovable property from the administrator's right to choose; rather, a right of termination (subject to a notice period) is given as well as the possibility of releasing the lease.[250]

C. Termination Clauses

4.85 Even though the various laws usually stipulate that a contract is not terminated solely due to the commencement of insolvency proceedings, the same consequence may often arise through contractual provisions made by the parties. The agreement might include an *ipso facto* clause allowing one party to terminate or to modify the executory contract on the basis of a predetermined event such as the counterparty's insolvency (or the initiation or commencement of proceedings).[251] Some jurisdictions accept such clauses and uphold their validity to ensure that commercial bargains that may be economically reasonable are respected.[252] A wide variety of reasons may support this approach, for example the belief that such clauses prevent harmful delays in the termination of contracts, thus preventing the increase of debts; the protection of the counterparty against the threat of its own insolvency; or the need for the creator of intellectual property to control the use of the insolvency practitioner (IP), etc.[253]

4.86 Such termination clauses deprive the administrator of the possibility to freely decide on the acceptance or rejection of contracts that could be crucial for a meaningful and profitable liquidation. For this reason, many legal systems provide for the supremacy

---

[247] *Re Oriental Bank Corp.* (1886) 32 ChD 366; van Zwieten, *Principles of Corporate Insolvency Law* (n 1) para. 5.24.

[248] Bork, *Corporate Insolvency Law* (n 1) paras 5.35 et seq.; UNCITRAL, *Legislative Guide on Insolvency Law* (n 2) 129 paras 137 et seq.; Westbrook et al., *A Global View of Business Insolvency Systems* (n 10) para. 3.9.8.

[249] For instance, in French, English, and US law; cf. Bork, *Corporate Insolvency Law* (n 1) paras 5.37 et seq.

[250] See §§ 108(1)(1) and 109(1) of the *Insolvenzordnung*; cf. Häsemeyer, *Insolvenzrecht* (n 6) paras 20.49 et seq.

[251] On such clauses, their treatment in different jurisdictions, and conflict of law, see J.F. Hoffmann, 'Executory Contracts, Ipso Facto Clauses and Licensing Agreements in Cross-Border Insolvencies', International Insolvency Review, 27 (2018) 300, 303 et seq., 309 et seq.

[252] UNCITRAL, *Legislative Guide on Insolvency Law* (n 2) 122 paras 114 et seq.

[253] ibid para. 115.

of insolvency law over contract law in this respect and consider such clauses to be invalid.[254] US law, for example, explicitly stipulates that an executory contract may not be terminated or modified solely because of a provision in such a contract that is conditioned on the insolvency, the commencement of proceedings, or the appointment of a trustee.[255] French law imposes a similar restriction on *ipso facto* clauses,[256] and German law also stipulates that the administrator's right to decide on pending contracts may not be circumvented by the contracting parties.[257] Although such provisions significantly interfere with general principles of contract law, they (and the resulting right to accept or reject) may be crucial to the success of the proceedings.[258]

VII. Swelling and Liquidation of the Assets

Achieving the main goal of the insolvency proceedings—settling the insolvency claims as comprehensively as possible—requires two preparatory steps: 'swelling'[259] the assets available to the creditors (especially through avoidance proceedings) and selling the assets at the best possible price (either in parts or as a unit).

4.87

A. Augmentation of the Estate and Avoidance Proceedings

The first step (i.e. increasing the insolvency estate) includes, for example, reclaiming assets that belong to the debtor but are in the possession of others. If, for example, the debtor is a lessor, the pending contracts must be rejected or terminated by the administrator in order to recover the leased property.[260] The insolvency estate is also increased through earnings generated by the administrator: If a (net advantageous) contract is fulfilled after the commencement, the fruits of performance will belong to the estate.[261] If an object was sold to the debtor under retention of title, the outstanding part of the sum could be paid and thus ownership be acquired, meaning that the asset would be part of the realizable estate.[262]

4.88

---

[254] Westbrook et al., *A Global View of Business Insolvency Systems* (n 10) para. 3.9.3; UNCITRAL, *Legislative Guide on Insolvency Law* (n 2) 122 paras 116 et seq. An overview of the following jurisdictions is provided by Hoffmann, 'Executory Contracts, Ipso Facto Clauses and Licensing Agreements in Cross-Border Insolvencies' (n 251) 300, 303 et seq.; on the discussion in English law, see van Zwieten, *Principles of Corporate Insolvency Law* (n 1) paras 7.14 et seq.

[255] See 11 U.S.C. §365(e); cf. Jackson, *The Logic and Limits of Bankruptcy Law* (n 224) 40 et seq., 119.

[256] See Arts 622-13(2)(1) and L 641-11-1(2)(1) of the *Code de Commerce*.

[257] See § 119 of the *Insolvenzordnung*; recently, and in detail on the treatment of termination clauses in German law, see BGH, 27 October 2022–IX ZR 213/21 = NJW 2023, 603.

[258] UNCITRAL, *Legislative Guide on Insolvency Law* (n 2) 122 para. 116.

[259] van Zwieten, *Principles of Corporate Insolvency Law* (n 1) paras 6.31 et seq.

[260] Such an executory contract may be subject to the administrator's general right to choose between accepting and rejecting performance or special provision may apply (e.g. 11 U.S.C. §365(h); §§ 108(1)(2) and 111 of the *Insolvenzordnung*).

[261] van Zwieten, *Principles of Corporate Insolvency Law* (n 1) para. 6.32.

[262] Retention of title would otherwise lead to the asset being excluded from the estate: see above, para. 4.31; cf. Bork, *Corporate Insolvency Law* (n 1) para. 5.33.

4.89 Another important factor for the swelling of the insolvency estate is the enforcement of outstanding claims: first, this, of course, concerns 'ordinary' claims the debtor has against third parties, for example customers, buyers, etc. Second, however, the main issue will often be asserting liability claims arising in connection with the insolvency. The various legal systems usually provide for the administrator to examine the causes of insolvency and whether the directors of the debtor company may have committed any wrongdoing in this regard.[263] Although there are considerable differences, in many jurisdictions, rules are in place according to which someone who has culpably caused or aggravated the insolvency situation may be held liable so that the damages of the creditors are partially compensated. Under English law, for example, a director guilty of fraudulent or wrongful trading may be ordered by the court to make compensating contributions to the company's assets as the court thinks proper.[264] Chinese law may require directors and managers to repay salaries, bonuses, or other rewards they received despite the insolvency of the company or on a fraudulent basis.[265] German law even stipulates, among other things, that (extraordinary) payments made by the directors on behalf of the company after insolvency has occurred are to be reimbursed by them.[266] Furthermore, liability may arise if creditors have been harmed by a belated filing for insolvency and as a result of fraudulent or intentional harmful conduct.[267]

4.90 A crucial, and often the most important, way to increase the estate lies in *avoidance proceedings*. Given its outstanding relevance, this possibility to reverse pre-insolvency outflows of assets is discussed and examined in detail in Chapter 6 'Transactions Avoidance Rules', therefore only a few aspects are briefly highlighted here. The commencement of insolvency proceedings results, in principle, in a clear cut: the estate is seized; from now on, only the administrator is entitled to act; and the debtor may no longer manage his or her assets, but transactions and payments made before the seizure are still acknowledged—at least, in principle. If the debtor has transferred an asset to another person before the commencement of proceedings, it will not be part of the estate and therefore cannot be realized for the benefit of the creditors. This would mean that a creditor who received payments or goods (shortly) before the opening of proceedings would be unaffected by the insolvency, while another creditor who may have had a similar claim would only receive the quota. The problem becomes particularly apparent in the case of transactions that are intentionally fraudulent, favour a closely related party, or are made below value.

---

[263] Westbrook et al., *A Global View of Business Insolvency Systems* (n 10) para. 3.3.1.2; Anderson, *The Framework of Corporate Insolvency Law* (n 3) paras 17.01 et seq.
[264] See ss 213(2) and 214(1) of the UK Insolvency Act; cf. van Zwieten, *Principles of Corporate Insolvency Law* (n 1) paras 6.36, 14.54 et seq; Anderson, *The Framework of Corporate Insolvency Law* (n 3) paras 17.14 et seq.
[265] See Art. 36 of the Enterprise Bankruptcy Law of the PRC; see Weiguo (n 102) National Report for the People's Republic of China, para. 6.16.1.
[266] See § 15b(1), (4) of the *Insolvenzordnung*.
[267] ibid § 15a(1); §§ 823(2) and 826 of the BGB; cf. Häsemeyer, *Insolvenzrecht* (n 6) paras 30.67 et seq.

SWELLING AND LIQUIDATION OF THE ASSETS 121

Therefore, practically all legal systems provide for transactions avoidance rules. In very **4.91** different ways, and for various reasons, certain transactions are reversed so that the assets are returned to the estate. As a result, the affected counterparty is usually not entitled to full satisfaction, but must join the ranks of the insolvency creditors, and is only satisfied according to the *pari passu* principle.[268] At the same time, the procedure leads to a swelling of the insolvency estate resulting in increased value being available for the creditors as a whole.[269]

The insolvency law generally contains provisions that apply retroactively to a specific **4.92** point in time, such as the initiation or the commencement of proceedings, and specify a certain 'suspect' period—going back months or even years—in which transactions may be void or voidable.[270] The exact conditions that must be met for the transaction to be reversed vary greatly; both objective and subjective elements may be considered and combined in different ways,[271] resulting in a variety of 'avoidance grounds'.[272] Objective grounds that could result in avoidance are, for example, that an asset was transferred after substantive insolvency had occurred or after the application for proceedings had been made or that the transaction benefited someone who did not have an enforceable claim against the debtor or was at an undervalue.[273] A subjective reason that may underlie avoidance is, in particular, the intent of defrauding creditors, which represents a modern form of the *actio pauliana* found in Roman law.[274] Often, objective and subjective elements must come together in a certain way, for instance that there is an objective preference of a creditor as well as the subjective knowledge regarding the debtor's financial problems.[275]

---

[268] See above, paras 4.56 et seq. and below paras 6.01 and 6.08. In many, though not all, cases, it is a matter of reversing the (full) satisfaction of a creditor.

[269] van Zwieten, *Principles of Corporate Insolvency Law* (n 1) paras 6.35 and 13.03; R. Bork and M. Veder, *Harmonisation of Transactions Avoidance Laws* (Intersentia 2022) paras 2.99 et seq.; this 'swelling' is, of course, always subject to limitations: the fundamental trust in the stability of performances always has to be considered; cf. Bork and Veder, ibid paras 2.105 et seq.

[270] UNCITRAL, *Legislative Guide on Insolvency Law* (n 2) 135 para. 150, 147 paras 188 et seq.; Radley-Gardner et al., *Fundamental Texts on European Private Law* (n 37) § 8.1 of the Principles of European Insolvency Law; Westbrook et al., *A Global View of Business Insolvency Systems* (n 10) para. 3.10.1.

[271] UNCITRAL, *Legislative Guide on Insolvency Law* (n 2) 137 et seq. paras 156 et seq.; McCormack, Keay, and Brown, *European Insolvency Law* (n 2) para. 4.8.

[272] See below, paras 6.29 et seq.; a comprehensive overview of the various avoidance grounds is given in Bork and Veder, *Harmonisation of Transactions Avoidance Laws* (n 269) paras 3.28 et seq.; in depth at paras 4.54 et seq.

[273] See Radley-Gardner et al., *Fundamental Texts on European Private Law* (n 37) § 8.2 of the Principles of European Insolvency Law; UNCITRAL, *Legislative Guide on Insolvency Law* (n 2) 137 para. 157; Westbrook et al., *A Global View of Business Insolvency Systems* (n 10) paras 3.10.3 et seq.; van Zwieten, *Principles of Corporate Insolvency Law* (n 1) paras 13.11 et seq.

[274] Cf. the Digests 22,1,38,4 (Paulus, Ad Plautius 6); Bork and Veder, *Harmonisation of Transactions Avoidance Laws* (n 269) paras 3.33, 3.54 et seq., 4.155 et seq.; Radley-Gardner et al., *Fundamental Texts on European Private Law* (n 37) § 8.2(a) of the Principles of European Insolvency Law; Westbrook et al., *A Global View of Business Insolvency Systems* (n 10) para. 3.10.2.

[275] See, e.g. ss 239 et seq. of the UK Insolvency Act (only focusing on the *debtor's* 'desire'); § 130(1) of the *Insolvenzordnung* (requiring the *creditor's* knowledge of the debtor's inability to pay or of the application for proceedings).

B. Realization of the Assets

4.93 An integral part of any insolvency procedure aimed at winding up is the liquidation of the debtor's assets. In order to distribute the seized estate among all creditors, all non-cash assets must be converted into money; the creditors are entitled only to the value of the debtor's property, not to the assets themselves.[276] The 'realization' of the estate's value is typically done by the insolvency administrator selling the various assets;[277] particularly significant realization decisions may require the consent of the creditors or the court.[278] In some insolvency laws, the courts take the decisive position in the sale of assets so that the administrator only plays a subordinate role, for example, collecting offers or obtaining the opinions of the creditors.[279] Either way, realization is aimed at generating the highest possible return in a timely manner. For this reason, most legal systems also have provisions allowing the administrator to 'disclaim' worthless or onerous property that does not promise a meaningful return when liquidated.[280]

4.94 In many jurisdictions, and in many cases, the administrator has a broad discretion; that is, he or she can decide to whom the assets will be given and in which way the sale should be carried out.[281] For example, English law stipulates that the liquidator has the power to sell any assets by public auction or private contract, with power to transfer the whole of it to any person or to sell the property in parcels; in addition, he or she is authorized to take all other measures necessary for the purpose of winding up the company and distributing its assets.[282] German law also gives the administrator wide discretion in realization so that he or she can sell via contract as well as via auction;[283] measures of 'particular importance' require the consent of the creditors.[284] Similar provisions can be found in US law, which allow the trustee to realize property of the estate outside the ordinary course of business by private sale or public auction but only after notice and a hearing.[285] Under Chinese law, the value of an insolvent company is generally to be realized through an auction; only if the creditors' meeting decides otherwise can the sale be carried out in a different form.[286]

---

[276] Bork, *Corporate Insolvency Law* (n 1) para. 7.39.

[277] ibid; Radley-Gardner et al., *Fundamental Texts on European Private Law* (n 37) § 12(1) of the Principles of European Insolvency Law; UNCITRAL, *Legislative Guide on Insolvency Law* (n 2) 106 paras 79 et seq.; Anderson, *The Framework of Corporate Insolvency Law* (n 3) paras 19.05 et seq.

[278] On this, see above, para. 4.53.

[279] UNCITRAL, *Legislative Guide on Insolvency Law* (n 2) 106 para. 80.

[280] McCormack, Keay, and Brown, *European Insolvency Law* (n 2) para. 5.4.4; see, e.g. 11 U.S.C. § 554; s. 178(3)(b) of the UK Insolvency Act; cf. van Zwieten, *Principles of Corporate Insolvency Law* (n 1) paras 6.26 et seq.; Bork, *Corporate Insolvency Law* (n 1) paras 4.17 et seq.

[281] UNCITRAL, *Legislative Guide on Insolvency Law* (n 2) 106 paras 79 et seq.

[282] See Sch. 4 paras 6 and 13 of the UK Insolvency Act; cf. Anderson, *The Framework of Corporate Insolvency Law* (n 3) para. 19.06; van Zwieten, *Principles of Corporate Insolvency Law* (n 1) para. 5.06.

[283] See §§ 159 et seq. of the *Insolvenzordnung*; cf. Häsemeyer, *Insolvenzrecht* (n 6) paras 13.36 et seq.

[284] See § 160 of the *Insolvenzordnung*; see above, para. 4.53.

[285] See 11 U.S.C. §363; US Bankruptcy Rule 6004; cf. J.J. Wielebinski and D. Rukavina in Lobo, *World Insolvency Systems* (n 166) Overview of the Bankruptcy Code in the US, 741 et seq.

[286] See Art. 112(1), (2) of the Enterprise Bankruptcy Law of the PRC.

A particular problem arises when the asset to be sold is subject to conflicting claims, **4.95**
such as ownership, leasehold, and especially lien.[287] If the disputes over these matters
had to be fully resolved first, the realization could be delayed at great length; the assets could be sold subject to those rights, but with such a caveat, the realizable proceeds would be very low. Therefore, some insolvency laws provide for the right of the
administrator to sell assets of the debtor *free and clear* of interests.[288] Certain conditions typically have to be met for this to be possible, for example that the holder of the
interest is notified in advanced, that he or she consents to such realization, or that his or
her consent is replaced by a court decision.[289] In this way, the assets being sold will be
'stripped' of all conflicts, meaning that potential buyers will be willing to pay more so
that—ideally—both the interest holders and the insolvency creditors will receive more
proceeds.[290]

Since the realization of the insolvency estate ultimately serves the interests of the cred- **4.96**
itors, it is important to ensure that the assets will be sold at a reasonable price. For this
purpose, the legal systems may provide for various safeguard mechanisms, such as demanding valuations by neutral, independent experts, ensuring proper notification of
creditors and potential buyers, or requiring a pre-bid qualification in order to establish
a minimum price.[291] Special provisions are often applicable when the sale is made in favour of *persons close to the debtor*, for example managers or shareholders. Such a sale to
insiders is usually not prohibited in principle; in fact, the related parties may have a special interest in the acquisition and are therefore willing to offer a good price. However,
in order to ensure that the appropriate and best possible price is paid in such a case, the
sale has to be adequately supervised and carefully scrutinized.[292]

C. Sale of the Debtor's Business in Particular

Compared to the piecemeal sale, a more sophisticated and, if possible, very lucrative **4.97**
way of realization is the sale of the debtor's business as a whole.[293] Although insolvency
proceedings are aimed at winding up the debtor, this does not mean that his or her
business must be dismantled as well; survival of the business and liquidation are not
necessarily mutually exclusive.[294] If the administrator succeeds in keeping the company running despite the financial distress and despite the insolvency proceedings, he
or she may be able to realize the *going-concern value* and thus generate significantly

---

[287] Cf. Westbrook et al., *A Global View of Business Insolvency Systems* (n 10) para. 3.8.
[288] See, e.g. 11 U.S.C. §363(f); cf. UNCITRAL, *Legislative Guide on Insolvency Law* (n 2) 108 paras 85 et seq.;
Westbrook et al., *A Global View of Business Insolvency Systems* (n 10) para. 3.8.
[289] UNCITRAL, *Legislative Guide on Insolvency Law* (n 2) 108 para. 85.
[290] Westbrook et al., *A Global View of Business Insolvency Systems* (n 10) para. 3.8.
[291] ibid para. 3.8.
[292] UNCITRAL, *Legislative Guide on Insolvency Law* (n 2) 106 para. 81, Recital 61; Eidenmüller, 'Comparative
Corporate Insolvency Law' (n 7) 24; see, e.g. § 162 of the *Insolvenzordnung*.
[293] Anderson, *The Framework of Corporate Insolvency Law* (n 3) paras 19.06 et seq.
[294] Westbrook et al., *A Global View of Business Insolvency Systems* (n 10) para. 4.1.2.

124 FORMAL INSOLVENCY PROCEEDINGS

higher proceeds than if all the individual parts were sold separately. Such a business-preserving 'asset deal' must not be mistaken for the reorganization and rescue of the debtor;[295] it is a form (albeit special) of liquidation: the debtor will lose all the assets and—in the case of a legal entity—will ultimately be dissolved.[296] While a genuine restructuring process 'removes the debt from the business, asset-deal restructuring removes the business from its debt'.[297]

4.98 Such an approach can, of course, only be considered if there is still a running business to be kept open. If the proceedings have been initiated too late, the essential contracts already terminated, warehouses emptied, and the employees dismissed, only a disruptive liquidation will be possible. But even if there is a going concern, the continuation is a highly difficult task for the administrator, for example because there will hardly be any liquid funds available to pay for necessary goods in the short term. If the administrator wants to take out a loan, the lender will demand special security and preferential treatment in order to provide fresh capital. Some jurisdictions therefore privilege 'new money' and provide for the possibility of super-priorities that take precedence not only over insolvency claims but also over secured creditors.[298] Priority over ordinary insolvency creditors is often also given to those who contract with the administrator after the commencement and thus provide the necessary goods and services for the continuation of the business.[299]

4.99 Another crucial factor is the ability to hold together the assets that are necessary for the business to operate. The items used to run the business will rarely all belong to the debtor and be free of security interests: real estate and factory buildings might be leased, manufacturing equipment might be the subject of security rights. If the holders of such rights immediately seized these objects, it would be impossible to continue the business and thus to realize the going-concern value. Insolvency laws must strike a balance between the conflicting interests of the affected right holders and the interests of the insolvency creditors as a whole; neither should property and security rights be devalued too much, nor should a liquidation via asset deal be made impossible from the outset.[300]

4.100 Special provisions might be laid down, for example, regarding the moratorium: even if a debtor would normally have a right to separation (e.g. of an encumbered asset) and

---

[295] See section IX on this alternative.

[296] Cf. Radley-Gardner et al., *Fundamental Texts on European Private Law* (n 37) § 12.1(2) of the Principles of European Insolvency Law; Westbrook et al., *A Global View of Business Insolvency Systems* (n 10) para. 4.1.2; UNCITRAL, *Legislative Guide on Insolvency Law* (n 2) 26 para. 20.

[297] Bork, *Corporate Insolvency Law* (n 1) para. 1.4.

[298] See, e.g. 11 U.S.C. §364(c)(1); Arts L 611-11(1) and L 622-17(2) of the *Code de Commerce*; cf. UNCITRAL, *Legislative Guide on Insolvency Law* (n 2) 106 before Recital 63; McCormack, Keay, and Brown, *European Insolvency Law* (n 2) para. 3.9.

[299] See, e.g. §§ 53 and 55(1) of the *Insolvenzordnung*; Westbrook et al., *A Global View of Business Insolvency Systems* (n 10) para. 3.7.3; see above, para. 4.60.

[300] UNCITRAL, *Legislative Guide on Insolvency Law* (n 2) 84 para. 27; McCormack, Keay, and Brown, *European Insolvency Law* (n 2) para. 6.5.

SWELLING AND LIQUIDATION OF THE ASSETS   125

would therefore generally not be subject to the automatic stay,[301] a different regime may apply if the asset in question is part of the ongoing business. Individual enforcement may be temporarily prohibited in order to keep the business together as a functioning unit for the time being.[302] Similar rules might govern the right of realization: German law, for example, provides that movable property which is subject to security rights may, by way of exception, be realized by the administrator if the asset is in the debtor's possession.[303] The idea behind this is that such an asset will be an integral part of the debtor's business; in order to enable the sale of the business as a whole and to allow for the realization of the going-concern value, the secured creditor's right is restricted.

In order to ensure that the sale of a business is not started too late (i.e. at a time when there is no longer an active business to be realized), some jurisdictions use what is known as a 'pre-pack': this practice is based on the insight that a long, cost-intensive, and public procedure will destroy a large part of the values and goodwill, that is that a quick, quiet sale process will lead to higher proceeds.[304] This type of approach, which is common, for example, in the United Kingdom and France, has similarities to a pre-packed insolvency plan, which aims to restructure and save the debtor (and not just his or her business).[305] Typically, the sale is prepared and negotiated in a first step prior to the insolvency proceedings and executed in a second step shortly after the commencement of proceedings.[306]   **4.101**

A critical aspect of selling a business is determining the best or appropriate selling price; this is often achieved through an auction, where the highest-bidding investor prevails and receives the debtor business—that is the assets without debt. In particular, insiders will participate in the bidding and often submit the highest bid. Therefore, it is important to ensure that the best possible price is obtained, for example through consent of the creditors, supervision of courts, or fault-based liability of the administrator.[307] Transparency and publicity, in particular, can help accomplish this task and ensure that many buyers are attracted and collusion is prevented.[308]   **4.102**

---

[301] See above, para. 4.37.

[302] UNCITRAL, *Legislative Guide on Insolvency Law* (n 2) 77 paras 7 et seq., 88 paras 39 et seq.; Dupoux and Nerguararian (n 57) National Report for France, para. 9.3.2.

[303] See § 166(1) of the *Insolvenzordnung*, deviating from the general right of realization of the secured creditor (ibid § 173(1)).

[304] McCormack, Keay, and Brown, *European Insolvency Law* (n 2) para. 5.4.1; cf. the comments of the EU Commission in the Proposal for a directive harmonising certain aspects of insolvency law, COM(2022) 702 final, 15 et seq.

[305] Cf. Westbrook et al., *A Global View of Business Insolvency Systems* (n 10) para. 4.5.4.

[306] van Zwieten, *Principles of Corporate Insolvency Law* (n 1) paras 11.38 et seq.; Anderson, *The Framework of Corporate Insolvency Law* (n 3) paras 18.01 et seq.; McCormack, Keay, and Brown, *European Insolvency Law* (n 2) para. 5.4.2. This approach is adopted by the EU Commission in the Proposal for a directive harmonising certain aspects of insolvency law, COM(2022) (n 304) Art. 19 et seq.: a preparation phase, which aims to find an appropriate buyer, is followed by the liquidation phase, which aims to approve and execute the sale of the business and to distribute the proceeds.

[307] Eidenmüller, 'Comparative Corporate Insolvency Law' (n 7) 24 et seq. See also above, para. 4.96.

[308] Westbrook et al., *A Global View of Business Insolvency Systems* (n 10) para. 3.8.

VIII. Final Steps of the Liquidation Proceedings

4.103 Once all the debtor's assets have been liquidated, all rights and claims have been asserted for the benefit of the estate, and it has been determined which creditors must be satisfied and in what order, the final steps of the proceedings have to be taken. With the distribution of the insolvency estate among the creditors, the insolvency procedure fulfils its core function.[309] At this point, priorities and subordinate ranks of creditors will take effect: the highest-ranking creditors are satisfied first, and only if the estate is sufficient to pay them in full will the next category of creditors receive payment, and so on.[310] Within the respective groups, the *pari passu* principle applies. Typically, one group of creditors, often the ordinary insolvency creditors, will not be repaid in full; thus, everyone is entitled to a portion of the remaining estate by way of dividend. Subordinated groups, such as the shareholders, do not receive any pay-out in this case.[311]

4.104 If—as is the norm—not all creditors can be satisfied in full, the question arises as to what happens to the remaining outstanding claims. As these are, in principle, not affected by the termination of proceedings, they continue to exist so that the creditors could take action against the debtor in the future if he or she had acquired new assets.[312] However, this principle is significantly limited in two ways: by *dissolution* and by *discharge*.

4.105 If the debtor is a legal entity, the final procedural steps include its dissolution, which results in the debtor and the outstanding claims ceasing to exist.[313] A special problem arises when the debtor is an entity whose owners have unlimited liability, which could result in them having to pay for unsatisfied claims after the proceedings,[314] possibly leading to their own insolvency. The dissolution of a company often follows *ipso jure* from the closure of the insolvency proceedings; by contrast, US law provides that after the distribution of the insolvency estate, a second, different process must be carried out for the final dissolution of the company.[315] In all cases, however, formal measures will usually need to be taken. If, for example, the company is listed in a

---

[309] See, e.g. § 1(1) of the *Insolvenzordnung*; Anderson, *The Framework of Corporate Insolvency Law* (n 3) paras 19.01 et seq.

[310] UNCITRAL, *Legislative Guide on Insolvency Law* (n 2) 274 para. 80; Radley-Gardner et al., *Fundamental Texts on European Private Law* (n 37) § 12.2(2) of the Principles of European Insolvency Law; on this 'waterfall', cf. above, para. 4.57.

[311] Bork, *Corporate Insolvency Law* (n 1) paras 7.40 et seq.; Westbrook et al., *A Global View of Business Insolvency Systems* (n 10) para. 4.2.6; UNCITRAL, *Legislative Guide on Insolvency Law* (n 2) 273 para. 76.

[312] Bork, *Corporate Insolvency Law* (n 1) paras 7.40 et seq.

[313] See Radley-Gardner et al., *Fundamental Texts on European Private Law* (n 37) § 13.2(3) of the Principles of European Insolvency Law; UNCITRAL, *Legislative Guide on Insolvency Law* (n 2) 274 para. 80; Bork, *Corporate Insolvency Law* (n 1) para. 7.42.

[314] Cf. UNCITRAL, *Legislative Guide on Insolvency Law* (n 2) 281 para. 3.

[315] Kilborn (n 9) National Report for the United States, para. 20.26.

register, the registrar must be informed, and the dissolution must be recorded in the register.[316]

If a natural person is insolvent, and the proceedings do not lead to the satisfaction of all creditors, the debtor would, in principle, have to pay the outstanding debts in the future without any restrictions. The consequence would be that the debtor would have practically no incentive to earn anything at all in the future, because all income would be given to his or her creditors; he or she could be driven into illicit work or end up unemployed and dependent on the welfare system.[317] For this reason, many—though not all—jurisdictions provide for the possibility of a *fresh start* by discharge of debt, with regulations varying widely.[318] **4.106**

The question of when, why, and under what conditions a person can escape his or her debts (at the expense of others) is politically very controversial, which is reflected in the great differences between the legal systems. While some jurisdictions do not provide for statutory discharge at all or only after a relatively long period of time, others provide for a fresh start immediately after the insolvency proceedings.[319] Often, a discharge is granted after a 'compliance period' following the proceedings, during which the debtor must cooperate and make a good-faith effort to pay his or her creditors.[320] Virtually all legal systems provide for certain restrictions, for example where the debtor has acted in a criminal, fraudulent way or withheld or concealed relevant information.[321] Significant differences concern the questions of which conditions must be met for a relief from debt, which persons are eligible for it, and whether specific claims are exempt from the discharge.[322] **4.107**

The final step of insolvency proceedings is their (usually formal) closure, which may be followed by the dissolution of the debtor or the discharge. In most jurisdictions, the conclusion of proceedings is declared by a judicial decision.[323] The insolvency administrator will often request such a declaration; before that, he or she may have had to inform the creditors or hold a last creditors' meeting and present the final accounting.[324] **4.108**

---

[316] See, e.g. Art. 121 of the Enterprise Bankruptcy Law of the PRC; ss 146(4) and 205 of the UK Insolvency Act; cf. Bailey and Groves, *Corporate Insolvency Law* (n 120) paras 19.2 et seq.

[317] Bork, *Corporate Insolvency Law* (n 1) para. 9.2; Jackson, *The Logic and Limits of Bankruptcy Law* (n 224) 230 et seq.

[318] McCormack, Keay, and Brown, *European Insolvency Law* (n 2) para. 7.3.1; Radley-Gardner et al., *Fundamental Texts on European Private Law* (n 37) § 13.2(1) of the Principles of European Insolvency Law; UNCITRAL, *Legislative Guide on Insolvency Law* (n 2) 282 paras 4 et seq.

[319] UNCITRAL, *Legislative Guide on Insolvency Law* (n 2) 282 paras 4 et seq.

[320] See, e.g. §§ 287(2) and 287b of the *Insolvenzordnung*; on this and US law, see Bork, *Corporate Insolvency Law* (n 1) paras 9.14 et seq.; UNCITRAL, *Legislative Guide on Insolvency Law* (n 2) 282 para. 5.

[321] UNCITRAL, *Legislative Guide on Insolvency Law* (n 2) para. 6; Bork, *Corporate Insolvency Law* (n 1) para. 9.10.

[322] UNCITRAL, *Legislative Guide on Insolvency Law* (n 2) 282 et seq. paras 7 et seq.; McCormack, Keay, and Brown, *European Insolvency Law* (n 2) para. 7.3.1; Bork, *Corporate Insolvency Law* (n 1) paras 9.6 et seq.

[323] See, e.g. Art. L 643-9(2) of the *Code de Commerce*; § 200(1) of the *Insolvenzordnung*; Art. 120 of the Enterprise Bankruptcy Law of the PRC; 11 U.S.C. §350(a); US Bankruptcy Rule 5009(a).

[324] UNCITRAL, *Legislative Guide on Insolvency Law* (n 2) 285 paras 16 et seq.

IX. Restructuring as an Alternative to Liquidation

4.109 In most jurisdictions, the traditional approach of liquidation proceedings, central to this chapter, is not the only way to respond to insolvency. The international trend is to establish restructuring procedures, aimed particularly at preserving insolvent companies, as a veritable alternative to (value-destroying) liquidation.[325] Although the legal systems differ significantly in their general approaches and specific provisions, some common key elements can be identified.[326] Very briefly summarized, the debtor company will receive certain advantages under such proceedings; the creditors waive part of their claims so that solvency is restored; and the company can rehabilitate itself, remain as a going concern, and generate profits in the future with which the creditors can be satisfied.

4.110 In many cases, such an approach is practically unfeasible: if there is no prospect of things getting better in the future; if the debtor simply does not run a good, competitive business; and if operations have already ceased, the only option is, in fact, liquidation.[327] However, if there is reasonable prospect of survival, restructuring can offer considerable advantages for creditors as well as for the shareholders and the society: creditors may have an interest in rescuing the debtor company because going-concern values are thus preserved. In a dissolution and liquidation scenario, the (unsecured) creditors often receive only a very small satisfaction quota as the assets may be worth very little as individual parts and are often encumbered with liens. For these creditors, it could therefore be profitable to waive a (large) portion of their claims to ensure that at least the rest is paid in the future by the rescued company. Compared to the sale of the business in an asset deal,[328] the rescue of the business *and* the debtor can have crucial advantages, for example, as special rights ('dedicated assets') may be tied to the individual debtor and cannot be transferred.[329] Society may also have an interest in saving viable companies—jobs are preserved, the market does not lose a competitor, subsequent insolvencies of contracting partners can be prevented, taxes continue to be paid, etc.[330] For shareholders, this approach is particularly attractive because it is the only way for them to keep their investment; in a liquidation scenario, the company is dissolved, and they virtually always end up empty-handed.[331]

4.111 The two paths are rooted in different traditions: the liquidation procedure is closely related to individual enforcement proceedings carried out with the assistance of state

---

[325] On the history and evolution, see M. Brouwer, 'Reorganization in US and European Bankruptcy Law', European Journal of Law and Economics, 22 (2006) 5, 15 et seq.; Westbrook et al., *A Global View of Business Insolvency Systems* (n 10) para. 4.1.

[326] A concise overview is given by UNCITRAL, *Legislative Guide on Insolvency Law* (n 2) 28 para. 28.

[327] Bork, *Corporate Insolvency Law* (n 1) para. 8.2; on the legal and economic justifications for liquidation, see UNCITRAL, *Legislative Guide on Insolvency Law* (n 2) 31 paras 35 et seq.

[328] See above, paras 4.97 et seq.

[329] Eidenmüller, 'Comparative Corporate Insolvency Law' (n 7) 24.

[330] Bork, *Corporate Insolvency Law* (n 1) para. 8.3.

[331] ibid paras 4.103 and 4.105.

courts, whereas restructuring is related to an informal settlement of debts through an agreement between the parties concerned.[332] The statutory insolvency-related restructuring proceedings often combine both aspects: Formal proceedings are initiated, often involving state bodies, and the rights of creditors may be affected by statutory provisions, for example when a moratorium prevents the enforcement of security rights, thus giving the debtor 'breathing space'.[333] However, at the core of these proceedings is the *restructuring plan*, negotiated between the parties involved; the (binding) results, the issue of payments, etc. are based—at least, in principle[334]—on the consent of the creditors.[335]

Some laws make a relatively clear distinction between liquidation and restructuring. US law, for example, provides for two different entry points and two separate procedures (Chapter 7 and Chapter 11); theoretically, any liquidation proceeding could be turned into a reorganization proceeding, but such conversions rarely happen in practice.[336] Other systems, such as German law, provide for a unitary approach and a single type of procedure, which could lead to restructuring (especially if initiated early enough) or could result in the debtor's liquidation.[337]   **4.112**

Some typical elements and instruments that are important for restructuring of debt can be found throughout many jurisdictions: unlike in a typical liquidation scenario, the debtor may be left in control of the business, especially when substantive insolvency has not yet arisen.[338] Such a debtor-in-possession approach has the advantage that the debtor (respectively, the directors) will have an incentive to initiate such proceedings (at an early stage).[339] Furthermore, this has the benefit of retaining the expertise and knowledge of the debtor to continue the business and of reducing the publicity of the financial difficulties.[340] However, reasonable protection may have to be implemented, such as supervision of the debtor and provision for displacement in specified circumstances.[341] Restructuring proceedings are usually aimed at preparing and implementing a plan, which may contain a variety of provisions, typically concerning the reduction of debt and the intended satisfaction of creditors, on the question of whether the shareholders can keep their shares and what contribution they may have to provide.[342]   **4.113**

---

[332] Westbrook et al., *A Global View of Business Insolvency Systems* (n 10) para. 4.0.

[333] UNCITRAL, *Legislative Guide on Insolvency Law* (n 2) 27 para. 24, 84 para. 28; McCormack, Keay, and Brown, *European Insolvency Law* (n 2) paras 6.5 et seq.

[334] Such procedures cannot be based on contract law alone, as the plans can generally be implemented against the resistance of minorities and still be binding—even for the dissenting creditors.

[335] Bork, *Corporate Insolvency Law* (n 1) paras 8.32 et seq.; UNCITRAL, *Legislative Guide on Insolvency Law* (n 2) 209 et seq. paras 1 et seq. ('reorganization plan').

[336] Kilborn (n 9) National Report for the United States, para. 20.25.

[337] Westbrook et al., *A Global View of Business Insolvency Systems* (n 10) para. 4.1.3; Bork, *Corporate Insolvency Law* (n 1) paras 8.7 et seq.

[338] Bork, *Corporate Insolvency Law* (n 1) paras 8.23 et seq.

[339] Eidenmüller, 'Comparative Corporate Insolvency Law' (n 7) 24; Bork, *Corporate Insolvency Law* (n 1) para. 8.21.

[340] Bork, *Corporate Insolvency Law* (n 1) para. 8.21; cf. *In re Marvel Entertainment Group*, 140 F.3d 463 (1998).

[341] UNCITRAL, *Legislative Guide on Insolvency Law* (n 2) 173 Recital 112.

[342] See, e.g. 11 U.S.C. §1123; Art. 81 of the Enterprise Bankruptcy Law of the PRC; Art. L 626-10 of the *Code de Commerce*; §§ 217, 220 et seq. of the *Insolvenzordnung*.

4.114 Such arrangements would be possible outside of formal procedures on the basis of a contractual agreement, but they would affect only those who accept them. Insolvency law usually helps to overcome this problem: typically, a plan will be adopted if a certain majority of the affected parties (i.e. in particular, the creditors) have approved it; the voting procedure will be subject to specific rules, such as the quorum requirement, the requirement of a qualified majority, whether the affected parties vote in separate groups, and whether there are any veto rights.[343] Once confirmed by the required majority, the plan will generally have binding effect on all persons affected by it, including dissenting creditors (and even dissenting groups)[344] and those who have not filed their claims.[345] To ensure that the plan was adopted in the correct procedural manner and that all statutory requirements were taken into account, some jurisdictions require a court to confirm the plan.[346] Finally, the plan is implemented, often involving some kind of external monitoring.[347] If everything goes as hoped and planned, the debtor recovers, settles his or her debts to the specified extent, and the financial collapse is avoided. If, on the other hand, the company subsequently becomes insolvent again, traditional insolvency proceedings may follow sooner or later.

---

[343] See Radley-Gardner et al., *Fundamental Texts on European Private Law* (n 37) § 11.3(2) of the Principles of European Insolvency Law; Bork, *Corporate Insolvency Law* (n 1) paras 8.32 et seq.

[344] On cramdown, see UNCITRAL, *Legislative Guide on Insolvency Law* (n 2) 226 paras 54 et seq; Eidenmüller, 'Comparative Corporate Insolvency Law' (n 7) 22.

[345] UNCITRAL, *Legislative Guide on Insolvency Law* (n 2) 218 paras 28 et seq., 229 para. 64; Radley-Gardner et al., *Fundamental Texts on European Private Law* (n 37) § 11.4 of the Principles of European Insolvency Law; Bork, *Corporate Insolvency Law* (n 1) paras 8.36 et seq., 8.40.

[346] See, e.g. §§ 248(1), 250 et seq. of the *Insolvenzordnung*; Art. 87 of the Enterprise Bankruptcy Law of the PRC.

[347] Westbrook et al., *A Global View of Business Insolvency Systems* (n 10) para. 4.5.6.

5

Security Rights and Creditors' Priority and Ranking: Realizable Priority in Rescue

Edward J. Janger

I. Introduction

Central to understanding value allocation in bankruptcy is a careful disaggregation **5.01** of the concept of distributional priority—or more accurately, 'priorities'. Stakeholder claims of distributional priority come in different flavours, arise from different legal sources, and serve different functions: some arise out of pre-bankruptcy entitlements, corporate structure, or jurisdictional limitations, while others are rooted in bankruptcy law; some are designed to protect certain creditors against bankruptcy, while others are designed to make the bankruptcy system work better; some are affected by bankruptcy, while others, at least ostensibly, are not. These distinctions have relatively little practical effect in a system based on liquidation, and hence, they are easy to miss. However, they are essential to understanding how insolvency law's concept of equitable (or fair) distribution works in a system that seeks to rescue a firm. (In this chapter, the term 'bankruptcy' takes the US law useage. Therefore, depending on the relevant context, in this chapter 'bankruptcy' means 'insolvency', 'insolvency law', 'insolvency law proceedings', or 'insolvency law case'.)

This chapter will proceed in a somewhat circular fashion. First, it will distinguish the **5.02** two major types of priority—*in personam* and *in rem*—and explain a few important differences. Second, this chapter will describe the major systems of security rights, as they exist in the United States, and the United Kingdom, with some attention to continental systems. It will then describe a variety of 'security devices' that are not, strictly speaking, lien based but rely on corporate structure and asset partitions to create priority. Third, it will explore a common confusion that arises when one overlooks the disparate bases for these two major types of priority. It is often mistakenly assumed that *in rem* security can be situated on a single waterfall with *in personam* priority; it cannot.[1]

---

[1] Melissa B. Jacoby and Edward J. Janger, 'Tracing Equity: Realizing and Allocating Value in Chapter 11 Cases', Texas Law Review, 96 (2018) 673; Edward J. Janger, 'The Logic and Limits of Liens', University of Illinois Law Review, 2 (2015) 589, 592.

Edward J. Janger, *Security Rights and Creditors' Priority and Ranking: Realizable Priority in Rescue* In: *The Anatomy of Corporate Insolvency Law*. Edited by: Reinhard Bork and Renato Mangano, Oxford University Press. © Edward J. Janger 2024. DOI: 10.1093/oso/9780198852094.003.0005

132 SECURITY RIGHTS AND CREDITORS' PRIORITY AND RANKING

Claims against the firm itself can be ranked hierarchically; claims of security are asserted against property of the firm rather than the firm itself.[2] Finally, it will discuss how these various types of creditor rankings interact with *in personam priorities* in the context of rescue-oriented regimes.

II. Security and Priority Inside and Outside of Bankruptcy

5.03 As a preliminary matter, several types of priority coexist uneasily within a bankruptcy system. Most claims and their priorities are creatures of non-bankruptcy law, but their treatment is determined within the bankruptcy system.[3] Claims of security generally rest on property law, while the priority of debt over equity is a creature of corporate and contract law. Some priorities, however, exist only in bankruptcy. Some employee protections fall into this category, as do priorities for post-petition obligations of the bankruptcy estate/trustee.[4] It is important to note that these basic features of priority exist in all national systems. For the purpose of this discussion, I will divide the types of priorities as follows: (a) firm based, (b) property or lien based, and (c) insolvency priorities. They can be broadly understood as follows.

A. Firm-Based (*in Personam*): The Waterfall

5.04 Firm-based priorities inhere in the nature of the claim against or interest in the firm (as a juridic person). The most obvious of these priorities is the priority of debt over equity. The owner's variable residual interest is 'junior' to the fixed claims of contract and tort claims against the firm. But modern firms are rarely structured in such a simple fashion. Just as certain issues of 'stock' may be given distributional preference, financial creditors may agree to take junior or senior positions relative to other debt. All of these claims, however, are against the debtor itself, and they can be arrayed hierarchically based on the entity's capital structure.

5.05 They are not, strictly speaking, creatures of bankruptcy. These priorities exist and can operate any time a solvent firm or partnership winds up; the estate is liquidated—reduced to a pot of money. The proceeds are distributed in order from most senior to most junior, with the junior-most class (the owners) sharing pro rata in proportion to their ownership of shares. The pro rata and variable nature of the junior-most class

---

[2] Jacoby and Janger, 'Tracing Equity' (n 1) 689. One source of confusion in this regard is the concept of a 'floating charge' in the United Kingdom. The 'floating charge' is a lien on circulating assets, but it is generally treated as a functional lien on the enterprise itself. This aspect of UK law will be discussed below.

[3] United Nations Commission on International Trade Law (UNCITRAL), 'Legislative Guide on Insolvency Law' (2005) Recommendations 30-34, 71–72, <https://uncitral.un.org/sites/uncitral.un.org/files/media-docume nts/uncitral/en/05-80722_ebook.pdf> accessed 10 January 2024.

[4] See 11 U.S.C. §§507(a)(2), (3).

is inherent in the concept of ownership—the owner bears the risks and benefits of changes in value.

The twist introduced by insolvency is that when a company is insolvent, the money runs out before all the debts are paid. This means that nothing is left over for equity, and the junior-most class of debt claims is now variable, sharing pro rata in the residuum. Pro-rata distribution to creditors treats junior creditors like stockholders, receiving a distribution based on the proportion of outstanding debt (instead of outstanding shares). **5.06**

B. Property-Based Priority (*in Rem*): Not the Waterfall

A second type of priority arises when a creditor takes an interest in property of the debtor as an alternative source of repayment of their claim. The most familiar mechanism is through a consensual lien in the form of a 'mortgage' on real estate or a 'security interest' (chattel mortgage) on personal property.[5] But such interests can arise in other ways. A judgment creditor may obtain a lien when the sheriff seizes the property.[6] A builder might obtain a mechanics lien on real estate or improvements. An automobile mechanic might obtain an artisan's lien. The key feature here is that the lien–property interest is not created so that the interest holder can use the property. Nor does the lien holder share in the risks and benefits of ownership (unless the value of collateral is less than the debt).[7] The interest is limited to the amount of the debt (or, if undersecured, the value of the collateral) and only if the debtor defaults. **5.07**

Functional security can, and is, created in other ways as well. For example, many firms finance operations through arrangements ostensibly based on a sale rather than security *per se*.[8] Factoring operates when a debtor sells its receivables to a factor for collection.[9] Securitization operates when a debtor sells its receivables or other assets to a special-purpose vehicle, which, in turn, issues its own debt securities.[10] A lease may be used instead of a mortgage to allow the lessor to retain title to the leased asset.[11] Sometimes, the boundaries between security and ownership are blurred, as with conditional sales (retention of title) and lease-to-own (hire-purchase) arrangements.[12] In each case, the seller purports to retain title to the goods until the purchase price is paid. **5.08**

---

[5] Restatement of the Law (3rd) of Property—Mortgages (2022); Uniform Commercial Code—Article 9—Secured Transactions (2010).

[6] See, e.g. § 5234 of the New York Civil Practice and Legal Rules.

[7] See Uniform Commercial Code (UCC) §9-615.

[8] ibid § 1-201(35). See Steven L. Schwarcz, 'The Alchemy of Securitization', Stanford Journal of Law, Business & Finance, 1 (1994) 133–54; Peter V. Pantaleo, Herbert S. Edelman, Frederick L. Feldkamp et al., 'Rethinking the Role of Recourse in the Sale of Financial Assets', Business Law, 52 (1996) 159, 185; Edward J. Janger, 'The Death of Secured Lending', Cardozo Law Review, 25 (2004) 1759–88.

[9] Factoring has a long history in the United States in the garment industry. See *Benedict v Rather*, 268 US 353 (1925), which involved New York's 1905 factoring statute.

[10] Schwarcz, 'The Alchemy of Securitization' (n 8) 135–6.

[11] See UCC §1-203.

[12] ibid §§1-201(35) (Retention of title treated as security interest), 1-203 (Lease distinguished from security interest).

5.09   Another 'quirk' introduced by insolvency, however, is that characterizing a financing as a sale or a lease may affect bankruptcy treatment. Whether the property is treated as part of the bankruptcy estate may depend on whether the property is treated as having been sold, leased, or liened as collateral for a financing. In some systems and contexts, the label chosen by the parties is all that matters. However, in the United States, for example, courts will look to the substance of the transaction rather than its form to determine whether it is a true sale, true lease, or a security interest.[13] Again, these property-based priorities exist without reference to insolvency *per se*. If a solvent firm were to wind up, these property arrangements would be respected, with each creditor being paid out of the proceeds of their particular collateral; where, however, the estate is sufficient to pay debt claims, recourse to collateral rights will not matter.

C. Bankruptcy-Based Priorities: A Different Waterfall

5.10   Finally, there are priorities that arise only in the event of an insolvency proceeding. They can come in either the *in rem* or the *in personam* variety.

To offer a set of US-based examples, 11 U.S.C. §507 offers a list of priorities amongst unsecured claims. They start at the top, with administrative expenses of the estate, and continue through a variety of other debts that are given priority above general unsecured claims. These include employee wage claims, spousal support claims, and tax claims, for example, and the funds flow through in a ranked waterfall.[14] But the hierarchy can be even more complicated. Within the top layer of administrative expense priorities, super-priority can be given to a post-petition lender, with court approval.[15] Claims of lien holders whose interests were not adequately protected during the case come ahead of ordinary administrative claims as well.[16]

5.11   Bankruptcy law can also create liens or alter the rights of existing lien holders. § 506(c) allows the trustee to deduct costs of realizing on the collateral from any distribution to a secured creditor. This right is uncontroversial and mirrors a foreclosure trustee's rights outside of bankruptcy law. More controversial, in the United States, the court may allow a post-bankruptcy loan to be secured by a lien that 'primes' (takes priority over) an existing lien, so long as the lien holder's rights are adequately protected by an equity cushion, a replacement lien, or payments.[17]

---

[13] ibid §§1-201(35) and 1-203.
[14] See 11 U.S.C. §507.
[15] ibid §364.
[16] ibid §507(b).
[17] ibid §§361, 362(d), 364(d).

D. Liquidation v. Rescue

For solvent debtors, priority doesn't matter: the debtor pays its debts, claims against assets are not invoked, and the priority waterfall does not come into play. Further, when an insolvent debtor liquidates, the differences among these types of priorities may not become apparent. Encumbered assets can be identified and liquidated. Priorities of competing claims against assets can be determined, and the remaining funds can be distributed according to the priority waterfall.

5.12

Modern bankruptcy practice, however, is oriented towards rescue through either a recapitalization or going-concern sale. In rescue, the business continues to operate. The encumbered assets are not sold in a manner that establishes a liquidated value. This considerably complicates the process of value allocation, both as a practical and conceptual matter. In a recapitalization under Chapter 11 in the United States, or pursuant to a scheme of arrangement in the United Kingdom, the debtor's value is determined and allocated amongst the creditors but without selling off the assets or allocating that value between assets and going-concern value. Similarly, in a going-concern sale, the value of the firm in operation is determined by the purchase price, but the allocation between claims against assets and claims against the firm must be established through negotiation around competing appraisals. The remainder of this chapter will seek to explore how the goal of 'rescue' complicates a distributional priority scheme where entitlements were developed under a regime premised on liquidation.

5.13

III. Security Rights

'Secured debt' merges two concepts—'security' and 'debt'—in a way that frequently confuses creditors, debtors, and courts. The first analytic task of this section is to distinguish 'security' from 'debt'. It is generally understood that secured creditors receive preferred treatment in bankruptcy, but the actual mechanism is poorly understood and often ignored. While secured debt is often confused with priority debt, it is not the same. Priority ranks one debt over another debt. This priority can be created by la, or by agreement with the debtor or other creditors.

5.14

The basis for the distributional advantage of secured debt is entirely different. The debt itself enjoys no special priority. Instead, the creditor has a separate claim against property of the debtor; the property guaranties the debt. The secured creditor's preferred distribution comes from the claim against property (a right *in rem*) not because of some special characteristic of the *in personam* debt obligation. This confusion is, perhaps, exacerbated by a linguistic peculiarity in the Uniform Commercial Code. Art. 9 defines a

5.15

136 SECURITY RIGHTS AND CREDITORS' PRIORITY AND RANKING

'debtor' as the owner or seller of the collateral.[18] The 'debtor' need not even owe a debt ('be an obligor').[19]

5.16 In liquidation, or in personal bankruptcy cases, this distinction is not confusing. An automotive lender, whose loan is secured by the car, will repossess the car, sell it, and credit the proceeds to the debt. A residential mortgage lender whose loan is secured by the debtor's house will foreclose on the house. To the extent that there is a deficiency, it can be pursued against the debtor as ordinary (often worthless) debt. This conceptual distinction is built into the structure of the Bankruptcy Code. Allowance of *in personam* debt 'claims' are governed by 11 U.S.C. §502, but US law is not an anomaly.[20] A 'claim' is defined in § 101(a)(5) as a '*right to payment*, whether or not such right is reduced to judgment, liquidated, unliquidated, fixed, contingent, matured, unmatured, disputed, undisputed, legal, equitable, secured, or unsecured'.[21] The definition is broad, and it acknowledges the possibility of security, but the 'claim' is the 'right to payment'. Security, by contrast is governed by § 506, which determines the extent to which an 'allowed' claim will be considered a 'secured' claim. Definitionally, a claim is secured only if it is 'secured by an interest in property' or 'subject to set-off'. § 506 focuses only on the value of the claim against the property or the amount subject to set-off. In other words, security only exists to the extent it is tied to a particular piece of property or offsetting claim. It is not a priority; it is a property right. Conceptually, it is more about what the creditor owns than about what they are owed. The amount of the debt is important, only because it fixes the amount of the claim against the asset (unless the value of the asset is insufficient).

5.17 This focus on specific assets is highlighted when one looks at the variety of 'secured' financing arrangements that are not based on liens. As discussed below, lenders may structure their secured loans in the form of 'sales', 'conditional sales', 'leases', and 'leases to own'. Sometimes, these transactions are true sales, where the buyer obtains all the risks and benefits of ownership. Sometimes, they are true leases, where the lessor retains a significant residual interest in the leased asset. Sometimes, however, those transactions are merely disguised secured loans, where the purchaser is simply guaranteed a fixed return on its investment, no more, no less, or where the lessor never expects to see the leased asset again (unless there is a default). As will be discussed below, one difference among legal systems is the extent to which courts will look to substance over form. But for the purpose of this discussion, the point is to illustrate that for there to be security, there must be property.

---

[18] See UCC §9-102(28).
[19] ibid.
[20] See 11 U.S.C. §502.
[21] ibid §101(a)(5) (emphasis added).

A. Lien Systems

Priority intersects with security in a way that is not entirely obvious. In bankruptcy, the **5.18** word 'priority' is used to reflect a distributional priority. Asset value is distributed first to claimant A and what is left, to claimant B. But priority in the context of security is not hierarchical; it is temporal. While temporal priority is linked to distributional priority, the two are not the same. Indeed, understanding the concept of lien priority has more to do with how the timing of the petition affects the 'content' of 'the estate' than it has to do with 'claims against' the estate.

Priority in connection with liens is not tied to the distributional waterfall but, instead, **5.19** to the '*nemo dat*' maxim: '*Nemo dat quod non habet*' ('No one has the power to give that which they do not own'). So, priority in property law relates to the order of conveyances, and the key question is at what point in time a conveyance becomes effective against the bankruptcy estate/trustee. These timing rules are not measured by the intent of the parties. They are measured by the rules of the particular property system involved. For real estate, timing rules are determined by the jurisdiction's recording acts and the steps necessary to put a potential purchaser on notice. That is usually recording the interest in the land records of the relevant county.[22] For cars, the owner must obtain a certificate of title, and the lien holder must note its lien on the certificate.[23] For cars held in inventory, by contrast, a lien holder may perfect its interest by filing a financing statement in the Art. 9 records of the Secretary of State.[24] For most personal property, filing a financing statement with the Secretary of State will suffice. But for fixtures (goods affixed to real estate), local filing at the county level may also be sufficient.[25] In common law systems, some form of public notice in a registry is required. In civil law jurisdictions, this is not always the case. The result of the multiplicity of property regimes is a multiplicity of lending patterns. Many secured loans focus on a particular asset or class of assets as security. Mortgage loans, accounts receivables financing, vendors' liens, etc. all rest on the idea that a particular asset will serve as collateral.

B. Quasi-Security

Priority can be created through other forms of asset partitioning: sales, leases, set-off **5.20** rights, and corporate structure. In this regard, sales and leases fall into one category for treatment, while structural priority must be addressed somewhat differently.

---

[22] See, e.g. § 291 of the New York Real Property Law (2020).
[23] See, e.g. §§ 2118 and 2119 of the New York Vehicle and Traffic Law, Title X (Uniform Vehicle Certificate of Title Act).
[24] See UCC §9-501.
[25] ibid.

1. Sales and leases

5.21 Some lenders seek to elevate their priority, even above that given by security, by characterizing finance transactions as 'sales', 'retentions of title', or 'leases'. In each of these transactions, the goal may be to actually exclude the subject asset from the bankruptcy estate. The goal with these transactions is not so much to improve bankruptcy treatment but to avoid bankruptcy altogether—to be able to exercise remedies against the 'collateral' without regard to the automatic stay:

- If a debtor sells a refrigerator and receives the purchase price, then it is no longer the debtor's property. The buyer need not worry about the seller's bankruptcy.
- If the debtor buys a refrigerator, and the seller retains title to goods until the purchase price is paid, then ostensibly, it can exercise its repossession rights without regard to the stay, as the goods are not the property of the debtor.
- If the debtor leases a refrigerator, the lessor retains title to the leased item. Again, it can simply take back its property on default.

Different legal systems take different approaches to these devices inside and outside of bankruptcy. For example, Art. 9 of the Uniform Commercial Code elevates substance over form. It treats a retention of title as a security interest.[26] It distinguishes true leases from leases intended as security.[27] It similarly distinguishes a true sale of accounts receivable from an interest in accounts receivable that 'secure an obligation', though it calls both a 'security interest'. At the same time, it recognizes a true sale of accounts receivables as a sale (though also calling it a security interest).[28] Many civil law jurisdictions recognize reservations of title as excluding the property from the bankruptcy estate.[29] Airframe leases receive special treatment in US law and under the Cape Town Convention.[30]

5.22 Generalization about the bankruptcy treatment of these devices is difficult across (and even within) legal systems. Some of them are effective to create bankruptcy remoteness. Others are assimilated into the general treatment of security. These devices share a common feature. They are all rooted in non-bankruptcy property law and are tied to specific assets of the firm. Attempts have been made to 'securitize' entire firms and hence render them bankruptcy remote. This is sometimes referred to as 'whole business securitization'. Whether true bankruptcy remoteness can be achieved is open to question.

5.23 Two examples are helpful here. In the *LTV* bankruptcy, a steel company sought to securitize both its accounts receivable and its inventory. The debtor asserted that notwithstanding the characterization of the transactions as 'sales', the debtor retained an

---

[26] ibid §1-201(35).

[27] ibid. §1-203.

[28] ibid.

[29] John Wires, 'Retention of Title Clauses in International Trade Law' (11 September, 2009) <https://ssrn.com/abstract=1471990> accessed 10 January 2024.

[30] See 11 U.S.C. §1110; Protocol to the Cape Town Convention on International Interests in Mobile Equipment on Matters Specific to Aircraft Equipment (16 November 2001).

equitable interest in the assets. The bankruptcy court found that there were sufficient issues as to the characterization of the entity to issue a temporary injunction.[31] In *General Growth Properties*, Judge Gropper similarly allowed real-estate partnerships that had securitized their assets to file for bankruptcy and upstream assets, notwithstanding the sale of their assets to securitization vehicles.[32] Apparently, whole-business securitization is used to describe transactions in the food services industry, where franchisee royalties are held in a securitization vehicle.[33] Notwithstanding that this is called 'whole-business securitization', this should not be confused with securitizing the firm. It merely means that the volatile income stream from the franchisees has been placed in a securitization vehicle.

In sum, the use of sale-and-lease transactions to create ostensibly bankruptcy-remote asset partitions emphasizes the *in rem*, non-hierarchical nature of these forms of security. The claim to priority lies in the value of the collateral, not in the value of the firm. To the extent that the investor might seek to receive more than the value of its collateral, that power comes from the situational leverage created by the power to exit notwithstanding the bankruptcy stay.

5.24

2. Set-off rights

Another form of priority derives from set-off or netting rights, often referred to as a banker's lien. Sometimes, a debtor is also owed money by a creditor. The two obligations need not be related. For example, a debtor might hold $1,000 in a household bank account and have borrowed $1,500 for their business. Thus, the bank owes the debtor money, and the debtor owes money to the bank. The two transactions are unrelated. Depending on whether set-off is allowed, the treatment is very different. Assume that the debtor is paying a dividend to unsecured creditors at 20%. In a world where netting is prohibited, the bank would owe the debtor $1,000 but would receive $300 back on its $1,500 claim. By contrast, in a world where set-off is allowed, the bank would sweep the deposit account and receive a further payment of $100 on the deficiency.

5.25

Both the United States and the United Kingdom respect the existence of the right to set-off if it exists under non-bankruptcy law. In the United States, § 553 preserves any existing set-off rights, and § 506 treats any set-off right so preserved as an allowed secured claim. In other words, the set-off right is treated as if it were a security interest. At least in the United States, this also means that the exercise of set-off rights is subject to the automatic stay.[34] There are exceptions, however, for certain financial contracts in the United States,[35] and the scope and timing of a creditor's right to exercise set-off varies from jurisdiction to jurisdiction.

5.26

---

[31] *In re LTV Steel Co.*, 274 BR 278 (Bankr. ND Ohio 2001).

[32] *In re General Growth Properties, Inc.*, 409 B.R. 43 (Bankr. SDNY 2009).

[33] Percent, 'Whole Business Securitization in 2020' in 'Cadence Private Credit Yearbook 2020' (26 January 2021) <https://percent.com/blog/whole-business-securitization-2020> accessed 10 January 2024.

[34] See 11 U.S.C. §362(a)(7).

[35] ibid §§555, 556, 559–62.

140 SECURITY RIGHTS AND CREDITORS' PRIORITY AND RANKING

3. Corporate form: Structural priority

5.27 Corporate structure can also be used to allocate priority among creditors. Just as a single debtor may transfer an interest in property as security, assets can be located in particular entities, and recourse to those assets can be limited to particular creditors. It can be used in a number of different ways. For example, in a holding company structure, where the assets of the parents consist of stock in the subsidiaries, any creditors of the holding company would be subordinate to the creditors of the operating companies. By contrast, where the subsidiaries routinely sent dividends upstream such that the cash in the business was held at the holding company level, creditors of the operating entities would effectively be subordinated to the creditors (and shareholders) of the holding company. Finally, particular assets, operations, and debt can be organized functionally so that particular businesses and finances would have their own liabilities and sources of income. Corporate structure can be used both appropriately and inappropriately. For example, bail-in structures were developed in the United States developed by the Federal Deposit Insurance Corporation (FDIC) in response to the 2008 financial crisis. There, corporate structure was used to assure that the holding company could serve as a source of capital and liquidity to the operating companies should one of the affiliates suffer a shock.[36] By contrast, Johnson and Johnson recently rearranged its corporate structure, using a device called the Texas two-step, to potentially subordinate tort creditors asserting product liability claims based on exposure to asbestos in baby powder.[37]

5.28 As a general rule, these decisions about corporate structure will be respected both inside and outside of bankruptcy. So long as the debtor observes the corporate formalities and is transparent about its structure with investors, corporate partitions can be a helpful means for clarifying creditor expectations about recourse. But there are limits. Doctrinally, the lines are policed by corporate veil piercing, substantive consolidation, fraudulent conveyance law, and fiduciary duties.

IV. Distinguishing Asset-Based (*in Rem*) and Firm-Based (*in Personam*) Claims of Priority: The Scope of Security

5.29 While this introduction to priority as temporal and asset-based may seem obvious, it runs counter to the facile and common assumption that the secured creditor sits comfortably atop the distributional waterfall. Many law and economics scholars have argued that a hierarchical capital structure is economically efficient, because it mimics the incentives of a single owner.[38] Colloquially, creditors frequently speak of loans as

---

[36] Federal Deposit Insurance Co., *Resolution of Systemically Important Financial Institutions: The Single Point of Entry Strategy*, 78 FR 76614 (18 December 2013).

[37] *In re LTL Mgmt LLC*, Case No. 21-30589 (MBK) [Docket No. 1572] (Bankr. DNJ 2021).

[38] Douglas G. Baird, 'A World without Bankruptcy', Law and Contemporary Problems, 50 (Spring 1987) 173–93; Alan Schwartz, 'The Sole Owner Standard Reviewed', Journal of Legal Studies, 17 (1988) 231–5.

being secured by a blanket lien on the firm.[39] In many discussions about priority, the existence of such a blanket lien on the value of the firm is simply assumed.[40] But the asset-based and temporal nature of security described above is antithetical to the concept of a hierarchical priority in the value of the firm, at least one that is rooted in security.[41] This failure to distinguish *in rem*- from *in personam*-based claims creates many of the complexities discussed below.

The essential element of such a hierarchical capital structure is an all-encompassing security interest that comprises the entire value of the firm—the going-concern value as well as the asset value.[42] The problem is that, at least under US law, such a blanket lien on the value of the firm is a fiction.[43] It is not attainable as a practical matter for the reasons described above. Moreover, even if a creditor were able to lien all, or substantially all the assets of a firm, as they are in the United Kingdom, it is not clear that this extends to the 'going-concern' value of the firm. Indeed, even the scholars who think that a hierarchical capital structure is desirable as a normative matter, acknowledge, when pressed, that it is not possible as a matter of positive law in the United States.[44] I have explored this issue previously[45] and will draw on that analysis here.

5.30

A. The Blanket Lien in the United States

Investors and economists often speak of 'blanket liens' as if there is such a thing.[46] It is true that loan documents are often structured to manifest an intention to encumber all assets in favour of a secured lender:[47] mortgages are granted against all real property; leases are assigned, and an Art. 9 security interest is granted in all property that comes

5.31

---

[39] See Christopher W. Frost, 'Secured Credit and Effective Entity Priority', Connecticut Law Review, 51 (2019) 575.

[40] See Anthony J. Casey, 'The Creditors' Bargain and Option-Preservation Priority in Chapter 11', *University of Chicago Law Review*, 79 (2011) 759; American Bankruptcy Institute (ABI), 'Final Report and Recommendations—Commission to Study the Reform of Chapter 11: 2012–2014 Final Report and Recommendations' at (2014) 207–24, <https://abiworld.app.box.com/s/vvircv5xv83aavl4dp4h> accessed 10 January 2024.

[41] Jacoby and Janger, 'Tracing Equity' (n 1) 709, 734; Janger, 'The Logic and Limits of Liens' (n 1) 592.

[42] Jay Westbrook, 'The Control of Wealth in Bankruptcy', Texas Law Review, 82 (2004) 792

[43] See Jacoby and Janger, 'Tracing Equity' (n 1); Janger, 'The Logic and Limits of Liens' (n 1); Frost, 'Secured Credit and Effective Entity Priority (n 39); Baird, 'A World without Bankruptcy' (n 38) 26; Douglas G. Baird, 'The Rights of Secured Creditors after Rescap', Illinois Law Review 2015 849.

[44] See Douglas G. Baird and Thomas H. Jackson, 'Bargaining after the Fall and the Contours of the Absolute Priority Rule', University of Chicago Law Review, 55 (1988) 738, 782–3. Baird and Jackson argued that a secured creditor should be able to bargain for its security interest to include the going-concern (or enterprise) value of the debtor, although they did not assert that this view reflected the law at the time of their publication: 'Thus, we believe, a secured creditor with a security interest in specific "hard" assets should be treated as having a claim to the asset's liquidation value. Its secured claim should reach no further', ibid 782–3. This conclusion, however, does not undercut the idea that a creditor should be able to bargain for a priority interest in the going-concern surplus in priority to other creditors. See also Douglas G. Baird and Anthony J. Casey, 'No Exit? Withdrawal Rights and the Law of Corporate Reorganizations', Columbia Law Review, 113 (2013) 1, 17 fn. 59.

[45] See Janger, 'The Logic and Limits of Liens' (n 1).

[46] See 11 U.S.C. §363(f); Carole Patemen, 'Self Ownership and Property in the Person: Democratization and a Tale of Two Concepts', Journal of Political Philosophy, 10 (2002) 20, 25.

[47] See above, fn. 45. See also Jay L. Westbrook, 'The Control of Wealth in Bankruptcy', Texas Law Review, 795 (2004) 818. ('A second-lien loan is a loan secured by a lien on part or all of the borrower's assets').

within the scope of Art. 9 of the Uniform Commercial Code ('UCC').[48] This package of conveyances is then described as a 'blanket lien'. It is not by any means clear, however, that such a conveyance actually creates a lien on the value of the 'firm' itself as distinct from the value of its assets. Indeed, in a recent article, Chris Frost explores this question in detail and concludes that the best that can be said is that, while 'effective entity priority is both practically and theoretically possible, the creation of that priority under an asset-based system relies on a doctrinal structure that is both ill-fitting and fragile'.[49] Whether a purported conveyance of property is effective is determined by state property law, not contract law, so one must look beyond the stated intent of the parties to determine the legal effect of the transaction, especially with regard to third parties.

5.32 To create a mortgage on real property, one must comply with the mortgage law of the state in which the real property lies.[50] This may seem reasonably straightforward, but as evidenced by the 2010 'robo-signing' crisis and the role of the Mortgage Electronic Registration System ('MERS'), it can still go horribly wrong. In 2010, a variety of procedural failures with mortgage recording, tracking, and foreclosure caused the United States' foreclosure apparatus to grind to a halt in the middle of a financial crisis.[51]

5.33 For personal property, Art. 9 makes the lien creation process more straightforward.[52] One can create the lien by creating an authenticated record memorializing the intended conveyance.[53] One can perfect it by filing a financing statement, taking possession of certain types of collateral, and taking control of certain other types of collateral.[54] However, the scope of Art. 9 is not all-encompassing. It is worth listing a few examples, as the gaps are not trivial.

5.34 First, s. 9-109 excludes a variety of types of property from the scope of Art. 9. These include many tort claims, real estate, recoupment and set-off, insurance claims, and so on.[55] As such, a blanket 'Art. 9' security interest may not be as all-encompassing as it

---

[48] See UCC §9-109.
[49] Frost, 'Secured Credit and Effective Entity Priority' (n 39) 575, 623.
[50] See Restatement of the Law (3rd) of Property—Mortgages (n 5) intro:

   [T]here can be no doubt that legal differences from state to state act as a serious impediment to the carrying out of these business arrangements. A major goal of this Restatement [...] is to assist in unifying the law of real property security by identifying and articulating legal rules that will meet the legitimate needs of the lending industry while at the same time providing reasonable protection for borrowers.

[51] See Gretchen Morgenson, 'Mortgage Registry Muddles Foreclosures', New York Times (1 September 2012), <http://www.nytimes.com/2012/09/02/business/fair-game-mortgage-registry-muddles-foreclosures.html?_r=0 accessed 10 January 2024.
[52] See UCC §§9-109, 1-201(b)(35), 9-203(a)–(b).
[53] ibid §§9-109, 1-201(b)(35), 9-203(a)–(b).
[54] ibid §§9-308, 9-310–9-316.
[55] ibid §9-109(d) excludes from the scope of Art. 9:

   (1) a landlord's lien, other than an agricultural lien;
   (2) a lien, other than an agricultural lien, given by statute or other rule of law for services or materials, but Section 9-333 applies with respect to priority of the lien;
   (3) an assignment of a claim for wages, salary, or other compensation of an employee;
   (4) a sale of accounts, chattel paper, payment intangibles, or promissory notes as part of a sale of the business out of which they arose;

DISTINGUISHING ASSET-BASED AND FIRM-BASED CLAIMS OF PRIORITY   143

sounds. Even if many of the excluded items could be encumbered by other methods, this highlights the fact that a statement of intent to create a blanket lien by the lender and the borrower, coupled with the filing of an all-encompassing financing statement, does not necessarily make it so.

A second limitation on the scope of liens can be described as 'inalienable property' or 'nonproperty'. Not all of a firm's value can be separated from the firm itself. For example, judicial lien creditors have been held unable to levy on domain names.[56] Some elements of firm value may not be property at all,[57] for example some government-granted licences that are personal in nature and non-transferrable. Similarly, accumulated corporate goodwill simply may not be subject to liens.[58] There have been both judicial and statutory attempts to work around this type of gap, but none have been universally accepted. For example, a number of cases involving Federal Communications Commission (FCC) licences have deemed the value of transferred licences (realized in bankruptcy) as proceeds, notwithstanding that the underlying licence was not collateral.[59]

5.35

(5) an assignment of accounts, chattel paper, payment intangibles, or promissory notes which is for the purpose of collection only;

(6) an assignment of a right to payment under a contract to an assignee that is also obligated to perform under the contract;

(7) an assignment of a single account, payment intangible, or promissory note to an assignee in full or partial satisfaction of a pre-existing indebtedness;

(8) a transfer of an interest in or an assignment of a claim under a policy of insurance, other than an assignment by or to a health-care provider of a health-care-insurance receivable and any subsequent assignment of the right to payment, but Sections 9-315 and 9-322 apply with respect to proceeds and priorities in proceeds;

(9) an assignment of a right represented by a judgment, other than a judgment taken on a right to payment that was collateral;

(10) a right of recoupment or set-off, but:

(A) Section 9-340 applies with respect to the effectiveness of rights of recoupment or set-off against deposit accounts; and

(B) Section 9-404 applies with respect to defenses or claims of an account debtor;

(11) the creation or transfer of an interest in or lien on real property, including a lease or rents thereunder, except to the extent that provision is made for:

(A) liens on real property in Sections 9-203 and 9-308;

(B) fixtures in Section 9-334;

(C) fixture filings in Sections 9-501, 9-502, 9-512, 9-516, and 9-519; and

(D) security agreements covering personal and real property in Section 9-604;

(12) an assignment of a claim arising in tort, other than a commercial tort claim, but Sections 9-315 and 9-322 apply with respect to proceeds and priorities in proceeds; or

(13) an assignment of a deposit account in a consumer transaction, but Sections 9-315 and 9-322 apply with respect to proceeds and priorities in proceeds.

[56] See *Network Solutions, Inc. v Umbro Int'l, Inc.*, 529 SE 2d 80, 80 (Va 2000).

[57] See *Straffi v New Jersey (In re Chris-Don, Inc.)*, 308 BR 214, 217 (Bankr. DNJ 2004).

[58] Some things of value to the enterprise (such as government-granted licences) have been construed not to be property to which an Art. 9 security interest can attach. See *New Jersey v Div of Taxation (In re Chris-Don, Inc.)* 367 F. Supp. 2d 696, 696–7 (DNJ 2005) (finding that a liquor licence is not property for Art. 9 purposes under New Jersey law); *Banc of America Strategic Solutions, Inc. v Cooker Rest. Corp.*, No. 05AP-1126, 2006 WL 2535734, at *7 (Ohio Ct App. 5 September 2006) (finding that liquor licences are not property under Ohio law).

[59] Compare *New Bank of New England, NA v Tak Commc'ns, Inc. (In re Tax Commc'ns, Inc.)*, 138 BR 568, 568 (WD Wis. 1992) (holding that the value of a broadcast licence is not proceeds of a secured creditor's collateral), *with In re Ridgley Commc'ns, Inc.*, 139 BR 374, 374 (Bankr. D. Md 1992) (holding that the value of a broadcast licence is proceeds of a secured creditor's collateral).

5.36 When Art. 9 of the UCC was amended in 2000, the drafters sought to turn some non-property into lienable property. §§ 9-406 and 9-408 of the UCC[60] override non-assignment clauses contained in contracts, intellectual property licences, and government licences. While § 9-406 is a complete override for the types of property it covers, § 9-408 overrides non-assignment provisions only to the extent necessary to allow a security interest to attach. It does not confer a power to enforce the lien. As such, § 9-408 does not alter the fact that these rights would not be realizable by the secured party outside of bankruptcy. Nonetheless, the drafters sought to ensure that any value realized in bankruptcy would be allocated to the secured party as proceeds.[61] However, since federal bankruptcy law defines property of the estate and supercedes state law, there is no particular reason to treat this result as a given or even as permitted by the Bankruptcy Code. Further, 11 U.S.C. §506 measures an allowed secured claim by the 'value of the creditor's interest' in the collateral. Here, the realizable value of the lien (outside of bankruptcy) would be zero.

5.37 A third limitation on a secured creditors' lien is technical failure to establish priority through perfection.[62] Liens are property rights, and the question in bankruptcy is not whether these property rights are enforceable against the debtor but whether they are enforceable against third parties.[63] Sometimes, a mere paper grant is sufficient,[64] but for many types of property interests, a public filing, the taking of possession or control, may be required to ensure priority over later lien creditors under state law or the bankruptcy trustee.[65] Again, loan documents may reflect an intent to convey a property interest, but unless the appropriate steps are followed, the promise may be ineffective. Property may fall through the cracks.

5.38 A fourth limitation is the concept of traceable proceeds. Under Art. 9 of the UCC, a security interest automatically covers proceeds of the collateral if it is sold or otherwise disposed of.[66] That concept of identifiable proceeds is extended by equitable tracing rules but only as far as those rules themselves can reach.[67] To claim property as proceeds, one must be able to trace the proceeds to original collateral, subject to a perfected security interest.[68] Sometimes, this is possible, but often it is not. Where a blanket lien is involved, outside of bankruptcy, tracing rules may not matter much because as

---

[60] See UCC §§9-406 and 9-408.

[61] Whether this will work will turn on the nature of proceeds in bankruptcy. Compare *In re Wiersma*, 283 BR 294, 294 (Bankr. D. Idaho 2002) (holding that insurance claims arising out of electrocution of cattle are proceeds) with *Helms v Certified Packaging Corp.* 551 F.3d 675, 678 (7th Cir. 2008) (holding that claims for failure to obtain business interruption insurance were not proceeds of collateral). Also, Art. 9's concept of proceeds only reaches property: *Straffi v New Jersey (In re Chris-Don, Inc.)* (n 57).

[62] See U.C.C. §§9-308, 9-310–9-317, 9-320, 9-322–9-324.

[63] See 11 U.S.C. §544.

[64] *Bluxome St Assocs v Fireman's Fund Ins. Co.*, 254 Cal. Rptr. 198, 198 (Cal. Ct App. 1988).

[65] See UCC §§9-308, 9-310–9-316.

[66] ibid §9-203(f).

[67] ibid §9-315(b)(2).

[68] *See In re Oriental Rug Warehouse Club, Inc.*, 205 BR 407, 407 (Bankr. D. Minn. 1997); UCC §§9-102(a)(64)(A), (C), 9-315(a)(2), (c), (d).

DISTINGUISHING ASSET-BASED AND FIRM-BASED CLAIMS OF PRIORITY 145

property changes from one form to another, it may simply float between and among collateral types, changing from inventory to an account, then to a deposit account, and back to inventory. So long as the security agreement covers after-acquired property of the relevant type, no value slips out of the security interests.[69] Similarly, when an employee develops intellectual property or provides services, the value becomes collateral as an after-acquired general intangible.[70]

If the debtor files for bankruptcy, however, tracing becomes crucial. Under § 552(a) of the Code, liens on after-acquired property no longer attach.[71] To put it another way, floating liens stop floating.[72] By contrast, if the prepetition security interest covers post-petition proceeds of pre-petition collateral (when property is sold by the debtor), the security interest will attach to the proceeds.[73] After-acquired property only becomes collateral if it is proceeds of prepetition collateral. The interest in proceeds is only perfected if the interest in the original collateral was perfected.[74]

5.39

It is not uncommon for a putative 'blanket-lien' creditor to assert that since it has a lien on all of the debtor's prepetition property, any post-petition value of the firm must, by definition, be proceeds.[75] Such creditors often get away with it, but they should not. First, post-petition value may not be a product of pre-petition collateral. Just to offer one example, imagine that an at-will employee of a software company develops an algorithm that is extremely valuable post petition. It is work for hire, so it belongs to the firm, but it is difficult to figure out how that intellectual property is proceeds of prepetition collateral.[76] In a restaurant, the value contributed by the line cooks and waiting staff is not proceeds of inventory, even though a customer technically pays for a meal.[77] § 552 of the Code recognizes this limitation on proceeds when it says that the proceeds can be limited as required by the 'equities of the case'.[78] Again, the secured

5.40

---

[69] See U.C.C. §9-204(a). As discussed in section IV.B, in the United Kingdom, this would be accomplished through a floating charge rather than a floating lien.

[70] See U.C.C. §§9-102(a)(42) and 9-204.

[71] See 11 U.S.C. §552(a).

[72] ibid §552(a).

[73] ibid §552(b).

[74] See UCC §9-315(c).

[75] In *DBSD I*, the bankruptcy court permitted secured creditors to make a 'gift' of the distributions to which they were entitled to junior classes of creditors: see *In re DBSD N. Am., Inc.*, 419 BR 179, 212 (Bankr. SDNY 2009), aff'd, No. 09 Civ. 10156 (LAK), 2010 WL 1223109 (SDNY 24 March 2010), aff'd in part, rev'd in part, 627 F.3d 496 (2d Cir. 2010). The Second Circuit reversed the bankruptcy court's finding and held that 'the bankruptcy court erred in confirming the plan of reorganization', which included the gift: *In re DBSD N. Am., Inc.*, 634 F.3d 79, 100–01 (2d Cir. 2011). The Second Circuit specifically noted 'Congress [...] did not create any exception for "gifts" like the one at issue [in *DBSD I*]': *In re DBSD N. Am., Inc.*, 634 F.3d 79, 100–01 (2d Cir. 2011). See also Jacoby and Janger, 'Tracing Equity' (n 1) 923–4.

[76] The argument that the employee was paid with cash collateral does not help. The algorithm would be property acquired by the debtor when created. The employee would be paid in arrears, well after the algorithm was created. Similarly, cases involving restaurants distinguish the extent to which food sold is a product of inventory and the extent to which it is a product of services.

[77] *In re Cafeteria Operators, LP*, 299 BR 400, 410 (Bankr. ND Tex. 2003). Some courts conclude that the food is not proceeds at all: *In re Inman*, 95 BR 479, 480 (Bankr. W.D. Ky. 1988) ('[T]he degree of service is not the significant factor for our consideration. Rather, the meritorious fact we should note is that the restaurant industry, in general, is a service-oriented industry').

[78] See 11. U.S.C. §552(b).

146 SECURITY RIGHTS AND CREDITORS' PRIORITY AND RANKING

party is entitled to the collateral value that they had as of the petition date, and that value may be traced through multiple forms, but that does not eliminate the fact that there is no such thing as 'proceeds in the air'. Proceeds must be traceable to prepetition collateral in order for the secured party to be entitled to the value to be attributable to those proceeds/that collateral.[79] In short, even if the debtor and secured creditor intend to create a blanket lien, the lien holder may not 'own' all of the firm's value. For better or for worse, this has significant governance implications. If the secured creditor is not the sole owner of the insolvent firm, then it does not have a unilateral right to decide what to do with the firm's assets.

B. The Floating Charge in the United Kingdom

5.41 The law in the United Kingdom is different, or at least apparently so. Security in the United Kingdom is asset-based as well, but it uses two distinct mechanisms for taking security over property, the 'fixed charge' to deal with specific assets, and a floating charge to deal with circulating assets that remain under the control of the debtor.[80] While US law contemplates liens that float over changing masses of collateral, these 'floating liens' attach and perfect with regard to assets as the debtor acquires them, and they receive priority as of the date of filing, without a separate registration. UK law, by contrast, distinguishes between liens on fixed assets and liens on circulating collateral such as inventory and accounts receivable. Those assets can be liened but only as a practical matter, through a 'floating charge'. The floating charge remains inchoate until the debtor defaults or opens a proceeding.

5.42 The floating charge is, thus, at once broader and weaker than the floating lien under US law. It does not appear to be limited in what it can cover so that it can, apparently, create a lien, albeit inchoate, on the entire firm. At the same time, the floating charge is subject to a number of 'carveouts'. These include certain preferential creditors (including the cost of administration), as well as a carveout—the prescribed part—to make provision for payments to unsecured creditors.[81]

5.43 As a practical matter, however, the power of the floating charge comes from the power it gives to choose the administrator and thereby to control the manner in which the firm is sold and the value distributed. Historically (i.e. before the Enterprise Act of 2002),[82] the floating charge holder had the power to appoint a receiver to liquidate the enterprise. After the Enterprise Act, the power to appoint the receiver shifted to the

---

[79] See above, fn. 55.

[80] R. Goode and L. Gullifer, *Goode and Gullifer on Legal Problems of Credit and Security* (6th edn, Thompson Reuters 2017) 126 (4-02); Adrian Walters, 'Statutory Erosion of Secured Creditors' Rights: Some Insights from the United Kingdom', Illinois Law Review 2015, 543, 548. See *Holroyd v Marshall* [1862] 10 HL Cas. 191; *Re Spectrum Plus* [2005] UKHL 41, [2005] 2 AC 680.

[81] *Re Spectrum Plus* (n 80).

[82] See c. 40 (Eng.) of the Enterprise Act 2002.

unsecured creditors but with a secured creditor veto. The result was that the floating charge holder still had the power to control the appointment of the receiver, though the receiver was now under a duty to the estate as a whole, not to the secured lender.[83] Apparently, as a practical matter, little changed. The administration remained oriented towards a quick sale of the firm as a going concern.[84] The value of the fixed assets was paid over to the fixed charge holders and the remainder, subject to carveouts, to the floating charge holder.[85] Indeed, through the use of 'pre-packaged' administrations or 'pre-packs', the secured creditors in the UK have managed to preserve a system where all of the value of a going-concern sale is passed along to the fixed lien holders and the floating charge holder, subject to carveouts.

V. Asset-Based Claims and Value-Based Claims in Rescue

The discussion above shows that in both the United States and the United Kingdom, **5.44** secured creditors assert that their priority as secured creditors extends to the entire value of the firm. In the United States, this assertion rests on the vitality of the concept of a 'blanket lien'. In the UK, it rests on the scope of the 'floating charge'. Both systems assume the equivalence between two forms of rescue: (a) going concern and (b) recapitalization. Both assertions—the enterprise lien and the equivalence of sale and restructuring—are problematic, and both rest on the failure to make a distinction between the value of the firm as an operating enterprise and the value of its assets—the things it owns. These two assertions will be discussed in reverse order.

A. Firm Value v. Asset Value: Going-Concern Value as Collateral

The value of the firm is not necessarily coextensive with the value of its property. The **5.45** value of the firm may be greater than or less than the value of its accumulated assets. The shareholder's interest is, on the one hand, junior to the claims of the creditors, so the value of the firm may be less than the value of its assets. On the other hand, however, the value of the firm may lie in the way in which those assets are used to produce income. In that instance, the value of the firm will be greater than the value of its assets. For example, imagine a small business, like a pizza shop or a plumber's business. The assets of the pizza shop may consist of a lease (which might be above market, below market, transferable or not), pizza ovens (which would be sold on the used restaurant equipment market), and inventory (flour, water, cheese, tomato sauce, drinks). Winding up the business would yield, hypothetically, tens of thousands of dollars. The same would

---

[83] Walters, 'Statutory Erosion of Secured Creditors' Rights' (n 80) 564–5.
[84] ibid.
[85] ibid.

be said for the plumber's business. But, assume that the pizza shop was famous and popular, with lines around the block. By making pizza, the business might be worth hundreds of thousands of dollars in cash flow. All that value, however, is embodied in the reputation of the pizzaiola or the plumber. It is not, and would not be, realizable by the creditors in a liquidation. So, the question arises, how much of the value of the business is embodied in its assets, and how much in the cash stream that they produce. It is not obvious that the cash stream should be considered collateral, even if the sale of the business is characterized as an asset sale. While the pizzaiola may have a contract with the business he or she owns, he or she might not. If part of the sale transaction is the drafting of a key person employment contract, it would be hard to characterize that as value attributable to the collateral.

5.46   Notwithstanding this seemingly obvious point, in both the United States and the United Kingdom, 'secured creditors' are often treated as atop a single waterfall and therefore entitled to all the value of the firm until they are paid in full.

B.   Sale v. Recapitalization: The Paradox of Rescue

5.47   This failure to distinguish firm value from asset value leads to a crucial false equivalence in practice. A firm can be rescued in two different ways—by recapitalization or sale. When the firm recapitalizes, the creditors end up as the owners of the firm, bearing the risks, but also reaping the benefits of any upside in the value of the firm. When the firm is sold, the creditors receive money, but the purchaser gets, and presumably pays for, the risks and benefits of ownership. When the firm is recapitalized, the new shareholders (the old creditors) retain both the going-concern value and the upside and allocate it. The line is not always clean. Sometimes, a recapitalization under a plan may involve the sale of some or all of the equity. But there is an important difference. The sale by an administrator in the United Kingdom, or under 363(b) in the United States, lacks the procedural protections that allocate the going concern and upside (option) value between the secured creditors and the other claimants against the estate. In short, a quick sale can have the effect of reordering priority between secured and unsecured creditors by (a) sweeping gaps in the security under the rug and (b) allowing secured creditors to capture going-concern value at the expense of other claimants.[86] For example, imagine that the realizable value of the assets of a firm was $100,000. Further, imagine that the discounted value of the cash flow produced by the firm was $250,000. It is a puzzle how to allocate the $150,000 in going-concern surplus, because in a rescue, the realizable value of the

---

[86] Melissa B. Jacoby and Edward J. Janger, 'Ice Cube Bonds: Allocating the Price of Process in Chapter 11 Bankruptcy', Yale Law Journal, 123 (2014) 862, 869, 915, 922–5. See also Janger, 'The Logic and Limits of Liens' (n 1) 592.

assets is never determined by an actual sale. The sale price of the business will be known but not the value of the component parts.

C. Priority and Process in Rescue

This was the puzzle that confronted the drafters of the Bankruptcy Code in 1978: in liquidation, one learns the value of the assets but not the value of the firm; in rescue (either by recapitalization or sale), one learns the value of the firm, but not the assets. Indeed, this has always been the puzzle faced by debtors and creditors in deciding whether to liquidate a business or restructure debt. As has frequently been observed, distress produces two alternative dysfunctional scenarios. If a firm has diffuse creditors and no dominant secured lender, coordination problems (principally holdouts) are likely to spell doom for a restructuring.[87] If a firm has a dominant secured creditor, that creditor's power over assets is likely to allow them to capture all the going-concern value, whether it is tied to collateral or not.[88]

5.48

The solution in the United States is a structured bargaining process that deals with holdout problems by providing for class voting that binds objectors and provides an entitlement back-stop for both secured and unsecured creditors (cramdown). If negotiations with the secured creditor fail, the debtor can buy out the secured creditor at the judicially determined value of the collateral. If negotiations over the share of equity or junior creditor classes fail, they face the alternative of being wiped out by the absolute priority rule.[89] The solution in the United Kingdom is to place the restructuring in the hands of an independent fiduciary—the administrator. And, after the Enterprise Act of 2002, that administrator's duties run to the unsecured, rather than the secured, creditors.

5.49

However, as noted above, these processes and duties are under threat, both in the United States and the United Kingdom, because of the practical power held by secured creditors. In the United States, this is because of the asserted blanket lien. In the United Kingdom, it is because of the power given to the holder of the floating charge to control the selection of the administrator. In both cases, there has been tremendous hydraulic pressure exerted by secured creditors to shortcut the processes provided for by statute by maintaining control over the sale process. This is accomplished in the United Kingdom, through the use of so-called 'pre-packs', and in the United States through all-asset sales under § 363(b).[90]

5.50

---

[87] T.H. Jackson, *The Logic and Limits of Bankruptcy Law* (Harvard University Press 1986) 7–19.
[88] Jacoby and Janger, 'Tracing Equity' (n 1) 917.
[89] See 11 U.S.C. §§1122 (classification), 1125 (disclosure), 1126 (voting), 1129(a) (negotiated confirmation), 1129(b) (cramdown).
[90] For the United Kingdom, see Walters, 'Statutory Erosion of Secured Creditors' Rights' (n 80); for the United States, see Jacoby and Janger, 'Ice Cube Bonds' (n 86).

150 SECURITY RIGHTS AND CREDITORS' PRIORITY AND RANKING

5.51 In both cases, the incumbent debtor and the key creditors negotiate the terms of sale in advance of filing and move the case quickly through to sale. The result is that the negotiation contemplated by the US Bankruptcy Code, and the independent judgment contemplated by the appointment of an administrator in the UK, never happens. The advantage of these quick realization techniques is that going-concern value is preserved. But this may come at the cost of fairness, in that value may be appropriated by the secured party or shared with the purchaser in a sweetheart deal.

D. Competing Approaches to Priority in Rescue

5.52 One might think that for a topic as crucial as the valuation of a secured creditor's claims, there would be broad agreement on the method of calculation, but this could not be further from the truth. Both in academic discussions and in public policy debates, there are multiple approaches to valuing a secured creditor's claim in bankruptcy. The confusion lies, at least in part, in the failure to distinguish claims against assets from claims against the firm mentioned. Broadly speaking, there are four approaches to secured creditor priority that can be used in rescue cases. I will describe each of them briefly, with a numerical example. They are (a) single waterfall absolute priority, (b) single waterfall relative priority (United States), (c) relative priority (European Union (EU)), and (d) equitable (asset-value-based) priority (United States). Choice amongst these methodologies is crucial, because it determines not just value allocation but also control over the case and the relevance of process.

1. Single waterfall absolute priority

5.53 'Single waterfall absolute priority' is the regime that is often assumed. The assumption of single waterfall absolute priority is that the blanket lien holder or floating charge holder has a senior lien on the value of the firm. As such, they are entitled to payment in full before any junior lien holders or unsecured creditors get paid anything. The problem with this approach as a positive matter is that it ignores the distinction between liens on property and debt claims against the firm. Normatively, it allows the secured creditors to squeeze out all junior creditors (including employees, tort claimants, and suppliers), while continuing the firm in operation.

5.54 As a numerical example, imagine the following firm: the realizable value of the liened assets (substantially all) is $100,000. The secured creditors are owed $300,000. Unsecured claims of employees, tort claimants, suppliers, and the taxing authority total $500,000. Further assume that the discounted value of current cash flows is $200,000. However, because of a promising business opportunity that is only realizable if the business continues, a buyer is willing to pay $250,000. Under single waterfall absolute priority, all of that value goes to the secured creditor who asserts a blanket lien, even though the value of the liened assets is only $100,000. Further, it is not, by any means, clear that the additional increment of value relates to the liened assets.

2. Single waterfall relative priority

Baird and Casey have expressed discomfort with this version of absolute priority.[91] **5.55**
Their concern, however, is not with valuation or the blanket lien. It is, instead, with the
concept of forced realization because of the absolute priority rule. They are troubled by
the fact that by selling the company, or buying it through a credit bid, the secured creditors, by asserting absolute priority, will impose realization on the unsecured creditors
at a moment when their interest is under water, thus depriving them of any potential
upside should the business improve. In their view, the unsecured creditors are entitled
to 'the option value' associated with that upside. However, because they too assume a
single waterfall and a blanket lien, the strike price of that option is the full amount of
the debt.

As a numerical example using the same firm: the realizable value of the liened assets **5.56**
(substantially all) is $100,000. The secured creditors are owed $300,000. Unsecured
claims of employees, tort claimants, suppliers, and the taxing authority total $500,000.
Further assume that the discounted value of current cash flows is $200,000. However,
because of a promising business opportunity that is only realizable if the business continues, a buyer is willing to pay $250,000. Under relative priority, as envisioned by Baird
and Casey, the lien holder would have to cash out the unsecured credit's option value,
which they describe as the value of an option to purchase the company for $300,000 at
some point in the future.

How to calculate the value of that option and implement the priority is a matter of some **5.57**
difficulty, but it is significant that Baird and Casey acknowledge that not all of the value
goes to the secured creditor. What is unclear about the Baird and Casey approach is
why the secured creditor's claim is entitled to priority beyond the value of the encumbered assets. Baird and Casey make a simplifying assumption that they then treat as
if it was positive law. They assume, contrary to the discussion above, that a secured
creditor can lien all of the value of the firm or, at least, all of its assets. They sit the first
lien lender atop the distributional waterfall and apply 'absolute priority' as if such an
all-encompassing lien was possible and 'absolute priority' applied. Even here, the only
value to slip through is the so-called 'option value'.

3. Relative priority: EU Directive

The issue of priority has been front and centre as jurisdictions have promulgated le- **5.58**
gislation to comply with the recent EU Directive on Preventive Restructuring
Frameworks.[92] The Directive recommends that enacting legislation contain the possibility of 'cross-class cramdown'. In describing the minimum cramdown entitlement,

---

[91] See Baird and Casey, 'No Exit?' (n 44) 32. They attribute it to Justice Douglas, who emphasized the importance of absolute priority when criticizing the then current practice in equity receiverships involving railroads. It
is important to recognize here, though, that the priority that Douglas was focused on was the priority of debt over
equity, not the priority of secured creditors, which, indeed, to Douglas, was part of the problem.

[92] See Art. 11 of Directive (EU) 2019/1023 of the European Parliament and of the Council, <https://eur-lex.eur
opa.eu/legal-content/EN/TXT/PDF/?uri=CELEX:32019L1023> accessed 10 January 2024.

152 SECURITY RIGHTS AND CREDITORS' PRIORITY AND RANKING

the directive uses the term 'relative priority' but not in the same way as Baird and Casey or Jacoby and Janger. The Directive sets forth minimum creditor protections in the case of cross-class cramdown. The priority creditor is entitled to at least the amount that they would realize in the 'next best' alternative scenario. This does not necessarily mean liquidation value but incorporates the possibility of multiple going concern options. With regard to ranked creditors, seniors must receive more than juniors, but the Directive does not specify a standard or determining those increments.

5.59   Where asset-based claims are involved, the 'next-best-alternative' approach may, under certain circumstances, offer the secured claimant more than the value of their collateral. Where non-asset-based claims are involved, the Directive offers little guidance.

4. Equitable (asset v. value-based) priority

5.60   At least insofar as Chapter 11 is concerned, Baird and Casey misread the statute and its treatment of secured claims in comparison to unsecured claims. 11 U.S.C. §1129(b) allows approval of a plan over a creditor's objection if the distribution being received is 'fair and equitable'. It defines 'fair and equitable' for three different types of claimants: holders of secured claims, unsecured claims, and ownership interests. For the plan to be fair and equitable with regard to claims against and interests in the firm, the absolute priority rule applies. But for secured creditors, the cramdown standard is different. The allowed secured claim (the amount of the claim entitled to priority) is measured by the value of the collateral, not by a position atop the distributional waterfall with respect to firm value.

5.61   The key to understanding the secured creditor's entitlement under US bankruptcy law is understanding the definition of a 'secured claim'. Under § 506(a), a claim is a 'secured claim' to 'the extent of the value of such creditor's interest in the estate's interest in such property'.[93] The secured creditor's entitlement in cramdown as determined under § 1129(b)(2)(A) is measured by the 'allowed amount' of the secured claim. A plan of reorganization can be approved over the secured creditor's objection, so long as the secured creditor retains a lien on the property with a value equal to its value on the effective date of the plan and is entitled to payments with a present value of at least the value of the collateral.[94] The creditor is also entitled to 'adequate-protection' payments to compensate for any decline in value of the collateral during the pendency of the case.[95] In other words, the secured creditor's priority as a secured creditor is only protected to the extent of the value of the collateral, and that value is realized as of the effective date of the plan of reorganization. To the extent that there is a deficiency, it is an unsecured claim.[96] As Melissa Jacoby and I have discussed elsewhere, the effect

---

[93]   See 11 U.S.C. §506(a).
[94]   ibid §1129(b)(2)(A).
[95]   ibid §§362(d)(1), 507(b).
[96]   ibid § 506(a).

of a bankruptcy filing is to fix the relative position of creditors and the pool of liened assets.[97]

To repeat the numerical example from above, using 1129(b)(2)(A): the realizable value of the liened assets (substantially all) is $100,000. The secured creditors are owed $300,000. Unsecured claims of employees, tort claimants, suppliers, and the taxing authority total $500,000. Further assume that the discounted value of current cash flows is $200,000. However, because of a promising business opportunity that is only realizable if the business continues, a buyer is willing to pay $250,000. Under the Bankruptcy Code's approach, the allowed secured claim of the secured creditor would be $100,000. The secured creditor would have a deficiency of $200,000. This would be added to the unsecured claims, which would total $700,000 and receive a pro rata distribution of 21.4%. So, instead of receiving $250,000 or $250,000 minus option value, the lienholder would receive $148,000, and the unsecured creditors would distribute the remaining $102,000 of the purchase price.

5.62

Under this approach, the secured creditor never has a lien on the value of the firm, only on the value of the assets. In a piecemeal liquidation, the two will be the same. In rescue, however, the result is different. The secured claimant has a claim on the value of the pool of assets that made up its collateral at the time of filing. The unsecured claimants are entitled to the remaining value of the firm. This includes the unencumbered assets of the firm but also any additional value created by continuing the firm in operation— the going-concern surplus.

5.63

As such, any time there is going-concern value, that value is allocated to the estate, not to the secured creditor.

5.64

E. Some Conclusions about Priority

This distinction between asset-based claims and firm-value-based claims has implications that are not generally, or at least consistently, understood for jurisdictions, like the United States and civilian jurisdictions, that adhere to the distinction between a lien on assets and a lien on the enterprise:

5.65

(1) To the extent that priority is based on a lien, the extent of the priority is based on the value of the collateral, not the value of the firm.

(2) In rescue, the secured creditor is entitled to the value of its collateral and not more. If there is a deficiency, it is an unsecured claim. This means that in rescue, the reorganization surplus, as well as any option value, are not tied to the assets and, hence, are not part of the secured creditor's priority claim.

---

[97] ibid §§502, 506, 541, 552.

154 SECURITY RIGHTS AND CREDITORS' PRIORITY AND RANKING

(3) The secured creditor's priority is fixed by the realizable value of its prepetition collateral. Undersecured creditors may be entitled to some share of the upside but only to the extent of an increase in value in prepetition collateral during the course of the case.

(4) This means that even when the value of the firm is not sufficient to pay the secured claimants in full, reorganization surplus and option value will flow through to the unsecured creditors (including the secured creditor's deficiency claim).

(5) This highlights the allocative difference between a going-concern sale and a recapitalization. In a going-concern sale, the purchaser pays for the reorganization surplus as well as any 'upside' or option value. In a recapitalization, the creditors retain that as part of the distribution.

(6) Therefore, even if, when a firm is sold as a going concern, the secured creditors are not paid in full, the value of the firm must be allocated between secured and unsecured creditors.

In jurisdictions like the United Kingdom, where the floating charge is thought to act like a lien on the enterprise, the result may be different. However, this is not necessarily the case for several reasons. First, a floating charge is still a lien on assets; it was created to capture circulating assets that were under the debtor's dominion and control. Second, even though it is generally understood that the floating charge will cover after acquired property even after it has crystallized. This does not necessarily imply that the value of the charge holder's collateral is the same as the capitalized value of the income stream produced by the firm's operations. Nonetheless, under current practice, the floating charge holder's lien is treated as capturing the going-concern value of a firm when it is recapitalized or sold as a going concern. As a positive matter, this concern is addressed through the so-called carve-outs and prescribed part, which are placed ahead of the floating charge holders in the distributional waterfall.

VI. Realizable Priority in Rescue: Asset Value and Firm Value

5.66 The discussion so far has drawn a distinction between claims against the property of the firm and claims against the enterprise itself. In Chapter 11, this distinction gives rise to two different ways of calculating priority entitlements. For asset-based claims, the entitlement for the purposes of cross-class cramdown is the value of the collateral (with a floor of the value on the petition date and a ceiling of the value on the effective date of the plan). For claims against the firm, priority is determined by the hierarchical ranking in the distributional waterfall—absolute priority. This leads to an anomaly. Where secured creditor priority is involved, value that is not tied to assets will flow through to unsecured creditors. But where firm based claims are involved, out-of-the-money creditors and equity are wiped out.

A. Critiques of Absolute Priority: Relative Priorities

When *in personam* claims are given priority, however the priority functions differently. **5.67** It operates like a true waterfall, with top-ranked claims paid first and junior claims paid only after the senior class is paid in full. Where *in personam* claims are involved, we are dealing with true priority rankings rather than entitlements to the value of property. The simplest of these priorities is debt ahead of equity, but all systems provide some additional priority rights, for example to administrative expenses of the estate, to employees, and often to tax claims. It is for these types of claims that the rule of 'absolute priority' comes into play. For these types of priority, US law applies the so-called absolute priority rule.[98]

As discussed above, the absolute priority rule has come under criticism in both the **5.68** United States and Europe. In the United States, Douglas Baird has pointed out that the absolute priority rule gives senior creditors the power to wipe out junior creditors at a point where there is a realistic chance that the firm may return to profitability. This has led him to propose a form of relative priority that would preserve that 'option value' for the junior claimants or interest holders.[99] The EU Directive's form of relative priority is more generous to the unsecured creditors. It would permit a country to limit the seniority of waterfall claims. The difference is that the EU Directive does not focus on 'option value' but instead on a floor based on the 'next best alternative'.[100]

B. Existing Approaches: The 'New-Value' Corollary

While these new approaches may address shortcomings of the absolute priority rule, **5.69** there is a pair of approaches under existing law that allow junior interests (equity) to retain an interest in a firm that is restructuring, even if senior classes object. The most obvious one is for the juniors to simply buy out the seniors at par. This is what would happen in a foreclosure sale, and that approach remains available in bankruptcy. A second approach, under US law, is referred to as the 'new-value' corollary to the absolute priority rule, or the *Case v Los Angeles Lumber* exception.[101] Under the new-value exception, the court may approve a distribution to junior claims or interests so long as the distribution is not 'on account of' the old junior claim or interest. The concept is that when the firm is recapitalized, the old junior interests are cancelled, but the former junior interest holders purchase the new equity in the reorganized firm. This approach has risks, because there is the possibility that the arrangement might be a sweetheart deal, so the courts must scrutinize the value of the equity being provided.[102] In the

---

[98] ibid §1129(b)(2)(B); *Boyd v United States*, 116 US 616 (1886).
[99] See Douglas G. Baird, 'Priority Matters: Absolute Priority, Relative Priority, and the Cost of Bankruptcy', University of Pennsylvania Law Review, 165 (2017) 785.
[100] See above, fn. 92.
[101] *Case v Los Angeles Lumber Products Co., Ltd*, 308 US 106 (1939).
[102] *Bank of America Nat. Trust and Sav. Assn v 203 North LaSalle Street Partnership*, 526 US 434 (1999).

156 SECURITY RIGHTS AND CREDITORS' PRIORITY AND RANKING

United States, in large-company Chapter 11s, the equity must be exposed to the market to assure that the price is fair.[103] Recently, a special version of this corollary was adopted for small businesses, where the 'sweat equity' of the owners is treated as an equity contribution such that the debtor must commit all of the disposable income of the business to payments under the plan, but once that period is complete, the obligations under the plan are satisfied.[104]

C. Realizable Priority for Asset-Based and Value-Based Claims

5.70   In a previous article, Stephan Madaus and I have argued for an approach to asset-based and structural priority that limits the entitlement to the value that could be realized in the absence of a restructuring or going-concern sale. We argue that the creditor claiming priority should have the burden of establishing the realizable value of its claim and argue that this would considerably reduce the level of hold-out power given to priority claimants in complex cases.[105] We did not, in that article, discuss the proper approach to waterfall-based claims, and we essentially left it out of the 'realizable priority' framework. The 'new-value' corollary to the absolute priority rule, discussed above, closes the circle, with only a small twist. The 'new-value' corollary recognizes that there are reasons to be suspicious of old equity participation. So, just as a senior must establish its entitlement to priority, a junior must establish its entitlement to participate in the new entity, either by establishing that they are in the money or that they are contributing fair value of the interest that they are purchasing. To do this, they will have to establish the realizable value not of the assets but of the firm.

VII. Conclusion

5.71   A rescue-oriented insolvency regime adds a layer of complexity to ascertaining the entitlements of creditors who seek priority. The value of asset-based claims must be established without a sale. The value of the firm must be established either to evaluate a sale price or allocate value in a recapitalization. The solution in the United States, the United Kingdom, and the 'pre-insolvency' regimes emerging in the EU is bargaining against the backstop of entitlement. If the parties agree to an allocation, then no hearing is necessary. If they cannot agree, senior creditors claiming priority will have to prove the realizable value of their assets. Junior creditors seeking to avoid being wiped out will have to establish the value of the firm or their proposed contribution. This basic

---

[103] ibid.

[104] See HR 3311 s. 2 of the Small Business Reorganization Act of 2019, codified in relevant part at 11 U.S.C. §1191.

[105] Edward J. Janger and Stephan Madaus, 'Value Tracing and Priority in Cross-Border Group Bankruptcies: Solving the Nortel Problem from the Bottom Up', University of Miami International and Comparative Law Review, 27 (2020) 331.

structure exists, to a varying degree in the United States, the United Kingdom, and continental systems. However, its outline is often obscured by the difficulties of translating common terms across systems. Security is not as all-encompassing as it may seem. Even absolute priority is not quite as absolute as is generally understood. Once these nuances are captured, it is possible to take a realist's view of priority and introduce a dose of common sense into negotiations towards corporate rescue.

6

Transactions Avoidance Rules

Reinhard Bork

I. Introduction

6.01 Insolvency[1] proceedings are primarily aiming at distributing the (proceeds of the) insolvent debtor's insufficient asset pool among the creditors on a pro rata basis. Under the principle of equal treatment of creditors, all claims shall be satisfied in collective enforcement proceedings in the same way, i.e. all creditors shall receive the same share of the proceeds as a percentage of their claim (*pari passu* rule). However, creditors who received satisfaction of their claims prior to the opening of insolvency proceedings do not participate in the collective proceedings and have managed to escape from the application of the *pari passu* rule. This is perceived as unjust, since it is, in many cases, more or less a matter of coincidence whether insolvency proceedings are commenced and opened before or after the payment. The remedy to correct this result—thereby enforcing basic principles of insolvency law[2]—is transactions avoidance law. Hence, in nearly all jurisdictions, certain transactions performed prior to the opening of insolvency proceedings can be avoided[3] after the opening of the proceedings when certain conditions are met. Although they are valid under general civil law,[4] national laws permit avoidance where transactions are detrimental to the general body of creditors and contrary to certain principles of insolvency law. This includes not only payments to existing creditors but also, for instance, gifts to a spouse and the collaborative creation of a security right to a hitherto unsecured creditor.

6.02 The following text will evolve the policies behind transactions avoidance law, the general prerequisites, and the special requirements (avoidance grounds), and it will also explain the legal consequences. However, it is not possible to consider all national

---

[1] As regards terminology, this chapter follows the English tradition where 'bankruptcy' is reserved for individuals (cf. s. 264(1) of the Insolvency Act 1986) whilst 'insolvency' is the legal term for legal entities.

[2] See more below at para. 6.07 et seq. See also Thomas H. Jackson, 'Avoiding Powers in Bankruptcy', Stanford Law Review, 36 (1984) 725 et seq.

[3] The term 'avoidance' is a customary expression in English legal language. It will be used here as representative for other expressions such as 'challenge', 'claw-back', or 'setting aside'.

[4] Note, however, that the validity of the transaction is not a necessary requirement. Since it can be easier to prove the prerequisites of transactions avoidance than those of invalidity under general civil law, courts have the choice as to whether to base their decision on grounds of (e.g.) contract law or company law (cf. *Re London Oil & Gas Ltd* [2022] EWHC 1672 (Ch)) or of transactions avoidance law (cf. BGH, 14 October 2010–IX ZR 16/10 = NZI 2011, 189).

Reinhard Bork, *Transactions Avoidance Rules* In: *The Anatomy of Corporate Insolvency Law*. Edited by: Reinhard Bork and Renato Mangano, Oxford University Press. © Reinhard Bork 2024. DOI: 10.1093/oso/9780198852094.003.0006

insolvency laws. References to national laws will thus be restricted in this chapter to the laws of England and Wales, France, Germany, and the United States because these jurisdictions represent leading systems internationally as it concerns insolvency law, albeit with typical differences, and their laws are role models for many other states.

II. Basics

A typical effect of the opening of insolvency proceedings is the shift of the power of disposal from the debtor to the insolvency practitioner. Hence, transactions made by the debtor *after* this point in time are not valid, since the debtor no longer has the power of disposal, and individual enforcement acts by single creditors are prohibited and invalidated by insolvency law. As opposed to this, transactions performed *prior* to the commencement of insolvency proceedings are normally not affected, since the estate is not seized retroactively.[5] This leaves performances of the debtor (e.g. gifts to the spouse or payments to creditors) unviolated. However, almost all national laws share the opinion that, under certain conditions, this might be contrary to foundational principles of insolvency law. They therefore mitigate the harsh consequences of the clear cut-off date (opening of the proceedings)[6] and allow the challenging of certain transactions in order to tackle unacceptable displacements of assets to the benefit of a third party.[7] This is in the pursuit of creditor protection,[8] primarily—yet not exclusively—to ensure the equal treatment of creditors. Relevant rules are suggested in the United Nations Commission on International Trade Law (UNCITRAL) *Legislative Guide*[9] and in the *Principles of European Insolvency Law*[10] and can be found in nearly all jurisdictions,[11] for example in England and Wales (ss 238–45, 339–48, 423–5 of the Insolvency Act 1986), France (Art. L. 632-1–632-4 of the *Code de Commerce*), Germany (§§ 129–47 of the *Insolvenzordnung*), and the United States (11 U.S.C. §§544–53). Since most of these rules are typically only applicable in opened insolvency proceedings, such opening is a

6.03

---

[5] For an exception, cf. below in fn. 41.

[6] Cf. *Angove's Pty Ltd v Bailey* [2016] UKSC 47.

[7] In the following text, the beneficiary of a vulnerable transaction will also be labelled as 'counterparty', 'opponent', or 'defendant'.

[8] In this regard, transactions avoidance law can supplement other instruments of creditor protection, e.g.such of company law; cf. Court of Justice of the European Union (CJEU) Case C-394/18 *I.G.I. Srl v Maria Grazia Cicenia, Mario Di Pierro, Salvatore de Vito, Antonio Raffaele*, ECLI:EU:C:2020:56 paras 61 et seq.

[9] UNCITRAL, *Legislative Guide on Insolvency Law* (UNCITRAL, New York 2005) 135 paras 148 et seq. with Recommendations 93 et seq.

[10] William W. McBryde, Axel Flessner, and Sebastian Kortmann, *Principles of European Insolvency Law* [abbreviated here as 'PEIL'], (Kluwer, Deventer 2003) (new edn 2005) §8.1(1): 'A juridical act unfairly detrimental to the creditors performed by the debtor within a certain period of time before the opening of the proceeding, is subject to reversal.'

[11] Extensive descriptions of the transactions avoidance laws of the Member States of the European Union are available in Reinhard Bork, and Michael Veder, *Harmonisation of Transactions Avoidance Laws*, (Intersentia, Cambridge/Antwerp/Chicago 2022) ch. 4. See further the national reports in Dennis Faber, Niels Vermunt, Jason Kilborn and Tomáš Richter, *Commencement of Insolvency Proceedings* (Oxford University Press, Oxford 2012) each at para. 24.1.

160 TRANSACTIONS AVOIDANCE RULES

prerequisite for transactions avoidance, and the nullity or voidability of such transactions is a further effect of the opening of insolvency proceedings.

6.04 The idea of such transactions avoidance goes back to Roman law, where the *praetor* was enabled to grant the so-called *actio Pauliana*, that is to order the claw-back of transactions that were fraudulent in respect of creditors.[12] The Latin expression '*actio Pauliana*' can be found in many languages (e.g. *Pauline (or Paulian) action* in English or *action paulienne* in French) and is still used in modern laws. However, in some jurisdictions, it is not (or not exclusively) part of insolvency law but rather located in general civil law,[13] and it is not always restricted to insolvency proceedings but also applicable outside such proceedings, for example in private enforcement proceedings.[14]

6.05 The effect of transactions avoidance cannot be summarized in one word. It depends on the case at hand and varies from country to country. Sometimes, the legal result is that the respective transaction is declared null and void by force of law; sometimes, the legal consequence is a claim of rescission or compensation, regularly to be enforced by the insolvency practitioner; sometimes, it suffices to simply ignore the transaction (e.g. when a creditor tries to enforce a security right that was created in a voidable way); and sometimes, the legal effects are left to the discretion of the court. We will deal with this variety of legal consequences in more detail below.[15] At this point of this chapter, it may suffice to highlight that transactions avoidance law primarily aims to remove the disadvantage for the general body of creditors caused by the vulnerable transactions from the estate.[16]

6.06 It goes without saying that not all transactions performed prior to the opening of insolvency proceedings are subject to avoidance rules. Principally, persons dealing with the subsequent debtor can trust in the stability of performances and have no need to take a future insolvency of their counterparty into account. Hence, insolvency-triggered transactions avoidance needs to be restricted to the necessary measure, and legislators have to find the right balance between the interest of the general body of creditors in 'swelling the assets' and improving their return from the estate, on the one hand, and the legitimate interests of the persons who have benefited from the transaction to keep

---

[12] The Digest 22, 1, 38, 4:

> *In Fabiana quoque actione et Pauliana, per quam quae in fraudem creditorum alienata sunt revocantur, fructus quoque restituuntur: nam praetor id agit, ut perinde sint omnia, atque si nihil alienatum esset: quod non est iniquum (nam et verbum 'restituas', quod in hac re praetor dixit, plenam habet significationem), ut fructus quoque restituantur.*

> (In both the Fabian and Paulian Actions, by means of which property which has been disposed of for the purpose of defrauding creditors, is recovered, the produce of said property must also be returned; for the Praetor uses his authority to place everything in the same condition as if nothing had been alienated; and this is not unjust, for the words, 'you shall return,' which the Praetor makes use of in this matter, have a broad signification, so that the produce of the property must also be surrendered.)

[13] Examples are Bulgaria, France, Greece, Italy, the Netherlands, Poland, Portugal, and Spain.
[14] Examples are the Czech Republic, Germany, the Netherlands, Slovakia, and Slovenia.
[15] At paras 6.58 et seq.
[16] See Bork and Veder, *Harmonisation of Transaction Avoidance Laws* (n 11) para. 4.215 and § 8.1(2) of PEIL (n 10): 'The administrator can recover or seek annulment of any benefit which has been obtained from the debtor.'

what they have received on the other hand. Insolvency laws do that by binding transactions avoidance to objective and subjective requirements, which narrows the scope of voidable transactions from 'all' to 'some'.

III. Underlying Principles

This leads us to the the principles[17] upon which transactions avoidance law is based.[18] **6.07** The first principle to be taken into account is the fixation principle. It supports all norms of insolvency law which aim to demarcate the personal and substantive scope of insolvency proceedings, i.e. distinguishing assets, creditors, and creditors' rights that are subject to the insolvency proceedings from those that are not. Transactions avoidance law is also seen as a consequence of the fixation principle, more specifically of the fixation of the estate, since it can be seen as a means of 'reconstructing' the estate to the size that it should have been at the moment of fixation.[19] It thus contributes to the development of the *de facto* estate (which the insolvency practitioner takes into possession when assuming the office) to the *de iure* estate (which is determined to be distributed among the ordinary creditors and which includes, among others,[20] assets transferred to the opponent in a voidable way).

Principles of transactions avoidance law can be grouped in those which support transactions **6.08** avoidance and those which require restrictions. As regards supportive principles, the principle of best possible satisfaction of the creditors' claims must be mentioned in particular. Insolvency proceedings are collective enforcement proceedings and aim to satisfy the creditors' claims in an optimal way. Another basic tenet is the principle of equal treatment of creditors. Where creditors have benefited from a challengeable transaction and are obliged to return the received under transactions avoidance law, they have anew an unsatisfied and unsecured claim against the debtor with which they compete with all other ordinary creditors for the debtor's estate. The opponent will now be satisfied on a pro rata basis under the *pari passu* rule from the proceeds, which is the purest enforcement of the principle of equal treatment of creditors. Further, the principle of collectivity also supports transactions avoidance law decisively. Avoidance actions aim to compensate transactions that caused a disadvantage for the general body of creditors. *Vice versa*, enforcing avoidance rules augments the estate for the benefit of the general body of creditors. Claims to compensation for the disadvantage caused for

---

[17] The term 'principles' is understood here as fundamental and basic standards, not as important topics or major issues.

[18] For extensive and groundbreaking insight into the principles or transactions avoidance law, see Bork and Veder, *Harmonisation of Transaction Avoidance Laws* (n 11) ch. 2.

[19] About this, see M.J.M. Franken, *Het insolventiepassief* (Wolters Kluwer, Deventer 2019) para. 3.2.

[20] On its way to the *de iure* estate, the *de facto* estate is mainly augmented by collecting receivables and by transactions avoidance. It is diminished by serving rights to separation, by satisfaction of secured and preferential creditors, and by set-off, because all these acts occupy assets which thus cannot be used to satisfy the unsecured creditors.

162 TRANSACTIONS AVOIDANCE RULES

the creditors are part of the estate and are collected by the insolvency practitioner as the official body of the collective proceedings. Hence, transactions avoidance law is designed to protect the collective interests of the creditors, thereby putting the individual interests of the opponent last. Finally, the principle of efficiency is of some importance, since rules on transactions avoidance should be shaped in such a way that they can 'bite' and be efficiently enforced.

6.09   As opposed to that, various principles claim attention when it comes to restrictions. Most notably, the principle of protection of trust must be observed. Taking account of the legitimate expectations of the opponents (in particular that they may keep what they have received) is of the essence when shaping and applying transactions avoidance law. However, the challenging task will be to evaluate which expectations are legitimate and how they can be best protected. In addition, the principle of predictability (legal certainty) deserves a closer look, since transactions avoidance law as such impairs the predictability and legal certainty of substantive rights, which must be countered by pruning avoidance grounds to a reasonable extent. Further, the principles of social protection and of protection of the debtor's rights can support restricting rules, albeit in very special constellations only. And finally, the principle of proportionality is helpful in restricting transactions avoidance law to the necessary extent.

6.10   Since various opposing principles are involved, weighing and balancing them in accordance with the principle of proportionality is necessary. None of the relevant principles reigns supreme. In particular, this holds true for the principles of best possible satisfaction of the creditors' claims and for the principle of protection of trust. Both deploy strong forces. However, a boundless enforcement of the satisfaction principle would lead to unacceptable uncertainty and would neglect the legitimate interests of the opponent completely, and an unrestricted application of the principle of protection of trust would render transactions avoidance law ineffective. Transactions avoidance as such is a well-founded and generally accepted instrument of insolvency law, supported by the principle of best possible satisfaction of the creditors' claims and the principle of equal treatment of creditors. But it needs a balanced tailoring, enforcing the principle of protection of trust and the principle of predictability in the first place.

IV. Effectiveness

6.11   It follows from the above that transactions avoidance law is based on certain principles of insolvency law, on the one hand, and is also destined for enforcing these principles on the other hand. This raises the question as to effectiveness.[21] While it can be said that

---

[21] For more on this, see Reinhard Bork, 'Ökonomische Analyse des Insolvenzanfechtungsrechts' in Thomas Eger, Jochen Bigus, Claus Ott, and Georg von Wangenheim (eds), *Internationalization of the Law and its Economic Analysis* (Gabler, Wiesbaden 2008) 593–603; John C. McCoid, 'Bankruptcy, Preferences, and Efficiency: An Expression of Doubt', Virginia Law Review, 67 (1981) 249–73.

transactions avoidance law, where properly designed, can be very efficient in enhancing the debtor's estate *ex post* (i.e. after the opening of the insolvency proceedings), it is questionable whether it is similarly efficient in deterring creditors *ex ante* from snaring the last available assets of a substantively insolvent debtor in the run-up to insolvency proceedings. As regards the latter, it is generally agreed that transactions avoidance law, although aiming to have a deterrent effect,[22] is not very efficient, since the recipients of a (later on vulnerable) transaction typically hope for the avoidance of insolvency proceedings, for at least escaping the relevant suspect period, or for the transaction remaining undetected by the insolvency practitioner.

V. General Prerequisites

Many jurisdictions distinguish between general requirements which must be met in all transactions avoidance cases and specific avoidance grounds, which stand abreast so that only one of them must be realized.[23] Not all of the general prerequisites dealt with in this part can be found in all jurisdictions. Some national insolvency laws can do without such requirements, and in others, they cannot be found in the wording of the statute but in case law only. However, there is an overlap which proves the common idea of transactions avoidance law. **6.12**

A. Transaction

Typically, insolvency laws do not define the term 'transaction'.[24] It should be clear that this comprises all human acts which have legal consequences. Given that rules on transactions avoidance law are supposed to have a deterrent effect, they aim at behavioural control. Debtors, creditors, and other parties involved shall be incentivized to refrain from actions that are detrimental to the general body of creditors.[25] This speaks in favour of describing the term 'transaction' with human behaviour. This human behaviour must have legal consequences. Transactions avoidance law aims to reverse the detrimental results of human behaviour. Where these results are not of a legal nature, transaction avoidance law is either useless (because mere facts cannot be reversed) or not necessary (because no harm is done). However, further clarification is necessary. **6.13**

---

[22] Cf. Bork and Veder, *Harmonisation of Transaction Avoidance Laws* (n 11) paras 2.81 and 2.86.

[23] More on these below, at paras 6.29 et seq.

[24] For an exception, see 11 U.S.C. §101(54):

> The term 'transfer' means (A) the creation of a lien; (B) the retention of title as a security interest; (C) the foreclosure of a debtor's equity of redemption; or (D) each mode, direct or indirect, absolute or conditional, voluntary or involuntary, of disposing of or parting with (i) property; or (ii) an interest in property.

[25] See, however, above, at para. 6.11.

164 TRANSACTIONS AVOIDANCE RULES

6.14 First, voidable transactions are, in many jurisdictions, not only acts of disposition (e.g. payment or transfer of title) but also real acts, which have legal consequences. For example, where brewing beer generates (under national tax law) a security right on the beer as a security for the state's beer tax claims, a mere factual behaviour (brewing beer) has caused legal effects (creation of a security right). It is irrelevant that the security right was not caused by an agreement between debtor (brewer) and creditor (tax authorities) but by operation of law.[26]

6.15 Second, forbearance can also be a challengeable transaction. The principle of equal treatment of creditors supports such inclusion, at least if the debtor behaved wilfully, i.e. decided to remain passive, despite the foreseeable legal consequences. In the end, it makes no significant difference whether a debtor (e.g.) actively waives a claim against his or her obligor or whether he or she remains passive and accepts the claim to become time-barred. The detriment to the general body of creditors might be the same, since, in both cases, the value of the debtor's claim against the obligor cannot be realized. Hence, there is no justification to treat opponents who benefited from the debtor's passivity (e.g. by accepting a debtor's claim to be time-barred) better than those who benefited from the debtor's active performance (e.g. by waiving the claim). The detriment to the general body of creditors and the advantage for the opponent is the same in both variants.

6.16 Third, a distinction can be made according to the person performing the transaction. In many jurisdictions, only transactions of the debtor are subject to avoidance law, whereas others include performances of a creditor or a third party.[27] From a principle-based perspective, avoidance rules should not be restricted *per se* to performances of the debtor but should include performances of the opponent (e.g. satisfaction by individual enforcement, transactions based on court orders applied for by the opponent, or the operation of a right to set-off by a creditor) and third parties (e.g. payment by a subsidiary of the debtor where they are disadvantageous for the debtor's estate[28]). The principle of best possible satisfaction of the creditors' claims supports this proposal, since the more transactions are covered, the greater the chance of enriching the *de facto* estate. Further, the principle of collectivity deals with the dividing line between individual and collective enforcement and supports the inclusion of satisfaction by individual enforcement, i.e. a transaction by the opponent. The principle of equal treatment of creditors suggests treating all creditors equally whose claims have been satisfied,

---

[26] Cf. for details, the decision of the German *Bundesgerichtshof*, 9 July 2009–IX ZR 86/08, NZI 2009, 644.

[27] It may occasionally be difficult to assess whether a transaction is one of the debtor or of a third party. Directors and other representatives of the debtor do not act on their own behalf. They are proxies, and their behaviour, at least where they act within their powers, are performances of the represented debtor. Beyond that, the allocation of transactions to the debtor for the purposes of transactions avoidance law depends on the contribution of the debtor to this transaction. Where the third party has paid autonomously and voluntarily, he or she is the originator of the transaction, and the debtor is not involved. Where the third party has paid on the behest of the debtor, it is the latter who initiated the transaction, and it is thus justified to characterize the payment as a transaction of the debtor.

[28] See more below, at para. 6.26.

regardless of whether the satisfaction resulted from a payment of the debtor, from an action by the creditor, or from a contribution by a third party.

National laws proceed quite differently in this respect. In Germany, all human acts with **6.17** legal consequences are covered, which includes not just acts of disposition but of all kinds, including forbearance (§ 129(2) of the *Insolvenzordnung*) and transactions of creditors and third parties. The same holds true for France (Art. L. 632-1, 632-2 of the *Code de Commerce*[29]) and the United States, where 11 U.S.C. §§547(b) and 548(a)(1) require a 'transfer' and 11 U.S.C. §101(54) defines this term very broadly,[30] including non-debtor performances such as foreclosure[31] (provided they result in a diminution of the debtor's assets) but excluding acts that extinguish the debtor's rights as this is not seen as a transfer.[32] As opposed to this, in England and Wales, where the term 'transaction' is defined in s. 436(1) of the Insolvency Act 1986 as including 'a gift, agreement or arrangement', only performances of the debtor are challengeable (ss 238(2), 239(2), 423(1) of the Insolvency Act 1986).[33]

The definition of relevant transactions has consequences for the avoidance of set-off. **6.18** In many jurisdictions, granting a right to set-off or operating such a right can be challenged as a preference. Subject to some modifications, this holds true for France (under the conditions of Art. L. 632-2 of the *Code de Commerce*), Germany (§§ 94–6, 130, 131 of the *Insolvenzordnung*), and the United States (11 U.S.C. §553), and also for England and Wales, provided the debtor participated in the transaction (s. 239 of the Insolvency Act 1986). However, it must be thoroughly described which transaction shall be attacked: the creation of the right to set-off (i.e. of the set-off situation) or the enforcement of the right to set-off by declaring both claims to be accounted against each other.

B. Prior to the Opening of Insolvency Proceedings

It follows from the restricting effects of the opening of insolvency proceedings[34] that **6.19** transactions avoidance is not necessary for transactions performed after the opening since they are invalid anyway.[35] It is for this reason that some laws draw a clear line and

---

[29] Individual enforcement is voidable according to Art. L. 632-2(2) of the *Code de Commerce*; cf. *Cour de Cassation (chambre commerciale)*–12 October 1999–96-13133 = Bull. Civ. 1999 IV No. 166. Only where French law requires 'payments', these can only be made by the debtor, not by a third party.

[30] Cf. above (n 24).

[31] *BFP v Resolution Trust Corp.*, 511 US 531, 114 S. Ct 1757, 128 L. Ed. 2d 556 (1994); *Boberschmidt v Society Nat'l Bank (In re Jones)*, 226 F.3d 917 (7th Cir. 2000).

[32] See *In re Wey*, 854 F.2d 196 (7th Cir. 1988).

[33] As for individual enforcement, it follows from s. 346 of the Insolvency Act 1986 that avoidance is not possible in bankruptcies if the enforcement was completed before the commencement of bankruptcy proceedings. See, however, below at para. 6.34: for preferences; it suffices that the debtor 'suffered anything to be done', which, in insolvencies, includes individual enforcement by a creditor.

[34] The term 'opening' is used in this chapter regardless of the fact that, in some jurisdictions, insolvency proceedings are not formally opened through a court decision but rather by an initiating act of the debtor or a creditor. A good example is the law of England and Wales, where administration proceedings can be commenced by the debtor appointing a liquidator (s. 91 of the Insolvency Act 1986) or an administrator (ibid para. 22 Sch. B1).

[35] Cf. above, at para. 6.03.

166 TRANSACTIONS AVOIDANCE RULES

restrict the scope of transactions avoidance law to acts performed before the opening of proceedings.[36] Examples are Germany, where § 129(1) of the *Insolvenzordnung* expressly states that 'transactions made prior to the opening of insolvency proceedings and disadvantaging the insolvency creditors may be contested by the insolvency administrator under §§130–146'. In other jurisdictions, it is decided by the requirement that the transaction must be made during a certain suspect period, which runs backwards from the application for, or the opening of, the insolvency proceedings.[37] However, this raises two questions.

6.20 The first question is whether post-petition transactions (i.e. transactions performed between the application for and the opening of insolvency proceedings) are covered by the relevant transactions avoidance law. It follows from the wording of § 129(1) of the *Insolvenzordnung*[38] that the answer is 'Yes' in Germany unless a preliminary insolvency practitioner pays debts created by him- or herself. The answer is also 'Yes' in France[39] and in the United States, where 11. U.S.C. §549 enables the trustee generally (subject to some exceptions) to avoid a transfer of property of the estate that occurs after the commencement of the case.[40] In England and Wales, transactions avoidance law also covers the time between the application for and the opening of administration and winding-up proceedings[41] (ss 127, 240(3)(d)/(e), 284(3) of the Insolvency Act 1986).

6.21 The second question regarding timing is at which point in time a transaction is deemed to be performed.[42] For example, where a debtor dispatches an envelope with cash before the opening of proceedings and the creditor receives the money after the opening of proceedings[43] (or, in more modern terms, where the debtor instructs his or her bank before the opening of proceedings to transfer money to a creditor and the creditor's account is only credited after the opening of proceedings[44]), is this payment subject to transactions avoidance (because the debtor acted before the opening) or is it invalid anyway (because the satisfying effect of the payment occurred after the opening of proceedings and is therefore subject to the rules on shift of disposition powers)? German

---

[36] For § 8.1 of PEIL see above (n 10).

[37] Cf. 11 U.S.C. §547(b)(4)(A) (90 days before the date of the filing of the petition) and s. 240(1)(a) of the Insolvency Act 1986 (period of 2 years ending with the onset of insolvency). The same holds true for France, where the '*période suspecte*' is defined from the day the debtor ceased payments (Art. L. 632-1 of the *Code de Commerce*) until the opening decision of the court. See general remarks in UNCITRAL, *Legislative Guide on Insolvency Law* (n 9) 147 paras 188 et seq. and Recommendation 89.

[38] Cited in para. 6.19.

[39] Cf. above (n 37).

[40] See also 11 U.S.C. §552.

[41] For bankruptcy proceedings, s. 284(3) of the Insolvency Act 1986 prepones the effects of the bankruptcy order. Hence, transaction avoidance is not necessary, since transactions after the application for bankruptcy proceedings are void anyway; cf. *Re Jagde v Singh Wasu, a Bankrupt, Darren Edwards (TiB of Jagdev Singh Wasu) v Aurora Leasing Limited and Howard de Walden Estates Limited* [2021] EWHC 96 (Ch). For a validation order by the court under s. 284 of the Insolvency Act 1986, see *Hood v HRMC and JD Classics Limited* [2019] EWHC 2236 (Ch).

[42] The same topic arises regarding the question as to whether the transaction lies outside or within the suspect period (cf. below at para. 6.32) and at which point in time the prerequisites of avoidance grounds (e.g. substantive insolvency of the debtor or knowledge of the opponent) must be met.

[43] Cf. the English case *Alderson v Temple* (1768) (1746–79) 1 Black W 660, 96 ER 384.

[44] See the German case BGH, 28 January 2021–IX ZR 64/20 = ZRI 2021, 282.

law answers this question expressly in § 140 of the *Insolvenzordnung* (which, in principle, refers to the effect and not to the performance of the transaction[45]) and US law in 11 U.S.c. §§547(e) and 548(d)(1) (which principally refer to the perfection of the transaction).[46] The French *Code de Commerce* is silent on this matter, but it is generally agreed that the point in time when the transaction was effected is relevant.[47] In contrast, in England and Wales, statute refers to the point in time when the debtor 'enters into' the transaction (ss 240(1) and 341(1) of the Insolvency Act 1986), which presumably—the definition of 'transaction' in s. 436(1) of the Insolvency Act 1986 is not very helpful in this respect, and authorities are silent on this matter—refers to the (irrevocable) departure of the asset rather than to its arrival.

C. Disadvantage for the General Body of Creditors

The idea of transactions avoidance law is to enable the insolvency practitioner to rescind the advantages from the benefited person in order to compensate the estate for the disadvantage[48] caused by the voidable transaction and thus to improve the pro rata satisfaction of the creditors' claims. This is not possible if the transaction in question did not diminish the (future) estate, because if the estate was not diminished, the clawback cannot enhance it. In other words, compensating the estate through transactions avoidance is not necessary if no disadvantage was caused.   **6.22**

It is for this reason that some jurisdictions expressly require that the transaction was disadvantageous for the general body of unsecured creditors.[49] In Germany, for example, § 129(1) of the *Insolvenzordnung*[50] postulates the transaction to be disadvantageous for the creditors. Similarly, 11 U.S.C. §547(b)(5) requires the transaction to enable the creditor to receive more than such creditor would receive without the transaction in insolvency proceedings. This wording indicates that transactions to the benefit of another person put this person in a better position and, at the same time, deprive the estate of assets which, in opened insolvency proceedings, are missing for the satisfaction of the creditors' claims.[51] Vice versa, if the recipient is not put in a better position, the transaction is normally not detrimental to the general body of creditors.[52] In England and Wales, the Insolvency Act 1986 is silent on this matter. However, it is generally agreed   **6.23**

---

[45] See above (n 44).

[46] Cf. *Mottaz v Oswald (In re Frierdich)*, 294 F.3d 864 (7th Cir. 2002).

[47] See for an assignment of claims, *Cour de Cassation (chambre commerciale)*–6 June 2001–98-14355.

[48] In the following text, the terms 'detriment/detrimental' will be used as synonyms for 'disadvantage/disadvantageous' (see also Art. 7(2) lit. m, 16 of the European Insolvency Regulation (EIR)). However, this must not be misinterpreted as assigning transactions avoidance law to tort law!

[49] For § 8.1 of PEIL, see above (n 10).

[50] Cited above, at para. 6.19.

[51] Cf. *Abramson v St Regis Paper Co.*, 715 F.2d 934 (5th Cir. 1983); *Nat'l Bank of Newport v Nat'l Herkimer County Bank of Little Falls*, 225 US 178, 32 S. Ct 633, 56 L. Ed. 1042 (1912).

[52] See also 11 U.S.C. §550(a): the recovery must benefit the estate; cf. *Mellon Bank, NA v Dick Corp.*, 351 F.3d 290 (7th Cir. 2003).

168 TRANSACTIONS AVOIDANCE RULES

that transactions avoidance law is drafted in order to tackle acts detrimental to the general body of creditors.[53] Only in France is it not necessary to establish a disadvantage for the creditors, although Art. L. 632-4(2) of the *Code de Commerce* prescribes that the avoidance action shall result in reforming the debtor's assets.

6.24   However, 'disadvantage for the general body of creditors' is a rather fuzzy and indistinct term. Under the principle of predictability (legal certainty) it needs some concretization, if not in the wording of the statute then at least in explanatory notes. Some examples can illustrate what could be regarded as being disadvantageous for the general body of creditors and what cannot.

6.25   In this respect, it should be self-evident that transactions are covered which are directly disadvantageous because the counter-performance does not balance the debtor's value and does not constitute fair value. Where the debtor gives an asset as a gift or sells the asset for an unusually low price, this reduces the value of the estate and is therefore detrimental to the general body of creditors. The same holds true where a security right is granted subsequently for a hitherto unsecured claim.[54] Direct disadvantage can also be created by an increase of debts, since the fact that the up-to-now creditors have to shared the proceeds of the estate with an additional creditor reduces the dividend for all of them. Hence, such instant and immediate disadvantage is embraced without doubt.

6.26   Transactions by third parties can also be disadvantageous. For example, where a subsidiary pays the debts of the parent company, this is normally not disadvantageous for the general body of creditors because the subsidiary pays from its own estate. This is either gratuitous or merely entails a change of creditors (third party with a claim for reimbursement instead of the creditor with the satisfied claim). However, things can be different where the third party's claim for reimbursement is secured whilst the creditor's claim is not or where the debtor had a right to set-off against a creditor who is him- or herself insolvent, which is now thwarted by the third party's payment.

6.27   Further, it has to be discussed whether indirect disadvantages (i.e. detriments that do not have an immediate effect to the value of the debtor's estate but develop such an effect subsequently) can also be included. For example, where the debtor sells real estate against fair value and subsequently hides the money from his or her creditors or spends it bit by bit, this is detrimental to the general body of creditors because it is more difficult to detect and seize money than it is with real estate. Money is a transient asset; real estate is not. Although the nominal value of the estate has not been changed, the situation for the general body of creditors is less comfortable after the transaction than

---

[53] Cf. *Doyle v Saville* [2002] BPIR 947; *Rubin v Eurofinance SA* [2012] UKSC 46; Rebecca Parry and Sharif Shivji, 'Preferences (Insolvency Act 1986, sections 239 and 340)' in Rebecca Parry, James Ayliffe, and Sharif Shivji (eds), *Transactions Avoidance in Insolvencies* (3rd edn, Oxford University Press, Oxford 2018) paras 5.51 et seq.

[54] However, where the collateral is already encumbered with other security rights, the amount of which exceeds the value of the asset, granting a further security right for the same asset does not have an immediate disadvantageous effect. In the further course, though, a mediate detriment can occur; for example, where a creditor with a higher ranking security right is satisfied, the hitherto worthless security right rises in rank and is now perceptible for the general body of unsecured creditors.

it was before. The same holds true where the debtor buys shares of a listed company against stock exchange price and the shares depreciate afterwards. Another example is the change of ranks. Where the position of a creditor is changed from ordinary to preferential creditor, now ranking senior to his or her so far equal-ranking fellow creditors,[55] this is disadvantageous for the latter. One could argue that such indirect disadvantages seem to open the door to transactions avoidance too far. However, it has to be taken into account that avoidance grounds serve as a narrowing corrective, rendering most, albeit not all, indirect detriments unchallengeable.

Many examples can be given of performances that are not disadvantageous for the general body of creditors, the most important being the satisfaction of a secured claim. In this case, the detrimental act is the creation of the security right, which reduces the asset pool available for the unsecured creditors, not the payment of the secured claim to the creditor, since the reduction of the asset pool by paying the creditor is compensated by the collateral reverting to the estate unencumbered. The same holds true for the realization of an as such not challengeable security right through a sale of the encumbered asset. This is not a new disadvantage for the creditors but only the manifestation of the detriment already caused by creating the security right. This also holds true where a security right is given in exchange for an already existing security right for the same claim and with the same value. The same applies to the execution of a right to set-off, unless, of course, this right of set-off is challengeable itself. Not disadvantageous is the sale or encumbrance of valueless assets[56] or assets which are not part of the insolvency estate (e.g. because they are not seizable[57]), since such assets do not enhance the dividend for the creditors anyway. **6.28**

VI. Avoidance Grounds

The above-mentioned general prerequisites are not sufficient to narrow the scope of transactions avoidance law in an adequate manner; they alone cannot enforce the principle of protection of trust and protect the legitimate expectations of persons dealing with the (future) debtor that they can keep what they have received.[58] The task is therefore to define which expectations are legitimate and need protection against claw-back and **6.29**

---

[55] For example, in the German *Karstadt* case, the debtor had given a guarantee to the benefit of the owner of department stores that other group companies would rent these stores and pay the rent. Later on, in the vicinity of insolvency, owner and debtor agreed that the debtor should be the tenant with immediate effect. As a result, the owner had now a privileged claim (rents due after the opening of insolvency proceedings are privileged under German law as expenses of the proceedings) instead of an ordinary claim (guarantee), which was assessed as being disadvantageous for the general body of creditors by the German *Bundesgerichtshof* (26 April 2012–IX ZR 146/11, NZI 2012, 562).

[56] However, see n 54.

[57] In some jurisdictions, unseizable assets are exempted from the debtor's insolvency estate in order to protect the debtor. Where the debtor disposes of such assets, which would not be included in the estate after the opening of insolvency proceedings, no harm to the general body of creditors is done, since the creditors could not take hold of these assets anyway, either in individual or in collective enforcement proceedings.

[58] Cf. above, at paras 6.06 and 6.09.

170 TRANSACTIONS AVOIDANCE RULES

which are not. National laws typically do this by establishing certain avoidance grounds, i.e. rules which put transactions avoidance under additional prerequisites in order to balance the principles of optimal satisfaction of the debtor's claims and of protection of trust. Typical avoidance grounds, available in most jurisdictions, tie on the granting of (a) preferences, (b) transactions at an undervalue, and (c) intentionally fraudulent transactions.[59]

6.30 Most jurisdictions alleviate the conditions for transactions avoidance where the opponent is a closely related party.[60] If persons who benefited from the transaction are closely connected with the debtor, it can be presumed that they knew of the debtor's financial difficulties and used this insider knowledge to feather their own nest. Insolvency laws are therefore sceptical about closely related parties and react by prolonging suspect periods or by shifting the burden of proof regarding the debtor's insolvency or required mental elements to the defendant. Typical addressees of such rules are (where the debtor is a natural person) spouses, partners, relatives, or housemates and (where the debtor is a legal entity) directors, shareholders (at least, shareholders with a significant influence), and contractual partners with special insight into the debtor company's financial affairs. Details are regulated in England and Wales in sss 249 and 435 of the Insolvency Act 1986, in Germany in § 138 of the *Insolvenzordnung*, and in the United States in 11 U.S.C. §101(31). In France, no insider rules are available in transactions avoidance law.

A. Preferences

6.31 Preferences can be defined as performances to the benefit of a creditor who, as a result of this performance, is better off compared to other creditors than he or she would otherwise have been.[61] Preferences are, by definition, transactions to the benefit of creditors only; transactions to third parties (e.g. a gift to a spouse) are not included. Transactions

---

[59] See also UNCITRAL, *Legislative Guide to Insolvency Law* (n 9) 141 paras 170 et seq. (with Recommendation 87) and § 8.2 of PEIL (n 10):

Juridical acts subject to reversal include:

a) A transaction with the intent of defrauding creditors;
b) A transaction for inadequate countervalue;
c) A transaction with a creditor for which no enforceable obligation existed;
d) A transaction with a creditor after the filing of the insolvency application or in a situation of imminent insolvency;
e) The creation of a security right to secure a pre-existing obligation.

[60] Cf. UNCITRAL, *Legislative Guide to Insolvency Law* (n 8) 145 paras 182 et seq. with Recommendations 90 et seq.; Bork and Veder, *Harmonisation of Transaction Avoidance Laws* (n 11) paras 4.200 et seq.

[61] See also s. 239(4) of the Insolvency Act 1986 (England and Wales):

For the purposes of this section and section 241, a company gives a preference to a person if

(a) that person is one of the company's creditors or a surety or guarantor for any of the company's debts or other liabilities, and
(b) the company does anything or suffers anything to be done which (in either case) has the effect of putting that person into a position which, in the event of the company going into insolvent liquidation, will be better than the position he would have been in if that thing had not been done.

in favour of creditors are preferences if these creditors receive a better treatment than they would have received in insolvency proceedings without the performance. A typical example is a payment to a creditor in the vicinity of insolvency proceedings. By this payment, the creditor's claim is fully satisfied, whereas in insolvency proceedings, the creditor, would he or she not have received the payment, would only be entitled to a pro rata distribution. Hence, by receiving the payment, the recipient is preferred to other creditors who were in the same position before the payment and who do not get full satisfaction of their claims. It follows from this that the underlying tenet of the avoidance of preferences is the principle of equal treatment of creditors. Without the payment, all creditors—including the recipient—would be paid the same share of their claims and would be satisfied on a pro rata basis according to the *pari passu* principle. Where insolvency laws allow explicitly for the avoidance of preferences, they undertake to enforce this principle of equal treatment of creditors by preponing its application to a certain time period prior to the opening of insolvency proceedings.[62]

6.32 However, recognizing the adverse need for protection of legitimate expectations under the principle of protection of trust, avoidance of preferences is typically bound to additional prerequisites. Such protection of trust can be granted in various ways. First, means are *suspect periods*, requiring the preference to be performed within a certain time span (e.g. three months or one year) prior to the application for insolvency proceedings, leaving all transactions outside this time span unchallengeable. A second typical requirement is the *substantive insolvency* of the debtor at the point in time when the transaction was performed, which is reasonable, since the principle of equal treatment of creditors is a principle of insolvency law[63] and is only applicable where the debtor is insolvent. Protection of trust can further be granted by the requirement of *mental elements* (subjective prerequisites, such as knowledge of the creditor of the debtor's substantive insolvency or good faith as a defence). We will see below[64] that nearly all transactions avoidance laws use these means singly or conjunctly.

6.33 Even if all these objective and subjective prerequisites are met, national laws provide for exceptions from the avoidance of certain preferences. Typical appearances of such exceptions are transactions that are part of a contemporaneous exchange for adequate new value, transactions in the ordinary course of business,[65] and transactions in the context of a serious restructuring attempt.

6.34 Taking a closer look to the rules on preferences in national insolvency laws,[66] communalities and differences become visible. To begin with, in England and Wales, s. 239 of

---

[62] *Canright v General Finance Corp.*, 35 F. Supp. 841 (E.D. Ill. 1940). For details, see the Conference on European Restructuring and Insolvency Law (CERIL) Report 2017-1 on Transactions Avoidance Laws: 'Clash of Principles: Equal Treatment of Creditors vs. Protection of Trust' (2017) <https://www.ceril.eu/news/ceril-statement-2017-1-on-transactions-avoidance-laws> accessed 10 January 2024.

[63] See above, at para. 6.08.

[64] At paras 6.34 et seq.

[65] For them, cf. UNCITRAL, *Legislative Guide to Insolvency Law* (n 9) 140 paras 164 et seq.

[66] Cf. also ibid 143 paras 177 et seq.; Bork and Veder, *Harmonisation of Transaction Avoidance Laws* (n 11) paras 4.55 et seq.

172 TRANSACTIONS AVOIDANCE RULES

the Insolvency Act 1986 allows for the avoidance of preferences under several conditions.[67] First, the term 'preference' is defined very broadly in s. 239(4) of the Insolvency Act 1986, which states that

> a company gives a preference to a person if (a) that person is one of the company's creditors or a surety or a guarantor for any of the company's debts or other liabilities, and (b) the company does anything or suffers anything to be done which (in either case) has the effect of putting that person into a position which, in the event of the company going into insolvent liquidation, will be better than the position he would have been in if that thing had not be done.

Second, the transaction must be performed within a suspect period, which is six months prior to the opening of insolvency proceedings (ss 240(1)(b) and 341(1)(c) of the Insolvency Act 1986). Third, ss 240(2) and 341(2) of the Insolvency Act 1986 require the debtor's inability to pay debts[68] at the point in time when the preference was given. The fourth prerequisite is a mental element: the debtor's decision to grant the preference must be influenced by a desire to put the creditor in a better position (ss 239(5) and 340(4) of the Insolvency Act 1986). If the recipient is closely connected to the debtor, the suspect period is two years (ss 240(1)(a) and 341(1)(b) of the Insolvency Act 1986) and the debtor's desire is presumed (ss 239(6) and 340(5) of the Insolvency Act 1986). The creditor's knowledge or intent is irrelevant. Although there is no general exception for transactions performed in the ordinary course of business, the exchange of assets against cash payments or other new-value transactions are not challengeable if they can be judged as not being detrimental to the general body of creditors.[69] Transactions made as a means of saving the debtor's business are assumed to be performed without the required intent.[70] In such cases, the court may also refuse to make a repayment order (or make a validation order).[71]

6.35 German insolvency law addresses preferences in §§ 130 and 131 of the *Insolvenzordnung*. These rules distinguish between 'congruent' and 'incongruent coverages'. According to § 131(1) of the *Insolvenzordnung*, a transaction granting or facilitating a security or satisfaction to a creditor is incongruent if the creditor had no entitlement to such security or satisfaction or to the kind, or date, of such security or satisfaction. In both cases, the suspect period is three months prior to the application for insolvency proceedings (or after such application but before the opening of proceedings). Congruent coverages are only voidable if the debtor was substantively insolvent at the point in time when

---

[67] For an example, see *Darty Holdings SAS (as successor to Kesa International Ltd) v Carton-Kelly as Liquidator of CGL Realisations Ltd (in liquidation)* [2021] EWHC 1018 (Ch).

[68] In bankruptcy proceedings, overindebtedness is sufficient (s. 341(3)(b) of the Insolvency Act 1986).

[69] *Re Fairway Magazines Ltd* [1992] BCC 924; *Re Ledingham-Smith* [1993] BCLC 635; Parry and Shivji, 'Preferences (Insolvency Act 1986, Sections 239 and 340)' (n 53) paras 5.67 et seq. See also *Express Electrical Contractors Ltd v Beavis* [2016] EWCA Civ. 765.

[70] *Re Lewis of Leicester Ltd* [1995] BCC 514; Parry and Shivji, 'Preferences (Insolvency Act 1986, Sections 239 and 340)' (n 53) paras 5.107 et seq.

[71] See for the legal consequences, below, at para. 6.58.

AVOIDANCE GROUNDS **173**

the transaction was made, and a further (subjective) prerequisite is the knowledge of the creditor of the debtor's inability to pay debts (§ 130(1) of the *Insolvenzordnung*). If the creditor is a closely related person, this knowledge is rebuttably presumed (§ 130(3) of the *Insolvenzordnung*). For incongruent coverages, there are no subjective requirements. The only additional prerequisite is the debtor's inability to pay debts; if the payment has been made during the last month before (or after) the application for insolvency proceedings, even this is not necessary (§ 131(1) of the *Insolvenzordnung*); it then suffices that the transaction was incongruent. An exception in the context of restructuring attempts is available for performances carrying out a court-confirmed restructuring plan,[72] and § 142 of the *Insolvenzordnung* exempts congruent coverages from the avoidance rule in § 130 of the *Insolvenzordnung*[73] if the debtor instantaneously received an equitable consideration (so-called '*Bargeschäft*').

In the United States, preferences are dealt with in 11 U.S.C. §547. The rule defines pref- **6.36** erences as any transfer of an interest of the debtor in property to or for the benefit of a creditor, for or on account of an antecedent debt owed by the debtor before such transfer was made, that enables such creditor to receive more (not earlier) than such creditor would receive otherwise (11 U.S.C. § 547(b)(1)/(2)/(5)). It is required that the transaction was made while the debtor was insolvent (i.e. overindebted within the meaning of 11 U.S.C. §101(32)), which is rebuttably presumed (11 U.S.C. §547(b)(3)/(f)).[74] The suspect period is 90 days before the filing of the petition, one year for insiders (11 U.S.C. §547(b)(4)).[75] Mental elements are not required. However, US law provides for many exceptions in 11 U.S.C. §547(c). Particularly, transactions made against contemporaneous or subsequent exchange of new value (11 U.S.C. §§547(c)(1)/(4)/(a)(2) and 549(b)), made in the ordinary course of business (11 U.S.C. §547(c)(2)), or of minor value ($600 in consumer and $6,425 in non-consumer cases, 11 U.S.C. §547(c)(8)/(9)) are not challengeable.

The system is different in France. French insolvency law has no special rule for prefer- **6.37** ences. Instead, Art. L. 632-1(1) of the *Code de Commerce* lists—quite straightforwardly— certain types of transactions and declares them generally void, provided the debtor had ceased payments. Generally speaking, the transactions listed in Art. L. 632-1(1) of the *Code de Commerce* appear to concern unusual legal acts. As far as preferences are concerned, particularly the numbers 3 (payments on non-mature debts), 4 (payments through unusual payment means) and 6 and 9 (granting securities for as yet unsecured debts)[76] from this list are important.[77] The only additional prerequisite for these types

---

[72] See § 90 of the Act on the Framework for Stabilisation and Restructuring of Enterprises (*Gesetz über den Stabilisierungs- und Restrukturierungsrahmen für Unternehmen*, StaRUG).

[73] However, avoidance as an intentionally fraudulent transaction (§ 133 of the *Insolvenzordnung*) remains possible.

[74] Cf. *In re Imagine Fulfillment Services, LLC* 489 BR 136, 144 et seq. (Bankr. CD Cal. 2013).

[75] This insider-rule is safeguarded by 11 U.S.C. §550(c).

[76] Numbers 1 and 2 concern transactions at an undervalue; cf. below, at para. 6.43.

[77] They all would be deemed 'incongruent' under German law, cf. above, at para. 6.35.

174 TRANSACTIONS AVOIDANCE RULES

of transactions is that they have occurred since the date of the cessation of payments[78] (which refers to Art. L. 631-8 of the *Code de Commerce*, according to which the court shall state the day the debtor ceased payments, without going back more than eighteen months before the opening decision). Other payments (i.e. payments on mature debts and payments made in exchange for valuable consideration) appear to be made in a normal way of business. They are—at the discretion of the court—only voidable if the debtor's counterparty knew of the cessation of payments (Art. L. 632-2 of the *Code de Commerce*).

6.38   In summary, it can be said that the four jurisdictions evaluated here have rules on preferences. All are sceptical for transactions benefiting creditors in the vicinity of insolvency proceedings, particularly unusual performances ('incongruent coverages'); all require the substantive insolvency of the debtor; and all provide for a suspect period, albeit with different length: 3 months in Germany and the United States, 6 months in England and Wales (but 2 years if the opponent is a closely related party), and up to 18 months in France. Only with respect to mental elements does a colourful picture become apparent: German insolvency law requires the creditor's knowledge of the debtor's insolvency, albeit only for 'congruent coverages'. A similar rule can be found in France. The law of England and Wales requires the debtor's desire to put the creditor in a better position, and US law on preferences has no subjective prerequisites at all. As regards exceptions, transactions for new value are protected in England and Wales, Germany, and the United States, but in France only if the creditor acted in good faith. A special exception for transactions made in the ordinary course of business (other than such for new value) is only available in the United States. Alleviations as it concerns proving the applicability of the transaction avoidance provisions with respect to closely connected parties are contained in English, German, and US law but not in French law.

6.39   Hence, where a supplier who refuses to deliver goods urgently needed for the continuation of the debtor's business unless outstanding debts are paid receives satisfaction for his or her outstanding claims after the application for insolvency proceedings, the payment can be successfully challenged as a preference in England and Wales under ss 239 and 240 of the Insolvency Act 1986. However, this only holds true if the court is convinced that the debtor did act with the necessary desire to put the supplier in a better position, given that the debtor paid old debts in order to get new deliveries. Under French law, all depends on the supplier's knowledge of the debtor's cessation of payments (Art. L. 632-2 of the *Code de Commerce*). Also, in Germany, the supplier has to pay the money back, provided he or she knew of the debtor's inability to pay debts or of the insolvency application (§ 130 of the *Insolvenzordnung*). The *'Bargeschäft'*-exception of § 142 of the *Insolvenzordnung* cannot be applied, since the debtor paid outstanding debts, not the purchase price for new deliveries. The same results are likely in the United States, since it is not in the ordinary course of business (11 U.S.C. §547(c)(2)) if an outstanding debt is paid after the application for insolvency proceedings.

---

[78]   This term is defined as 'being unable to pay its accrued liabilities with it's quick assets' (Art. L. 631-1(1)(1) of the *Code de Commerce*).

B. Transactions at an Undervalue

Legislators are also sceptical of transactions at an undervalue,[79] which can be defined as 'performances to the benefit of the opponent which result in a reduction of assets without (or with no compensating) counter-performance'. The policy behind this avoidance ground is not the principle of equal treatment of creditors, since the recipient of (for instance) a gift is not necessarily a creditor. It also does not aim to prevent the debtor from being generous to the detriment of their creditors,[80] since gifts are not suspicious as such and are not an appearance of fraudulent behaviour.[81] Rules on transactions at an undervalue are rather based on the conviction that someone who has received a performance without consideration is not—or not in the same way as a person who granted a compensating counter-performance—worthy of protection of trust. Hence, the limitations for the avoidance of gratuitous transactions are less strict compared to the avoidance of preferences. Typically, suspect periods are longer, and neither insolvency of the debtor nor mental elements are required.

6.40

A decisive point is the definition of 'undervalue'. There is no dissent that gifts are captured by these avoidance rules, albeit typically with an exception for conventional gifts of minor value, such as birthday gifts or donations to charities, churches, or political parties. However, (partly) gratuitous are also mutual transactions if the value of the debtor's performance significantly exceeds the counter-performance of the opponent, that is more than a reasonable assessment of market value would judge as exchange for fair value. Notwithstanding a margin of discretion, a transaction against an unusually low compensation should be deemed gratuitous.

6.41

In England and Wales,[82] ss 238(4) and, 339(3) of the Insolvency Act 1986 define transactions at an undervalue as such without any consideration or with a consideration the value of which is significantly less than the value of the transaction provided by the debtor company. Transactions at an undervalue are voidable if they were entered into by the debtor within a suspect period of two years prior to the commencement of insolvency proceedings (ss 238(2) and 240(1)(a) of the Insolvency Act 1986), in bankruptcies five years prior to the commencement of the proceedings (s. 341(1) of the Insolvency Act 1986). Surprisingly, there is not only the requirement of substantive insolvency of the debtor (s. 240(2) of the Insolvency Act 1986)[83] but also the opponent's

6.42

---

[79] Cf. also UNCITRAL, *Legislative Guide to Insolvency Law* (n 9) 143 paras 174 et seq.; Bork and Veder, *Harmonisation of Transaction Avoidance Laws* (n 11) paras 4.136 et seq.

[80] However, it is frequently stated that the requirement for debtors is to 'be just before you are generous', that is 'pay your creditors from the assets with which you are liable for your debts before you make gifts'; cf. Robert C. Clark, 'The Duties of the Corporate Debtor to Its Creditors', Harvard Law Review, 90 (1976/77) 505, 510. See also, for Germany, BGH, 27 June 2019–IX ZR 167/18 = BGHZ 222, 283 = NJW 2019, 2923; BGH, 18 July 2018–IX ZR 307/16 = NZI 2018, 80.

[81] See differently US law and partly the law of England and Wales; cf. below, at paras 6.42 and 6.45.

[82] A comparison between English and German law is given by Reinhard Bork, 'Transactions at an Undervalue', Journal of Corporate Law Studies 14 (2014) 453–77.

[83] Substantive insolvency is rebuttably presumed if the opponent is a party closely connected to the debtor (s. 240(2) of the Insolvency Act 1986); see for this, above at para. 6.30. In bankruptcies, substantive insolvency is only

176 TRANSACTIONS AVOIDANCE RULES

defence that the debtor acted in good faith and for the purpose of carrying on business, provided there were reasonable grounds for believing that the transaction would benefit the company (s. 238(5) of the Insolvency Act 1986).[84] Note, however, that transactions at an undervalue can also be challenged as intentionally fraudulent transactions under s. 423 of the Insolvency Act 1986.[85] In all cases, an exception for conventional gifts is not available.

6.43 France enables the avoidance of transactions at an undervalue under the same conditions as for the avoidance of preferences.[86] According to Art. L. 632-1(1) Nos 1 and 2 of the *Code de Commerce*, transactions of the debtor are void upon the opening of insolvency proceedings if they were performed against no consideration (No. 1) or if the debtor's obligations significantly exceeded those of the other party (No. 2), provided that they were performed during the cessation-of-payments period fixed by the court. Hence, insolvency of the debtor is necessary. However, it is at the discretion of the court to prolong this suspect period for a maximum of six months if there was no consideration at all (Art. L. 632-1(2) of the *Code de Commerce*). In all cases, mental elements are not required, and exceptions for conventional gifts are not available.

6.44 In Germany, transactions at an undervalue are challengeable under § 134 of the *Insolvenzordnung*. This norm is quite straightforward. Nothing more is required than a gratuitous performance (which is not specified in the statute but construed in the sense explained above at para. 6.41) by the debtor in the suspect period of four years prior to the application for insolvency proceedings. It is not relevant whether the debtor was substantively insolvent when the transaction was performed, and neither intent of the debtor nor knowledge of the beneficiary is necessary. 'Usual casual gifts of minor value'[87] are exempted from transactions avoidance by § 134(2) of the *Insolvenzordnung*.

6.45 Quite differently, US law classifies transactions at an undervalue under certain prerequisites as fraudulent transactions (11 U.S.C. §548(a)(1)(B)). Since there are no subjective requirements, these cases are labelled 'constructive fraud'.[88] Fraudulent in this sense are transactions of the debtor performed within two years prior to the commencement of insolvency proceedings (11 U.S.C. §548(a)(1)), provided that the debtor received no reasonable consideration (11 U.S.C. §548(a)(1)(B)(i))[89] and (a) was substantively insolvent,[90] (b) was left with unreasonably small

---

required if the transaction was performed not less than two years prior to the commencement of the proceedings (ibid s. 341(2)).

[84] In bankruptcies, no such defence is possible, which means that mental elements are of no importance.
[85] See below, at para. 6.49.
[86] Cf. above, at para. 6.37.
[87] According to case law, the limit is 200 € per gift and 500 € per year for the same recipient, cf. BGH, 4 February 2016–IX ZR 77/15 = NJW 2016, 2412.
[88] As opposed to 'actual fraud', cf. below, at para. 6.52.
[89] This is sometimes seen very harshly; cf. *DeGiacomo v Sacred Heart Univ., Inc. (In re Palladino)*, 942 F.3d 55 (1st Cir. 2019), where the court held that payment of college tuition for an adult child was a constructive fraudulent transfer because the payment 'depleted the estate and furnished nothing of direct value to the creditors who are the central concern of the code provisions at issue'.
[90] Which, in the United States, means overindebtedness, cf. above, at para. 6.36.

capital,[91] (c) intended to incur debts beyond the debtor's ability to pay when due,[92] or (d) made the transaction with an insider under an employment contract and not in the ordinary course of business (11 U.S.C. §548(a)(1)(B)(ii)). Charitable contributions— yet not conventional gifts—are exempted by 11 U.S.C. § 548(a)(2). Note, however, that fraudulent conveyances are also voidable under state laws.[93]

In sum, all national insolvency laws covered here enable the tackling of transactions at   **6.46** an undervalue by the debtor and all include in this term not only gifts but also trans- actions against no adequate consideration. Suspect periods are quite long: two years in the United States, England and Wales for insolvencies, and (at the utmost) France, four years in Germany, and five years in England and Wales for bankruptcies. Substantive insolvency is required in England and Wales as well as in France, to some extent in the United States, and not in Germany. Most jurisdictions refrain from subjective prerequisites, England and Wales being the only exception where the defence of the debtor's good faith is granted.

Conventional gifts are exempted in Germany, charitable contributions in the United   **6.47** States. Hence, where the debtor presents a precious birthday gift to his wife and be- comes bankrupt 30 months later, this can only be challenged in Germany, where the mere transaction at an undervalue suffices and the exception for usual casual gifts does not apply, since the gift is not of minor value. In France and the United States, the trans- action was outside the relevant suspect period. Further, the debtor was not substan- tively insolvent when presenting the gift, which is necessary in England and Wales, France, and the United States. Subjective prerequisites are not applicable, since they are only relevant in England and Wales and in corporate insolvencies only (s. 238(5) of the Insolvency Act 1986), not in personal bankruptcies (cf. ss 338 and 341 of the Insolvency Act 1986).

C. Internationally Fraudulent Transactions

A third group of voidable performances are intentionally fraudulent transactions,[94]   **6.48** roughly defined as 'any act performed with the (as the case may be: implied) intent to disadvantage the general body of creditors (or similar mental elements, such as know- ledge)'. This type is the modern form of the *actio Pauliana*,[95] the appearance of which can be established in nearly all jurisdictions. However, rules on defrauding creditors are not, or not exclusively, included in insolvency law in many national laws but also

---

[91] This is the case where the debtor is 'technically solvent but doomed to fail'; cf. *MFS/Sun Life Tr.-High Yield Series v Van Dusen Airport Servs Co.*, 910 F. Supp. 913, 944 (SDNY 1995).

[92] This is seen as an appearance of inability to pay debts: *Burtch v Opus LLC (In re Opus East LLC)*, 698 Fed. Appx. 711 (3d Cir. 2017).

[93] See for details, below, at para. 6.52.

[94] See also UNCITRAL, *Legislative Guide to Insolvency Law* (n 9) 142 paras 172 et seq.; Bork and Veder, *Harmonisation of Transaction Avoidance Laws* (n 11) paras 4.155 et seq.

[95] Cf. above, at para. 6.04.

178 TRANSACTIONS AVOIDANCE RULES

in general civil law, which raises the question as to whether they can be enforced by the insolvency practitioner. *Actio Pauliana*-type rules are typically marked by intensive mental elements, long suspect periods, and little objective criteria. However, wording and location of the relevant rules vary from country to country.

6.49 For example, in England and Wales, s. 423 of the Insolvency Act 1986, which applies to insolvencies as well as bankruptcies, allows for the avoidance of transactions defrauding creditors, albeit with significant restrictions.[96] First, it is only applicable to transactions at an undervalue (s. 432(1) of the Insolvency Act 1986), which narrows the scope of the rule considerably.[97] Second, although there is no suspect period,[98] and the debtor need not to be substantively insolvent, there must be a 'victim' of the transaction under s. 423 of the Insolvency Act 1986, and creditors will not be victims if the debtor company can, nevertheless, pay all creditors in full at the point in time when the transaction was performed. Further, the debtor is required to act for the purpose of putting assets beyond the reach of—or otherwise prejudicing—current or future creditors (s. 423(3) of the Insolvency Act 1986).[99] As regards standing, the avoidance can be enforced by the insolvency practitioner or a creditor disadvantaged by the transaction (s. 424(1)(a) of the Insolvency Act 1986). In the latter case, the creditor acts on behalf of all prejudiced creditors (s. 424(2) of the Insolvency Act 1986), which is no incentive to pursue this. The burden of proof for all prerequisites is with the claimant, even where closely related parties are involved.

6.50 France has no rule on transactions defrauding creditors in its insolvency law. As reported above,[100] purpose or intent on the debtor's side is generally irrelevant. Only knowledge of the opponent authorises the court to set aside transactions not voidable by force of law (Art. L. 632(1) of the *Code de Commerce*). However, Art. 1167 of the French *Code de Civil* enables a creditor to challenge fraudulent actions entailing personal damage for this creditor. There is no hardening period, and special knowledge of the counterparty is not required. In insolvency proceedings, this claim can be enforced by the insolvency practitioner.

6.51 Under German law, fraudulent transactions can be challenged under § 133 of the *Insolvenzordnung*. All acts of the debtor disadvantageous for the general body of creditors and granted within ten years (or four years in the case of congruent or incongruent coverages) prior to (or after) the application for insolvency proceedings can be avoided if the debtor acted in bad faith (i.e. with the intent to disadvantage the general body of creditors) and the opponent knew of this intention. Substantive insolvency

---

[96] For an example, see *BTI 2014 LLC v Sequana SA and ors* [2022] UKSC 25; *BTI 2014 LLC v Sequana SA and ors* [2019] EWCA Civ. 112; on the latter, see Reinhard Bork, 'Sequana I: Struggling with Section 423 of the Insolvency Act 1986', International Insolvency Review, 31(1) (2022) 8 et seq.

[97] For example, payments on existing claims can never be tackled as a transaction defrauding creditors.

[98] Only general limitation periods apply.

[99] Cf. *Domco SICA Ltd and ors v SBL Carston Ltd and ors* [2021] EWHC 3209 (Ch); *Hinton (as Trustee in Bankruptcy of John Wotherspoon) v Gillian Wotherspoon* [2022] EWHC 2083 (Ch); *The Deposit Guarantee Fund for Individuals (as liquidator of National Credit Bank PJSC) v Bank Frick & Co. AG* [2022] EWHC 2221 (Ch).

[100] At paras 6.37 and 6.43.

of the debtor is not required. However, since this rule is dominantly characterized by mental elements, which are difficult to prove, the German *Bundesgerichtshof* has found a wide range of circumstantial evidence. Especially if the debtor knew that he or she was (at least imminent) insolvent, the subjective requirements are indicated provided the debtor knew or at least accepted that he or she would also not be able to fully satisfy the (other) creditors at a later date.[101] It is then for the opponent to prove that the debtor acted in good faith or that the debtor's intent was unknown to him or her. In addition, § 133(4) of the *Insolvenzordnung* presumes the mental elements for closely related parties if an exchange contract causes an immediate disadvantage for the general body of creditors, a rule that covers not only disadvantageous contracts but also payments.

In the United States, fraudulent transfers and obligations are covered by 11 U.S.C. § 548, provided they are made by the debtor within two years prior to the commencement of insolvency proceedings. This rule, which covers all transactions,[102] distinguishes between actual fraud and constructive fraud. 'Actual fraud' is given where the debtor acted with the actual, subjective intent to hinder, delay, or defraud current or future creditors (11 U.S.C. §538(a)(1)(A)). Although statute is silent on this matter, such intent can be indicated by the opponent's close relationship to the debtor.[103] 'Constructive fraud' means that this intent is irrebuttably presumed for transactions at an undervalue where certain additional prerequisites, particularly substantive insolvency of the debtor, are met (11 U.S.C. §548(a)(1)(B)).[104] For actual fraud, substantive insolvency of the debtor is not required, yet grants circumstantial evidence for the debtor's intent.[105] In addition, fraudulent conveyances can also be tackled by the insolvency practitioner if an unsecured creditor is entitled to do so under State law[106] (11 U.S.C. §544(b)). **6.52**

Summing up, all jurisdictions explored here have rules on transactions defrauding creditors. They can mostly be found in insolvency law, but in some countries they are additionally (United States) or exclusively (France) implemented in general civil law. With the exception of England and Wales (transactions at an undervalue only), all transactions are covered, and substantive insolvency of the debtor is not required. Suspect periods are either rather long (ten/four years in Germany, two years in the United States) or not provided for at all (England and Wales, France, in the United States according to State law). The decisive prerequisite is the debtor's purpose or intent to prejudice creditors (England and Wales, Germany, United States, not explicitly in France), the proof of such mental elements being sometimes alleviated where closely connected parties are involved (Germany, the United States). Entitled to enforce the **6.53**

---

[101] The leading case is BGH, Urt. v. 6 May 2021–IX ZR 72/20 = BGHZ 230, 28.
[102] For some important exceptions, see 11 U.S.C. §548(a)(2)/(c).
[103] *Reade v Livingston*, 8 Am. Dec. 520 (NY Ch. 1818).
[104] For details, see above, at para. 6.45.
[105] See, for the 'badges of fraud', s. 4(b)(9) of the Uniform Voidable Transactions Act and *Liquidation Trust of Hechinger Inv. Co. of Delaware v Fleet Retail Finance Group (In re Hechinger Inv. Co. of Delaware)*, 327 BR 537 (D Del. 2005); *United States v Theall*, 609 Fed. Appx. 807 (5th Cir. 2015).
[106] States laws cannot be explained in detail here. However, it should be mentioned that no suspect periods but only general limitation periods apply.

180 TRANSACTIONS AVOIDANCE RULES

avoidance rules is the insolvency practitioner (all jurisdictions), in some countries with a concurrent standing of every disadvantaged creditor (England and Wales, France, the United States).

6.54 Differences can be highlighted when it comes to challenging payments to existing creditors as transactions defrauding creditors. For example, let it be given that a heavily insolvent debtor pays a creditor who knows of the debtor's insolvency and puts significant pressure on the debtor to receive performance. One year later, insolvency proceedings are opened against the debtor. Challenging the payment will be fruitless in England and Wales, since it was not a transaction at an undervalue (as required in s. 423 of the Insolvency Act 1986) and cannot be challenged as a preference because it was performed outside the suspect period.[107] In France, the payment can be tackled as a preference (Art. L. 632-2 of the *Code de Commerce*).[108] The insolvency practitioner will also succeed in Germany, where the mutual knowledge of the debtor's substantive insolvency is assessed as circumstantial evidence for the subjective prerequisites[109] as required in § 133 of the *Insolvenzordnung*. Under US law, the payment can be challenged as 'actual fraud' under 11 U.S.C. §548(a)(1)(A).

D. Others

6.55 The typical avoidance grounds described here are frequently accompanied by further rules that either modify or supplement the basic norms for special situations.[110] For example, the law on preferences is sometimes altered for payments on cheques,[111] the law on intentionally fraudulent transactions for extortionate credit transactions.[112]

6.56 Most jurisdictions class the creation of security rights as voidable transactions,[113] and some even have special norms for avoiding such rights.[114] For example, in England and Wales, s. 245 of the Insolvency Act 1986 intervenes into the law of credit securities and directly voids (and thereby spares the office-holder the trouble of challenging) 'late floating charges' insofar as they exceed the value of a simultaneously or subsequently rendered counter-performance (a line of credit, delivery of goods, performance of services) over which the debtor had free disposal (s. 245(2)/(6) of the Insolvency Act

---

[107] Cf. above, at para. 6.34.

[108] See above, at para. 6.37.

[109] References above (n 101).

[110] Cf. Bork and Veder, *Harmonisation of Transaction Avoidance Laws* (n 11) paras 4.179 et seq.

[111] See, for France, Art. L. 632-3 of the *Code de Commerce*, for Germany § 137 of the *Insolvenzordnung*.

[112] An example is s. 244 of the Insolvency Act 1986. According to this norm, the insolvency practitioner may apply to the court to adjust or set aside the terms of an extortionate credit arrangement that was concluded within the three years leading up to the insolvency proceedings. Section 244(3) of the Insolvency Act 1986 defines credit as extortionate if it demands vastly exorbitant payments from the debtor relative to the amount of risk taken on by the creditor or in some other way represents a gross violation of the principles of fair dealing.

[113] See also UNCITRAL, *Legislative Guide to Insolvency Law* (n 9) 145 paras 180 et seq. with Recommendation 88; see further, Gerard McCormack and Reinhard Bork (eds), *Security Rights and the European Insolvency Regulation* (Intersentia, Cambridge/Antwerp/Portland 2017) ch. 4, 121 paras 367 et seq.

[114] Cf. 11 U.S.C. §545(3)/(4), which enables the insolvency practitioner to challenge statutory landlords' liens.

1986).[115] The charge must have been issued in the year leading up to the opening of insolvency proceedings (s. 245(3)(b)/(5) of the Insolvency Act 1986), and the company must have been unable to pay its debts or rendered so by the issuance of the security (s. 245(4) of the Insolvency Act 1986). If the security-holder is a closely connected person, the relevant time is two years (s. 245(3)(a)/(5) of the Insolvency Act 1986), and there is no requirement that the company must be unable to pay its debts (arguably s. 245(4) of the Insolvency Act 1986). In addition, s. 874 of the Companies Act 2006 declares certain securities, such as floating charges, void against the estate if the registration requirements of s. 859A of the Companies Act 2006 are not met. Similar rules can be found in 11 U.S.C. §§544(a), 545(2), 547(e), 548(d). The reason for such rules is that unregistered security rights can be set aside by a bona fide purchaser and that creditors who were not aware of the 'secret charge' might have given credit which they would not have given had they known of the charge.

A special case are shareholder loans.[116] Payments to shareholders (e.g. distribution of **6.57** profits) can be void if they lack the necessary basis in company law, for example a resolution of the shareholders' meeting.[117] In these cases, they can be rescinded as unjust enrichment as well as transactions at an undervalue.[118] Shareholder loans are a different matter. Shareholders tend to finance their company with loans instead of equity capital, expecting a return of the loan in full (in good times) or at least on a pro rata basis (if the company is insolvent). It can frequently be observed that such loans are— suspiciously[119]—paid back in the vicinity of insolvency. Reacting to this phenomenon, transactions of the debtor company made with regard to shareholder loans can be challenged in Germany under § 135 of the *Insolvenzordnung* without further requirements if (a) the debtor is a company that does not have a natural person as a general partner and neither does it have a general partner which is a company that has a natural person as its own general partner and (b) performance was rendered no more than one year (for the granting of security rights over collateral ten years) prior to the insolvency application. Compared to the regular rule on 'congruent coverages',[120] neither substantive insolvency of the debtor nor mental elements of the parties are required, and the suspect period is significantly longer (one year or ten years instead of three months). Similar rules can be found, albeit sometimes in company law, in the laws of Austria, Croatia, Italy, and Portugal. In Slovakia, all payments of dividends to shareholders can be contested unless the company has fully satisfied all registered unsecured claims. US law provides for the avoidance of transactions benefiting the general partner of an insolvent partnership[121] (11 U.S.C. §548(b)). However, such rules are rare. In the end,

---

[115] See *Crumpler and anor (liquidators of Peak Hotels and Resorts Ltd) v Candey Ltd* [2019] EWCA Civ. 345.
[116] Cf. Bork and Veder, *Harmonisation of Transaction Avoidance Laws* (n 11) paras 4.180, 4.182 et seq.
[117] For an example, see *Burnden Holdings (UK) Ltd v Fielding* [2019] EWHC 1566 (Ch).
[118] *BTI 2014 LLC v Sequana SA and ors* (n 96).
[119] It is presumed that the shareholders took advantage of their insider knowledge of the company's financial crisis; cf. *Berisford, Inc. v Stroock & Stroock & Lavan (In re 1634 Assocs)*, 157 BR 231 (Bankr. SDNY 1993).
[120] Cf. above, at para. 6.35.
[121] As opposed to corporations, see *Jacobs v Altorelli (In re Dewey & LeBoeuf LLP)*, 518 BR 766 (Bankr. SDNY 2014).

182 TRANSACTIONS AVOIDANCE RULES

they are special appearances on rules on preferences which account to the fact that shareholders are less worthy of being protected against transactions avoidance than ordinary creditors. Most jurisdictions are satisfied without such special rules and restrict themselves to treating (influential) shareholders as closely related parties.[122]

VII. Legal Consequences

6.58 Transactions avoidance law aims to compensate the estate for the disadvantage caused by the challengeable transaction. Under the principle of efficiency, the legal consequences must be shaped in a way that this objective can be reached as simply as possible. At the same time, the principle of legal certainty must be taken into account. This requires the legal consequences to be as predictable and clear as possible. Also, the principle of proportionality has an impact, since the consequence should not put more burden on the opponent than necessary for compensating the estate for the disadvantaged suffered. Against this background, the result of transactions avoidance can primarily be described as an obligation of the opponent to compensate the estate for the disadvantage. This can be done in various ways: by returning an asset transferred by the debtor, by paying the amount of money the estate is lacking, by surrendering surrogates and emoluments, by waiving a right acquired from the debtor, or by simply ignoring the legal position that resulted from the challengeable transaction. Which option fits the case at hand best needs thorough consideration.

6.59 Although there are many similarities regarding the avoidance grounds, national laws[123] diverge substantially as regards the legal consequences. A first important aspect in this respect is whether the legal consequences are determined by statute or are left at the discretion of the court. In the latter case, it is difficult to predict what the outcome of the avoidance action might be. Hence, legal certainty and efficiency plead in favour of statutory regulation. However, while the legal consequences are determined by statute in Germany (§§ 143 et seq. of the *Insolvenzordnung*) and the United States (11 U.S.C. §§546 and 550), they are at the court's discretion in England and Wales (ss 238(3), 239(3), 339(2), 340(2) of the Insolvency Act 1986)[124] and partly in France (Art. L. 632-1(2), 632-2 of the *Code de Commerce*).

6.60 A second relevant aspect is whether transactions subject to avoidance law are—upon opening of insolvency proceedings, as the case may be—automatically void by force of law or voidable by court decision. Most national laws require a decision of the court. This is certainly true for jurisdictions where the legal consequences are at the discretion

---

[122] See more on this above, at para. 6.30.

[123] For § 8.1(2) of PEIL, see above (n 16). See further UNCITRAL, *Legislative Guide to Insolvency Law* (n 9) 148 paras 192 et seq., 151 paras 202 et seq. and Recommendations 93 et seq.; Bork and Veder, *Harmonisation of Transaction Avoidance Laws* (n 11) paras 4.212 et seq.

[124] This includes the decision not to order any legal consequence at all; cf. *Integral Petroleum SA v Petrogat FZE and ors* [2023] EWHC 44 (Comm).

of the court (England and Wales) but also for countries where the legal consequences result in a claim of the estate (to be enforced by the insolvency practitioner) against the defendant for returning the received (Germany, the United States). In France, the wording of the statute is ambiguous. On the one hand, Art. L. 632-1(1) of the *Code de Commerce* declares that certain transactions 'shall be considered null and void', which indicates nullity by force of law. On the other hand, Art. L. 632-4 of the *Code de Commerce* mentions an 'action for annulment', which speaks in favour of voidability. It is prevailing opinion that the wording of the statute does address the discretion of the court to set voidable transactions aside (given under Art. L. 632-1(2), 632-2 of the *Code de Commerce*, not under Art. 632-1(1)) rather than the distinction between 'void' and 'voidable'.

The next question is whether defendants may allege lapse of enrichment. Opponents **6.61** who, under transactions avoidance law, are obliged to compensate the estate for the disadvantage caused by the voidable transaction tend to defend themselves by claiming that they are unable to satisfy the claim because they have sold, spent, or consumed the received. However, this is not a serious problem where the legal consequence is a claim for compensation. If the recipient has sold, spent, or consumed the received, he or she is obliged to compensate the disadvantage for the estate by paying an amount equivalent to the value of the received. Nevertheless, the defence of lapse of enrichment may be valid under the principle of protection of trust, albeit under strict conditions only. For example, where the debtor transferred a car in a challengeable way and the opponent sold the car, he or she cannot claim lapse of enrichment because the opponent's estate does still comprise the purchase price, which has to be handed over to the insolvency practitioner as compensation for the disadvantage for the estate. Things are no different where the opponent received money and spent it. If he or she had to meet the relevant expenses anyway, this also does not cause lapse of enrichment, since other financial means have been spared by using the money from the voidable payment. Hence, where the object of the voidable transaction is still available in the opponent's estate (either *in natura* or in value), lapse of enrichment cannot be established. It is thus only in rare cases that the opponent can claim that he or she is no longer enriched, for example where he or she gave the received as a present or a donation to a third party (to whom the opponent was not obliged to give something anyway) or where he or she consumed it as (or transformed it in) a luxury which the opponent could not have afforded without the voidable transactions. This sums up to the question as to whether (a) lapse of enrichment can be established and (b) the national insolvency law permits the defence of lapse of enrichment. For example, Germany allows it, albeit only for transactions at an undervalue (§ 143(2) of the *Insolvenzordnung*). US law is very restrictive in this respect: if the defendant is unable to return the received, the court may order to pay the value of the received (11 U.S.C. § 550(a)), and the same holds true for England and Wales,[125] and France.

---

[125] In accordance with the restrictively applicable principle 'change of position'; cf. *Skandinaviska Enskilda Banken AB (Publ.) v Conway* [2019] UKPC 36; see further, *Re Fowlds (a bankrupt), Bucknall and anor v Wilson* [2021] EWHC 2149 (Ch).

184   TRANSACTIONS AVOIDANCE RULES

6.62 Finally, legal consequences for third parties must be discussed. It is of particular importance whether insolvency practitioners can challenge voidable transactions against persons other than the recipient[126] where they have profited from the transactions. In Germany, a transaction may be contested against not only the heir or another comprehensive legal successor of the recipient but also other legal successors if they were aware of the circumstances giving rise to the enrichment of the recipient (which is rebuttably presumed for closely related persons) or received the enrichment by way of a gratuitous transfer (§ 145 of the *Insolvenzordnung*). A similar rule can be found in the United States, where 11 U.S.C. §550(a)(2)/(b) entitles the insolvency practitioner to recover the property transferred from the immediate or mediate successor of the transferee unless this person acted for value, in good faith, and without knowledge of the voidability of the predecessor's transaction.[127] The same holds true in England and Wales, where the court can proceed against third parties unless they acted in good faith and for value (ss 241(2) and 342(2) of the Insolvency Act 1986). In France, the nullity of the challengeable transaction can also be held out towards third parties such as successors, even if they acted in good faith.[128]

6.63 Taking a closer look to national laws, England and Wales is a special case. Here, statute does not give the insolvency practitioner a substantive-law claim against the opponent for the reversal of the transaction. Instead, they merely accrue the right to ask the court (ss 238(2), 239(2), 339(1), 340(1) of the Insolvency Act 1986), which then uses its discretion to decide what remedies are best suited to restoring the parties to the position they would be in if the transaction had never taken place (ss 238(3), 239(3), 339(2), 340(2) of the Insolvency Act 1986). The discretion of the court is wide and includes the power to make no order at all. Although ss 241 and 342 of the Insolvency Act 1986 contain a number of examples by way of guidance, the list is not exhaustive. The court can order the reversal of the transaction or the renunciation of securities, but it can also order counter-performance or relieve the obligation to render agreed counter-performance, adjust the amount of performance due, and order the payment of additional compensation. The decision is made based on the interests of the creditors who benefit from the reversal, not of the parties to the transaction. Hence, lapse of enrichment can be taken into account.[129] It is at the discretion of the court whether it orders compensation, makes no order at all, or makes an order against a successor, that is a third party to whom the recipient has transferred the received. However, the latter is not possible if the third party acted in good faith and for value (ss 241(2) and 342(2) of the Insolvency Act 1986), the absence of good faith being presumed where the third

---

[126] It should be noted that a 'third party' can, in actual fact, be the 'recipient', e.g. where the debtor gives money to someone who is an agent for the recipient only; cf. *Skandinaviska Enskilda Banken AB (Publ.) v Conway* (n 125). The determination of the recipient has priority to the question of transactions avoidance against third parties.

[127] See below, at para. 6.64.

[128] *Cour de Cassation (chambre commerciale)*–3 February 1998–95-20389 = Bull. Civ. 1998 IV No. 53. See also above (n 112).

[129] Under the—restrictively applied—principle of 'change of position'; see, for details, *Skandinaviska Enskilda Banken AB (Publ.) v Conway* (n 125).

party had notice of the relevant surrounding circumstances and of the relevant proceedings or was connected with, or was an associate of, either the company in question or the person with whom that company entered into the transaction (ss 241(2A) and 342(2A) of the Insolvency Act 1986).

French law declares transactions void by force of law if they meet the prerequisites **6.64** of Art. L. 632-1(1) of the *Code de Commerce*. Although Art. L. 632-4 of the *Code de Commerce* mentions an 'action for annulment', this is merely declarative as far as Art. L. 632-1(1) of the *Code de Commerce* is concerned. As opposed to Arts L. 632-1(2) and 632 of the *Code de Commerce*, the court has no discretion. It is bound to treat the transaction as null and void (retroactively and with *erga omnes* effect) and has to decree the legal consequences resulting from this nullity, for example obliging the recipient to return the received or obliging a surety to indemnify the creditor who has to return the payment that has been received in a challengeable way. According to Art. L. 632-4 of the *Code de Commerce*, the action for annulment shall result in reforming the debtor's assets.

In Germany, the legal consequence of the challengeable transaction is a claim against **6.65** the recipient (or—under the conditions of § 145 of the *Insolvenzordnung*—against a successor of the recipient) to return the received to the estate (§ 143(1) of the *Insolvenzordnung*). This claim emerges with the opening of insolvency proceedings, no matter whether the insolvency practitioner has knowledge of the voidable transaction or not. As a consequence, any property of the debtor sold, transferred, or relinquished under the contestable transaction must be restituted to the insolvency estate. Lapse of enrichment is only relevant where a transaction at an undervalue shall be reversed (§ 143(2) of the *Insolvenzordnung*).

In the United States, challengeable transactions are not void by force of law but voidable by court order. Hence, avoidance needs litigation, which follows from the rule on the limitation period in 11 U.S.C. §546(a).[130] However, by avoidance, the transaction is set aside, which does not automatically lead to a claim for recovery. It is for this reason that 11 U.S.C. §550 enables the insolvency practitioner to recover, for the benefit of the estate, the property transferred from the initial transferee of such transfer, or the entity for whose benefit such transfer was made, or any immediate or mediate transferee of such initial transferee. Once recovered from the opponent, the property becomes the property of the estate (11 U.S.C. §541(a)(3)). The value of such property can only be recovered if the court so orders. However, such an order prevents the defendant from claiming lapse of enrichment. Third parties can also be obliged, since 11 U.S.C. §550(a)(2)/(b) entitles the insolvency practitioner to recover the property transferred from the immediate or mediate successor of the transferee unless this person acted for value, in good faith, and without knowledge of the voidability of the predecessor's transaction.[131]

---

[130] On this time bar, see *Kelley v Stone & Baxter, LLP (In re Brownlee)*, 606 BR 109 (Bankr. MD Ga. 2019).
[131] Cf. *Matter of Bernard L. Madoff Inv. Sec. LLC*, 548 BR 13 (Bankr. SDNY 2016).

186 TRANSACTIONS AVOIDANCE RULES

6.67 The differences between the national laws can be exemplified by a case where the debtor assigns a claim against an obligor to a creditor in a challengeable way and the obligor pays the creditor. Under French law, the insolvency practitioner can demand a second payment from the obligor, since the assignment is null and void under Art. L. 632-1(1) of the *Code de Commerce*, and third parties affected by this nullity are not protected, even if they acted in good faith.[132] Under German law, the obligor would be protected under § 407 of the *Bürgerliches Gesetzbuch*, provided good faith can be established. As a result, the creditor is obliged to pay the amount received from the obligor to the estate. In the United States, third parties are only liable if they are successors, and they are protected if they acted in good faith (11 U.S.C. §550(a)(2)/(b)). Hence, the creditor would be ordered to hand over the amount received from the obligor to the estate. In England and Wales, the same result seems most likely, albeit at the discretion of the court only (ss 241(2A) and 342(2A) of the Insolvency Act 1986).

VIII. Cross-Border Avoidance

6.68 In a globalized world, insolvency proceedings have increasingly international connotations, which will be dealt with extensively in Chapter 9 'Cross-Border Insolvency Law'. In the present context, an important question regards the transactions avoidance law applicable to cross-border transactions, for example where a debtor pays a foreign creditor, grants a security right to a creditor domiciled in another jurisdiction (over collateral that is situated in a third country, as the case may be), or gifts a friend living abroad. In all these situations, the question arises as to which transactions avoidance law is applicable: the law of the debtor's country, where insolvency proceedings have been opened (*lex fori concursus*), or the law of the state the recipient is living in, or the law of a third country. Since it follows from the above that national transactions avoidance laws differ in many respects, it may well be that the *lex fori concursus* is more avoidance-friendly than another transactions avoidance law coming into question. Hence, the topic of the applicable law is decisive.

6.69 In cases to which the European Insolvency Regulation (EIR) applies, all Member States[133] have to utilise Art. 7(2) lit. m of the EIR, according to which the *lex fori concursus* is applicable to transactions avoidance. This means that the transactions avoidance law of the Member State where insolvency proceedings have been opened (opening state) applies, even if the opponent or the asset in question is situated abroad. However, opponents may defend themselves under Art. 16 of the EIR by proving that the transaction is subject to the law of a Member State other than that of the opening state and that the law of that Member State (i.e. the *lex causae*) does not allow any means

---

[132] *Cour de Cassation (chambre commerciale)*–11 October 2011–10-11938 = Bull. Civ. 2011 IV No. 155.
[133] Except Denmark, where the EIR is not applicable: see Recital 88 of the EIR.

of challenging that act in the relevant case.[134] For example, where a German debtor refunded a loan granted by a French shareholder, this is challengeable in German insolvency proceedings under the *lex fori concursus*.[135] However, where the loan is governed by French law, the opponent can defend him- or herself under Art. 16 of the EIR by claiming that the payment is only challengeable as a preference under the conditions of Art. L. 632-1, 632-3 of the *Code de Commerce*.[136]

These rules apply indubitably, where both the debtor/insolvency practitioner and the opponent are situated in a Member State of the European Union (EU). However, where the opponent is located in, or the transaction concerned is governed by the laws of, a Non-Member State ('third country'), the application of rules of the EIR is debatable. It is not decided yet whether Art. 16 of the EIR, which refers to the law of a Member State, applies in relation to third countries. In another view, similar protection might at least be provided for by national private international law. As opposed to this, Art. 7 of the EIR does not mention any relationship to another Member State. Since the same holds true for Art. 3 of the EIR and the CJEU has ruled that Art. 3 of the EIR applies also in relation to third countries,[137] and given that EU Regulations are directly applicable in all Member States without any transforming legal act (Art. 288(2) of the Treaty on the Functioning of the European Union (TFEU)), much can be said for applying Art. 7 of the EIR even if there is no link to another Member State. If one follows this path, national laws do not need specific cross-border rules on the law applicable to transactions avoidance. They are only necessary where the scope of Art. 7 of the EIR is restricted to Inter-Member State relationships.

6.70

As regards national laws, many Member States of the EU have mirrored both Art. 7(2) lit. m of the EIR and Art. 16 of the EIR in their national cross-border insolvency laws, be it expressly by statute or by case law. Others accept the transactions avoidance law of the *lex fori concursus* without any proviso. Hence, the application of the *lex fori concursus* is the rule and an Art. 16-type defence is the exception.

6.71

Outside the EU, many national laws have adopted the UNCITRAL Model Law on Cross-Border Insolvency. This holds particularly true for England and Wales[138] and the United States.[139] These recommendations deal with transactions avoidance in s. 23, which, upon recognition of the foreign insolvency proceedings, permits the foreign insolvency practitioner to challenge transactions not under the *lex fori concursus* but under national law. If the insolvency practitioner has sued the opponent in the opening state, a judgment against the opponent should be recognized in the creditor's

6.72

---

[134] For criticism of this norm, see Reinhard Bork, *Principles of Cross-Border Insolvency Law* (Intersentia, Cambridge/Antwerp/Portland 2017) paras 6.83 et seq.

[135] Cf. above, at para. 6.57.

[136] See above at para. 6.37.

[137] See the groundbreaking CJEU Case C-328/12 *Schmid v Hertel*, ECLI:EU:C:2014:6; see, in particular, at para. 24 of this judgment (which concerned jurisdiction for a transactions avoidance case).

[138] Here, the UNCITRAL Model Law has been transformed into national law by the Cross-Border Insolvency Regulation 2006.

[139] See Chapter 15 of the Bankruptcy Code.

188 TRANSACTIONS AVOIDANCE RULES

jurisdiction, even if it is based on the *lex fori concursus*.[140] However, these recommendations have not been transformed entirely into national laws.

6.73   For example, in the United States, a foreign insolvency practitioner can only challenge transactions under US transactions avoidance law in (secondary) insolvency proceedings formally opened in the United States (11 U.S.C. §1523(a)).[141] However, according to the majority of court decisions,[142] US transactions avoidance law has no extraterritorial effect and is therefore only applicable if the transaction in question occurred largely in the United States, that is was a domestic transfer. Things are easier if the insolvency practitioner sued the opponent in the opening state. In this case, a foreign decision against the opponent is recognizable and enforceable in the United States under the principle of comity.[143]

6.74   In England and Wales, it is just the other way around. Foreign insolvency practitioners are entitled to bring avoidance actions under English transactions avoidance law (Sch. 1 Art. 23 of the Cross-Border Insolvency Regulations (CBIR) 2006). But avoidance decisions of foreign courts under foreign transactions avoidance law are only recognizable if the foreign court had international jurisdiction according to the 'Dicey rule'[144].[145]

---

[140] This is recommended by the UNCITRAL Model Law on Recognition and Enforcement of Insolvency-Related Judgments.

[141] See *In Re Awal Bank, BSC* (Bankr. SDNY 2011], 455 BR 73. In *Fogerty v Petroquests Resources Inc (In Re Condor Insurance Co.)* (5th Cir. 2010), 601 F.3d 319, however, the court permitted an action to avoid a foreign transaction brought by a foreign insolvency practitioner under foreign transactions avoidance law. For criticism, see Gerald McCormack, 'Conflicts, Avoidance and International Insolvency 20 Years On: A Triple Cocktail', Journal of Business Law 2 (2013) 141, 151 et seq.

[142] See *Re CIL Ltd*, 582 BR 46 (SDNY 2018); *Re Maxwell Communication Corp. plc*, 186 BR 807 (Bankr. SDNY 1995); *Barclay v Swiss Fin. Corp. Ltd (In re Midland Euro Exch. Inc.)*, 347 BR 708 (Bankr. CD Cal. 2006); opposing *Re French*, 440 F.3d 145 (2006).

[143] *Re Metcalfe & Mansfield Alternative Investments*, 421 BR 685. (Bankr. SDNY 2010).

[144] Albert Venn Dicey, John Humphrey Carlile Morris, and Lawrence Anthony Collins, *Conflict of Laws* (15th edn, Sweet & Maxwell, London 2012) para. 14R-054:

> a court of a foreign country outside the United Kingdom has jurisdiction to give a judgment in personam capable of enforcement or recognition as against the person against whom it was given in the following cases:
>
> *First Case*—If the person against whom the judgment was given was, at the time the proceedings were instituted, present in the foreign country.
>
> *Second Case*—If the person against whom the judgment was given was claimant, or counter-claimed, in the proceedings in the foreign court.
>
> *Third Case*—If the person against whom the judgment was given submitted to the jurisdiction of that court by voluntarily appearing in the proceedings.
>
> *Fourth Case*—If the person against whom the judgment was given had before the commencement of the proceedings agreed, in respect of the subject matter of the proceedings, to submit to the jurisdiction of that court or of the courts of that country.

[145] *Rubin v Eurofinance SA* (n 53) paras 88 et seq. This may change, once the UNCITRAL Model Law on Recognition and Enforcement of Insolvency-Related Judgments has been implemented into English law.

7

Directors' Duties in the Vicinity of Insolvency, Disqualification, Piercing the Veil

Renato Mangano

I. The Limits of Limited Liability

Limited liability is at the very core of modern business law, since it allows the members of an organization running a firm to protect their own assets from the claims of the firm's creditors.[1] This explains why limited liability is, nowadays, a standard feature of any corporate organization and why this is increasingly present in many unincorporated entities.[2]

7.01

However, limited liability has a dark side, since it shifts the risk of business failure from those who have invested in a business to the debtor's creditors; indeed, some scholars highlight the fact that limited liability may incentivize investors to bet with creditors' money. For example, as regards English law, *Brian Cheffins* writes:

7.02

> [t]ake the example of a company which has an issued share capital of £100, which means that the members have paid this amount to receive the shares which the company has issued to them. Those running the company then borrow £10,000 on its behalf. If everything goes well, the shareholders reap much of the benefit since they are the residual claimants. On the other hand, if things go awry the shareholders only lose the value of their £100 investment while the creditors might end up receiving

---

[1] John Armour, Henry Hansmann, Reinier Kraakman, and Mariana Pargendler, 'What Is Corporate Law?' in Reinier Kraakman, John Armour, Paul Davies et al., *The Anatomy of Corporate Law. A Comparative and Functional Approach* (3rd edn, OUP 2009) 9, who state:

> [l]imited liability shields the firm's owners—the shareholders—from creditors' claims [...] The 'owner shielding' provided by limited liability is the converse of the 'entity shielding' [...] Entity shielding protects the assets of the firm from the creditors of the firm's owners, while limited liability protects the assets of the firm's owners from the claims of the firm's creditors. Together, these forms of asset shielding (or 'asset partitioning') ensure that business assets are pledged as security to business creditors, while the personal assets of the business's owners are reserved for the owners' personal creditors.

[2] Larry E. Ribstein, *The Rise of the Uncorporation* (OUP 2010) 119 et seq. Moreover, nowadays, the feature of limited liability is also present in those legal creations according to which a sole proprietor segregates for business purposes a portion of his or her personal wealth and achieves, for the activity carried out through this portion of assets, the feature of limited liability but not that of legal personality. Here, a reference is made to the *patrimoine affecté* under Art. L 526-6(1) of the French *Code de Commerce*. This expansion of limited liability beyond the borders of corporate law should not come as a surprise, since it has been demonstrated that, historically, there is no necessary coincidence between corporate form and limited liability. On this point, see John Armour, Henry Hansmann, Reinier Kraakman, and Mariana Pargendler, 'What Is Corporate Law?' (n 1) 8–9.

Renato Mangano, *Directors' Duties in the Vicinity of Insolvency, Disqualification, Piercing the Veil* In: *The Anatomy of Corporate Insolvency Law*. Edited by: Reinhard Bork and Renato Mangano, Oxford University Press. © Renato Mangano 2024.
DOI: 10.1093/oso/9780198852094.003.0007

190 DIRECTORS' DUTIES IN THE VICINITY OF INSOLVENCY

little, if any, of the £10,000 which the company owes. Because of these circumstances, investing in a company as a shareholder can be characterized as a 'heads we win, tails creditors lose' situation.[3]

Scholars, policymakers, and lawmakers are aware of the limits of limited liability, but they are also aware that when the company is flourishing, the pros of limited liability outnumber its cons, including the risk that the situation may take a turn for the worse. Moreover, to give creditors adequate protection, jurisdictions adopt many legal devices that operate throughout the company's life. The following are just a few of many such devices: mandatory disclosure, regulations on capital, policies restricting distributions to shareholders, directors' duties owed to the company, and regulations on related party transactions. These are dealt with in textbooks about company law.

7.03 However, the feature of limited liability becomes more toxic when the firm is in the vicinity of insolvency, since in this case, the undesirable incentives of limited liability even become perverse. In fact, if a firm is distressed and shareholders have lost their hope not only of receiving dividends but also even of recovering their initial investment, directors might have more incentive to undertake very risky operations. To be more realistic, if a company has lost all or most of its subscribed capital, directors tend to focus on the upside of their projects, even if there is only a remote possibility of these projects being successful.[4] Of course, this problem is even more pronounced in the case of closely held companies (i.e. in those companies whose stock is held by a small number of people), since in this case, shareholders tend to have a strong influence on directors or even to be appointed as directors themselves.

7.04 This chapter will deal with the legal devices that jurisdictions adopt to protect creditors from the limits of limited liability when companies are in the vicinity of insolvency, or even when they are actually insolvent, but insolvency procedures or proceedings have not yet been commenced. These devices vary from jurisdiction to jurisdiction, but looked at from a functional point of view, they may be grouped under the general labels of 'Directors' liability in the vicinity of insolvency', 'Directors' disqualification', and 'Piercing the corporate veil'. The present chapter, however, will not deal with similar problems and solutions that may occur in unincorporated organizations that are provided with limited liability, even though some considerations that are expressed here will be applicable also to these, *mutatis mutandis*. Further, the present chapter does not examine the obligations and liability of directors that may apply under criminal law.

7.05 Some specifications are of paramount importance for a better understanding of what is discussed in this chapter. In particular, some jurisdictions, such as Germany and Italy, have two distinct types of limited liability companies. In one type, the company's capital

---

[3] Brian R. Cheffins, *Company Law. Theory, Structure, Operation* (OUP 1997) 497–8.
[4] Paul Davies, 'Directors' Creditor-Regarding Duties in Respect of Trading Decisions Taken in the Vicinity of Insolvency' in Horst Eidenmüller and Wolfgang Schön (eds), *The Law and Economics of Creditor Protection. A Transatlantic Perspective* (T.M.C. Asser Press 2008) 303 et seq., at 308.

is necessarily divided into shares that are of identical size and content (at least, within the same class of shares), while this is not so in the other type, where there is even a prohibition against such a division. In the latter case, each member can have only one single stake, whose size and content are proportional to his or her contribution, unless otherwise agreed. The former type of company may also issue bonds; in addition, their shares and, if any, their bonds are usually—but not necessarily—bought and sold in stock exchanges. For the purposes of this chapter, the companies whose capital is divided into shares will be called 'joint stock companies', while the companies whose capital cannot be divided into shares will be called 'private companies'. However, for the sake of simplicity, the members of both types of companies will henceforth be called 'shareholders', even when they hold no shares but only stakes. These two types of company are regulated by two different sets of rules. In Germany, joint stock companies are regulated by the *Aktiengesetz*, while private companies are regulated by the *Gesetz betreffend die Gesellschaften mit beschränkter Haftung*. In Italy, both types of company are regulated by two distinct parts of the *Codice civile*.

Again, for the purposes of this chapter, the term 'director' will be employed regardless of the way the company's management is structured. Therefore, the term 'director' will include both a sole director and each executive director who acts without being a member of any board of directors; a member of a board of directors, whether he or she acts as a member of the board or as a person delegated by the board; and, in the case of a German joint stock company (*Aktiengesellschaft*) when a two-tier corporate structure is compulsory, each member of the management board (*Vorstand*).[5]

Last but not least, when a reference is made to UK law, the analysis will cover the law of England and Wales only. Indeed, throughout this chapter, 'England' is used to signify 'England and Wales' and 'English law' to signify 'the law of England and Wales'.

II. Directors' Liability in the Vicinity of Insolvency

A. Overview

In the past few years, it has become a moot point whether companies' directors should **7.06** look after shareholders' interests only or whether they should balance shareholders' interests with other constituencies.[6] Nevertheless, when companies are on the brink

---

[5] In the German joint stock company, §§ 76 et seq. and 95 et seq. of the *Aktiengesetz* impose the adoption of a two-tier corporate structure, which consists of a management board and a supervisory board. The management board, whose members are appointed by the supervisory board, are in charge of the daily management of the company. The supervisory board, whose members are representatives of both the company's shareholders and employees, are in charge of appointing and removing the members of the management board, supervising the management board, and approving the management board's business when this goes beyond simple, day-by-day management.

[6] Determining the purpose of a solvent company has become a very topical issue. In effect, while, in the past 25 years, it has commonly been maintained that companies exist principally to serve their shareholders (but, for

of insolvency, it is accepted throughout the world that directors must change their approach to decision-making and show enhanced regard for creditors. Indeed, on this point, it is still appropriate to quote a case decided by the English House of Lords, the *Winkworth v Edward Baron Development Co. Ltd* case. Here, Lord Templeman clearly stated:

> [a] company owes a duty to its creditors, present and future. The company is not bound to pay off every debt as soon as it is incurred and the company is not obliged to avoid all ventures which involve an element of risk, but the company owes a duty to its creditors to keep its property inviolate and available for the repayment of its debts [...] A duty is owed by the directors to the company and to the creditors of the company to ensure that the affairs of the company are properly administered and that its property is not dissipated or exploited for the benefit of the directors themselves to the prejudice of the creditors.[7]

7.07 These policies are known worldwide under various labels, such as the 'doctrine of the shift of directors' duties', 'directors' duties and liability in the vicinity of insolvency', 'directors' duties and liability in the twilight zone', 'directors' obligations in the period approaching insolvency', or other similar classifications. Moreover, depending on the relevant jurisdiction, the idea of protecting creditors from the limits of limited liability when the company is distressed has been developed in various ways. For example, while in some countries, these policies are rooted in statutes, in others, they are rooted in general principles; moreover, while in some jurisdictions, these forms of liability are grounded in company law, in others, they are grounded in insolvency law or tort law. Indeed, in this respect, the use of the above-mentioned labels may even be misleading. For example, while the INSOL International Report 'Directors in the Twilight Zone V'[8] includes forms of liability based on company law and tort law, the United Nations Commission on International Trade Law (UNCITRAL) *Legislative Guide on Insolvency Law—Part Four: Directors' Obligations in the Period Approaching Insolvency*[9] specifies that '[t]his part does not deal with the obligations of directors that may apply under

a variation of the traditional shareholder value theory, see s. 172 of the UK Companies Act 2006, which required, and still requires, directors to promote the success of the company), this point has recently been placed at the core of a vivid debate according to which the traditional conception is opposed by those who support the view that directors must take into account every stakeholder. For this new conception of a company's purpose, which includes generating jobs, a strong and sustainable economy, innovation, and a healthy environment, see especially the 2019 Statement of the US Business Roundtable (<https://opportunity.businessroundtable.org/ourcommitment> accessed 11 January 2024), the 2020 study by EY, 'Study on Directors' Duties and Sustainable Corporate Governance', for the European Commission (<https://op.europa.eu/it/publication-detail/-/publication/e47928a2-d20b-11ea-adf7-01aa75ed71a1/language-en> accessed 11 January 2024), and the new version of Art. 1833 of the French *Code Civil*. The latter (also) states that '[t]he company is managed in its corporate interest, taking into consideration the social and environmental issues relating to its business'.

[7] *Winkworth v Edward Baron Development Co. Ltd* [1986] 1 WLR 1512, at 1516.
[8] This is available at <https://unov.tind.io/record/66583?In=en> accessed 27 March 2024.
[9] This is available at <https://uncitral.un.org/sites/uncitra.un.org/files/media-documents/uncitral/en/19-112 73_part_4_ebook.pdf> accessed 27 March 2024.

criminal law, company law or tort law, focussing only on those obligations that may be included in the law relating to insolvency and become enforceable once insolvency proceedings commence'.

This explains why, for the purposes of this chapter, the policies at issue will be dealt with under the following headings: 'Liability for Breach of the Duty to Show Enhanced Regard to Creditors', 'Liability for Wrongful Trading', 'Other Forms of Liability Based on Tort Law', and 'Overlapping and Twisted Strategies'.

B. Liability for Breach of the Duty to Show Enhanced Regard to Creditors

1. Concept and rationale

The special regime for the 'twilight zone' is present in both common law and civil law **7.08** jurisdictions. In common law jurisdictions, this trend originated in a 1976 Australian case where a judge stated *obiter* that when a company is distressed, directors must shift their focus from shareholders to creditors.[10] Subsequently, this concept was judicially developed under the name of the 'doctrine of the shift of directors' duties' and is well illustrated in *Nicholson v Permakraft (NZ) Ltd*,[11] which is the most important case in New Zealand; in *Kinsela v Russell Kinsela Pty Ltd*,[12] the most famous case in Australia; and, later on, in *Liquidator of West Mercia Safetywear v Dodd*,[13] in England, and, more recently, in *BTI 2014 LLC v Sequana SA*, in England as well.[14]

This picture is functionally comparable to what happens in civil law jurisdictions, **7.09** where, however, the policy of creditor protection in the twilight zone may be based on either statutes or general principles.

In particular, an example of statutory regime for the 'twilight zone' is well illustrated **7.10** by Italian law. Here, Arts 2394 and 2476(6) of the Italian *Codice Civile* explicitly lay down that directors of both joint stock companies and private companies have a duty to preserve the integrity of a company's assets so that when a company's assets prove

---

[10] *Walker v Wimborne* (1976) 137 CLR 1. Here, however, the doctrine of duty shifting was expressed *obiter* only.
[11] *Nicholson v Permakraft (NZ) Ltd* (1985) 3 ACLC 453.
[12] *Kinsela v Russell Kinsela Pty Ltd* (1986) 4 ACLC 215.
[13] *Liquidator of West Mercia Safetywear v Dodd* (1988) 4 BCC 30. Moreover, even though, in the United Kingdom, the doctrine of directors' duty shifting is still regarded as a doctrine grounded in common law, this was, to a certain extent, recognized by s. 172(3) of the UK Companies Act 2006. This section, on the one hand, lays down that '[a] director of a company must act in the way he considers, in good faith, would be most likely to promote the success of the company for the benefit of its members as a whole' and, on the other hand, that '[t]he duty imposed by this section has effect subject to any enactment or rule of law requiring directors, in certain circumstances, to consider or act in the interests of creditors of the company'. As already mentioned, the UK Companies Act 2006 preserves, but does not replace, the common law duty-shifting rule. This is because, as regards the whole regulation on directors' duties, s. 179(4) lays down that '[t]he general duties shall be interpreted and applied in the same way as common law rules or equitable principles, and regard shall be had to the corresponding common law rules and equitable principles in interpreting and applying the general duties'. On this point, see Paul Davies and Sarah Worthington, *Gower's Principles of Modern Company Law* (10th edn, Sweet & Maxwell 2016) para 9-11.
[14] *BTI 2014 LLC v Sequana SA* [2022] UKSC 25.

194 DIRECTORS' DUTIES IN THE VICINITY OF INSOLVENCY

insufficient to satisfy the company's creditors, the company's directors are liable towards the company's creditors.

7.11   Something similar happens in Germany, as regards joint stock companies. First, the new formulation of § 93(1) of the *Aktiengesetz* lays down that directors must focus not only on shareholders' interests but also on the company's wealth (*Wohl der Gesellschaft*), which is regarded as including creditor protection.[15] Second, the combination of §§ 93(5) and 93(3) of the *Aktiengesetz* lays down that when the company's creditors cannot obtain satisfaction from the company, they may take steps to ensure that the company's directors are liable towards the company's creditors, provided that

- either the company's directors have breached 'the due care of a prudent manager faithfully complying with his duties' owed towards the company in situations where either contributions are restituted to the shareholders; or shareholders have been paid interest or have participated in the company's profits in violation of para. 58(4) of the *Aktiengesetz*; or treasury shares of stock in the company or in some other companies have been subscribed to, purchased, accepted in pledge, or redeemed; or preference or premium shares have been issued; or the company's assets have been distributed; or remunerations have been granted to members of the supervisory board; or loans have been granted; or shares of a new issue are issued in the context of the conditional capital increase and this is done outside of the purpose specified therefore or prior to the equivalent value having been fully paid;
- or, alternatively, the company's directors have grossly neglected their duty to exercise the due care of a prudent manager faithfully fulfilling his duties.

7.12   On the contrary, German law on private companies offers an example of a regime for the 'twilight zone' based on general principles. Even though § 43(1) of the *Gesetz betreffend die Gesellschaften mit beschränkter Haftung* lays down only that '[t]he directors shall conduct the company's affairs with the due care of a prudent businessman', it is commonly accepted that when a private company is distressed, directors must show enhanced regard to creditors.[16]

7.13   The above-mentioned common law doctrine and the civil law regulations also share their rationale, which, in both cases, is rooted in the awareness that when the company is distressed, shareholders have less, or even nothing, to lose, and directors are inclined to favour very risky projects in the hope that these may restore the company to solvency. Moreover, at least in the case of some US States and France, this convergence also extends to the way the above-mentioned rationale is put into operation. In

---

[15] On this point, Thomas Raiser and Rüdiger Veil, *Recht der Kapitalgesellschaften* (6th edn, Verlag Franz Vahlen 2015) 168 para. 70 maintain that Germany does not need a case-law policy of duty shifting similar to that endorsed by the US case *Credit Lyonnais Bank Nederland, NV v Pathe Communications Co.* 1991, Del. Ch WL 277613. This will be briefly discussed in n 15 below.

[16] Christoph Thole, *Gesellschaftsrechtliche Maßnahmen in der Insolvenz* (3rd edn, RWS 2020) § 419.

these jurisdictions, a company's distress has been regarded as a trigger event for the company's assets to be 'segregated' for the benefit of the company's creditors.

Consider, first, US law. Here, in some States, the common law idea that when a company is distressed, directors must have enhanced regard to creditors is based on the centuries-old 'trust fund doctrine'. This is well summarized in a passage of the *Bovay v HM Byllesby & Co.* case, where the court held that

> [a]n insolvent corporation is civilly dead in the sense that its property may be administered in equity as a trust fund for the benefit of creditors. The fact which creates the trust is the insolvency, and when that fact is established, the trust arises, and the legality of the acts thereafter performed will be decided by very different principles than in the case of solvency. The execution of a trust and the following and administering of trust funds are immemorial heads of equity jurisprudence.[17]

Consider, now, French law. Here, there has never been a trust fund doctrine, but old scholars elaborated something that was functionally comparable with it, that is the collective pledge doctrine (*théorie du gage commun*). This doctrine held that when a person became a creditor of a trader or a company, the creditor participated *pro quota* in a collective pledge encumbering all the assets of the debtor. When the debtor was flourishing, this collective pledge produced no effects; by contrast, when the debtor became insolvent, this gave the debtor's creditors some collective powers over the debtor's assets, whether or not insolvency proceedings had been opened.[18]

Unfortunately, there is not sufficient evidence to give a precise date to when this doctrine was employed in France to justify the doctrine of duty shifting and to determine whether, and to what extent, this idea was related to similar contemporary doctrines elaborated across Europe.[19] Nevertheless, it is certain that a French scholar recently resumed the collective pledge theory and, accordingly, held that when insolvency proceedings have been opened, the insolvency practitioner appointed to them has a right to enforce the collective pledge; this right also includes the power to restore the debtor's

---

[17] *Bovay v HM Byllesby & Co.*, 38 A.2d 808, at 813 (Del. 1944). The same position is held in the State of New York, for which see *New York Credit Men's Adjustment Bureau Inc. v Weiss* (1953) 110 NE.2d 397. By contrast, the courts of other US States justified the duty-shifting policy by ruling that directors owe a duty to the whole corporate enterprise, which includes all its constituencies and, therefore, the enterprise's creditors. In this respect, see *Credit Lyonnais Bank Nederland, NV v Pathe Communications Co.* 1991 (n 13).

[18] On this point see, e.g. Augustin-Charles Renouard, *Traité des faillites et banqueroutes*, vol. 1 (3rd edn, Guillaumin et C., 1857) 344 et seq., who distinguishes between '*dessaisissement de fait*' and '*dessaisissement de plain droit*' (*de facto* divestment, i.e. before the opening of proceedings and *de jure* divestment, i.e. after, and as a result of, the opening of proceedings). The reference to a trader or a company depends on the fact that, in the past, French insolvency law was restricted to traders and companies only.

[19] For example, in the same period in Germany, Karl Ziebarth, *Die Realexecution und die Obligation mit besonderer Rücksicht auf die Miethe erörtet nach römischem und deutschem Recht in Vergleich mit dem Preußischen* (Verlag der Buchhandlung des Waisenhauses 1866) 30–1, at 42 held that the unsecured creditors of a debtor had a right of pledge over all the assets of their debtor. Moreover, in Austria Ernst Demelius, *Das Pfandrecht an beweglichen Sachen nach österreichishen bürgerlichen Recht mit besonderer Berücksichtigung des bürgerlichen Gesetzbuches für das Deutsche Reich*, vol. 1 (Braumüller 1897) 31 ss, distinguished between a special pledge and a collective pledge.

196 DIRECTORS' DUTIES IN THE VICINITY OF INSOLVENCY

assets as they were prior to the emergence of insolvency; for such a purpose, the insolvency practitioner may employ both transaction avoidance actions and actions to make the company's directors liable; from a functional point of view, these forms of action diverge only because the former provides creditors with a compensation in kind, while the latter provides them with a compensation in money.[20]

2. Prescription addressees, 'twilight zone', and BJR

7.14 The common law doctrine of duty shifting and the parallel regulations in civil law countries are addressed to both *de jure* directors and *de facto* directors, that is to both those persons who are formally appointed as directors and those who play this role in practice only. In some jurisdictions, the extension to the *de facto* directors is grounded in statutes. For example, this is the case in England, where s. 250 of the UK Companies Act 2006 lays down that '[i]n the Companies Acts "director" includes any person occupying the position of director, by whatever name called'. By contrast, in other jurisdictions, this extension is the achievement of the relevant case law. For example, this is the case in Germany, where the Supreme Court holds that the duties imposed on the directors of private companies should be regarded as also addressed to those persons who act as directors.[21] Similarly, this extension occurs in Italy, where the civil liability of *de facto* directors is based on case law.[22]

7.15 Some jurisdictions extend *de jure* directors' duties also to those persons who instruct directors without playing the role of de facto directors. This happens in England, where the UK Companies Act 2006, on the one hand, lays down that '[t]he general duties [of a *de jure* director] apply to a shadow director of a company where and to the extent that they are capable of so applying' (s. 170(5)) and, on the other hand, specifies that a 'shadow director' is any 'person in accordance with whose directions or instructions the directors of the company are accustomed to act' (s. 251(1)). In the past, the exact contours of the 'shadow director' were considered obscure, and the ascertainment in the real world of the existence of this third category gave rise both to confusion with the figure of the *de facto* director and to concerns about the risks of any excessive extension of directors' liability. Nowadays, however, this problem seems to have been solved for two reasons. First, the judiciary has clarified that, in this matter, the distinction between *de facto* directors and shadow directors must not be the main focus. Here, the real point is that the duties imposed on *de jure* directors should be extended to those persons who have a real influence on the company's decision-making. Second, the UK Small Business, Enterprise and Employment Act 2015 modified the contents of s. 251(2) of the UK Companies Act 2006 and clarified that

---

[20] Marc Sénéchal, *L'effet réel de la procédure collective: Essai sur la saisie collective du gage commun des créanciers* (Litec 2002) 707 ss.

[21] BGHZ 104, 44, 47f.

[22] Cass. civ. 21567/2017. By contrast, in Italy, the criminal liability of de facto directors is provided for by Art. 2639 of the *Codice civile*.

[a] person is not to be regarded as a shadow director by reason only that the directors act: (a) on advice given by that person in a professional capacity; (b) in accordance with instructions, a direction, guidance or advice given by that person in the exercise of a function conferred by or under an enactment; (c) in accordance with guidance or advice given by that person in that person's capacity as a Minister of the Crown.[23]

7.16 Those jurisdictions that have not elaborated the category of 'shadow director' travel by other routes to protect creditors from the influence of persons who instruct the directors. For example, this happens in Germany and Italy, where—under certain conditions—the directors' liability is extended to those people or entities who/that have influenced the directors' decision making. This point will be dealt with in paras 7.78–7.79 below, text and accompanying footnote, and in paras 7.80–7.81.

7.17 Both the common law doctrine and the parallel regulations in civil law countries are based on a concept of the vicinity of insolvency or a twilight zone. However, determining the extent of this period of time is proving to be difficult. It is clear when this period of time ends, as this date coincides with the date of the request for the opening of insolvency proceedings,[24] but it is debatable when this period of time actually starts. In this respect, courts and policymakers strive to strike a balance between an interest in not excessively discouraging directors from undertaking operations that may prove profitable for the company and an interest in protecting creditors as soon as possible. For example, in one case at common law, the court regarded as relevant the point in time when the company became insolvent,[25] while in another case, the court referred to the point in time of 'a course of action which would jeopardize solvency'.[26]

7.18 The same uncertainty is present in some civil law jurisdictions whose regulations—at least textually—do not mention the term 'insolvency' in order to bring creditor protection forward to a point in time that is prior to the date when the company becomes insolvent. For example, in Germany, § 93(5) of the *Aktiengesetz* refers to a point in time when the company's creditors cannot obtain satisfaction from the company. In Germany, the fact that, at a certain point in time, a company's creditors cannot obtain satisfaction from the company does not necessarily prove that the company is insolvent since, for this to be the case, the inability to pay must be of long duration.[27] In Italy, Arts 2394 and 2476(6) of the Italian *Codice civile* refer to a point in time when the company's assets prove insufficient to satisfy the company's creditors—in Italy, a situation where

---

[23] Davies and Worthington, *Modern Company Law* (n 11) paras 16-9 and 16-10.

[24] However, the fact that a company enters into insolvency proceedings (or procedures) does not necessarily mean that directors will lose their power completely. This is because many jurisdictions allow the debtor company to remain totally, or at least partially, in control of its assets and affairs in accordance with the 'debtor-in-possession' (DIP) scheme. On this point, refer to Chapters 3 'Debt Restructuring Outside Formal Insolvency Proceedings' and 4 'Formal Insolvency Proceedings'.

[25] *West Mercia Safetywear v Dodd* (n 11) at 33.

[26] *Nicholson v Permakraft (NZ) Ltd* (n 9). In Europe, Art. 19 of the recent Directive (EU) 2019/1023 refers to a situation of likelihood of insolvency. However, to determine the point in time when this situation starts, Art. 2(2) of the Directive (EU) 2019/1023 refers to national laws. On this point, see para. 7.28.

[27] Reinhard Bork, *Einführung in das Insolvenzrecht* (10th edn, Mohr Siebeck 2021) 54–5 para. 102.

198 DIRECTORS' DUTIES IN THE VICINITY OF INSOLVENCY

there is a balance sheet deficit does not necessarily qualify as insolvency. However, in practice, the difference between the prerequisites adopted and the concept of insolvency endorsed by the above-mentioned jurisdictions is more formal than substantial so that both the German and the Italian prescriptions usually apply when the company is formally declared insolvent and insolvency proceedings have been opened.[28]

7.19 The difficulty in determining the twilight zone is not the only hurdle that creditors must overcome. In some countries, company directors are protected against legal allegations concerning the way they conduct business through the so-called 'business judgment rule' (BJR). Basically, this rule contains a presumption according to which directors are assumed to have acted in 'good faith', with the result that the courts cannot review or question their decisions. For example, this happens in the United States, under Delaware case law,[29] or in Germany under § 93(1) of the *Aktiengesetz*. This specifies that '[n]o dereliction of duties shall be given in those instances in which the member of the management board, in taking an entrepreneurial decision, was within his rights to reasonably assume that he was acting on the basis of adequate information and in the best interests of the company'. In Germany, this rule, moreover, applies by analogy to private companies.[30] It goes without saying that when a jurisdiction has endorsed the BJR, this also protects directors from any misconduct that has injured creditors in the twilight zone.

3. Standing, damages, and ancillary prescriptions

7.20 At common law, the policy of duty shifting does not change the rules on standing. This implies that the liability for breach of duties owed to creditors can be enforced by the company and, derivatively, by one of its shareholders, but not by its creditors.[31] The situation is different when insolvency procedures or proceedings have been opened. In these cases, the decisive factor is what is laid down by the relevant insolvency law and, in particular, whether or not this divests the debtor company of its powers. Of course, if it does, the standing is given to the insolvency practitioner appointed to the procedures or proceedings, and he will act on behalf of the company. For example, this happens in England.[32]

7.21 The situation is more variegated in civil law jurisdictions, where some regulations give creditors not only standing but also a direct claim against a company's directors. For example, this happens in Germany as regards the action provided for by § 93(5) of the

---

[28] As regards § 93(5) of the German law regulating joint stock companies, see Wolfgang Hölters, '§ 93' in Wolfgang Hölters (ed.), *Akiengsetzt Kommentar* (3rd edn, Beck/Vahlen 2017) § 93 para. 322, while as regards Arts 2394 and 2476(6) of the Italian *Codice civile*, see Gian Franco Campobasso, *Diritto commerciale, vol. 2, Diritto delle società* (10th edn, Utet 2020) 389 ss, 391, 593.

[29] Robert A.G. Monks and Nell Minow, *Corporate Governance* (5th edn, John Wiley & Sons Ltd 2011) 268 ss.

[30] Detlef Kleindiek, '§ 43' in Marcus Lutter and Peter Hommelhoff (eds), *GmbH-Gesetz Kommentar* (20th edn, Verlag Dr. Otto Schmidt 2020) § 43 para 23.

[31] Davies and Worthington, *Modern Company Law* (n 11) para. 9-15.

[32] Kristin van Zwieten, *Goode on Principles of Corporate Insolvency Law* (5th edn, Sweet & Maxwell 2019) para. 14-15.

Aktiengesetz. This also happens in Italy, as regards the actions regulated by Arts 2394 and 2476(6) of the Italian *Codice civile.* By contrast, when the relevant regulations do not give creditors a direct claim, the company has both a substantial claim and a procedural standing. For example, this occurs in Germany as regards the action laid down by § 43(1) of the *Gesetz betreffend die Gesellschaften mit beschränkter Haftung.* By contrast, both these jurisdictions converge in the fact that when insolvency proceedings have been opened and the debtor companies have been divested of their assets, the standing for enforcing directors' liability in the vicinity of insolvency is handed over to the insolvency practitioners who have been appointed.[33]

Directors who have been declared liable must compensate for the harm produced. **7.22** However, when this liability protects the company's creditors only indirectly, the damages are regarded as compensatory in relation to the company and not to its creditors. This holds true in common law jurisdictions where compensation is measured in relation to the whole loss suffered by the company. However, this common law rule may clash with the existence of a security right, granted by the company to a specific creditor, which encumbers the whole of the company's assets. A case in point might be a floating charge under English law. When this situation occurs, the enforcement of the directors' liability will benefit just the secured creditor, whose security right will absorb all the proceeds of the liability action.[34]

The same remedy applies in Germany as regards the action laid down by § 43(1) of **7.23** the *Gesetz betreffend die Gesellschaften mit beschränkter Haftung.* Here, courts calculate damages by comparing the hypothetical value that the company would have had if its directors had not injured it, with the value of the same company at the date when the liability action was brought. The difference between the (putative) former value and the latter value gives the amount of the compensation.[35]

In Italy, the way compensation should be calculated is controversial, since the nature **7.24** of the action is controversial too. In particular, those who maintain that the actions regulated by Arts 2394 and 2476(6) of the *Codice civile* were originally conceived as belonging to creditors maintain that damages should be compensatory in relation to the injured creditors; by contrast, those who maintain that the actions regulated by Arts 2394 and 2476(6) of the *Codice civile* allow creditors, exceptionally, to bring the actions belonging to the company, when and because the company fails to bring them, also maintain that damages should be compensatory in relation to the company. However, this dispute is more theoretical than practical, since the actions at issue are usually brought in insolvency proceedings where damages are regarded as compensatory in

---

[33] See: as regards private German companies, Kleindiek, '§ 43' (n 28) § 43 para. 37a; as regards joint stock Italian companies, Art. 255 of the Italian *Codice della crisi d'impresa e dell'insolvenza* and Art. 2394-*bis* of the Italian *Codice Civile*; and, as regards private Italian companies, Art. 255 of the Italian *Codice della crisi d'impresa e dell'insolvenza.*

[34] Davies and Worthington, *Modern Company Law* (n 11) para. 9-15.

[35] Kleindiek, '§ 43' (n 28) § 43 para. 46.

200   DIRECTORS' DUTIES IN THE VICINITY OF INSOLVENCY

relation to the overall loss to the company.[36] In this case, indeed, the Italian Supreme Court, aiming to ease the insolvency practitioner's burden of proof, has ruled that, whenever it is difficult to determine the exact amount of the harm caused (e.g. because no balance sheets have been kept), a company's directors should be considered liable for the whole deficit of the company.[37]

7.25   The policy of duty shifting and the parallel regulations in civil law jurisdictions are sometimes supplemented by the provision of additional duties aiming to give additional protection to creditors. These duties vary to a great extent, but the following are prominent examples:

- the duty to recapitalize or liquidate the distressed company,
- the duty to initiate insolvency proceedings,
- the duty to rescue the company,
- the prohibition against making payments.

7.26   The duty to recapitalize or liquidate the distressed company is typical of European legislations. In Europe, not only was this rule part of the legal tradition of some Member States, but also, in 1976, it was adopted by the European Economic Community (EEC, the organization subsequently transformed into the European Union). Article 17 of the Second Directive 77/91/EEC of 13 December 1976 laid down that '1. In the case of a serious loss of the subscribed capital, a general meeting of shareholders must be called within the period laid down by the laws of the Member States, to consider whether the company should be wound up or any other measures taken' and that '2. The amount of a loss deemed to be serious within the meaning of paragraph 1 may not be set by the laws of Member States at a figure higher than half the subscribed capital.'[38]

Since the European instrument was a directive, Member States transposed Art. 17 of the Second EEC Directive in various ways. For example, in Italy, it is laid down that this duty arises both in joint stock companies and private companies, when these have

---

[36] As regards the dispute concerning Art. 2394 of the Italian *Codice civile*, see Campobasso, *Diritto delle società* (n 26) 389–91. Since the more recent Art. 2476(6) of the *Codice civile,* added in 2019, reproduces the contents of Art. 2394 of the *Codice civile,* the debate concerning Art. 2394 also refers to Art. 2476(6). On this point, see Campobasso, *Diritto delle società* (n 26) 593.

[37] Cass., Sez. Un., 9100/2015 and, more recently, Cass. 24431/2019. In practice, this tendency produces a result similar to what happens in France in accordance with Art. L651-2 of the French *Code de Commerce.*

[38] Second Council Directive 77/91/EEC of 13 December 1976, OJ L 26, 31 January 1977, 1–13. Subsequently, this EEC directive was replaced by the Directive (EU) 2012/30/EU of 25 October 2012, OJ L 315, 14 November 2012, 74–97, which, in its turn, was replaced by the Directive (EU) 2017/1132 of 14 June 2017. With reference to the duty at issue, Art. 58 of this last directive lays down that

> 1. In the case of a serious loss of the subscribed capital, a general meeting of shareholders shall be called within the period laid down by the laws of the Member States, to consider whether the company should be wound up or any other measures taken. 2. The amount of a loss deemed to be serious within the meaning of paragraph 1 shall not be set by the laws of Member States at a figure higher than half the subscribed capital.

Recently, Art. 32 of the Directive (EU) 2019/1023 has laid down that Member States must derogate from Art. 58(1) of the Directive (EU) 2017/1132 to the extent and for the period of time that such derogations are necessary in order to set up the preventative restructuring frameworks provided for in the Directive (EU) 2019/1023.

lost one-third of their subscribed capital (Arts 2446(1) and 2482-*bis*(1) of the Italian *Codice civile*). By contrast, in Germany, it is laid down that this duty arises in joint stock companies only, when these have lost one-half of their subscribed capital (§ 92 of the *Aktiengesetz*). At any rate, in both jurisdictions, the breach of these duties is sanctioned through actions that aim to enforce the director's liability towards both the company and its creditors.

Some countries also impose on directors a duty to initiate insolvency proceedings. For example, this happens in Germany. Here, if distress consists in insolvency, company directors have a duty to file for the opening of insolvency proceedings. Paragraph 15a(1) of the German *Insolvenzordnung* lays down that **7.27**

> [w]here a legal person becomes illiquid or overindebted, the members of the board of directors or the liquidators shall file a request for the opening of proceedings without culpable delay, at the latest, however, either three weeks after the commencement of the debtors' inability to pay or six weeks after the commencement of overindebtedness.

In accordance with the German regulation, these proceedings could result in either liquidation or rescue. The violation of this duty is punished under criminal law. By contrast, under civil law, the duty to file is sanctioned through an action grounded in tort law. This will be dealt with in paras 7.42–7.44 below.

Directors' liability in the twilight zone was conceived, at least originally, as a way of protecting the creditors of those companies that were about to be liquidated. However, the more rescue culture has prevailed over liquidation culture, the more liability in the twilight zone has been employed to support rescue culture. This explains why Art. 19 of Directive (EU) 2019/1023 lays down that **7.28**

> Member States shall ensure that, where there is a likelihood of insolvency, directors have due regard, as a minimum, to the following:
>
> (a) the interests of creditors, equity holders and other stakeholders;
> (b) the need to take steps to avoid insolvency; and
> (c) the need to avoid deliberate or grossly negligent conduct that threatens the viability of the business.

Basically, Art. 19 of Directive (EU) 2019/1023 aims to harmonize national laws on directors' liability in the twilight zone across Europe. This explains why this prescription applies under the condition that there is an objective situation of the likelihood of insolvency, even though the existence of this situation must be determined in accordance with the relevant national law. On this point, Art. 2(2) of Directive (EU) 2019/1023 lays down that '[f]or the purposes of this Directive, the following concepts are to be understood as defined by national law: (a) insolvency; (b) likelihood of insolvency'.

Further, Art. 19 of Directive (EU) 2019/1023 aims to accommodate national laws to rescue culture. This explains why Art. 19 of Directive (EU) 2019/1023 has enlarged the scope of legal protection from a company's creditors to all of its constituencies—the

202 DIRECTORS' DUTIES IN THE VICINITY OF INSOLVENCY

soundness of every constituency may be crucial for the company's rescue; and this explains why Art. 19 of Directive (EU) 2019/1023 has introduced a new behavioural duty and a new prohibition—directors of companies that are in a situation where there is a likelihood of insolvency must take steps to avoid insolvency and must refrain from deliberate or grossly negligent conduct that threatens the viability of the business.[39]

7.29 Since this European law act is a directive, Member States must transpose it into national law by adopting the means which, from State to State, are considered most apt to achieve the goals of the directive. On 22 December 2020, Germany transposed the Directive (EU) 2019/1023 by adopting a new law instrument that, with some exceptions, which are irrelevant to the topic at issue, entered into force on 1 January 2021 under the title of *Gesetz zur Fortentwicklung des Sanierungs- und Insolvenzrechts*. This act aims to make the German legal framework more rescue-friendly. As regards the topic at issue, § 42 of the *Gesetz zur Fortentwicklung des Sanierungs- und Insolvenzrechts* lays down that when a company—that is still viable—becomes illiquid or overindebted, directors are exempted from the duty to file provided for by § 15a of the *Insolvenzordnung* and must report the situation to the competent court in order to plan restructuring. Moreover, § 43 of the same *Gesetz zur Fortentwicklung des Sanierungs- und Insolvenzrechts* lays down that if this situation occurs, the company's directors have a duty to look after the company's restructuring with a duty of care similar to that of a diligent manager. If the company's directors are not compliant with this duty, § 43 continues, they will be obliged to compensate the company with a sum of money equal to the harm sustained by the company's creditors.[40]

7.30 Article 5(9) of the German *Gesetz zur Fortentwicklung des Sanierungs- und Insolvenzrechts* has, moreover, added to the *Insolvenzordnung* a new paragraph, namely § 15b. This paragraph, which accommodates a previous prescription to rescue culture, lays down that after the company has become unable to pay its debts as they fall due, or after the company has become overindebted, the company's directors are prohibited from making any payments, unless these are compatible with the standard of due care of a diligent and conscientious manager. The same prescription adds that the payments that have been made by those directors who have illicitly failed to file for the commencement of insolvency proceedings should be considered illegal. Finally, § 15b

---

[39] On this point, see also Giorgio Corno, 'Art. 19—Duties of Directors Where There Is a Likelihood of Insolvency' in Christoph G. Paulus and Reinhard Dammann, *European Preventive Restructuring. Directive (EU) 2019/1023 Article-by-Article Commentary* (Beck-Hart-Nomos 2021) 242 para 12. Moreover, as regards the law of the European Union, see Art. 36 of the 'Proposal for a Directive of the European Parliament and of the Council harmonising certain aspects of insolvency law' of 7 December 2022 (COM(2022) 702 final). The text of this recommended prescription, which is entitled 'Duty to request the opening of insolvency proceedings', reads:

> Member States shall ensure that, where a legal entity becomes insolvent, its directors are obliged to submit a request for the opening of insolvency proceedings with the court no later than 3 months after the directors became aware or can reasonably be expected to have been aware that the legal entity is insolvent.

[40] The tenor of §§ 42 and 43 of the German *Gesetz zur Fortentwicklung des Sanierungs- und Insolvenzrechts* implies that, at least as regards this form of liability, the twilight zone starts when the company is already insolvent.

of the German *Insolvenzordnung* lays down that the directors who have violated the prohibition must compensate the company for the payments made.

C. Liability for Wrongful Trading

1. Concept and rationale

The limits of the duty-shifting policy and parallel regulations in civil law jurisdictions, and especially the difficulty in determining the extension of the twilight zone, explain why some policymakers tend to protect creditors in a more flexible manner. Here, the challenge in law-making consists in protecting the creditors of distressed companies in a way that does not require the determination of a (theoretically) clear-cut twilight zone. **7.31**

A prominent example of these new-generation devices is the English regulation on 'wrongful trading', which is laid down by ss 214 and 246ZB of the UK Insolvency Act 1986.[41] In essence, s. 214 of the UK Insolvency Act 1986 lays down that when a company has gone into liquidation proceedings, its director (including a *de facto* and a shadow director) might be made liable for the loss suffered by the company's creditors, provided that: 'at some time before the commencement of the winding up of the company, that person knew or ought to have concluded that there was no reasonable prospect that the company would avoid going into insolvent liquidation'. The director may avoid this liability by demonstrating that he or she 'took every step with a view to minimizing the potential loss to the company's creditors as [...] he ought to have taken'. *Mutatis mutandis*, this regulation has been extended to administration procedure (s. 246ZB of the UK Insolvency Act 1986). **7.32**

The difference between the duty-shifting policy and the wrongful trading policy is evident. While the former is based on the existence of a clear-cut twilight zone, which is regarded as something that can be determined objectively, the latter pivots around the subjective evaluation of a director's business judgement—here, what is required is a culpable failure to act properly with a view to minimizing the potential loss to creditors.[42] This point explains why s. 214(4) lays down that, for the purposes of this regulation, **7.33**

> the facts which a director of a company ought to know or ascertain, the conclusions which he ought to reach and the steps which he ought to take are those which would be known or ascertained, or reached or taken, by a reasonably diligent person having both—(a) the general knowledge, skill and experience that may reasonably be expected of a person carrying out the same functions as are carried out by that director

---

[41] In its turn, this device is the evolution of the regulation on 'fraudulent trading', which is now regulated by s. 213 of UK Insolvency Act 1986.

[42] van Zwieten, *Principles* (n 30) para. 14-33.

204 DIRECTORS' DUTIES IN THE VICINITY OF INSOLVENCY

in relation to the company, and (b) the general knowledge, skill and experience that that director has.

7.34 This reference to the subjective evaluation of the skills of a company's director, even though these must be evaluated in accordance with the objective criteria laid down by s. 214(4), makes this regulation particularly flexible and, therefore, rescue-friendly. Indeed, on this point, it has been observed that the clause 'took every step with a view to minimizing the potential loss to the company's creditors as [...] he ought to have taken' does not necessarily imply a duty for the director to cease business, because— depending on the case at issue—the opposite might be true.[43]

2. Prescription addressees, standing, and damages

7.35 The English device against 'wrongful trading' was conceived as an action that could be brought in insolvency proceedings or procedures. This explains why the standing for this is given to the relevant insolvency practitioners only. However, in England, this choice of policy has proved to be disadvantageous for the general body of creditors, since this action must be brought at the expense of the insolvency assets—when the chances of success are uncertain, insolvency practitioners are reluctant to pay for an action that might not increase the insolvency assets. Therefore, in 2015, a law reform allowed insolvency practitioners to assign the wrongful trading claims to third parties in order that actions against culpable directors might be taken not by the more prudent insolvency practitioners themselves but by more aggressive companies, specialized in this kind of litigation (s. 246ZD of the UK Insolvency Act 1986).[44]

7.36 The 'wrongful trading' action aims to make culpable directors liable for damages. Indeed, s. 214 of the UK Insolvency Act 1986 lays down that the court applied to should declare the directors in question liable to contribute to the company's assets 'as the court thinks proper'. Moreover, unlike what happens in the case of a liability action based on duty shifting, on this point, s. 176ZB of the UK Insolvency Act 1986 lays down that 'the proceeds of the claim or assignment [...] are not to be treated as part of the company's net property'. This prevents a potential floating charger encumbering the company's assets from sweeping them out.

7.37 The liability for wrongful trading is certainly an innovative device in creditor protection. Nevertheless, in England, scholars and practitioners are not wholly enthusiastic about its outcomes; as a result, other jurisdictions, which had adopted similar regulations, have further improved this model by giving standing also to creditors, by simplifying the onus of proof imposed on the claimant, and by clarifying the content of the defendant's defence. The recent regulation of Singapore is a conspicuous case in point.[45]

---

[43] ibid para. 14-47.

[44] Davies and Worthington, *Modern Company Law* (n 11) para. 9-10.

[45] See s. 239 of the Insolvency, Restructuring and Dissolution Act 2018 (IRDA). By contrast, in the past, the device regulated by s. 214 of the UK Insolvency Act 1986 was particularly appreciated in Continental Europe. For example, the 2003 'Report of the High-Level Group of Company Law Experts on a Modern Regulatory Framework

D. Other Forms of Liability Based on Tort Law

Some jurisdictions have developed additional forms of directors' liability, which are **7.38** based on tort law. For example, this is the case in some US States and Germany.

1. US liability for deepening insolvency
In the United States, cases of directors' liability under the common law doctrine of duty **7.39** shifting are rare, because most US States adopt the BJR. Moreover, in the United States, there is no device similar to the UK regulation on wrongful trading. This context explains why, in the *Lafferty* case, the US Court of Appeals for the Third Circuit (which has appellate jurisdiction *inter alia* over the three district courts of Pennsylvania) ruled that improperly prolonging the life of an insolvent corporation through new finance can deepen company insolvency and, especially, that this wrongdoing may be regarded as a valid cause of action under Pennsylvania state law. In particular, in this respect, the Third Circuit ruled that

> [u]nder federal bankruptcy law, insolvency is a financial condition in which a corporation's debts exceed the fair market value of its assets. 11 U.S.C. § 101(32). Even when a corporation is insolvent, its corporate property may have value. The fraudulent and concealed incurrence of debt can damage that value in several ways [...] Aside from causing actual bankruptcy, deepening insolvency can undermine a corporation's relationships with its customers, suppliers, and employees. The very threat of bankruptcy, brought about through fraudulent debt, can shake the confidence of parties dealing with the corporation [...] In addition, prolonging an insolvent corporation's life through bad debt may simply cause the dissipation of corporate assets. These harms can be averted, and the value within an insolvent corporation salvaged, if the corporation is dissolved in a timely manner, rather than kept afloat with spurious debt.[46]

In actual fact, the Third Circuit dismissed the *Lafferty* case in accordance with the *in* **7.40** *pari delicto* doctrine, since the defendant proved that the company had taken part in the alleged wrongdoing. However, the decision given in the *Lafferty* case influenced other US courts, not just of the State of Pennsylvania. This decision further developed the concept that keeping an insolvent company afloat by assuming new obligations that waste corporate assets is a specific cause of action in tort law.[47] Some courts, moreover,

---

for Company Law' in Europe suggested that the European Union should introduce a form of liability for wrongful trading. 'If the directors ought to foresee that the company cannot continue to pay its debts', the Report states, 'they must decide either to rescue the company (and ensure future payment of creditors) or to put it into liquidation. Otherwise, the directors will be liable fully or in part to creditors for their unpaid claims.' This report (4 November 2002) is available at <https://ecgi.global/sites/default/files/report_en.pdf> accessed 11 January 2024. However, the EU Commission, in drawing up Art. 19 of the Directive (EU) 2019/1023, did not accept this suggestion and preferred to reshape the traditional concept of directors' liability in the twilight zone in order to accommodate it to rescue culture.

[46] *Official Committee v R.F. Lafferty Co.*, 267 F.3d 340, at 349–50.

[47] See the analysis carried out by David C. Thompson, 'A Critique of "Deepening Insolvency", New Bankruptcy Tort Theory', *Stanford Journal of Law, Business, and Finance*, 12(2) (2007) 536, at 539 ss.

206 DIRECTORS' DUTIES IN THE VICINITY OF INSOLVENCY

have made a further step forwards and employed this doctrine also to determine the damages to be recovered. In particular, on this point, some courts have ruled that in cases of liability for deepening insolvency, the culpable directors are liable for the whole amount of the wrongfully incurred debts that the company is unable to pay.[48]

7.41 However, the deepening insolvency doctrine is not universally accepted across the US States—for example, it is not accepted by the courts of the State of New York.[49] Moreover, this doctrine has been severely criticized since it is regarded as a new way of circumventing the BJR.[50] These criticisms have been even stronger when directed towards the version of this theory that also aims to determine the harm suffered by the injured company and its creditors.[51]

2. German liability for the delayed opening of insolvency proceedings

7.42 As already noted, § 15a(1) of the German *Insolvenzordnung* lays down that

> [w]here a legal person becomes illiquid or overindebted, the members of the board of directors or the liquidators shall file a request for the opening of proceedings without culpable delay, at the latest, however, either three weeks after the commencement of the debtors' inability to pay or six weeks after the commencement of overindebtedness.

However, since this rule is sanctioned under criminal law only, German courts have judicially developed under tort law the so-called liability for the delayed opening of insolvency proceedings (*Insolvenzverschleppungshaftung*).

7.43 In particular, German courts have ruled that the intentional or negligent violation of the duty to file for the opening of insolvency proceedings is a cause of action in accordance with para, 823(2) of the *Bürgerliches Gesetzbuch* (BGB). The combination of subsections 1 and 2 of these prescriptions lays down that

> [a] person who, intentionally or negligently, unlawfully injures the life, body, health, freedom, property or other right of another person is liable to make compensation to the other party for the damage arising from this. The same duty is incumbent on a person who commits a breach of a statute that is intended to protect another person. If, according to the contents of the statute, it may also be breached without fault, then liability to compensation only exists in the case of fault.

7.44 The German doctrine on liability for the delayed opening of insolvency proceedings follows the general rules of tort law. This explains why the insolvency practitioner intending to bring an action against company directors must prove that the delay in filing

---

[48] James B. Heaton, 'Deepening Insolvency', Journal of Corporate Law, 30 (2005) 465 ss, at 480, where the author analyses the relevant case law to demonstrate the existence of this variation in doctrine.

[49] *In re Global Service Corporation*, 316 BR 451, 460 (Bankr. SDNY 2004).

[50] Thompson, 'Deepening Insolvency' (n 45) 546–7.

[51] Heaton, 'Deepening Insolvency' (n 46) 491 ss.

for insolvency proceedings is the consequence of either intentional or negligent conduct on the part of a director, that this conduct has caused loss to creditors, and that between the directors' conduct and the loss caused to creditors there exists a causal link. As regards compensation, German courts, however, distinguish between a debtor's old and new creditors ('*alte*' and '*neue Gläubiger*'), that is between those who were already creditors when the director's duty arose (old creditors) and those who became creditors after that point in time (new creditors). In particular, courts hold that old creditors are entitled to receive a compensation that equals the difference between the dividend that they expected to receive at that point in time and the dividend that they have actually achieved. This claim can be enforced by the insolvency practitioners appointed to the insolvency proceedings. By contrast, courts hold that new creditors might receive a compensation that only equals the harm that these suffered from the fact that they became creditors in good faith, relying on the debtor's ability to pay debts when they fell due.[52] Here, the insolvency practitioner has no standing, and the relevant claim may be enforced by any single creditor who has been injured.[53]

E. Overlapping and Twisted Strategies

7.45 The comparative analysis which has been carried out demonstrates that, at least in some jurisdictions, there are areas where the devices examined tend to overlap, with the result that—in some cases and under certain conditions—these could be employed interchangeably. For example, in England, a situation of functional overlap exists between the claim related to breach of duties owed to creditors and the claim related to wrongful trading—both devices aim to recoup the loss to the company so as to benefit the creditors as a whole.[54]

7.46 Theoretically, no overlap could exist between liability for breach of duties owed to creditors and preference law because a breach harms the company and only indirectly its creditors, while a preference transaction alters the position of a creditor *vis-à-vis* another creditor. In addition, while, in the case of liability for breach of duties, the remedy consists in ordering the culpable director to compensate the company, the remedy within preference law consists in ordering the preferred creditor to give back to the

---

[52] Reinhard Bork, '§ 64' in Reinhard Bork and Carsten Schäfer, *Kommentar zum GmbH-Gesetz* (5th edn, RWS, 2022) § 64 a.F. ('*alte Fassung*', i.e. old version) paras 86 and 88. Up until 2008, this duty was laid down by § 64 of the *Gesetz betreffend die Gesellschaften mit beschränkter Haftung*; German commentaries on § 64 provide comments on § 15a(1) of the *Insolvenzordnung*.

[53] Kleindiek, '§ 64' (n 28) Appendix to § 64 GmbHG, para. 101. For a different position according to which the insolvency practitioner would also be entitled to bring actions on behalf of new creditors, see what is reported by Kleindiek, ibid Appendix to § 64 GmbHG, para. 102.

[54] Even though the former claim could be brought even before the opening of insolvency procedures, while the latter requires that these procedures should already exist, in practice, this distinction is blurred since data demonstrate that a breach is most likely to be proved within insolvency proceedings. Moreover, in English law, there is a partial overlap with Arts 15A–15C of the UK Company Directors Disqualification Act 1986. These prescriptions, which, in 2015, were added to the 1986 disqualification statute, also provide for compensation orders and the acceptance of compensation undertakings. On this point, see below, n 53.

208 DIRECTORS' DUTIES IN THE VICINITY OF INSOLVENCY

insolvency practitioner the sum received from the debtor. Nevertheless, since common law jurisdictions courts have great flexibility in accommodating the law to each single case, the claim related to breach of duties can be employed as a substitute for a preference action. For example, this happened in the *West Mercia* case, where the director of *West Mercia* authorized the payment of a debt that this company owed to its parent company, when both companies were insolvent.[55]

III. Directors' Disqualification

A. Concept, purpose, and terminology

7.47   In most jurisdictions, the legal framework regarding directors' duties and liability is supplemented by a set of rules that prohibit dishonest directors from managing companies—these rules prohibit directors not only from continuing to manage the company where they had been appointed before they proved to be 'dishonest' but also from managing other companies that are based in the same jurisdictions.[56] These regulations usually refer to *de jure*, *de facto*, and, if provided for, *shadow directors*. In addition, this set of rules also prohibits 'dishonest' people from being appointed as company directors, even though they have never actually been appointed as directors.

7.48   This area of law is traditionally dealt with in corporate governance textbooks since these regulations aim especially to improve corporate standards and prevent further misconduct by directors. For example, in the English case *Re Blackspur Group plc, Secretary of State for Trade and Industry v Davies*, Lord Woolf MR stated:

> [t]he purpose of the *1986 Act* [i.e. the Company Directors Disqualification Act 1986] is the protection of the public, by means of prohibitory remedial action, by anticipated

---

[55] In this respect, Kristin van Zwieten, 'Director Liability in Insolvency and Its Vicinity', Oxford Journal of Legal Studies, 38(2) (2018) 382 ss, at 393–4, clearly wrote:

> [i]n West Mercia it appears to have been accepted that the payment made to the parent was vulnerable to being unwound as a preference under the precursor to s 239, but no such action was apparently brought. This was presumably because the £4,000 payment was made by crediting the parent's overdrawn bank account (thus being applied immediately to discharge the parent's debt to the bank), and the parent was insolvent: the company had 'no other assets available to repay the £4,000'. Instead, the liquidator took an alternative route to a remedy: rather than look to the parent to repay the subsidiary, the liquidator looked to the director who had (self-interestedly) authorized the payment to do so. The making of such an order would, however, have put the unsecured creditors of the subsidiary in a better position than they would have been in had the parent not been paid: the assets of the subsidiary would be swelled by payment from the director, without any corresponding increase in liabilities (since the debt to the parent would remain discharged). To avoid this result, the Court of Appeal ordered the director to repay the £4,000 to the subsidiary (with interest), but also ordered that the remaining debt owed by the subsidiary to the parent be notionally increased by £4,000 for the purpose of calculating the parent's entitlement to a distribution in the subsidiary's liquidation, with any dividend attributable to the notional increase to be recouped by the director rather than paid to the parent. The overall effect was to produce a similar result for unsecured creditors to that which would have been obtained had the payment been set aside as a preference.

[56] Therefore, director disqualification is different from director removal.

deterrent effect on further misconduct and by encouragement of higher standards of honesty and diligence in corporate management, from those who are unfit to be concerned in the management of the company.[57]

Nevertheless, disqualification has some points of contact with insolvency law, since most jurisdictions regard as grounds for disqualification both the fact that the relevant person was personally insolvent and that a director committed a criminal offence related to insolvency law. For example, he or she may have intentionally delayed the opening of insolvency proceedings.

Legislations vary to a great extent, and the language employed in English-speaking countries is not always consistent. For example, while in England (and in other jurisdictions influenced by English law, such as Australia and Canada), this ban is called 'disqualification', in the United States, it is called 'suspension' or 'debarment'. **7.49**

B. Taxonomies

Despite these diversities, the regulations concerning directors' disqualification (broadly understood) may be grouped, from a functional point of view, into three main regimes, depending on the way disqualification is provided for. These main regimes may be called 'Automatic disqualification', 'Disqualification ordered by a court', and 'Disqualification imposed by an administrative body'. Sometimes, the same jurisdiction features more than one regime. **7.50**

1. Automatic disqualification

Many jurisdictions provide for some forms of 'automatic disqualification'. This form of disqualification implies that when a director commits an act which violates a rule that provides for disqualification, he or she is disqualified by operation of law and, if he or she is appointed as a director despite the disqualification, he or she commits an illicit or even a criminal offence. For example, this happens in England in accordance with Art. 11 of the Company Directors Disqualification Act 1986. The same happens in Germany, where, however, there is no specific act devoted to disqualification, and the cases of automatic disqualification are classified by company law statutes as cases of the **7.51**

---

[57] *Re Blackspur Group plc, Secretary of State for Trade and Industry v Davies* [1998] 1 BCLC 676, 680. Usually, the regulations on disqualification do not contain rules on compensation. However, the revised UK Company Directors Disqualification Act 1986 allows the Secretary of State to apply to a court for an order of compensation (Arts 15A–15C). This possibility was introduced in 2015 in order to make this regulation more attractive. As already said (n 52 above), the provisions on compensation laid down by the revised Company Directors Disqualification Act 1986 only partially overlap with both the legal framework concerning directors' duties and liability and the regulation on wrongful trading. This is because both the legal framework on directors' duties and liability and that on wrongful trading oblige courts to order a compensation in favour of all the debtor's creditors (it does not matter if some of them have benefited from the director's misconduct), while the revised regulation on disqualification is more selective since it allows a court to decide which entity must be compensated.

210 DIRECTORS' DUTIES IN THE VICINITY OF INSOLVENCY

non-eligibility of company directors. In particular, as regards limited companies, § 6(2) No. 3, of the *Gesetz betreffend die Gesellschaften mit beschränkter Haftung* states:

> [w]hoever has been convicted on account of one or more intentionally committed criminal offences, consisting either a) of failing to file an application for the opening of insolvency proceedings (delay in filing for insolvency), or b) of committing the criminal facts that are punished in sections 283 to 283d of the *Strafgesetzbuch* [Criminal Code] (offences in the state of insolvency) […] may not be appointed as director; this debarment shall apply for a period of five years after the judgment becomes final, which period shall exclude the period in which the actor was detained in an institution upon an official order.

The same holds true for joint stock companies, the topic at issue being regulated by § 76(3) of the *Aktiengesetz*.

7.52 In both England and Germany, the above-mentioned cases are prominent examples of automatic disqualification. However, while in England, the regulation features a certain degree of flexibility (in England, the court may grant a leave that excludes the commitment of a criminal offence, s. 11(1) of the Company Directors Disqualification Act 1986), in Germany, civil disqualification is still influenced by criminal law and the relevant concerns about constitutional law. Therefore, in Germany, neither courts nor administrative bodies have any discretion in applying this regulation; and disqualification for having committed criminal offences is provided for in situations only where directors have violated criminal law intentionally—it does not matter if the relevant criminal offence is also punishable because of mere negligence.[58]

2. Disqualification ordered by court order

7.53 Some countries lay down rules according to which disqualification is the outcome of an order issued by a court.

7.54 This happens, for example, in England, where, on demand of the Secretary of State (in s. 6(1) and, as regards the application, s. 7(1) of the Company Directors Disqualification Act 1986),

> [t]he court shall make a disqualification order against a person in any case where, on an application under this section, it is satisfied—(a)that he is or has been a director of a company which has at any time become insolvent (whether while he was a director or subsequently), and (b) that his conduct as a director of that company (either taken alone or taken together with his conduct as a director of one or more other companies or overseas companies) makes him unfit to be concerned in the management of a company.

---

[58] Andreas Rühmkorf, 'The United Kingdom' in Jean Jacques du Plessis and Jeanne Nel de Koker (eds), *Disqualification of Company Directors. A Comparative Analysis of the Law in the UK, Australia, South Africa, the US and Germany* (Routledge 2017) 173 ss.

This regulation is particularly strict. In fact, if the court ascertains that the director at issue was really 'unfit', it must necessarily disqualify him or her. The court, however, has discretionary powers as regards the length of the ban, which, in accordance with s. 6(4) of the Company Directors Disqualification Act 1986, may range from 2 to 15 years. **7.55**

This regulation does not contain any definition of a director's unfitness. However, Sch. 1 of the Company Directors Disqualification Act 1986 provides courts with some guidance by listing a series of factors that have to be taken into account. *Inter alia*, these are: the extent to which the person was responsible for the causes of a company becoming insolvent, the nature and extent of any loss or harm caused or any potential loss or harm which could have been caused, and any misfeasance or breach of any fiduciary duty by the director. **7.56**

Section 8ZA of the Company Directors Disqualification Act 1986, moreover, lays down that the court that has disqualified a director in accordance with s. 6 of the Company Directors Disqualification Act 1986 may make a disqualification order against any person that has exercised any 'amount of influence' over the disqualified director. **7.57**

Section 10 of the Company Directors Disqualification Act 1986 provides for another case of disqualification that is related to insolvency law. In particular, this section lays down that **7.58**

> [w]here the court makes a declaration under sections 213 or 214 of the Insolvency Act 1986 that a person is liable [because of fraudulent or wrongful trading] to make a contribution to a company's assets, then, whether or not an application for such an order is made by any person, the court may, if it thinks fit, also make a disqualification order against the person to whom the declaration relates.

The same prescription, moreover, lays down that, in this case, the maximum period of disqualification under this section is 15 years.

Both ss 6 and 10 of the Company Directors Disqualification Act 1986 provide for cases of disqualification by court order. However, between the two regimes, there are some differences. First, under s. 6, the court acts on application by the Secretary of State, while under s. 10, it may act on its own motion. Second, under s. 6, the court must disqualify the unfit director, while under s. 10, it may do so. **7.59**

Germany does not have a specific case of disqualification by court order that is applicable to cases relating to insolvency. However, § 70(1) of the German *Strafgesetzbuch* (Criminal Code) lays down that **7.60**

> [p]ersons who have been convicted of an unlawful act which they committed in abuse of their profession or trade or in gross breach of the attendant duties, or persons who have committed the same acts, but who have not been convicted merely because their criminal responsibility has been or can be ruled out, may be issued with an order disqualifying them from exercising that profession, branch of profession, trade or branch of trade for a period of between one year and five years if an overall evaluation of the

212 DIRECTORS' DUTIES IN THE VICINITY OF INSOLVENCY

offender and the offence shows that by further exercising the profession, branch of profession, trade or branch of trade there is a danger that they will commit serious unlawful acts of the type indicated. The disqualification order may be made in perpetuity if there is reason to believe that the statutory maximum period will not suffice to avert the danger posed by the offender.

7.61 Certainly, this regulation is not specifically devoted to directors of insolvent companies. Nevertheless, it allows a court imposing a criminal sanction on a director to supplement this punishment with a ban on his or her being appointed as a director.

3. Disqualification imposed by an administrative body

7.62 Some jurisdictions lay down rules according to which an administrative authority has the power to disqualify a director without the need for a court order.

7.63 For example, this happens in the United States, as regards companies that are obliged to file periodic reports to the Securities and Exchange Commission (SEC). Section 1105 of the Sarbanes–Oxley Act 2002 lays down that the SEC may prohibit persons from serving as officers and directors in the cease-and-desist proceedings under s. 21C of the Securities and Exchange Act 1934.

7.64 A special form of disqualification by an administrative decision exists also in England, where, under certain conditions, the Secretary of State may accept an undertaking given by a director who is on the verge of being subject to a disqualification order. Here, the court does not intervene at all, and the Secretary of State accepts the director's undertaking in which the latter proposes the length of the period of time for disqualification (s. 7 of the Company Directors Disqualification Act 1986).

C. Enforcement and Registration

7.65 Disqualification is enforced in various ways. Usually, countries that only rely on automatic disqualification do not have a body that is obliged to check whether disqualified directors observe the relevant prohibition. By contrast, countries that have a more sophisticated system of disqualification usually have an authority that is responsible for enforcement and registration.

7.66 For example, in England, the online 'Individual Insolvency Register' (IIR) allows people to know in real time about anyone who has been the subject of a bankruptcy order, a debt relief order, or other restrictions that prevent him or her from being a director of a company.[59] Moreover, the online 'Companies House Disqualified Directors Register' includes details of directors disqualified by the courts and the Secretary of State.[60]

---

[59] See <https://www.insolvencydirect.bis.gov.uk/eiir> accessed 11 January 2024.
[60] See <https://find-and-update.company-information.service.gov.uk/search/disqualified-officers> accessed 11 January 2024.

In England, registering is an important part of disqualification: first, because this makes **7.67** the ban visible to everyone and, consequently, prevents companies from appointing as a director a person who has been disqualified; second, because registering is also a form of punishment in accordance with the logic of naming and shaming. However, registering may also give rise to concerns, especially when the register is accessible to everyone. In fact, this policy may interfere with the privacy of the disqualified persons and may even make it difficult for them, as private individuals, to borrow money from banks—in England, there is evidence that banks have prejudices against those who are disqualified.[61]

IV. Piercing the Corporate Veil

A. Concept, Scope, and Terminology

Limited liability is the outcome of a well-considered choice of policy, which is based on **7.68** the general assumption that limited liability is beneficial to the company and its constituencies. Therefore (at least, in principle), this statement should imply that when the costs of limited liability exceed its benefits, a court ought to have the power to disregard a company's limited liability and regard its shareholders as unlimitedly liable for the company's liabilities. Indeed, this operation ought to be performed also within groups of companies, which, by design, magnify both the benefits and the costs of limited liability. However, with the exception of the United States, where judicial intervention against limited liability has a long tradition in many fields of law, including insolvency law, these operations are exceptional in other countries and, when permitted, are allowed only under strict conditions. In fact, against the above-mentioned reasoning, one could object that a cost–benefit analysis of the limited liability of each single company is no easy matter, that any judicial intervention disregarding limited liability may produce uncertainties about the very tenet of limited liability and its legal basis, and that these uncertainties might produce a cost for the whole economy that would certainly exceed the benefit that any single intervention might produce.

In this field, the terminology may also be slightly confusing. In Europe, and especially **7.69** in continental Europe, scholars, courts, and practitioners adopt the US expression 'piercing (or lifting) the corporate veil' or similar idioms to denominate interventions disregarding limited liability in all the relevant areas of law, including insolvency law. By contrast, their US colleagues prefer to restrict the expression 'piercing (or lifting) the corporate veil' to tort law, contract law, environmental law, and other fields, but excluding insolvency law. By contrast, in US insolvency law, the more usual expression

---

[61] Tom Reker, 'Unqualified Directors in Insolvency: A Comparative Study on the Desirability of Civil Law Director's Disqualification in the Netherlands', International Insolvency Review, 23(2) (2014) 142 ss, at 165, quoting analyses carried out on the UK regulation.

214 DIRECTORS' DUTIES IN THE VICINITY OF INSOLVENCY

is 'substantial consolidation', which, in Europe, is only employed to denominate the application of veil piercing to groups of distressed companies. See Chapter 8 'Corporate Groups in Rescue', para. 8.36.

7.70 The present section will adopt continental European terminology in dealing with legislation and case laws, which allow courts to disregard limited liability in insolvency law cases in order to give better protection to a company's creditors. These experiences are grouped under the heading 'Real Veil Piercing'. In addition, this section deals with some laws that—at least, in principle—do not disregard limited liability but employ different mechanisms to achieve functionally comparable results. These experiences, which are usually more selective and less problematic, are grouped under the heading 'Functional Veil Piercing'.

B. Real Veil Piercing

7.71 The worldwide picture on veil piercing is exceedingly variegated, and, while English law is reluctant to pierce the corporate veil,[62] France has a well-established tradition of abuse of rights (*abus des droits*), according to which rights must be understood by looking more at their function than at their content. This doctrine, which may be dated back to seminal studies carried out at the beginning of the twentieth century, has been applied to many fields of law, where it is still alive. Even though there is no coincidence between the doctrine of abuse of rights and the regulations on veil piercing, it goes without saying that the above-mentioned climate has facilitated the work of the French lawmaker. As a result, Art. L. 621-2 of the French *Code de Commerce* regulates an action that aims to extend the scope of already opened insolvency proceedings to persons who have a specific relation with the debtor (*action en extension*). Article L. 621-2 lays down that, on demand of the insolvency practitioner, the debtor, or the public prosecutor, a court may extend the scope of some insolvency proceedings that have been already opened against a debtor to other persons, provided that either the debtor is a fictive legal entity and these other persons are misusing its organization to achieve their own purposes or the debtor's assets and the other persons' assets are commingled.

7.72 In actual fact, this prescription does not refer exclusively to companies—according to Art. L. 621-2 of the French *Code de Commerce*, a court may extend the proceedings opened against a sole trader or a partnership if assets have been amalgamated. In any case, this prescription plays a crucial role when a company has misused its limited liability, provided that either the company is fictive or the company's assets and the shareholders' assets are commingled. Moreover, Art. L. 621-2 of the French *Code de Commerce* is also worth noting as regards the remedy adopted, which here consists in a drastic substantive consolidation of all the relevant assets and liabilities. This means

---

[62] Davies and Worthington, *Modern Company Law* (n 11) paras 8-1 and 8-17.

that when this prescription is applied, the single set of insolvency proceedings that has already been opened against the company will include all the assets and liabilities of the shareholders affected by the extension with all the possible unintended redistributive effects that this 'sanction' may imply. For example, consider the negative impact that this remedy may have on a shareholder, or on a personal creditor of this shareholder, when this shareholder has many assets but few liabilities.

Germany has no regulation on veil piercing, but German courts have always been **7.73** particularly sensitive to this issue. In particular, in the past, German courts came to standardize a quite generous list of symptomatic cases where shareholders were to be regarded as having abused limited liability and, when these situations occurred, it was ruled that limited liability should be disregarded. This list included assets amalgamation, the plundering of a company's assets so that the company risked termination, undercapitalization, and similar abuses perpetrated within a group of companies (such as cases where the amalgamation refers to the parent's and a subsidiary's assets or where a parent company had plundered the assets of one of its subsidiaries).[63] However, this case law was considered too strict and capable of discouraging business initiatives so that, in deciding the *Trihotel* case in 2007, the German Supreme Court overruled the above-mentioned case law and restricted veil piercing only to cases where a company's assets and shareholders' assets were commingled. Nowadays, as regards these situations only, a court may apply, by analogy, § 128 of the German *Handelsgesetzbuch* ('Trade Code'). This prescription, which textually refers to partnerships, lays down that '[t]he partners shall be personally and jointly and severally liable to the creditors for the partnership's obligations.'[64]

The United States stands apart in this picture. Here, courts have developed a doctrine **7.74** of substantial consolidation that is applicable whenever the administration of a case requires the involvement of a debtor's related persons or entities, whether or not fraud or misconduct has been committed. For example, this doctrine is applicable whenever a corporate business is run through a group of companies whose financial architecture is so intricate that, in the event of the companies' insolvency, the insolvency practitioners appointed to the various proceedings are unable to disentangle the assets and liabilities of each company. However, because the US doctrine is mainly applied within a group of companies, this will be dealt with in Chapter 8 'Corporate Groups in Rescue'.

---

[63] The approach taken by the German Supreme Court to this topic has changed many times. After the 1985 *Autocran* case (BGHZ 95, 330) this Court justified this form of liability by exploiting the prescriptions regulating groups of companies (paras 291 ss and 311 ss of the *Aktiengesetz*). Later on, the Supreme Court justified its position by referring to the principle of capital maintenance and its importance for creditor protection. See the 2001 *Bremer Vulkan* case (BGHZ, 149,10). Finally, in the 2007 *Trihotel* (BGHZ 173, 246), the Supreme Court again changed its position, as reported in the text.

[64] BGHZ 173, 246, para 27. For this trajectory in Germany and the related theories, see Raiser and Veil, *Kapitalgesellschaften* (n 13) 490 et seq. paras 3 et seq.

216 DIRECTORS' DUTIES IN THE VICINITY OF INSOLVENCY

C. Functional Veil Piercing

7.75 In some cases, the devices adopted to protect creditors from the risks of limited liability do not imply disregarding the corporate veil but produce some effects that are functionally equivalent to this remedy, even though to a limited extent.

1. Shareholders' liability

7.76 Basically, shareholders risk their contributions only, and usually neither case law nor regulations impose on them personal liability. However, this statement is not absolute, and across the world it is possible to find some rare examples of shareholders' liability. This happens, for example, in China. In particular, Art. 20 of the Chinese Company Law Act lays down that '[w]here a shareholder of a company abuses the independent status of the company as a legal person or the limited liability of shareholders, evades debts and thus seriously damages the interests of the creditors of the company, he shall assume joint and several liability for the debts of the company'. The Chinese regulation is quite different from both the French regulation and the above-mentioned more recent German case law as regards both prerequisites and remedy. In particular, as regards prerequisites, Art. 20 of the Chinese Company Law Act requires that it be proved that (a) the company shareholders have abused the company, (b) this abuse consisted in an evasion of the payments of the company to its creditors, (c) this misconduct injured the company's creditors seriously, and (d) a causal link existed between the shareholders' misconduct and the loss suffered by the creditors. Moreover, as regards remedy, the Chinese regulation does not imply that the court must disregard the company's 'veil', or even treat the company as a partnership, but simply entails that the shareholders at fault must be held jointly liable for the company's liabilities.[65]

7.77 Something similar has happened in Germany since the above-mentioned *Trihotel* case. In that case, the Federal Supreme Court ruled that, under certain conditions, one or more shareholders of a private company might be made liable because they had plundered the company's assets and, by doing so, created the conditions for the termination of the company's existence. However, since the *Trihotel* case, the Federal Supreme Court has ruled that this form of liability should be based on tort law.[66]

This liability, which is called liability for the termination of a company's existence (*Existenzvernichtungshaftung*), is grounded in § 826 of the German *Bürgerliches Gesetzbuch* ('Civil Code'). This paragraph, which is entitled 'Intentional damage contrary to public policy', lays down that '[a] person who, in a manner contrary to public policy, intentionally inflicts damage on another person is liable to the other person to make compensation for the damage'.

---

[65] Cheng-Hang Tan, Jiangyu Wang, and Christian Hofmann, 'Piercing the Corporate Veil: Historical, Theoretical & Comparative Perspectives', Berkeley Business Law Journal, 16(1) (2019) 140 ss, at 186 ss. These authors, however, adopt a very broad concept of veil piercing, including both real and functional veil piercing, which therefore includes the Chinese regulation too.

[66] BGHZ 173, 246, 2 ruling.

This shift from true veil piercing to functional veil piercing grounded in tort law has **7.78** complicated the burden of proof for the claimant, who nowadays must prove that (a) one or more of a company's shareholders have misused the company' resources, including employees and chances of profit, without any consideration for the company's financial situation; (b) this conduct has caused the company's insolvency and inflicted on it harm, corresponding to the difference between the putative value that the company would have had if the shareholders had not injured it and the value that the same company has at the date when the liability action must be brought; (c) the shareholders' conduct was contrary to public policy (e.g. because the culpable shareholders acted for selfish interests only); and (d) the culpable shareholders acted with intent to damage the company or, at least, with awareness that their activity would damage the company in a manner contrary to public policy. Since this action requires the insolvent company to be put into insolvency proceedings, the insolvency practitioner appointed to these proceedings has exclusive standing.[67]

The application of liability for the termination of a company's existence grounded in **7.79** tort law is very rare. Nevertheless, this doctrine has also been employed in some cases of blatant undercapitalization (*qualifizierte materielle Unterkapitalisierung*), that is where the company's capital structure is heavily leveraged by debts. The *Gamma* case was the most prominent example in this respect.[68]

The concept of *Existenzvernichtungshaftung* influenced, to a certain extent, Art. 2476(8) **7.80** of the Italian *Codice civile*. This article, which refers to private companies, lays down that 'when the company directors are liable in accordance with the regulation laid down by the previous subsections [i.e. by the sections regulating directors' duties and liability], they are jointly liable together with those shareholders who intentionally decided or authorized the execution of any act which has proved harmful to the company, to its shareholders or third parties'. This regulation was introduced in 2003 in order to involve in the liability of directors those shareholders who, even though not playing the role of *de facto* directors, have influenced the directors' decision-making with the specific intent to damage the company, its shareholders, or third parties. It is precisely this choice of policy that explains why this regulation on shareholders' misconduct applies under three conditions: (a) that one or more directors are liable in accordance with the relevant regulation on directors' duties and liability; (b) that one or more shareholders decided or authorized the performance of those acts which have proved harmful to the company, to its shareholders, or third parties; (c) that this decision or authorization was performed 'intentionally'. Here, 'intentionally' means that the shareholders' activity was performed with intent to damage either the company, its shareholders, or third

---

[67] Marc-Philippe Weller and Markus Lieberknecht in Bork and Schäfer, *GmbH-Gesetz Kommentar* (n 50) § 13 paras 45–56. The fact that this action is based on tort law also has some pros. For example, the tortious nature of this device allows the insolvency practitioner to sue not only the culpable shareholders but also other individuals or entities, such as advisors, lawyers, and banks, who/which have intentionally contributed to the occurrence of harm in accordance with § 830(2) of the German *Bürgerliches Gesetzbuch*.

[68] BGHZ, 176, 204.

218 DIRECTORS' DUTIES IN THE VICINITY OF INSOLVENCY

parties or, along the lines of the German approach to the intent required by § 826 of the German *Bürgerliches Gesetzbuch* ('Civil Code'), with the awareness that the shareholders' activity would damage the company, its shareholders or third parties.

7.81 However, the Italian regulation diverges from the German regulation in many respects. First, the Italian regulation is based on company law. Second, the Italian regulation requires that at least one of the company's directors should be liable. And, third, the Italian regulation requires no situation of insolvency so that an action may be brought outside insolvency proceedings. However, when the company is subject to insolvency proceedings, the appointed insolvency practitioner will have standing. At any rate, the cases where Art. 2476(8) has been successfully applied, whether outside or inside insolvency proceedings, are very rare.

2. The subordination of shareholders' claims

7.82 Sometimes, shareholders lend money to the company that they belong to instead of contributing to its capital stock. This situation occurs especially when the company is distressed. It is precisely in this context that shareholders are concerned that when the company is subject to insolvency proceedings, their contribution to the capital stock will be paid back only after the satisfaction of the company's creditors. By contrast, if they have lent money, they will better ranked in insolvency proceedings, since they will be sharing their position with the other creditors of the company.

7.83 In principle, jurisdictions do not prohibit shareholders from lending money to their companies. By contrast, some jurisdictions lay down devices which aim to ensure that when the company is distressed and contributions to capital stock would be appropriate, shareholders do not create conditions whereby they might fraudulently jump the queue. For example, this happens in Germany in accordance with § 39(1) No. 5 of *Insolvenzordnung*. According to this provision, all claims for the repayment of a shareholder's loan are subordinated when a company is insolvent. 'Subordination' means that subordinated claims may only be satisfied after the claims of all the other unsecured creditors of the company have been fully satisfied. Subordination also applies to claims resulting from legal transactions that are comparable to a shareholder's loan in financial terms. As a result, subordination will basically apply to all claims resulting from circumstances in which a shareholder has given credit to its company in any form. Something similar happens in Italy, even though this regulation textually applies only to private companies or within groups of companies, regardless of the nature of the companies involved.[69]

7.84 The United States has a comparable regime. 11 U.S.C. §510(c) lays down that 'the court may under principles of equitable subordination, subordinate for purposes of distribution all or part of an allowed claim to all or part of another allowed claim'. Unlike the German and the Italian prescriptions, the US prescription gives courts more discretion

---

[69] See Arts 2467 and 2497-*quinquies* of the Italian *Codice civile*.

in subordinating one claim to another, and 11 U.S.C. §510(c) requires for this decision no specific prerequisite. Nevertheless, in the United States, it is commonly accepted that this remedy may be used only when the claimant is culpable of any wrongdoing that confers an unfair advantage on the claimant or, more frequently, when the claimant's misconduct disadvantages the debtor's other claimants participating in the same insolvency proceedings. Indeed, in accordance with US case law, this situation *inter alia* occurs when the company has been undercapitalized and some insiders, such as the company's shareholders, have lent money to the company instead of contributing to its share capital.[70]

---

[70] Jeffrey Ferriel and Edward J. Janger, *Understanding Bankruptcy* (4th edn, Carolina Academic Press 2019) 349–50.

8

Corporate Groups in Rescue

Edward J. Janger

I. Introduction

8.01 Modern business enterprises rarely do business through a single legal entity. For example, even a neighbourhood delicatessen may be structured as three corporations: the restaurant, the catering company, and the management company. Each may hold its own assets and have a distinct set of creditors. All may be wholly owned by a single parent or may have distinct ownership structures and investors. The structures may be straightforward or a tangled web. Disentangling these relationships and allocating value can be complex if the business fails. It is yet more complex if the business enterprise seeks to restructure in insolvency.

8.02 Two questions will run through this chapter and reappear at various points: (a) what does it mean to respect the 'corporate form' in a liquidation and (b) how does that change in rescue, where the firm continues in business through a restructuring or going-concern sale? Each of these questions circles back to a more fundamental question about corporate groups: how does one situate enterprise value within the corporate group? Title to a piece of equipment may be held by one entity, but it may be used by another. Indeed, the value of the piece of equipment owned by one entity may be specific (and tailored) to its use by another entity. It may have virtually no resale value to the creditors of Entity A, but without it, Entity B will be unable to generate large amounts of income. Is that excess value located in Entity A (with the machine) or Entity B (the manner in which it is used)?

8.03 The puzzle of corporate groups is made more complicated because the group is not, in and of itself, an entity, but much of the value produced by the group enterprise may be a product of the sum of its parts—impossible to situate in, or trace to, any one group member. This going-concern or group surplus is homeless value. When all group members are solvent, this is not a problem, because the excess value flows up to the holding company as equity. Where the group or its members are insolvent, however, this 'homeless' value cannot be characterized as equity and does not belong to the shareholders. If it is preserved in a restructuring, it must be allocated among the creditors of the various entities. Yet, fights over allocation may swallow, or even destroy value. Historically, these fights have been waged over the question of substantive consolidation—whether to disregard the corporate form. This chapter argues that there is a better—less disruptive—approach to value allocation in rescue that respects the

---

Edward J. Janger, *Corporate Groups in Rescue* In: *The Anatomy of Corporate Insolvency Law*. Edited by: Reinhard Bork and Renato Mangano, Oxford University Press. © Edward J. Janger 2024. DOI: 10.1093/oso/9780198852094.003.0008

corporate form without fetishizing it. The key concept is that a creditor's baseline entitlement is established by realizable, rather than formal, priority.

The concept of realizable priority is developed more fully in Chapter 5 'Security Rights **8.04** and Creditors' Priority and Ranking: Realizable Priority in Rescue', but to put it succinctly: in a going-concern sale or restructuring, if a creditor or the holder of rights *in rem* seeks to claim a distributional priority (beyond its pro rata share of enterprise value), it has the burden of establishing that the value of such priority is realizable in the absence of the restructuring, by exercising its legal remedies. These priorities may derive from claims of ownership or security in particular assets of the firm, from the firm's capital structure (debt over equity) or statutory priority waterfall for claims against the firm,[1] or from corporate entity structure. The particular focus of this chapter is priority arising from corporate group structure, but the other forms of priority play a role as well.

In a group case, the compound nature of the enterprise creates a special problem for **8.05** the 'realizable-priority' approach.[2] Some value—the going-concern increment in particular—may be a collective good. No single group member will be able to realize on the reorganization increment going it alone. But if individual group members can assert claims to priority in their full value against a group member, their effective veto rights will doom any effort to restructure. Therefore, the 'group equity' will be preserved if, and only if, the group member's claims of structural priority are reduced to their realizable value. To the extent that enterprise value remains, that 'group value' can, and should, be treated as a 'rump estate', applied to any deficiency claims of creditors, sharing pro rata.

This chapter proceeds in the following order. In section II, it identifies basic attributes **8.06** and patterns for corporate groups under corporate or company law. Section III discusses the issues that arise for corporate groups and their members when they experience financial distress. Section IV explores issues that arise when seeking to administer a group case and coordinate a group restructuring. Section V explores the difficulties of setting a baseline entitlement when allocating enterprise value in a group restructuring. To what extent can enterprise value be traced to group members, and what should be done about homeless or untraceable value? This section proposes the functional solution described above. Finally, section VI considers the problem of group restructuring in cross-border cases. In particular, this section considers the recently promulgated United Nations Commission on International Trade Law (UNCITRAL) Model Law on the Insolvency Legislative Groups as a model.

---

[1] In cross-border cases, claims of priority may arise from multiple statutory priority schemes.
[2] The ideas developed here, in this regard, are spelled out more fully in Edward J. Janger and Stephan Madaus, 'Value Tracing and Priority in Cross-Border Group Bankruptcies: Solving the Nortel Problem from the Bottom Up', University of Miami International & Comparative Law Review 27 (7 December 2020) 331, <https://ssrn.com/abstract=3744233> accessed 11 January 2024.

II. Group Structures

8.07 It is impossible to identify all the ways and reasons that corporate groups may structure the relationships among their various entities. Different industries and types of companies may structure themselves along geographic lines, along functional lines to allocate managerial responsibility, or by business-line to allocate profits and risk. The permutations are endless.

8.08 For example, real estate developers are often structured on a project-by-project basis. Each building or development is set up as a separate partnership or corporation with its own financing, usually secured by the real estate and its rents. Where developers are relying on bank financing, a typical feature is for the project entity to have its debt guaranteed by the developer. These 'relational' guaranties are designed to bind the interest of the developer to the interest of the lender. In those instances, a default by the developer on one project may trigger a default on other projects. By contrast, where capital markets financing is being used, the structure may be designed to do the opposite—to insulate and partition the project from the fortunes of the developer and the group as a whole.

8.09 Sometimes, developers mix and match. One example can be seen in the insolvency of the *General Growth Properties*, a prominent developer of destination shopping malls in the United States. Its flagship properties included Faneuil Hall in Boston, South Street Seaport in Lower Manhattan, and Fells Point in Baltimore. When the group needed to restructure, different entities and projects had relied on different modes of financing: the entities with secured financing held guaranties from the parent; those that were financed through mortgage-backed securities were structured to maintain their financial independence from the fortunes of the group.[3]

8.10 Other enterprises use a group structure to distinguish business lines. Sometimes, this is to accommodate different regulatory regimes. For example, financial institutions may separate the broker dealer business from the insurance company from the investment bank. Indeed, the Federal Deposit Insurance Corporation (FDIC), in implementing its post-financial crisis reforms to address systemic risk, has regulated the group structure of financial institutions to encourage predictability and limit systemic risk should a financial institution fail.[4] This structuring may be expressly done with the goal of creating

---

[3] *In re General Growth Properties, Inc.*, 409 BR 43 (Bankr. SDNY 2009). The problem faced by the debtor in General Growth Properties (GGP) was that many of the group members had been structured to be 'bankruptcy remote', with directors pledged never to file for bankruptcy (irrespective of their fiduciary duties). Prior to the bankruptcy filing, those directors were replaced, and the group members joined the restructuring.

[4] FDIC, 'Resolution of Systemically Important Financial Institutions: The Single Point of Entry Strategy', 78 FR 76614 (18 December 2013) <https://www.federalregister.gov/documents/2013/12/18/2013-30057/resolution-of-systemically-important-financial-institutions-the-single-point-of-entry-strategy> accessed 11 January 2024. See Randall Guynn, '"Single Point of Entry" Resolution Strategy for U.S. Global Systemically Important Banking Groups (G-SIBs), 18th Annual International Conference on Policy Challenges for the Financial Sector World Bank—IMF—Federal Reserve (6 June 2018) <https://thedocs.worldbank.org/en/doc/857691528991163692-013 0022018/original/GuynnDavisPolkSessionTwo.pdf> accessed 11 January 2024. The single-point-of-entry strategy was designed to use a holding company group structure to give the debt of operating companies structural priority

predictable insolvency outcomes. At other times the dividing lines may be functional, separating sales from manufacturing from finance, as in automotive companies, or locating customer-facing aspects of the business in one subsidiary, production in another, and financial assets in another. Finally, when companies operate internationally, they may create a national subsidiary or set of subsidiaries to conduct operations in each jurisdiction.

From the debtor/creditor perspective, the key feature of the group structure is that each **8.11** group member is treated as a discrete juridic person, with its own assets and liabilities. Formally, at least, priority within the group is determined structurally. Creditors have recourse against their particular debtor, and their asset-based priority is asserted against the assets of the group member, while their *in personam* claims follow the priority waterfall as to the value of that member. As between group members, the equity (owned by the corporate parent) is junior to the debts of the subsidiary.

However, corporate groups are like families of real people; it is not always obvious **8.12** who owns what or whether family members are acting individually or on behalf of the whole family. Corporate personality can be clarifying, obscuring, or both—clarifying for some creditors and obscuring for others. These attributes of corporate groups are not just issues in insolvency law. Group structure implicates aspects of contract law, property law, and corporate law, while the interactions among these non-bankruptcy areas of law also affect the treatment of groups in bankruptcy. (In this chapter, the term 'bankruptcy' is used according to the US law useage. Therefore, depending on the relevant context, in this chapter, 'bankruptcy' means 'insolvency', 'insolvency law', 'insolvency law proceedings', or 'insolvency law case'.)

III. Corporate Groups in the Vicinity of Insolvency: Fiduciary Duty, Avoidance, and the Liquidation Baseline

When considering these interactions in insolvency and business rescue, one must step **8.13** back a bit, to the moments in time prior to opening a proceeding, to consider (a) the single entity liquidation entitlement baseline, (b) the obligations of officers and directors to a single firm in the vicinity of insolvency, and (c) the effect of group structure on those entitlements and obligations. In all three cases, the starting point for analysing groups begins by ignoring the group entirely and looking at each member individually.

---

over debt of the bank holding company. Further, the group structure was used to position the parent holding company as a source of capital and liquidity for the corporate group such that if an operating entity suffered a shock, the pain would be felt by the creditors of the holding company, not the operating company, and that insolvency law, if used at all, would only be used by the holding company (Guynn, '"Single Point of Entry" Resolution Strategy', ibid). This strategy is not just a US phenomenon. The 'bail-in' approach to bank resolution has been identified as a 'best practice' in Europe and by key international organizations: Elke Konig, 'Single Point of Entry—A Resolution Strategy Addressing the Home–Host Issue in Europe's Banking Union' (27 April 2021) <https://www.srb.europa.eu/en/content/single-point-entry-resolution-strategy-addressing-home-host-issue-europes-banking-union> accessed 11 January 2024.

A. The Single Entity Liquidation Baseline

8.14   The duties of the directors in the vicinity of insolvency are the same for a group member as for a stand-alone entity. These duties may vary from country to country. Some jurisdictions recognize a duty to creditors in the vicinity of insolvency;[5] others do not.[6] But the directors' duty is always to the stand-alone entity. The same is true for measuring baseline distributional entitlements. The starting point for measuring the baseline entitlements of shareholders and creditors is the single entity and the outcome if the entity were to seek to address its insolvency alone. As a result, there are national differences as to how that baseline should be measured—liquidation value in some jurisdictions, 'next best alternative' in others,[7] and perhaps even reorganization value, if possible. The valuation methods may differ, but the single company baseline is the default. Further, when exercising their discretion as officers and directors, the single-firm, stand-alone outcome is the baseline against which alternatives must be judged.

B. Regulating Decisions in the Vicinity of Insolvency

8.15   Broadly speaking, there are three related bodies of law that police decision-making when a group or group members enter the vicinity of insolvency: (a) fiduciary duty, (b) avoidance, and (c) veil piercing or consolidation. Each has its own elements and quirks, but they can all be understood as safeguarding two basic principles—the priority of debt over equity and the principle of equitable treatment of similarly situated members of any class that is not being paid in full.[8] Directors' duties consider the actions of corporate officers and directors. Fraudulent conveyance and avoidance look at both the debtor's actions and those of the recipient of the transfers. All three seek to draw a distinction between transactions that are value creating and those that are either being used to reconfigure the risk attributes of other people's investments or shift value from one corporate constituency to another. The officers and directors have a duty not only to maximize value but, because of the cumulative effect of these rules, to do so equitably.

8.16   This common through-line is obvious when the debtor is insolvent: it is a breach of fiduciary duty to continue incurring credit when the debtor does not have a reasonable

---

[5]   *BTI 2014 LLC v Sequana SA* [2019] EWCA Civ 112. On this point, see also Chapter 7 'Directors' Duties in the Vicinity of Insolvency, Disqualification, Piercing the Veil' in this volume, paras 7.08 et seq.

[6]   *North American Catholic Educational Programming Foundation, Inc. v Gheewalla*–930 A.2d 92 (Del. 2007).

[7]   Compare 11 U.S.C. §1129(a)(7) with the Directive (EU) 2019/1023 of the European Parliament and of the Council of 20 June 2019 on preventive restructuring frameworks, on discharge of debt and disqualifications, and on measures to increase the efficiency of procedures concerning restructuring, insolvency and discharge of debt, and amending Directive (EU) 2017/1132 (Directive on Restructuring and Insolvency).

[8]   Edward J. Janger, 'Equitable Duty: Regulating Corporate Transactions in the Vicinity of Insolvency from a Comparative Perspective' in Arthur Laby and Jacoby Hale Russell (eds), *Fiduciary Obligations in Business* (CUP 2021) 152. As regards fiduciary duties and veil piercing, see also Chapter 7 'Directors' Duties in the Vicinity of Insolvency, Disqualification, Piercing the Veil' in this volume, paras 7.08 et seq., and paras 7.68 et seq., respectively. By contrast, as regards avoidances, see also Chapter 6 'Transactions Avoidance Rules' in this volume.

belief that it will be able to repay, it is a preference for an insolvent debtor to pay one creditor in full when others will be forced to take a haircut, it is a fraudulent conveyance when a debtor transfers assets to another in order to frustrate collection efforts, and using the corporate form to accomplish any of the above transfers and/or to deceive investors or creditors may lead a court to disregard the corporate form.

Each of these bodies of law (fiduciary duty, avoidance, and veil piercing) take on a common, and generally underappreciated feature in insolvency—governance. They force the owners, fiduciaries, and transferees to consider whether actions by the debtor seek to maximize value or only to redistribute. They accomplish this sorting by measuring each corporate action taken to continue the business against the alternative—liquidation. Together, the regulatory effect of duty, avoidance, and veil piercing is to impose a duty to behave equitably with regard to creditors—to respect the pre-bankruptcy entitlement, and to preserve their relative positions (and distributions) in rescue, and to protect their entitlements should the firm ultimately liquidate.

8.17

Here, the single-firm liquidation baseline is crucial. Prior to the advent of rescue regimes, in the absence of a contractual workout, insolvency was followed by liquidation.[9] In liquidation, value is realized for the stakeholders and is then distributed based on legal entitlements. Breach of fiduciary duty, preference, fraudulent conveyance, and veil piercing are each measured against the distribution that would have incurred in liquidation absent the transfer or misbehaviour—to wit, the baseline entitlement.[10] Liquidation establishes the entitlement baseline, the minimum distribution that would be considered equitable. This is true for individual entities but also for groups. The complexities in restructuring a group all spring from sorting between transactions within the group that increase the value of the entity and the group and those that inequitably alter the distribution of value.

8.18

1. Directors' duties in the vicinity of insolvency

Different legal systems take different approaches to the duties of officers and directors when a firm is in the vicinity of insolvency. There are three major approaches: US, Commonwealth, and civilian. They array on a spectrum from most to least permissive. The framing of the conversation is over whether there is a shift of duty from the shareholders to the creditors in the vicinity of insolvency. There is disagreement in corporate law as to whether the officers and directors of a solvent firm owe their duty to the shareholders or the corporation itself. How a jurisdiction approaches this question will affect the importance of these questions.[11]

8.19

---

[9] Even now, that is the default.
[10] 11 U.S.C. §547(b).
[11] Jared Ellias and Robert Stark, 'Bankruptcy Hardball', California Law Review, *108* (2019) 745. Compare Larry Edward Ribstein and Kelli Alces Williams, 'Directors' Duties in Failing Firms', Journal of Business and Technology Law, 1 (2007) 529, <https://ssrn.com/abstract=880074 > accessed 11 January 2024 with Stephen M. Bainbridge, 'Much Ado about Little? Directors' Fiduciary Duties in the Vicinity of Insolvency', Journal of Business and Technology Law, 1 (2007) 335, <https://digitalcommons.law.umaryland.edu/jbtl/vol1/iss2/7)> accessed 11 January 2024.

226 CORPORATE GROUPS IN RESCUE

8.20 In the United States, the tone is set by Delaware. It has evolved over time. In 1991, the Delaware Court of Chancery suggested that when a debtor enters the vicinity of insolvency, the duty of officers and directors may expand to include the interest of creditors.[12] In 2007, the court clarified that there was no independent duty to creditors and that the duty did not shift in the vicinity of insolvency.[13] Later, they further clarified that the fiduciary duties were always owed to the corporation itself, not to a particular corporate constituency.[14] By contrast, in the United Kingdom and the British Commonwealth, in the vicinity of insolvency, there is a duty to minimize harm to creditors. And, if the debtor continues to do business after becoming insolvent, there may be liability for 'wrongful trading' or 'trading while insolvent'.[15] While wrongful trading occurs only when the company continues trading after there is no reasonable prospect of avoiding insolvent liquidation, a debtor who is in the vicinity of insolvency must act with regard to creditors.[16] In civil law countries, liability for trading while insolvent may even be criminal.[17]

2. Avoidance

8.21 Pre-petition transfers to insiders can be a breach of fiduciary duty, but they may also be avoidable transfers as preferences or fraudulent conveyances. The *Purdue Pharma* case in the United States is illustrative. *Purdue* manufactured and distributed a very popular and addictive painkiller called oxycontin. It became the target of personal injury cases, as well as cases brought by State attorneys general for damages. In response, the officers and directors engaged in a concerted effort to 'milk' the company of its value and transfer it to the insider stockholders as dividends.[18] These dividends were the basis for avoidance actions that has yielded a settlement for the debtor worth billions of dollars.

8.22 Avoidance is available on one of three theories, each of which maps onto a behaviour that could constitute a breach of fiduciary duty: (a) preferring one creditor at the expense of another,[19] (b) transferring property at an undervalue while insolvent,[20] or (c) intentionally transferring or hiding assets from creditors.[21] The difference is that the avoidance does not seek to recover from the officer or director but, instead, from the transferee. In summary, together, fiduciary duty and avoidance enforce a set of common principles. If a debtor is in the vicinity of insolvency, the priority of debt over equity

---

[12] *Credit Lyonnais Bank Nederland v Pathe Communications Corp.*, No. 12150, 1991 WL 277613 (Del. Ch. 30 December 1991).

[13] *North American Catholic Educational Programming Foundation Inc. v Gheewalla* (n 6).

[14] *Quadrant Structured Products Co., Ltd v Vertin*, 115 A.3d 535 (Del. Ch. 2015).

[15] See s. 214 of the Insolvency Act of 1986.

[16] *BTI 2014 LLC v Sequana SA* (n 5).

[17] United Nations Commission on International Trade Law (UNCITRAL), *Legislative Guide On Insolvency Law—Part Four: Directors' Obligations in the Period Approaching Insolvency (including in Enterprise Groups)*(2nd edn, UNCITRAL 2020), 7, 11 <https://uncitral.un.org/sites/uncitral.un.org/files/media-documents/uncitral/en/19-11273_part_4_ebook.pdf> accessed 27 March 2024.

[18] *In re Purdue Pharma*, Decision and Order on Appeal, <https://portal.ct.gov/-/media/AG/Press_Releases/2021/Judge-McMahon-Decision-121621.pdf> accessed 11 January 2024.

[19] 11 U.S.C. §547.

[20] ibid §548(1)(A). See also § 5 of the Uniform Voidable Transactions Act 1998.

[21] 11 U.S.C. §548(1)(B). See also § 4 of the Uniform Voidable Transactions Act 1998.

should be respected, and enterprise value should not be transferred (as a dividend) to owners or their nominees. Further, if the business is to be continued, it should not be done at the expense either of the creditors or of particular creditor constituencies.

C. Directors' Duties and Avoidance for Groups

So far, the focus has been on the individual firm. However, the collective nature of the enterprise cannot be ignored. The *sine qua non* of group structures is that the whole is greater than the sum of its parts. That is where the complexities arise. Groups complicate the decisions faced by directors in the vicinity of insolvency. To what extent can group members take steps to assist the group that may or may not benefit the group member itself? The key point for all discussions of groups is that the use of a group structure creates a two-step decision process: (a) Does an action benefit or harm the group as a whole? (b) Does the action benefit or harm the group member and its relevant stakeholders? In other words, corporate decision must be judged both based on benefit to the group member and to the collective. **8.23**

1. The entity and the group: Value maximization and equity

For a solvent group, these two questions do not constrain decision-making to any significant degree. In most cases, the stock of the subsidiaries will be owned by the parent. This means that any differential effect of an action on subsidiaries will wash out, as equity is dividended upstream to the parent. Similarly, intra-group transfers and intra-group guaranties can be used to move money around. But in the aggregate, the value will flow to the parent. Further, in considering the effect of an action in relation to the group on the entity itself, the business judgment rule will allow great latitude. If the duty is to the shareholders, the subsidiary is wholly owned, and the entity is solvent, then all value flows upward. **8.24**

However, when there is a meaningful probability that the group or its members may not be able to satisfy their debts in full, these simplifying assumptions no longer work. First, risk of non-payment is borne not by the shareholders but by the creditors of the group member. Second, any 'upside' will be captured first by the creditors (up to payment in full), not the shareholders.[22] **8.25**

To put the point more generally, when creditors who are ostensibly 'fixed' claimants of a group member face a meaningful risk of non-payment in full, the consequences of any decision for the individual group member loom larger. Also, if the whole group is teetering, the subsidiary may not be as likely to benefit from its contributions to the larger **8.26**

---

[22] Similar issues arise if the entity is not wholly owned by the parent; one must consider the interest of the entity in addition to the interest of the group. This situation is beyond the scope of this chapter but would be addressed by the corporate law regarding oppression of minority shareholders: F. Hodge O'Neal, Robert B. Thompson, and Douglas K. Moll, *O'Neal and Thompson's Oppression of Minority Shareholders* (Clark, Boardman, Callaghan 2022).

228 CORPORATE GROUPS IN RESCUE

group. To what extent is group membership a source of value for the single entity's stakeholders? To what extent is group membership a liability? Could the group member survive as a stand-alone entity, or is its value wrapped up in the common group enterprise? Worse yet, to what extent does group structure create opportunities for abuse?

2. Fiduciary duty and the 'Texas two-step'

8.27 For example, group structure can be used to manipulate recourse. Such recourse manipulation raises issues of both duties and avoidance. Whether this implicates fiduciary duty depends on whether there is a duty to creditors. The issue is a live one, in current cases. A strategy has emerged, in both the United States and United Kingdom, to manipulate group structure to affect the recourse available to creditors of a particular group member.

8.28 In the United States, a recent (and controversial) example is the 'Texas two-step'. A number of debtors have used Texas's 'divisive merger' statute to divide a company into two pieces, placing the liabilities in one entity, while leaving the assets and productive business operations in another.[23] The most prominent example of this is its use by the pharmaceutical giant Johnson and Johnson to isolate product-liability claims based on injury from allegedly carcinogenic talc in baby powder in a single subsidiary, which then filed for bankruptcy. The process required the reincorporation of Johnson and Johnson in Texas, execution of the merger/split, then reincorporation of the talc entity—LTL— in North Carolina, where it filed for bankruptcy. The North Carolina bankruptcy court found that this venue was inappropriate (because the operations of the company were based in New Jersey), so the case was transferred to the Bankruptcy Court in Trenton, NJ.[24] The bankruptcy court in New Jersey was then faced with the question of whether the bankruptcy filing by LTL was in good or bad faith. Notwithstanding the tortured (and transparent) procedural history, the bankruptcy court found that, even though Johnson and Johnson was not insolvent and even though it had created a financially distressed subsidiary solely for the purpose of entering bankruptcy, the filing was in 'good faith' and not just a litigation tactic.[25] If this had worked, the next step would have been to couple the Two-Step with a series of so-called 'third-party releases' to insulate the corporate parent and siblings. The goal was to manipulate the group structure and corporate personality of the enterprise to insulate J&J's business and investors from the talc liabilities. In the end, J&J's tactic failed. Third Circuit court of appeals subsequently

---

[23] See, e.g. *In re Bestwall LLC*, 71 F.4th 168 (4th Cir. 2023); *In re DBMP LLC*, No. 20-30080, 2021 WL 3552350 (Bankr. W.D.N.C. 11 August 2021).

[24] *In re LTL Mgmt*, LLC, 64 F.4th 84 (3d Cir. 2023) For discussions of the Texas two-step, see <https://bankruptc yroundtable.law.harvard.edu/2023/02/14/texas-two-step-and-the-future-of-mass-tort-bankruptcy-series-pos tscript-and-analysis-of-third-circuit-dismissal-of-ltl-managements-bankruptcy> accessed 11 January 2024.

[25] *In re LTL Mgmt*, LLC, 637 B.R. 396 (Bankr. D.N.J. 2022), rev'd and remanded, 58 F.4th 738 (3d Cir. 2023), and rev'd and remanded, 64 F.4th 84 (3d Cir. 2023). See also Edward Janger, 'Aggregation and Abuse: Mass Torts in Bankruptcy', Fordham Law Review, 91 (2022) 362, <http://fordhamlawreview.org/wp-content/uploads/2022/11/ Janger_November.pdf> accessed 11 January 2024.

reversed the finding of good faith, finding that the filing subsidiary was not in financial distress and had no need of bankruptcy.[26]

At the moment, the law surrounding both the Texas-Two Step and third-party releases in mass-tort cases are in flux. A number of senators have encouraged the US Supreme Court to grant *certiorari* in an earlier Two-Step case,[27] and the manoeuvre has been challenged in Texas bankruptcy courts.[28] Meanwhile, the availability of third-party releases is before the US Supreme Court in the *Purdue Pharma* case, where an opioid manufacturer obtained third-party releases of direct tort claims against officers, directors, and shareholders.[29]

The goal of the Two-Step transaction in *LTL* was to limit the recourse of the talc creditors to the (solvent) corporation's assets. If the manoeuvre survives, it has fiduciary duty implications. While Delaware case law takes the view that directors of the corporate parent have no duty to the creditors of a subsidiary, manoeuvres like the Texas two-step raise questions about whether this rule is appropriate.[30] Meanwhile, in the United Kingdom, a recent government consultation considered a similar question— whether the officers and directors of a corporate parent had a duty to the creditors and other stakeholders of an insolvent subsidiary.[31] The answer was instructive. The conclusion was that directors of a parent corporation could be held liable for breach of fiduciary duty for a sale of a subsidiary that had the effect of impairing the recourse of the subsidiary's creditors. Such a rule would significantly limit the hazard associated with transactions like the 'two-step'.

8.29

3. Avoidance: Guaranties and the Texas two-step

Intra-group guaranties and transfers can also pose issues in insolvency. When a group member borrows money, other members of the group may guarantee the debt with contractual recourse or *in rem* security. Where the corporate parent guaranties a debt of

8.30

---

[26] *In re LTL Mgmt*, LLC, 64 F.4th 84 (3d Cir. 2023). The court focused on a key feature of the arrangement between J&J and LTL, an agreement that the new operating entity and the corporate parent would fund any adjudicated talc liabilities.

[27] Dietrich Knauth, 'Senators, States Ask US Supreme Court to Curb 'Two-Step' Bankruptcy Abuse', Reuters (23 January 2024) <https://www.reuters.com/legal/government/senators-states-ask-us-supreme-court-curb-two-step-bankruptcy-abuse-2024-01-23> accessed 27 March 2024. See *In re Bestwall LLC*, 71 F.4th 168 (4th Cir. 2023).

[28] *Akiko Matsuda*, 'Judge in Prison Healthcare Contractor's Bankruptcy Intends to Keep Narrow Focus', Wall Street Journal (4 March 2024)<https://www.wsj.com/articles/judge-in-prison-healthcare-contractors-bankruptcy-intends-to-keep-narrow-focus-d9f2de24?st=ypj2bpxazic1wyt&reflink=desktopwebshare_permalink> accessed 27 March 2024.

[29] *In Re Purdue Pharma L.P.*, 69 F.4th 45 (2d Cir.), cert. granted sub nom; *Harrington v Purdue Pharma L.P.*, 144 S. Ct 44, 216 L. Ed. 2d 1300 (2023).

[30] Ellias and Stark, 'Bankruptcy Hardball' (n 11).

[31] UK Department of Business, Energy and Industrial Strategy, 'Consultation on Insolvency and Corporate Governance: Government Response' (26 August 2018) <https://www.gov.uk/government/consultations/insolvency-and-corporate-governance> accessed 11 January 2024. For a collection of news stories about Carillion, see Financial Times, 'FT Collections: Carillion's Collapse: Risk and Failure' <https://www.ft.com/content/2cab2ac2-fb83-11e7-9b32-d7d59aace167> accessed 11 January 2024. A discussion of the Board's role can be found at <https://www.ft.com/content/2095beca-fb8b-11e7-a492-2c9be7f3120a> accessed 11 January 2024; Ian Clark, 'The British Home Stores Pension Scheme: Privatised Looting?', Industrial Relations Journal, 50(4) (2019) 331, 331–2.

230 CORPORATE GROUPS IN RESCUE

a subsidiary (a downstream guaranty), the issue is unproblematic, as the parent receives value for the transaction through the increased value of its stock. However, where the subsidiary guaranties a debt of the parent (upstream), or a group member guarantees the debt of another group member (cross-stream), issues may arise. The transaction might be characterized as a fraudulent conveyance in the United States[32] or a transaction at undervalue in the United Kingdom. The basic elements are that the debtor transferred an asset or obligation without receiving fair value, while insolvent. In the case of upstream and cross-stream guarantees, it may be difficult to demonstrate that the guarantor received any value at all. So, if the guarantor is insolvent, fraudulent conveyance liability may arise. Similarly, to the extent that one group member satisfied an intra-corporate debt on the eve of insolvency, preference liability may arise, regardless of whether it would constitute a fraudulent conveyance.[33]

8.31 In the *Johnson and Johnson* insolvency case discussed above, the divisive merger may be subject to challenge as a fraudulent conveyance due to its potential effect on the recourse of talc claimants to Johnson and Johnson's assets. Indeed, while the Trenton bankruptcy court was receptive to the Johnson and Johnson case, as was the Fourth Circuit in *Bestwall*,[34] the Third Circuit was not, and a bankruptcy judge in Minnesota has looked askance at a similar manoeuvre involving defective ear plugs, in the *3M* bankruptcy.[35]

IV. Administering a Group Case in Liquidation and Rescue

8.32 The same issues that bedevil officers and directors in the vicinity of insolvency arise when a multi-entity enterprise enters an insolvency proceeding. As a formal matter, liquidation of a corporate group should be fairly straightforward. Each entity liquidates its assets and distributes value to its particular stakeholders. But even in liquidation, there are complexities introduced by group structure. Group members may have a network of debits and credits within the group. Creditors of one entity may have claims of avoidance against another. Further, notwithstanding group structure, many businesses are operated, as a practical matter, as a consolidated enterprise. The lines between entities, assets, and claims may not be distinct. These questions become even more complicated if an effort is being made to rescue the business, and they become even yet more complicated if the case crosses national borders. This section addresses each of these layers of complexity in order.

---

[32] See §§ 4 and 5 of the Uniform Voidable Transactions Act 1998; 11 U.S.C. §548.
[33] 11 U.S.C. §547.
[34] *In re Bestwall LLC*, 71 F.4th 168 (4th Cir. 2023).
[35] *In re Aearo Techs. LLC*, 642 B.R. 891 (Bankr. S.D. Ind. 2022). The court denied the debtor's motion to stay product liability litigation against the corporate parent. The debtor appealed, but the case ultimately settled, with the debtor proposing a settlement that allowed dissenting creditors to opt out: <https://www.lawsuit-information-center.com/13-million-3m-earplug-verdict.html> accessed 27 March 2024.

A. Administrative Consolidation

In the United States, it is not unusual for all members of a group to open proceedings **8.33** in the same bankruptcy court. Under 28 U.S.C. §1408, a bankruptcy court has jurisdiction, and venue is proper if an affiliate has a case pending in that court. When cases are administratively consolidated, each entity retains its corporate form and is administered separately. As a formal matter, each entity has a separate case. Even in administrative consolidation, however, the lines may be blurred. Arguably, each group member should have its own counsel, its own creditors' committee, its own schedules, and so on. For many companies, however, the proliferation of professionals is not only unaffordable, but it may also be unnecessary, depending on which entities have separate assets and separate creditors. The judge, in these cases, has some discretion with regard to appointing committees and professionals in each case, though managing issues of conflicting interest can be difficult. Further, allocating enterprise value to group members may be problematic. Issues may arise in determining which entity owns a particular asset, and therefore which creditors can claim it. This is true in liquidation, even without the added complexity of rescue.

The *Lehman*[36] and *Nortel*[37] insolvency law cases provide excellent examples. For ex- **8.34** ample, in *Lehman*, the corporate group operated its cash management system on a global basis, with the cash handled by a subsidiary based in the United Kingdom. Each day, cash would be distributed, as needed, to group members, and in the evening, accounts would be settled. This raised an important question when the company filed for bankruptcy: where was the money? Creditors of the global subsidiaries took the view that the cash was in the subsidiaries. Creditors of the central entity said the money was in London. The English Supreme Court ultimately held that the funds were held in trust for the customers, leaving the affiliates holding the bag.[38] The resolution of the dispute is not of consequence for this discussion. The point is that in a complex corporate group, the location of assets may be difficult to ascertain.

Nortel raised a similar issue. The principal asset of the Nortel enterprise was an inven- **8.35** tory of broadcast-spectrum licences. The case was a liquidation, so the decision was made to sell the licences in a coordinated auction. The auction succeeded beyond the creditors' wildest imagination. But without any agreement about how that value would be distributed amongst the claimants against members of the global group considerable

---

[36] *Lehman Bros Special Fin. Inc. v BNY Corp. Tr. Serv. Ltd* (*In re Lehman Bros Holdings Inc.*), 422 BR 407, 416 (Bankr. SDNY 2010).

[37] *Nortel Networks Corp. (Re)*, [2015] ONSC 2987 (Can. Ont. Sup. Ct); see Michael Barrett, 'Substantive Consolidation After Nortel: The Treatment of Corporate Groups in Canadian Insolvency Law', Insolvency Institute of Canada, <https://www.insolvency.ca/en/whatwedo/resources/SubstantiveConsolidationAfterNortel_TheTreatmentofCorporateGroupsinCanadianInsolvencyLaw.pdf> accessed 11 January 2024.

[38] See Reuters, 'UK Court Rules Lehman Bros Clients Can Claim Cash' (29 February 2012) <https://www.reuters.com/article/lehman-clients/uk-court-rules-lehman-bros-clients-can-claim-cash-idUSL5E8DTAX220120229> accessed 11 January 2024.

232 CORPORATE GROUPS IN RESCUE

wrangling ensued. The result was that the court decided to treat all of the creditors pro rata—by estate.[39]

8.36 The court in *Nortel* characterized its action as 'modified pro rata distribution', but as we discuss below, cases like *Nortel* and *Lehman* illustrate a more fundamental problem that is pervasive in rescue cases—asset ownership cannot always be attributed to a particular group member in a manner that is enforceable against third parties. Multiple group members may have legitimate claims to the asset. Further, corporate groups are not entities that can own assets; only group members are able to do so. Even where cases are jointly administered, there may be assets, particularly intangible assets, that cannot be located within the group. The cash in *Lehman* and the intellectual property licences in *Nortel* are just two examples.

B. Substantive Consolidation

8.37 In extreme cases, a solution to the problem described above is the remedy of 'substantive consolidation'—the insolvency law equivalent of veil piercing. Courts in the United States have used a number of different formulations. The Second Circuit, in *Augie Restivo*, suggested that courts should order substantive consolidation in two types of cases: (a) where the debtor has dealt with creditors on a consolidated basis and (b) where the debtor has disregarded the corporate form, to the extent that it is impossible to unscramble the egg.[40] Other federal courts have stated the standard slightly differently, saying that consolidation should be ordered if: '(i) there is a substantial identity between the entities to be consolidated; and (ii) consolidation is necessary in order to avoid some harm or realize some benefit'.[41] In either case, the focus is on creditor expectations.

8.38 Substantive consolidation is, however, an extraordinary remedy. Though it is often invoked to vindicate creditor expectations, it may just as often defeat them. As a result, it is only available after a finding of some sort of fraud or mismanagement, commingling of funds, disregard of the corporate form, or other inequitable behaviour. Where such problems exist, the remedy is powerful. Indeed, while it remains controversial, some US courts have even used it to consolidate the assets of non-debtor entities with those of the entity in bankruptcy.[42]

8.39 Substantive consolidation is also available when the various creditors can agree on a consensual solution. It is not uncommon in the United States for corporate groups to agree to consensual substantive consolidation for the purpose of approving a

---

[39] *In re Nortel Networks, Inc.*, 532 BR 494, 500 (Bankr. D Del. 2015); *Nortel Networks Corp. (Re)* (n 32).
[40] *Union Savings Bank v Augie/Restivo Baking Co., Ltd (In re Augie/Restivo Baking Co., Ltd)*, 820 F.2d 515 (2d Cir. 1988).
[41] *Eastgroup Properties v Southern Motel Assoc., Ltd*, 935 F.2d 245 (11th Cir. 1991). See also *Drabkin v Midland Ross Corp. (In re Auto-Train Corp., Inc.)*, 810 F.2d 270 (DC Cir. 1987).
[42] *Kapila v S & G Fin. Servs, LLC (In re S & G Fin. Servs of S. Fla., Inc.)*, 2011 WL 96741 (Bankr. SD Fla. 2011).

consensual plan of reorganization. In such a case, the classes of creditors in each case will vote on the plan and consider their distributions. If the plan of reorganization meets the requirements for confirmation (including best interest), and all classes consent by the appropriate majorities, there is little reason to object to consolidating the firm for the purposes of distributing its value. Indeed, Bill Widen has noted that such consolidations are relatively common.[43]

If a class objects, however, consensual consolidation is not available, and, in the absence **8.40** of bad behaviour, non-consensual substantive consolidation may not be available either. Even in liquidation, allocation of value can present a problem in corporate groups. In *Nortel*, the debtor auctioned off its intellectual property and spectrum licences, but then faced significant and costly questions about how the value of the intellectual property should be allocated. Was the value situated in the entity or jurisdiction where the intellectual property was located or in the entity or jurisdiction where it was used, for example? As noted above, the Delaware and Toronto courts agreed to a distribution that was 'pro rata by estate'. Both the US and Canadian courts went to great lengths to point out that this was not a substantive consolidation, as the corporate forms were retained and arguably respected. But the proceeds of the sale were treated, in effect, as a common aspect of the group.

The key point from *Nortel* is that 'substantive consolidation', as it is generally under- **8.41** stood, is not a particularly useful concept in large-group cases, even when the value is produced through a sale of assets. The problem is that even where the corporate form is respected, and intra-corporate accounts are carefully managed, some of the value of a coordinated sale may derive from the coordination itself. In other words, the ability to liquidate as a group may create value that cannot be situated in any one entity. This may not justify disrespecting the corporate form. However, since the group is not an entity, there is no obvious place to situate that incremental value; neither is there an obvious way to allocate it among group members. Where the value is generated by continuing operations, this problem looms even larger.

C. Corporate Groups in Rescue

Locating group value is an even bigger problem in rescue. When a group or members of **8.42** a corporate group find themselves in financial distress and struggle to survive, difficult questions of governance and value allocation arise for both group members and the group as a whole.

---

[43] William H. Widen, 'Corporate Form and Substantive Consolidation', George Washington Law Review, 75 (2007) 237.

234 CORPORATE GROUPS IN RESCUE

1. Governance

8.43 For group members, the vicinity of insolvency raises the difficult governance questions, whether to continue in operation or liquidate, and more importantly, whether to support the group. Even in Delaware, where the duty never shifts to creditors, the officers and directors may need to be able to justify difficult choices, particularly whether it is ever appropriate to privilege the interest of the group over that of a group member or its creditors.

8.44 As noted in the introduction of this chapter, this is not a problem for a solvent group member, at least where the subsidiary is 100% owned by the holding company. The subsidiary can allocate its equity any way it wants. However, when the business is in distress, it may not be obvious whether it is appropriate for the group member to fund the reorganization. Sometimes, the issue is clear-cut. If the group member is a stand-alone entity, it can go it alone. But if the financial survival of the member is tied to the fate of the group, the choices are more difficult. To what extent is it in the best interests of the group member to transfer assets? Again, if the group member is solvent, then this can be handled as a dividend. However, if the group member itself is in distress, the transfer must be justified by reference to its benefit to the member, and in a way, that does not unduly shift risk to the member's creditors.

8.45 The UNCITRAL *Legislative Guide on Insolvency Law*[44] has offered some insights into how to approach this problem, though the answer that it provides is incomplete. Recommendation 267(b) states that the fiduciary of the group member may act in the interest of the group, so long as it is in the best interests of the group member, or at least
8.46 does no harm:

> It may take *reasonable steps* to promote a *group insolvency solution* that addresses the insolvency of the enterprise group as a whole or some of its parts. In so doing, the person may take into account the possible benefits of maximizing the value of the enterprise group as a whole, *while taking reasonable steps to ensure that the creditors of the enterprise group member and its other stakeholders are no worse off* than if that enterprise group member had not been managed so as to promote such a group insolvency solution [emphasis added].[45]

8.47 Of course, this leaves open the question of what constitutes, 'reasonable steps'. Recommendation 268(1)addresses this question, suggesting that the fiduciary might engage in the following analysis: (a) compare the future of the member going it alone with participating in a 'group insolvency solution', (b) compare whether the interrelationship of its finances with other group members would justify participating in a group financing arrangement, (c) consider whether participating in the group solution would

---

[44] UNCITRAL *Legislative Guide on Insolvency—Part 3: Treatment of Enterprise Groups in Insolvency* (2012) <https://uncitral.un.org/sites/uncitral.un.org/files/media-documents/uncitral/en/leg-guide-insol-part3-ebook-e.pdf> accessed 27 March 2024; UNCITRAL, *Legislative Guide on Insolvency—Part 4: Directors' Obligations in the Period Approaching Insolvency (Including in Enterprise Groups)* (n 17).

[45] UNCITRAL *Legislative Guide on Insolvency—Part 4* (n 17) Recommendation 267, at 38.

benefit the member's creditors, (d) consider various ways of cooperating and assisting in the group solution.[46] It also suggests that the fiduciary should consider the necessity of opening formal insolvency proceedings for the group member. This last recommendation, of course, carries with it a further set of nested questions relating to whether the particular jurisdiction imposes a duty to open a proceeding and the possible consequences of opening such a proceeding.

The *Legislative Guide* approach captures both the need for pragmatism in a group **8.48** rescue situation and the myriad questions raised for the group member, particularly when the member itself is in the vicinity of insolvency. As a practical matter, the Recommendations place a compliance duty on the officers and directors of the member to look at any transactions within the group from the perspective of the group member and then further consider whether they can be justified as in the best interests of the group member itself and its stakeholders.

Whether it is possible to justify participation in the group solution from the group **8.49** member perspective will depend on a wide variety of factors. These include, the integrated nature of the enterprise's operations, the extent to which the finances of the group members are integrated or kept separate, and the exigencies of timing. When an enterprise group finds itself in financial distress, two dynamics pull in opposite directions. The group as a whole may be searching for sources of funds, but the group members may have enhanced duties to consider the interests of their own particular creditors. This is particularly true where individual group members may have been set up specifically as 'asset partitions' to assure the recourse of favoured creditors. Worse, when things unravel, they may unravel quickly, so what might, in the moment, seem a reasonable decision to keep the business afloat may, after the fact, look like robbing Peter to pay Paul.

2. Avoidance

Avoidance amplifies the concerns faced by officers and directors of a group member. **8.50** Transactions that guaranty or fund 'upstream' or 'cross-stream' activities, may, after the fact, be subject to challenge as fraudulent conveyances or transactions at undervalue. To the extent that a group member transfers value to the group, in service of the group solution, that transaction must be evaluated from the perspective of the transferor. In most jurisdictions, a transfer made while insolvent is avoidable, unless the transferor received 'reasonably equivalent value' in return.[47]

3. Value allocation

Therefore, when the officers and directors, consider participating and contributing to **8.51** a group solution, they must also consider the manner in which the member will be compensated for any increase in value. Here is where negotiations outside of a formal

---

[46] ibid Recommendations 267–8.
[47] See, e.g. § 5 of the Uniform Voidable Transactions Act 1998.

236 CORPORATE GROUPS IN RESCUE

proceeding may become virtually impossible. Assets might be loaned upstream to the parent but assuring repayment may be difficult. To what extent should a group member bargain for favourable terms on behalf of its own stakeholders? To the extent that there is 'upside' for the group, how should it be shared amongst group members? To what extent can that allocation be established and assured outside of the opening of a formal proceeding. That question is faced by different legal systems in a variety of ways: (a) in the United States, Chapter 11 allows the opening of a judicial proceeding without signalling the end of the business; (b) in the United Kingdom, a scheme of arrangement seeks judicial approval of a restructuring after the fact; and (c) in Europe, the advent of so-called 'pre-insolvency' or 'protective restructuring' regimes seek to accomplish this value allocation through the use of a variety of bespoke tools.

8.52 It is here, however that the corporate form can become a significant obstacle to restructuring a business as a going concern. The group structure can be a valuable tool for locating assets and liabilities. By placing operations in one entity and assets in another, creditors and shareholders can allocate the risks and benefits of the enterprise. This can be done with care and transparency or intentionally or unintentionally to obscure. Enterprises may take great care with corporate niceties and asset locations, or (more often) day-to-day operations may obscure the corporate boundaries. This can create difficulties along two dimensions: legal entitlements and practical vetoes.

V. Allocating Group Value in Rescue

8.53 Rescue requires coordination. Modern rescue regimes provide tools for crafting a going-concern restructuring. Often, there is a fair amount of pre-filing planning, and perhaps even the execution of a restructuring support agreement. But inevitably, closing the deal and binding hold-outs may require some degree of judicial assistance. These tools range from the moratorium on debt collection to mechanisms for binding hold-outs to the restructuring. Each of these tools is geared towards overcoming the coordination problems faced by creditors when seeking to consummate a value-maximizing restructuring. Restructuring is hard enough with a single debtor, but group structures can complicate restructurings in two ways. First, the corporate group structure may create expectations about entitlements. Certain claimants may see themselves as having structural claims of priority with regard to either assets or group member value. Second, group structure and the law's respect for the corporate form may give legal heft to these claims in the form of legal vetoes that allow them to block any group solution unless their particularized entitlement to priority is satisfied. These entitlement-based vetoes can add significantly to the cost and likelihood of success of any restructuring.[48] Third, these vetoes can be practical rather than legal. A group member may control a key asset or business relationship. As is discussed below, this practical leverage can be

---

[48] Janger and Madaus, 'Value Tracing and Priority in Cross-Border Group Bankruptcies' (n 1).

multiplied when the group members are organized around national lines. Such practical leverage can also create obstacles to a value-maximizing restructuring. This section explores the problem of such vetoes and proposes a pragmatic solution.

A. Group Structure and Coordination Problems: *Nortel* (again)

On the one hand, *Nortel* offers an example of a successful group case—at least along **8.54** the value-maximization axis. Instead of liquidating the assets of the group members separately—as they were spread around the world, Nortel's administrators followed a coordinated strategy and pooled the firm's key assets (spectrum and intellectual property licences), which allowed them to sell these assets in a single auction. Here, competing bids of major market participants drove the price up to unforeseen levels and generated about $7 billion in cash.[49] Value maximization happened. The modified universalist idea worked. But the *Nortel* bankruptcy also provides a stunning example of how group structure (compounded by cross-border issues) can complicate a bankruptcy. In *Nortel*, this fight lasted for more than 8 years and generated costs estimated at $2.6 billion.[50] A significant piece of that fight was due to US bondholders, who hoped to receive larger distributions in the United States than their Canadian or European counterparts. After a costly attempt at mediation failed,[51] the Canadian and US courts solved this problem through modified pro-rata distribution that respected the corporate form but not necessarily the structural claims to priority.[52] The various estates shared pro rata in the value of the assets of the company. Equality of distribution trumped claims to priority based on nationality.[53]

Nortel was essentially a coordinated liquidation. The difficulties associated with group **8.55** structure can be even more problematic when the goal is to preserve a going-concern business. Fights over the location of key assets may disrupt operations and, hence, give creditors of a particular group member the power to hold the restructuring hostage. The hostage value associated with practical vetoes endangers value-maximizing restructurings and distorts equitable distribution.

A second example of the problem of proving the location of assets can be found in **8.56** *Lehman*.[54] Lehman's business was global,[55] but in order to keep track of its money, it

---

[49] ibid 2.
[50] ibid 16.
[51] Steven Church, 'Nortel Mediation over Splitting $9 Billion Extended by Judge', Bloomberg (22 January 2013) <https://www.bloomberg.com/news/articles/2013-01-22/nortel-mediation-over-splitting-9-billion-extended-by-judge-1-> accessed 11 January 2024; Donald L. Swanson, 'The Monstrous Cost of Mediation Failures (the Nortel Networks Bankruptcy, Part One)', American Bankruptcy Institute, <https://www.abi.org/feed-item/the-monstrous-costs-of-mediation-failures-the-nortel-networks-bankruptcy-part-one> accessed 11 January 2024.
[52] Swanson, 'The Monstrous Cost of Mediation Failures' (n 44) 1–2.
[53] Peg Brickley, 'Nortel Creditors Fail to Reach Deal on How to Split $7.3 Billion', *Wall Street Journal* (7 October 2016) <https://www.wsj.com/articles/nortel-creditors-fail-to-reach-deal-on-how-to-split-7-3-billion-1475876 175> accessed 11 January 2024.
[54] *Lehman Bros Special Fin. Inc. v BNY Corp. Tr. Serv. Ltd (In re Lehman Bros Holdings Inc.)* (n 31).
[55] Richard Herring, 'The Challenge of Resolving Cross-Border Financial Institutions', Yale Journal on Regulation, 31 (2014) 853, 867.

238   CORPORATE GROUPS IN RESCUE

had a centralized cash-management system.[56] Operating funds were disbursed to subsidiaries on a daily basis, but overnight, they were returned to a central account, managed out of London.[57] When Lehman failed, disputes arose as to whether funds were located in the subsidiaries all over the world or centralized in the subsidiary in London that operated the cash-management system. The money was in the firm but not, predictably, in any one subsidiary at any one moment. The location of cash varied with the time of day.

8.57   The difficulty in both cases was that money could not be distributed to creditors until these disputes over priority were resolved. On the one hand, the cases were successful at liquidating the businesses without disputes over allocation standing in the way. On the other hand, the absence of a robust set of rules for allocation made it extremely expensive to figure out how to distribute the proceeds.

8.58   *Nortel* and *Lehman* demonstrate that, in global group cases, the increment of untraceable value can be quite large, even when the value is in the form of relatively discrete assets—cash, or the proceeds from the sale of spectrum licences. For many firms, much of the firm's value will inhere in income generated by operations—the 'going-concern value' of the firm. The increment of extra value that is generated by continuing the operation of the business will often, by definition, be impossible to allocate to a particular piece of property or to situate in a particular subsidiary or country. When there are multiple claims to an undifferentiated pot of money, then it is worth fighting over. And, when there is no principled basis for distributing that pot, the allocation is necessarily arbitrary. Moreover, negotiations among multiple claimants about 'dividing the dollars' frequently end in what game theorists call an 'empty core', with the various stakeholders caught in an endless cycle of negotiation.[58]

B. Entitlements within the Group Structure

8.59   Thus, the greatest difficulty with value allocation within a group structure is the problem of the group itself; the group is not an entity. A group is a collection of entities. But if the group is engaged in a common enterprise, the value of the sum should be greater than the value of the parts. Group members working together are worth more than the group members going it alone, but this value is both ephemeral and common. It exists only if the group continues to operate the business, but it is not equity, which flows up to the

---

[56] ibid 870.

[57] ibid. *In re Lehman Brothers Holdings Inc.*, 404 B.R. 752 (Bankr. S.D.N.Y. 2009) >https://www.mayerbrown.com/public_docs/cashmanagementmotion.pdf> accessed 27 March 2024.

[58] See generally, Kenneth A. Shepsle, *Analyzing Politics: Rationality, Behavior, and Institutions* (2nd edn, W.W. Norton 2010) (explaining the idea about empty core and the divide of the dollars claim). See Douglas G. Baird and Robert K. Rasmussen, 'Antibankruptcy', Yale Law Journal 119 (2010) 648, 687–98; Edward J. Janger, 'The Costs of Liquidity Enhancement: Transparency Cost, Risk Alteration, and Coordination Problems', Brooklyn Journal of Corporate, Financial & Commercial Law, 4 (2009) 39.

holding company, at least when members of the group are not able to pay their creditors in full. As noted above, the 'reorganization surplus' is homeless value. It is common to all but owned by none. This problem is compounded by the vetoes discussed above.

Each group member may have the power to destroy the reorganization surplus, but none has the right to claim it. In the absence of a mechanism for allocating the going-concern surplus, the result is likely to be an anticommons. Multiple creditors of multiple group members may have leverage within a key group member or within the group as a whole. Each may have a claim to priority, but more importantly, they may have the power to obstruct. The use of hostage leverage by multiple claimants will inevitably lead to the destruction of any going-concern surplus. *There are essentially two ways out of the box created by multiple vetoes: the single waterfall and tracing. Both have the power to preserve going-concern value, but they reflect diametrically opposed approaches to distributional equity.* **8.60**

1. The single waterfall: Metaphor and myth

For over 40 years, bankruptcy scholars of the law and economics stripe have been invested in the idea of a hierarchical capital structure as the solution to the anticommons problem described above. The theory behind the hierarchical capital structure is that a dominant senior lender will be able to recreate the incentives of a single owner to maximize the value of the firm.[59] As Jay Westbrook has pointed out, the mechanism for accomplishing such a structure, under current practice, is to create a single, all-encompassing, unitary security interest.[60] While some of the leading law and economics scholars have stepped back from the idea that a 'strict' hierarchical capital structure may not be ideal,[61] they have not retreated from the metaphor of (and assumed desirability of) the single waterfall, where the secured creditor sits atop unsecured creditors, who sit atop equity.[62] The author of this chapter has written extensively about the problems of the single waterfall metaphor, both as a positive matter and as a normative matter.[63] **8.61**

---

[59] Paul M. Shupack, 'Preferred Capital Structures and the Question of Filing', Minnesota Law Review, 79 (1995) 2064, <https://scholarship.law.umn.edu/mlr/2064> accessed 11 January 2024; Alan Schwartz, 'A Theory of Loan Priorities', Journal of Legal Studies, 18 (1989) 209, 216–18, 240–1.

[60] Jay L. Westbrook, 'The Control of Wealth in Bankruptcy', Texas Law Review, 82 (2004) 795.

[61] Douglas G. Baird, 'Priority Matters: Absolute Priority, Relative Priority, and the Costs of Bankruptcy', University of Pennsylvania Law Review, 165 (2017) 785.

[62] In Baird's more recent work, along with Casey, they have advocated what they call 'relative' priority, where the secured creditor sits atop the distributional waterfall, but junior creditors retain the value of an option to cash out the senior lender at par (ibid). A similar approach to an 'option preservation priority' was discussed by the American Bankruptcy Institute Commission to Study the Reform of Chapter 11 in their final report: ABI, *American Bankruptcy Institute Commission to Study the Reform of Chapter 11 (Final Report)* (ABI 2014) 207–24.

[63] Melissa B. Jacoby and Edward J. Janger, 'Ice Cube Bonds: Allocating the Price of Process in Chapter 11 Bankruptcy', Yale Law Journal, 123 (2014) 862, 874–83; Edward J. Janger, 'The Logic and Limits of Liens', University of Illinois Law Review 2015, 589; Melissa B. Jacoby and Edward J. Janger, 'Tracing Equity: Realizing and Allocating Value in Chapter 11', Texas Law Review, 96 (2018) 673, 682–709; Edward J. Janger, 'The Creditors' Bargain Reconstituted: Comments on Barry Adler's The Creditors' Bargain Revisited', University of Pennsylvania Law Review, Online, 167 (2019) 47 <https://scholarship.law.upenn.edu/penn_law_review_online/vol167/iss1/3> accessed 27 March 2024; Edward J. Janger and Adam J. Levitin, 'The Proceduralist Inversion', Yale Law Journal Forum, 130 (2020–21) 335.

240   CORPORATE GROUPS IN RESCUE

8.62   The key normative points are familiar. A super-senior fixed claimant does not have the proper incentives to maximize value. A super-senior variable claimant has the power, often in conjunction with incumbent management or old equity, or a stalking horse, to roll up or squeeze out operating creditors, employees, and tort claimants. This externalization of risk may lead the senior investors to take excessive risk at the expense of others. Further, to the extent that seniority, under this approach, confers control, the result may be an effort to accomplish transactions at excessive speed, thereby exacerbating any existing information asymmetries.

8.63   As a positive matter, the availability of a hierarchical structure varies from jurisdiction to jurisdiction. In the United States, and in civil law jurisdictions, a secured creditor's interest in the firm is limited to the value of the assets and does not include the going-concern value of the firm.[64] In the United Kingdom and other Commonwealth countries, the floating charge *may* confer a lien on all of the value of the firm.[65] Regardless, whether that lien interest covers going-concern value that arises after the opening of a proceeding remains open to question.[66] More importantly, where corporate groups are involved and, as shall be discussed below, where international corporate groups are involved, the corporate form, as well as jurisdictional boundaries create multiple entitlement waterfalls within the same integrated enterprise. Respect of the corporate form creates multiple distributional hierarchies within the same integrated enterprise.

8.64   In the United States, a common approach to this problem, at least in consensual plans of reorganization, is to agree to a consensual substantive consolidation.[67] It is impossible to tell, however, to what extent the distributions in the plan reconstitute the distributional hierarchy through the classification of claims. But, as the *Nortel* case illustrates, in many cases, such bargaining can be costly, and in other cases, the bargaining can be short-circuited by the dominant secured creditor taking control of the transaction.[68]

2. Realizable priority: A functional solution to the problem of multiple waterfalls

8.65   These two scenarios—hierarchy and consolidation—illustrate seemingly diametrically opposed approaches to value allocation in rescue: either transfer all of the value to a dominant secured creditor, without regard to equity, or disregard the corporate form, possibly defeating legitimate creditor expectations.

8.66   But there is a middle way that holds the potential to respect the corporate form, legitimate creditor expectations, and create appropriate governance incentives. The starting

---

[64] Jacoby and Janger, 'Tracing Equity' (n 56).

[65] Adrian Walters, 'Statutory Erosion of Secured Creditors' Rights: Some Insights from the United Kingdom', University of Illinois Law Review 2015, 543.

[66] Jacoby and Janger, 'Tracing Equity'(n 56). In the United States, under 11 U.S.C. §552, floating liens stop floating over new collateral, and continue only in proceeds. In the United Kingdom, the floating charge crystallizes upon the opening of a proceeding. The effect of such crystallization on the rights of the secured creditor in rescue has not been thoroughly explored.

[67] Widen, 'Corporate Form and Substance Consolidation' (n 38).

[68] Jacoby and Janger, 'Ice Cube Bonds' (n 56).

point is respect of the asset-based and structural priorities discussed above. But it is necessary to go further, to recognize both the practical and legal limits on the scope of property rights and the extent to which they confer ownership on income from continued operations. This approach requires a focus on three additional concepts: (a) enterprise value and the 'rump estate', (b) value tracing, and (c) burden of proof.

a. Enterprise value and the rump estate

8.67 The first step is to disaggregate enterprise value from the value of particular assets or entities. As noted earlier, for a solvent firm, reorganization value flows up the corporate structure to the holding company in the form of dividends or share value. But if an entity, or the group as a whole, is insolvent, the going-concern increment no longer flows upwards. Going-concern value can be preserved by continuing operations, but that increment remains within the operating company for the benefit of creditors— it does not flow upstream to equity holders (who are under water). Further, in many cases, preservation of the going-concern increment may be contingent on continued participation in, and continued operation of, the group.

8.68 In other words, there is enterprise value that remains at the operating entity level but does not belong to any particular operating entity, only to the collective. As noted above, there is no place in traditional corporate structure to locate this collective but homeless value—preserved by rescue, but not allocated. In previous writing, this author has referred to this value as the 'rump estate'. It is not a product of substantive consolidation or disregard of the corporate form. It is an asset created by rescue that must be shared equitably.

8.69 The second step is to recognize that assets and their value can be homeless as well. At the entity level, assets may be owned by a particular entity, and they may be subject to property-based claims of priority. To the extent that claims to asset or entity-based priority can be established, they should be respected: a perfected security interest, a true lease, a real estate mortgage, or a true sale to a special-purpose vehicle should be respected.

8.70 However, in any enterprise of any complexity, there may be assets that fall through the cracks. Perfection might be disputed. Priority might be disputed. The nature of a sale as a true sale or a lease as a true lease might be subject to challenge. To the extent that assets cannot be located, or claims cannot be proven, those assets fall into the rump estate as well. The *Lehman* case, discussed above, offers an example, where the centralized cash-management system created a situation where the operating cash in the corporate group was both everywhere and nowhere at once. Again, such homeless assets fall conceptually into the rump estate.

b. Value tracing: Allocating group value in rescue

8.71 In liquidation, value is realized by the sale of the assets and allocated by adjudicating claims of ownership or priority. The claims are administered, estate by estate. There

242   CORPORATE GROUPS IN RESCUE

may be some homeless assets, where title cannot be established, but these disputes do not interfere with value realization, and they are not time sensitive. The *sine qua non* of rescue is that the encumbered assets are not sold, and the entities are not liquidated. Instead, either the assets and operations are sold as a going concern or the enterprise is recapitalized in place. There is no receipt of sale with regard to the various encumbered assets. The assets are transferred to a buyer or to the reorganized debtor, but the assets are commingled. The value of the business is determined by its earnings. So, how should the encumbered assets be valued? How should the encumbrance on those assets be valued? And most importantly, should priority confer a veto over use or sale of the asset?

8.72   In rescue, value is realized from a cash stream, but claims to priority are based on the value of the assets or entities. This creates a choice: should this governance question about how to realize value be answered from the top down (assets) or from the bottom up (value)? Chapter 11, in the United States, seeks a middle path, bargaining in the shadow of entitlement. The parties are expected to bargain over their distributions, and then, if all goes well, the plan is approved by the requisite majorities of each class of claimants.[69] But if agreement is not possible, then the claimant can be 'cashed out' by payment of their statutory entitlement. For unsecured creditors and equity holders, the entitlement is to 'absolute priority'. For creditors who base their priority in an asset, however, the entitlement is the value of their collateral on the effective date. In summary, their priority is limited to the value they could realize in the absence of the reorganization by selling the collateral.

8.73   This answers part of the value-allocation question. To the extent that claims to priority are based on security or title, then the value is the value that can be traced to those assets. Nothing about group structure changes this. But it is important to recognize that, even if all of the assets of an entity are encumbered, to the extent that the going-concern value exceeds the realizable value of the assets, that increment is unencumbered.

8.74   Where claims to priority are structural, rather than asset-based, the answer is similar. To the extent that value can, or could be, realized by the entity going it alone, either through liquidation or operation, that value is allocated first to the claimants of that entity. But to the extent that enterprise value hinges on the combined efforts of the group members, again, their priority is limited to that traceable value.

c. Burden of proof

8.75   If the claim of priority is limited to the realizable value of the claim against assets or a group entity going it alone, the question remains as to who has the burden of proving priority. Is it the debtor's obligation to prove that a claim of priority has been satisfied, or is it the claimant's burden to establish the realizable value of their priority? Here, the question would seem to answer itself. A claim to priority is a claim to special treatment.

---

[69] See 11 U.S.C. §1129(a).

The confounding aspect of debtor/creditor law is that the claims to priority arise out of a promise or relationship between the debtor and the creditor. But giving effect to the priority involves not a dispute between the debtor and the creditor but a dispute amongst the creditors. In other words, when a claimant seeks priority, it is not sufficient to show that the debtor made a particular promise or that the creditor believed that the transaction was being structured a particular way. Instead, the creditor must establish that its claim to priority is entitled to be honoured vis-à-vis other creditors, who may be recipients of similar promises. The claimant to priority has the burden of establishing that their claim is enforceable against third parties and that its value is not dependent on the reorganization.

An excellent example of this approach can be found in the Second Circuit's recent **8.76** opinion in the *Sears* bankruptcy.[70] In that case, the secured lenders holding a second lien on Sears assets sought compensation for a decline in the value of their collateral during the course of the Chapter 11, pursuant to 11 U.S.C. §507(b). They claimed that their interest in the collateral, and hence their allowed secured claim, had not been adequately protected. The creditor made claims with regard to three types of collateral: (a) inventory; (b) 'non-borrowing base' inventory (i.e. inventory that the secured creditor was not prepared to lend against because it was perishable, in transit, or unsaleable); and (c) letters of credit. The court, in valuing these assets, put the burden of establishing value on the second lien lenders. With regard to the inventory, the court, after hearing evidence, valued the inventory based on a 'net orderly liquidation value', in other words the amount that would be realized in an orderly going-out-of-business sale. Given that this was how Sears actually realized the value of its inventory, the Court of Appeals found this to be a reasonable valuation method. In other words, the creditor had established the realizable value of the inventory. With regard to the non-borrowing base inventory, the creditors presented no evidence of realizable value, other than book value. The court found that the lenders had not presented credible evidence of valuation and, hence, valued the non-borrowing base inventory at zero. Similarly, where no evidence was given as to the likely draws on the letters of credit, the bankruptcy court found that the creditor had not met its burden and valued the allowed secured claim at zero. The Second Circuit affirmed all of these rulings.[71]

3. Realizable priority in group cases
The concept of realizable priority captures the reality of negotiating over bankruptcy- **8.77** created value—the going-concern increment that is preserved by a successful restructuring. Creditors who have bargained for priority have an entitlement, but it is a practical entitlement, not a metaphysical one. They are entitled to what they would have got going it alone. A rescue is only worth the effort if there is value, beyond that

---

[70] *ESL Investments, Inc. v Sears Holdings Corporation (In re Sears)* (Case 20-3343, Document 166-1, 14 October 2022) <https://www.govinfo.gov/content/pkg/USCOURTS-ca2-20-03343/pdf/USCOURTS-ca2-20-03343-0.pdf> accessed 11 January 2024.
[71] ibid.

244 CORPORATE GROUPS IN RESCUE

realizable by creditors on their own, that can only be realized by cooperation. The restructuring should do no harm, but harm is measured by what the creditor could actually obtain, not some romanticized idea of their contractual remedies. The court in *Nortel* recognized that, as to the increment of added value, no particular creditor had a special claim; the homeless value should be shared pro rata.

8.78 There is at least one structure that might be used to implement realizable priority in a 'consensual' plan of reorganization. In a consensual plan, presumably, each group member would be recapitalized at its realizable value. This would leave equity to flow up to the corporate parent. Provable claims of priority could be satisfied within the member. Any deficiencies would be asserted by the member against the parent and satisfied with a stock distribution. In cramdown, a similar result might be obtained, with secured creditors being paid the value of their assets. The absolute priority rule might present a bit of a problem. The key would be that the parent would have to purchase the equity of the member through its contribution of stock.

8.79 Crucially, participation in the reorganization surplus would not be swallowed by a priority claim and, instead, would be a benefit associated with cooperating in the restructuring.

VI. Cross-Border Issues: Administering a Global Restructuring

8.80 The discussion above shows that restructuring a corporate group can be devilishly complex. However, an additional wrinkle is added by the fact that many corporate groups operate across borders. Group structures are often set up so that a global business can operate in multiple jurisdictions and across legal systems. Differences in fiduciary duties discussed above, and the different rules for when it is necessary to open an insolvency proceedings proceeding, may lead a business to try to organize its group structure along national lines.

8.81 This may simplify operations when things are running normally, but when trying to coordinate a global restructuring, the proliferation of entities and national boundaries can cause opportunities for strategic behaviour to proliferate. For this reason, in a global case, there needs to be both a forum for developing a 'group solution' and a mechanism for achieving recognition. For the process of recognition to work smoothly, there must be a mechanism for distinguishing objections based on strategy from legitimate objections based on claims of inequitable treatment. This section suggests that the recently promulgated UNCITRAL Model Law on the Insolvency of Enterprise Groups (MLEG), when implemented in conjunction with the UNCITRAL Model Law on Cross-Border Insolvency, with an eye upon 'realizable priority', offers a workable framework and is an important step forward. A similar approach is followed by the European Union (EU) Insolvency Regulation (Recast), but, since it is designed for use within the EU, it lacks the somewhat more developed and important structure for recognition.

The key features that matter, for the purpose of this discussion, are the concept of a **8.82** 'planning proceeding', the 'group insolvency solution', 'recognition', and 'adequate protection'. The term 'adequate protection' is not defined, and admittedly, it has some play in the joints. However, embedded within the concept of 'adequate protection' is the entitlement to 'realizable priority' and 'equitable treatment'. These entitlements are given effect through the mechanism of 'synthetic treatment'. Each of these concepts will be explained in order.

A. The Planning Proceeding

The first concept is the 'planning proceeding'. That term is defined in Art. 2(g) of the **8.83** MLEG as 'a main proceeding commenced in respect of an enterprise group member' that 'is likely to be a necessary and integral participant in that group insolvency solution', where 'a group representative has been appointed'. This definition serves a number of functions. It allows for the creation of a single proceeding that can operate as a forum for negotiating a restructuring for the enterprise as a whole. It also limits the extent of venue shopping by requiring the planning proceeding to be the main proceeding in respect of an essential group member.[72] The planning proceeding does not come into being until a 'group insolvency representative' has been chosen.[73]

B. The Group Insolvency Solution

Once the planning proceeding has been opened, and a group representative appointed, **8.84** the group members can go about formulating a 'group insolvency solution'. This is what might be referred to in the United States as a plan of reorganization. However, the process of negotiating and confirming the group insolvency solution within the planning proceeding is left to the local law of the jurisdiction where the proceeding is pending. Instead, the MLEG creates a mechanism for recognition[74] and implementation of relief necessary to continue the business enterprise[75] and to seek approval of the group solution in the relevant jurisdictions—in most cases, the centre of main interest of the group member.[76]

[72] The definition contemplates that the planning proceeding could be the proceeding of that group member or a separate proceeding opened in the court where the group member's case is pending: ibid.
[73] See Art. 19 of the MLEG.
[74] ibid Art. 21.
[75] ibid Arts 21, 23, 24.
[76] ibid Art. 26.

C. Recognition

8.85 The MLEG leaves open the nature of approvals that a receiving jurisdiction would follow in ratifying or giving effect to the group insolvency solution.[77] The key point, though, is that the relief granted is subject to the requirement of 'adequate protection'.[78] The term 'adequate protection' is not defined, and given the general goal of cooperation and coordination, it cannot demand identical treatment to that available under local law. It does carry with it the idea that the relief must be subject to sufficient procedural safeguards and contain a substantive result that it is entitled to comity. It is important to note that, as written, Art. 27 imposes a requirement that is both specific to the group member and horizontal across the group.[79] Finally, the MLEG contains a mechanism for allowing a planning proceeding to provide adequate protection to creditors of group members who might be entitled to particular treatment in the country where they are organized and/or operate. Articles 28 and 29 of the MLEG allow the planning proceeding to issue an undertaking to grant local treatment to a group member who would be entitled to priority or special protection in a local proceeding.

D. Adequate Protection and Realizable Priority

8.86 This, of course, brings us back to the question of how to give practical effect to such local priorities. When a receiving court considers adequate protection, what are the appropriate criteria? This is where the concept of realizable priority offers guidance. The concept of local priority can be given formal effect, but if it does so, it operates as a veto. When evaluating a 'group insolvency solution', a receiving court should ask the question, 'What would local creditor receive in the absence of the proposed solution?' That should establish the lower threshold for a claim of priority when evaluating the group insolvency solution. But Art. 27 also requires the receiving jurisdiction to ask whether the interests of 'each group member' are adequately protected. This carries with it a requirement of horizontal equity—that the going-concern increment be shared fairly amongst group members. As discussed above, this can be accomplished by allowing the creditor of a group member to assert its deficiency against the common value held by the rump estate.

8.87 In summary, the MLEG offers a procedural mechanism for administering group cases across national boundaries. But also, through the concept of 'adequate protection', it provides a basis for establishing an entitlement baseline for creditors of group members and for distribution of the surplus value that inheres in the group enterprise.

---

[77] ibid Art. 26.

[78] ibid Art. 27.

[79] ibid Art. 27 provides: 'In granting, denying, modifying or terminating relief under this Law, the court must be satisfied that the interests of the creditors of each enterprise group member subject to or participating in a planning proceeding and other interested persons, including the enterprise group member subject to the relief to be granted, are adequately protected.'

VII. Conclusion

Business enterprises divide themselves into discrete corporate entities for a variety of **8.88**
reasons and purposes. It can be functional, to separate businesses and organize functions. It can be transactional, allocating risks and benefits among investors. It can be
territorial, to accommodate differences among geographic markets and legal systems. When a firm finds itself in financial distress, the group structure can be a source
of clarity, but it can also create confusion and opportunities for strategic behaviour.
Keeping the ship afloat may require difficult choices, and the interests of group members may conflict. Effectuating the rescue of a complex corporate group presents a host
of difficult issues. This chapter has canvassed, albeit briefly, the related issues of duty
and value allocation and sought to offer an approach to both fiduciary duty and value
allocation that can guide decision-making in rescue. The key concept in the vicinity
of insolvency is to do no harm. The key concept in rescue is to give effect to the harm
principle based on a functional, rather than formal, approach to priority rooted in realizable value. Establishing realizable value can be costly, particularly where asset value
or group member value is being allocated across an integrated enterprise that is being
reorganized as a group. Here, the key point is that, while the burden of satisfying the
creditor's baseline entitlement is on the debtor, the baseline entitlement is pro rata, and
the burden of establishing the value of a priority entitlement is on the creditor.

9

Cross-Border Insolvency Law

Reinhard Bork

I. Introduction

9.01 Increasingly, insolvency proceedings have international connotations. Debtors have assets abroad, are obliged to foreign creditors, are engaged in contractual relationships with counterparties in other jurisdictions, or have other cross-border affairs, for example offices, branches, or subsidiaries in a different country. This not only holds true for entrepreneurs but also for consumers who order goods from abroad or own a holiday home in a foreign State. As soon as other jurisdictions are involved, we can speak of cross-border insolvencies, and the rules that deal with this phenomenon can be consolidated as cross-border (or international) insolvency law.[1]

A. Issues

9.02 Cross-border insolvency law deals with typical problems. The first question concerns the number of proceedings: is there only one single set of insolvency proceedings, or should there be separate proceedings in each jurisdiction involved? If there is only one single set of proceedings, which State has international jurisdiction to open such proceedings? What are the trans-border effects of 'outgoing' domestic insolvency proceedings; for example, does the seizure of the estate include assets located abroad? Are 'incoming' foreign proceedings recognised domestically; for example, does a foreign insolvency practitioner have the power to dispose of assets located inland? Which law does apply to the insolvency proceedings; for example, is the insolvency law of the opening State[2] applicable to security rights encumbering collateral located in another State, and what are the effects on employment contracts of employees hired abroad? Where there are multiple proceedings, how are they coordinated?

---

[1] See extensively on international insolvency law, R. Bork, Cross-Border Insolvency Law, (Edward Elgar Publishing 2023); R. Bork, Einführung in das Insolvenzrecht (11th edn, MohrSiebeck 2023) § 38; R. Dammann and M. Sénéchal, Le droit de l'insolvabilité international (Joly 2018); Fletcher, The Law of Insolvency (Sweet & Maxwell 2107) chs 28 et seq.; Le Corre, Droit et pratique des procédúres collectives (12th edn, Dalloz 2022); Mélin, La faillite international (Librairie Général de Droit 2004); Sheldon, Cross-Border Insolvency (4th edn, Bloomsbury Professional 2015); C.J. Tabb, Law of Bankruptcy (5th edn, West Academic Publishing 2020) § 1.27(e); B. Wessels, International Insolvency Law (5th edn, Kluwer 2022) Pt I; K. van Zwieten, Goode on Principles of Corporate Insolvency Law (5th edn, Sweet & Maxwell 2018) chs 15, 16.

[2] Henceforth, the meaning of 'opening State' is the State where insolvency proceedings have been opened.

Reinhard Bork, *Cross-Border Insolvency Law* In: *The Anatomy of Corporate Insolvency Law.* Edited by: Reinhard Bork and Renato Mangano, Oxford University Press. © Reinhard Bork 2024. DOI: 10.1093/oso/9780198852094.003.0009

INTRODUCTION 249

B. Codifications

In searching for a codification (or various codifications) of international insolvency **9.03**
law, a wealth of suitable material can be found. Internationally binding laws, which
apply to more than one State, and thus do not constitute purely national law but rather transnational law, belong within the first group of laws to be depicted here. The
first transnational law to be named is the European Insolvency Regulation (EIR[3]),
which was first adopted in 2000, recast in 2015, and applies to all Member States of the
European Union, with the exception of Denmark.[4] Alongside this, there are—among
others—the Nordic Bankruptcy Convention,[5] which applies to the Scandinavian countries of Denmark, Finland, Iceland, Norway, and Sweden; the Treaties of Montevideo,[6]
which were ratified by Argentina, Bolivia, Columbia, Paraguay, Peru, and Uruguay;
the Havana Convention of 20 February 1928, which was signed by 15 South American
States[7] and is better known as the Code Bustamante;[8] and finally Art. 247 of the Uniform
Act Organising Collective Proceedings for Wiping off Debts,[9] which is binding for the
17 Member States[10] of the Organisation for the Harmonisation of Business Law in
Africa (OHBLA).

---

[3] Regulation (EU) 2015/848 of the European Paliament and of the Council, of 20 May 2015 on insolvency proceedings (recast), OJ 2015 L 141/19, <https://eur-lex.europa.eu/legal-content/EN/TXT/?uri=CELEX%3A320
15R0848> accessed 23 August 2021. For details, see Bělohlávek, *EU and International Insolvency Proceedings,
Regulation (EU) 2015/848 on Insolvency Proceedings Commentary* (Lex Lata 2020); R. Bork and R. Mangano,
European Cross-Border Insolvency Law (2nd edn, OUP 2022); R. Bork *and* K. van Zwieten (eds), Commentary
on the EIR (2nd edn, OUP 2022); M. *Brinkmann* (ed.), EIR (Verlag C.H. Beck/Hart Publishing/Nomos
Verlagsgesellschaf, 2019); Marshall and Herrod, European Cross-Border Insolvency (Sweet & Maxwell, loose-
leaf as of 2023); *Moss, Fletcher,* and *Isaacs* (eds), The EC Regulation on Insolvency Proceedings (3rd edn, Oxford
University Press 2016); Virgós and Garcimartín, The European Insolvency Regulation (Kluwer Law International
2004); B. Wessels and S. Madaus, International Insolvency Law (5th edn, Kluwer 2022) Pt II.
[4] See Recital 88 of the EIR. See, for this exception, *Re Arena Corporation Ltd* [2003] EWHC 3032 (Ch); see further, *Global Maritime Investments Cyprus Limited v O.W. Supply & Trading A/S (under konkurs)* [2015] EWHC
2690 (Comm) (where the English court reported the recognition of Danish proceedings under the Cross-Border
Insolvency Regulations (CBIR) 2006, which would not have been possible if the EIR was applicable); *SwissMarine
Corporation Limited v O.W. Supply & Trading A/S (in bankruptcy)* [2015] EWHC 1571 (Comm).
[5] Of 7 November 1933, also called the 'Copenhagen Convention', with amendments on 11 October 1977 and
11 October 1982 (English text available in B. Wessels and Boon, Cross-Border Insolvency Law—International
Instruments and Commentary (2nd edn, Wolters Kluwer 2015) Annex 38.
[6] See Title X Arts 35 et seq. of the Montevideo Treaty on Commercial International Law of 12 March 1889
(English text available at Wessels and Boon, *Cross-Border Insolvency Law* (n 5) Annex 45); Arts 40 et seq. of the
Montevideo Treaty on International Commercial Terrestrial Law of 19 March 1940 (English text available in the
American Journal of International Law 37(3) (1943) Supp., 132 et seq.); Arts 16 et seq. of the Montevideo Treaty
of International Procedural Law of 19 March 1940 (English text available in the American Journal of International
Law, 37(3) (1943) Supp., 116 et seq.).
[7] Bolivia, Brazil, Chile, Costa Rica, Cuba, the Dominican Republic, Ecuador, El Salvador, Guatemala, Haiti,
Honduras, Nicaragua, Panama, Peru, and Venezuela. The convention was also signed but not ratified by Argentina,
Colombia, Mexico, Paraguay, and Uruguay.
[8] See Title IX Art. 414 et seq. (English text available at 86 (1929) League of Nations—Treaty Series, 362 et seq.);
also at Wessels and Boon, *Cross-Border Insolvency Law* (n 5) Annex 46 and at <http://www.worldlii.org/cgi-bin/
download.cgi/download/int/other/LNTSer/1929/47.pdf> accessed 23 August 2021.
[9] Of 10 April 1998, revised on 10 September 2015; French text available at <http://www.ohada.com/actes-
uniformes/1668/1743/titre-vii-procedures-collectives-internationales.html> accessed 20 April 2023).
[10] Benin, Burkina Faso, Cameroon, Central African Republic, Chad, the Comoros, the Democratic Republic
of the Congo, Equatorial Guinea, Gabon, Guinea, Guinea-Bissau, Ivory Coast, Mali, Niger, the Republic of the
Congo, Senegal, and Togo.

9.04 A second group consists of non-binding recommendations for the legislature and for those involved in cross-border insolvency proceedings. A prominent example is the United Nations Commission on International Trade Law (UNCITRAL) Model Law on Cross-Border Insolvency,[11] which has been incorporated into the national law of 49 States.[12] In addition, different recommendations by international organisations should be mentioned, such as the Principles of Cooperation in Transnational Insolvency Cases among the North American Free Trade Agreement (NAFTA) Countries (NAFTA Principles),[13] which were formulated in 2000 by the American Law Institute, or the Cross-Border Insolvency Concordat of 31 May 1996, which was created by the International Bar Association.[14] Cooperation guidelines are helpful for practice, particularly the Global Principles for Cooperation in International Insolvency Cases (Global Principles) of 30 March 2012, jointly drafted by Ian Fletcher and Bob Wessels and published by the American Law Institute in cooperation with the International Insolvency Institute,[15] and the European Communication and Cooperation Guidelines for Cross-Border Insolvencies, presented by INSOL Europe.[16]

9.05 National rules on international insolvency law belong to the third group.[17] Examples to be named include §§ 335 et seq. of the *Insolvenzordnung* (Germany),[18] which leans heavily on the European Insolvency Regulation, as well as Chapter 15 of the US Bankruptcy Code, which builds upon the UNCITRAL Model Law. Other examples from Europe include Spain (Arts 721 et seq. of the *Ley Concursal*)[19] and the Netherlands (Arts 203 et seq. of the Netherlands Bankruptcy Act).[20] The United Kingdom had four legal regimes operating regarding cross-border insolvency cases. During the European Union (EU) membership of the United Kingdom, in relation to other Member States

---

[11] United Nations Commission on International Trade Law (UNCITRAL), *Model Law on Cross-Border Insolvency Law with Guide to Enactment and Interpretation* (United Nations Publications 2014). See further, Ho (ed.), *Cross-Border Insolvency* (4th edn, Global Law and Business 2017).

[12] Cf. <https://uncitral.un.org/en/texts/insolvency/modellaw/cross-border_insolvency/status> accessed 20 April 2023.

[13] American Law Institute, *Principles of Cooperation in Transnational Insolvency Cases among the NAFTA Countries* (Juris Publishing 2003); for the genesis of these principles, see J.L. Westbrook, 'Creating International Insolvency Law', American Business Law Journal, *70* (1996), 563, 564 et seq.

[14] Text available at <https://www.yumpu.com/en/document/view/37628562/committee-j-cross-border-insolvency-concordat-international> accessed 20 April 2023. For the use of the concordat by courts, cf. Nielsen, Sigal, and Wagner, 'The Cross-Border Insolvency Concordat: Principles to Facilitate the Resolution of International Insolvencies', American Business Law Journal, *70* (1996) 533 et seq.

[15] Available at <https://www.ali.org/publications/show/transnational-insolvency> (accessed 20 April 2023) and in International Insolvency Review, 23 (2014) 221 et seq. The American Law Institute (ALI) Annual Meeting adopted the text on 23 May 2012, the 3rd Annual Conference on 22 June 2012.

[16] Text, edited by B. Wessels, available in Bork and van Zwieten, *Commentary on the EIR* (n 3) Appendix 5; extensively on these principles and guidelines, see B. Wessels, 'A Glimpse into the Future: Cross-Border Judicial Cooperation in Insolvency Cases in the European Union', International Insolvency Review, *24* (2015) 96 et seq.; B. Wessels, 'Towards A Next Step in Cross-Border Judicial Cooperation', Insolvency International, *27* (2014) 100 et seq.; B. Wessels, 'EU Courts Can Rely on Soft Law Principles for Cooperation in International Insolvency Cases', International Insolvency Law Review, (2015) 145 et seq.

[17] For references, cf. above (n 1).

[18] Insolvency Regulation: English text at <http://www.gesetze-im-internet.de/englisch_inso/index.html> accessed 20 April 2023. All mentions of '*Insolvenzordnung*' in this text are related to this statute.

[19] Ley 4859/2020 of 5 May 2020; Spanish text available at <https://www.boe.es/buscar/act.php?id=BOE-A-2020-4859#dd> accessed 20 April 2023.

[20] English text at <http://www.dutchcivillaw.com/bankruptcyact.htm> accessed 20 April 2023.

of the EU, the EIR was applicable. In relation to Commonwealth States, s. 426 of the Insolvency Act 1986 is applied. And in relation to all other States, the provisions of the Cross-Border Insolvency Regulation 2006 (henceforth CBIR 2006) apply, which incorporated the UNCITRAL Model Law into national English insolvency law. In addition, duties to cooperate can be derived from the common law. In France, however, cross-border insolvency law is not codified but handled on a case-by-case basis under general legal principles (*droit commun*), unless the EIR or bilateral treaties apply.[21] It is for this reason that French cross-border insolvency law will not be considered in detail in this chapter.

C. Principles

We have learned about the principles of insolvency law, which can be identified as basic tenets for insolvency law in general and transactions avoidance law in particular.[22] Similarly, the principles of cross-border insolvency law deserve attention.[23] Especially in an area where there are few common rules, the recognition that there are common legal principles which shape and systematise international insolvency law is of great importance. These principles of cross-border insolvency law can be summarised in three groups: jurisdictional, procedural, and substantive principles. In the following part of this chapter, the principles will be briefly introduced and illustrated with some examples. **9.06**

1. Jurisdictional principles
Jurisdictional principles of cross-border insolvency law take account of the circumstance that, in cross-border insolvencies, the territories of at least two sovereign, equal-ranking States are concerned.[24] Against this background, no State can impose any legal consequences as provided for in insolvency law on another State. This would, in and of itself, argue for separate insolvency proceedings in each State concerned. Modern international insolvency laws, though, generally base themselves on principles that point in a different direction. **9.07**

The first principle to be named here is the principle of unity. It supports the idea that there shall fundamentally be no more than one single insolvency procedure governing the debtor's insolvency. This was clearly stated by Lord Hoffmann in the UK Supreme Court decision *Re HIH Casualty*, where it is explained that **9.08**

> [D]espite the absence of statutory provision, some degree of international co-operation in corporate insolvency had been achieved by judicial practice. This was

---

[21] Le Corre, *Droit et pratique des procédures collectives* (n 1) para. 093.091; see extensively, Dammann and Sénéchal, *Le droit de l'insolvabilité international* (n 1) paras 2038 et seq.

[22] See Chapter 6 'Transactions Avoidance Rules' at paras 6.07 et seq.

[23] See extensively, R. Bork, *Principles of Cross-Border Insolvency Law* (Intersentia 2017).

[24] Details in ibid paras 1.29, 2.1 et seq.

252   CROSS-BORDER INSOLVENCY LAW

based upon what English judges have for many years regarded as a general principle of private international law, namely that bankruptcy (whether personal or corporate) should be unitary and universal. There should be a unitary bankruptcy proceeding in the court of the bankrupt's domicile which receives world-wide recognition and it should apply universally to all the bankrupt's assets.[25]

9.09   With this quote, a second important jurisdictional principle is referred to—the principle of universalism (or universality): if there is only one unified set of proceedings opened against an insolvent debtor (unity), these proceedings should have worldwide scope. The latter applies in any case from the perspective of the State opening the proceedings, which demands worldwide application of its 'outgoing' proceedings, while it is another story as to whether other affected States will recognise the 'incoming' insolvency proceedings as requiring recognition. This can nicely be illustrated by Art. 5 of the UNCITRAL Model Law, and in its lead by Art. 5 Sch. 1 of the CBIR 2006, 11 U.S.C. §1505, which states that a domestic insolvency practitioner 'is authorized to act in a foreign State [i.e. 'outgoing universalism'[...], as permitted by the applicable foreign law [i.e. 'incoming universalism']'.[26] Subject to some restrictions, the principle of universalism is nowadays enforced in nearly all jurisdictions, thus replacing the principle of territoriality according to which the effects of insolvency proceedings do not go beyond the territory of the opening State.[27]

9.10   In addition, the principle of equality of States precludes a State from forcing worldwide application of its law on another. It can be found in the Preamble and in Art. 2(1) of the Charter of the United Nations (UN). Under this principle, 'incoming universalism' requires a respective decision of the State on the territory of which the legal consequences of foreign insolvency proceedings shall take effect. These effects must be recognized by this State, either generally in international or bilateral regulations or treaties or individually through (typically, court) decisions in each relevant case.

9.11   It is the principle of mutual trust between States that facilitates such decisions. This principle proposes that, if the insolvency law and the handling of the insolvency proceedings in the original State meet the required standards, the relevant State should be urged to trustfully recognize it. This tenet, which has been repeatedly acknowledged by the Court of Justice of the European Union (CJEU),[28] is of particular importance within

---

[25] *Re HIH Casualty & General Insurance Ltd* [2008] UKHL 21.

[26] Parts in brackets added.

[27] An illustrative example for the change from territoriality to universalism is Japanese insolvency law. Until 2001, it adhered strictly to the principle of territorialism for both outgoing and incoming insolvency proceedings (according to Art. 3 of the Insolvency Statute). In 2010, the Japanese legislature adopted the UNCITRAL Model Law (cf. above para. 9.04) through its Act on Recognition of and Assistance for Foreign Insolvency Proceedings (ARAFIP); Act No. 129 of 29 November 2000). Since then, Japanese cross-border insolvency law has enforced the principle of universalism. Cf. Krohe, 'Insolvenzverfahren' in Baum and Bälz (eds), *Handbuch Japanisches Handels- und Wirtschaftsrecht* (Carl Heymanns Verlag 2011) paras 106 et seq. with further references; Matsushita, 'UNCITRAL Model Law and the Comprehensive Reform of Japanese Insolvency' in Basedow and Kono (eds), *Legal Aspects of Globalization* (Kluwer Law International 2000) 151 et seq.

[28] Examples are CJEU Case C-341/04 *Eurofood IFSC Ltd*, ECLI:EU:C:2006:281; CJEU Case C-444/07 *MG Probud Gdynia sp. z o.o.*, ECLI:EU:C:2010:24; CJEU Case C-723/20 *Galapagos BidCo. Sàrl*, ECLI:EU:C:2022:209.

the EU, since this union is built on the principle of mutual trust. It is for this reason that Recital 65 of the EIR—on the basis of Art. 67 of the Treaty on the Functioning of the European Union (TFEU) and in line with Recital 26 of the Brussels Ia-Regulation[29]— reads: 'The recognition of judgments delivered by the courts of the Member States should be based on the principle of mutual trust.'

Regardless, the principle of cooperation and communication between the different **9.12** official bodies taking part in the proceedings is generally recognized with regard to cross-border insolvency proceedings. The EIR acknowledges this principle with special norms on cooperation and communication, for example in Arts 41 et seq. regarding the relationship between main and secondary insolvency proceedings and in Arts 56 et seq. regarding group insolvency proceedings; the UNCITRAL Model Law already recognizes it in its Preamble, which names as its significant goal the encouragement of cooperation between procedural organs of the affected States, and also refers to it in Arts 25 et seq., which concern themselves extensively with the cooperation of courts and insolvency practitioners.

In the context of international insolvency law, the principle of subsidiarity deserves **9.13** mentioning. It can be traced back to the seventeenth century, where it found its classical wording in the social encyclical *Quadramesimo anno*, issued by Pope Pius XI on 15 May 1931,[30] and requires that a central authority should perform only those tasks that cannot be performed effectively at a more immediate or local level. For example, Recital 86 of the EIR reads:

> Since the objective of this Regulation cannot be sufficiently achieved by the Member States but can rather, by reason of the creation of a legal framework for the proper administration of cross-border insolvency proceedings, be better achieved at Union level, the Union may adopt measures in accordance with the principle of subsidiarity as set out in Article 5 of the Treaty on European Union.[31]

However, the CJEU has accepted, in many cases, that the basic decisions of the EIR must be complemented by national laws on matters such as the admissibility of insolvency

---

[29] Regulation (EU) 1215/2012 of the European Parliament and of the Council of 12 December 2012 on jurisdiction and the recognition and enforcement of judgments in civil and commercial matters, [2012] OJ L351/1.

[30] English text available at <http://w2.vatican.va/content/pius-xi/en/encyclicals/documents/hf_p-xi_enc_19 310515_quadragesimo-anno.html> accessed 20 April 2023. The salient passages can be found at paras 79 and 80:

> 79. As history abundantly proves, it is true that on account of changed conditions many things which were done by small associations in former times cannot be done now save by large associations. Still, that most weighty principle, which cannot be set aside or changed, remains fixed and unshaken in social philosophy: Just as it is gravely wrong to take from individuals what they can accomplish by their own initiative and industry and give it to the community, so also it is an injustice and at the same time a grave evil and disturbance of right order to assign to a greater and higher association what lesser and subordinate organizations can do. For every social activity ought of its very nature to furnish help to the members of the body social, and never destroy and absorb them.

> 80. The supreme authority of the State ought, therefore, to let subordinate groups handle matters and concerns of lesser importance, which would otherwise dissipate its efforts greatly.

[31] Cf. also B. Wessels and S. Madaus, *International Insolvency Law* (Pt II) (n 3) para. 10433.

254 CROSS-BORDER INSOLVENCY LAW

applications,[32] the capacity of the debtor to be subject to insolvency proceedings[33] and the entitlement of creditors to apply for secondary proceedings.[34]

9.14 Finally, the principle of subsidiarity is often accompanied by the principle of proportionality. For example, with regard to Art. 5 of the Treaty on European Union (TEU), Recital 86 of the EIR reads: 'In accordance with the principle of proportionality, as set out in that Article, this Regulation does not go beyond what is necessary in order to achieve that objective.' Accordingly, the CJEU has mentioned this principle in various cases. For example, in *Nortel*, the court has explained that the EIR does not contain a complete set of harmonized conflict-of-laws rules but rather restricts these rules to the extent that they are necessary, due to the principle of proportionality.[35]

2. Procedural principles

9.15 The second group of principles of cross-border insolvency law takes account of the fact that insolvency proceedings are—by their very labelling—procedures that are supported and shaped by procedural principles.

9.16 A very important procedural principle is the principle of efficiency: proceedings must be shaped in such a way as to ensure that the legal protection that the procedure seeks to provide can be granted as quickly and as comprehensively as possible. This tenet influences procedural law in general and the law of (cross-border) insolvency proceedings in particular. In *Nike*,[36] for example, the CJEU had to deal with the burden of proof concerning the prerequisites of (what is now) Art. 16 of the EIR. The court pointed out that neither the EIR nor harmonized law contained any provisions on the procedural details and then continued:

> [28] According to settled case-law, in the absence of harmonisation of such rules under EU law, it is for the national legal order of each Member State to establish them in accordance with the principle of procedural autonomy provided, however, that those rules are not less favourable than those governing similar domestic situations (principle of equivalence) and that they do not make it excessively difficult or impossible in practice to exercise the rights conferred by EU law (principle of effectiveness) ...

> [29] In particular, in so far as the principle of effectiveness mentioned in paragraph 28 above is concerned, that principle precludes, first, the application of national rules of procedure that would make reliance on Article 13 of Regulation No 1346/2000[37] impossible or excessively difficult by providing for rules which are too onerous, especially in connection with proof of the negative, namely that certain circumstances did not exist. Second, that principle precludes national rules of evidence that are not

---

[32] CJEU Case C-396/09 *Interedil*, ECLI:EU:C:2011:67.
[33] CJEU Case C-112/10 *Zaza Retail BV*, ECLI:EU:C:2011:743.
[34] CJEU Case C-327/13 *Burgo Group SpA v Illochroma SA and Jérôme Theetten*, ECLI:EU:C:2014:2158.
[35] *CJEU Case C-649/13 Comité d'entreprise de Nortel Networks SA and ors v Cosme Rogeau and Cosme Rogeau v Alan Robert Bloom and ors*, ECLI:EU:C:2015:384.
[36] *CJEU Case C-310/14 Nike European Operations Netherlands BV v Sportland Oy*, ECLI:EU:C:2015:690.
[37] Now Art. 16 of the EIR.

sufficiently rigorous, the application of which would, in fact, have the effect of shifting the burden of proof laid down in Article 13 of the regulation.

Further, the principle of transparency requires that insolvency proceedings are conducted publicly and transparently in order to strengthen public confidence in the correctness, fairness, and legitimacy of proceedings; to enable the parties to the proceedings to enforce their procedural and substantive rights; and to give the public the chance to control the proceedings.[38] In international insolvencies, this requires transborder publication and information. For example, the principle of transparency is enforced by Procedural Principle 13 of the NAFTA Principles, which reads as follows:

9.17

> When a bankruptcy proceeding is likely to include claims from another NAFTA country where no parallel proceeding is pending, the court should make such special orders concerning the giving of notice to foreign creditors, to the extent permitted by governing law, as will afford them a fair chance to file claims and participate in the bankruptcy.

Of utmost significance is the principle of predictability (or legal certainty). Every person involved in legal affairs must be able to foresee (or be reliably advised on) not only their legal position but also how they can exercise their rights, what amount of support they are entitled to from public authorities, and which steps they must take to access such support. Parallel to the legal implications, predictability can render economic benefits by contributing to a reduction of transaction costs. Although these interdependencies must not be overrated,[39] one may assume that creditors calculating the risks of a foreign contract partner becoming insolvent will reasonably include the procedural hurdles concerning receiving their share of the debtor's asset pool in their assessment. This assessment is much easier, and the result is much more reassuring, where the law provides for predictable proceedings so that creditors are able to judge from an *ex ante* perspective how the proceedings will be conducted, how the creditors themselves are expected to contribute, and what economic effects this will have. 11 U.S.C. §1501(a) (2), for example, highlights 'greater legal certainty for trade and investment' as one of several objectives of US cross-border insolvency law, as contained in Chapter 15 of the US Bankruptcy Code,[40] thus following the Preamble of the UNCITRAL Model Law. Regarding international jurisdiction under Art. 3 of the EIR 2000, the CJEU held, in *Eurofood*, that the 'centre of main interests' (COMI) presumption 'can be rebutted only if factors which are both objective and ascertainable by third parties enable it to be established that an actual situation exists which is different from that which the location

9.18

---

[38] Cf. *Re Cozumel Caribe, SA de CV*, 508 BR 330, 338 (Bankr. SDNY 2014); there is a useful analysis of this decision by Good, ' "Stress Testing" Chapter 15 of the US Bankruptcy Code', Corporate Rescue and Insolvency, 7 (2014) 192 et seq.

[39] J.L. Westbrook, 'A Global Solution to Multinational Default', Michigan Law Review, *98* (2000) 2276, 2326 et seq.

[40] See also *In re Bear Stearns High-Grade Structured Credit*, 389 BR 325, 333 (SDNY 2008): 'By establishing a simple, objective eligibility requirement for recognition, Chapter 15 promotes predictability and reliability.'

256 CROSS-BORDER INSOLVENCY LAW

of the registered office is deemed to reflect'.[41] In the present context, the following passage from the judgment, referring to Recital 13 of the EIR 2000, is worth quoting:

> That definition shows that the centre of main interests must be identified by reference to criteria that are both objective and ascertainable by third parties. That objectivity and that possibility of ascertainment by third parties are necessary in order to ensure legal certainty and foreseeability concerning the determination of the court with jurisdiction to open main insolvency proceedings. That legal certainty and that foreseeability are all the more important in that, in accordance with Article 4(1) of the Regulation, determination of the court with jurisdiction entails determination of the law which is to apply.[42]

9.19 Another important principle of insolvency law is the principle of procedural justice. Under the rule of law, all proceedings have to be fair and just. The absence of arbitrariness; the equal treatment of all parties involved in the proceedings; and the adequate and fair organization and administration of the proceedings, including granting the right to be heard, are all necessary for accepting the result of the proceedings. It has been convincingly explained by Niklas Luhmann that only parties that have had the chance to make their legal position clear and to participate in fair and just proceedings will be willing to accept the (potentially negative) decision that terminates the proceedings and is binding on these parties.[43] This also holds true for insolvency proceedings, regardless of whether they have cross-border effects or not. The importance of procedural justice is acknowledged in quite a few cross-border insolvency laws, most prominently by the Preamble of the UNCITRAL Model Law, which declares 'fair and efficient administration of cross-border insolvencies that protects the interests of all creditors and other interested persons, including the debtor' as being one of the scheme's main objectives. Similar provisions can be found in national cross-border insolvency laws, these being based on the UNCITRAL Model Law, such as 11 U.S.C. §1501(a)(3). For the EU, it is generally accepted and expressly stated in Recital 83 of the EIR that the right to fair proceedings can be based on Art. 47 of the EU Charter of Fundamental Rights.[44] Accordingly, the CJEU, in *Eurofood*, clearly pointed out that 'the general principle of Community law that everyone is entitled to a fair legal process' is also applicable to cross-border insolvency proceedings.[45]

9.20 Finally, the procedural principle of priority (*lis pendens*) must be mentioned. In the law of civil procedure, it is widely accepted that the commencement of proceedings

---

[41] CJEU Case C-341/04 *Eurofood IFSC Ltd* (n 28).
[42] CJEU Case C-341/04 *Eurofood IFSC Ltd* (n 28). See also CJEU Case C-1/04 *Susanne Staubitz-Schreiber*, ECLI:EU:C:2006:39; CJEU Case C-328/12, *Schmid v Hertel*, ECLI:EU:C:2014:6; *McKellar v Griffin and anor* [2014] EWHC 2644 (Ch); *Re Northsea Base Investment Ltd* [2015] EWHC 121 (Ch), and on this judgment, Tett and Jones, 'In the Matter of Northsea Base Investment Limited & Ors' [2015] EWHC 121 (Ch); Birss J, 26 January 2015', ICR, 12 (2015) 325 et seq.
[43] N. Luhmann, *Legitimation durch Verfahren* (Luchterhand 1969).
[44] Cf. also Art. 6 of the European Convention on Human Rights.
[45] CJEU Case C-341/04 *Eurofood IFSC Ltd* (n 28).

INTRODUCTION 257

blocks a second set of proceedings on the same subject matter. This is known as the general procedural principle of priority or *lis pendens*. This principle is also applicable in insolvency law in general and in cross-border insolvency law in particular. Once insolvency proceedings have been opened, a second set of proceedings must be avoided. Under the principles of unity and universality, insolvency proceedings are supposed to cover the estate in its entirety, which renders parallel proceedings for the same debtor superfluous. They would only cause unnecessary costs and would unavoidably lead to a conflict of powers and responsibilities of the official bodies of the proceedings. Hence, to enforce the principles of unity and universality, it is also necessary to avoid parallel insolvency proceedings in different countries regarding the same debtor, and a way to ensure this is through the application of the procedural principle of priority, which depicts priority as being ancillary to unity. In Germany, for example, Art. 102 § 3 of the EGInsO[46] reads: 'Where the court of another Member State of the European Union has opened main insolvency proceedings, the lodgement of an application with a domestic insolvency court for opening such proceedings regarding assets which belong to the insolvency estate is not admissible as long as the main insolvency proceedings are pending.'[47] With regard to Art. 16 of the EIR 2000,[48] it has also been acknowledged by the CJEU in *Eurofood* that

> [a]s is shown by the 22nd recital of the Regulation,[49] the rule of priority laid down in Article 16(1) of the Regulation, which provides that insolvency proceedings opened in one Member State are to be recognised in all the Member States from the time that they produce their effects in the State of the opening of proceedings, is based on the principle of mutual trust.'[50]

In *Soundview Elite*, the US Bankruptcy Court Southern District of New York was tasked with deciding whether insolvency proceedings applied for in the Cayman Islands prior to the petition for Chapter 11 proceedings in the United States would hinder the opening of such Chapter 11 proceedings. The court acknowledged that the application to the Cayman Islands court did not trigger a stay and therefore could not ban the US court from opening Chapter 11 proceedings. On the contrary, a stay was triggered by the application in the United States and should therefore hinder the Cayman Islands court in opening insolvency proceedings. The court, however, granted some relief from

---

[46] '*Einführungsgesetz zur Insolvenzordnung*' ('Introductory Act to the Insolvency Regulation').
[47] Cf. BGH, 29 May 2008–IX ZB 102/07 = NZI 2008, 572 and *AG Düsseldorf*, 12 March 2004–502 IN 126/03 = NZI 2004, 269, 270: no parallel main proceedings in Germany after the opening of main proceedings in England.
[48] Now Art. 19(1) of the EIR 2015.
[49] Now ibid Recital 65.
[50] *CJEU* Case C-341/04 *Eurofood IFSC Ltd* (n 28); see also *CJEU* Case C-444/07 *MG Probud Gdynia sp. z.o.o.* (n 28); *Cour d'Appel (Versailles) Klempka v ISA Daisytek SA* [2003] BCC 984, 989 et seq.; *Re ARM Asset Backed Securities SA (No. 2)* [2014] EWHC 1097 (Ch); *Re Daisytek-ISA Ltd* [2003] BCC 562; *Václav Fischer v D.l. sro*, Usnesení Nejvyššího soudu České republiky sp.zn. 31 January 2008–R 87/2008, [2008] EIRCR(A) 73. In *Galapagos*, the Court of Justice of the European Union (CJEU) ruled that an application for insolvency proceedings in one Member State blocks further applications in other Member States, but the CJEU did not expressly employ the principle of priority but rather assigned exclusive jurisdiction to the first court: *CJEU* Case C-723/20 *Galapagos BidCo. Sàrl* (n 28).

258 CROSS-BORDER INSOLVENCY LAW

this US stay, thus being considerate towards the Cayman Islands court.[51] The decision of the Bankruptcy Court was later confirmed by the District Court.[52]

3. Substantive principles

9.21 Among the substantive principles, which are primarily designed to protect the substantive interests of the parties involved, the most important one is the principle of equal treatment of creditors belonging to the same class, also known as the *pari passu* rule. On the one hand, it has a procedural dimension, because all creditors must be granted the same procedural rights. On the other hand, it has a substantive dimension, since all creditors of the same class deserve the same share in the proceeds of the debtor's assets. In cross-border insolvency proceedings, this principle requires (*inter alia*) that the distribution of the proceeds of main and secondary proceedings are coordinated. For example, this is acknowledged in Art. 32 of the UNCITRAL Model Law (and consequently in Art. 32 Sch. 1 of the CBIR 2006 and 11 U.S.C. §1532) and in Art. 23 (2) of the EIR, which reads:

> In order to ensure the equal treatment of creditors, a creditor which has, in the course of insolvency proceedings, obtained a dividend on its claim shall share in distributions made in other proceedings only where creditors of the same ranking or category have, in those other proceedings, obtained an equivalent dividend.

9.22 The second substantive principle to be mentioned here is the principle of optimal realization of the debtor's assets, 'optimal' meaning that costs must be kept low, market value of assets must be preserved and realized, and delays must be avoided. This is acknowledged, for example, by the Preamble of the UNCITRAL Model Law, which declares that one of its purposes is '[p]rotection and maximization of the value of the debtor's assets', and this is mirrored *inter alia* by 11 U.S.C. §1501(a)(4). Another example is Recital 48 of the EIR, which states, in the context of coordinating main and secondary proceedings,

> Main insolvency proceedings and secondary insolvency proceedings can contribute to the efficient administration of the debtor's insolvency estate or to the effective realisation of the total assets if there is proper cooperation between the actors involved in all the concurrent proceedings.

9.23 The flipside of this coin is the principle of best possible satisfaction of the creditors' claims. Maximizing the value of the debtor's assets is not an end in itself but serves the optimal satisfaction of the creditors' claims. This principle must also be taken into account in cross-border insolvency proceedings. Hence, all rules which aim to preserve or even maximize the estate are based on two pillars: the principle of optimal

---

[51] *Re Soundview Elite Ltd, et al., Debtors,* 503 BR 571, 583 et seq. (Bankr. SDNY 2014).
[52] *Re Soundview Elite Ltd, et al., Debtors,* (SDNY, 12 December 2014), <https://www.leagle.com/decision/infdco20141229351> accessed 20 April 2023).

realization of the debtor's assets and the principle of best possible satisfaction of the creditors' claims.

However, not only the creditors' but also the debtor's substantive rights need protec- **9.24**
tion in international insolvency law. For example, the Preamble of the UNCITRAL Model Law states that one of its objectives is to protect 'the interests of all creditors and other interested persons, including the debtor', and this is reflected in Art. 22 of the UNCITRAL Model Law, where, regarding decisions on relief that may be granted upon recognition of foreign proceedings, courts are prompted to 'be satisfied that the interests of the creditors and other interested persons, including the debtor, are adequately protected'. The programmatic clause in the Preamble is mirrored in 11 U.S.C. §1501(a) (3), and the wording of Art. 22 of the UNCITRAL Model Law is borrowed by Art. 22(1) Sch. 1 of the CBIR 2006[53] and 11 U.S.C. §1522(a).

Of specific importance is the principle of protection of trust, particularly with respect to **9.25**
creditors' or contractual partners' expectations that their legal position is not inflicted by the debtor's insolvency proceedings. In cross-border insolvencies, this comprises the protection of trust in the certainty of transactions, in the stability of substantive rights, and in the applicability of a certain legal regime. We will deal with this principle at various points below. For now, one example may suffice. The CJEU, in the context of Art. 16 of the EIR, ruled that this provision is an

> exception, which, as stated in recital 24[54] of that regulation, aims to protect legitimate expectations and the certainty of transactions in Member States other than that in which proceedings are opened, must be interpreted strictly, and its scope cannot go beyond what is necessary to achieve that objective.[55]

Further, the principle of social protection plays an important role in cross-border in- **9.26**
solvency law. This concerns the debtor, on the one hand, and special groups of contractual partners, on the other hand, namely employees and tenants. For example, where international insolvency laws declare the law applicable to employment contracts as relevant even where insolvency proceedings have been opened abroad, this is supported by the principle of social protection rather than by the principle of protection of trust.[56]

---

[53] Albeit only 'if appropriate'.

[54] Now Recital 67 of the EIR 2015.

[55] CJEU Case C-310/14 *Nike European Operations Netherlands BV v Sportland Oy* (n 36); cf. also CJEU Case C-557/13 *Hermann Lutz v Elke Bäuerle*, ECLI:EU:C:2015:227 paras 34, 54; European Free Trade Association (EFTA) Court Case E-28/13 *LBI h. f. v Merrill Lynch International Ltd.*

[56] Cf. R. Bork in Bork and Mangano, *European Cross-Border Insolvency Law* (n 3) para. 4.91; F. Garcimartín and M. Virgós in R. Bork and K. van Zwieten, *Commentary on the EIR* (n 3) para. 13.3; Mélin, *La faillite international* (n 1) para. 225; Moss and T. Smith in Moss, Fletcher, and Isaacs, *The EC Regulation on Insolvency Proceedings* (n 3) para. 8.245; Arnold in Sheldon, *Cross-Border Insolvency* (n 1) para. 2.102; Wessels and Madaus, *International Insolvency Law* (Pt II) (n 3) paras 10678, 10696. However, see also United Nations Commission on International Trade Law (UNCITRAL), *Legislative Guide on Insolvency Law* (UNCITRAL 2005) 70 para. 87, which refers to the 'reasonable expectations of employees'.

9.27 The fixation principle supports the distinction between assets, creditors, and creditors' rights that are subject to the insolvency proceedings and those that are not. Typically, the point in time when insolvency proceedings are opened marks a very important time bar. Principally, creditors are only entitled to participate in insolvency proceedings where their claims have been established before the opening of insolvency proceedings. This is based on the fixation principle, which can be assigned to the substantive principles and is the underlying tenet of all norms demarcating the personal and substantial scope of insolvency proceedings. In cross-border insolvency law, a good example is Art. 19(1) of the EIR, which provides for the recognition of foreign insolvency proceedings as soon as the judgment opening insolvency proceedings has become effective in the opening State. This is flanked by Art. 34 of the EIR, which states that, from this moment on, the courts of any other Member States can only open secondary proceedings.

9.28 Finally, the principle of proportionality should be mentioned. According to this general principle, all legal measures must pursue a legitimate objective, must be suitable to attain this goal, and must not go beyond what is necessary to achieve this goal. This principle has its effects also in cross-border insolvency laws. It is recognized by the CJEU[57] and finds it expression *inter alia* in Art. 60(1)(b) of the EIR which, for insolvency proceedings of members of a group of companies, assigns to all insolvency practitioners appointed for one group member the right to

> request a stay of any measure related to the realisation of the assets in the proceedings opened with respect to any other member of the same group, provided that:
>
> (i) a restructuring plan for all or some members of the group for which insolvency proceedings have been opened has been proposed under point (c) of Article 56(2) and presents a reasonable chance of success;
> (ii) such a stay is necessary in order to ensure the proper implementation of the restructuring plan".

4. Conflict of principles

9.29 We will see in the further course of this chapter that not only rules but also court decisions are mostly based on more than one principle. These can be—and mostly are—conflicting principles, and it is then the task of lawmakers and legislators, as well as judges, to weigh and balance the principles involved in order to find an adequate and acceptable solution. At this point, one example may suffice. As already explained above,[58] many international insolvency laws grant special protection for employees by assigning the treatment of employment contracts not to the *lex fori concursus* but to the law governing the employment contract. Such rules are opposed by the principles of universalism, mutual trust, procedural justice, and efficiency, but they are supported by the principle of social protection and, to some extent, by the principle of protection

---

[57] Cf. above (n 55).
[58] At para. 9.26.

of trust.[59] When weighing and balancing the principles involved, the principle of social protection must prevail.

II. Details

When insolvency proceedings have cross-border effects, typical questions arise. The first **9.30** concerns international jurisdiction: the courts of which State are competent to open and to administer the proceedings? The second question deals with the law applicable to the proceedings and its effects: are affairs and relationships abroad governed by the law of the opening State or is this law superseded by the local law? Finally, how about recognition? Are decisions of domestic insolvency courts recognized abroad and, if so, under which conditions? However, cross-border insolvency law is a very complex matter and a field of law of its own. In this chapter, only basic features can be addressed. For more detailed information, reference must be made to specialized literature.[60]

A. Jurisdiction

The matter of international jurisdiction is closely connected to two fundamental principles **9.31** of cross-border insolvency law: unity and universalism (universality).[61]

1. Main, secondary, and territorial proceedings

A logical consequence of these principles is that the opening of insolvency proceedings **9.32** in one State hinders the opening of a second insolvency procedure in another State (which, by the way, is supported by the procedural principle of priority[62]). As a consequence, only one single set of insolvency proceedings with worldwide effect is possible. Although this is principally accepted in many regulations, significant exceptions can be found. A second set of proceedings is unavoidable if State B does not recognize the opening decision of State A; in this case, two 'main proceedings' compete—a result that is not acceptable under the principles of unity and universalism. Another reason for two (or more) insolvency proceedings for the same debtor may arise from the complexity of the debtor's affairs abroad. In such cases, it may be reasonable not to include these affairs in the domestic ('main') insolvency proceedings of State A but to open another procedure in State B as a second set of proceedings. Where this a permitted,

---

[59] See extensively, Bork, *Principles of Cross-Border Insolvency Law* (n 23) paras 6.100 et seq. See also below at para. 9.51.

[60] For references, see on international insolvency law above (n 1); for European law, above (n 3).

[61] For details, see above at paras 9.08 and 9.09.

[62] For this, see above at para. 9.20.

262 CROSS-BORDER INSOLVENCY LAW

the underlying principle is enforced in a modified way only, which is why one speaks of 'modified universalism'.[63]

9.33 For example, this is permitted in Arts 3(2), 34 et seq. of the EIR, which provide for so-called 'secondary proceedings' in another Member State of the EU if the debtor has an establishment within the territory of that other Member State.[64] Such secondary proceedings are conducted alongside the main proceedings, a distinction that is also well known to the UNCITRAL Model Law[65] and many national laws.[66] The main feature of secondary proceedings is that their effects are restricted to the assets of the debtor situated within the territory of the State in which those proceedings have been opened,[67] whereas all other assets are subject to the main proceedings. Vice versa, the main proceedings do not cover the assets located in the State where secondary proceedings have been opened.[68] This is an exception to the principle of universalism[69] and justifies the term 'modified universalism'.

9.34 In very rare cases, 'secondary' proceedings can be opened prior to the main proceedings. They are then labelled 'territorial proceedings'. They have the same effects, and are typically only available under the same prerequisites, as secondary proceedings. Advanced international insolvency laws provide for further restrictions. For example, Art. 3(4)(a) of the EIR permits territorial proceedings only where main insolvency proceedings cannot be opened because of the conditions laid down by the law of the Member State that would have jurisdiction.

2. Jurisdiction

9.35 Against this background, the question arises as to the courts of which State have jurisdiction to open (main) insolvency proceedings. This is an important feature not only of the two principles discussed above but also of the principle of predictability.[70] While the UNCITRAL Model Law is silent on this matter, a leading example is given by Art. 3(1) of the EIR, which—binding for parties and courts[71]—states:

---

[63] This label has been coined by J.L. Westbrook, 'Choice of Avoidance Law in Global Insolvencies', Brooklyn Journal of International Law, *17* (1991) 499, 517. For comparable terms, see R. Mangano, 'Introduction' in Bork and Mangano, *European Cross-Border Insolvency Law* (n 3) para. 1.61.

[64] Similar provisions are Arts 28 et seq. of the UNCITRAL Model Law;, in England and Wales, Arts 28 et seq. Sch. 1 of the CBIR 2006; in Germany, §§ 354 et seq. of the *Insolvenzordnung*; in the United States, 11 U.S.C. §§1528 et seq.

[65] See Art. 2 of the UNCITRAL Model Law.

[66] See, for Germany, § 343 of the *Insolvenzordnung*; for the United States, 11 U.S.C. §1505; for France, *Cour de Cassation (chambre commerciale)*–21 March 2006–04-17869 = Bull. civ. 2006, IV No. 74; for England and Wales, Art. 5 Sch. 1 of the CBIR 2006; *Sturgeon Central Asia Balanced Fund Ltd (in liquidation)* [2019] EWHC 1215 (Ch).

[67] Cf. Art. 34 sentence 3 of the EIR.

[68] See Art. 20(1) of the EIR; Art. 28 of the UNCITRAL Model Law; Art. 28 of the CBIR 2006; 11 U.S.C. §1528; for the latter, see *In Re Awal Bank*, 455 BR 73 (Bankr. SDNY 2011).

[69] Cf. CJEU Case C-444/07 *MG Probud Gdynia sp. z.o.o.* (n 28).

[70] See above at para. 9.18.

[71] Cf. CJEU Case C-493/18 *UB v VA, Tiger SCI, WZ and Banque patrimoine et immobilier SA*, ECLI:EU:C:2019:1046.

The courts of the Member State within the territory of which the centre of the debtor's main interests is situated shall have jurisdiction to open insolvency proceedings ('main insolvency proceedings'). The centre of main interests shall be the place where the debtor conducts the administration of its interests on a regular basis and which is ascertainable by third parties. In the case of a company or legal person, the place of the registered office shall be presumed to be the centre of its main interests in the absence of proof to the contrary. That presumption shall only apply if the registered office has not been moved to another Member State within the 3-month period prior to the request for the opening of insolvency proceedings. In the case of an individual exercising an independent business or professional activity, the centre of main interests shall be presumed to be that individual's principal place of business in the absence of proof to the contrary. That presumption shall only apply if the individual's principal place of business has not been moved to another Member State within the 3-month period prior to the request for the opening of insolvency proceedings. In the case of any other individual, the centre of main interests shall be presumed to be the place of the individual's habitual residence in the absence of proof to the contrary. This presumption shall only apply if the habitual residence has not been moved to another Member State within the 6-month period prior to the request for the opening of insolvency proceedings.

9.36 It follows from this wording that the Regulation, assisted by comprehensive case law,[72] refers basically to the COMI and endeavours to assist the courts in determining the debtor's COMI by various rebuttable presumptions.[73] The COMI concept is also addressed by the UNCITRAL Model Law[74] and many other national laws,[75] albeit for recognition purposes only and not in the context of international jurisdiction, where many States rely on their regular insolvency law[76] or general civil procedural law.

9.37 A famous example is the *Galapagos* case. Galapagos SA (D), a company with a registered office in Luxembourg, was the subsidiary of an Italian Holding company. D was tasked to generate financial means for the group by borrowing money from banks and issuing bonds and to forward the money as a loan to other group companies. The directors of D moved the office of the company in Luxembourg, from which they ran the company, to London and applied for administration proceedings. Before the High

---

[72] See the leading judgments of the CJEU Case C-341/04 *Eurofood IFSC Ltd* (n 28); CJEU Case C-723/20 *Galapagos BidCo. Sàrl* (n 28); CJEU Case C-1/04 *Susanne Staubitz-Schreiber* (n 42); CJEU Case C-396/09 *Interedil* (n 32).

[73] See for Art. 3(1) (subparas 1 and 4) of the EIR, *CJEU Case C-253/19 MH and NI v OJ and Novo Banco SA*, ECLI:EU:C:2020:585; see further, *Re Melars Group Ltd* [2022] EWCA Civ 1419.

[74] See Arts 2(b), 16(3), 17(2)(a) of the UNCITRAL Model Law. Cf. *Re Videology Ltd* [2018] EWHC 2186 (Ch).

[75] See, for England and Wales, Arts 2(g), 16(3), 17(2)(a) Sch. 1 of the CBIR 2006; for the United States, 11 U.S.C. §§1502(4), 1516(c), 1517(b) and *In re Serviços de Petróleo Constellation SA*, 600 BR 237 (Bankr. SDNY 2019).

[76] In Germany, the general rule for insolvency courts in § 3 of the *Insolvenzordnung* is applied ('centre of the debtor's business activity'). The same holds true for France (reference to Art. R. 600-1 of the *Code de Commerce*: 'centre of main interests').

264 CROSS-BORDER INSOLVENCY LAW

Court could decide upon this application, the shareholders dismissed the directors and appointed a new director, who instantly moved the office to Düsseldorf (Germany) and applied for insolvency proceedings in Düsseldorf. The court in Düsseldorf appointed a preliminary insolvency practitioner and ordered preliminary measures, among others by binding transactions of the debtor company to the consent of the preliminary insolvency practitioner. This raised the question as to international jurisdiction of the court in Düsseldorf. Since all States involved were (at the time) members of the EU, Art. 3 of the EIR was applicable. Given that the directors of D were the only employees and that financial affairs could be dealt with from any office in the world, it must be conceded that D moved its COMI first from Luxembourg to London and then to Düsseldorf, thereby rebutting the presumption, which refers to the registered office in Luxembourg. Hence, the court in Düsseldorf had international jurisdiction under Art. 3(1) of the EIR. However, this would not have hindered the court in London opening insolvency proceedings, since the COMI of D was in London at the time of the application to the High Court, and the subsequent COMI shift was irrelevant under the *perpetuatio fori* rule.[77] What *was* relevant was the decision of the court in Düsseldorf to appoint a preliminary insolvency practitioner, since this was an opening decision (Art. 2 No. 7(ii) of the EIR), which was automatically recognized in all other EU Member States (Art. 19(1) of the EIR) and hindered further opening decisions under the *lis pendens* rule.[78] However, the *Bundesgerichtshof* suspended the case and asked the CJEU for a preliminary ruling under Art. 267 of the TFEU.[79] The CJEU held that the court first seized in a Member State has exclusive jurisdiction in relation to all other Member States until it has ruled on the opening but that this no longer applies in relation to the United Kingdom after Brexit.[80] The *Bundesgerichtshof* therefore declared the court in Düsseldorf to have exclusive jurisdiction.[81]

9.38 As explained above,[82] a pragmatic approach to cross-border insolvency law suggests permitting secondary proceedings with effect to one country only alongside main proceedings with otherwise worldwide effect, thus enforcing the principle of 'modified universalism'. Where a legal system provides for such secondary proceedings, the question as to the prerequisites for a court to open such proceedings must be answered. In some jurisdictions, it suffices that the debtor has assets in the State where secondary proceedings shall be opened.[83] The EIR, however, remains acutely aware of the hampering side effects of such additional proceedings[84] and therefore restricts the availability of secondary proceedings by requiring that the debtor has an establishment

---

[77] CJEU Case C-1/04 *Susanne Staubitz-Schreiber* (n 42).
[78] CJEU Case C-341/04 *Eurofood IFSC Ltd* (n 28).
[79] BGH, 17 December 2020–IX ZB 72/19 = NZI 2021, 187 et seq.
[80] CJEU Case C-723/20 *Galapagos BidCo. Sàrl* (n 28).
[81] BGH, 8 December 2022–IX ZB 72/19 = NZI 2023, 183 (R. Bork).
[82] At para. 9.32 et seq.
[83] See Art. 28 of the CBIR 2006, 11 U.S.C. §1528, both following the lead of Art. 28 of the UNCITRAL Model Law. Cf. *In Re SPhinX, Ltd*, 351 BR 103 fn. 17 (Bankr. SDNY 2006).
[84] Cf. Recital 41 of the EIR.

in the Member State in which secondary proceedings are to be opened (Art. 3(2), 34 of the EIR). The term 'establishment' is defined in Art. 2(1) of the EIR with 'any place of operations where a debtor carries out or has carried out in the 3-months period prior to the request to open main insolvency proceedings a non-transitory economic activity with human means and assets'.[85] As an exception to the principle of universalism, this definition must be applied in a narrow and restrictive interpretation.[86] This means that it is not sufficient if the debtor only has assets in the second State but no organizational unit acting on its behalf.[87]

3. Annex procedures

International jurisdiction is frequently regulated not only for the opening of insolvency proceedings but also for annex procedures. For example, according to Art. 6 of the EIR, the courts of the Member State within the territory of which insolvency proceedings have been opened shall have jurisdiction 'for any action which derives directly from the insolvency proceedings and is closely linked with them'. Typical examples of such trials stemming from the insolvency proceedings are actions on transactions avoidance,[88] on directors' liability for wrongful trading,[89] on the allocation of assets to main and secondary proceedings,[90] and on the recognition of claims to the insolvency schedule,[91] but not actions regarding the performance of a contract concluded prior to the commencement of the insolvency proceedings[92] or actions regarding pre-insolvency claims stemming from tort law. The issue of annex procedures is not addressed in the UNCITRAL Model Law. However, in 2018, UNCITRAL recommended a Model Law on Recognition and Enforcement of Insolvency-Related Judgments which, in its Art. 2(d), states:

9.39

> Insolvency-related judgment: (i) Means a judgment that: a. Arises as a consequence of or is materially associated with an insolvency proceeding, whether or not that insolvency proceeding has closed; and b. Was issued on or after the commencement of that insolvency proceeding; and (ii) Does not include a judgment commencing an insolvency proceeding.

---

[85] Similarly, Art. 2(f) of the UNCITRAL Model Law; 11 U.S.C. §1502(2).

[86] CJEU Case C-327/13 *Burgo Group SpA v Illochroma SA and Jérôme Theetten* (n 34); Case C-396/09 *Interedil* (n 32); Case C-112/10 *Zaza Retail BV* (n 33). See also for the UK, *The Trustees of the Olympic Airlines SA Pension and Life Assurance Scheme v Olympic Airlines SA* [2015] UKSC 27; for the United States, *In Re Basis Yield Alpha Fund (Master)*, 381 BR 37 (Bankr. SDNY 2008); *In re Bear Stearns High-Grade Structured Credit* (n 40) 325, 338 et seq.

[87] CJEU Case C-327/13 *Burgo Group SpA v Illochroma SA and Jérôme Theetten* (n 34); Case C-396/09 *Interedil* (n 32).

[88] Cf. Art. 6(1) of the EIR and CJEU Case C-339/07 *Seagon v Deko Martium Belgium NV*, ECLI:EU:C:2009:83; Case C-493/18 *UB v VA, Tiger SCI, WZ and Banque patrimoine et immobilier SA* (n 71).

[89] CJEU Case C-295/13 *H. v H.K.*, ECLI:EU:C:2014:2410.

[90] CJEU Case C-649/13 *Comité d'entreprise de Nortel Networks SA and ors v Cosme Rogeau and Cosme Rogeau v Alan Robert Bloom and ors* (n 35).

[91] CJEU Case C-47/18 *Skarb Pánstwa Rzeczpospolitej Polskiej—Generalny Dyrektor Dróg Krajowych i Autostrad v Stephan Riel*, ECLI:EU:C:2019:754.

[92] See also CJEU Case C-198/18 *CeDe Group AB v KAN sp. z.o.o. (in liquidation)*, ECLI:EU:C:2019:1001.

266 CROSS-BORDER INSOLVENCY LAW

This Model Law does not provide for rules on international jurisdiction but at least for the recognition of judgments handed down in annex procedures.

B. Applicable Law

9.40 A second set of issues concerns the law applicable to the insolvency proceedings.

1. Basics

9.41 To begin with, insolvency proceedings are national proceedings conducted by national courts and must therefore be governed by national insolvency law, generally referred to as *lex fori concursus*. This does not change automatically just because the debtor has assets or creditors abroad. It is therefore generally accepted under not only the principles of unity and universalism but also the principle of predictability[93] that insolvency proceedings are conducted under the law of the opening State and that this also holds true for cross-border affairs. In the end, this aims to guarantee a synchronization of international jurisdiction and applicable law.[94]

9.42 Corresponding rules are Art. 7 of the EIR, which explains in great detail which affairs are governed by the *lex fori concursus*. In Germany, § 335 of the *Insolvenzordnung* states that, unless provided otherwise, the insolvency proceedings and their effects shall be subject to the law of the State in which the proceedings have been opened. The UNCITRAL Model Law is silent on this matter, and so are many national laws, particularly those that are based on the Model Law. Yet, the reason for this silence is that these laws take it for granted that official bodies apply their national law to both domestic and foreign assets, creditors, contracts, etc.[95]

9.43 However, many special constellations exist, which call the application of the *lex fori concursus* into question. For example, where insolvency proceedings have been opened in Sweden against a Swedish debtor, this debtor has an employee (sales agent) in Italy, and the employment agreement is governed by Italian law, it is not self-evident that this contract should be subject to (the rules on employment contracts in) Swedish insolvency law. The same holds true for collateral encumbered with security rights for the benefit of a foreign creditor, at least where the collateral is not located in the opening State. Other examples are tenancy agreements where the premises are located in another State and transactions that are governed by foreign law but shall be challenged under the transactions avoidance law of the *lex fori concursus*. Many regulations that

---

[93] For details, cf. Bork, *Principles of Cross-Border Insolvency Law* (n 23) paras 3.47 et seq.
[94] See CJEU Case C-198/18 *CeDe Group AB v KAN sp. z.o.o. (in liquidation)* (n 92).
[95] Cf. UNCITRAL, *Legislative Guide on Insolvency Law* (n 57) 69 para. 83 and Recommendation 31; for England, Dicey, Morris, and Collins, Conflict of Laws (15th edn, Sweet & Maxwell 2012) paras 31-084 et seq.; for France, Dammann and Sénéchal, *Le droit de l'insolvabilité international* (n 1) paras 2164 et seq.

DETAILS   267

address the problems of applicable law provide for exceptions or modifications to the *lex fori concursus* and declare other legal regimes applicable.[96] This particularly holds true for the EIR, where Arts 8–18 provide for special rules on the applicable law. Some—not all—of these rules shall be introduced below as examples for typical exception provisions.

2. Security rights

A very important and, to some extent, peculiar exception concerns rights *in rem*. According to Art. 8(1) of the EIR, collateral that is encumbered with security rights and is located in a Member State different from the opening State is not affected by the opening of insolvency proceedings.[97] It is prevailing opinion in case law[98] and literature[99] that this insulates such collateral from any insolvency law (i.e. from the *lex fori concursus* as well as from the insolvency law of the state where the collateral is located, *lex situs*) and subjects it to the substantive law on security rights of the *lex situs*. This is justified with reference to the principles of predictability, efficiency, and protection of trust.   **9.44**

A good example is the decision of the CJEU in *Erste Bank Hungary*.[100] D, an Austrian company, had pledged shares in a Hungarian subsidiary as a security for a loan granted by the Hungarian bank C. After the opening of insolvency proceedings in Austria concerning D's estate, C filed a lawsuit in Hungary against D seeking a declaratory judgment to the effect that it had a security right over the shares. The Hungarian court declined the request, arguing that, under Austrian insolvency law as the applicable *lex fori concursus*, actions against the debtor of insolvency proceedings are impermissible. Indeed, lawsuits regarding security rights must be filed against the insolvency practitioner, not against the debtor. However, this is only true under national insolvency laws. As opposed to that, Art. 8 of the EIR exempts security rights from the application of each insolvency law whatsoever, provided the collateral (here, the shares) are situated in another Member State of the EU (here, Hungary) than the opening State (here, Austria). Hence, the pledge was treated as if insolvency proceedings would not exist, and C's lawsuit against D was permissible.   **9.45**

---

[96] However, French law only reluctantly accepts such exceptions; cf. Dammann and Sénéchal, *Le droit de l'insolvabilité international* (n 1) paras 2165 et seq.

[97] Provisions similar to Art. 8(1) of the EIR can be found, for instance, in Germany (§ 351(1) of the *Insolvenzordnung*, albeit regarding foreign insolvency proceedings only) and Austria (ibid § 11(2)); on this, see Kodek, 'The Treatment of Security Rights', International Insolvency Law Review (2015) 10 et seq.

[98] See CJEU Case C-527/10 *ERSTE Bank Hungary Nyrt v Magyar Állam and ors*, ECLI:EU:C:2012:417; CJEU Case C-557/13 *Hermann Lutz v Elke Bäuerle* (n 55).

[99] Cf. (among others) Snowden in Bork and van Zwieten, *EIR* (n 3) paras 8.09 et seq.; Dahl and Kortleben in Brinkmann, *EIR* (n 3) Art. 8 paras 25 et seq.; Fletcher, Insolvency in Private International Law (2nd edn, OUP 2005) para. 7.87; Fletcher in Moss, Fletcher, and Isaacs, *The EC Regulation in Insolvency Proceedings* (n 3) paras 4.11 et seq.; Arnold in Sheldon (n 56) para. 2.76.

[100] CJEU Case C-527/10 *ERSTE Bank Hungary Nyrt v Magyar Állam and ors* (n 98).

9.46 However, the rule in Art. 8 of the EIR is overprotective. It is difficult to see how it can be upheld in light of other principles.[101] The principle of universalism requires all collateral to be subject to the insolvency proceedings, no matter whether the assets are located inland or abroad. The principle of equal treatment of creditors speaks in favour of applying the same rules to all secured creditors. And regarding the principle of protection of trust, the secured creditors' expectations not to be affected by the insolvency proceedings are not legitimate, since lenders that grant credit to a foreign debtor must be aware that the debtor's insolvency will be administered in foreign insolvency proceedings under foreign insolvency law. Hence, they can only trust in the application of the *lex fori concursus*. Beyond, Art. 8(1) of the EIR identifies the wrong point in time regarding the formation of these expectations. The expectations of a secured creditor that are relevant here (if at all) are those that were formed when the *right in rem* was created and not, as provided by Art. 8(1) of the EIR, those that manifested themselves when the insolvency proceedings were opened. In the end, it is hardly convincing that secured creditors with collateral in another Member State are not affected by the insolvency proceedings at all and are treated differently from creditors with collateral in the opening State.[102]

9.47 Similar deliberations are due for the rule on the right to set-off in Art. 9 of the EIR.[103] A right to set-off can be seen as a special security right, since it has the same effects as a pledge or lien on the debtor's claim against the creditor.[104] Therefore, it does not come as a surprise that Art. 9 of the EIR—although Art. 7(2)(d) of the EIR provides for the application of the *lex fori concursus* to set-off—protects rights to set-off similarly to rights *in rem*, stating that 'the opening of insolvency proceedings shall not affect the right of creditors to demand the set-off of their claims against the claims of a debtor, where such a set-off is permitted by the law applicable to the insolvent debtor's claim'. Subject to transactions avoidance law (Art. 9(2) of the EIR), creditors with a right to set-off enjoy the application of a 'most favourable' principle, since combining Art. 7(2)(d) of the EIR with Art. 9(1) of the EIR produces the following result.[105] Where the *lex fori concursus* permits set-off, the creditor needs no further protection; he or she can declare set-off and will thus receive full satisfaction of their claim. However, where the *lex fori concursus* does not permit set-off, the creditor gets a second chance: provided that the debtor's (principal) claim is subject to a law different from the *lex fori concursus*, the creditor may still demand set-off if this law (the *lex causae*) permits set-off after the

---

[101] See more in Bork, *Principles of Cross-Border Insolvency Law* (n 23) paras 4.21, 6.12 et seq.

[102] For criticism, see ibid; K. van Zwieten in Bork and van Zwieten, *Commentary on EIR* (n 3), para. 0.56; van Galen, André, Fritz et al., *Revision of the EIR*, (INSOL Europe 2021) 52 at 5.6 et seq.; C. Paulus, 'Security Rights in Cross-Border Insolvency Proceedings', International Insolvency Law Review (2014) 366, 369 et seq.; M. Veder, 'The Future of the European Insolvency Regulation', International Insolvency Law Review (2011) 285, 289 et seq.; M. Veder, *Cross-Border Insolvency Proceedings and Security Rights* (Kluwer 2004) 338 et seq.; Virgós and Garcimartín, *EIR* (n 3) para. 164; Wessels and Madaus, *International Insolvency Law* (Pt II) (n 3) para. 10640.

[103] Similarly, § 338 of the *Insolvenzordnung*.

[104] *Stein v Blake (No. 1)* 2 WLR 710.

[105] For the effects of Art. 9 of the EIR, see Snowden (n 99) para. 9.2.

opening of insolvency proceedings against the debtor. Although the provision is frequently defended,[106] many authors plead for a return to the pure application of the *lex fori concursus*,[107] a solution that is also backed by the *UNCITRAL Legislative Guide on Insolvency Law*[108] and is supported by the principles of unity, mutual trust, efficiency, predictability, optimal realization of the debtor's assets, and equal treatment of creditors.[109] The same applies here as with Art. 8 of the EIR.[110]

The same approach is appropriate for the rule on reservation of title in Art. 10 of the EIR.[111] For this norm, a distinction must be made between insolvency of the purchaser and insolvency of the seller. In the latter case, contract law must be taken into account, which will be dealt with below.[112] As regards the former, Art. 10(1) of the EIR states that

9.48

> the opening of insolvency proceedings against the purchaser of an asset shall not affect sellers' rights that are based on a reservation of title where at the time of the opening of proceedings the asset is situated within the territory of a Member State other than the State of the opening of proceedings.

The effect of this rule is that the seller may enforce his or her property rights as regulated by the *lex situs*, on the one hand, and the purchase contract between debtor and purchaser, on the other hand, without any limitations being imposed on the transactions by the fact of insolvency at all: neither the insolvency law of the *lex fori concursus* nor of the *lex situs* or the *lex contractus* is applicable.[113] This follows the example of Art. 8 of the EIR and must be subject to the same concerns as Art. 8 of the EIR.[114]

3. Contracts

The question of the law applicable to contractual relationships arises in various constellations, the first being the contractual position of an insolvent seller who delivered under retention of title. According to Art. 10(2) of the EIR, 'the opening of insolvency proceedings against the seller of an asset, after delivery of the asset, shall not constitute grounds for rescinding or terminating the sale and shall not prevent the purchaser from acquiring title where at the time of the opening of proceedings the asset sold is

9.49

---

[106] Fletcher, *Insolvency in Private International Law* (n 99) para. 7.97; I. Fletcher(n 99), 'Choice of Law Rules', paras 4.22 and 4.24; Moss and Smith (n 56), 'Regulation 1346/2000 on Insolvency Proceedings', para. 8.233; Wessels and Madaus, *International Insolvency Law* (Pt II) (n 3) para. 10663.

[107] Bork, *Principles of Cross-Border Insolvency Law* (n 23) paras 6.43 et seq.; Gruber in Haß, Huber, Gruber, and Heiderhoff (eds), *EU-Insolvenzverordnung* (C.H. Beck 2005) Art. 6 para. 2; Reinhart, *Münchener Kommentar zur Insolvenzordnung, Art. 9 EuInsVO* (2015) para. 1. See also Snowden (n 99) para. 9.2: 'Certainly, the rule in Article 9 is a generous one.'

[108] UNCITRAL, *Legislative Guide on Insolvency Law* (n 57) para. 91 and Recommendations 31 et seq., 73 et seq.

[109] For details, see Bork, *Principles of Cross-Border Insolvency Law* (n 23) paras 6.43 et seq.

[110] Cf. above at para. 9.46.

[111] See Bork, *Principles of Cross-Border Insolvency Law* (n 23) paras 6.70 et seq.

[112] At para. 9.49.

[113] Virgós and Garcimartín, *EIR* (n 3) para. 173.

[114] Cf. above at para. 9.46.

270 CROSS-BORDER INSOLVENCY LAW

situated within the territory of a Member State other than the State of the opening of proceedings.'[115] This norm overrules Art. 7(2)(e) of the EIR and prevents the application of the *lex fori concursus*. It aims to protect the interests of the purchaser to acquire title, provided he or she pays the remaining part of the purchase price to the seller's insolvency practitioner. However, it is questionable under various principles whether such expectations are legitimate,[116] since he who buys an asset from a foreign seller must take the seller's insolvency, and thus the application of the *lex fori concursus*, into account. Further, Art. 10(2) of the EIR protects the purchaser only where the sold asset is located in a Member State different from the opening State, which leads to unequal treatment of sellers whose assets are in a different Member State compared to sellers whose assets are located in the opening State or in a non-EU Member State

9.50 As opposed to that, Art. 11 of the EIR, which assigns purchase and tenancy agreements on immovables to the law of the Member State within the territory of which the immovable property is situated,[117] is less problematic.[118] Although the policy of this rule is not clear, it can be justified under the principle of social protection,[119] albeit for tenancy agreements only where the tenant is a consumer who deserves protection against 'surprises from abroad', that is interference of foreign insolvency law in a domestic tenancy agreement. For all other contracts, there is no need and no justification for exempting them from the *lex fori concursus*.

9.51 Similar deliberations are due for other norms, which assign certain contracts to the *lex contractus*, namely Art. 13 of the EIR.[120] Deviating from Art. 7(2)(e) of the EIR, this norm supersedes the *lex fori concursus* and provides for the application of the *lex contractus* to employment contracts in order to protect employees against foreign (insolvency related) labour law under the principle of social protection.[121] This comes very close to the protection of trust, since employees who have been hired under a certain law can legitimately expect to be protected (only) by this law. However, social protection as granted by Art. 13 of the EIR is insufficient, for several reasons.[122] First, it is restricted to those rules dealing with the effects of the insolvency proceedings on the employment contract, omitting protection by priority rules or social security.[123]

---

[115] Some national cross-border insolvency laws contain similar rules, e.g. Austria (§ 224(2) of the *Insolvenzordnung*); Poland (Art. 463(2) of the BRA, albeit for bank insolvencies only).

[116] For criticism, see Bork, *Principles of Cross-Border Insolvency Law* (n 23) paras 6.74 et seq.

[117] See also § 336 of the *Insolvenzordnung*.

[118] Cf. Bork, *Principles of Cross-Border Insolvency Law* (n 23) paras 6.114 et seq.

[119] See above at para. 9.26.

[120] Similarly, § 337 of the *Insolvenzordnung*.

[121] Details in Bork, *Principles of Cross-Border Insolvency Law* (n 23) paras 6.100 et seq.; see also Fletcher, *Insolvency in Private International Law* (n 99) para. 7.110; Mélin, *La faillite international* (n 1) para. 120; Arnold (n 56) para. 2.102; Virgós and Garcimartín, *EIR* (n 3) para. 207; Wessels and Madaus, *International Insolvency Law* (Pt II) (n 3) paras 10678, 10695 et seq.

[122] See Bork, *Principles of Cross-Border Insolvency Law* (n 23) para. 6.112.

[123] Cf. Bork, 'Law applicable' (n 56) para. 4.95; Pfeiffer in Hess, Oberhammer, and Pfeiffer, *European Insolvency Law* (C.H. Beck/Hart Publishing/Nomos Verlagsgesellschaft 2014) para. 814.

Second, the rule dictates that the *lex contractus* will apply to the employment relationship, regardless of whether this law grants more or less protection for the employee than other potentially relevant legal systems, such as the *lex fori concursus*.[124] The principle of social protection could be better enforced if the employee was given a choice between the two competing jurisdictions. If employees opt for the application of the *lex fori concursus*, they bolster the principles of universalism, mutual trust, procedural justice, and efficiency. Hence, when it comes to taking social protection seriously, better solutions are conceivable.

4. Transactions avoidance

Finally, the exception for transactions avoidance should be mentioned. Transactions avoidance laws interfere massively in the legal position of the opponent, that is the person who received something from the debtor in a voidable way.[125] Hence, there is a typical clash between various principles, in particular between the principles of equal treatment of creditors and optimal satisfaction of the creditors' claims, on the one hand, and of the principle of protection of trust on the other hand.[126] Where a creditor receives a performance from a foreign debtor, the expectations of the creditor that he or she may keep the received can be disappointed not only by the law applicable to the performance in question but also by the *lex fori concursus*. For example, where a French bank grants a loan to a Russian debtor under French law, the debtor pays instalments, and insolvency proceedings are opened in Russia shortly after the payments, the question arises as to whether the payments are challengeable under the *lex fori concursus* (Russian transactions avoidance law) or under the *lex causae* (French transactions avoidance law). This question is of specific importance, since what is challengeable under the laws of State A may be safe under the laws of State B.

9.52

The UNCITRAL Model Law does not expressly address this problem, since it does not deal with the applicable law. However, Art. 23(1) of the UNCITRAL Model Law assigns the standing to initiate avoidance proceedings to a foreign insolvency practitioner as soon as the foreign insolvency proceedings are recognized. As a result, jurisdictions that have adopted the Model Law open their courts for avoidance claims to foreign insolvency practitioners. However, they do no apply foreign transactions avoidance law (i.e. the *lex fori concursus*) but their own domestic transactions avoidance law, provided there is sufficient connection with this jurisdiction.[127] Moreover, in the United States, this gateway is closed unless the foreign insolvency practitioner applies for (secondary)

9.53

---

[124] See, however, Garcimartín and Virgós in Bork and van Zwieten (n 56) para. 13.7: 'This principle of the most favourable law also applies in the context of Article 13 of the Insolvency Regulation.'

[125] For details on transactions avoidance law, see above, Chapter 6 'Transactions Avoidance Rules'.

[126] Cf. Bork, *Principles of Cross-Border Insolvency Law* (n 23) paras 6.83 et seq.

[127] Cf. for Australia, *King v Linkage Access Ltd* [2018] FCA 1979; *Wild v Coin Co. International plc* [2015] FCA 354; for the United Kingdom, Art. 23(1) of the CBIR 2006 and *Galbraith v Grimshaw* [1910] AC 508; *Re Paramount Airways Ltd* [1993] Ch 223 (CA); *UBS AG New York and ors v Fairfield Sentry Ltd (in liquidation)* [2019] UKPC 20.

insolvency proceedings in the United States (11 U.S.C. § 1523(a)), typically under the rules of Chapter 7 (Bankruptcy) or Chapter 11 (Reorganization) of the US Bankruptcy Code, and the case has a connection to the United States.[128] An alternative might be to challenge the transaction under the *lex fori concursus* before the courts of the opening State and ask for recognition of the judgment abroad.[129]

9.54 For the EU, the question as to the applicable transactions avoidance law finds its answer in Arts 7(2)(m) and 16 of the EIR. According to Art. 7(2)(m) of the EIR, the transactions avoidance rules of the *lex fori concursus* are to be applied. However, this is subject to Art. 16 of the EIR, according to which the *lex fori concursus*

> shall not apply where the person who benefitted from an act detrimental to all the creditors provides proof that (a) the act is subject to the law of a Member State other than that of the State of the opening of proceedings; and (b) the law of that Member State does not allow by any means of challenging that act in the relevant case.[130]

The effect of this provision is that the benefited person enjoys the application of the 'most favourable' principle. If the detrimental act is not challengeable under the *lex fori concursus*, the creditor can keep what he or she has received. If it is challengeable, they get a second chance: they are permitted to overturn the challenge by proving that the act would be neither void nor voidable under any provision of the *lex causae*,[131] provided the *lex causae* is the law of a Member State of the EU. Hence, Art. 16 of the EIR grants a 'safe harbour'[132] by permitting a defence against the application of the *lex fori concursus*. However, this is overprotective.[133] It has repeatedly been argued that protection of trust as granted by Art. 16 of the EIR is not justifiable, since the challenging of the act in question is a 'foreseeable risk'.[134] It is suggested that creditors who enter into

---

[128] For details, see *In re CIL Ltd*, 582 BR 46 (2018); *In re Condor Insurance Ltd*, 601 F.3d 319 (5th Cir. Miss. 2010); *In re Fairfield Sentry*, 485 BR 665 (SDNY 2006); *In Re French*, 440 F.3d 145 (4th Cir. 2006); *In Re International Banking Corp. BSC*, 439 BR 614 (SDNY 2010); *In Re Maxwell Communications Corp.*, 93 F.3d 1036 (2d Cir. 1996).

[129] More on this below at para. 9.61. An interesting example is described by A.A. Kostin, 'Avoidance of the Debtor's Transactions within the Framework of a Foreign Insolvency before a Russian Court', <https://conflic toflaws.net/2021/avoidance-of-the-debtors-transactions-within-the-framework-of-a-foreign-insolvency-bef ore-a-russian-court/?utm_source=feedburner&utm_medium=email&utm_campaign=Feed%3A+conflictofl aws%2FRSS+%28Conflict+of+Laws+.net%29> accessed 16 September 2021.

[130] For case law of the CJEU, see the decisions in C-73/20 *ZM in his capacity as liquidator in the insolvency of Oeltrans Befrachtungsgesellschaft mbH v E.A. Frerichs*, ECLI:EU:C:2021:315; C-310/14 *Nike European Operations Netherlands BV v Sportland Oy* (n 36); C-54/16 *Vinyls Italia SpA (in liquidation) v Mediterranea di Navigazione SpA*, ECLI:EU:C:2017:433; Case C-557/13 *Hermann Lutz v Elke Bäuerle* (n 55).

[131] An example is, among others, the Italian case *Volare SpA v WLFC*, Tribunale di Busto Arsizio–10 July 2012 – [2012] EICR(A) 350.

[132] Garcimartín and Virgós in Bork and van Zwieten, *Commentary on EIR* (n 3) para. 16.9.

[133] Cf. Bork, *Principles of Cross-Border Insolvency Law* (n 23) paras 6.83 et seq.

[134] Bork (n 56), 'Law Applicable', para. 4.104; M. Brinkmann, 'Avoidance Claims in the Context of the EIR', International Insolvency Law Review (2013) 371, 378; M. Veder in Hess, Oberhammer, and Pfeiffer, *European Insolvency Law* (n 123) 577 et seq.; Veder, *Cross-Border Insolvency Proceedings* (n 102) 315 et seq.; M. Veder, 'Party Autonomy and Insolvency' in Westrik and van der Weide (eds), *Party Autonomy in International Property Law* (Sellier 2011) 261, 267; Veder, 'The Future of the European Insolvency Regulation' (n 102) 285, 294 et seq.

transactions with a debtor (who is, in most cases, subject to insolvency proceedings shortly after the transaction) have to take into account the possibility that they cannot keep what they have received due to the debtor's national transactions avoidance law.

The impact of Art. 16 of the EIR can be illustrated by the following example. C, the Luxembourg-based only shareholder of the German D GmbH, grants a loan to her company. The loan agreement is governed by French law. Five months before the application for insolvency proceedings, D GmbH pays the loan back. After the opening of insolvency proceedings in Germany, the insolvency practitioner tackles the payment under German transactions avoidance law. This would be successful according to § 135 of the *Insolvenzordnung*, which provides for the avoidance of payments on shareholder loans.[135] However, since the loan agreement is governed by French law, C may prove that the payment is not voidable under French transactions avoidance law, which does not contain any rules on shareholder loans and requires the creditor's knowledge of the debtor's cessation of payments at the relevant time (Art. L. 632-2 of the *Code de Commerce*).[136] **9.55**

C. Recognition

An important and difficult topic is the recognition of (the effects of the opening of) (a) foreign insolvency proceedings and (b) judgments handed down in the course of such proceedings. **9.56**

1. Proceedings

It follows from the principle of universalism, as well as from the principle cooperation and coordination,[137] that 'outgoing' insolvency proceedings, which claim to have worldwide effect, are expected to be recognised in all other affected jurisdictions. This recognition (which refers to the effects of the opening of insolvency proceedings rather than to the proceedings themselves), is necessary in order to extend the effects of the opening decision to assets situated in another State and to enable insolvency practitioners to act on foreign soil. It goes without saying that the courts of State A have no power to produce legal effects on the territory of State B. Hence, it needs a recognition of foreign insolvency proceedings, either by statute or by court decision. Such recognition not only enforces the principles mentioned above but also the principle of mutual trust between States,[138] since by recognizing a foreign State's insolvency procedure, **9.57**

---

[135] Cf. above, Chapter 6 'Transactions Avoidance Rules' at para. 6.57.
[136] ibid para. 6.37.
[137] See Bork, *Principles of Cross-Border Insolvency Law* (n 23) paras 2.52 et seq.
[138] On this, cf. above at para. 9.11.

274 CROSS-BORDER INSOLVENCY LAW

the official bodies of the recognizing State express their trust that the insolvency law and the handling of the insolvency proceedings in the original State meet the required standards.

9.58 However, many States—examples are Norway or Switzerland—have decided to generally refuse recognition. They would not deny that insolvency proceedings have been opened abroad, but they do not accept the legal consequences of such opening decision of a foreign court on their territory. Hence, where a foreign insolvency practitioner intends, for example, to sell assets located in such a State, he or she would not be recognized as being entitled to dispose of the assets. As a consequence, the insolvency practitioner needs a proxy of the debtor, who may be obliged, under the *lex fori concursus*, to support and to cooperate with the insolvency practitioner and to make out the necessary documents.[139] The same holds true where the opening State does not enforce the principles of unity and universalism but sticks to the (outmoded[140]) principle of territoriality. Effects of a decision that the opening State does not require to have cannot be recognized by any other State.

9.59 Where the opening State claims for 'outgoing universalism', most jurisdictions grant recognition, although there are many differences in the details, depending on the level of mutual trust (among other factors). On a procedural level, some regulations provide for automatic recognition by statute (albeit with the possibility of refusing recognition on application where certain conditions are met, the most important being questions concerning international jurisdiction of the foreign court or the public policy exception[141]). Examples include Arts 19 et seq., 32, 33 of the EIR and § 343 of the *Insolvenzordnung*. The latter rule, by the way, is the result of a longer development. The German *Bundesgerichtshof*, taking a somewhat schizophrenic approach, used to favour the principle of universalism for outgoing German insolvency proceedings whilst not accepting cross-border effects of incoming foreign insolvency proceedings.[142] It was not until 1985 (i.e. before the EIR came into force) that the *Bundesgerichtshof*—provoked by the Belgian *Tribunal de Commerce de Bruxelles*, which, as a reprisal, refused to acknowledge the competencies of a German insolvency practitioner in defiance of Belgian law (which pursues the principle of universalism),[143] changed its mind and also applied the principle of universalism to foreign proceedings.[144] Today, German national cross-border insolvency law is firmly based

---

[139] Cf. for Germany, BGH, 25 February 2016–IX ZB 74/15 = NZI 2016, 365.

[140] See more above at para. 9.09.

[141] The latter entitles states to refuse recognition or enforcement 'where the effects of such recognition or enforcement would be manifestly contrary to that State's public policy, in particular its fundamental principles or the constitutional rights and liberties of the individual' (Art. 33 of the EIR).

[142] BGH, 4 February 1960–VII ZR 161/57 = NJW 1960, 774.

[143] *Tribunal de Commerce de Bruxelles*, 20 June 1975 = KTS 1978, 247 (German) = JCB 1976-IV-629 (French). The court applied—hardly convincingly—the public policy exception, stating that universalism is part not only of Belgian cross-border insolvency law but also of Belgian public policy and that recognition of German insolvency proceedings, which follow territorialism for incoming proceedings, would be against this public policy.

[144] BGH, 11 July 1985–IX ZR 178/84 = BGHZ 95, 256, 263 et seq.

on the principle of universalism for domestic as well as for foreign insolvency proceedings (§§ 335, 343 of the *Insolvenzordnung*).

Other jurisdictions require predetermined recognition proceedings and a recognition decision from the court, sometimes even on the condition that reciprocity is guaranteed.[145] Court decisions are primarily[146] required in those countries, which follow Art. 15 of the UNCITRAL Model Law, for example England (Art. 15 Sch. 1 of the CBIR 2006)[147] and particularly the United States (11 U.S.C. §§1504, 1505,[148] 1509, 1515[149]), where 'Section 1509 of the Code, captioned "Right of direct access", effectively establishes the bankruptcy court as a gatekeeper for a foreign representative's access to the U.S. courts, with recognition as the means to open the gate'.[150] The court decision prerequisite is clearly deficient from a universalistic point of view, not only because it results in additional costs and expenditure of effort due to the recognition proceedings but also because it is a gateway to territorialistic *caveats* based on mistrust among States. Recognition of foreign proceedings by domestic courts is not a 'rubber stamp exercise'[151] but opens the door for domestic courts to control foreign proceedings from scratch, which at least means checking whether they are procedurally fair and whether they contravene domestic laws or public policy.[152] However, this may be acceptable at least in relation to those foreign States where equal standards are not guaranteed by mutual binding laws, such as bilateral treaties or multilateral conventions.[153] On a substantive level, some courts may merely recognize that insolvency proceedings

9.60

---

[145] See Art. 5 of the Enterprise Bankruptcy Law (China) and, on this, *Beijing No. 1 Intermediate People's Court*, 16 January 2023 [2022] Jing 01 Po Shen No. 786; see further, Yamauchi, 'Should Reciprocity Be a Part of the UNCITRAL Model Cross-Border Insolvency Law?', International Insolvency Review, 16 (2007) 145, 167 et seq.; for Russia, Savina and Mukhametgaliev, 'Recognition of Foreign Insolvency-Related, Judgments in the Russian Federation', International Corporate Rescue,*16* (2019) 271 et seq.

[146] Also in France; cf. Dammann and Sénéchal, *Le droit de l'insolvabilité international* (n 1) paras 2103 et seq., 2112 et seq.

[147] Cf. *Leite v Amicorp* [2020] EWHC 3560 (Ch) and, on this decision, *Cooper, Leite v Amicorp* [2020] EWHC 3560 (Ch), (2021), 18 ICR, 137 et seq.

[148] This provision deviates from Art. 5 of the UNCITRAL Model Law, which provides for automatic recognition of foreign insolvency practitioners; see Gilhuly, Posin, and Malatesta, 'Bankruptcy without Borders', American Bankruptcy Institute Law Review, *24* (2016) 47, 67.

[149] Cf. *In re Iida*, 377 BR 243, 257 et seq. (9th Cir. BAP 2007); *In re Loy*, 380 BR 154, 164 (Bankr. ED Va. 2007); *In re OAS SA, et al.*, 533 BR 83, 92 et seq. (Bankr. SDNY 2015). For statistics on recognition of foreign proceedings in US courts, see Gilhuly, Posin, and Malatesta, 'Bankruptcy without Borders' (n 148) 47 et seq.; J.L. Westbrook, 'An Empirical Study of the Implementation in the United States of the Model Law on Cross Border Insolvency', American Bankruptcy Law Journal, 87 (2013) 247, 254 et seq.

[150] *In re Millard*, 501 BR 644, 653 fn. 27 (Bankr. SDNY). Cf. also *In re Ran*, 390 BR 257, 290 (Bankr. SD Tex. 2008); D.G. Epstein, Markell, Nickles, and Ponoroff, Bankruptcy (4th edn, West Academic Publishing 2015) 419; Glosband, Kelakos, Lifland et al., Cross-Border Insolvency in the United States (American Bankruptcy Institute 2008) 17.

[151] *In re Basis Yield Alpha Fund (Master)* (n 86), citing *In re Bear Stearns High-Grade Structured Credit Strategies Master Fund, Ltd* (Bankr. SDNY 2007) 122, 126/130.

[152] For the United States, cf. *In re Compañia de Alimentos Fargo, SA*, 376 BR 427, 434 (Bankr. SDNY 2007); *In re Irish Bank Resolution Corp. Ltd*, Case No. 13-12159 (Bankr. D Del. 2014); *In re Northshore Mainland Services, Inc.*, 537 BR 192, 207 (Bankr. D Del. 2015); *J.P. Morgan Chase Bank v Altos Hornos de Mexico, SA de CV*, 412 F.3d 418 (2d Cir. 2005).

[153] Independent recognition proceedings are heavily supported by Kolmann, Kooperationsmodelle im Internationalen Insolvenzrecht (Gieseking 2001) 517 et seq., 527 et seq.; L. LoPucki, Courting Failure (University of Michigan Press 2005) 254 et seq. An overview of the opinions on this matter can be found in M. Veder, 'Bob's "Unvollendete"?' in Santen and van Offeren (eds), Tribute to Bob Wessels (Kluwer 2014) 139, 145 et seq.

276 CROSS-BORDER INSOLVENCY LAW

have been opened, while in other countries, the court may recognize some or all of the worldwide effects of foreign proceedings (provided that the *lex fori concursus* claims that such worldwide effects exist).[154]

2. Judgments

9.61 A different matter is the recognition of judgments closely related to insolvency proceedings.[155] In principle, this is a matter of recognition under international civil procedure law. However, some insolvency laws—encouraged by the UNCITRAL Model Law on Recognition and Enforcement of Insolvency-Related Judgments[156]— include such judgments into their recognition rules. A leading example is Art. 32 of the EIR, which provides for automatic recognition of all judgments that concern the course and the closure of insolvency proceedings. This includes preliminary measures, the approval of a restructuring plan, and judgments deriving directly from the insolvency proceedings, which are closely linked with them (which refers particularly to judgments on transactions avoidance). Other countries recognize preservation measures ordered by the insolvency court in the same way as they recognize the opening decision,[157] but cross-border insolvency laws are otherwise silent on the matter[158] and thereby rely on cross-border civil procedure law rather than on cooperation rules.

9.62 In England, the Court of Appeal in *New Cap Re*[159] had to decide on the recognition of a transactions avoidance judgment of an Australian court and found that such a judgment could be recognised and enforced on both a procedural and a cross-border insolvency law basis—at least according to s. 426(4) of the Insolvency Act 1986, and most likely also according to common law. This outcome was heavily criticized,[160] and on appeal, the Supreme Court decided that the cooperation rule in s. 426(4) of the Insolvency Act 1986 was not applicable to the enforcement of foreign judgments on transactions avoidance and that common law was set aside by the applicable cross-border procedural law.[161]

9.63 However, it should be highlighted that the recognition of judgments closely related to the conduct of insolvency proceedings, or at least the recognition of the insolvency proceedings themselves, frequently includes the recognition of decisions of the

---

[154] Examples are the European Union, Art. 20(1) of the EIR; Germany, §§ 343 and 335 of the *Insolvenzordnung* (cf. BGH, 24 June 2014–VI ZR 315/13 = ZIP 2014, 1997); furthermore, post-Art. 20 of the UNCITRAL Model Law, England, Art. 20 Sch. 1 of the CBIR 2006; United States, 11 U.S.C. §1520 and the resultant *ratio* of *In re Rede Energia SA*, 515 BR 69 (Bankr. SDNY 2014).

[155] For them, see above at para. 9.39.

[156] Of 2 July 2018, <https://uncitral.un.org/en/texts/insolvency/modellaw/mlij> accessed 15 February 2024.

[157] This holds true for Germany (§ 343(2) of the *Insolvenzordnung*), even if, following the distinction between recognition and enforcement, an execution judgment is necessary according to ibid § 353(2).

[158] This is especially accurate regarding the UNCITRAL Model Law, as well as national laws of countries that have adopted the Model Law. However, for the exception of judgments approving compositions, see below, para. 9.62.

[159] *New Cap Reinsurance Corp. v Grant* [2011] EWCA Civ. 971.

[160] *Ho*, CRI 2011, 157 et seq.

[161] *Rubin v Eurofinance SA* [2012] UKSC 46.

insolvency court sanctioning compositions such as insolvency plans or schemes of arrangement, especially if they are drafted in order to enable the reorganization of the debtor's company. This is an important topic, since many companies, at least outside Europe, use the restructuring proceedings of Chapter 11 of the US Bankruptcy Code because there are no similar means available under their domestic laws.[162] However, this only makes sense if the restructuring plan (11 U.S.C. §§1121 et seq.) or the court decision confirming such a plan (11 U.S.C. §1129) will be recognized domestically. The wording of Art. 32(1) of the EIR expressly mentions compositions approved by the court that opened the proceedings, and this wording must be construed widely.[163] The UNCITRAL Model Law, although it does not mention compositions expressly, can be said to facilitate the recognition of insolvency plans under the general rules of Art. 21(1) ('any appropriate relief') and Art. 7 ('additional assistance'),[164] depending on the facts of the case in question and the limits of national law, and this is also true of national cross-border insolvency laws which are moulded in the image of the Model Law.[165] A third group of regulations accepts judgments sanctioning compositions as decisions terminating the proceedings, of which § 343(2) of the *Insolvenzordnung* is a good example.[166]

The complexity of the legal situation can be illustrated by the following example. **9.64**
German D GmbH is in financial turmoil because in four months a bond will become due and follow-up financing is not in sight. The directors of D GmbH develop a rescuing plan, which provides for a prolongation of the bond, for a cutback of the bondholders' claims, and for a reduction of interest rates. Since a minority opposes this plan, D GmbH commences administration proceedings in London, claiming that the United Kingdom has international jurisdiction because the bond is governed by English law and the majority of bondholders are based in England. The insolvency practitioner starts a scheme of arrangement procedure,[167] which is eventually sanctioned by the High Court.[168] C, a German bondholder, files a lawsuit for full payment in Germany, claiming that the English insolvency proceedings and the scheme are not recognisable

---

[162] In the aftermath of the COVID-19 crisis, this held particularly true for airline companies, such as South-American LATAM Airlines Group or Philippine Airlines, Inc.

[163] P. Oberhammer and F. Scholz-Berger in Bork and van Zwieten, *Commentary on EIR* (n 3) para. 32.12.

[164] See also Art. X of the UNCITRAL Model Law on Recognition and Enforcement of Insolvency-Related Judgments.

[165] Cf. for the UK *Cambridge Gas Transportation Corp. v Official Committee of Unsecured Creditors of Navigator Holdings plc* [2006] UKPC 26; T. Smith in Sheldon, *Cross-Border Insolvency* (n 1) paras 6.104 et seq.; for the United States, *In re Metcalfe & Mansfield Alternative Investments*, 421 BR 685 (Bankr. SDNY 2010); *In re Vitro SAB de CV*, 701 F.3d 1031 (5th Cir. 2012).

[166] For this interpretation, see BGH, 24 June 2014–VI ZR 315/13 = ZIP 2014, 1997.

[167] See details above, in Chapter 8 'Corporate Groups in Rescue', para. 8.51.

[168] English courts are not very reluctant to confirm their international jurisdiction; groundbreaking in the context of schemes of arrangement is *Re Drax Holdings Ltd* [2003] EWHC 2743 (Ch); see further *Re ColourOz Investment 2 LLC* [2020] EWHC 1864 (Ch); *Re DAP Holding NV* [2005] EWHC 2092 (Ch); *Re DTEK Energy BV and DTEK Finance plc* [2021] EWHC 1456 (Ch); *Re Haya Holdco 2 plc* [2022] EWHC 1079 (Ch) and [2022] EWHC 2732 (Ch); *Re MAB Leasing Ltd* [2021] EWHC 152 (Ch) and [2021] EWHC 379 (Ch); *Re OJSC Ank Yugraneft* [2008] EWHC 2614 (Ch); *Re Rodenstock GmbH* [2011] EWHC 1104 (Ch); *Re Safari Holding Verwaltungs GmbH* [2022] EWHC 781 (Ch) and [2022] EWHC 1156 (Ch); *Re Sovereign Marine & General Insurance Co. Ltd* [2006] EWHC 1335 (Ch); *Re Steinhoff International Holdings NV* [2021] EWHC 184 (Ch).

in Germany. This would not be successful under the EIR, since the insolvency proceedings were to be recognised under Art. 19(1) of the EIR.[169] The same holds true for the scheme (Art. 32(1) of the EIR). However, after Brexit, the EIR is no longer applicable unless any exit treaties provide otherwise. As a consequence, German cross-border insolvency law applies, which is recognition-friendly but requires international jurisdiction of the English court under German cross-border insolvency law (§ 343(1), (2) No. 1 of the *Insolvenzordnung*). Since D GmbH has its COMI (Art. 3 of the EIR[170]) and its centre of business activities (§ 3 of the *Insolvenzordnung*) in Germany, English courts have no jurisdiction under German law, and neither the insolvency proceedings nor the scheme decision (as a judgment) are recognisable in Germany. However, since the bond is governed by English law, the amendments to C's substantive rights effected by the scheme have to be accepted in Germany under private international law, in this case Art. 12(1)(d) of the Rome I Regulation.[171] Hence, in the end, C's lawsuit would be dismissed.

9.65 The recognition of a foreign discharge goes without saying under the EIR, which not only covers separate discharge proceedings under its Art. 1(1)[172] but also includes discharge decisions in insolvency proceedings through the automatic recognition of judgments closely related to them under Art. 32(1) of the EIR. Some national laws, however, are more reluctant. While German[173] and US[174] courts recognise foreign discharge decisions consistently (only subject to the public policy exception), English law, for example, accepts a foreign discharge only if this is in accordance with the proper law of the contract pursuant to which the debt was incurred. Yet, a debt will not be discharged where the proper law of the contract is not the law of the jurisdiction in which the proceedings are taking place, making the position of English law rather restrictive. This was decided early on by the Court of Appeal in *Gibbs v La Societé Industrielle*,[175] which was criticised as constituting a 'paradigm of territoriality'[176] but was confirmed in many other judgments.[177]

---

[169] This holds true regardless of the fact that D GmbH's COMI was not in England, which cannot be examined on the recognition stage: CJEU Case C-341/04 *Eurofood IFSC Ltd* (n 28).

[170] The European Insolvency Regulation is part of German insolvency law and also applicable in relation to non-EU Member States; cf. CJEU Case C-328/12 *Schmid v Hertel* (n 42).

[171] *Re DTEK Energy BV and DTEK Finance plc* (n 168).

[172] See also Linna, 'Cross-Border Debt Adjustment', International Insolvency Review, 23 (2014) 20 et seq.

[173] E.g. BGH, 14 January 2014–II ZR 192/13 = NZI 2014, 238; BGH, 18 September 2001–IX ZB 51/00 = NJW 2002, 960.

[174] The leading case is *Canada Southern R. Co. v Gebhard*, 109 US 527, 3 S. Ct 363, 27 L. Ed. 1020 (1883). See also *Barclays Bank plc v Kemsley*, 992 NYS 2d 602 (NY Sup. Ct 2014); *Re Modern Land (China) Co., Ltd*, 18 July 2022, Case No. 22-10707 (MG) (Bankr. SDNY 2022).

[175] *Gibbs v La Societé Industrielle et Commercial des Metaux* [1890] 25 QBD 399, 406 (CA). See extensively on English law in this context, Dicey, Morris, and Collins, *Conflict of Laws* (n 95), paras 31R-092 et seq.; J Goldring in Sheldon, *Cross-Border Insolvency* (n 1) paras 13.1 et seq.

[176] Tregear, 'More Than One Way to Skin a Cat', Corporate Rescue Insolvency, 7 (2014) 51.

[177] See, e.g. *Adams v National Bank of Greece* [1961] AC 255; *Fen v Cosco Shipping (Qidong) Offshore Ltd* [2021] CSOH 94 and 95; *Joint Administrators of Heritable Bank plc v The Winding-Up Board of Landsbanki Islands hf* [2013] UKSC 13; *National Bank of Greece and Athens SA v Metliss* [1958] AC 509 (HL); *Re OJSC International Bank of Azerbaijan* [2018] EWHC 59 (Ch); *Wight v Eckardt Marine GmbH* [2003] UKPC 37.

D. Cooperation and Coordination

In cross-border insolvencies, particularly where there are multiple proceedings, co-operation of the official bodies and coordination of the procedures is necessary.[178] There are four typical cases. First, there is only one single set of insolvency proceedings, opened in State A, but the debtor has assets in State B and the insolvency practitioner needs the support of the courts or enforcement institutions of State B to recover these assets. Second, concurrent insolvency proceedings are opened in two States, which do not apply the principle of universalism or do not recognise the competing proceedings. Third, main proceedings are opened in State A and secondary proceedings in State B. Fourth, a group of companies has group members in various jurisdictions and insolvency proceedings are opened for each group member in its COMI state. All these proceedings must be coordinated, at least in order to ensure that proceeds distributed in State A are taken into account when it comes to distributions in State B, since it must be guaranteed that all ordinary creditors are treated equally and that no creditor receives more than the full amount of his or her claim. Hence, it is necessary that the official bodies—courts[179] as well as insolvency practitioners—involved in multiple proceedings communicate and coordinate their actions where necessary.

9.66

Rules on coordination and cooperation can be found in many regulations. The EIR provides for such rules in Arts 41 et seq. for the coordination of main and secondary proceedings and in Arts 56 et seq. for group insolvencies.[180] Similarly, the UNCITRAL Model Law aims to ensure coordination and cooperation between the official bodies of multiple insolvency proceedings in various countries, which follows from its preamble and particularly from Arts 25 et seq.[181] Further, many 'soft laws' endeavour to suggest and to support coordination and cooperation.[182] They all aim to promote the efficiency and justice of the proceedings, particularly under the principles of equal treatment of creditors and best possible realization of the debtor's assets by encouraging judges and insolvency practitioners in the jurisdictions concerned to communicate, to coordinate the proceedings, and to support the efforts of the other side where necessary and possible under domestic law.

9.67

---

[178] See extensively, Bork, *Principles of Cross-Border Insolvency Law* (n 23) paras 2.39 et seq.

[179] On this, see Vallender and Nietzer, 'Cooperation and Communication of Judges in Cross-Border Insolvency Proceedings' in Santen and van Offeren (eds), Tribute to Bob Wessels (n 153) 127 et seq.

[180] See B. Wessels and Kokorin, 'Communication and Cooperation in Cross-Border Restructuring and Insolvency Matters in the EU', American Bankruptcy Institute Journal, 37 (2018) 32.

[181] See also UNCITRAL, *Practice Guide on Cross-Border Insolvency Cooperation* (United Nations Publications 2010).

[182] Cf. above, at para. 9.04.

280   CROSS-BORDER INSOLVENCY LAW

9.68   A highly illustrative example is the cooperation of two bankruptcy courts in the United States and Canada in the *Nortel* case. The Nortel Networks group was a leading enterprise in the telecom market, with worldwide business activity and highly integrated subsidiaries in over 100 countries. On 14 January 2009, insolvency applications were lodged simultaneously in Delaware for the United States, in Toronto for Canada and in London for Europe, the Middle East, and Africa. Three mediation attempts on an international scale concerning how to distribute the proceeds of 7.3 bn USD among the group's worldwide creditors failed. Finally, the courts in the United States and in Canada organized a 21-day joint trial with video-conference-calling facilities, facilitating the participation of all involved parties. Nearly 40 witnesses testified, deposition testimony of 130 witnesses was designated, and the parties admitted more than 2,200 exhibits into evidence. On 12 May 2015, the courts ultimately decided on the distribution of the proceeds simultaneously and reached the same conclusions, holding that the allocation of sales proceeds to all debtor entities should take place on a pro rata basis.[183]

9.69   In practice, cooperation and coordination is frequently organised on the basis of so-called 'protocols':[184] insolvency agreements between the courts and/or insolvency practitioners determining how to coordinate the proceedings in a manner that serves the best interests of all creditors. They were first developed as 'best practices' by courts and insolvency practitioners in order to solve practical problems of cross-border cooperation and communication and to fill the gap in insolvency legislation, which failed to provide detailed guidance. They are welcomed by judges, who believe that such agreements are 'clearly a proper and common-sense business arrangement to make, and manifestly for the benefit of all parties interested'.[185] They are nowadays also backed by

---

[183]   In Canada, *Re Nortel Networks Corporation* [2015] ONSC 2987; confirmed in *Re Nortel Networks Corporation* [2015] ONSC 4170; *Re Nortel Networks Corporation* [2016] ONCA 332; *Re Nortel Networks Corporation* [2015] ONCA 681; in the United States, *In re Nortel Networks Inc.* 532 BR 494 (Bankr. D Del. 2015). See extensively on this case Harlang and Vininsky, 'Nortel Networks', American Bankruptcy Institute Journal, 34(8) (2015) 18 et seq.; Peacock, 'The Novel Cross-Border Bankruptcy Trial', American Bankruptcy Institute Law Review, 23 (2015) 543 et seq.; Tillman and Bullen, '*Nortel*: Cross-Border Decisions Points the Way to Distributions', Insolvency International, 28 (2015) 91 et seq.; Tillman and Bullen, 'The *Nortel* "Allocation" Decisions: *Nortel Networks Corporation (Re)*, 2015 ONSC 2987 and *In re Nortel Networks Inc. et al.*, 09–10138 (Delaware Bankruptcy Court)', International Corporate Rescue, 12 (2015) 202 et seq.; J.L. Westbrook, '*Nortel*: The Cross-Border Insolvency Case of the Century', Journal of International Banking and Financial Law, 30 (2015) 498 et seq.

[184]   On this, see Adler, *Managing the Chapter 15 Cross-Border Insolvency Case* (2nd edn, Federal Judicial Center 2014) 33 et seq.; Bellissimo and Johnston, 'Cross Border Insolvency Protocols: Developing an International Standard' in *Norton Annual Review of International Insolvency* (2010) 37 et seq.; Clark, *Ancillary and Other Cross-Border Insolvency Cases under Chapter 15 of the Bankruptcy Code* (LexisNexis Matthew Bender 2008) 98 et seq.; Kokorin and B. Wessels, *Cross-Border Protocols in Insolvencies of Multinational Enterprise Groups* (Edward Elgar Publishing 2021); Leonhard, 'A Creative Application of Chapter 15', American Bankruptcy Institute Journal, 33(12) (2014) 48 et seq.; Peck, 'Cross-Border Observations Derived from My Lehman Judicial Experience', Journal of International Banking and Financial Law, 30 (2015) 131 et seq.; B. Wessels, Markell, and Kilborn, *International Cooperation in Bankruptcy and Insolvency Matters* (OUP 2009) 176 et seq.; Zumbro, 'Cross-Border Insolvencies and International Protocols—An Imperfect But Effective Tool', Business Law International, 11 (2010) 157 et seq. Plenty of material is available on the matter at <https://www.universiteitleiden.nl/en/research/research-projects/law/insolvency-protocols-project> accessed 20 April 2023.

[185]   *P Macfadyen & Co. Ex p. Vizianagaram Co. Ltd, Re* [1908] 1 KB 675.

many binding or soft law regulations, such as Recital 49 of the EIR and Arts 41(1)(2) and 56(1)(2) of the EIR; Procedural Principle 14 of the NAFTA Principles;[186] Chapter III of the UNCITRAL *Practice Guide on Cross-Border Insolvency Cooperation*;[187] Principles 2.1., 23.3., 26.1 of the Global Principles for Cooperation in International Insolvency Cases;[188] and Principles 4.1 and 16.5 of the EU Cross-Border Insolvency Court-to-Court Cooperation Principles (2015).[189]

Rules on cooperation and communication have also been developed through case law. **9.70** This holds especially true for the United Kingdom, where cooperation has been depicted as an common law obligation of (and stemming from) the courts.[190] As early as 1764, Bathurst J, in his famous decision *Solomons v Ross*,[191] accepted *de facto* the principle of universalism and granted assistance to Dutch insolvency proceedings by recognizing the effects of these proceedings on English assets. This was the starting point for an extensive evolution of common law-based case law concerning comity in cross-border insolvency proceedings, resulting in the very well-reasoned decision of the Privy Council in *Cambridge Gas*[192] (granting assistance by implementing a creditors' plan relating to an insolvent company, which had been approved by a New York bankruptcy court). The most recent case law took a significantly more restrictive approach: the Supreme Court in *Rubin v Eurofinance SA*[193] and the *obiter dicta* of two Lords of the Privy Council in *Singularis*.[194] Unfortunately, this has significantly limited the courts' freedom to assist in foreign insolvency proceedings through use of common law.

---

[186] See above (n 13), with examples in Appendix C to those Principles.

[187] (New York 2010) 27 et seq.

[188] See above (n 15).

[189] Text, edited by B. Wessels, in Bork and van Zwieten, *Commentary on EIR* (n 3) Appendix 6.

[190] For the history of this development, see Fletcher in Santen and van Offeren (eds), *Tribute to Bob Wessels* (n 153) 55 et seq.; for the four sources of English cross-border insolvency law, see Bowen, 'An Introduction to the Fundamental Principles Governing Cross-Border Insolvency in an English Law Context', International Insolvency Law Review (2013) 121 et seq.; Moss in Santen and van Offeren (eds), *Tribute to Bob Wessels* (n 153) 95 et seq.; Taylor, 'International Insolvency When the EU Regulation Is Not Applicable: The Case of the United Kingdom' in Affaki (ed.), *Faillite internationale et conflit de juridiction—Regards croisés transatlantique* (FEC/Bruylant 2007) 125 et seq. For criticism on this, see Williams and Walters, 'The Model Law: Is It Time for the U.K. to Change Tack?', American Bankruptcy Institute Journal, 35(1) (2016) 16 et seq.

[191] *Solomons v Ross* [1764] 1 H Bl 131n and 126 ER 79; for more on this decision, see Nadelmann, '*Solomons v Ross* and International Bankruptcy Law', Modern Law Review 9 (1946) 154 et seq.

[192] *Cambridge Gas Transportation Corp. v Official Committee of Unsecured Creditors of Navigator Holdings plc* (n 163) by Lord Hoffmann.

[193] *Rubin v Eurofinance SA* (n 161); see criticism by Omar, 'Cross-Border Insolvency and Principles of Judicial Assistance: Recent Themes and Developments' in Santen and van Offeren (eds), Tribute to Bob Wessels (n 153) 103, 111 et seq.

[194] *Singularis Holdings Ltd v PricewaterhouseCoopers (Bermuda)* [2014] UKPC 36.

282 CROSS-BORDER INSOLVENCY LAW

9.71 However, there are also less convincing judgments. An illustrative example is the Canadian case *Antwerp Bulkcarriers NV v Holt Cargo Systems, Inc.*[195] *Antwerp Bulkcarriers* was a Belgian company facing Belgian insolvency proceedings. The company owned a ship and US stevedores attached a lien under US maritime law to this ship. The ship sailed to Canada, where the stevedores opened a Canadian admiralty proceeding. The Belgian administrator sought for the ship to be turned over to him. The Canadian Supreme Court denied this application, the reason being that foreign bankruptcy law should 'faithfully mirror the provisions of Canadian bankruptcy law', according to which 'protection of secured creditors is a strong public policy in [Canadian] bankruptcy scheme'. In the parallel case of *Holt Cargo Systems*,[196] the Supreme Court ruled that 'the need for such international cooperation in bankruptcy and insolvency has been evident for a very long time' but that 'only some of the key components of the universalist approach have been reflected in Canadian law'. 'Given the almost infinite variations in circumstances that can occur in an "international bankruptcy", the pragmatism of the "plurality" approach continues to recommend itself. International coordination is an important factor, but it is not necessarily a controlling factor.' This decision is a sad relapse to territorialism.[197]

---

[195] *Antwerp Bulkcarriers NV v Holt Cargo Systems, Inc.* [2001] 3 SCR 951; see also the illuminating analysis of this decision by Pottow, Greed and Pride in International Bankruptcy: The Problems of and Proposed Solutions to "Local Interests"', Michigan Law Review, *104* (2006) 1899, 1922 et seq.
[196] *Holt Cargo Systems Inc. v ABC Containerline NV (Trustee of)* [2001] 3 SCR 907.
[197] Cf. Bork, *Principles of Cross-Border Insolvency Law* (n 23) paras 2.64 et seq.

10

Aspects of Tax Law

Günter Kahlert

I. Introduction

Individual enforcement is governed by the principle of priority: the first creditor to access   **10.01**
a particular asset of the debtor to satisfy its claim has priority in obtaining satisfaction.[1] If
the debtor is no longer in a position to satisfy all claims against it, the principle of priority
loses its intrinsic justification.[2] A resulting race among the creditors would be unjustifiable.
In this kind of unsatisfactory situation, individual enforcement is therefore replaced by
insolvency proceedings: collective enforcement in which the creditors form a community
of losses.[3]

The State assumes a dual role in insolvency proceedings. On the one hand, it is obliged to   **10.02**
protect the rights of the debtor (rights of freedom) and of the creditors (rights of claim); on
the other, it is obliged to enforce the taxes against the debtor. The relationship between insolvency proceedings and tax law is marked by this tension within the State's dual responsibility. Regarding the enforcement of taxes in insolvency proceedings, a distinction must
be made between taxes arising before and taxes arising after the opening of insolvency
proceedings. In principle, it is up to the national legislature to balance the rights and obligations involved considering constitutional law, thereby resolving the tension.[4]

However, the Member States of the European Union must also comply with Union law   **10.03**
in insolvency proceedings. Thus, the Court of Justice of the European Union (CJEU)
has ruled that the partial satisfaction by an insolvent trader of a value-added tax (VAT)
claim based on the VAT Directive is permissible under Union law only if it does not
constitute a general and indiscriminate waiver of collecting VAT.[5] Furthermore,

---

[1] Seer, *DStR* (2016) 1289 (1289).
[2] Stürner in *MüKoInsO* (4th edn, 2019) introduction marginal no. 77 with further references.
[3] BGH, 22 January 2004–IX ZR 39/03 = BGHZ 157, 350 (353). See H. Eidenmüller, *ZIP* (2016), 145 (151) on the
cross-border impact of insolvency proceedings.
[4] On the fundamentals, see Krumm, *Steuervollzug und formelle Insolvenz* (2009) 52 ff. Also Seer, *DStR* (2016)
1289 (1289 f.). On tax claims in cross-border insolvency proceedings, see Piekenbrock, *EWS* (2016) 181. On the
position of the German state as a tax creditor in insolvency proceedings outside Germany, see Mankowski, *DStR*
(2019) 1927. On the recognition of foreign insolvency decisions in Germany and their impact on the German state
as a tax creditor, see Mankowski, ibid 1979.
[5] CJEU Case C-546/14 *Degano Trasporti*, ECLI:EU:C:2016:206.

Günter Kahlert, *Aspects of Tax Law* In: *The Anatomy of Corporate Insolvency Law*. Edited by: Reinhard Bork and Renato Mangano,
Oxford University Press. © Günter Kahlert 2024. DOI: 10.1093/oso/9780198852094.003.0010

284 ASPECTS OF TAX LAW

irrespective of the type of tax, the prohibition of State aid under Union law must be observed in connection with the restructuring of companies in insolvency proceedings.[6]

10.04 How a State decides to resolve the tension within its dual responsibility is also likely to depend on the purpose of that State's national insolvency proceedings. The decisive factors should be not only whether insolvency proceedings aim to secure the interests of the creditors or the debtor but also whether their purpose is to liquidate or reorganize the company.[7] The outcome may additionally be influenced by whether jurisdiction is held by the insolvency courts or the specialized courts, in particular the tax courts. In Germany, for example, it is the tax courts that have jurisdiction for disputes concerning the determination of tax claims in the insolvency schedule pursuant to ss174 et seq. of the Insolvency Code (*Insolvenzordnung*, InsO). In Austria, the civil courts hold that jurisdiction.[8]

10.05 Tax law is regularly linked to structures under civil law.[9] Therefore, how a State resolves the tension within its dual responsibility depends on how the specific insolvency proceedings are structured and whether special tax regulations or the general tax regulations apply. In insolvency proceedings in Germany, for example, the general tax regulations generally apply. The question of how those regulations are to be applied to insolvency proceedings is generally answered by the tax courts. In Germany, the legislature has not created an insolvency tax law. In this context, a distinction must be made between States in which—as in Germany—insolvency proceedings are uniform and States—such as the United States or England and Wales—in which specific insolvency proceedings are conducted for specific purposes. If insolvency proceedings vary in accordance with the purpose, the tax consequences may vary too. In addition, each type of tax and each type of taxation of the taxpayer in question must be considered for each insolvency proceeding. Taxes that the debtor collects or withholds in the interest of the State, especially VAT and wage tax, take on particular importance in this context. This is because the debtor's function as a tax collector or tax withholder for the benefit of the State is often used to justify fiscal privileges, even if the dogmatic justifications vary.

10.06 It follows from the above that potential tax issues arising in relation to insolvency proceedings are many, varied, and frequently complex, and the complexity is amplified when looking across countries. This chapter aims to simplify the complexity described. It takes the legal situation in Germany as its starting point. By comparing Germany with other States, it will show, from a tax perspective, where the tension within a State's

---

[6] CJEU Case C-203/16 *P. Andres (Insolvenz Heitkamp BauHolding)*, ECLI:EU:C:2018:505 on the recognition of loss carryforwards pursuant to s. 8c(1a) of the *Körperschaftsseuergesetz* (KStG) (German Corporate Income Tax Act).

[7] See Fries, *Fiskusprivilegien* (Verlag Dr Otto Schmidt 2020) 19ff.

[8] Engelhart in Konecny, *Kommentar zu den Insolvenzgesetzen*, instalment 48a (Manz Verlag 2012) § 46 marginal no. 6.

[9] See BVerfG, 27 December 1991–2 BvR 72/90 = BStBl. II 1992, 212; BFH, 6 March 2008–VI R 6/05 = BStBl. II 2008, 530; BFH, 29 January 2015–V R 5/14 = BStBl. II 2015, 567, marginal no. 36.

dual responsibility becomes apparent in insolvency proceedings and how this tension can be conceptually resolved.

II. Basic Principles

In Germany, the idea that the insolvency estate—rather than the debtor—could be **10.07** treated as a separate entity for tax purposes was briefly discussed in the case law of the Reich Fiscal Court in the 1930s but immediately rejected.[10] Since then, there has been agreement in the case law of the Federal Fiscal Court and in the literature that the opening of insolvency proceedings does not cause the debtor to lose its status as a tax debtor. Even if an insolvency administrator is appointed, the income and sales revenue continue to be assigned to the debtor.[11] When an individual in the United States files for insolvency under Chapter 12 (Adjustment of Debts of a Family Farmer or Fisherman with Regular Annual Income) or Chapter 13 (Adjustment of Debts of an Individual with Regular Income) of the Bankruptcy Code, the insolvency estate is not treated as a separate entity. This also applies for tax purposes. However, the insolvency estate is treated as a separate entity for tax purposes (see 11 U.S.C. §§541(a) and 346) when an individual files for insolvency under Chapter 7 (Liquidation) or 11 (Reorganization) of the Bankruptcy Code. The transfer (other than by sale or exchange) of an asset from the debtor to the insolvency estate and vice versa in the event of termination or dissolution of the insolvency proceedings is not treated as a disposition for income tax purposes. An insolvency estate is not created as a separate entity, including for tax purposes, when a partnership or a corporation files an insolvency petition.[12]

In resolving the tension within the State's dual responsibility, a distinction must be made **10.08** between the substantive tax claim and the tax assessment notice by which this claim is enforced under procedural law. Since insolvency law regularly deals with the enforcement of a substantive claim, it does not, in principle, affect the constituent elements of the substantive (public) tax claim. In Germany, § 15b(8) of the InsO, which applies to insolvency proceedings filed on or after 1 January 2021, provides for an exception to this principle. According to this provision, non-payment of taxes does not constitute a breach of tax obligations under § 34 of the German Fiscal Code (*Abgabenordnung*, AO) in the event the debtor is illiquid (*Zahlungsunfähigkeit*, § 17 of the InsO) or over-indebted (*Überschuldung*, § 19 of the InsO), and the managing director is not liable for taxes under § 69 of the AO if the insolvency petition is filed in good time and the insolvency proceedings are properly conducted.

---

[10] RFH, 22 June 1938–VI 687/37 = RFHE 44, 162 (164 f.).

[11] BFH, 1 October 2015–X B 71/15 = BFH/NV 2016, 34 marginal no. 27 on income tax and BFH, 21 October 2015–XI R 28/14 = BFH/NV 2016, 873 marginal no. 33 on VAT.

[12] Internal Revenue Service (IRS), 'Bankruptcy Tax Guide', Publication 908 (IRS February 2023) 5f., 9, 23, <https://www.irs.gov/publications/p908> accessed 13 January 2024.

286   ASPECTS OF TAX LAW

10.09   Furthermore, the legal effects of the insolvency proceedings may influence whether the constituent elements for a substantive tax claim are met. According to the case law of Germany's Federal Fiscal Court, the appointment of a preliminary insolvency administrator with a reservation of consent from the controlled company has the effect that the fiscal unity with the controlling company for VAT purposes is terminated.[13] Pursuant to § 276a(3) of the InsO, which applies to insolvency proceedings filed on or after 1 January 2021, this also applies in the event that preliminary self-administration proceedings are ordered. In a similar vein, the Court of Appeal of England and Wales held, in 2017, that the appointment of a receiver at the controlled company ends the control by the controlling company required for a consolidated tax group for income tax purposes.[14] For Germany, the Federal Fiscal Court has ruled that the appointment of the same insolvency administrator over both the assets of the controlling company and the assets of the controlled company does not terminate the profit-and-loss transfer agreement required for a consolidated tax group for income tax purposes, but it does constitute good cause for termination. Furthermore, the Federal Fiscal Court is of the opinion that the legal effects of the insolvency proceedings over the assets of the controlled company terminate the execution required for a consolidated tax group for income tax purposes.[15]

10.10   The legal effects of the insolvency proceedings can also influence whether a tax assessment notice may be issued. In Germany, the Federal Fiscal Court has ruled that tax assessment notices may not be issued in respect of tax claims that qualify as insolvency claims under § 38 of the InsO.[16] The Court's reasoning is that the tax assessment notice prepares the individual enforcement of the substantive tax claim, which is inadmissible in insolvency proceedings (s. 89 of the InsO). According to the case law of the Federal Fiscal Court, exceptions exist in the case of tax refunds[17] and tax assessments to zero (except income tax)[18] as well as after the termination of insolvency plan proceedings.[19] In Austria, however, tax claims that qualify as insolvency claims (s. 51 of the Austrian Insolvency Code (*Insolvenzordnung*, IO) may be determined by tax assessment notice.[20] Note, though, that in Austria, as in Germany, the underlying tax claims must be satisfied as insolvency claims in the distribution of the insolvency estate. In both Germany[21] and Austria,[22] tax claims that do not qualify as insolvency claims (§ 38 of the InsO and § 51 of the IO) but as preferential liabilities (§ 55 of the InsO and § 46 of the IO) may be determined by means of a tax assessment notice. In the United

---

[13]   BFH, 8 August 2013–V R 18/13 = BStBl. II 2017, 543, marginal no. 30 ff.

[14]   Court of Appeal of England and Wales, 13 June 2017–UT/2016/0185, UT/2016/0186.

[15]   BFH, 2 November 2022–I R 29/19 = DStR 2023, 264.

[16]   BFH, 18 December 2002–I R 33/01 = BStBl. II 2003, 630.

[17]   BFH, 5 April 2022–IX R 27/18 = BStBl. II 2022, 703.

[18]   ibid.

[19]   BFH, 8 March 2022–VI R 33/19 = BStBl. II 2023, 98.

[20]   Supreme Administrative Court, 19 February1985, 84/14/0126; Supreme Administrative Court, 12 July 1990, 89/16/0054.

[21]   BFH, 11 April 2018–X R 39/16 = BFH/NV 2018, 1075 marginal no. 23.

[22]   The tax assessment procedure is not affected by the opening of insolvency proceedings in Austria; see Kofler and Kristen, *Insolvenz und Steuern* (Orac 2000) 11.

States, the automatic stay pursuant to 11 U.S.C. §362 due to a petition or application applies to all entities, including governmental units. The automatic stay does not prohibit assessing a tax and sending a notice and demand for payment. As in Austria, the underlying tax claims must be satisfied as insolvency claims in the distribution of the insolvency estate, unless privilege applies.[23]

The legal effects of the insolvency proceedings can interrupt appeal periods and appeal proceedings as well as action periods and action proceedings regarding tax claims. In Germany, this is justified by a corresponding application of § 240 of the German Code of Civil Procedure (*Zivilprozessordnung*—ZPO).[24] **10.11**

Tax law can influence insolvency law. In Germany, for example, under § 270b(2) No. 1 of the InsO, preliminary self-administration measures are ordered in the event of significant payment arrears to tax creditors only if, despite this circumstance, the debtor is expected to be willing and able to align its business management with the interests of the creditors. Section 270b(2) No. 1 of the InsO, in principle, applies to insolvency proceedings filed on or after 1 January 2021. **10.12**

The tension within the State's dual responsibility is also demonstrated by the managing director's tax liability. This is because successful tax liability has the economic effect of enforcing the underlying tax claim in favour of the State. **10.13**

III. Resolving the Tension in the Relationship between the State and Creditors

A. Insolvency Law Regulations

The starting point is the fact that the State's tax claim is regularly included in the creditors' community of losses by way of the insolvency proceedings. However, on this basis, States vary in their approach to resolving the tension within their dual responsibility. **10.14**

One concept for resolving the tension within the State's dual responsibility is to take into account tax claims that qualify as insolvency claims in proportion to all other claims that qualify as insolvency claims when the insolvency estate is distributed using the insolvency rate. This concept has been the basis of German insolvency law since the Insolvency Code came into force on 1 January 1999. Section 1 sentence 1 of the InsO enshrined the principle of equal treatment of creditors, thereby abolishing the priority of tax claims in the distribution of the insolvency estate previously contained in § 61(1) No. 2 of the German Bankruptcy Act (*Konkursordnung*, KO). According to a 2016 study, the privileged treatment of tax claims in the distribution of the insolvency estate was also abolished in Austria, the United Kingdom, Croatia, the Czech Republic, Denmark, **10.15**

---

[23] IRS, 'Bankruptcy Tax Guide' 25 ff.
[24] BFH, 27 February 2014–V R 21/11 = BStBl. II 2014, 501 marginal no. 14 (concerning a lawsuit).

288   ASPECTS OF TAX LAW

Estonia, Finland, and Sweden.[25] The same occurred in Australia.[26] In Germany, the concept of equal treatment of creditors was later breached with the introduction of § 55(4) of the InsO.[27] According to this provision, which applies to insolvency proceedings filed on or after 1 January 2011, tax liabilities established in the preliminary insolvency proceedings were upgraded to preferential liabilities. Section 55(4) of the InsO was amended for insolvency proceedings filed on or after 1 January 2021. The new version no longer covers income taxes but only VAT and certain withholding taxes, in particular wage tax. Put simply, § 55(4) of the InsO aims to prevent the insolvency estate from being enriched by VAT. When the debtor, as the party performing the service, receives the consideration, including the calculated VAT portion contained therein, in the (preliminary) insolvency proceedings, the resulting VAT must be classified as a preferential liability and adjusted from the insolvency estate as a priority.[28] The Federal Fiscal Court justifies its case law on the basis of European Union (EU) statutory requirements.[29] The Advocate General's opinion in *Degano Trasporti* shows that the European Commission takes the view that, in insolvency proceedings, VAT should rank first within the category of preferential claims, both in form and in substance.[30] The Advocate General disagreed with this view. As far as can be seen, French case law has not yet dealt with this VAT issue.[31] In England and Wales, the concept of equal treatment of creditors was later breached with the introduction of the Finance Act 2020.[32] For a business entering an insolvency procedure on or after 1 December 2020, His Majesty's Revenue & Customs (HMRC) now ranks as a 'secondary' preferential creditor (see ss 175 and 386 of the Insolvency Act 1986, 15D of Sch. 6 to this Act) when the insolvency estate is distributed in relation to outstanding VAT and relevant tax deductions described in the Insolvency Act 1986 (HMRC Debts: Priority on Insolvency) Regulations 2020. These regulations, which entered into force on 1 December 2020,[33] cover pay-as-you-earn (PAYE) income tax, employee national insurance contributions, student loan repayments, and construction industry scheme deductions. This means that VAT and other relevant tax deductions will be paid in advance of creditors who hold floating charges and other non-preferential debts rather than ranking equally with any other unsecured creditors of the insolvent company. HMRC's preferential claim does not include other tax liabilities and penalties and interest; corporation tax liabilities, for example, continue to be treated as unsecured debts. The government rationale

---

[25] 'Study on a New Approach to Business Failure and Insolvency' (2016) 129, <https://op.europa.eu/en/publication-detail/-/publication/3eb2f832-47f3-11e6-9c64-01aa75ed71a1/language-en> accessed 13 January 2024.

[26] See Fries, *Fiskusprivilegien* (2020) 61f.

[27] Section 55(4) of the *Insolvenzordnung* applies to a foreign tax claim; see Kahlert in Paulus and Wimmer-Amand (eds), *Festschrift Wimmer* (Nomos Verlaggesellschaft 2017) 356.

[28] For details see Kahlert, Kayser, and Bornemann, *Perspektiven für eine kohärente und praxisgerechte Verzahnung von Steuerrecht und Insolvenzrecht* (Verlag Dr Otto Schmidt KG 2020) marginal no. 91ff.

[29] BFH, 27 September 2018–V R 45/16 = BFHE 262, 214 marginal no. 14.

[30] Opinion of Advocate General E. Sharpston delivered on 14 January 2016, CJEU Case C-546/14 *Degano Trasporti*, ECLI:EU:C:2016:13 marginal no. 32.

[31] See Fries, *Fiskusprivilegien* (2020) 81ff.

[32] According to the Finance Act 2020, this applies also to Scotland and Northern Ireland.

[33] Insolvency Act 1986 (HMRC Debts: Priority on Insolvency) Regulations 2020, <https://www.legislation.gov.uk/uksi/2020/983/contents/made> accessed 13 January 2024.

behind this policy is that taxes that employees and customers have paid to businesses in good faith should be used to fund public services rather than be distributed to creditors. The government estimates that the change could raise extra revenue up to GBP 185 million annually.[34]

Another concept for resolving the tension within the State's dual responsibility is to give priority to tax claims in the distribution of the insolvency estate. As shown above, Germany and England and Wales have enacted this concept but limited it to certain taxes collected (especially VAT) or withheld (certain withholding taxes) by the debtor in the interest of the state. As can be seen from the CJEU ruling of 3 June 2021, Art. 123 of the Insolvency Law in Romania provides for a privileged first rank of (all) tax claims in the distribution of the insolvency estate.[35] What is more, this provision apparently contains no time restriction regarding the due date of tax claims in order for them to obtain first-rank status. In contrast, § 61(1) No. 2 of the KO was subject to the condition that the tax claims had become due in the last year before the commencement of proceedings. In this respect, tax claims enjoy greater protection in Romania because all tax claims qualifying as insolvency claims are taken into account in the priority distribution. In the United States,[36] certain unsecured federal tax claims arising before the insolvency case was filed are classified as eighth priority claims. This concerns certain income taxes; withholding taxes; the employer's share of employment taxes on wages, salaries, or commissions; and excise taxes on transactions. In a Chapter 7 case, eighth-priority tax may be paid out of the assets of the insolvency estate to the extent that assets remain after paying the claim of secured creditors and other creditors with higher priority claims. Different rules apply to payments of eighth-priority pre-petition taxes under Chapters 11, 12 and 13. A Chapter 11 plan can provide for payment of these taxes, with post-confirmation interest, over a period of five years from the date of the order for relief issued by the bankruptcy court (this is the bankruptcy petition date in voluntary cases) in a manner not less favourable than the most favoured non-priority claims (except for convenience claims under 11 U.S.C. §1122(b)). In a Chapter 12 case, the debtor can pay such tax claims in deferred cash payments over time. However, certain priority taxes may be paid as general unsecured claims if they result from the disposition of a farm asset, but only in cases where the debtor receives discharge. In a Chapter 13 case, the debtor can pay such taxes over three years or over five years with court approval. Certain taxes are assigned a higher priority for payment. Taxes incurred by the insolvency estate are given second-priority treatment, as administrative expenses. In an involuntary bankruptcy case, taxes arising in the ordinary course of business or the debtor's financial affairs (after the filing of the bankruptcy petition but before the earlier of the appointment of a trustee or the order for relief) are included in the third-priority

10.16

---

[34] See L. Conway, 'Insolvency: Return of HMRC Preferential Creditor Status', House of Commons Library, Briefing Paper, No. 8800 (31 January 2020) <https://researchbriefings.files.parliament.uk/documents/CBP-8800/CBP-8800.pdf> accessed 13 January 2024.

[35] CJEU Case C-182/20 *Administraţia Judeţeană a Finanţelor Publice Suceava*, ECLI:EU:C:2021:442.

[36] See, in connection with the following explanations, IRS, 'Bankruptcy Tax Guide' (n 12) 29ff.

290 ASPECTS OF TAX LAW

payment category. If the debtor has employees, fourth-priority treatment is given to the employees' portion of employment taxes on the first USD 13,650 (this amount is adjusted every 3 years) of wages that they earned during the 180-day period before the date of the bankruptcy filing or the cessation of the business, whichever occurs first. However, the debtor's portion of the employment taxes on these wages, as the employer, is given eighth-priority treatment. In France, there is no distribution order that applies to tax claims in insolvency only.[37] Note that insolvency-proof legal positions apply to taxes in the United States and France; see section III.B below.

10.17 If the tension within the State's dual responsibility is balanced by classifying the tax claim as an insolvency claim or as a preferential liability, the criteria for this classification under insolvency law are fundamental. The interpretation under tax law criteria can be more advantageous for the state. In Germany, for example, according to the case law of the Federal Fiscal Court, the decisive factor for classifying a tax claim as an insolvency claim within the meaning of § 38 of the InsO is the time at which the substantive (dependent) chargeable event occurs; the accrual or due date of the tax on expiry of the assessment period (in the case of income taxes)[38] or tax period (in the case of VAT)[39] is irrelevant. If the chargeable event occurs after insolvency proceedings are opened, the tax in question is classified not as an insolvency claim but as a preferential liability pursuant to § 55(1) No. 1 of the InsO, ranking ahead of all other claims for settlement out of the insolvency estate pursuant to § 53 of the InsO.[40] In this context, the Federal Fiscal Court takes the view that a legal act by the insolvency administrator is not required for the classification of a tax claim as a preferential liability pursuant to § 55(1) No. 1 of the InsO.[41] If the taxable event occurs before the opening of the insolvency proceedings, and the proceedings are opened intra-year, the uniform income tax must be allocated to the periods before and after the insolvency proceedings commence.[42] According to this interpretation, income taxes triggered by the liquidation of hidden reserves, in particular the sale of real estate in insolvency proceedings, do not qualify as insolvency claims.[43] In Austria, an interpretation such as that in Germany, in which the time of the realization of the chargeable event is decisive for the classification of a tax claim as an insolvency claim, is, in principle, not possible. This is because the Austrian Insolvency Code (s. 46 No. 2 of the IO) stipulates that the circumstances triggering the tax liability are decisive for the classification of a tax claim as an insolvency claim.[44] This is in line with the case law of Germany's Federal Court of Justice.[45]

---

[37] See Fries, *Fiskusprivilegien* (2020) 59ff.
[38] BFH, 16 May 2013–IV R 23/11 = BStBl. II 2013, 759.
[39] BFH, 9 December 2010–V R 22/10 = BStBl. II 2011, 996.
[40] BFH, 9 December 2014–X R 12/12, BStBl. II 2016, 852.
[41] BFH, 7 July 2020–X R 13/19 = BStBl. II 2021, 174 (income tax); BFH, 10 July 2019–X R 31/16 = BFHE 265, 300 (income tax); BFH, 5 April 2017–II R 30/15 = BStBl. II 2017, 971 (inheritance tax); BFH, 3 August 2016–X R 25/14 = BFH/NV 2017, 317 (income tax); BFH, 9 February 2011–XI R 35/09 = BStBl. II 2011, 1000 (VAT). See also Onusseit's criticism concerning income tax, *ZInsO* (2021) 894.
[42] BFH, 27 October 2020–VIII R 19/18 = BFHE 271, 15.
[43] BFH, 16 May 2013–IV R 23/11 = BStBl. II 2013, 759 marginal no. 23ff.
[44] See Supreme Court of Justice of 24 August 2011, 3 Ob 103/11.
[45] BGH, 22 September 2011–IX ZB 121/11 = NZI 2011, 408.

According to this, only the basis of the claim under the law of obligations must have arisen before the opening of the insolvency proceedings; it is irrelevant whether the claim itself has already arisen or is due. In France,[46] the classification of a tax claim as an insolvency claim or as a preferential liability is not determined solely by the realization of the substantive chargeable event. Rather, it is also necessary for the claim to have arisen in a certain way with regard to the proceedings in order to qualify as a preferential liability. As far as can be seen, the details have not yet been clarified by case law.

In balancing the tension within the State's dual responsibility, a further relevant aspect is whether the avoidance in insolvency covers taxes. The Seventh Senate of Germany's Federal Fiscal Court answered in the negative with reference to the inadmissibility of set-off under § 96(1) No. 3 of the InsO in conjunction with §§ 129 et seq. of the InsO.[47] It reasoned that tax claims arise by operation of law pursuant to § 38 of the AO, and thus the legal act required for the insolvency avoidance was lacking. The Ninth Civil Senate of Germany's Federal Court of Justice later ruled that tax claims are linked to legal acts—such as the brewing of beer in connection with beer tax or the provision of services in connection with VAT/input tax—and are thus subject to avoidance in insolvency.[48] The Seventh Senate of Germany's Federal Fiscal Court then followed the case law of the Ninth Civil Senate of the Federal Court of Justice.[49] However, the Fifth Senate of Germany's Federal Fiscal Court takes the view that the tax calculation pursuant to § 16 of the German VAT Act (*Umsatzsteuergesetz*, UStG) does not constitute a set-off that may be avoided.[50] In the tax calculation pursuant to § 16 of the UStG, all VAT claims, input tax claims, and adjustment claims must be netted as dependent tax bases, and only after this netting does a substantive tax claim arise. If the tax calculation were contestable, the input tax claims could be added to the insolvency estate, whereas the State would have to declare its VAT claims in the insolvency schedule. This would also be the case if the result of the netting was zero.[51]

10.18

The balancing of the tension within the State's dual responsibility is also influenced by the inadmissibility of set-off under insolvency law. On the prohibition of set-off pursuant to § 96(1) No. 3 of the InsO in conjunction with § 129 et seq. of the InsO in Germany, see the explanations above. Pursuant to § 96(1) No. 1 of the InsO, if the principal claim (tax refund claim of the debtor) against which the insolvency creditor (the State as the holder of a tax claim) wants to set off is established only after commencement of insolvency proceedings, there is no trust that is worthy of protection, and the set-off is inadmissible. The Federal Fiscal Court interprets this provision from a tax perspective and considers it decisive whether the debtor's tax refund claim arose under

10.19

---

[46] See Fries, *Fiskusprivilegien* (2020) 84ff.

[47] BFH, 16 November 2004–VII R 75/03 = BStBl. II 2006, 193.

[48] BGH, 9 July 2009–IX ZR 86/08 = ZIP 2009, 1674.

[49] BFH, 2 November 2010–VII R 6/10 = BStBl. II 2011, 374 and BFH, 2 November 2010–VII R 62/10 = BStBl. II 2011, 439.

[50] BFH, 24 November 2011–V R 13/11 = BStBl. II 2012, 298.

[51] On contesting insolvency proceedings on taxes in Germany, France, the United States, and Australia, see the overview in Fries, *Fiskusprivilegien* (2020) 90ff.

292 ASPECTS OF TAX LAW

substantive law before the opening of insolvency proceedings (set-off is not prohibited) or afterwards (set-off is prohibited). In particular, the Federal Fiscal Court is of the opinion that a tax refund claim—regardless of the type of tax—based on an overpayment prior to the insolvency proceedings, as a claim subject to a condition precedent, is already established prior to the insolvency proceedings according to § 96(1) No. 1 of the InsO, with the consequence that an offset with an insolvency claim—regardless of the type of tax—is admissible.[52] In practice, this interpretation reduces the scope of application of the set-off prohibition under § 96(1) No. 1 of the InsO.[53] If the automatic stay has been applied in an insolvency proceeding in the United States under 11 U.S.C. §362, the Inland Revenue Service (IRS) generally cannot use its right of set-off without obtaining relief from the stay. The Bankruptcy Abuse Prevention and Consumer Protection Act of 2005 changed this to allow the IRS to offset pre-petition income tax liabilities against pre-petition income tax overpayments without obtaining relief from the automatic stay pursuant to 11 U.S.C. §362(b)(26). Note that 11 U.S.C. §362(b)(26) is limited to income tax. Courts have held that an income tax overpayment becomes property of the taxpayer 'at midnight on December 31 on the taxable year in which the payment occurred'. Thus, some courts have ruled that set-off is inadmissible if the insolvency petition was filed before that time. In contrast, some courts have held that income tax overpayments are contingent property interests that do not become part of the insolvency estate if the tax overpayment is less than the pre-existing debt owed.[54]

B. Regulations on Insolvency-Proof Legal Positions

10.20   The balancing of the tension within the State's dual responsibility in the distribution of the insolvency estate described above results in economic disadvantages for the State. This applies regardless of whether the tax claim has prior ranking in the distribution of the insolvency estate. In Germany, the disadvantages become particularly evident when the insolvency court is notified of a deficiency of assets pursuant to §§ 208 et seq. of the InsO. In this case, the tax claims that are treated as preferential claims are satisfied subordinately in the distribution of the insolvency estate. Therefore, it is more advantageous for the state if certain assets of the debtor are assigned to its tax claim, because these assets are then available to satisfy the tax claim in the event of insolvency. Such assignments can take one of two forms: collecting or holding taxes in trust for the State or automatically creating collateral in the debtor's assets for the benefit of the tax claim.

10.21   Germany's tax laws do not provide for collecting or holding taxes in trust. Case law has not considered this in connection with VAT and wage tax, although the entrepreneur owes these taxes in the interest of the State. Regarding VAT, the CJEU has explicitly ruled that the entrepreneur is 'acting as a tax collector on behalf of the state and in the

---

[52] BFH, 15 October 2019–VII R 31/17 = BStBl. II 2023, 262.
[53] See Kahlert, *DStR* (2020) 1993.
[54] See *In re: Larry Edward Wood et al.*, No. 5:2019cv00302 (S.D.W. Va. 2019).

interest of the state'.[55] Accordingly, the taxpayer is only formally the debtor of VAT and must therefore be taxed in a neutral manner.[56] If the State were the trustee, it would be entitled to segregation pursuant to § 47 of the InsO, and it would not have to rely on the insolvency quota as part of the distribution of the assets. According to the case law of Germany's Federal Court of Justice, the segregation of an asset as trust property requires that the asset has been transferred directly from the settlor's assets to the trustee's assets.[57] This requirement was not met in the case of wage tax because the wage tax was paid from the employer's assets and not from the employee's assets. Germany's Federal Court of Justice did not consider whether the State could be entitled to segregation because the employer could hold the trust property in the interest of the State.[58] However, the direct transfer of assets required by Germany's Federal Court of Justice would also be lacking in this respect. The same applies to VAT. This is because neither the service recipient nor the State transfers its own assets to the entrepreneur: the service recipient owes a dependent purchase price share in the amount of the turnover tax,[59] and the entrepreneur owes the turnover tax as a monetary obligation.[60] In principle, Germany's tax laws do not provide for the automatic creation of collateral in the debtor's assets for tax claims. There are only two exceptions. First, according to § 76 of the AO, goods liable to excise, import, or export duty shall serve as a guarantee for the taxes due on those goods (liability *in rem*), irrespective of any third-party rights. Pursuant to § 51(1) No. 4 of the InsO, § 76 of the AO gives rise to a right of segregation. However, the creation of the liability *in rem* pursuant to § 76 of the AO is contestable pursuant to §§ 129 et seq. of the InsO because it is linked to a legal act, for example brewing beer in connection with beer tax.[61] Second, according to § 12 of the Real Estate Tax Act (*Grundsteuergesetz*, GrStG), the real estate tax rests as a public charge on the taxable object. Since the owner must tolerate compulsory enforcement against the property pursuant to § 77(2) sentence 1 of the AO, § 12 of the GrStG has the effect of a real estate lien. Unlike the liability *in rem* under § 76 AO, the public charge under § 12 of the GrStG is not enforceable under §§ 129 et seq. of the InsO, as it is linked not to a legal act but exclusively to the ownership of a real estate item.

In the United States, § 7501(a) of the Internal Revenue Code stipulates: **10.22**

> Whenever any person is required to collect or withhold any internal revenue tax from any other person and to pay over such tax to the United States, the amount of tax so collected or withheld shall be held to be a special fund *in trust for* the United States.

---

[55] CJEU Case C-271/06 *Netto Supermarkt*, DStR 2008, 450 marginal no. 21; CJEU Case C-10/92, EuGHE 1993, I-5105 marginal no. 25.

[56] CJEU Case C-664/16 *Vadan*, ECLI:EU:C:2018:933 marginal no. 38.

[57] BGH, 10 February 2011–IX ZR 49/19 = BGHZ 188, 317, III.1.a).

[58] BGH, 22 January 2004–IX ZR 39/03 = BGHZ 157, 350, II.4.b.

[59] See BGH, 8 May 2008–IX ZR 229/06 = ZIP 2008, 1127 marginal no. 9.

[60] Also Fries, *Fiskusprivilegien* (n 7) 39; Witfeld, *Das Umsatzsteuerverfahren und die Insolvenz* (Verlag C.H. Beck oHG 2016) 52–74. For another opinion see Stadie, '§18' in Rau and Dürrwächter (Verlag Dr Otto Schmidt KG 2020) § 18 Appendix 2, marginal no. 81ff. (as of April 2020).

[61] BGH, 9 July 2009–IX ZR 86/08 = ZIP 2009, 1674.

294   ASPECTS OF TAX LAW

The amount of such fund shall be assessed, collected, and paid in the same manner and subject to the same provisions and limitations (including penalties) as are applicable with respect to the taxes from which such fund arose [emphasis by the author].

Payroll taxes (ss 3401 et seq. of the Internal Revenue Code) fall under this provision.[62] Whether the sales taxes regulated by the federal government fall under this provision depends on their structure in the relevant State.[63] If the retained funds are still in the assets of the company, they do not belong to the insolvency estate, and the State has a right of segregation. This follows from a decision of the US Supreme Court according to which, in the case of a trust under § 7501(a) of the Internal Revenue Code, the voluntary payment of taxes from the retained funds is not contestable under 11 U.S.C. §547. According to the US Supreme Court, a separation of assets, which is, in principle, required for the recognition of a trust under US law, is not necessary. The court reasoned that § 7501(a) of the Internal Revenue Code refers to a specific sum of money and not to specific funds.[64] § 6321 of the Internal Revenue Code reads:

If any person liable to pay any tax neglects or refuses to pay the same after demand, the amount (including any interest, additional amount, addition to tax, or assessable penalty, together with any costs that may accrue in addition thereto) *shall be a lien* in favor of the United States upon all property and rights to property, whether real or personal, belonging to such person [emphasis by the author].

A tax lien under § 6321 of the Internal Revenue Code does not create a first-priority right. Thus, the tax creditor shall not be placed in a better position than under the catalogue of privileges in 11 U.S.C. §507 in a Chapter 7 proceeding, and the order of priority under 11 U.S.C. §724(b) shall be observed. A prerequisite for the accrual of a tax lien under § 6321 of the Internal Revenue Code is the disclosure of the tax lien. According to § 547(c)(6) of the Internal Revenue Code, the creation of a statutory lien is generally not contestable. However, this is the case only if it was published in time before the opening of the proceedings (11 U.S.C. §§544(a)(1), 545(2) and 6323(a)).[65]

10.23   The trust in France (Arts 2011 et seq. of the *Code Civil*) corresponds to the trust in Germany. Comparable to Germany, VAT and wage tax—as far as can be seen—are not treated as trust property in France and are therefore not subject to a right of segregation.[66] The mortgage regulated in Art. 1929 ter of the *Code Général des Impôts* (*hypothèque légale du Trésor public*) secures all types of taxes, arises automatically by operation of law at the same time as the tax claim, and is not contestable. Its ranking

---

[62]   Supreme Court of the United States 4 June 1990, *In re Harry P. Begier*, 496 US 53, 54.

[63]   For the California affirmative, see United States Court of Appeals for the Ninth Circuit 18 June 1986, *In re Shank*, 792 F.2d 829, 831. In the negative, for Washington, see United States Bankruptcy Appellate Panel for the Ninth Circuit 30 September 1994, *In re Raiman*, 172 B.R. 933, 940.

[64]   Supreme Court of the United States, *In re Harry P. Begier* 54.

[65]   United States District Court for the Eastern District of New York 2 June 1993, *In Re Federation of Puerto Rico Organizations of Brownsville, Inc.* 155 BR 44, 48.

[66]   See Fries, *Fiskusprivilegien* (2020) 42.

is determined by the time of entry in the register, which is possible only when the recovery of the tax claim begins, with certain creditors, in particular employees, having priority.[67] Another privilege (*privilège du Trésor public*) arises by operation of law at the time the claim arises and also favours the State. With regard to the form and ranking, Art. 2327 of the *Code Civil* refers to the Tax Code, in particular to Arts 1920 et seq. of the *Code Général des Impôts*. According to this, in favour of direct and indirect taxes, there is a general privilege over movable property, which, however, is preceded by certain other claims. These are claims of employees, claims of social security funds, court fees, and claims that have been established after the opening of proceedings. In certain cases, according to Art. 1929 ter of the *Code Général des Impôts*, the State must have its privilege entered in a public register, otherwise the State is to be treated as an unsecured creditor.[68]

C. Regulations on the Managing Director's Tax Liability

Even if, as described above, (a) tax claims—whether prior ranked or not—are included **10.24** in the distribution of the insolvency estate and (b) insolvency-proof legal positions exist for tax claims on certain assets of the debtor, the question arises as to whether the duty to secure insolvency estate associated with the ordering of (preliminary) insolvency proceedings takes priority over the duty to pay taxes under public law. The answer to this question determines whether the managing director is subject to tax liability if he or she complies with the duty to secure insolvency estate, that is no taxes are paid. In Germany, this question arose primarily with regard to preliminary insolvency proceedings.[69] For insolvency proceedings filed on or after 1 January 2021, § 15b(8) of the InsO solves the managing director's conflict of duties in the event that the debtor is illiquid (*Zahlungsunfähigkeit*, § 17 of the InsO) or overindebted (*Überschuldung*, § 19 of the InsO) by withdrawing the duty to pay tax if the insolvency filing is in time and the insolvency proceedings are properly conducted, in which case, the managing director is not subject to tax liability. Australian law contains a comparable regulation (s. 588FGA of the Corporation Act 2001), under which the managing director must pay wage taxes and VAT or initiate insolvency proceedings.[70] If the managing director settles a tax claim that would have been contestable, which constitutes a breach of duty under insolvency law, he or she is liable.

---

[67] See Fries, *Fiskusprivilegien* (2020) 43f.
[68] See ibid 44 ff.
[69] For details see Kahlert, *Restrukturierungssteuerrecht—Steuerliche Aspekte einer Restrukturierung nach StaRUG und InsO* (Verlag C.H. Beck oHG 2022) marginal no. 390 ff.
[70] See Fries, *Fiskusprivilegien* (2020) 127ff.

296 ASPECTS OF TAX LAW

D. Taxes Arising during the Insolvency Proceedings

10.25 In Germany, as mentioned in section III.A above, a tax claim is classified as a preferential liability pursuant to § 55(1) No. 1 of the InsO if the chargeable event arises after insolvency proceedings are opened or, in a case covered by § 55(4) of the InsO, during the period of provisional insolvency administration. In England and Wales, taxes arising during a liquidation or an administration are classified as expenses[71] and expenses in England and Wales rank higher in the order of payments than taxes classified as preferential debts. Thus, taxes classified as expenses enjoy greater protection than in Germany. The disadvantage is also evident when the insolvency court is notified of a deficiency of assets pursuant to §§ 208 et seq. of the InsO. In this case, tax claims that are treated as preferential claims are satisfied subordinately in the distribution of the insolvency estate.

IV. Resolving the Tension in the Relationship between the State and the Debtor

A. Restructuring

10.26 Balancing the tension within the State's dual responsibility plays an important role when the debtor is restructured. In Germany, the restructuring of a company in insolvency proceedings can be carried out by means of an insolvency plan (ss 217 et seq. of the InsO). In this case, the legal entity remains in existence. Otherwise, the restructuring can be carried out by transferring the assets of the company to a purchaser that continues the company. In this case, the legal entity is liquidated in the insolvency proceedings (see section IV.B below). Debt relief is a key restructuring tool in the event of an insolvency plan. A distinction must be made between taxes that have arisen up to the debt relief and taxes that arise due to the debt relief of private creditors. From a tax perspective, a debt relief of private creditors regularly releases the liability to income, which could trigger an income tax burden. This would regularly call the restructuring of the enterprise into question.

10.27 In Germany, a new act on the further development of restructuring and insolvency law (*Sanierungsrechtsfortentwicklungsgesetz*, SanInsFoG) entered into force on 1 January 2021 pursuant to Art. 25 of the SanInsFoG.[72] Under Art. 1 of the SanInsFoG, the German legislature created the Corporate Stabilization and Restructuring Act (*Unternehmensstabilisierungs- und Restrukturierungsgesetz*, StaRUG). The legislation

---

[71] See LexisNexis, 'Restructuring in Insolvency: Tax—Overview', <www.lexisnexis.com/uk/lexispsl/tax/docum ent/393773/5KKK-F3G1-F18C-V461-00000-00/Restructuring_and_insolvency__tax_overview> accessed 13 January 2024.

[72] Act on the Further Development of Restructuring and Insolvency Law (*Sanierungsrechtsfortentwicklungss etz*, SanInsFoG) of 22 December 2020, BGBl. I 2020, 3256.

contains two new instruments to prevent insolvency, namely the restructuring plan (§§ 2–93 StaRUG) and the restructuring settlement (§§ 94–100 StaRUG). The restructuring plan serves to implement Title II of the EU Restructuring Directive.[73] Neither the provisions on the restructuring plan nor the provisions on the restructuring settlement are assessed as insolvency proceedings. This is primarily based on the fact that the debtor may choose to include one, multiple, or all creditors in these proceedings and that individual enforcement applies or continues to apply. Therefore, the tax consequences described above, which are linked to insolvency proceedings, in principle, cannot apply accordingly. Rather, the relationship between the StaRUG and tax law must be determined separately. Since the StaRUG does not contain any special tax regulations, this determination rests on general principles.[74] The rules on the tax exemption of restructuring gains (ss 3a, 3c(4) of the the German Income Tax Act (*Einkommensteuergesetz*, EStG), § 7b of the German Trade Tax Act (*Gewerbesteuergesetz*, GewStG)) outlined below are excepted. These rules apply, in principle, regardless of the legal form of the debtor and how the debt relief comes about. The explanatory memorandum to § 3a of the EStG therefore rightly assumes that, in addition to debt relief in insolvency proceedings, debt relief based on the Restructuring Directive is also covered.[75]

In Germany, an insolvency plan (ss 217 et seq. of the InsO) covers all claims that classify as insolvency claims within the meaning of § 38 of the InsO. Thus, all tax claims classified as insolvency claims and covered by the insolvency plan are dischargeable. Germany's Federal Tax Court held that an income tax claim due to debt relief in an insolvency plan is classified not as an insolvency claim but as a preferential claim that is not dischargeable.[76] The decisive factor is therefore whether any tax burden can be prevented. In Germany, this has always been the case for restructuring a business under certain conditions, regardless of the legal form of the business and how the debt relief comes about.   **10.28**

As early as the 1920s, the German Reich Fiscal Court examined whether, even if creditors waive claims in order to rescue their business partner (the debtor), taxable income arises for the debtor on the basis of the determination of profit by comparison of business assets, thereby triggering income tax or corporation tax and trade tax.[77] The Court found that no tax liability arose, thus creating a framework that, notwithstanding changes in the dogmatic justifications for tax exemption over time, remains valid and is now regulated by § 3a of the EStG. This regulation, in principle, applies regardless   **10.29**

---

[73] Directive (EU) 2019/1023 of the European Parliament and of the Council of 20 June 2019 on preventive restructuring frameworks, on discharge of debt and disqualifications, and on measures to increase the efficiency of procedures concerning restructuring, insolvency and discharge of debt, and amending Directive (EU) 2017/1132 (Directive on Restructuring and Insolvency), Official Journal 2019 L 172, 18.

[74] For details see Kahlert, *Restrukturierungssteuerrecht* (n 69) marginal no. 140ff. See Kahlert and Schumann, *DStR* (2021) 2741, and Kahlert, *Restrukturierungssteuerrecht* (n 69) marginal no. 461ff. on the cross-border impact of restructuring plans and restructuring settlements regarding tax claims.

[75] See *Beschlussempfehlung und Bericht des Finanzausschusses*, BT printed paper 18/12128, 30f.

[76] BFH, 15 November 2018–XI B 49/18 = BFH/NV 2019, 208.

[77] See Kahlert, *ZIP* (2016) 2107 and Seer, *FR* (2014) 721.

298 ASPECTS OF TAX LAW

of the legal form of the debtor and how the debt relief comes about; pursuant to § 8(1) of German Corporate Income Tax Act (*Körperschaftsteuergesetz*, KStG), § 3a of the EStG applies to the taxation of corporations. Thus, even according to the explanatory memorandum to the law, debt relief in an insolvency plan (ss 217 et seq. of the InsO) is covered by § 3a(1) sentence 1 of the EStG, unless it is not aimed at breaking up the company.[78] This means that the tax exemption of the restructuring proceeds is not automatically linked to the insolvency plan. Various conditions must be met for the gains from a debt discharge to be tax-exempt under § 3a of the EStG and not subject to income tax or corporation tax. Section 7b of the GewStG contains a corresponding provision for trade tax that refers to

- the enterprise's need to be restructured,
- the enterprise's ability to be restructured,
- the suitability of the debt discharge for operational reasons, and
- the creditors' intention to restructure.

10.30   However, in Germany, the tax exemption for the restructuring gains comes at a price for the debtor. Thus,

- under § 3a(1) sentence 2 of the EStG, tax options must be exercised in the enterprise to be restructured in the year in which a restructuring gain is achieved (restructuring year) and in the following year, reducing profits;
- under § 3a(3) of the EStG, tax-reducing items (including loss carryforwards) must be reduced under the conditions specified therein;
- under § 3c(4) of the EStG, reductions in business assets or business expenses that are directly economically related to tax-exempt restructuring gains within the meaning of § 3a of the EStG, irrespective of the assessment period in which the restructuring gain arises, may be deducted only under the conditions set out in that provision.

10.31   The European Commission issued a comfort letter to conclude the notification procedure initiated by Germany in connection with §§ 3a and 3c(4) of the EStG and § 7b of the GewStG.[79] This letter sets out the view that these provisions in any case constitute 'old' aid that is protected because the criteria for tax exemption have been in force in Germany since the 1920s. The European Commission has thus refrained from commenting on whether the provisions on the tax exemption of restructuring gains constitute inadmissible aid under substantive law. In the literature, it is rightly argued that the balancing of the tension within the State's dual responsibility in the relationship between the State and the debtor is required by constitution and based on the criteria set out by the Reich Fiscal Court and regulated today in §§ 3a and 3c(4) of the EStG

---

[78] See *Beschlussempfehlung und Bericht des Finanzausschusses,* BT printed paper 18/12128, 31.
[79] See BT printed paper 19/5595, 92.

and § 7b of the GewStG.[80] According to the case law of the CJEU, the examination of aid under Union law pursuant to Art. 107(1) of the Treaty on the Functioning of the European Union (TFEU) first requires the reference system to be determined. This involves identifying the generally applicable or 'normal' tax regime of national tax law. If the regulation in question does not deviate from the reference system, no inadmissible aid exists for this reason alone. Any justification of a deviation from the reference system is irrelevant.[81] In my opinion, the constitutionally required balancing described is the generally applicable or 'normal' tax regulation, which is why inadmissible aid is ruled out.[82]

The German restructuring clause in § 8c(1a) of the KStG stipulates that the non-deductibility of losses in the event of an acquisition of an equity interest pursuant to § 8c(1) of the KStG does not apply if the equity interest is acquired for the purpose of restructuring the business operations of the corporation. The European Commission and the European General Court found that the restructuring clause constituted inadmissible aid.[83] In 2018, the CJEU ruled that the restructuring clause resulted in a return to the generally applicable or 'normal' tax regime, namely the use of losses pursuant to § 10d of the EStG.[84] Since the European Commission had overlooked this and thus used the wrong reference system as a basis, the Court declared the European Commission's decision null and void for this reason alone. In a press release in 2020, the European Commission stated that it had examined § 8c(1a) of the KStG on the basis of the broader frame of reference provided by the CJEU and had come to the conclusion that this provision did not deviate from the general rules and thus did not give distressed enterprises any selective advantages over other enterprises.[85]

10.32

In Austria, a gain from a debt relief in a restructuring plan arises from the fulfilment of the agreed quota. Any resulting tax claim is not covered by the restructuring plan as a future income tax claim.[86] Section 36 of the Austrian Income Tax Act (*Einkommensteuergesetz*, EStG) and § 23a of the Austrian Corporate Income Tax Act (*Körperschaftsteuergesetz*, KStG) provide for a different tax assessment or tax calculation, which is intended to relieve the tax burden on restructuring. According to these rules, the tax with and without the debt relief is calculated and the difference is multiplied by a relief ratio. The amount is deducted from the tax result, including the profits from the debts relieved. The prerequisite is that the tax is based on debt relief for the purpose of restructuring.

10.33

---

[80] Krumm in Brandis and Heuermann, *Ertragsteuerrecht* (Verlag Franz Vahlen 2022) s. 3a EStG marginal no. 10 (as of December 2022).

[81] CJEU Case C-203/16 *P. Andres (Insolvenz Heitkamp BauHolding)*.

[82] For details see Kahlert, *Restrukturierungssteuerrecht* marginal no. 116ff.

[83] CJEU Case T-287/11 *Heitkamp BauHolding/Kommission*, ECLI:EU:T:2016:60.

[84] CJEU Case C-203/16 *P. Andres (Insolvenz Heitkamp BauHolding)*.

[85] See <https://germany.representation.ec.europa.eu/news/eu-wettbewerbsaufsicht-gibt-deutsche-sanierungs klausel-frei-2020-01-22_de> accessed 13 January 2024.

[86] See VwGH, 24 May 1993, 92/15/0041.

300 ASPECTS OF TAX LAW

10.34 In the United States, under Chapter 11 (Reorganization) of the Bankruptcy Code, the scope of discharge regarding tax claims depends, among other factors, on whether the debtor is an individual or a corporation. For individuals in Chapter 11 cases, the following tax debts (including interest) are non-dischargeable (see 11 U.S.C. §523): taxes entitled to eighth priority, taxes for which no return was filed, taxes for which a return was filed late after two years before the bankruptcy petition was filed, taxes for which a fraudulent return was filed, and taxes that the debtor wilfully attempted to evade or defeat. Different rules apply to corporations. A corporation in a Chapter 11 case may receive a broad discharge when the reorganization plan is confirmed; however, secured and priority claims must be satisfied under the plan. The reorganization plan can provide payment of unsecured eighth-priority taxes, with post-confirmation interest, over a period of five years from the date of the order relief issued by the bankruptcy court. There is an exception to discharge for cases in which the debtor filed a fraudulent tax return or wilfully attempted to evade or defeat taxes.[87] According to § 108(a)(1)(A) of the Internal Revenue Code, debt cancelled in a title 11 case is not included in the income. In return, pursuant to § 108(b) of the Internal Revenue Code, the amount excluded from gross income shall be applied to reduce the tax attributes of the taxpayer as provided in para. (2), especially any net operating loss for the taxable year of the discharge and any net operating loss carryover to such taxable year.

B. Liquidation

10.35 In Germany, after insolvency proceedings are opened for a corporation, liquidation taxation pursuant to § 11(7) of the KStG in conjunction with § 11(1)–(6) of the KStG may be considered instead of profit determination by comparison of business assets pursuant to § 8(1) of the KStG in conjunction with § 5(1) of the EStG. According to Germany's Federal Fiscal Court, liquidation taxation applies if the company is not continued but the liquidation of the company is initiated.[88] If the corporation is continued (in which case, § 8(1) of the KStG in conjunction with § 5(1) of the EStG applies), Germany's Federal Fiscal Court takes the view that its liabilities are not to be dissolved with an effect on income. The mere fact that the debtor is insolvent does not mean that a legally existing obligation must be removed from the commercial or tax accounts, because the decisive factor is whether the creditor is determined to assert its existing claim.[89] If the corporation is not continued (in which case, § 11(7) of the KStG in conjunction with § 11(1)–(6) of the KStG applies), Germany's tax authorities are of the opinion that its liabilities remaining after the final distribution and termination of the insolvency proceedings are not to be dissolved with an effect on income, notwithstanding the subsequent deletion of the company from the commercial register

---

[87] IRS, 'Bankruptcy Tax Guide' 31 ff.
[88] BFH, 23 January 2013–I R 35/12 = BStBl. II 2013, 508, marginal no. 9.
[89] BFH, 19 August 2020–XI R 32/18 = BFHE 270, 344, marginal no. 24 ff.

pursuant to § 394 of the German Act on Proceedings in Family Matters and in Matters of Non-Contentious Jurisdiction (*Gesetz über das Verfahren in Familiensachen und in den Angelegenheiten der freiwilligen Gerichtsbarkeit*, FamFG). The tax authorities justify their view by stating that the economic burden required for the (remaining) liabilities to be recognized as liabilities continues to exist because the creditors can assert corresponding (remaining) claims even after the insolvency proceedings have been terminated in accordance with § 201(1) of the InsO.[90] This view is correct because, in the event that assets later come to light, a supplementary liquidation can be considered in which these assets can be used to satisfy the creditor's claim.[91] If the (remaining) claims had been extinguished, this would be ruled out. Against this background, it is possible to reorganize a corporation in such a way that it is transferred to an investor by means of an asset deal without dissolving the liabilities. If certain rights that are necessary for the continuation of the corporation (e.g. rental agreements) would be lost through an asset deal, a conversion can be considered: assets of the corporation are first spun off to a subsidiary (universal legal succession instead of single legal succession), and then the shares in the subsidiary are transferred to an investor.[92] In both cases, the tax consequences of the asset deal must be considered.

In Austria, too, liabilities continue to exist in the context of an insolvency-related liquidation due to liquidation taxation. Unlike in reorganization proceedings, insolvency proceedings do not lead to a relief of debts. They continue to be recognized, and there is no impact on income. Austria's Federal Administration Court upheld this view against the view of the tax authorities in 2019.[93] **10.36**

---

[90] OFD Frankfurt/M., 3 August 2018–S 2743 A–12–St 525 = juris; OFD NRW, Kurzinformation ESt Nr 46/2014, 21 November 2014 = DStR 2015, 699; see also Kahlert, *DStR* (2014) 1906.

[91] See Haas in Noack, Servatius, and Haas, *GmbH-Gesetz* (23rd edn, Verlag C.H. Beck oHG 2022) § 60 marginal no. 104ff.

[92] For details see Hölzle and Kahlert, *ZIP* (2017) 510.

[93] VwGH, 4 September 2019–Ro 2017/130009. See also Kanduth-Kristen and Komarek, *ÖStZ* (2015) 506.

11

Aspects of Labour Law

Laura Carballo Piñeiro

I. Introduction

11.01 Insolvency and labour are two distinct fields of law that are obliged to interact in the event of the employer's (vicinity of) insolvency. However, such an interaction varies among countries, depending on the weight placed on the worker protection principle by the relevant State. The starting point is, nevertheless, the prevalence of insolvency law over other legal matters on account of the exceptionality of this regime developed to tackle an otherwise exceptional situation. This approach has not changed despite the socio-legal evolution of insolvency law towards becoming a preventative tool in order to avoid actual insolvency, among other reasons, to preserve employment. In this vein, the functions of insolvency law—liquidation or reorganization—dominate any labour law issue that might come up during the relevant proceedings, and the insolvency objectives are usually prioritized over the worker protection principle.[1] Notwithstanding this, important concessions are made to this principle, as discussed in this chapter.

11.02 A quick overview of the key objectives for an effective and efficient insolvency law as summarized, for example, by the United Nations Commission on International Trade Law (UNCITRAL) *Legislative Guide on Insolvency Law* reveals that none of them mention worker protection. However, the reference is implied in the objective of insolvency law to provide certainty in the market to promote economic stability and growth. To this end, national legislation should provide a toolkit capable of promoting the restructuring of viable businesses and thus the maintenance of jobs, as well as the efficient closure of non-viable businesses and, where appropriate, the transfer of assets, if possible, as a going concern.[2] In this vein, the implied relationship between insolvency and labour is well portrayed in the United Nations (UN) Sustainable Development Goal (SDG) No. 8 on Economic Growth and Decent Work, whose target 8.3 requests countries to 'promote development-oriented policies that support productive activities, decent job creation, entrepreneurship, creativity and innovation, and encourage the formalization and growth of micro-, small- and medium-sized enterprises, including

---

[1] Common law countries, in particular the United Kingdom, name the weak party to an employment contract 'employee' while 'worker' is a broader term than employee and includes self-employed people. However, and for our purposes, both worker and employee will be used as synonymous in this chapter.
[2] See UNCITRAL, *Legislative Guide on Insolvency Law* (UNCITRAL 2005) 10 para. 4.

Laura Carballo Piñeiro, *Aspects of Labour Law* In: *The Anatomy of Corporate Insolvency Law*. Edited by: Reinhard Bork and Renato Mangano, Oxford University Press. © Laura Carballo Piñeiro 2024. DOI: 10.1093/oso/9780198852094.003.0011

through access to financial services'.[3] COVID-19 pandemic-related measures, such as reforms on available insolvency proceedings and adoption of compensation schemes, including furloughed schemes,[4] vividly illustrate the obvious interaction between capital and labour when it comes to sustaining businesses in distress and avoiding liquidation.

As discussed in Chapter 1 'What Is Insolvency Law?', the main task of insolvency law is not the preservation of employment. As a debt collection device, insolvency law primarily focuses on balancing competing interests, seeking to protect creditors' rights while managing the interests of the debtor, shareholders, and customers. This narrative sets aside workers' rights, whose preservation is considered a collateral task, in particular because job security is seriously compromised by the employer's insolvency. At the same time, insolvency law cannot ignore that the company's workforce is a relevant asset and a serious liability and thus plays a critical role in any insolvency plan, be it in a positive or a negative manner. Against this backdrop, legislations might specifically address this situation by granting workers and their representatives information, participation, and consultation rights, as well as conditioning the transfer of the business as part of an insolvency plan to the continuation of employment contracts and relationships.

11.03

Workers' interests are mainly addressed from a creditors' rights perspective in insolvency law, that is as someone entitled to a claim against the debtor or the insolvency estate, being labour and employment law objectives only embedded in the type and extent of priority provided to these creditors. As indicated by the World Bank, '[w]orkers are a vital part of an enterprise and careful consideration should be given to balancing the rights of employees with those of other creditors'.[5] In practice, insolvencies result not only in job losses for workers but also in loss of wages and other related benefits. Workers are considered among the most vulnerable creditors because they lack the ability to diversify their risk, even in the event that they learn about their employer being in the vicinity of insolvency, due to a lack of prospects in the labour market and mobility restrictions as well as lack of a voice in insolvency matters.[6] This lack of agency places them in a passive position that forces them to wait to be paid until the insolvency proceeding is over. And their vulnerability does not shield them against the complexities of insolvency law with which they have to deal in order to claim for their rights. Against this backdrop, social policy considerations might inform the issuance of

11.04

---

[3] Tuula Linna, 'Insolvency Proceedings from a Sustainability Perspective', International Insolvency Review, 28(2) (2019) 210.

[4] See, among others, Emily Ghio, Gert-Jan Boon, David Ehmke, Jennifer Gant, Line Langkjaer, and Eugenio Vaccari, 'Harmonizing Insolvency Law in the EU: New Thoughts on Old Ideas in the Wake of the COVID-19 Pandemic', International Insolvency Review, 30 (2021) 1, where the six countries subjected to examination have introduced different variations of furloughed schemes.

[5] World Bank, *Principles and Guidelines for Effective Insolvency and Creditor Rights Systems* (World Bank 2016) Principle C.12.4 (revised).

[6] Gordon Johnson, 'Insolvency and Social Protection: Employee Entitlements in the Event of Employer Insolvency', Organisation for Economic Co-operation and Development (2006) 1, 2.

304   ASPECTS OF LABOUR LAW

income safeguards such as employee priorities and insurance or guarantee protections. Depending on whether, and to what extent, these safeguards are regulated, they reflect the approach taken by a domestic insolvency law to worker protection in the event of an employer's insolvency.

11.05   This chapter next discusses the treatment granted to employment contracts from a comparative and a private international law perspective, which will take into consideration not only the legal approach to collective redundancies but also employment protection in the event of the business transfer, or part of it, as a result of an insolvency proceeding. The chapter then examines whether workers have a priority as regards other creditors and to what extent this is granted, followed by an examination of the role of insurance or guarantee schemes for workers made redundant because of the employer's insolvency in their protection. To this end, countries might opt for different combinations of employee priorities and guarantee schemes, as analysed in section V. The chapter ends by examining the director's liability as regards employees as a useful means to protect them in the event of the company's insolvency.

II. Employment Contracts and Employers' Insolvency

11.06   In the advent of the Fourth Industrial Revolution, economic growth still relies on workers' productivity, which is the most valuable asset of a country. For example, high levels of employment, productivity, and social cohesion, are interconnected objectives in 'Europe 2020: A European Strategy for Smart, Sustainable and Inclusive Growth', which seeks to address the challenges posed by a globalized economy that puts enormous pressure upon businesses to be competitive and significantly increases their risk of becoming insolvent. While the stigma associated with insolvency is still an issue in many countries, the regulatory framework has changed to facilitate entrepreneurship and address business failure. The focus is thus on the rescue of the company or the debtor's recovery, also as a means to preserve employment.[7] Nevertheless, that might happen through the sacrifice of the workers employed by the debtor at the time of the insolvency.

11.07   As a type of executory contract,[8] employment contracts and relationships are subject to the powers granted to the insolvency practitioner (IP) or the debtor in possession (DIP) to terminate or modify them with a view to achieving the insolvency objectives. Workers might be a burden for business reorganization or liquidation and thus would have to be made redundant or their conditions changed in order to make the

---

[7] Empirical studies point out that, in addition to creditors' interests, employment preservation is the main reason for restructuring. See Reinout D. Vriesendorp and Martin A. Gramatikov, 'Impact of the Financial Crisis: A Survey' (January 2010) European Banking Center Discussion Paper No. 2010–12; Center Discussion Paper Series No. 2010–42, <https://ssrn.com/abstract=1546987> accessed 14 January 2024.

[8] Jason Chuah, 'A Thematic and Comparative Critique' in Jason Chuah and Eugenio Vaccari (eds), *Executory Contracts in Insolvency Law: A Global Guide* (Edward Elgar 2019) 1, 4.

business viable again. The use of these powers by the IP/DIP is, nevertheless, a controversial decision, whose basis might be geared by statutory interventions, for example to protect workers and their information, participation, and consultation rights on company matters.[9] Again, this approach might have a downside (i.e. to be a restraint on the efforts to rehabilitate the business due to costly and time-consuming measures),[10] which has given rise to a discussion as to the real benefits of these mechanisms in terms of employment protection.[11] In short, the question to be answered by policymakers is whether worker protection should be suspended or abolished as part of the restructuring efforts, the objective being to make sure that the (new) company actually recovers and can create jobs.

More often than not, employers in distress would need to terminate employment contracts in order to increase the chances of their underperforming business or simply as a result of closing it down. However, and regardless of the insolvency situation, the termination of an employment contract is usually subject to certain conditions, as laid down by the International Labour Organization (ILO) Termination of Employment Convention, 1982 (No. 158). In addition to making dismissals fair only in specific circumstances,[12] employers are requested to provide workers with a reasonable notice for termination of employment contracts, or compensation is otherwise required.[13] More specifically, the convention calls for direct participation and consultation of worker representatives if terminations are due to reasons of an economic, technological, structural, or similar nature. In particular, consultation rights are granted with a view to monitoring any measures that might avert or minimize the number of redundancies but also to discussing measures that might alleviate the consequences of such

11.08

---

[9] For example, the European Union has been active in this field: Directive 98/59/EC of 20 July 1998 on the approximation of the laws of the Member States relating to collective redundancies [1998] OJ L 225/6 (Collective Redundancies Directive); Directive 2001/23/EC of 12 March 2001 on the approximation of the laws of the Member States relating to the safeguarding of employees' rights in the event of transfers of undertakings, businesses or parts of undertakings or businesses [2001] OJ L 82/16 (Acquired Rights Directive); Directive 2002/14/EC of 11 March 2002 establishing a general framework for informing and consulting employees in the European Community—Joint declaration of the European Parliament, the Council and the Commission on employee representation [2002] OJ L 80/29; Directive 2008/94/EC of the European Parliament and of the Council of 22 October 2008 on the protection of employees in the event of the insolvency of their employer [2008] OJ L 283/36 (Protection of Employees Directive); Directive 2009/38/EC of 6 May 2009 on the establishment of a European Works Council or a procedure in Community-scale undertakings and Community-scale groups of undertakings for the purposes of informing and consulting employees (Recast) [2009] OJ L 122/28; Directive (EU) 2019/1023 of 20 June 2019 on preventive restructuring frameworks, on discharge of debt and disqualifications, and on measures to increase the efficiency of procedures concerning restructuring, insolvency and discharge of debt, and amending Directive (EU) 2017/1132 (Directive on Restructuring and Insolvency) [2019] OJ L172/18.

[10] For a discussion of this matter in relation to the impact of the Acquired Rights Directive (n 9) on the efficacy of business rescue, see Jennifer L.L. Gant, *Balancing the Protection of Business and Employment in Insolvency: An Anglo-French Perspective* (Eleven International Publishing 2017).

[11] See, mong others, Chrispas Nyombi, 'Employees' Rights during Insolvency', International Journal of Law and Management, 55 (2013) 417–28; Nicolae Stef, 'Bankruptcy and the Difficulty of Firing', International Review of Law and Economics, 54 (2018) 85–94; Henrick Aalbers, Jan Adriaanse, Gert-Jan Boon, Jean-Pierre van der Rest, Reinout Vriesendorp, and Frank Van Wersch, 'Does Pre-Packed Bankruptcy Create Value? An Empirical Study of Postbankruptcy Employment Retention in the Netherlands', International Insolvency Review, 28 (2019) 320.

[12] See Arts 4–6 of the Termination of Employment Convention, 1982 (No. 158) (Termination of Employment Convention).

[13] See ibid Art. 11.

306 ASPECTS OF LABOUR LAW

terminations, such as finding alternative employment.[14] These rights have been implemented by countries depending on their political and socio-economic environment,[15] leading to divergences among them, also in respect of non-ratifying countries, which might only acknowledge information rights.[16]

11.09 From a comparative law perspective, the European Union provides an example of strong worker protection while striving for a 'balanced social and economic development' through the Collective Redundancies Directive.[17] Participation and consultation rights are not exhausted in this directive, but extended in particular by the Acquired Rights Directive.[18] More specifically, the former strives to level the playing field across the Union where, at the time of its adoption, two countries, France and Germany, already provided for employee protection in the event of the business transfer.[19] This protection might thus be triggered in a rescue by a firm sale, by a firm reorganization, or by any other transfer of the business within a liquidation or an out-of-court insolvency plan.[20] However, and in view of the fact that existing job preservation might collide with insolvency objectives, the question is whether an insolvency exception should be applied in these situations and thus exclude the safeguards in place in non-insolvency scenarios, in particular the obligation of the buyer to take over existing jobs and respect terms and conditions of employment agreed upon with the seller.

11.10 Support for the development of an insolvency exception is found on the flexibility embedded in restructuring toolkits, which should not be restrained by worker protection mechanisms. The latter are particularly weak in the United States, where the Model Employment Termination Act (1991) has not achieved harmonization purposes across the country and the powers of the IP/DIP to terminate employment contracts in insolvency proceedings, including those under Chapter 11 of the US Bankruptcy Code, are

---

[14] See ibid Art. 13. The following provision supplements this latter, requesting the employer to notify the competent authority of his or her intention to terminate any employment contracts because of the particular reasons mentioned in text such as insolvency.

[15] The Termination of Employment Convention (n 12) has been ratified by only 35 countries.

[16] See the Worker Adjustment and Retraining Notification (WARN) Act approved by the 100th United States Congress, Pub. L. 100-379 102 Stat 890, which requires notification of plant closings and mass lay-offs in advance.

[17] Collective Redundancies Directive (n 9), Recital 2. In contrast, the WARN Act (n 16) does not require consultations but only 60-day-in-advance notice to employees by employers with more than 100 workers of which different categories are excluded. The implementation of the Directive across the EU diverges, with some countries being close to the minimum standards therein enshrined, such as Hungary and the United Kingdom, and others being more pro-employee, as is the case of France. Although the latter has introduced reforms to speed up the consultation process, the employer still has to provide a job protection plan in any type of rescue proceeding. See Arts L-1233-1 and L 1233-91 of the French Labour Code, as amended by *Loi 2013-504 du 14 juin 2013 relative à la sécurisation de l'emploi*. See further, Nicola Countouris, Simon Deakin, Mark Freedland, Aristea Koukiadaki, and Jeremias Prassl, 'Report on Collective Dismissal. A Comparative and Contextual Analysis of the Law of Collective Dismissals in 13 European Countries' (International Labour Office 2016).

[18] While recalling former directives such as the Acquired Rights Directive (n 9) (see Recitals 60 and 62 and Art. 13), the Directive on Restructuring and Insolvency (n 9) stresses that 'workers whose claims are affected by a restructuring plan should have the right to vote on the plan. For the purposes of voting on the restructuring plan, Member States should be able to decide to place workers in a class separate from other classes of creditors.' See Recital 62 and Art. 9(4) thereof.

[19] Nick Adnett, 'The Acquired Rights Directive and Compulsory Competitive Tendering in the UK: An Economic Perspective', European Journal of Law & Economics, 6 (1998) 69–81, 71.

[20] See a taxonomy of insolvency proceedings in Chapter 1 'What Is Insolvency Law?'

not constrained by statutory provisions. Accordingly, employees cannot only be dismissed 'at will', but also their employment terms and conditions can be changed for rescue purposes; that is, such flexibility is meant to increase the chances of the debtor's recovery and, in the end, maintain a high employment rate.[21] Nevertheless, it highlights that worker protection in this jurisdiction is also weak in non-insolvency cases, signalling that not only economic but also historical and political reasons play a role in the presence of these employee safeguards in insolvency law.

In contrast, the Acquired Rights Directive secures jobs by requiring buyers or the new company to take on those employed by the company subject to restructuring and respect their contractual terms of employment,[22] creating a sort of job property right.[23] The latter includes the respect for pre-existing collective agreements, although Member States are entitled to limit the period during which compliance with this is mandatory.[24] In this vein, modifications in contractual arrangements have to be agreed upon with employees or worker representatives; otherwise, workers are entitled to resign on grounds of the employer's breach of contract.[25] Nevertheless, the Acquired Rights Directive does include an insolvency exception,[26] in principle designed with liquidation proceedings in mind, where collective redundancies are usually expected because the business is meant to be terminated.

11.11

In implementing the Acquired Rights Directive, some countries have opted for not applying the insolvency exception, such as France and Germany, while others have made use of it, such as Belgium,[27] the United Kingdom, [28] and the Netherlands.[29] Since their issuance, the Court of Justice has been active in interpreting the meaning of this exception, that is which type of insolvency proceedings is covered by it, in particular whether those aiming to restructure of the company are.[30] From a social perspective,

11.12

---

[21] Suggesting that this flexibility has contributed to a faster economic recovery in the United States than in the EU, see Jennifer L.L. Gant, 'Studies in Convergence? Post-Crisis Effects on Corporate Rescue and the Influence of Social Policy: The EU and the USA', International Insolvency Review, 25 (2015) 72–96.

[22] See Art. 3 of the Acquired Rights Directive (n 9). According to this provision, both buyer and seller are jointly and severally liable in respect of obligations arising out of the transfer.

[23] See Stephen Hardy and Nick Adnett, 'Entrepreneurial Freedom versus Employee Rights: The Acquired Rights Directive and EU Social Policy Post-Amsterdam', Journal of European Social Policy, 9 (1999) 127–37, 127; Jennifer L.L. Gant, 'Employees as Stakeholders in Restructuring and Insolvency: Acquired Rights and Business Transfers' in Paul J. Omar (ed.), *Research Handbook on Corporate Restructuring* (Edward Elgar 2021) 166.

[24] See Art. 3(3) of the Acquired Rights Directive (n 9).

[25] See ibid Art. 6(1).

[26] See ibid Art. 5.

[27] See Art. 61(3) of the *Wet betreffende de continuïteit van de ondernemingen* of 31 January 2009.

[28] See reg. 8 of the UK Transfer of Undertakings (Protection of Employment) Regulations 2006, SI 2006/246, amended in 2014.

[29] See Art. 7:666 of the Dutch Civil Code.

[30] This was the situation before the redrafting of the Acquired Rights Directive (n 9) in 2001, whose amendment was triggered by the case law of the Court of Justice in these matters: *HBM Abels v The Administrative Board of the Bedrijfsvereniging voor de Metaalindustrie en de Electrotechnische Industrie* [1985] ECLI:EU:C:1985:55; *D'Urso and ors v Ercole Marelli Eletromeccanica Generale SpA and ors* [1991] ECLI:EU:C:1991:326; *Spano and ors v Fiat Geotech and Fiat Hitachi* [1995] ECLI:EU:C:1995:421; *Jules Déthier Equipement SA v Jules Dassy* [1998] ECLI:EU:C:1998:99; *Eurpiéces SA (in liquidation) v Wilfried Sanders and Automotive Industries Holding Company SA* [1998] ECLI:EU:C:1998:532; *First Steps Federatie Nederlandse Vakvereniging and ors v Smallsteps BV* [2017] ECLI:EU:C:2017:489.

308 ASPECTS OF LABOUR LAW

the application of the rights embedded in the Acquired Rights Directive should prevail, and the insolvency exception is to be narrowly interpreted, excluding restructuring proceedings. In contrast, another interpretation suggests that debtor companies
not bound by transfer provisions would increase their recovery chances, and thus the
exception is to be broadly interpreted, thus including restructuring proceedings. The
Dutch pre-pack procedure is a case in point: seeking the application of the insolvency
exception, and thus the avoidance of difficulties and costs associated with the termination of contracts in accordance with Dutch employment law,[31] the pre-pack mechanism is construed within a procedure with liquidation purposes that ends up with the
dissolution of the debtor company.[32]

11.13   The interpretation issue (i.e. whether the business transfer provisions on employment
matters are applicable to Dutch pre-pack procedures or not) was brought before the
Court of Justice on the occasion of the purchase by Smallsteps of the Estro's business
consisting in day-care centres.[33] The reasoning was that the insolvency exception in
the Acquired Rights Directive as implemented in the Netherlands does not cover these
procedures because their intention is not the liquidation of the business but its continuation, at least in part and in the hands of a third party. In line with its previous case law,
the Court of Justice agreed with this rationale, highlighting, on the one hand, that the
establishments' transfer had been carefully planned to ensure their immediate operation afterwards and thus not with a liquidation in mind, while, on the other hand, the
lack of pre-pack's supervision by a competent authority made it impossible to classify
this procedure within the insolvency exception as envisaged by the Acquired Rights
Directive.[34] A Belgian provision indicating that the transferee has the right to choose
which employees to take over, provided that the decision is based on economic, technical, or organization reasons, was also rejected by the Court of Justice in the *Plessers*
case.[35] These findings have provided national courts with some room to apply a fact-
based approach and examine whether the insolvency exception is applicable or not on a
case-by-case basis,[36] signalling that the discussion as to whether job property rights are
applicable to pre-packs or not is still open in the European Union. It is thus to be seen
whether the *Heiploeg* case will settle the matter.[37] Contrary to what was sustained in

---

[31] Peter Vas Nunes, 'Do the Rules on Transfer of Undertaking Apply in a "Pre-Pack" Insolvency? A Dutch Court
Asks the ECJ for Guidance', European Employment Law Cases (2016) 4, 4.

[32] See *Wet Continuïteit Ondernemingen I, Kamerstukken II* 2014/15, 34 218, 2. This procedure is greatly influenced by the United Kingdom, although the same cannot be predicated of the type of proceedings in which
pre-package procedures are embedded. See Alexandra Kastrinou and Stef Vullings, ' "No Evil Is without Good": A
Comparative Analysis of Pre-Pack Sales in the UK and the Netherlands', International Insolvency Review, 27(3)
(2018) 320, 328.

[33] *Smallsteps* (n 31).

[34] ibid paras 49–50 and 55.

[35] *Christa Plessers v PREFACO NV and the Belgian State* [2019] ECLI:EU:C:2019:424.

[36] Gant, 'Employees as Stakeholders' (n 23) 166; Gina Gioia, 'La tutela legislative eurounitaria del lavoratore
nella crisi d'impresa', Diritto Fallimentare e delle Società Commerciali, 97(2) (2022) 349, 362.

[37] *Federatie Nederlandse Vakbeweging v Heiploeg Seafood International BV, Heitrans International B* [2022]
ECLI:EU:C:2022:321 (*Heiploeg*). Prior to its release, see the comments by Barend Vos and Gert-Jan Boon, 'Getting
the Dutch Pre-Pack Done: The Options after Heiploeg', Leidenlawblog (5 May 2020) <https://www.leidenlawblog.
nl/articles/getting-the-dutch-pre-pack-done-the-options-after-heiploeg> accessed 27 March 2024.

Smallsteps, the Court of Justice concluded that the Dutch fish and seafood-related business transfer, negotiated prior to the opening of a liquidation proceeding but concluded thereafter, could be considered covered by the said insolvency exception, 'provided that that *pre-pack* procedure is governed by statutory or regulatory provisions'.[38]

As said, there is a lively debate, mostly framed in economic terms, as to whether rescue proceedings would benefit from the exclusion of these workers' rights or not. However, the significance of historical and political reasons in this discussion cannot be neglected, as can be learnt from those countries that have not resorted to the insolvency exception enshrined in the Acquired Rights Directive, signalling the existence of a strong social dialogue in the country. Against this backdrop, whether to include an insolvency exception to job protection in the event of employer's change might well depend on whether such a protection is strong or not beyond the insolvency realm, as the US and the UK cases illustrate. More specifically, while transfer provisions seem to be generally applicable to UK pre-packs, the impact of these employee safeguards in the event of the employer's default has not been as relevant as it has been in the case of the Dutch pre-packs, where worker protection beyond insolvency is much stronger than the one provided by UK employment and labour law.[39]

11.14

The divergent approaches to worker protection in the event of the employer's default raise the question as to which law governs employment contracts and relationships in cross-border insolvencies. As discussed in Chapter 9 'Cross-Border Insolvency Law', the effects of insolvency proceedings on executory contracts are submitted to the *lex fori concursus*.[40] However, an exception to this rule is usually made in employment matters; that is, contract termination or modification is subject to the *lex laboris*[41] for worker protection purposes.[42] The ranking of unpaid wage claims and other related entitlements are, nevertheless, subject to the law governing the insolvency proceedings.

11.15

The law applicable to insolvency proceedings is thus set aside, with the aim of avoiding conflicts between the mandatory rules laid down by the *lex fori concursus* and the *lex laboris* and thus reducing the legal complexity attached to these matters. Against this backdrop, the IP/DIP is in charge of terminating, modifying, or transferring the employment contracts to a new employer in accordance with the labour and employment provisions of a country other than the one where insolvency proceedings are opened. These actions might request a complex procedure involving a competent authority in

11.16

---

[38] *Heiploeg* (n 37) para. 55. See Bob Wessels, 'Heiploeg—European Commission: Your Move!' (19 May 2022) <http://www.bobwessels.nl> accessed 14 January 2024.

[39] Aalbers et al., 'Does Pre-Packed Bankruptcy Create Value?' (n 11).

[40] See Art. 7(2)(e) of Regulation (EU) 2015/848 of the European Parliament and of the Council of 20 May 2015 on insolvency proceedings (EIR Recast), OJ [2015] L 141/19 (EIR Recast) and Rule 12 of the Global Rules on Conflict of Laws Matters in International Insolvency Cases (the Global Rules), included in the American Law Institute (ALI) and the International Insolvency Institute (III), *Transnational Insolvency: Global Principles for Co-operation in International Insolvency Cases* (ALI-III, 2012).

[41] See Art. 13 of EIR Recast (n 38) and Rule 20 of the Global Rules.

[42] Miguel Virgós and Jan Schmit, Report on the Convention on Insolvency Proceedings (EU Council of the European Union, 1995) para. 118.

310 ASPECTS OF LABOUR LAW

charge of approving the social plan, raising the question whether this authority should be the insolvency court, a local court, or another public authority. The answer is provided by the law governing the employment contracts, but it might require solving adaptation problems if the *lex fori concursus* does not contemplate such a complex procedure, and thus, there is no obligation on the side of the insolvency court or any other authority to approve the social plan. The solution might be allocating the jurisdiction upon the authorities of the country where the debtor's establishment is seated,[43] although a pro-worker approach allowing for a choice between the two jurisdictions has also been advocated.[44]

III. Worker Entitlements and Priority of Payment

11.17 The employer's insolvency might lead not only to job losses but also to outstanding worker entitlements arising out of the employment contract or relationship. Among them, the main distinction is between wage and pension claims to the extent that the latter might not only concern active workers but also retired employees and not always be considered for insolvency purposes. As to wage claims, they include not only salaries and wages but also other related benefits such as holiday pay, vacation pay, severance pay, termination pay, and other emoluments arising out of the employment contract such as bonuses, premiums, travel expenses, or privately funded insurance benefits.[45]

11.18 Pension claims might be taken into consideration in insolvency law along with wage claims, depending on the type of arrangements made by the relevant country in terms of social welfare. Building upon the World Bank's classification,[46] pensions can be organized in three pillars: a first pillar that is run by the State and funded through contributions linked to earnings, on a pay-as-you-go basis or through general tax revenues; a second pillar that relies on occupational pension plans funded by employers and/or employees; and a third pillar based on personal savings plans. Legal divergence on these matters is certainly significant across countries, with many not providing any type of social security benefits to their citizens.[47] Nevertheless, the classification helps to understand the impact

---

[43] As it is suggested now in Art. 13(2) of the EIR Recast (n 38). An example of the abovementioned situation can be found in the Netherlands, where the dismissal of employees by the IP/DIP has to be approved by the supervising court, as was reported in Burkhard Hess, Paul Oberhammer, and Thomas Pfeiffer (eds), *European Insolvency Law. The Heidelberg–Luxembourg–Vienna Report* (C.H. Beck/Hart/Nomos 2014) 480, which preceded the amendment of the EIR Recast (n 38).

[44] Francisco Garcimartín and Miguel Virgós, 'Article 13-Contracts of Employment' in Reinhard Bork and Kristin van Zwieten (eds), *Commentary on the European Insolvency Regulation* (2nd edn, OUP 2022) para. 13.17.

[45] Still actual, it can be consulted: ILO, 'General Survey of the Reports concerning the Protection of Wages Convention (No. 95) and the Protection of Wages Recommendation (No. 85), 1949' (ILO 2003) on national provisions in these matters.

[46] World Bank, *Averting the Old Age Crisis: Policies to Protect the Old and Promote Growth* (OUP 1994) 15.

[47] While only one-quarter of the world population has access to any sort of social security benefits, target 1.3 of SDG No. 1 requests countries to 'Implement nationally appropriate social protection systems and measures for all, including floors, and by 2030 achieve substantial coverage of the poor and the vulnerable', in particular, women and old people.

of the employer's insolvency in the attempts to fight poverty during old age. More specifically, the discussion on pension claims and their payment during insolvency proceedings concerns the abovementioned second pillar to the extent that neither old-age benefits nor personal savings claims entail workers' claims against the debtor employer.[48] On the other hand, occupational pension plans might have been made mandatory by countries as a means to administer their social security scheme.

11.19 The significance of pension claims in the event of the employer's default has significantly decreased as a result of the shift, with the change of millennium, from defined benefits schemes towards defined contribution schemes. Unlike the former, the latter frames the employer's responsibility on the contributions made to a pension plan, placing the investment responsibility upon households; that is, while funds are fuelled on a regular basis on behalf of employees, the company is not obliged to provide a guaranteed payment to the individual at retirement based on a previously established formula depending on years of service and salary history.[49] The latter is the case in defined benefit schemes that are managed by the company itself or an intermediary on its behalf, and thus they are critically affected by the employer's insolvency. Against this backdrop, two types of pension claims, unfunded pension liabilities and outstanding pension contributions, are likely to arise in the latter scenario, while the resort to defined contribution schemes has the benefit of limiting these claims to the second type and for a limited period of time.[50]

11.20 In terms of ranking of claims, worker claims are, in principle, on the same footing as any other unsecured creditor. As elaborated in Chapter 5 'Security Rights and Creditors' Priority and Ranking: Realizable Priority in Rescue', creditors are essentially classified into secured and unsecured. Creditors whose claims are secured by a right *in rem* are entitled to be satisfied from specific assets in the event of insolvency, contrary to unsecured creditors, whose (non-)contractual rights and claims to payment can only be realized against the general assets of the debtor and thus after secured creditors have been satisfied. Both the World Bank's *Principles and Guidelines for Effective Insolvency and Creditor Rights Systems* and UNCITRAL's *Legislative Guide on Insolvency Law*[51] suggest that the general terms of this classification, as well as the ranking of claims that it implies, should be respected to the extent that this ensures the legitimate expectations of creditors and fosters predictability in commercial matters by honouring, where feasible, the pre-insolvency entitlements, in particular those arising out of private arrangements such as pledges, mortgages, and other security rights.[52]

---

[48] Although the first pillar, consisting of State-run pensions, might be funded via social contributions, their non-payment by the debtor employer would give rise to a tax claim as it can be learned in Chapter 10 devoted to 'Aspects of Tax Law'.

[49] See Paul M. Secunda, 'An Analysis of the Treatment of Employees Pension and Wage Claims in Insolvency and under Guarantee Schemes in OECD Countries: Comparative Law Lessons for Detroit and the United States', Fordham Urban Law Journal, 41 (2014) 867–997, 880.

[50] See ibid 893.

[51] See World Bank, *Principles and Guidelines for Effective Insolvency and Creditor Rights Systems* (n 5) Principle C12.1 and UNCITRAL, *Legislative Guide on Insolvency Law* (n 2) 275 para. 80.

[52] This principle can be also found in Thomas H. Jackson, *The Logic and Limits of Bankruptcy Law* (Harvard University Press 1986) 21–5.

11.21 However, the respect for the pre-insolvency status quo is only one aspect of the distributional question that arises out of debtor's default,[53] and whose answer is usually politically motivated.[54] To this end, statutory priorities are the preferred tool when it comes to the distribution of the debtor's estate to the extent that they transfer value from some creditors to the preferred class by altering the payment order of pre-insolvency entitlements. This distributional effect might only involve unsecured creditors shifting value from one class to another,[55] but it can also concern secured creditors if a so-called super-priority is granted. In doing so, legal jurisdictions manage to address social policy consideration instead of resorting to general tax revenues.[56]

11.22 In view of this distributional question, social policy considerations inform a differential treatment for worker claims as regards to other unsecured creditors.[57] As already mentioned, they are particularly vulnerable in the event of the employer's insolvency on account of their lack of sophistication and, in particular, ability to react to the employer's adverse circumstances, even if they had been made aware of the insolvency situation. Other contractual creditors are not in this situation because they are not in a subordinate position as regards to the debtor and usually have different sources of income.[58] By the same token, these creditors have access to financial and economic data, usually unavailable to workers, and can make informed decisions as to whether to trade with the debtor or not.[59] Moreover, employees' ties to their workplace and likely only means to earn their bread facilitate opportunistic behaviours on the side of the employer, such as the non-payment of wages and contributions in the vicinity of the insolvency.[60] Interestingly, the allocation of priority status to workers' claims might curtail the employer's attempts to avoid his or her labour obligations by resorting to the opening of an insolvency proceeding.[61]

---

[53] See José María Garrido, 'The Distributional Question in Insolvency: Comparative Aspects', International Insolvency Review, 4 (1995) 25.

[54] See Federico M. Mucciarelli, 'Not Just Efficiency: Insolvency Law in the EU and Its Political Dimension', European Business Organization Law Review, 14 (2013) 175; Jennifer L.L. Gant, 'Optimising Fairness in Insolvency and Restructuring. A Spotlight on Vulnerable Stakeholders', International Insolvency Review, 31 (2022) 3.

[55] Garrido, 'The Distributional Question' (n 53) 32–6.

[56] Federico M. Mucciarelli, 'Employee Insolvency Priorities and Employment Protection in France, Germany and the United Kingdom', Journal of Law and Society, 44 (2017) 255.

[57] Johnson, 'Insolvency and Social Protection' (n 6) 1.

[58] This reasoning is not applicable to non-contractual claims for obvious reasons. However, there are not systemic reasons supporting the construction of a priority for them as it happens in the case of employees. For sustainability reasons, the case has been made as regards to environmental claims, but the reality is that they are considered unsecured claims in all insolvency laws. See Linna, 'Insolvency proceedings' (n 3) 210.

[59] The transformations experienced by the world of work reveal that this reasoning is not applicable anymore to all trade creditors, but many of them (such as suppliers to the debtor's company) have a subordinated position similar to the one of employees, for which reason different attempts are being made to extend the protection granted to the latter to the former. See, e.g. Martin Risak and Thomas Dullinger, 'The Concept of "Worker" in EU Law. Status Quo and Potential for Change', European Trade Union Institute, Report No. 140, Brussels (2018).

[60] Eric Tucker, 'Shareholder and Director Liability for Unpaid Workers' Wages in Canada: From Condition of Granting Limited Liability to Exceptional Remedy', Law and History Review, 26 (2008) 58–98,, although only discussing the case of limited liability companies.

[61] Mucciarelli, 'Employee Insolvency Priorities' (n 56) 265. In a similar vein, the Directive on Restructuring and Insolvency (n 9) extends this protection to the pre-insolvency stage:

Given the need to ensure an appropriate level of protection of workers, Member States should be required to exempt workers' outstanding claims from any stay of individual enforcement actions,

WORKER ENTITLEMENTS AND PRIORITY OF PAYMENT   313

From a macro-economic perspective, supporting employees is a critical means to achieving social cohesion and avoiding social unrest. Both objectives lie behind the approach to business failure that seek to avoid the stigma traditionally linked to insolvency in order to provide debtors with a second opportunity, and thus the ability to support themselves, but also to create employment again.[62] The latter is critical, in particular in those countries with high unemployment rates and weak social protection systems for the unemployed, a combination that might lead to social unrest. Accordingly, the said objectives should also inform a policy prioritizing workers' claims in the distribution of the debtor's assets, although there are important objections to this approach that point to a counter-reaction to such a priority on the part of trade creditors. The latter might increase the prizes of their goods and services in exchange for their subordination to worker claims in the event of the debtor's default, thereby putting the business at risk and indirectly hampering job creation.[63]   **11.23**

Priorities granted to employees for their claims cover those arising prior to the opening of insolvency proceedings. Post-filing entitlements should be considered administrative expenses of the insolvency estate and thus enjoy priority in payment as regards to any other pre-filing claims except for secured debts.[64] As to pre-filing workers' claims, their priority, if any, varies from country to country, as examined in section IV below on the comparative approach to these matters. A Tuscany insolvency statute of 1713 seems to be the first documented case of employee priorities,[65] although the most well-known provisions are those enshrined in the French Civil Code, which codified pre-existing customary law in 1804.[66] Remarkably, this form of worker protection has been expanded via a critical convention for our purposes. In accordance with Art. 11(1) of the Protection of Wages Convention (No. 95) issued by the ILO as early as 1949:   **11.24**

> irrespective of the question of whether those claims arise before or after the stay is granted. A stay of enforcement of workers' outstanding claims should be allowed only for the amounts and for the period for which the payment of such claims is effectively guaranteed at a similar level by other means under national law. Where national law provides for limitations on the liability of guarantee institutions, either in terms of the length of the guarantee or the amount paid to workers, workers should be able to enforce any shortfall in their claims against the employer even during the stay period. Alternatively, Member States should be able to exclude workers' claims from the scope of the preventive restructuring frameworks and provide for their protection under national law. (Recital 61 and Arts 1(5)(a) and 6(5))

[62] For example, Recital 16 of the Directive on Restructuring and Insolvency (n 9) claims, inter alia, that 'Removing the barriers to effective preventive restructuring of viable debtors in financial difficulties contributes to minimising job losses and losses of value for creditors in the supply chain, preserves know-how and skills and hence benefits the wider economy.'

[63] Johnson, 'Insolvency and Social Protection' (n 6) 3.

[64] This is, for example, the case under 11 U.S.C. §503(b)(1)(A). Nevertheless, it is to note the case of Chile, which exempts employees from participating in insolvency proceedings with the side effect that this type of protection is not considered, and thus, pre- and post-filing entitlements are treated equally. See Eduardo Jequier Lehuedé, 'Créditos laborales y trabajadores en el procedimiento de reorganización judicial, Ley No. 20.720', Revista chilena de derecho, 44(3) (2017) 805–30, 806.

[65] Riforma degli Statuti di Mercanzia, issued motu proprio by the Grand Duke of Tuscany Cosimo III on 11 April 1713, as documented by Garrido, 'The Distributional Question' (n 53) 22 fn. 51.

[66] See Arts 2101 and 2104 of the French Civil Code and Arturo S. Bronstein, 'The Protection of Workers' Claims in the Event of the Insolvency of Their Employer', International Labour Review, 126 (1987) 715, 718–20.

314   ASPECTS OF LABOUR LAW

> [i]n the event of the bankruptcy or judicial liquidation of an undertaking, the workers employed therein shall be treated as privileged creditors either as regards wages due to them for service rendered during such a period prior to the bankruptcy or judicial liquidation as may be prescribed by national laws or regulations, or as regards wages up to a prescribed amount as may be determined by national laws or regulations.

It is to be noted that a similar provision is enshrined in Art. 11 of the Workmen's Compensation (Accidents) Convention, 1925 (No. 17), but this refers only to the payment of compensation for personal injury or death in case of industrial accident. Both conventions specifically place the establishment of the relative priority of wage claims as regards to other creditors in the hands of Member States,[67] with a view to providing room for adjustment to local circumstances and different degrees of welfare systems.

11.25 The compromise embedded in Art. 11 of the 1949 Protection of Wages Convention is that workers' claims have to be granted priority, or even super-priority, in respect of other creditors. However, another convention of the same title was issued by the ILO in 1992,[68] with a clear shift in the philosophy behind the said provision.[69] While the latter only took into consideration worker protection,[70] the 1992 Protection of Wages Convention is in line with the abovementioned principle that the pre-insolvency status quo should be respected with a view to protecting creditors' expectations and increasing market predictability. To this end, and although the possibility of granting a relative priority to workers is still enshrined in the convention, it only refers to other unsecured creditors, while secured creditors are not mentioned.[71] More dramatically, the convention opens the door to either reducing or altogether abolishing the priority in the event that 'workers' claims are protected by a guarantee institution',[72] the fine line being when an insurance or guarantee fund makes the need for workers' priorities redundant because it offers the same level of protection.

11.26 In view of the different options available as to employee priorities, countries' legislations vary as regards to (a) whether a priority is granted to workers' claims, (b) the type of priority granted to these creditors (i.e. whether it is absolute or relative priority), (c) whether the priority covers the claim in full or in part, (d) whether payments refer

---

[67] See Art. 11(3) of the Protection of Wages Convention, 1949 (No. 95). This convention has been ratified by 99 States, the latest one being Saudi Arabia, for whom it entered into force on 7 December 2021, and has been denounced only by the United Kingdom.

[68] ILO Protection of Workers' Claims (Employer's Insolvency) Convention, 1992 (No. 173) (1992 Protection of Workers' Claims Convention) and Protection of Workers' Claims (Employer's Insolvency) Recommendation, 1992 (No. 180), were issued in 1992; Convention No. 173 has only gathered 21 ratifications.

[69] Some countries have ratified both conventions (Albania, Armenia, Botswana, Bulgaria, Burkina Fasso, Chad, Madagascar, Mexico, Portugal, Russian Federation, Slovakia, Slovenia, Spain, Ukraine, and Zambia), which live together with the exception of Art. 11 of Convention No. 95, which has ceased to apply in favour of the provisions of Convention No. 173.

[70] Nevertheless, Art. 11 of the 1949 Protection of Wages Convention (n 67) is not free from criticism as elaborated by Bronstein, 'The Protection of Workers' Claims' (n 66) 719–24.

[71] See Art. 5 of the Protection of Workers' Claims Convention (n 69).

[72] See ibid Art. 8.

IV. Worker Entitlements and Guarantee Schemes

Providing workers with a priority over other unsecured creditors in the event of the **11.27** employer's insolvency might come with side effects such as reducing investments in companies, as indicated above. Accordingly, and with a view to securing creditors' expectations and market confidence, the establishment of an insurance or guarantee fund might be an alternative to wage and pension claims' priority. Moreover, such a fund might also play a key role in helping debtors in distress to avoid insolvency by taking over due wage claims during the restructuring stage.[74] They might also help to relieve pressure upon State social protection systems, although unemployment benefits and retraining would still have to be provided.[75] In practice, both priority and guarantee fund might work in a supplementary way, balancing the general body of creditors' interests with those of workers.

An insurance or guarantee scheme can be set up either to cover wage claims, or pen- **11.28** sion claims, or both. In this vein, domestic legislation lays down not only the type of claims covered but also the type of employees that might benefit from such a scheme. Directive 2008/94/EC of the European Parliament and of the Council of 22 October 2008 on the protection of employees in the event of the insolvency of their employer[76] provides Member States with discretion for such determinations. For example, and while specifically excluding domestic servants employed by natural persons from its scope of application,[77] Member States are entitled to exceptionally exclude claims by referring to certain categories of employees from the operation of the fund.[78] Moreover,

---

[73] For example, and according to ibid Art. 6:

The minimum coverage of the privilege coverage includes: I. Workers' claims for wages relating to a prescribed period of not less than three months prior to the insolvency or prior to the termination of the employment. II. Claims for holiday pay as a result of work performed during the year in which the insolvency or the termination of the employment occurred and in the preceding year. III. Claims for amounts due in respect of other types of paid absence (e.g. sick leave or maternity leave) relating to a prescribed period which may not be less than three months prior to the insolvency or prior to the termination of the employment. IV. Severance pay.

[74] For example, the Spanish Wage Guarantee Fund, *Fondo de Garantía Salarial* (FOGASA) is allowed to conclude agreements with companies by which the FOGASA pays the wages during a given period, and in exchange, the company provides for security rights that cannot be challenged later on by any means. See Order 20 August 1985 supplementing Art. 32 of the Royal Decree 505/1985, 6 March on the conclusion of restructuring agreements on debts owed to the Wage Guarantee Fund.

[75] Signalling the significance of this layer of social protection, Art. 25 of the European Social Charter specifically provides that workers' claims arising from contracts of employment or employment relationships should 'be guaranteed by a guarantee institution or by any other effective form of protection'.

[76] Protection of Employees Directive (n 9). This directive replaces Council Directive 80/987/EEC of 20 October 1980, which had already been amended several times: OJ [1980] L 283/23.

[77] See Art. 1(3) of the Protection of Employees Directive (n 9).

[78] See ibid Art. 1(2). Article 2(2) and (3) thereof further limits the discretion of States in implementing the Directive by requesting them not to discriminate part-time employees, employees with a fixed-term contract and with a temporary employment relationship, or those that have not been working for a minimum time for the

316   ASPECTS OF LABOUR LAW

the establishment of a guarantee fund might be linked just to the opening of liquidation proceedings or to any other type of insolvency proceedings.

11.29   The payment of outstanding wages and/or pensions might be further limited by referring to those earned in a period of time prior to the opening of an insolvency proceeding and/or after a given date determined by the relevant country.[79] The latter does not mean that outstanding pay claims will be covered in full by the guarantee fund because legislations might also cap the amount to be paid to the worker creditor.[80] As a matter of fact, the abovementioned social policy considerations should be informing the elaboration of these provisions, including their relationship with other options, such as insolvency priorities or social benefits, that might be available to employees.

11.30   In a similar vein, and while several measures might be in place to alleviate the plight of employees in the event of the employer's insolvency, an insurance or guarantee fund might make a significant contribution to their recovery if payments are made on time; that is, such schemes might be more beneficial for workers than a priority in the ranking of creditors because they might significantly reduce late payments usually associated with an insolvency proceeding. The latter can last for years, especially in the case of liquidations, with employees depending on social protection if another job is not available. For example, share fishers were excluded from the Protection of Employees Directive on the grounds that they were protected by a maritime lien attached to their wages and emoluments, at least in Greece, Italy, Malta, and the United Kingdom and in accordance with the International Conventions on Maritime Liens and Mortgages. However, a review undertaken by the European Commission concluded that this lien 'may not always offer a degree of protection equivalent' to that of a guarantee scheme.[81] That applies not only to the value that might (not) get recovered via the debtor's estate but also to the moment when employees get paid.[82]

11.31   However, the timing of payments also depends on legislations, meaning that they might choose to meet the outstanding pay claims only once the distribution of the

---

debtor before the opening of insolvency proceedings. As to Part III of the 1992 Protection of Workers' Claims Convention (n 68), it requests, as a minimum, the following:

> I. Workers' claims for wages relating to a prescribed period of not less than eight weeks prior to the insolvency or prior to the termination of the employment. II. Claims for holiday pay as a result of work performed during a prescribed period which may not be less than six months prior to the insolvency or the termination of the employment. III. Claims for amounts due in respect of other types of paid absence relating to a prescribed period which may not be less than eight weeks prior to the insolvency or prior to the termination of the employment. IV. Severance pay.

[79] See Arts 3 and 4 of the Protection of Employees Directive (n 9).

[80] See ibid Art. 4(3).

[81] Report from the Commission to the European Parliament and the Council on the implementation and application of certain provisions of Directive 2008/94/EC on the protection of employees in the event of the insolvency of their employer, 28 February 2011, COM (2011) 84 Final, 3. The concept of 'equivalent protection' is to be narrowly interpreted in accordance with *Elliniko Dimosio v Stefanos Stroumpoulis and ois* [2016] ECLI:EU:C:2016:116, para. 75.

[82] See Laura Carballo Piñeiro, 'Worker Protection in International Insolvency Law: The Limited Role of Maritime Liens' in José Manuel Martín Osante and Olga Fotinopoulou Basurko (eds), *New Trends in Maritime Law. Maritime Liens, Arrest of Ships, Mortgages and Forced Sale* (Thomson-Reuters Aranzadi 2017) 219.

debtor's assets has taken place. This approach not only undermines the worker protection principle but also ignores the subrogation rights of guarantee institutions and their better performance as participating creditors in insolvency proceedings than workers. As indicated in section I above, workers might get discouraged in claiming their rights because of the complexities of insolvency law, an obstacle that is not encountered by guarantee institutions. Accordingly, and while ensuring that workers are satisfied, subrogation rights provide these institutions with a means to keep pursuing their objectives by collecting unsatisfied claims from debtors. The latter is more feasible for these institutions than for workers not only because of their expertise but also because of the greater bargaining power that they have in the insolvency proceeding on account of a larger overall claim than the one in the hands of individual employees.[83] Generally, the subrogation rights also include the priority granted to workers' claims in the insolvency ranking of creditors,[84] but not necessarily.[85]

The funding of these institutions also varies from country to country. While both public and private[86] funds might exist side by side, payments made by employers seem to be the best option to the extent that they critically contribute to the establishment of a safety net in the event of default and, by this means, enhance the investment environment.[87] Moreover, contributions might be requested only from companies that meet specific standards with a view to reducing the impact on small businesses of this type of arrangement. Countries might also request employees to contribute to the system,[88] although it is questionable whether they should be paying for the employer's default. At any rate, and once insolvency has been opened, the guarantee fund must operate regardless of whether the employer in distress had actually made the mandatory payments or not. As mentioned, subrogation rights may critically contribute to the funding of these institutions, thereby making the priority granted to workers' claims relevant for the sustainability of the system. Otherwise, the guarantee fund might become financially unstable or request higher premium rates for remaining employers.[89] As to the system's structure, it might take the form of a financial security that employers are requested to take or a governmental body.

11.32

The significance of the guarantee funds' subrogation rights for their sustainability was made clear during the negotiations of the EIR Recast. Following a proposal of the

11.33

---

[83] See these considerations in Secunda, 'An Analysis' (n 49) 918–19.

[84] As is the case of Canada according to the Wage Earner Protection Program Act enacted by s. 1 of Chapter 47 of the Statutes of Canada, 2005, in force July 7, 2008 [SI/2008-78], Chapter 47, s. 36(1).

[85] For example, Denmark, Sweden, and Switzerland provide some priority to employees that is not included in the subrogation rights of their wage guarantee institutions.

[86] Canada funds the Wage Earner Protection Program (WEPP) created by the Act of the same name, with general tax revenues. Article 17 of the Wage Claim Guarantee Act of Korea also establishes a government-run and funded institution.

[87] This is the case in Germany, whose guarantee fund is industry funded. Payments are made depending on each company's expenditure on total wages paid to all insured employees, including quarterly advance payments and one final payment. Subrogation rights are, nevertheless, granted to the guarantee institution.

[88] This is the case of the United Kingdom in accordance with ss 166–9 of the Employment Rights Act 1996.

[89] Secunda, 'An Analysis' (n 49) 885.

318   ASPECTS OF LABOUR LAW

French delegation in the Council discussions,[90] public authorities are also entitled to request the opening of territorial proceedings if authorized by the law of the State within which the debtor's establishment is situated,[91] the reason being that wage guarantee funds would not otherwise have the right to act against the debtor in another State because they do not have the status of a creditor prior to the opening of such proceedings.[92] In a similar vein, and in order to increase legal certainty for those employed in companies with cross-border activities, conflict rules allocate the responsibility for settling employees' entitlements upon the guarantee institutions of the country where they (habitually) work[93] so that the law governing them also determines the extent of employees' rights without prejudice to giving proper consideration to decisions taken within the insolvency proceeding abroad.[94] It might be the case that workers have access to both wage guarantee funds, either in addition to or instead of, provided, however, that that guarantee results in a greater level of worker protection.[95] Should the *lex loci laboris* not contemplate such a fund, a worker should be covered by the fund established in the country where insolvency proceedings have been instituted.[96]

11.34   All in all, countries vary on the following issues: (a) whether they contemplate an insurance or guarantee fund, (b) the amount that the fund covers, (c) the period of time prior to the opening of the insolvency proceeding used as reference for claims covered, (d) the type of claims covered by the fund, and (e) whether the insurance or guarantee fund lives with a priority granted to workers' claims in the event of default or whether it operates separately from the latter.

V. Comparative Law Approaches to Worker Entitlements Protection

11.35   In view of the different comparative approaches to these issues, heavily dependent on the social, economic, and political background of the relevant country, the basic

---

[90]   European Council, Note from the French delegation to the Working Party on Civil Law Matters (Insolvency), Document 9080/13 ADD 9 (14 June 2013) 10.

[91]   See Art. 3(4)(b)(ii) of the EIR Recast (n 38).

[92]   See further discussion in Wolf-Georg Ringe, 'International Jurisdiction' in Bork and van Zwieten, *Commentary on the European Insolvency Regulation* (n 44) paras 3–217–3–219.

[93]   See Art. 9(1) of the Protection of Employees Directive (n 9). Note that the EIR Recast (n 38) is not applicable to the functioning of these public institutions. See Reinhart Bork, 'Law Applicable' in Reinhard Bork and Renato Mangano (eds), *European Cross-Border Insolvency Law* (OUP 2016) para. 4.95; Peter Mankowski, 'Artikle 13' in Peter Mankowski, Michael F. Müller, and Jessica Schmidt (eds), *Europäische Insolvenzverordnung* (C.H. Beck 2016) para. 31.

[94]   See Art. 9(2) and (3) of the Protection of Employees Directive (n 9).

[95]   See *Charles Defossez v Christian Wiart and ors* [2011] ECLI:EU:C:2011:134, para. 35, interpreting the 1980 Protection of Employees Directive (n 76). The case has not been contemplated in the in force Directive, whose Art. 10 lays down coordination mechanisms among institutions to determine who is responsible, making it doubtful whether a worker can now benefit from two funds. See this discussion in Carballo Piñeiro, 'Worker Protection' (n 82) 238.

[96]   According to *Stroumpoulis* (n 81) paras 29–42, Arts 1 and 2 of the Protection of Employees Directive (n 9) do not require employees' obligations to be discharged towards their employers in the Member State where insolvency proceedings are opened, to be covered by the relevant fund.

COMPARATIVE LAW APPROACHES   319

categorization of countries made by Gordon Johnson depending on how they combine wage protection mechanisms, either granting a priority, establishing a wage guarantee fund, or both, is adopted for this analysis.[97] A case in point in this classification was the pro-employee approach taken by Chinese insolvency law, which placed worker claims over secured claims without a cap. The exceptionality of this approach in comparative law finished with the passing of the new Corporate Insolvency Law in 2006,[98] which was delayed precisely because of the reluctance to embrace such a drastic departure from the previous approach.[99] Nowadays, secured creditors in this jurisdiction get a treatment distinct from unsecured creditors, including employee claims that have a priority only as regards to the latter.[100]

Once the Chinese pro-employee approach has been removed from the classifica-   **11.36** tion, three policy models remain, as can be also deducted from the structure of the Protection of Workers' Claims Convention, where States can choose to ratify either Part II on employee protection by means of a privilege, or Part III on employee protection by a guarantee institution, or both. Accordingly, a first category of countries provides workers only with an insolvency priority, such as the cases of Chile and Mexico illustrate. A second category of countries does not provide for an insolvency priority but only for a sort of insurance or guarantee fund, Finland and Germany being prominent examples. A majority of countries do provide for both (i.e. an insolvency priority and a wage guarantee fund), although there are significant divergences among these countries on the extent of the (super-)priority offered and that provided by the said wage guarantee funds. On account of these differences, further distinctions are made between those countries with a robust protection system versus those with a weaker sub-model.[101] This group of countries is the most numerous, and the model can be found in the majority of European Union (EU) Member States.

As indicated, some countries only provide for employee priorities in the event of the   **11.37** employer's default and do not contemplate any wage guarantee scheme. That is the case with Chile, whose Civil Code establishes a priority covering unpaid wages, family allowances, and social security contributions withheld from such wages, as well as severance pay accrued in favour of workers, in this case with a cap.[102] In addition to having ratified only Part II of ILO Convention No. 173, Art. 123 of the Mexican Constitution

---

[97] Johnson, 'Insolvency and Social Protection' (n 6) 1.

[98] Law on Corporate Insolvency promulgated by the National People's Congress on 27 August 2006, in force since 1 June 2007.

[99] See Steven J. Arsenault, 'The Westernization of Chinese Bankruptcy: An Examination of China's New Corporate Bankruptcy Law through the Lens of the UNCITRAL Legislative Guide to Insolvency Law', Penn State International Law Review, 27 (2008) 45, 57–8.

[100] See Art. 41 of the Chinese Corporate Insolvency Law. In accordance with Art. 132 thereof, and striving for a compromise between the old and new approaches, wages and medical payments and debts for medical, retirement, and insurance expenses for employees of the insolvent entity that were owed before 27 August 2006 were granted priority treatment over the secured creditors of the debtor.

[101] This adjustment in Johnson's classification can be found in Secunda, 'An Analysis' (n 49) 874.

[102] The relevant provision is Art. 2472(5) of the Chilean Civil Code, which submits to Art. 163bis(2) of the Code of Labour to establish, for severance pay, a cap of up to a maximum of three months' wages per year and up to ten years per employee. Vacation pay is included in the priority without limitations.

320   ASPECTS OF LABOUR LAW

lays down a super-priority for unpaid wages and seniority bonuses that is capped up to one year by Art. 113 of the Federal Labour Law. Both countries provide for the workers to be paid with the proceeds of the insolvency estate without them being required to file their claims in the proceedings.[103] In practice, this generous (super-)priorities encounter problems of lack of assets in the estate to cover all claims, late payments, and insolvencies of viable businesses precisely triggered by the payment of wage claims and which could have been alleviated by the existence of a guarantee fund.[104]

11.38   The benefits of a model that only relies on a wage guarantee fund to protect employees is the predictability that it instils to the ranking of claims and thus to the relationship between creditors/lenders and debtor. Against this backdrop, Germany issued a new *Insolvenzordnung* (InsO) in 1994 adhering to this philosophy and abolishing all pre-existing statutory priorities save the case of some statutory liens. More specifically, the new insolvency law put an end to a super-priority granted to claims for due wages over six months prior to the employers' insolvency, introduced in 1974.[105] In this year, a wage guarantee fund was also introduced,[106] which is in operation nowadays and compensates for the absence of employee priorities in the new system.[107] However, this social fund only covers outstanding workers' claims related to a three-month period prior to the opening of insolvency proceedings[108] and only up to an amount in line with the monthly unemployment benefit.[109] In the case of Finland, the Pay Security Act (866/1998) provides for a pay security system funded by the employer's contribution to unemployment insurance and that covers all workers' claims due within a three-month period prior to applying for guarantee, regardless of the duration of employment or the type of contract. However, the amount to be paid per employee is capped.

11.39   The most common approach to worker protection in the employer's insolvency is to provide for a hybrid system that includes both, employee priorities and an insurance or guarantee fund, although the level of protection greatly varies from country to country. On the upper end of the scale, the French jurisdiction is a case in point, and not just because of their historical role in introducing employee priorities as abovementioned. The system lays down a super-priority that covers any outstanding workers' claims, although capped at an amount that can be increased and updated by the government.[110]

---

[103] See Art. 148 of the Chilean Insolvency Act and Art. 114 of the Mexican Federal Labour Law.

[104] Jequier Lehuedé, 'Créditos laborales y trabajadores' (n 64) 805–30; Amayrani Zamorano Muñoz, 'Fondo de garantía salarial en caso de insolvencia del empleador', Hechos y Derechos, 33 (2016) <https://revistas.juridicas. unam.mx/index.php/hechos-y-derechos/article/view/10465/12631> accessed 15 January 2024.

[105] See §§ 59(1) No. 3-a, 60(1), and 61(1) No. 1-a of the *Konkursordnung*, introduced by Art. 2 § 1 No. 1-b of the Act of 17 July 1974, BGBl I, 1481.

[106] See § 141a of the *Arbeitsförderungsgesetz* (AFG) [1969] BGBl. I/582, as amended in 1974. The AFG was repealed in 1997 through the *Sozialgesetzbuch*, 3d book.

[107] See § 165 of the *Sozialgesetzbuch* [1997] BGBl, I/594.

[108] ibid. Wage claims include wages, holiday pay, bonuses, and pension contributions (*Insolvenzgeld*).

[109] ibid § 167.

[110] The super-priority only covers a monthly amount up to a maximum of twice the amount used to calculate social and social security contributions. See Art. L625-7 of *Code de Commerce* referring to Art. L143-10 of the *Code du Travail*. This rule was originally introduced by *Décret* 73-1046 of 15 November 1973 and, since 2008, is laid down in Art. L3253-2 of the *Code du Travail*.

The exceeding outstanding claims benefit from a fourth-rank general privilege over movable assets and a second-rank general privilege on immovable assets.[111] These priorities are supplemented with an insurance vehicle fed by employers' contributions that covers all due wages and pensions claims without time limitation up to a maximum amount that is updated every year.[112] It is to be noted that an excess of statutory priorities makes it difficult to get payment from the debtor's assets, making the role of the wage guarantee fund that nevertheless has subrogation rights more relevant.

On the other side of the scale, the UK jurisdiction is an example of a constrained worker protective hybrid system. Statutory priorities are exceptional in this insolvency law, with the exception of workers' claims earned for a four-month period prior to the opening of an insolvency proceeding.[113] The priority is capped at a maximum amount of £800, a figure that has remained unchanged since 1976.[114] Hence, the relevant protection is provided by the National Insurance Fund, which pays for a maximum eight-week pay claim and a maximum of six weeks' holiday pay, all at a rate of £464 a week, and a statutory redundancy payment.[115] Another example of weak worker protection is provided by the United States, where employee and pension claims earned in the 180 days prior to a Chapter 11 petition rank fourth in priority, but only up to an amount.[116]

11.40

In one way or another, legislations seem to acknowledge the need for worker protection in the event of the employer's insolvency. However, and since the 1949 Protection of Wages Convention, the situation has significantly changed, and not to the workers' benefit but placing other creditors, in particular secured ones, on a more prominent place. While the political connotations of employee priorities have been replaced by economic considerations that align the employer's recovery with securing investment opportunities, workers' singularity as creditors has been somehow realigned.[117] Moreover, the economics behind (not) supporting workers tend to resurface in the form of social protection mechanisms that transfer the costs to the whole economy.

11.41

---

[111] Respectively, Arts 2331 and 2375 of the *Code Civil*.

[112] See Arts L 3253-6 et seq. of *Code de Travail* governing the *Association pour la Gestion du Régime d'Assurance des Créances des Salaires*. As to the maximum amount to be paid, it depends on the seniority of the employee. The maximum for 2021 for contracts of up to more than a two-year seniority prior to the opening of insolvency proceedings was set up at 82,272€. See Ministére du Travail, de l'Emploi et de l'Insertion, 'La garantie en cas de sauvegarde, de redressement ou de liquidation judiciaire', <https://travail-emploi.gouv.fr> accessed 26 February 2024.

[113] See Sch. 6, Category 5 of the Insolvency Act 1986. According to s. 387 thereof, priority is triggered according to the specific procedure, the date on which the company entered administration, the date on which a voluntary arrangement takes effect, the date of the appointment of a provisional liquidator, or the date of the winding-up order.

[114] This amount was originally increased to £800 by Sch. 1 Pt 1 of the Insolvency Act 1976 (amending s. 33(1)(b) and (c) of the Insolvency Act 1914) and then, following the enactment of the Insolvency Act 1986, it was confirmed by s. 4 of the Insolvency Proceedings (Monetary Limits) Order 1986, SI 1986/1996.

[115] See ss 166–9 of the Employment Rights Act 1996.

[116] See 11 U.S.C. §507.

[117] See Mucciarelli, 'Employee Insolvency Priorities' (n 56) 263–4. Remarkably, there seems to be a trend towards placing them on an equal footing with trade creditors. To this end, it is worth reminding ourselves of the words of Lord Steyn: '[i]t is no longer right to equate a contract of employment with commercial contracts. One possible way of describing a contract of employment in modern terms is as a relational contract': see *Johnson v Unisys Ltd* [2001] IRLR 279 at para. 20.

322   ASPECTS OF LABOUR LAW

In the case of hybrid systems, insurance or guarantee funds may still benefit from the distributive effects implied in statutory priorities and get financed by the insolvency estate.[118] Against a backdrop of increasing inequality among societies, and the pressure exercised by the SDGs upon countries, it is to be noted that the 2015 EIR Recast acknowledges the different employee priorities across Member States, but suggests that the next review—due in 2022—should seek to 'improve preferential rights of employees at European level'.[119] In a similar vein, draft legislation to amend title 11 of the United States Code, with a view to improving protections for employees and retirees in business bankruptcies, has been introduced in the House of Representatives in 2020.[120] All in all, both ongoing legislative processes reveal that the distributional question in insolvency is far from being closed, showing that the debate is as lively as ever.

VI. Worker Entitlements and Directors' Liability

11.42   Directors' liability in the event of the company's insolvency might also include the payment of workers' entitlements. The rationale behind this approach is the role that they play in the operation of companies, that is the powers that they are granted by corporate law in order to run the business and thus lead it either to wealth creation or insolvency. In view of these powers, directors have a responsibility not only as regards to shareholders and the corporation but also towards society and economy, that compels them to minimize damage to the latter, especially in the vicinity of insolvency, as can be learnt from Chapter 7 'Directors' Duties in the Vicinity of Insolvency, Disqualification, Piercing the Veil'. Against this backdrop, and in view of workers' vulnerability, some jurisdictions have laid down their responsibility for workers' claims in the period leading up to insolvency proceedings.[121] However, directors' liability only arises on a subsidiary basis, that is after the insolvency proceedings over the debtor company reveals that there are no assets or insurance that can cover workers' claims and thus the director's estate becomes liable.[122]

11.43   The abovementioned devices operate in the framework of an insolvency proceeding and provided that the insolvency practitioner pursues the case. However, another device might encourage the payment of wages even in the event of employer's default.

---

[118] Highlighting the benefits of a hybrid model, see ILO, 'General Survey' (n 45) para. 353.

[119] See Recital 22 of EIR Recast (n 38).

[120] See H.R.7370—Protecting Employees and Retirees in Business Bankruptcies Act of 2020.

[121] In Australia, this problem is named 'fraudulent phoenix activity' and has given rise to litigation not only as regards directors' liability but also involving their counsellors. See Helen Anderson, 'Fraudulent Transactions Affecting Employees: Some New Perspectives on the Liability of Advisors', Melbourne University Law Review, 39 (2015) 1; Anne Matthew, 'The Conundrum of Phoenix Activity: Is Further Reform Necessary?', Insolvency Law Journal, 23 (2015) 116.

[122] See s. 214 of the UK Insolvency Act 1986. This is the case of Canada, whose s. 119 of the Business Corporation Act establishes director's subsidiary liability for six months' wages and related entitlements in the period leading up to insolvency. In case of several directors, liability is jointly and severally held by them. Art. 125 of the Chinese Corporate Insolvency Act lays down directors' liability in the vicinity of insolvency, including wage and pension claims.

A court in the United Kingdom can issue a director's disqualification order for 'unfitness' whenever evidence is submitted that a director's conduct 'makes him unfit to be concerned with the management of a company'.[123] Case law illustrates that this would be the case when directors pay in the vicinity of the insolvency only some classes of creditors but not others, such as employees.[124] Accordingly, directors have a strong incentive to pay workers' claims even if the company is on the verge of insolvency, that of avoiding a disqualification order for preferring some creditors over others.

---

[123] See s. 6 of the Company Directors Disqualification Act 1986.
[124] Although workers had been paid in these cases; see *Sevenoaks (Stationers) Retail* [1991] Ch 164; *Secretary of State for Trade and Industry v McTighe* [1997] BCC 224; *Official Receiver v Barnes* [2001] BCC 578; *Official Receiver v Roger Charles Gawn* [2014] Ch. WL 1219446.

Bibliography

Adler, Managing the Chapter 15 Cross-Border Insolvency Case, 2nd ed., Federal Judicial Center, 2014

Atkins/Luck, *Re Hydrodec Group* [2021] NSWSC 755 (case comment), (2021), 30 IIR, 460

Bellissimo/Johnston, Cross Border Insolvency Protocols: Developing an International Standard, in: Norton Annual Review of International Insolvency 2010, 37

Bělohlávek, EU and International Insolvency Proceedings, Regulation (EU) 2015/848 on Insolvency Proceedings Commentary, Lex Lata, 2020

Bender/Bovenzi/Pinkas, Scheme of Arrangement Confirming Nonconsensual Third-Party Releases Approved in Chapter 15s, (2018), 37 ABIJ 34

Berends, The UNCITRAL Model Law on Cross-Border Insolvency: A Comprehensive Overview, (1998), 6 Tulane Journal of International and Comparative Law, 309

Berger, The Creeping Codification of the New Lex Mercatoria, 2nd ed., Wolters Kluwer, 2010

de Boer/Wessels, The Dominance of Main Insolvency Proceedings under the European Insolvency Regulation, in: Omar (ed.), International Insolvency Law. Themes and Perspectives, Ashgate Publishing, 2008, 185

Bork, Corporate Insolvency Law, Intersentia, 2020

Bork, Einführung in das Insolvenzrecht, 10th ed., MohrSiebeck, 2021

Bork, Opening Statement on the New Rules for the Insolvency of Groups of Companies, in: Hess/Oberhammer/Bariatti/Koller/Laukemann/Isidro/Villata (eds), The Implementation of the New Insolvency Regulation, Nomos Verlagsgesellschaft/Hart Publishing, 2017, 284

Bork, Principles of Cross-Border Insolvency Law, Intersentia, 2017

Bork, The European Insolvency Regulation and the UNCITRAL Model Law on Cross-Border Insolvency, (2017), 26 IIR, 246

Bork/Harten, Die Niederlassung iSv Art. 2 Nr. 10 EuInsVO bei natürlichen Personen' (2018), 18 NZI, 674

Bork/Mangano, European Cross-Border Insolvency Law, 2nd ed., Oxford University Press, 2022

Bork/Veder, Harmonisation of Transactions Avoidance Laws, Intersentia 2022

Bork/van Zwieten (eds), Commentary on the EIR, 2nd ed., Oxford University Press, 2022

Bowen, An Introduction to the Fundamental Principles Governing Cross-border Insolvency in an English Law Context, (2013), 4 IILR, 121

Brinkmann, Avoidance Claims in the Context of the EIR, (2013) 4 IILR, 371

Brinkmann (ed.), European Insolvency Regulation, C. H. Beck/Hart Publishing/Nomos Verlagsgesellschaft, 2019

Brown, Kireeva v Bedzhamov, (2022), 15 CRI, 28

Brown, LBI hf v. Kepler Capital Markets SA [2013] EUECJ C.85/12, (2014), 11 ICR, 12

Bufford, Revision of the European Union Regulation on Insolvency Proceedings: Recommendations, (2012), 3 IILR, 341

Buxbaum, Rethinking International Insolvency: The Neglected Role of Choice-of-Law Rules and Theory, (2000), 36 Stan. J. Int'l L., 23

Carr/Peral, Landlords Without Borders: Challenges in Canadian/U.S. Cross-Border Retail Restructurings, (2022), 41 ABIJ, 20

Casasola, The Transaction Avoidance Regime in the Recast European Insolvency Regulation: Limits and Prospects, (2019), 28 IIR, 163

Clark, Ancillary and Other Cross-Border Insolvency Cases Under Chapter 15 of the Bankruptcy Code, LexisNexis Matthew Bender, 2008

Conolly/Rawson, Re Akkurate Ltd (in Liquidation) [2020] EWHC 1433 (Ch), (2020), 17 ICR, 400

Cooper, Leite v Amicorp [2020] EWHC 3560 (Ch), (2021), 18 ICR, 137

Countryman, Executory Contracts in Bankruptcy, (1973), 57 Minn. L. Rev., 439

326 BIBLIOGRAPHY

Crinson/FitzGerald, When Will Actions be Considered Sufficiently Closely Connected to Fall Within the Scope of the Insolvency Regulation in Light of the CJEU's Decision in *Tünkers Maschinenbau GmbH v Expert France?*, (2018), 11 CRI, 14

Crinson/Gallagher, Fighting on: the Rule in *Gibbs* Survives Another Day, (2019), 12 CRI, 47

Dammann/Sénéchal, Le droit de l'insolvabilité international, Joly, 2018

Davies, The Influence of Huber's *De Conflictu Legum* on English Private International Law, (1937), 18 BYBIL, 49

Dicey/Morris/Collins, Conflict of Laws, 15th ed., Sweet & Maxwell, 2012

Ebo/Gillingham, *Lekars Group Ltd v East-West Logistics LLP* [2021] EWHC 1523 (Ch), (2022), 19 ICR, 49

Eidenmüller, What is an Insolvency Proceeding?, (2018), 92 ABLJ 53

Epstein/Markell/Nickles/Ponoroff, Bankruptcy, 4th ed., West Academic Publishing, 2015

Faber/Vermunt/Kilborn/Richter, Commencement of Insolvency Proceedings, Oxford University Press, 2021

Fabok, Jurisdiction concerning annex actions in the context of the insolvency and Brussels Ibis regulations, (2020), 29 IIR, 204

Fennessy/Radia/Andronikou, The Restructuring of the DTEK Group: A Challenge to the International Effectiveness of a Scheme of Arrangement in a Post-Brexit Era, (2021), 18 ICR, 331

Fink/Barrett, Any Port in a Storm? The Applicability of Section 546(e)'s Safe Harbor in Chapter 15 Cases, (2021), 18 ICR, 353

Fink/Barrett, Is Chapter 15 a Prerequisite to Obtain Comity from a US Court with Respect to Foreign Insolvency Proceedings, (2022), 19 ICR, 38

Fletcher, Ancient and Modern: Mediations on the Anglo-Dutch Dimension in the Evolution of Cross-border Insolvency Law in: Santen/van Offeren (eds), Tribute to Bob Wessels, Kluwer 2014, 55

Fletcher, Insolvency in Private International Law, 2nd ed., Oxford University Press 2005

Fletcher, Spreading the Gospel: The Mission of Insolvency Law, and Insolvency Practitioners, in the Early 21st Century, (2014), 26 JBL, 535

Fletcher, The Law of Insolvency, 5th ed., Sweet & Maxwell, 2017

Fletcher, The Public Policy Exception under Article 6 of the UNCITRAL Model Law – Anglo-American Judicial Approaches, (2018), 31 Insolv. Int., 64

Fox/McIntosh/Yeong, Timing is Everything: Different Approaches to the Relevant Date for Determining COMI in Cross-border Recognition Proceedings, (2019), 12 CRI, 142

Fradley, Re Akkurate Ltd: The Territorial Limits of Section 236(3), (2021), 34 Insolv. Int., 43

Fu, Cross-Border Insolvency in Bermuda: Cambridge Gas Revisited, (2018), 31 Insolv. Int., 118

van Galen, The Recast Insolvency Regulation and Groups of Companies, in Parry/Omar (eds), Reimagining Rescue, INSOL Europe, 2016, 53

van Galen/André/Fritz/Gladel/van Koppen/Marks/Wouters, Revision of the EIR, INSOL Europe, 2021

Garcimartín, Cross-Border Vis Attractiva Concursus: the EU Approach, (2018), 31 Insolv. Int., 14

Garrido, Oversecured and Undersecured Creditors in Cross-border Insolvencies, (2014), 5 IILR, 375

Gilhuly/Posin/Malatesta, Bankruptcy Without Borders, (2016), 24 ABILR, 47

Glosband, Update on Third-Party Releases in Chapters 15 and 11, (2019), 32 Insolv. Int., 38

Glosband/Kelakos/Lifland/McEvoy/Melnik/Seamon/Silverman, Cross-border Insolvency in the United States, American Bankruptcy Institute, 2008

Good, *Jaffe v Samsung Electronics Co., Ltd.*: Exploring the Limits of 'Additional Relief' and 'Additional Assistance' under Chapter 15 of the US Bankruptcy Code, (2014), 11 ICR, 119

Good, 'Stress testing' Chapter 15 of the US Bankruptcy Code, (2014), 7 CRI, 192

Greenleaf, Is Substantive Consolidation a Viable Cause of Action Post-Law?, (2018), 37 ABIJ, 54

Gropper, The Curious Disappearance of Choice of Law as an Issue in Chapter 15 Cases, (2014), 9, Brook. J. Corp. Fin. & Comm. L., 57

Harlang/Vininsky, Nortel Networks, (2015), 34 ABIJ, 18

Haß/Huber/Gruber/Heiderhoff, EU-Insolvenzverordnung, C. H. Beck, 2005

Hawthorn, *Videology Ltd* and the Cross-Border Insolvency Regulations 2006: A Matter of Discretion, (2018), 11 CRI, 161

Hawthorn/Gass, The Importance of Full and Frank Disclosure in Seeking Assistance Under the CBIRs: A Look at *Re Dalnyaya Step LLC (In Liquidation)* [2017] EWHC 3153 (Ch), (2018), 11 CRI, 41

Hawthorn/Thompson, Re Agrokor DD: An Extraordinary Foreign Proceedings, but not too Extraordinary for Recognition under the Cross-Border Insolvency Regulations 2006, (2018), 11 CRI, 6

Hawthorn/Young, Remodelling the Model Law: The Model Law on Recognition and Enforcement of Insolvency Related Judgments, (2018) 11 CRI, 195

Herman/Zucker/Kaslow, Fundamental Procedural Fairness: The Sine Qua Non for the Enforcement of Third-Party Releases Authorized in a Foreign Proceeding, (2021), 40 ABIJ, 30

Hess/Oberhammer/Pfeiffer, European Insolvency Law, C. H. Beck/Hart Publishing/Nomos Verlagsgesellschaft, 2014

Ho (ed.), Cross-Border Insolvency, 4th ed., Global Law and Business, 2017

Ho, Enforcing Foreign Insolvency Judgments: *New Cap Re*, (2011), 4 CRI, 157

Hoffmann, Executory Contracts, *Ipso Facto* Clause sand Licensing Agreements in Cross-Border Insolvencies, (2018), 27 IIR, 300

Houmand/Ortiz, Substantive Consolidation Might Redefine a Debtor, (2018), 37 ABIJ, 30

Hrycaj, The Cooperation of Court Bodies of International Insolvency Proceedings, (2011), 2 IILR, 7

Huber, Praelectionum Juris Romani et Hodierni, Leonardus Strickius, Franeker 1689 (2nd ed., 1700)

Isidro, Cooperation, Communication, Coordination, in: Hess/Oberhammer/Bariatti/Koller/Laukemann/Isidro/Villata (eds), The Implementation of the New Insolvency Regulation, Nomos Verlagsgesellschaft/Hart Publishing, 2017, 139

Johnston/Werlen/Link, Set-Off Law and Practice, Oxford University Press, 3rd ed., 2018

Kaçar, Territorialism Embraced: Cross Border Insolvency in Turkey, (2018), 11 CRI, 20

Kodek, The Treatment of Security Rights, (2015), 6 IILR, 10

Kokorin/Wessels, COMIs Under Chapter 15 and EIR Recast: Brothers, but Not Twins, (2018), 37 ABIJ, 62 et seq.

Kokorin/Wessels, Cross-Border Protocols in Insolvencies of Multinational Enterprise Groups, Edward Elgar Publishing, 2021

Kolmann, Kooperationsmodelle im Internationalen Insolvenzrecht, Gieseking, 2001

Kostin/Rzyanina, Avoidance of the Debtor's Transactions Within the Framework of a Foreign Insolvency Before a Russian court, available at https://conflictoflaws.net/2021/avoidance-of-the-debtors-transactions-within-the-framework-of-a-foreign-insolvency-before-a-russian-court/?utm_source=feedburner&utm_medium=email&utm_campaign=Feed%3A+conflictofl aws%2FRSS+%28Conflict+of+Laws+.net%29

Kramer/Sogo, Switzerland – New International Insolvency Law, (2019), 16 ICR, 1

Krohe, Insolvenzverfahren, in: Baum/Bälz (eds), Handbuch Japanisches Handels- und Wirtschaftsrecht, Carl Heymanns Verlag, 2011, para. 106

Lagram-Taylor, Re Agrokor [2017] EWHC 2791 (Ch) (9 November 2017), (2018), 15 ICR, 303

Laughton, The Cross-Border Insolvency Regulations 2006: A Practical Guide to Opportunities for Cooperation now That the UK has Left the EU, (2021), 14 CRI, 149

Laukemann, Instruments to avoid or postpone secondary proceedings, in: Hess/Oberhammer/Bariatti/Koller/Laukemann/Isidro/Villata (eds), The Implementation of the New Insolvency Regulation, Nomos Verlagsgesellschaft/Hart Publishing, 2017, 106

Le Corre, Droit et pratique des procédúres collectives, 11th ed., Dalloz, 2021

Leonhard, A Creative Application of Chapter 15, (2014), 33 ABIJ, 48

Li, Substantive Consolidation of Bankruptcy Proceedings in China: A Critical Examination, (2021), 95 ABLJ, 537

Linna, Cross-border Debt Adjustment, (2014), 23 IIR, 20

LoPucki, Courting Failure, The University of Michigan Press, 2005

Lorenzen, Huber's de Conflictu Legum, (1919), 13 Ill. Law Rev., 375

Lowe/McNeil, COMI Manipulation in Chapter 15: Are There any Lessons for Other Jurisdictions?, (2018), 11 CRI, 133

Luhmann, Legitimation durch Verfahren, Luchterhand, 1969

328 BIBLIOGRAPHY

Lupton/Hecht/Nolan, Cayman Communications: The Grand Court of the Cayman Islands Approves Direct Court-to-Court Communications Protocol for the First Time *In Re LATAM Finance Ltd (and ors)*, (2020), 17 ICR, 422

Madaus, Insolvency Proceedings for Corporate Groups Under the New Insolvency Regulation, (2015), 6 IILR, 235

Madaus, Leaving the Shadows of US Bankruptcy Law, (2018), 19 EBOR, 615

Magalhaes, Chapter 15 Primer: Learning the Global Chess Game, (2019), 38 ABIJ 18

Magalhaes, Chapter 15 Revisited: Unpacking More Concepts from Recent Cases (2021), 40 ABIJ, 24

Mangano, The Puzzle of the New European COMI Rules: Rethinking COMI in the Age of Multinational, Digital and Glocal Enterprises', (2019), 20 EBOR, 780

Marshall/Herrod, European Cross-Border Insolvency, Sweet & Maxwell, loose-leaf, as of 2021

Martin/Speckhart, Chapter 15 for Foreign Debtors, American Bankruptcy Institute, 2015

Matsushita, UNCITRAL Model Law and the Comprehensive Reform of Japanese Insolvency, in: Basedow/Kono (eds), Legal Aspects of Globalization, Kluwer Law International, 2000, 151

McCormack, Conflicts, Avoidance and International Insolvency 20 Years on: A Triple Cocktail, (2013), 2, JBL, 141

McCormack, Set-off Under the European Insolvency Regulation (and English Law), (2020), 29 IIR, 100

McCormack, US Exceptionalism and UK Localism? Cross-border Insolvency Law in Comparative Perspective, (2016), 36 Legal Studies, 136

McCoy, The *Singularis* Work-around? Overcoming Limitations to the Common Law Power of Assistance for Foreign Insolvency Investigations, (2019), 16 ICR, 210

Mélin, La faillite international, Librairie Général de Droit, 2004

Mevorach, A Fresh View on the Hard/Soft Law Divide: Implications for International Insolvency of Enterprise Groups, (2019), 40 Michigan Journal of International Law, 505

Mevorach, Insolvency within Multinational Enterprise Groups, Oxford University Press, 2009

Mevorach, Prospects for an International Bankruptcy Court: My Conversations with Ian Fletcher, (2019), 32 Insolv. Int., 16

Mitchell-Fry/Çapani, Compromising English law debts: Has the Rule in *Gibbs* had its Days?, (2018), 11 CRI, 206

Mokal, What is an insolvency proceeding? *Gategroup* lands in gated community, (2022), 31 IIR, 418

Moss, The English Contribution to Cross-Frontier Recognition and Judicial Assistance, in: Santen/van Offeren (eds), Tribute to Bob Wessels, Kluwer 2014, 95

Moss, UNCITRAL Model Law on Recognition and Inforcement of Insolvency-related Judgments, (2019), 32 Insolv. Int., 21

Moss/Douglas, A US Perspective on *Agrokor*: Bankruptcy Court in Chapter 15 Case Refuses to Extend Comity to the Rule in *Gibbs*, (2019), 12 CRI, 90

Moss/Fletcher/Isaacs (eds), The EC Regulation on Insolvency Proceedings, 3rd ed., Oxford University Press, 2016

Münchener Kommentar zur Insolvenzordnung see *Stürner* et al.

Murray-Jones/Balmond, *In the Matter of Nektan (Gibraltar) Ltd* [2020] EWHC 65 (Ch), (2020), 17 ICR, 141

Nadelmann, *Solomons v Ross* and International Bankruptcy Law, (1946), 9 Modern Law Review, 154

Neder Cerezetti, Reorganization of Corporate Groups in Brazil: Substantive Consolidation and the Limited Liability Tale, (2021), 30 IIR, 169

Nielsen/Sigal/Wagner, The Cross-border Insolvency Concordat: Principles to Facilitate the Resolution of International Insolvencies, (1996), 70 ABLJ, 533

Oberhammer/Koller/Auernig/Planitzer, Insolvencies of Groups of Companies, in: Hess/Oberhammer/Bariatti/Koller/Laukemann/Isidro/Villata (eds), The Implementation of the New Insolvency Regulation, Nomos Verlagsgesellschaft/Hart Publishing, 2017, 185

Omar, Cross-Border Insolvency and Principles of Judicial Assistance: Recent Themes and Developments, in: Santen/van Offeren (eds), Tribute to Bob Wessels, Kluwer 2014, 103

Omar, Judicial Cooperation in the Post-*Singularis* World, (2018), 15 ICR, 22

Patrick, Gibbs Expansion in Prosafe Further Erdes Universalism in Cross-Border Insolvency?, (2022), 19 ICR, 25

Patella, Judge, I've Got a Feeling We're Not in Kansas Anymore (or Moscow, Either), (2019), 38 ABIJ 28

Paulus, Security Rights in Cross-Border Insolvency Proceedings, (2014), 5 IILR, 366

Peacock, The Novel Cross-Border Bankruptcy Trial, (2015), 23 ABILR, 543

Peck, Cross-border Observations Derived from my Lehman Judicial Experience, (2015), 30 JIBFL, 131

Pepels, Cross-border CoCo in group insolvencies under the Recast EIR and the existence of an 'overriding group interest' – One for all, and all for one?, EIRJ-2021-5

Pepels, Defining Groups of Companies Under the European Insolvency Regulation (Recast): On the Scope of EU Group Insolvency Law, IIR 30 (2021), 96

Pepels, Group Coordination Proceedings under the Recast EIR in practice – or not?, EIRJ 2022-2

Possinger/Stevens, *In re Fairfield Sentry II*: Testing the Brakes on Comity, (2018), 15 ICR, 170

Pottow, Greed and Pride in International Bankruptcy: The Problems of and Proposed Solutions to 'Local Interests', (2006), 104 Mich. L. Rev., 1899

Reumers, Cooperation between Liquidators and Courts in Insolvency Proceedings of Related Companies under the Proposed Revised EIR, (2013), 10 European Company and Financial Law Review, 588

Roberts/Williams, Australian Court Winds up UK Company and Dismisses Recognition Application by UK Monitors, (2021), 14 CRI, 118

Robinson/Duffy, *Stephen John Hunt v Transworld Payment Solutions U.K. Ltd (in liquidation)* [2020] Bda LR 17, (2021), 18 ICR, 175

Rogan, DTEK and International Recognition of the Scheme of Arrangement in the post-Brexit Era, (2021), 14 CRI, 130

Rordorf, Cross Border Insolvency, (2010) 1 IILR, 16

Sachdev, Choice of Law in Insolvency Proceedings: How English Courts' Continued Reliance on the Gibbs Principle Threatens Universalism, (2019), 93 ABLJ, 343

Sandberg, *Sturgeon* revisited: UK Courts Cannot Grant Recognition to Solvent Winding up Proceedings under the Cross-Border Insolvency Regulations 2006, (2020), 13 CRI, 21

Sandberg/Skupski, Cross-Border Insolvency Regulations 2006: UK Courts can Grant Recognition to Solvent Winding up Proceedings, (2019), 12 CRI, 167

Savigny, System des heutigen Römischen Rechts, vol. VIII, Veit, 1849

Savina/Mukhametgaliev, Recognition of Foreign Insolvency-related Judgments in the Russian Federation, (2019), 16 ICR, 271

Savković, Universalism and the Recognition of Group Proceedings under the UNCITRAL Model Law in Montenegro, (2019), 28 IIR, 103

Schmidt, Preventive Restructuring Frameworks: Jurisdiction, Recognition and Applicable Law, (2022), 31 IIR, 81

Schreurs, The Approval of European Synthetic Secondaries ('Undertakings') by Local Creditors, A Dutch Perspektive, (2020), 33 Insolv. Int., 78

Sheldon, Cross-Border Insolvency, 4th ed., Bloomsbury Professional, 2015

Shelly, Chapter 15 Court Balances Competing Comity Concerns and Grants Conditional Approval of Croatian Restructuring Plan (*In re Agrokor*, 2018 WL 5298403 (Bankr. S.D.N.Y.)), (2019), 16 ICR, 45

Shelley, Innovative Use of Chapter 15 of US Bankruptcy Code Helps Brazilian Debtors Reorganise (*In re Oi, S.A.*, 587 BR 253 (Bankr. S.D.N.Y.)), (2018), 15 ICR, 364

Shelley, Move It On Over: Intentional Prepetition COMI Shift Does Not Preclude Chapter 15 Recognition (*In re Ocean Rig UDW Inc.*, 570 B.R. 687 (Bankr. S.D.N.Y. 2017)), (2018), 15 ICR, 51

Shorr, Avoidance Actions Under Chapter 15: Was Condor Correct? (2016), 1, F. I. L. J., 351

Shuster/Loveland, Al Zawawi and § 109(a): Parsing What It Means to Be a 'Debtor' Under Chapter 15, (2022), 41 ABIJ, 30

Shuster/Loveland, Olinda Star Achieves Broad Intercompany Cross-Border Relief, (2020), 39 ABIJ 18

Shuster/Loveland, Seeing Double?, (2018), 37 ABIJ 18

de Soveral Martins, Groups of Companies in the Recast European Insolvency Regulation: Around and About the 'Group', (2019), 28 IIR, 354

330 BIBLIOGRAPHY

Stones, Hotchpot (or the Equality Rule), (2015), 8 CRI, 25

Stürner/Eidenmüller/Schoppmeyer (ed.), Münchener Kommentar zur InsO, vol. 4, 4th ed., C. H. Beck 2021

Tabb, Law of Bankruptcy, 4th ed., West Academic Publishing, 2016

Taylor, International Insolvency when the EU Regulation is not Applicable: The Case of the United Kingdom, in: Affaki (ed.), Faillite internationale et conflit de juridiction – Regards croisés transatlantique, FEC/Bruylant, Paris/ Bruxelles 2007, 125

Taylor/Cheema, Re Videology Ltd [2018] EWHC 2186 (Ch), (2019), 16 ICR, 119

Teong Ying Keat, What is Sauce for the Goose may not be Sauce for the Gander – Analysing the Principles Applicable to Recognition of Foreign Parallel Proceedings in Staying Local Proceedings, (2021), 34 Insolv. Int., 120

Tett/Jones, In the matter of Northsea Base Investment Limited & ors [2015] EWHC 121 (Ch); Birss J, 26 January 2015, (2015), 12 ICR, 325

Thole/Dueñas, Some Observations on The New Group Coordination Procedure of the Reformed European Insolvency Regulation, (2015), 24 IIR, 214

Thomas/Steel, A New Trend? US-Based Syncreon Opts for English Scheme of Arrangement with Canadian Court Recognition, (2019), 12 CRI, 213

Tillman/Bullen, Nortel: Cross-border Decision Points the Way to Distributions, (2015), 28 Insolv. Int., 91

Tillman/Bullen, The Nortel 'Allocation' Decisions: Nortel Networks Corporation (Re), 2015 ONSC 2987 and In re Nortel Networks Inc. et al., 09-10138 (Delaware Bankruptcy Court) (2015), 12 ICR, 202

Tregear, More Than One Way to Skin a Cat, (2014), 7 CRI, 51

Tribe/Baister, Lord Bathurst's Gift, (2019), 32 Insolv. Int., 7

United Nations Commission on International Trade Law, Digest of Case Law on the UNCITRAL Model Law on Cross-border Insolvency, United Nations 2021

Usmani/Small, Jain Group Successfully Navigates English Restructuring, (2021), 14 CRI, 183

Vallender/Nietzer, Cooperation and Communication of Judges in Cross- border Insolvency Proceedings, in: Santen/van Offeren (eds), Tribute to Bob Wessels, Kluwer, 2014, 127

Veder, Bob's 'Unvollendete'?, in: Santen/van Offeren (eds), Tribute to Bob Wessels, Kluwer 2014, 139

Veder, Cross-border Insolvency Proceedings and Security Rights, Kluwer, 2004

Veder, Party Autonomy and Insolvency, in: Westrik/van der Weide (eds), Party Autonomy in International Property Law, Sellier, 2011, 261

Veder, The Future of the European Insolvency Regulation, (2011), 2 IILR, 285

Virgós/Garcimartín, The European Insolvency Regulation, Kluwer Law International, 2004

Virgós/Schmit, Report on the Convention on Insolvency Proceedings, EC Council Document 6500/96 of 3 May 1996; text available in Bork/van Zwieten, (eds), Commentary on the EIR, 2nd ed., Oxford University Press, 2022, Appendix 4

Viswanathan/Kumar, Cross-Border Insolvency Protocols: A New Beginning in India, (2020), 17 ICR, 95

Walters, Modified Universalisms & the Role of Local Legal Culture in the Making of Cross-Border Insolvency Law, (2019), 93 ABLJ, 47

Warner, Conflicting Norms: Impact of the Model Law on Chapter 11's Global Restructuring Role, (2019), 28 IIR, 273

Warner, Cross-Border Cooperation in the United States: A Retreat or Merely a Pause?, in: Burdette/ Omar/Parry/Walters (eds), Festschrift in Honour of Prof Ian Fletcher QC, (2015), 3 NIBLeJ, 393

Welch/Jumbeck, Know Your Limits: An Approach for Rejecting Substantive Consolidation of Nondebtors, (2018), 37 ABIJ, 22

Wessels, A Glimpse into the Future: Cross-Border Judicial Cooperation in Insolvency Cases in the European Union, (2015), 24 IIR, 96

Wessels, EU Courts Can Rely on Soft Law Principles for Cooperation in International Insolvency Cases, (2015), 6 IILR, 1

Wessels, EU Cross-border Insolvency Court-to-court Cooperation Principles, eleven international publishing, 2015

Wessels, International Insolvency Law, 4th ed., Kluwer, Part I 2015, Part II 2017

Wessels, Towards A Next Step in Cross-border Judicial Cooperation, (2014), 27 Insolv. Int. 100

Wessels, What is an Insolvency Proceedings Anyway?, (2011), 2 IILR, 491

Wessels/Boon, Cross-border Insolvency Law – International Instruments and Commentary, 2nd ed., Wolters Kluwer, 2015

Wessels/Kokorin, Insolvency of Yukos and Public Policy in International Insolvency Cases, (2019), 16 ICR, 229

Wessels/Kokorin, Communication and Cooperation in Cross-Border Restructuring and Insolvency Matters in the EU, (2018), 37 ABIJ, 32.

Wessels/Markell/Kilborn, International Cooperation in Bankruptcy and Insolvency Matters, Oxford University Press, 2009

Wessels/Virgós, European Communication and Cooperation Guidelines for Cross-Border Insolvency, INSOL Europe, 2007

West, UNCITRAL Cross-border Insolvency Model Laws: And Then There Were Two …, (2019), 16 ICR, 82

Westbrook, A Global Solution to Multinational Default, (2000), 98 Mich. L. Rev., 2276

Westbrook, An Empirical Study of the Implementation in the United States of the Model Law on Cross Border Insolvency, (2013), 87 Am. Bankr. L. J., 247

Westbrook, Choice of Avoidance Law in Global Insolvencies, (1991), 17 Brook. J. Int'l L., 499

Westbrook, Creating International Insolvency Law, (1996), 70 ABLJ, 563

Westbrook, *Nortel*: The Cross-border Insolvency Case of the Century, (2015), 30 JIBFL, 498

Westbrook, Universalism and Choice of Law, (2005), 23, Penn State International Law Review, 625

Whibley/Cooper, *Kireeva (Trustee & Bankruptcy Manager in Russia of Bedzhamov) v Bedzhamov* [2021] EWHC 2281 (Ch), (2022), 19 ICR, 52

Wilfinger, Declaration of Claims in International Insolvency Proceedings, EIRJ-2021-2

Williams/Walters, The Model Law: Is it Time for the U.K. to Change Tack?, (2016), 35 ABIJ, 16

Williams/Walters, Modified Universalism in Our Time? A Look at Two Recent Cases in the U.S. and U.K., (2018), 37 ABIJ, 24

Yamauchi, Should Reciprocity Be a Part of the UNCITRAL Model Cross-Border Insolvency Law?, (2007), 16 IIR, 145

Zerjal, *In re B.C.I. Finances PTY Limited*: Further Insights on the Second Circuit Requirement of Having Property in the US to Obtain Recognition of a Foreign Proceeding in Chapter 15, (2019), 16 ICR, 107

Zerjal, UK Order Granting Non-consensual Third-party Releases is Enforced in US Chapter 15 Case, (2018), 15 ICR, 291

Zerjal/Daly, Syncreon: Using an English Scheme to Restructure Debt of a US-based Enterprise, (2020), 17 ICR, 126

Zerjal/Fink/Clements, Bad Faith Is Not a Bar to Chapter 15 Recognition of Foreign Proceedings, Says Southern District of New York Bankruptcy Court, (2022), 19 ICR, 108

Zerjal/Volin, Chapter 15: Appointing a Foreign Representative after the Conclusion of the Foreign Proceedings is not a Bar to Recognition, (2020), 17 ICR, 305

Zhen Qu/Godwin, Does the Common Law Power to Grant Cross-border Insolvency Assistance Apply to an Insolvency Winding-up that is Voluntary? The Reaction to *Singularis* from Singapore and Hong Kong, (2019), 28 IIR, 305

Zumbro, Cross-Border Insolvencies and International Protocols – An Imperfect but Effective Tool, (2010), 11 Bus. L. Int'l, 157

van Zwieten, Apperley Investments Ltd v Monsoon Accessorize Ltd, (2021), 34 Insolv. Int., 69

van Zwieten, Goode on Principles of Corporate Insolvency Law, 5th ed., Sweet & Maxwell, 2018

Index

ability to pay debts *see* inability to pay debts
absolute priority rule (APR) 1.64–1.77
  administrative expenses of the State 5.67
  asset-based (*in* rem) claims and value-based
    claims in rescue 5.49
  confirmation of restructuring
    plans 3.47–3.51
  distributional waterfall 5.66
  fair and equitable test 3.47, 5.60
  labour law 5.68
  pari passu principle 1.61
  realizable priority 5.66, 5.67–5.68, 5.71, 8.72,
    8.78
  relative priority rule (RPR) 1.71, 3.50,
    5.67–5.68
  reorganization process, conditions for debtors
    to enter the 2.35
  Restructuring Directive 3.50
  tax claims 5.68
Acquired Rights Directive 11.09, 11.11–11.13
actio Pauliana/Pauline actions 6.04, 6.48
administration
  consolidation 8.33–8.36
  expenses 3.71, 5.67
  groups
    global restructurings 8.80–8.87
    rescue, in 8.32–8.52
administrators *see* insolvency administrators,
    role and obligations of
admission of insolvency claims 4.64–4.68
after-acquired property 5.38–5.39
anticommons problem 3.14, 8.60, 8.61
applicable law 9.02, 9.30, 9.40–9.55 *see also lex
    fori concursus*
  avoidance of transactions 6.68, 9.52–9.55
  basics 9.41–9.43
  contracts 9.49–9.51
  efficiency, principle of 9.44, 9.47, 9.51
  European Insolvency Regulation (EIR) 9.42–
    9.51, 9.54–9.55
  labour law 11.15–11.16, 11.33
  lex causae 9.47, 9.52, 9.54
  lex loci laboris 11.16, 11.33
  lex situs 9.44, 9.48
  security rights 9.43, 9.44–9.48
approval of the restructuring plans by
    creditors 3.27–3.34

approval levels 3.34, 3.40
  class meetings, constituting 3.27–3.34
  imposition on dissenting creditors 3.28
  majority principle 3.27, 3.34
  minority protection 3.27–3.30
  votes by the creditors 3.27–3.34
asset-based (*in* rem) claims
  blanket liens 5.30, 5.31–5.40
  competing approaches to priority in
    rescue 5.52–5.64
  equitable (asset-value-based) priority 5.52,
    5.60–5.64
  firm-based (*in personam*) claims,
    distinguishing 5.02, 5.29–5.43
  going-concern value 5.44, 5.45, 5.47–5.48,
    5.51, 5.64
  priority 5.02, 5.03, 5.07–5.09, 5.48–5.64, 5.71,
    8.71–8.75
  recapitalization 5.44, 5.47–5.48, 5.65, 5.71
  rescue 5.44–5.65
  sale versus recapitalization 5.47, 5.48, 5.65
  security rights 5.15
  single waterfall absolute priority 5.52, 5.53–
    5.55, 5.57
  single waterfall relative priority 5.52, 5.55–5.57
  value-based claims in rescue 5.44–5.65, 5.70
  value of firm and value of assets, distinction
    between 5.44, 5.45–5.48, 5.52, 5.63
assets of the insolvency estate 4.29–4.34
    see also asset-based (*in* rem) claims; sale
      of businesses
auctions 3.01, 4.94, 4.102, 8.35, 8.40, 8.54
authority paradigm 1.13–1.15
avoidance of transactions *see* transactions
    avoidance rules

Baird, Douglas G 5.55–5.58, 5.60, 5.68
banker's liens 5.25
bankruptcy remoteness 5.22, 5.24
bargain theory 3.15
bargaining game 1.20, 1.73
best interests
  creditors, of the 1.72, 3.47
  groups, of the 8.45, 8.48
  rescue plans 1.67
best possible satisfaction, principle of 6.08,
    6.10, 6.16, 9.23

334 INDEX

blanket liens *see* United States, blanket liens in
brands 2.34, 2.39
Brussels Ia Regulation 9.11
burden of proof
avoidance of transactions 6.30
European Insolvency Regulation (EIR) 9.16
initiate proceedings, creditors' right
to 4.15–4.16
involvement of the creditors 4.67
liability 4.49
piercing the corporate veil 7.78
realizable priority in group cases 8.75–8.76
business distress distinguished from financial
distress 2.01
business judgment rule (BJR) 7.19, 8.24
business transfers 11.09, 11.11–11.13 *see also*
sale of businesses

carveouts 5.42–5.43
Casey, Thomas H 5.55–5.58, 5.60
centre of main interests (COMI)
presumption 8.84, 9.18, 9.35–9.37, 9.66
certainty *see* predictability/legal certainty,
principle of
cessation of payments 2.04, 2.09, 2.32–2.33, 2.36
continuing failure, as a 2.32
inability to pay, presumption of 2.32–2.33
indicators 2.32
initiate proceedings, creditors' right to 4.16
preferences 6.37, 6.39
chicken game 1.24–1.25, 1.73, 1.77
China
bankruptcy reconciliation procedure 2.35
Enterprise Bankruptcy Law 1.15, 1.21, 2.24,
2.36, 4.02, 4.04
guarantees 2.14
inability to pay debts 2.14, 2.19, 2.24, 2.30, 2.35
industry, type of 2.39
labour law 11.35–11.36
liability 4.47
reorganization process, conditions for debtors
to enter the 2.35, 2.39
salaries, bonuses or rewards of directors/
managers, repayment of 4.89
set-off 4.71
shareholders' liability 7.76
shell resources of public companies 2.43
submission and admission of insolvency
claims 4.65
United States, influence of 1.70
civil law systems
directors, duties of 7.08–7.10, 7.13–7.14,
7.17–7.18, 7.21, 7.25, 8.19–8.20
groups in rescue 8.19–8.20, 8.63

lien priority 5.19
tax law 10.05
wrongful trading, directors' liability for 7.31
closely held companies 7.03
closely related parties
avoidance of transactions 6.30, 6.57, 6.63
fraudulent transactions 6.51, 6.53
insiders 6.30, 6.36, 6.38, 6.45, 8.21
preferences 6.34, 6.35–6.36, 6.38
coercion 1.02, 1.11–1.27, 3.04, 3.13–3.20
comity 6.73, 8.85, 9.70
common law
cooperation and coordination 9.70
directors, duties of 7.08, 7.13–7.14, 7.17, 7.20,
7.22, 7.25, 7.46
lien priority 5.19
security rights 7.22
shifting, common law doctrine of duty 7.13–
7.14, 7.20, 7.25
common-pool problem 1.11, 1.23, 3.14, 3.26,
3.56
communicate, encouragement to 1.18–1.20
communication, principle of 9.12
compensation 4.13, 6.05, 6.08, 6.61, 11.02,
11.24 *see also* damages
conditions to enter insolvency liquidation
process 2.04, 2.08–2.46
auxiliary criterion 2.04, 2.09, 2.25–2.33
cessation of payments 2.04, 2.09, 2.32–2.33
core criterion 2.01, 2.03–2.04, 2.08–2.24
general conditions 2.09–2.33
inability to pay 2.01, 2.03–2.04, 2.08–2.24
likely inability to pay 2.09, 2.20–2.24
overindebtedness 2.01, 2.03–2.04, 2.09, 2.12,
2.25–2.31
confirmation of restructuring plans by the
court 3.14, 3.17, 3.35–3.54
absolute priority rule (APR) 3.47–3.51
appeal processes 3.54
cramdowns 3.38–3.53
dissent of whole groups 3.41–3.42
effect of confirmation 3.54
imposition of plans 3.39, 3.41
minority protection 3.37–3.40, 3.42, 3.44,
3.46–3.51
refusal to sanction plans 3.37
valuation 3.44–3.48, 3.52–3.53
connected claims 4.71
consolidation
realizable priority in group cases 8.65
substantive consolidation 8.37–8.42
constitution of the insolvency estate 4.28–4.32
assets of the insolvency estate 4.29–4.32
seizure of the debtor's assets 4.28, 4.33–4.34

consultation 4.53, 11.03, 11.08–11.09
contracts *see also* **contractual workouts;**
 pending and ongoing contracts
 applicable law 9.49–9.51
 employment, of 4.83, 11.05, 11.06–11.16
 European Insolvency Regulation
  (EIR) 9.49–9.51
 group structures 8.12
 insolvency practitioners, concluded by 1.59
 liquidation 1.29
 moratoriums 3.55–3.56, 3.58
 restructuring/reorganization 4.113–4.114
contractual workouts 3.04, 3.06–3.11
 advantages and disadvantages 3.08–3.11
 consent of all creditors to be bound 3.10–
  3.11, 3.14
 INSOL Principles 3.06
 London Approach 3.06
 negotiations 3.07, 3.09–3.10, 3.26
 priority 3.07
 refusal of consent 3.14
 repeat players 3.09, 3.26
 rescue 1.42–1.45
 restructuring plans 3.04, 3.14, 3.17, 3.26–
  3.27, 3.34
 subset of creditors, involving all or a 3.09,
  3.26
 waive part of claims, compromises where
  creditors 3.07
cooperation
 authority 1.13–1.15, 1.23
 case law 9.70–9.71
 collective and individual interests, tension
  between 1.08–1.10
 competing claimants, lack of cooperation
  between 1.02, 1.06–1.11
 coordination 8.53, 8.54–8.58, 9.04, 9.57,
  9.66–9.71
 encouragement 1.18–1.20
 European Insolvency Regulation (EIR) 9.12,
  9.67
 first-come, first-served 1.02, 1.07–1.08
 formal insolvency proceedings 4.35
 insolvency law, definition of 1.02
 main and secondary proceedings,
  coordination of 9.21–9.22, 9.66
 making it easier to co-operate 1.02, 1.11–1.27
 negative consequences of
  non-cooperation 1.18–1.20
 pay-offs 1.08–1.09
 recognition of judgments 9.61–9.62
corporate groups *see* groups
corporate structure 5.27–5.28, 8.04
costs 3.13, 3.23, 4.24

Covid-19 3.01, 11.02
cramdowns 3.38–3.53
 class meetings 3.28, 3.31, 3.40, 3.51
 confirmation 1.68, 3.38–3.53
 cross-class cramdowns 1.50, 3.28, 3.31, 3.38,
  3.41–3.53, 5.58, 5.66
 fair and equitable distribution 5.60
 minority protection 3.38–3.40
 priority 5.49, 5.66, 8.78
 relative priority rule (RPR) 1.73
 rescue 1.50–1.53, 1.68
 restructuring plans 3.20, 3.25
 sanctioning hearings, court's oversight of
  plans at 3.40
 within a class 3.38–3.53
creditors' committees 4.44, 4.74–4.75
creditors' meetings 4.55, 4.72–4.75
 class meetings
  approval levels 3.36
  constituting 3.27–3.34
  cramdowns 3.51
  voting 3.40
 general meetings 4.73
 insolvency administrators, role and
  obligations of 4.42, 4.54, 4.73
creditworthiness and level of
 indebtedness 2.42
criminal law 1.42, 4.13, 7.48, 7.51–7.52,
 7.60–7.61 *see also* **fraud; intentionally**
 fraudulent transactions
cross-border insolvency law 9.01–9.71
 see also **applicable law; jurisdiction;**
  UNCITRAL Model Law on Cross-
  Border Insolvency
 assets located abroad 9.02, 9.33, 9.43–9.46,
  9.49, 9.58
 codifications 9.03–9.05
 conflict of principles 9.29
 cooperation and coordination 9.04, 9.21–
  9.22, 9.66–9.71
 creditors, contacting and informing 4.64
 European Insolvency Regulation (EIR) 9.03,
  9.05, 9.16, 9.18–9.20, 9.25–9.28, 9.67
 fixation principle 9.27
 groups 8.80–8.87, 9.66–9.67
 incoming foreign proceedings, recognition
  of 9.02
 issues, examples of 9.02
 justice, principle of procedural 9.19, 9.29
 labour law 9.02, 9.26, 9.29, 11.15–11.16, 11.33
 main and secondary proceedings,
  coordination of 9.21–9.22, 9.66
 multiple proceedings 9.02, 9.66
 NAFTA Principles 9.04, 9.17, 9.69

336 INDEX

cross-border insolvency law (*cont.*)
  national laws 9.05
  outgoing domestic insolvency proceedings,
      trans-border effect of 9.02
  principles 9.06–9.29
    conflict of principles 9.29
    procedural 9.06, 9.15–9.20
    substantive 9.06, 9.21–9.28
  procedural principles 9.06, 9.15–9.20
  recognition of foreign insolvency
      proceedings 9.02, 9.56, 9.57–9.60
  recognition of judgments 9.56, 9.61–9.65
  recommendations 9.04
  substantive principles 9.06, 9.21–9.28
  transnational law 9.03
cross-class cramdowns 1.50, 3.28, 3.31, 3.38,
    3.41–3.53, 5.58, 5.66

damages 4.47, 7.22–7.24, 7.36 *see also*
    compensation
de facto and *de jure* insolvency, gap
    between 4.18–4.22
debt overhang *see* overindebtedness
debt-for-equity swaps 1.39–1.40, 3.07, 3.24
debt restructuring outside formal insolvency
    proceedings 3.01–3.73
  contractual workouts 3.04, 3.06–3.11
  distress 2.05–2.07, 3.01, 3.03, 3.73
  financial distress 3.01, 3.03, 3.73
  in-court procedures, linkage with 2.07
  moratoriums 3.55–3.68
  rescue finance 3.69–3.73
  restructuring plans 3.04, 3.12–3.54, 3.73
debtors in possession (DIP) 4.11, 4.113, 11.07,
    11.10, 11.16
descriptive law 1.04
deterrence 6.11, 6.13
directors *see* directors, disqualification of;
    directors, duties of; wrongful trading,
    directors' liability for
directors, disqualification of 7.47–7.67
  administrative bodies, imposed by the 7.50,
    7.62–7.64
  automatic disqualification 7.50, 7.51–7.52, 7.65
  concept 7.47–7.48
  court, ordered by the 7.50, 7.53–7.61
  criminal offences 7.48, 7.51–7.52, 7.60–7.61
  de facto directors 7.47
  de jure directors 7.47
  dishonesty 7.47
  influence, disqualification of people with 7.57
  length of bans 7.55, 7.60
  privacy 7.67
  purpose 7.47

registration 7.65–7.67
shadow directors 7.47
taxonomies 7.50–7.64
unfitness 7.55–7.56, 11.43
directors, duties of 3.13, 7.01–7.46
  avoidance of transactions 8.23–8.31
  challenging directors 3.68
  civil law systems 7.08–7.10, 7.13–7.14, 7.17–
    7.18, 7.21, 7.25, 8.19–8.20
  common law systems 7.08, 7.13–7.14, 7.17,
    7.20, 7.22, 7.25, 7.46
  contractual workouts 3.08
  director, definition of 7.14–7.15, 7.05
  enhanced regard to creditors, liability for
    breach of duty to show 7.08–7.30
  groups in rescue 8.15, 8.19–8.20, 8.23–8.31
  inability to pay 3.66
  labour law 11.42–11.43
  liability in the vicinity of insolvency 7.06–
    7.46, 8.19–8.20
  limited liability 7.01–7.07
  managing directors, tax liability of 10.24
  moratoriums 3.59, 3.66, 3.68
  overlapping and twisted strategies 7.45–7.46
  prescription addressees 7.14–7.19
  salaries, bonuses or rewards 4.89
  tort law 7.38–7.44
  wrongful trading, liability for 7.31–7.37, 7.45,
    8.20
discharge of debts 1.02, 4.104, 4.106–4.108, 9.65
disclaimer of worthless or onerous
    property 4.93
disclosure statements 3.23
disputes over debts 2.15, 2.18, 2.32
disqualification of directors *see* directors,
    disqualification of
dissolution of legal entities 4.104–4.105,
    4.107–4.108
distress and likelihood of insolvency 2.01–2.46
  business distress, definition of 2.01
  cessation of payments 2.04, 2.09, 2.32–2.33
  choice of ways to overcome distress 2.05–2.07
  conditions to enter insolvency liquidation
    process 2.04, 2.08–2.46
  financial distress 2.01–2.04, 2.12, 3.01, 3.03,
    3.73
  inability to pay debts 2.01, 2.03–2.04, 2.08,
    2.10–2.24
  out-of-court reorganization 2.05–2.07
  overindebtedness 2.01, 2.03–2.04, 2.09, 2.12,
    2.25–2.31
  reasons for distress 2.01
  restructuring/reorganization 2.04, 2.05–2.08,
    2.33–2.46

INDEX

distribution of debtor's resources 1.02, 1.54–
1.77 *see also* **distributional waterfall
(priority)**; *pari passu* **principle; priority**
core function, as 4.103
distributional advantage 5.15
insolvency administrators, role and
obligations of 4.45
insolvency law, definition of 1.02
insolvency rate, using the 10.15
liquidation 1.57–1.61
preferential creditors 1.58, 1.59, 1.61
pre-insolvency priority, reliance on 1.54–1.61
ranking 1.57, 1.59–1.61
tax law 10.15, 10.35
distributional waterfall (priority)
absolute priority rule (APR) 5.66, 5.68
asset-based (*in* rem) claims and firm-
based (*in personam*) claims,
distinguishing 5.29, 5.70
groups 8.04, 8.11
priority 5.02, 5.04–5.05, 5.12
multiple 8.65–8.76
realizable 5.66, 8.04, 8.65–8.76
secured creditors 5.46
single waterfall metaphor 5.52, 5.53–5.57,
8.61–8.64
unsecured creditors 5.55–5.56
due debts, non-payment of 2.15, 2.17–2.19,
2.32, 4.08

economics 1.04, 2.12–2.14, 2.26–2.27
effectiveness, principle of 6.10, 6.11, 9.16
efficiency principle
applicable law 9.44, 9.47, 9.51
avoidance of transactions 6.08, 6.11,
6.58–6.59
cross-border insolvency law 9.16, 9.29
organization theory 1.04
prisoner's dilemma game 1.08–1.09
regulated self-governance 1.16
employment *see* **labour law**
encumbered assets 4.32, 5.12–5.13, 8.71
enterprise value 8.67–8.70, 8.72
equal treatment of creditors principle 4.55, 4.71
applicable law 9.46, 9.47
avoidance of transactions 6.03, 6.08, 6.10,
6.15, 9.52
cooperation and coordination 9.67
groups 8.54–8.57, 8.81
pari passu principle 4.56, 4.60, 4.63, 6.08
preferences 6.31–6.32
tax law 10.15
equality of States, principle of 9.10
equity, debt over 5.03, 5.04–5.06, 5.67

European Insolvency Regulation (EIR)
annex procedures 9.39
applicable law 9.42–9.51, 9.54–9.55
avoidance of transaction 6.69–6.71,
9.54–9.55
burden of proof 9.16
centre of main interests (COMI)
presumption 9.18 , 9.35–9.37
contracts 9.49–9.51
cooperation and coordination 9.12, 9.67
cross-border insolvency law 9.03, 9.05, 9.16,
9.18–9.20, 9.25–9.28, 9.67
establishment, definition of 9.38
European Insolvency Regulation Recast 8.81,
9.03, 11.33, 11.41
fixation principle 9.27
groups 8.81
jurisdiction 9.12–9.14, 9.34–9.39
labour law 11.33, 11.41
recognition of foreign insolvency
proceedings 9.27, 9.59
recognition of judgments 9.61, 9.63,
9.64–9.65
retention of title 9.48, 9.49
secondary proceedings 9.33, 9.38
security rights 9.44–9.46
set-off, right to 9.47
territorial proceedings 9.34
European Union *see also* **European Insolvency
Regulation (EIR); Restructuring
Directive**
Acquired Rights Directive 11.09, 11.11–11.13
Brussels Ia Regulation 9.11
Collective Redundancies Directive 11.09
Preventive Restructuring Frameworks
Directive 5.58–5.59, 5.68
realizable priority 5.71
recapitalize or liquidate, duty to 7.25–7.27
relative priority rule (RPR) 1.71–1.73, 1.77
restructuring/reorganization 1.71–1.77
Rome I Regulation 9.64
Second Company Law Directive 7.26
tax law 10.03, 10.15–10.16, 10.21, 10.31–10.32
VAT Directive 10.03
expenses 3.71, 5.10, 5.67, 6.61, 10.16, 10.25,
10.30, 11.24
experts
insolvency administrators, role and
obligations of 4.40
liquidation 4.113
reorganization process, conditions for debtors
to enter the 2.34, 2.46
restructuring plans 3.22
valuation 2.34, 2.46, 4.96

338 INDEX

expropriation 3.16, 3.53, 3.73
extortionate credit transactions 6.55

factoring 5.08
fair and equitable test 3.47, 5.01, 5.60
fiduciary duties 8.15–8.18, 8.20–8.31, 8.80, 8.88
filing for insolvency proceedings 4.10–4.17
  creditors, right to initiate proceedings
    of 4.10, 4.15–4.16
  debtors, right to initiate proceedings of 4.10,
    4.11–4.14
  failure to comply with legal obligation 4.13
  incentives 4.10, 4.11–4.12
  involuntary filing 4.10, 4.12, 4.15
  pre-filing claims 11.24
  public authorities, right to initiate
    proceedings of 4.10, 4.17
  voluntary filing 2.23, 4.10
financial distress 2.01–2.04, 2.12, 3.01, 3.03, 3.73
  business distress distinguished 2.01
  inability to pay debts 2.01, 2.03–2.04, 2.12
  poverty 2.02
firm-based (*in personam*) claims 5.29–5.43
  asset-based (*in rem*) claims 5.02, 5.29–5.43
  blanket liens 5.30, 5.31–5.40
  equity, debt over 5.03, 5.04–5.06
  priority 5.02, 5.03, 5.04–5.05, 5.12, 5.29–5.43
  security rights 5.15–5.16
fixed charges 5.41, 5.43
Fletcher, Ian 9.04
floating charges *see* **United Kingdom, floating**
  charges in
forbearance 6.15, 6.17
foreseeability 2.22, 4.12, 6.15
formal insolvency proceedings 4.01–4.114
  collective enforcement 4.02
  consequences of commencement 4.26–4.38
  constitution of the insolvency
    estate 4.28–4.32
  cut-off date 4.27
  discharge of individuals' debts 4.104,
    4.106–4.108
  dissolution of legal entities 4.104–4.105,
    4.107–4.108
  distribution as a core function 4.103
  final steps of liquidation
    proceedings 4.103–4.108
  formal closure of proceedings 4.108
  initiation of proceedings 4.06–4.26
  insolvency administrators, role and obligations
    of 4.26–4.28, 4.39–4.54, 4.108
  involvement of creditors 4.55–4.75
  moratoriums 4.36–4.38
  opening of proceedings 4.23–4.25

  outstanding claims, continued existence
    of 4.103–4.108
  pari passu principle 4.02, 4.103
  pending contracts 4.27, 4.76–4.86
  priority 4.27, 4.103
  restructuring as an alternative to
    liquidation 4.109–4.114
  rights and obligations of debtors 4.33–4.35
  swelling and liquidation of assets 4.87–4.102
  termination of proceedings 4.103–4.108
forum shopping 8.83
France
  abuse of rights 7.71, 7.76
  Acquired Rights Directive 11.09, 11.12
  applicable law 9.55
  avoidance of transactions 6.02–6.03, 6.17,
    6.18–6.23, 6.30, 6.59–6.61, 6.64, 6.67
  cessation of payments 6.37, 6.39, 6.43
  challenging transactions 6.60, 6.64, 6.67
  closely related parties 6.30
  collective pledge doctrine 7.13–7.14
  cross-border insolvency 9.05
  European Insolvency Regulation (EIR) 9.05
  fraudulent transactions 6.50, 6.53, 6.54
  inability to pay debts 2.18
  insolvency administrators, role and
    obligations of 4.40
  judicial recovery proceedings 1.21
  judiciary liquidation 1.15, 4.02, 4.04
  knowledge of insolvency 6.37, 6.38, 6.39
  labour law 11.24, 11.39
  overindebtedness 4.13
  pending and ongoing contracts 4.83
  piercing the corporate veil 7.71–7.72, 7.76
  preferences 6.37, 6.38, 6.39
  pre-packs 4.101
  priority 11.24, 11.39
  protection proceedings 1.21
  public authorities, right to initiate
    proceedings of 4.17
  set-off 4.71
  shareholders' liability 7.76
  suspect periods 6.43, 6.46, 6.47
  tax law 10.23
  third parties 6.67
  transactions at an undervalue 6.43, 6.46, 6.47
  voidability of transactions 6.64
fraud 4.90, 4.92, 8.15–8.16, 8.18 *see also*
  intentionally fraudulent transactions
Frost, Chris 5.31
future claims 2.20–2.23, 4.66

game theory 1.04, 1.08–1.10, 1.19–1.20, 1.24–
  1.25, 1.68, 1.73, 1.77

Germany
absolute priority rule (APR) 1.74–1.75
Acquired Rights Directive 11.09, 11.12
applicable law 9.42, 9.55
avoidance of transactions 6.02–6.03, 6.17–
 6.23, 6.30, 6.57–6.62, 6.65, 6.67
centre of main interests (COMI) 9.37
cessation of payments 2.33
closely related parties 6.30, 6.35, 6.38, 6.51,
 6.53
congruent and incongruent coverages 6.35,
 6.38
delay in opening of insolvency proceedings,
 directors' liability for 7.42–7.44
directors
 de facto 7.14
 definition 7.05
 disqualification of 7.51–7.52, 7.60–7.61
 duties 7.11–7.12, 7.18–7.19, 7.21, 7.23,
  7.29–7.30, 7.42–7.44
 reimbursement of payments 4.89
double-track proceedings 1.15
European Insolvency Regulation (EIR) 9.05
filing 4.13
formal insolvency proceedings 4.02, 4.04
fraudulent transactions 6.51, 6.53, 6.54
good faith 6.51, 6.67
guarantee or insurance schemes 11.36
inability to pay debts 2.18, 2.21–2.22, 2.28,
 7.40, 6.35, 6.39
insolvency administrators, role of 4.41, 4.44,
 4.94
joint stock companies, directors of 7.05, 7.11,
 7.51
knowledge of insolvency 6.35, 6.38, 6.39
labour law 11.38
leases 4.84
limited liability 7.05
liquidation 4.112, 10.35
managing directors, tax liability of 10.24
moratoriums 3.57
negligence 7.52
opening of insolvency proceedings 4.24
pari passu principle 4.63
partnerships 7.73
pending contracts 4.83
piercing the corporate veil 7.73, 7.77
Plan Proceedings of restructuration 1.74
preferences 6.35, 6.38, 6.39
priority 9.20, 10.15, 11.38
recognition of foreign insolvency
 proceedings 9.59
recognition of judgments 9.64–9.65
rescue 1.15, 7.29–7.30

Restructuring Directive, transposition
 of 1.49, 1.71–1.77, 7.29–7.30
restructuring plans 3.13, 3.19–3.20, 3.41,
 3.49, 6.35
restructuring/reorganization 1.21, 1.71–1.77,
 4.112, 10.26–10.32
sale of businesses as a whole 4.100
schemes of arrangement 3.13
set-off, right to 4.71
shareholders 6.57, 7.76–7.84
specialized courts 10.04–10.05
standing 7.21, 7.44
successors, challenges by 6.62, 6.65
suspect periods 6.35, 6.38, 6.44, 6.46, 6.51
tax law 10.04–10.12, 10.15–10.32, 10.35
tort law 7.27, 7.42–7.44
transactions at an undervalue 6.44, 6.46, 6.47
United States, influence of 1.70
universalism, principle of 9.59
voidability of transactions 6.65
gifts/gratuitous transactions 6.40–6.47
global financial crisis 2008 3.01–3.02, 5.27
going-concern value
 asset-based (*in* rem) claims 5.30, 5.44, 5.45,
  5.47–5.48, 5.64
 groups in rescue 8.03, 8.63
 interim protection 4.19
 overindebtedness 2.27–2.28
 preservation 2.05, 4.109–4.110
 realizable priority 8.67, 8.73, 8.77
 relative priority rule (RPR) 1.73
 reorganization process, conditions for debtors
  to enter the 2.37
 rescue 1.63–1.64, 1.68–1.69, 5.13, 8.52, 8.55,
  8.58, 8.60
 restructuring plans, confirmation of 3.52
 sale of businesses as a whole 4.97, 4.99–4.101
 surplus 8.60
going concerns *see also* **going-concern value**
 increment 8.86
 moratoriums 3.66
 rescue 1.39, 1.63–1.64, 1.68–1.69, 3.66, 3.72,
  5.13
 restructuring plans 3.24
 sales 8.02, 8.04–8.05
 surplus 5.63
good faith 6.51, 6.62, 6.66, 6.67, 7.19
groups *see also* **administering group global
  restructurings; groups in rescue**
 avoidance of transactions 8.17, 8.21–8.31
 business lines 8.07, 8.10
 centre of main interests (COMI) 9.66
 collective and individual interests, tension
  between 1.10

340 INDEX

groups (*cont.*)
  contractual workouts 3.07
  cross-border insolvency 9.66–9.67
  functional lines 8.07, 8.10, 8.88
  geographic lines 8.07, 8.88
  structures 8.07–8.12
groups in rescue 8.01–8.88
  administering group cases 8.32–8.52,
    8.80–8.87
  administrative consolidation 8.33–8.36
  best interests of the group 8.45, 8.48
  coordination problems 8.53, 8.54–8.58
  cross-border issues 8.80–8.87
  directors, duties of 8.15, 8.19–8.20, 8.23–8.31
  entitlements 8.13, 8.59–8.79
  equality of distribution 8.54–8.57
  fiduciary duties 8.15–8.18, 8.20–8.21, 8.46–
    8.47, 8.88
  fraudulent conveyances 8.15–8.16, 8.18
  going concerns 8.02–8.04, 8.52, 8.55, 8.58,
    8.60, 8.63
  governance 8.43–8.49
  group value 8.05, 8.42
  hierarchical capital structure 8.61–8.63
  homeless value 8.03
  preferences 8.16, 8.18
  priority 8.03–8.05, 8.15, 8.22, 8.53–8.57,
    8.65–8.79, 8.88
  realizable priority 8.03–8.05, 8.65–8.79, 8.88
  reasonable steps to promote group
    insolvency 8.46–8.47
  regulating decisions in the vicinity of
    insolvency 8.13, 8.15–8.22
  rescue regimes 8.18, 8.51–8.79, 8.88
  restructuring/reorganization 8.02, 8.04, 8.18,
    8.80–8.87
  single entity liquidation baseline 8.13, 8.14,
    8.18, 8.88
  single waterfall metaphor 8.61–8.64
  substantive consolidation 8.37–8.42
  value, allocation of 8.03–8.05, 8.18, 8.51–
    8.79, 8.88
  veil, piercing the corporate 8.15, 8.17, 8.18,
    8.37
  vicinity of insolvency, obligations of
    officers and directors in the 8.13–8.31,
    8.43
guarantees
  avoidance of transactions 8.30–8.31, 8.50
  distress 2.03
  inability to pay debts 2.14
  insolvency administrators 4.79
  insolvency practitioners (IPs) 3.62
  labour law 11.04–11.05, 11.17–11.39, 11.41
  pensions 11.27–11.29, 11.39

  priority 11.17–11.39, 11.41
  subrogation rights 11.31–11.33
  wages 11.27–11.29, 11.33, 11.35–11.39

homeless assets 8.03, 8.70, 8.71

in rem **claims** *see* **asset-based (*in* rem) claims**
in personam **claims** *see* **firm-based (*in*
    personam) claims**
inability to pay debts 2.08–2.24 *see also* **likely
    inability to pay**
  balance-sheet test 2.12, 2.26–2.27
  cash-flow test 2.13, 4.08
  cessation of payments 2.32–2.33
  contingent liability test 2.14
  continuous state, as 2.10
  disputes over debts 2.15, 2.18
  due debts, non-payment of 2.15, 2.17–2.19,
    2.25, 4.08
  financial distress 2.01, 2.03–2.04, 2.12
  future contingent debts or undue debts 2.15
  guarantor for other debtors, acting as 2.14
  instalments, ability to pay in 2.10
  liquidity problems 2.03
  objective inability 2.10, 2.32
  overindebtedness 2.01, 2.03–2.04, 2.09, 2.12,
    2.17–2.18
  reasons 2.08
  reorganization process, conditions for debtors
    to enter the 2.35–2.36
  subjective inability 2.10
  technical inability 2.03
  temporary cash-flow problems/
    postponement 2.10
  time limits 2.10
independence and impartiality 4.39
information rights 11.03, 11.08
initiation of insolvency proceedings 4.06–4.26
  creditors, right to initiate proceedings
    of 4.10, 4.15–4.16
  debtors, right to initiate proceedings of 4.10,
    4.11–4.14
  defining insolvency 4.08
  directors, duties of 7.25, 7.27
  due debts, non-payment of 4.08
  filing for insolvency proceedings 4.10–4.17
  gap between *de facto* and *de jure*
    insolvency 4.18–4.22
  inability to pay 4.08
  interim administrators, appointment
    of 4.20–4.21
  interim protection 4.18–4.22
  opening of proceedings 4.23–4.26
  preliminary proceedings 4.18–4.22
  provisional moratoriums 4.22

public authorities, right to initiate
proceedings of 4.10, 4.17
starting point, insolvency as the 4.07–4.09
substantive insolvency 4.07
insolvency administrators, role and obligations
of 4.26–4.28, 4.39–4.54
appointment 4.41–4.44
approval of the court, duty to get 4.53
assets of the insolvency estate 4.29–4.30
authority and autonomy of creditors 4.54
avoidance of transactions 4.90
challenging decisions of administrator 4.52
closure of proceedings 4.108
consult, duty to 4.53
contacting and informing creditors 4.64
court, appointment by the 4.41, 4.44
creditors
challenge claims, right to 4.67
committees 4.74
involvement 4.64, 4.67–4.68
meetings 4.54, 4.73
voluntary liquidation 4.42
damages 4.47
discretion 4.94
duties and responsibilities 4.45–4.46
earnings generated by insolvency
administrators 4.88
employment contracts 4.83
encumbered assets, treatment of 4.32
enforcement of claims 4.39
expertise 4.40
formal insolvency proceedings 4.26–4.28,
4.39–4.54
guarantees 4.79
independence and impartiality 4.39
interim administrators, appointment
of 4.20–4.21
liability 4.39, 4.47–4.49, 4.79
list of responsibilities 4.45
moratoriums 4.37
pari passu principle 4.63
pending and ongoing contracts 4.27, 4.39,
4.78–4.84
qualifications 4.40–4.41
realization of assets 4.93–4.95
registered offices 4.50
rotation systems 4.41
sale of assets 4.93–4.95, 4.98–4.100
seizure of the debtor's assets 4.28
selection 4.41
submission and admission of insolvency
claims 4.64–4.67
supervision 4.50–4.54
swelling and liquidation of assets
4.88–4.90

termination clauses 4.82–4.83, 4.85–4.86
ultra vires 4.52
insolvency estate
assets of the insolvency estate 4.29–4.32
constitution of the insolvency
estate 4.28–4.32
insolvency exception 11.09–11.13
insolvency law, definition of 1.01–1.03
insolvency practitioners (IPs) *see also*
insolvency administrators, role and
obligations of
avoidance of transactions 6.03
contracts concluded by IPs 1.59
co-operation 1.13
fees 1.59
guarantees 3.62
labour law 11.07, 11.10, 11.16, 11.43
liquidation 1.29–1.30
moratoriums 3.62, 3.68
powers 11.07, 11.10, 11.16, 11.43
restructuring plans 3.13
insurance schemes 11.04–11.05, 11.17–11.39
intentionally fraudulent transactions 6.29,
6.48–6.54
avoidance of transactions 8.21, 8.30–8.31, 8.50
closely related parties 6.51, 6.53
enforcement 6.48–6.53
extortionate credit transactions 6.55
good faith 6.51
groups 8.21, 8.30–8.31, 8.50
mental elements 6.48, 6.51
modification of norms 6.55
objective factors 6.48
subjective factors 6.51, 6.54
suspect periods 6.48, 6.51, 6.53
transactions at an undervalue 6.42, 6.45,
6.49, 6.52, 6.53, 6.54
voidable transactions 6.48, 6.50
interference with creditors' rights 3.04, 3.13–
3.20, 3.62, 3.66
involvement of the creditors 4.55–4.75 *see also*
creditors' meetings
challenge claims, right to 4.67
creditors' committees 4.74–4.75
equal treatment principle 4.55, 4.71
excluded claims 4.68
insolvency administrators 4.64, 4.67–4.68,
4.73–4.74
meetings 4.55, 4.72–4.75
pari passu principle and ranking of
creditors 4.56–4.63
representation 4.55, 4.72–4.75
set-off, rights of 4.69–4.71
submission and admission of insolvency
claims 4.64–4.68

INDEX

ipso facto clauses 3.55, 3.62–3.63, 4.85–4.86
Italian guilds 1.06

Jackson, Thomas 1.07
Jacoby, Melissa B 5.58, 5.61
Janger, Edward J 5.58
Johnson, Gordon 11.35
judgments, recognition of *see* recognition of judgments
jurisdiction 9.30, 9.31–9.39
  annex procedures 9.39
  avoidance of transactions 9.39
  centre of main interests (COMI) 9.35–9.37
  European Insolvency Regulation (EIR) 9.12–9.14, 9.34–9.39
  exclusive jurisdiction 9.37
  main proceedings 9.32–9.35, 9.38
  opening insolvency proceedings 9.35
  outgoing domestic insolvency proceedings, trans-border effect of 9.09
  principles 9.06, 9.07–9.14, 9.35
  proportionality principle 9.14
  recognition 9.09–9.11
    incoming foreign proceedings 9.09
    treaties and regulations 9.10
  restructuring plans, confirmation of 3.36
  secondary proceedings 9.32–9.34, 9.38
  tax courts 10.04
  territorial proceedings 9.34
  territoriality, principle of 9.09
  unity, principle of 9.08–9.09, 9.20, 9.31–9.32
  universalism, principle of 9.08–9.10, 9.20, 9.31–9.33, 9.38
justice, principle of procedural 9.19, 9.29, 9.51

labour law 11.01–11.43 *see also* wages
  absolute priority rule (APR) 5.68
  Acquired Rights Directive 11.09, 11.11–11.13
  agency of workers, lack of 11.04
  applicable law 11.15–11.16, 11.33
  collective agreements 11.11
  comparative approaches 11.35–11.41
  compensation for personal injury and death 11.24
  consultation rights 11.03, 11.08–11.09
  continuation of contracts 11.03
  contracts of employment 9.51, 11.05, 11.06–11.16
    cross-border insolvency law 9.02, 9.26, 9.29
    pending and ongoing contracts 4.83
    social protection, principle of 9.29
    transactions at an undervalue 6.45
  Covid-19 11.02
  cross-border insolvency 11.15–11.16, 11.33

debtors in possession (DIPs), powers of 11.07, 11.10, 11.16
directors' liability 11.42–11.43
dismissals 11.10
employee benefits 11.17
entitlements of workers 11.17–11.34, 11.42–11.43
European Union
  Acquired Rights Directive 11.09, 11.11–11.13
  European Insolvency Regulation (EIR) Recast 11.33, 11.41
  guarantee schemes 11.28, 11.30, 11.36
functions of insolvency law 11.01, 11.03
globalization 11.06
guarantee or insurance schemes 11.04–11.05, 11.17–11.39, 11.41
hybrid systems 11.39–11.41
ILO Conventions 11.36–11.37
information rights 11.03, 11.08
insolvency administrators 4.83
insolvency exception 11.09–11.13
insolvency practitioners (IPs), powers of 11.07, 11.10, 11.16, 11.43
insurance protections 11.04–11.05, 11.17–11.39
legitimate expectations 11.20, 11.25, 11.27
lex fori concursus 9.29, 11.16
lex loci laboris 11.16, 11.33
liens 11.30, 11.38
liquidation 4.110, 11.01
maritime liens 11.30
objectives of insolvency 11.07, 11.09
opportunistic behaviour by employers 11.22
pari passu principle 4.61
participation rights 11.03, 11.09
pension payments 11.17–11.19, 11.40
  defined benefit schemes 11.19
  defined contribution schemes 11.19
  guarantee schemes 11.27–11.29, 11.39
  priority 11.17–11.19, 11.27, 11.40
personal injury and death, compensation for 11.24
pre-insolvency entitlements 11.20–11.21
pre-filing claims 11.24
pre-packs 11.12–11.14
preservation of jobs 11.01, 11.03, 11.06, 11.09
priority 5.03, 5.10, 11.04–11.05, 11.17–11.40
  guarantee funds 11.17–11.39, 11.41
  payments 11.17–11.24
  super-priority 11.21, 11.25, 11.36–11.37, 11.39
ranking 11.20, 11.31, 11.38
redundancies 11.05, 11.07–11.09, 11.11
  collective 11.05, 11.09, 11.11
  Collective Redundancies Directive 11.09

rescues 11.06, 11.10, 11.14
restructuring/reorganization 4.110, 11.01,
    11.09–11.12, 11.27
secured creditors 11.20–11.21, 11.24–11.25,
    11.35, 11.41
social policy 11.04, 11.21–11.23, 11.29
social protection principle 9.26, 9.51, 11.41
subrogation rights 11.31–11.33
tax law 10.16, 10.22
termination of employment contracts 11.08,
    11.12
terms and conditions 11.09–11.11
transactions at an undervalue 6.45
unemployment 2.34, 4.106, 11.23, 11.27, 11.38
unsecured creditors 11.20–11.22, 11.25, 11.35
workers' representatives, participation
    of 11.08, 11.11, 11.14
worker protection principle 5.03, 5.10,
    11.01–11.04, 11.07–11.11, 11.31, 11.33,
    11.36–11.40
leases
European Insolvency Regulation (EIR) 9.50
insolvency administrators 4.84
priority 5.08
quasi-security 5.20–5.24
sale of businesses as a whole 5.09
security rights 5.17
legal certainty see predictability/legal
    certainty, principle of
legitimate expectations
avoidance of transactions 6.09, 6.29, 9.52
European Insolvency Regulation (EIR) 9.46,
    9.49
labour law 11.20, 11.25, 11.27
preferences 6.32
realizable priority 8.65–8.66
substantive consolidation 8.37–8.38
lex fori concursus
avoidance of transactions 6.68–6.72
cross-border insolvency 9.29, 9.41–9.49,
    9.52–9.54, 9.58, 9.60
labour law 9.29, 11.16
recognition of foreign insolvency
    proceedings 9.58, 9.60
liability *see also* limited liability
contingent liability 2.14
deepening insolvency 7.39–7.41
delayed opening of insolvency
    proceedings 7.42–7.44
directors 7.08–7.37, 10.13, 10.24,
    11.42–11.43
insolvency administrators 4.39, 4.47–4.49,
    4.79
shareholders 7.76–7.84

tax liability 10.13, 10.24
vicinity of insolvency, in the 7.46
wrongful trading 7.31–7.37, 7.45
liens *see also* United States, blanket liens in
banker's liens 5.25
chattel mortgages on personal property 5.07
floating charges 5.41
floating liens 5.39, 5.41–5.42
labour law 11.30, 11.38
maritime liens 11.30
priority 5.07, 5.10–5.11, 5.17, 5.18–5.19
tax law 10.22
timing rules 5.18–5.19
likelihood of insolvency *see* distress and
    likelihood of insolvency
likely inability to pay 2.09, 2.20–2.24
abuse of applications 2.21
foreseeability 2.22
future claims 2.20–2.23
limited liability 7.01–7.07
advantages 7.01, 7.03
closely held companies 7.03
criticism 7.02–7.03
directors, duties of 7.01–7.37
overindebtedness 2.25, 2.29
private companies 7.05
vicinity of insolvency, firms in the 7.03–7.04
wrongful trading, directors' liability
    for 7.31–7.37
liquidation *see also* formal insolvency
    proceedings
concepts, taxonomies, and devices 1.28–1.31
conditions to enter insolvency liquidation
    process 2.04, 2.08–2.46
contractual agreements 4.113–4.114
distribution 1.57–1.61
insolvency administrators, role and
    obligations of 4.42
insolvency practitioners 1.29–1.30
labour law 4.110, 11.01
publicity 4.113
reasonable prospect of survival 4.110
recapitalize or liquidate, duty to 7.25–7.27
rescue, distinction from 1.11–1.27, 5.12–5.13
restructuring/reorganization, as an alternative
    to 4.109–4.114
sale of businesses as a whole 4.97–4.98
security rights, law on 1.29
shareholders, benefits to 4.110
swelling of assets 4.87–4.102
taxation 10.35–10.36
lis pendens 9.20
Lubben, Stephen J 3.49
Luhmann, Niklas 9.19

344 INDEX

Madaus, Stephan 5.70
main proceedings 9.21–9.22, 9.32–9.35, 9.38,
    9.66
majority principle 1.45–1.51, 1.72, 3.14–3.15,
    3.27, 3.34
meetings *see* creditors' meetings
minority protection 3.10, 3.23
    class meetings, constituting 3.27–3.30
    cramdowns 3.39–3.40
    initiation of insolvency proceedings 4.07
    restructuring plans 3.04, 3.16–3.17
    restructuring/reorganization 3.02, 3.04,
        3.37–3.40, 3.42, 3.44, 3.46–3.51
misconduct or misfeasance 4.47, 7.74
moratoriums 4.36–4.38
    advantages 3.58–3.59
    automatic stay 3.64, 4.36–4.38
    contractual rights 3.55–3.56, 3.58
    directors 3.59, 3.66, 3.68
    duration of stay 3.67
    insolvency administrators 4.37
    insolvency practitioners 3.62, 3.68
    interference with creditors' rights 3.62, 3.66
    ipso facto clauses 3.55, 3.62–3.63
    provisional moratoriums 4.22
    publicity 3.64
    restructuring moratoriums 3.55–3.68
    restructuring plans 3.14–3.15
    scope of the statutory stay 3.60–3.63
    set-off, right to 4.38
    standstill periods or informal
        moratoriums 3.07, 3.58, 3.64
    subsets of creditors 3.60, 3.68
    timing 3.65–3.66
    voluntary stays 3.64
most favourable principle 9.47, 9.54
mutual trust, principle of 9.11, 9.29, 9.47, 9.51,
    9.57, 9.59

negotiations
    contractual workouts 3.07, 3.09–3.10, 3.14
    incentives 1.02, 1.62–1.65
    priority 5.51
    regulated self-governance 1.18–1.20
    rescue finance 3.69
    restructuring/reorganization 4.111, 8.83
nemo dat principle 5.19
netting rights *see* set-off, right to
next-best-alternative approach 5.58–5.59, 5.68

objectives of insolvency procedure 2.05, 2.34,
    2.36, 4.04, 11.01, 11.03, 11.07, 11.09
onerous property, disclaimer of worthless
    or 4.93

ongoing contracts *see* pending and ongoing
    contracts
opening of formal insolvency
    proceedings 4.23–4.26
    avoidance of transactions 6.01–6.03,
        6.19–6.21
    delay, directors' liability for 7.42–7.44
    fees, payment of 4.24
    filing 4.10–4.17
    initiation of insolvency
        proceedings 4.23–4.26
    jurisdiction 9.35
    publicity 4.25
    recognition of foreign insolvency
        proceedings 9.02, 9.56, 9.57–9.60
    suspect periods 6.19, 6.30
opportunistic behaviour 1.02, 1.20, 1.73, 3.13,
    11.22
optimal realization principle 6.29, 9.22–9.23,
    9.47, 9.52
organization theory 1.04
outstanding claims, continued existence
    of 4.103–4.108
overindebtedness 2.01, 2.03–2.04, 2.09,
    2.25–2.33
    balance-sheet test 2.26–2.27, 4.08
    borrowing, ability to pay due to 2.25
    capital joint ventures, limited liability of 2.25,
        2.29
    cash-flow 2.25
    due debts, non-payment of 2.25
    economics 2.26–2.27
    errors, compensation payments for 4.13
    going-concern value 2.27–2.28
    inability to pay 2.01, 2.03–2.04, 2.09, 2.12,
        2.17–2.18, 2.25, 2.28–2.30
    initiation of insolvency proceedings 4.08
    knowledge of overindebtedness 2.30
    natural persons 2.26, 2.28–2.29
    proof requirement, no 2.31
    restructuring plans 3.24

pari passu principle 4.56–4.63
    absolute priority rule (APR) 1.61
    avoidance of transactions 4.56, 4.91, 6.01,
        6.08
    cross-border insolvency 9.21
    employees 4.61
    equal treatment of creditors 4.56, 4.60, 4.63,
        6.08
    exceptions 4.58–4.61
    formal insolvency proceedings 4.02, 4.103
    ordinary and subordinated claims 4.62–4.63
    preferences 1.61, 4.60, 4.62, 6.31

priority 4.58–4.61
ranking 4.56–4.63
separation, right to 4.58
set-off, right to 4.63, 4.69
social or political reasons, privileges
established for 4.61
participation rights 11.03, 11.08–11.09,
11.11, 11.14 *see also* **involvement of the
creditors**
Pauline actions 6.04, 6.48
pending and ongoing contracts 4.27, 4.76–4.86
acceptance or rejection of contractual
performance 4.78–4.81
assets of the insolvency estate 4.31, 4.33
cost-benefit analysis 4.78
crucial for continuation of debtor's business,
fulfilment of contracts that are 4.80
employment contracts 4.83
executory contracts 4.77, 4.85–4.86
formal insolvency proceedings 4.27, 4.76–4.86
general provisions 4.82–4.84
insolvency administrators, role of 4.27, 4.39,
4.78–4.86
ipso facto clauses 4.85–4.86
priority 4.77–4.79
pro rata basis, satisfaction of claims on a 4.78
social and economic difficulties, special
treatment of contracts associated
with 4.82–4.84
specific provisions 4.82–4.84
termination clauses 4.82–4.83, 4.85–4.86
underperformance 4.77
pensions 11.17–11.19, 11.27–11.29,
11.39–11.40
**personal injury and death, compensation
for** 11.24
piercing the corporate veil 7.68–7.84
burden of proof 7.78
cost-benefit analysis 7.68
functional veil piercing 7.70, 7.75–7.84
groups 7.68, 7.73–7.74, 8.15, 8.17, 8.18, 8.37
limited liability 7.68–7.84
real veil piercing 7.70, 7.71–7.74
shareholders' liability 7.76–7.84
standing 7.78
terminology 7.69–7.70
tort law 7.78–7.79
plans *see* **restructuring plans**
predictability/legal certainty, principle of
absolute priority rule (APR) 3.50–3.51
applicable law 9.41, 9.44, 9.47
avoidance of transactions 6.09, 6.10, 6.24,
6.58–6.59
cross-border insolvency 9.18, 9.25

European Insolvency Regulation (EIR) 9.18,
9.35
labour law 11.02
preferences 6.18, 6.29, 6.31–6.39
avoidance of transactions 6.69
cheque payments 6.55
closely related parties 6.34, 6.35, 6.38
contracts concluded by insolvency
practitioners 1.59
definition 6.31, 6.34, 6.36
directors, duties of 7.46
disadvantage requirement 6.34
equal treatment of creditors 6.31–6.32
exceptions 6.33
fees of insolvency practitioners 1.59
floating charges 5.41
groups 8.16, 8.18, 8.21–8.22, 8.30
legitimate expectations 6.32
mental elements 6.32, 6.34
modification of norms 6.55
new value, transactions for 6.33, 6.34, 6.36,
6.38
objective factors 6.33
ordinary course of business, transactions in
the 6.33, 6.34, 6.38, 6.39
pari passu principle 1.61, 4.60, 4.62, 6.31
restructuring attempts, transactions in
context of serious 6.33
security rights 5.14
shareholder loans 6.57
subjective factors 6.32–6.33, 6.35
substantive insolvency requirement 6.32
suspect periods 6.32, 6.34–6.36, 6.38
tax law 10.10, 10.15, 10.17, 10.20, 10.25, 10.28
pre-packs 2.04, 2.07, 4.101, 5.43, 11.12–11.14
principles
avoidance of transactions 6.07–6.10, 6.15–
6.16, 6.29, 6.58–6.61
conflict of principles 9.29
cross-border insolvency 9.06–9.29
jurisdiction 9.06, 9.07–9.14
procedure 9.06, 9.15–9.20
substantive principles 9.06, 9.21–9.28
weighing and balancing 6.10
priority *see also* **absolute priority rule (APR);
distributional waterfall (priority);
realizable priority; relative priority rule
(RPR)**
administrative expenses 3.71
applicable law 9.51
asset-based (*in* rem) claims 5.02, 5.03, 5.07–
5.09, 5.29–5.43, 5.48–5.64, 5.71
characterization a financing as a sale or
lease 5.09

346 INDEX

priority (*cont.*)
  corporate structure 5.27
  distributional waterfall 5.02, 5.04–5.05, 5.12
  equity, debt over 5.03, 5.04–5.06, 8.15, 8.22
  firm-based (*in personam*) claims 5.02, 5.03,
    5.04–5.05, 5.12, 5.29–5.43
  floating charges 5.41
  formal insolvency proceedings 4.27, 4.103
  groups in rescue 8.03–8.05, 8.15, 8.22, 8.54–
    8.57, 8.65–8.79, 8.88
  guarantee or insurance schemes 11.17–11.39,
    11.41
  insolvency priorities 5.01, 5.03, 5.10–5.11
  labour law 5.03, 5.10, 11.04–11.05,
    11.17–11.40
    employee benefits 11.17
    guarantee funds 11.17–11.39, 11.41
    payments 11.17–11.24
    pensions 11.17–11.19, 11.27, 11.40
    super-priority 11.21, 11.25, 11.36–11.37,
      11.39
    wages 11.17–11.18, 11.22, 11.24–11.25,
      11.35–11.38
  liens 5.10–5.11, 5.17, 5.18–5.19
  local priority 8.85, 8.86
  negotiations 3.07
  pari passu principle 4.58–4.61
  pending and ongoing contracts 4.77–4.79
  pensions 11.17–11.19, 11.27, 11.40
  post-petition obligations 5.03
  pre-insolvency priority, reliance on 1.54–1.61
  procedure 9.20
  ranking 4.103, 5.02, 5.10, 5.14
  relative priority 5.52, 5.55–5.59, 5.67–5.68
  rescue 3.71–3.72, 5.12–5.13, 5.52–5.64
  restructuring plans, confirmation of 3.45,
    3.50
  security rights 5.14, 5.18–5.19
  super-priority 5.10, 11.21, 11.25, 11.36–
    11.37, 11.39
  tax law 10.01, 10.15–10.16, 10.20, 10.22,
    10.24, 10.34
  value-based claims 5.52, 5.60–5.64
  wages 11.17–11.18, 11.22, 11.24–11.25,
    11.35–11.38
prisoner's dilemma game 1.08–1.10, 1.19
privatization 1.22–1.27
proportionality principle 6.09, 6.10, 6.58, 9.14,
  9.28
public authorities, right to initiate proceedings
  of 4.10, 4.17
public interest 1.15, 1.17, 2.34, 2.44–2.46, 4.10,
  4.17
publicity 3.64, 4.25, 4.102, 4.113

quasi-security 5.20–5.28
  bankruptcy remoteness 5.22, 5.24
  corporate structure 5.27–5.28
  leases 5.20, 5.21–5.24
  sales 5.20, 5.21–5.24
  set-off/netting rights 5.25–5.26
  whole-business securitization 5.22–5.23

ranking
  distribution 1.57, 1.59–1.61
  hierarchy 5.02, 5.10
  labour law 11.20, 11.31, 11.38
  pari passu principle 4.56–4.63
  priority 4.103, 5.14
realizable priority 8.65–8.79, 8.88
  absolute priority rule (APR) 5.66, 5.67–5.68,
    5.71, 8.72, 8.78
  adequate protection 8.81, 8.86
  asset-based priority 5.66–5.70, 8.71–8.75
  baseline entitlement 8.03
  burden of proof 8.75–8.76
  consolidation 8.65
  corporate entity structure 8.04
  corporate form, respecting the 8.66
  cramdowns 5.66, 8.78
  distributional priority 8.04
  encumbered assets 8.71
  enterprise value 8.67–8.70, 8.72
  firm-based (*in personam*) claims 5.66–5.70
  going concerns 8.04–8.05, 8.67, 8.73, 8.77
  group cases 8.65–8.79, 8.88
  hierarchy 8.54
  homeless assets 8.70, 8.71
  legitimate expectations 8.65–8.66
  Preventive Restructuring Frameworks
    Directive 5.68
  rescue 8.03–8.05, 8.65–8.79, 8.88
    realizable priority 5.66–5.70
    value allocation in 8.65, 8.71–8.74, 8.77,
      8.88
  restructuring/reorganization 8.04–8.05,
    8.77–8.79, 8.81, 8.86
  third parties, enforcement against 8.75
  value 5.70, 8.04, 8.65, 8.67, 8.71–8.74, 8.77
realization of the assets 4.93–4.96
recapitalization 5.44, 5.47–5.48, 5.65, 5.71,
  7.25–7.27
recognition *see* recognition of foreign
    insolvency proceedings; recognition of
    judgments
recognition of foreign insolvency proceedings
  automatic recognition 9.59
  cross-border insolvency 9.02, 9.56, 9.57–9.60
  groups 8.81, 8.82, 8.85

jurisdiction 9.09–9.11
opening of insolvency proceedings 9.02, 9.56, 9.57–9.60
proxies of debtors 9.58
reciprocity condition 9.60
refusal of recognition 9.58
territoriality, principle of 9.58
timing 9.27
recognition of judgments 9.56, 9.61–9.65
applicable law 9.53
automatic recognition 9.61, 9.65
avoidance of transactions 9.62
cooperation principle 9.61–9.62
cross-border insolvency 9.56, 9.61–9.65
discharge decisions 9.65
European Insolvency Regulation (EIR) 9.61, 9.63, 9.64–9.65
Germany 9.64–9.65
recognition of insolvency proceedings 9.63
Rome I Regulation 9.64
redundancies 11.05, 11.07–11.09, 11.11
collective 11.05, 11.09, 11.11
Collective Redundancies Directive 11.09
regulated self-governance 1.16–1.21, 1.23, 1.26–1.27
relative priority rule (RPR) 1.71–1.72
absolute priority rule (APR) 1.71, 3.50, 5.67–5.68
European Union 1.71–1.73, 1.77, 5.58–5.59
Preventive Restructuring Frameworks Directive 5.58–5.59
single waterfall relative priority 5.52, 5.55–5.57
reorganization process, conditions for debtors to enter the 2.08, 2.34–2.46
absolute priority rule (APR) 2.35
additional conditions 2.37–2.46
basic conditions 2.36
brands 2.34, 2.39
cessation of payments 2.36
commercial and market judgment 2.46
creditworthiness and level of indebtedness 2.42
exit route for strategic investors, importance of 2.45
experts, bringing in 2.34, 2.46
going-concern value 2.37
governance and internal culture 2.41
government licence qualification 2.43
inability to pay 2.35–2.36
industry, type of 2.39
intangible assets, value of 2.34
judge, role of the 2.46
large enterprises 2.34

market confidence 2.34
objectives 2.34, 2.36
operating value, whether there is a 2.34, 2.38–2.42
public-interest value 2.34, 2.44–2.46
qualification value, whether there is a 2.43
reasons for reorganization 2.36
shareholders, strength of 2.40
social welfare 2.34
unemployment 2.34
value 2.34–2.46
experts 2.34, 2.46
final-offer arbitration approach to disputes 2.46
judge, role of the 2.46
measurement 2.37–2.46
operating value, whether there is a 2.38–2.42
public-interest value, whether there is a 2.44–2.46
qualification value, whether there is a 2.43
verge of, or already in, financial distress 2.36
voluntary reconciliation 2.35
rescue
absolute priority rule (APR) 1.67
advantages of rescue 1.32
asset-based (in rem) claims and value-based claims in rescue 5.44–5.65
avoidance of transactions 8.50
best-interests-of-creditors test 1.67, 1.72
classes, division into 1.48–1.53
classification 1.41
concepts 1.32–1.41
contractual workouts 1.42–1.45
court approval 1.47
cramdowns 1.50–1.53, 1.68
criminal offences 1.42
culture 1.33, 7.28, 7.30
debt-equity swap 1.39–1.40
devices 1.42–1.53
directors, duties of 7.25, 7.28
discrimination 1.67, 1.72
distribution 1.55, 1.62–1.65
finance 3.69–3.73
firm sales 1.33, 1.34–1.36, 1.38, 1.41, 1.62
going-concerns 1.39, 1.63–1.64, 1.68–1.69, 3.66, 3.72, 5.13
incentives to negotiate 1.62–1.65
information asymmetries 3.72
labour law 11.06, 11.10, 11.14
liquidation distinguished 1.11–1.27, 5.12–5.13
majority principle 1.45–1.46, 1.48–1.51
moratoriums 3.66

348 INDEX

rescue (*cont.*)
  paradox of rescue 5.47
  plans 1.67–1.69, 1.72–1.73
  pre-insolvency priorities 1.62
  pre-packs 1.36
  priority 1.72, 3.71–3.72
  relative priority rule (RPR) 1.72
  restructuring/reorganization 1.33, 1.37–1.41,
    1.62–1.64
  signalling effect 3.69
  tax law 10.29
  taxonomies 1.32–1.41
  unanimous consent, principle of 1.45–1.46,
    1.50–1.51
  value allocation 8.65, 8.71–8.74, 8.77, 8.88
Restructuring Directive
  absolute priority rule (APR) 1.71, 3.50
  debt restructuring outside formal insolvency
    proceedings 3.02
  directors, duties of 7.28–7.30
  majority principle 1.49
  moratoriums 3.67
  privatization 1.25
  restructuring plans 3.20, 3.23–3.24, 3.34,
    3.50, 3.54
  tax law 10.27
  transposition 1.71–1.77, 7.29–7.30
restructuring plans 3.04, 3.12–3.54
  abuse of individual creditors 3.16
  advantages 3.13–3.14
  approval of creditors 3.27–3.34, 4.114
  binding effect 4.114
  coercion 3.04, 3.13–3.20
  commencement of plans 3.18–3.23
  confirmation by the court 3.14, 3.17, 3.35–3.54
  consent 3.22, 4.111, 8.78
  content of the plan 3.24–3.26, 4.113
  contractual workouts 3.04, 3.14, 3.17, 3.26
  court, involvement of the 3.04, 3.13–3.14,
    3.17, 3.20, 3.23, 3.35–3.54
  deadlock 3.14, 3.73
  early access to procedure 3.18
  experts, appointment of 3.22
  external monitoring 4.114
  financial conditions 3.19–3.20
  going concern, sale as a 3.24
  implementation 4.114
  imposition on dissenting creditors 3.14
  insolvency practitioners 3.13
  interference with creditor rights 3.04,
    3.13–3.20
  liquidation 4.111, 4.113–4.114
  majority approval mechanisms 3.14–3.15
  minority protection 3.04, 3.16–3.17, 3.23

  moratoriums 3.14–3.15
  negotiations 3.13, 4.111
  opportunistic behaviour 3.13
  overindebtedness 3.24
  Restructuring Directive 3.20, 3.23–3.24
  restructuring/reorganization 3.20, 3.23–
    3.24, 4.111, 4.113–4.114
  shareholders, involvement of 3.25
  SMEs, accessibility by 3.13, 3.17, 3.73
  stay of proceedings 3.14
  tax law 10.27, 10.29, 10.33
  timing 3.18–3.21
  uncoordinated creditor enforcement
    actions 3.15
restructuring/reorganization *see also*
    debt restructuring outside formal
    insolvency proceedings; moratoriums;
    reorganization process, conditions for
    debtors to enter the; restructuring plans
    (debt restructuring)
  Acquired Rights Directive 11.11–11.12
  alternative to liquidation 4.109–4.114
  collective and individual interests, tension
    between 1.10
  conditions 2.08, 2.34–2.46
  contractual agreements 4.113–4.114
  co-operation 1.21
  debt-equity swap 1.39–1.40
  debt relief 10.26–10.29, 10.33
  distress 2.04, 2.05–2.08, 2.33–2.46
  entry thresholds 2.04
  European Union 1.71–1.77
  financial structure, changes in 1.39–1.40
  groups 8.02, 8.04, 8.18, 8.59–8.60, 8.80–8.87
  incentives 1.62–1.65, 1.73
  initiate proceedings, debtor's right to 4.11
  labour law 4.110, 11.01, 11.09–11.12
  liquidation, as an alternative to 4.109–4.114
  preferences 6.33
  pre-packs 2.04, 2.07
  Preventive Restructuring Frameworks
    Directive 5.58–5.59
  publicity 4.113
  realizable priority 8.04–8.05, 8.77–8.79
  reasonable prospect of survival 4.110
  reasons 2.08
  recognition of judgments 9.63
  rescue 1.33, 1.37–1.41, 1.62–1.64
  shareholders, benefits to 4.110
  surplus 5.65, 8.59–8.60, 8.79
  tax law 10.03, 10.26–10.36
  toolkits 11.10
retention of title 4.30, 4.59, 4.88, 5.08, 5.21,
    9.48, 9.49

Roman law 6.04, 6.48
Rome I Regulation 9.64
rump estate 8.05, 8.67–8.70, 8.86

sale-and-lease transactions 5.24
sale of businesses
   Acquired Rights Directive 11.09, 11.11–11.13
   auctions 3.01, 3.43, 4.94, 4.102
   conflicting claims 4.94
   discretion 4.94
   free and clear of interests, consent to
      sales 4.95
   going-concern value 4.97, 4.99–4.101
   holding together assets, problems
      in 4.99–4.100
   insolvency administrators 4.98–4.100
   liquidation, as a form of 4.97–4.98
   parts of businesses 3.24
   pre-packs, use of 4.101
   price 4.96, 4.102
   quasi-security 5.20, 5.21–5.24
   realization of assets 4.93–4.95
   recapitalization 5.47, 5.48, 5.65
   rescue 1.33, 1.34–1.36, 1.38, 1.62
   restructuring plans 3.24, 3.43–3.44
   retention of title 5.21
   security rights 5.17, 5.21
   swelling and liquidation of assets 4.87,
      4.97–4.102
   whole, businesses as a 4.87, 4.97–4.102
secondary proceedings 9.21–9.22, 9.32–9.34,
   9.38, 9.66
secured creditors
   asset-based (*in* rem) claims and value-based
      claims in rescue 5.44–5.65
   distribution 1.58, 1.59, 5.46
   labour law 11.20–11.21, 11.24–11.25, 11.35,
      11.41
   pari passu principle 4.59
   single waterfall absolute priority 5.55–5.57
   single waterfall relative priority 5.55–5.56
securitization 5.08, 5.22–5.23
security devices 5.02
security rights 1.29, 5.14–5.43 *see also* liens;
      quasi-security; United Kingdom,
      floating charges in
   applicable law 9.43, 9.44–9.48
   avoidance of transactions 6.01, 6.25, 6.28,
      6.56
   common law systems 7.22
   encumbered assets, treatment of 4.32
   European Insolvency Regulation
      (EIR) 9.44–9.46
   ownership, boundaries with 5.08

   preferential treatment of secured
      debtors 5.14
   priority debt, confusion with 5.14
   property right, security as a 5.16
   retention of title 4.30, 4.59, 4.88, 5.08, 5.21,
      9.48, 9.49
   security and debt, distinguishing 5.14
   set-off, right to 4.70
segregation/separation of assets 4.31, 4.34,
   4.37, 4.58, 10.21–10.23
seizure of the debtor's assets 4.28, 4.33–4.34
self-governance 1.16–1.21, 1.23, 1.26–1.27
set-off, right to 4.69–4.71
   avoidance of transactions 6.18, 6.26, 6.28
   European Insolvency Regulation (EIR) 9.47
   moratoriums 4.38
   pari passu principle 4.63
   quasi-security 5.25–5.26
   tax law 10.18–10.19
shareholders
   distribution 1.58, 1.60
   interests 7.06
   liability 7.76–7.84
   liquidation 4.110
   loans 6.57
   reorganization process, conditions for debtors
      to enter the 2.40
   restructuring/reorganization 3.14, 3.25,
      4.110
   transactions at an undervalue 6.57
single entity liquidation baseline 8.13, 8.14,
   8.18, 8.88
social choice theory 1.17
social contract 3.15
social policy 11.04, 11.21–11.23, 11.29
social protection principle
   applicable law 9.50–9.51
   avoidance of transactions 6.09
   cross-border insolvency 9.26, 9.29
   European Insolvency Regulation (EIR) 9.50
   labour law 9.26, 9.51, 11.41
   tenancy agreements 9.50
social welfare 2.34, 11.18
specialized courts 10.04–10.05
standing 7.21, 7.35, 7.44, 7.78, 9.53
State in insolvency law, role of the 10.02–10.08,
   10.13–10.25
stay of proceedings *see* moratoriums
submission and admission of insolvency
      claims 4.64–4.68
subordination of claims 1.58, 1.59, 4.62–4.63,
   7.82–7.84
subrogation rights 11.31–11.33
subsidiarity, principle of 9.13–9.15

350 INDEX

support proceedings, duty to 4.35
suspect periods
    avoidance of transactions 4.92, 6.19, 6.30
    fraudulent transactions 6.48, 6.51, 6.53
    preferences 6.32, 6.34–6.36, 6.38
    transactions at an undervalue 6.40, 6.42–
        6.43, 6.46, 6.47
Sustainable Development Goals (SDGs) 11.02,
    11.41
swelling and liquidation of assets 4.87–4.102
    avoidance of transactions 4.90–4.92, 6.06
    insolvency administrators 4.88–4.90
    realization of the assets 4.93–4.96
    sale of debtor's business 4.87, 4.97–4.102

tax law 10.01–10.36
    absolute priority rule (APR) 5.68
    action periods and proceedings 10.11
    after opening of proceedings 10.02, 10.07,
        10.35
    appeals 10.11
    assessment notices 10.09–10.10
    avoidance of transactions 10.18
    basic principles 10.07–10.13
    before opening of proceedings 10.02, 10.17,
        10.22
    civil law as linked to structures under tax
        law 10.05
    constitutional law 10.02
    creditors
        rights of (claim rights) 10.02, 10.04, 10.12
    State and creditors, resolving tension in
        relationship between 10.14–10.25
    debtors
        rights of (freedom rights) 10.02, 10.04
    State and debtors, resolving tension in
        relationship between 10.25–10.36
    distribution 10.15, 10.35
    dual responsibility of States 10.02–10.08,
        10.13–10.20, 10.26, 10.31
    during insolvency proceedings, taxes
        arising 10.25
    employees 10.16, 10.22
    enforcement 10.02, 10.08, 10.13, 10.21, 10.27
    European Union 10.03, 10.15–10.16, 10.21,
        10.31–10.32
    insolvency law, tax law as influencing 10.12
    insolvency-proof legal positions, regulations
        on 10.20–10.23, 10.24
    liens 10.22
    liquidation taxation 10.35–10.36
    managing directors, tax liability of 10.13, 10.24
    overpayments 10.19
    preferences 10.10, 10.15, 10.17, 10.20, 10.25,
        10.28

    priority 10.01, 10.15–10.16, 10.20, 10.22,
        10.24, 10.34
    regulations 10.14–10.24
    restructuring/reorganization 10.03,
        10.26–10.36
    segregation of assets 10.21–10.23
    separate entity, insolvency date as a 10.07
    set-off 10.18–10.19
    specialized courts 10.04–10.05
    State in insolvency law, role of the 10.02–
        10.08, 10.13–10.25
    substantive claims 10.08
    trust, holding taxes in 10.21–10.23
    VAT 10.03, 10.15, 10.18, 10.21
tenancy agreements *see* **leases**
termination of insolvency
        proceedings 4.103–4.108
terminology 1.28–1.31, 7.49
territoriality, principle of 9.09, 9.58
Texas two-step 5.27, 8.28–8.31
third parties
    assets of the insolvency estate 4.31
    assignment of claims 7.35
    avoidance of transactions 6.16–6.17, 6.26,
        6.61–6.63, 6.66–6.67
    enforcement 8.75
    liens 5.31, 5.37
    wrongful trading, directors' liability for 7.35
tort law 7.27, 7.42–7.44, 7.78–7.79
tracing 5.38–5.40, 8.71–8.74
transactions at an undervalue 4.92, 6.29,
    6.40–6.47
    charitable gifts 6.41, 6.45, 6.47
    consideration 6.40, 6.42–6.45
    definition 6.40, 6.42
    fraudulent transactions 6.49, 6.52, 6.53, 6.54
    gifts/gratuitous transactions 6.40–6.47
    groups 8.22, 8.50
    intentionally fraudulent transactions 6.42,
        6.45
    lapse of enrichment 6.61, 6.65
    shareholders, payments to 6.57
    subjective factors 6.46, 6.47
    suspect periods 6.40, 6.42–6.43, 6.46
    undervalue, definition of 6.41
    voidable, as 6.42
transactions avoidance rules 4.30, 6.01–6.74
    see also **preferences; intentionally**
        fraudulent transactions; transactions at
        an undervalue
    assets of the insolvency estate 4.30, 4.33
    best possible transaction principle 6.08, 6.10,
        6.16
    burden of proof, shifting the 6.30
    business judgment rule (BJR) 8.24

closely related parties 6.30, 6.57, 6.63
collectivity, principle of 6.08
compensation 6.05, 6.08, 6.61
cross-border avoidance 6.68–6.74
debtors' rights, principle of 6.09
deterrence 6.11, 6.13
directors, duties of 8.23–8.31
disadvantage to general body of creditors,
    requirement for 6.01, 6.05–6.08, 6.22–
    6.28, 6.58, 6.61
  foreseeability 6.15
  indirect disadvantage 6.27
  no disadvantage, where there is
    no 6.22–6.23
  transaction, definition of 6.13
discretion of the court 6.05
effectiveness, principle of 6.10, 6.11
efficiency principle 6.08, 6.11, 6.58–6.59
equal treatment of creditors principle 6.03,
    6.08, 6.10, 6.15, 9.52
equity 8.24–8.26
European Insolvency Regulation
    (EIR) 9.54–9.55
fiduciary duties, breach of 8.21–8.22,
    8.27–8.29
fixation principle 6.07
fraud 4.90, 4.92
general prerequisites 6.02–6.03, 6.12–6.29
gifts, giving assets as 6.25
grounds 4.92, 6.02, 6.12, 6.29–6.57
groups 8.17, 8.21–8.31
guarantees 8.30–8.31, 8.50
insider rules 6.30, 8.21
insolvency administrators 4.90
jurisdiction 9.39
lapse of enrichment 6.61–6.63, 6.65–6.66
legal consequences 6.58–6.67
legitimate expectations 6.09, 6.29, 9.52
low prices, selling assets at 6.25
mental elements 6.30
objective requirements 4.92, 6.06
opening of insolvency proceedings 6.01–
    6.03, 6.19–6.21, 6.30
pari passu principle 4.56, 4.91, 6.01, 6.08
post-petition transactions 6.20
predictability/legal certainty, principle
    of 6.09, 6.10, 6.24, 6.58–6.59
principles 6.07–6.10, 6.15–6.16, 6.29,
    6.58–6.61
proportionality principle 6.09, 6.10, 6.58
recognition of judgments 9.62
recourse manipulation 8.27
rescue 8.50
restrictions 6.07, 6.09, 6.19
reversal of transactions 4.90–4.92

security rights for unsecured creditors,
    creation of 6.01, 6.25, 6.28, 6.56
set-off 6.18, 6.26, 6.28
shareholder loans 6.57
spouses, gifts to 6.01, 6.30
subjective requirements 4.92, 6.06
suspect periods 4.92, 6.19
swelling the assets 4.90–4.92, 6.06
tax law 10.18
third parties 6.16–6.17, 6.26, 6.61–6.63,
    6.66–6.67
timing as to when transaction is deemed to be
    performed 6.21
transaction, definition of 6.13–6.18, 6.21
trust, principle of protection of 6.09, 6.10,
    6.29, 6.61
value maximization 8.24–8.26
vicinity of insolvency, in the 8.15, 8.17, 8.21–8.31
voidability or nullity of transactions 6.03,
    6.05, 6.14, 6.22, 6.56, 6.60–6.65, 9.52
transfer of undertakings 11.09, 11.11–11.13 *see*
    also **sale of businesses**
transparency, principle of 4.102, 9.17
trust, holding taxes in 10.21–10.23
trust-like estates 4.28
trust, principle of mutual 9.11, 9.29, 9.47, 9.51,
    9.57, 9.59
trust, principle of protection of
  applicable law 9.44, 9.46
  avoidance of transactions 6.09, 6.10, 6.29, 6.61
  cross-border insolvency 9.25, 9.29
  predictability/legal certainty, principle of 9.26
  preferences 6.32
  transactions at an undervalue 6.40
twilight zone *see* **vicinity of insolvency, in the**
    (twilight zone)

unanimous consent, principle of 1.45–1.46,
    1.50–1.51
UNCITRAL *see also* UNCITRAL Legislative
    Guide on Insolvency Law: Parts one
    and two; UNCITRAL Legislative Guide
    on Insolvency Law: Part four: Directors'
    obligations in the period approaching
    insolvency (including in enterprise
    groups); UNCITRAL Model Law on
    Cross-Border Insolvency (MLCBI);
    UNCITRAL Model Law on Enterprise
    Group Insolvency (MLEGI); and
    UNCITRAL Model Law on Recognition
    and Enforcement of Insolvency-Related
    Judgments (MLIRJ)
UNCITRAL Legislative Guide on Insolvency
    Law: Parts one and two 2.32, 6.03, 9.47,
    11.02, 11.20

352 INDEX

UNCITRAL Legislative Guide on Insolvency
 Law: Part four: Directors' obligations
 in the period approaching insolvency
 (including in enterprise groups) 7.07,
 8.45, 8.46, 8.48
UNCITRAL Model Law on Cross-Border
 Insolvency (MLCBI) 9.04–9.05, 9.19,
 9.21–9.22, 9.24
 annex procedures 9.39
 applicable law 9.42, 9.53
 avoidance of transactions 6.74
 centre of main interests (COMI) 9.36–9.37
 cooperation and coordination 9.12, 9.67
 jurisdiction 9.09, 9.12, 9.33, 9.35–9.37, 9.39
 predictability/legal certainty, principle
  of 9.18, 9.35
 recognition of foreign insolvency
  proceedings 9.60
 standing 9.53
 UNCITRAL Model Law on Enterprise Group
  Insolvency (MLEGI) 8.81, 8.83, 8.84–8.87
 UNCITRAL Model Law on Recognition and
  Enforcement of Insolvency-Related
  Judgments (MLIRJ) 9.39, 9.61, 9.63
undervalue, transactions at an *see* transactions
 at an undervalue
United Kingdom *see also* United Kingdom,
 floating charges in; wrongful trading,
 directors' liability for
 Acquired Rights Directive 11.12
 administrative consolidation 8.34–8.36
 avoidance of transactions 6.02–6.03, 6.17–
  6.18, 6.56, 6.72, 6.74, 9.62
  challenging transactions 6.62–6.63, 6.67
  closely related parties 6.30, 6.56, 6.63
  disadvantage requirement 6.23
  legal consequences 6.59–6.63
  opening, transactions prior to 6.20–6.21
 better position, putting creditors in a 6.34,
  6.38, 6.39
 class meetings, constituting 3.28, 3.33
 closely related parties 6.30, 6.56, 6.63
 Commonwealth 8.19–8.20, 8.63, 9.05
 company voluntary arrangements
  (CVAs) 3.25
 compulsory winding up 4.42
 cooperation and coordination 9.70
 court, winding up by the 1.15
 cramdowns 1.51
 criminal offences 7.52
 cross-border insolvency 6.72, 9.05, 9.21, 9.24
 directors, disqualification of 7.48–7.49, 7.52,
  7.54–7.59, 7.64–7.67, 11.43
 directors, duties of 7.14–7.15, 7.20, 7.22, 7.45
 disputes over debt 2.15

equal treatment of creditors 10.15
European Insolvency Regulation (EIR) 9.05,
 9.64
fiduciary duties 8.29
fraudulent trading 4.89
fraudulent transactions 6.49, 6.53, 6.54
going-concern value 5.30
good faith 6.42, 6.46, 6.62, 6.63
inability to pay debts 2.15
insolvency administrators, role and
 obligations of 4.40
jurisdiction 9.08–9.09, 9.37
labour law 11.14, 11.40, 11.43
limited liability 7.02
liquidators, role of 4.42
majority principle 1.45
minority protection 3.51
moratoriums 3.57, 3.66
National Insurance Fund 11.40
new value, transactions for 6.34, 6.38
opening of insolvency proceedings 4.24
pending and ongoing contracts 4.83
piercing the corporate veil 7.71
preferences 6.34, 6.38, 6.39, 10.15
pre-packs 4.101
priority 5.71, 10.16, 11.40
public interest, petitions presented by
 Secretary of State in the 4.17
recognition of foreign insolvency
 proceedings 9.60
recognition of judgments 6.74, 9.62, 9.64
recourse manipulation 8.27
rescue 1.45, 1.47
restructuring plans 3.12, 3.13, 3.22, 3.35–
 3.36, 3.41, 3.52
restructuring/reorganization 3.28, 3.33–3.34
sale 4.94, 5.47, 5.65
schemes of arrangement 1.17, 1.45, 3.02,
 3.12, 3.13, 3.29–3.22, 8.51
set-off, right to 5.26
shareholders 3.25, 4.14
statutory demands 2.15
suspect periods 6.34, 6.38, 6.42, 6.46
tax law 10.09, 10.15–10.16, 10.25
transactions at an undervalue 6.42, 6.46,
 6.47, 6.49, 6.53, 6.54
UNCITRAL Model Law on Cross-Border
 Insolvency 6.72, 9.05
voluntary winding up 1.15
winding up 1.15, 4.02, 4.14, 4.42
United Kingdom, floating charges in 4.89,
 5.41–5.43, 5.49–5.51
administrators, appointment and selection
 of 5.50–5.51
after-acquired property 5.65

avoidance of transactions 6.56
crystallization and conversion to fixed
    charges 5.65
directors, duties of 7.22
fixed charges 5.41, 5.43, 5.65
groups in rescue 8.63
inchoate, as 5.41
liens 5.41
priority 5.41, 5.50
receiver, power of holders to appoint a 5.43
single waterfall absolute priority 5.53
United States, floating liens in 5.41–5.42
unsecured creditors 5.42–5.43
wrongful trading, directors' liability
    for 7.36
United States 1.15–1.18, 1.21 *see also* **absolute
    priority rule (APR); United States,
    blanket liens in**
abuse of insolvency 2.08, 2.35
administrative consolidation 8.33
airframe leases 5.21
asset-based (*in* rem) claims and value-based
    claims in rescue 5.46, 5.48–5.51, 5.65
avoidance of transactions 6.02–6.03, 6.17–
    6.23, 6.45, 6.72–6.73, 8.30, 9.53
    good faith 6.62, 6.66, 6.67
    insider rules 6.30
    lapse of enrichment 6.61, 6.66
    legal consequences 6.59–6.61, 6.66
    partners of insolvent partnerships,
        transactions benefiting 6.57
    security rights for unsecured creditors,
        creation of 6.56
    successors, challenges by 6.62, 6.66
bail-in structures 5.27
burden of proof 8.76
business judgment rule (BJR) 7.19
Chief Reorganization Office (CRO)
    system 2.34
claim, definition of 5.16
closely related parties 6.30, 6.52, 6.53
conditions to enter insolvency liquidation
    process 2.08, 2.09
cooperation and coordination 9.68
cramdowns 1.51, 1.68
cross-border insolvency 9.20–9.21, 9.24
debt restructuring outside formal insolvency
    proceedings 3.02
directors
    deepening insolvency, liability
        for 7.39–7.41
    disqualification of 7.49, 7.62–7.63
    duties 7.13, 7.19, 7.39–7.41, 8.18–8.20
disputes over debts 2.18
dissolution of legal entities 4.105

equitable (asset-value-based) priority 5.52,
    5.60–5.63
extraterritoriality 6.73
floating liens 5.39, 5.41–5.42
foreclosure 6.17
formal insolvency proceedings 4.02, 4.04
fraudulent transactions 6.45, 6.52, 6.53, 6.54,
    7.74, 8.30–8.31
good faith 6.62, 6.66, 6.67, 7.19
groups
    piercing the corporate veil 7.74
    regulation 8.10
    rescue 8.54–8.58, 8.63–8.65
    restructuring/reorganization 8.83–8.84
in pari delicto doctrine 7.40
inability to pay debts 2.15
influence on other jurisdictions 1.70
insiders 6.36, 6.38, 6.45
insolvency administrators, role and
    obligations of 4.43, 4.49
justice, principle of procedural 9.19
labour law 11.10, 11.14, 11.40–11.41
liens 5.11, 10.22
liquidation 4.112
moratoriums 3.64
new value, transactions for 6.36, 6.38
optimal realization of assets, principle of 9.22
ordinary course of business, transactions in
    the 6.36, 6.38, 6.39
overindebtedness 2.17
partners of insolvent partnerships,
    transactions benefiting 6.57
pending and ongoing contracts 4.83
pensions 11.40
piercing the corporate veil 7.68–7.69, 7.72,
    7.74
predictability/legal certainty, principle of 9.18
preferences 6.36, 6.38, 6.39, 8.30
priority
    equitable (asset-value-based) priority 5.52,
        5.60–5.63
    insolvency priorities 5.10–5.11
    realizable 5.66, 5.69, 5.71
    tax law 10.16
recognition of foreign insolvency
    proceedings 9.60
recognition of judgments 9.63, 9.65
recourse manipulation 8.27
rescue 1.47, 1.67–1.69, 3.71–3.72, 8.72
restructuring/reorganization 1.21, 1.66–1.71,
    1.77, 4.112, 8.84
    conditions 2.36–2.46
    outside formal insolvency proceedings 3.02
    plans 3.22, 5.61, 8.39
    tax law 10.34

354 INDEX

United States (*cont.*)
sale versus recapitalization 5.47
Sarbanes-Oxley Act 7.63
secured creditors 5.60–5.63
security rights for unsecured creditors,
creation of 6.56
set-off, right to 4.70–4.71, 5.26
shareholders' liability 7.84
short-term objective insolvency
standard 2.17
single waterfall relative priority 5.52
social choice theory 1.17
state law 7.39–7.41
substantive consolidation 7.72, 7.74,
8.37–8.41
successors, challenges by 6.62, 6.66
suspect periods 6.36, 6.38, 6.46, 6.47, 6.52,
6.53
tax law 10.07, 10.10, 10.16, 10.19,
10.22, 10.34
termination clauses 4.86
terms and conditions of employment, changes
in 11.10
Texas two-step 5.27, 8.28–8.31
third parties 6.66, 6.67
tort law 7.39–7.41
transactions at an undervalue 6.45, 6.47, 6.52
trust fund doctrine 7.13
UNCITRAL Model Law on Cross-Border
Insolvency 6.72, 9.05
US Trustee 4.43
value 2.36–2.46
voidability of transactions 6.66
United States, blanket liens in 5.30, 5.31–5.40,
5.44, 5.50
after-acquired property 5.38–5.39
asset-based (*in* rem) claims and firm-
based (*in personam*) claims,
distinguishing 5.30, 5.31–5.40
blanket lien, definition of 5.31
floating liens 5.39
government licences 5.35–5.36
inalienable property or
non-property 5.35–5.36
intellectual property licences 5.36
limitations 5.35–5.40
mortgages on real property, creation of 5.32
non-assignment clauses 5.36
personal property 5.33
pre-petition collateral 5.39–5.40
single waterfall absolute priority 5.53–5.55
single waterfall relative priority 5.55
statements of intent 5.34
third parties, enforcement against 5.31, 5.37
traceable proceeds 5.38–5.40

unity principle 9.08–9.09, 9.20, 9.31–9.32, 9.41,
9.47, 9.58
universalism, principle of
applicable law 9.41, 9.46, 9.51
conflict of principles 9.29
jurisdiction 9.08–9.10, 9.20, 9.31–9.33, 9.38
recognition of foreign insolvency
proceedings 9.57–9.60
secondary proceedings 9.32, 9.38
unsecured creditors
distribution 1.58, 1.59, 1.61
floating charges 5.42–5.43
labour law 11.20–11.22, 11.25, 11.35
priority 5.49, 5.55–5.56
single waterfall relative priority 5.55–5.56

value *see also* going-concern value
asset-based (*in* rem) claims and value-based
claims in rescue 5.44–5.65, 5.70
cash stream 8.72
discounted value, admission of claims
for 4.66
enterprise value 8.67–8.70, 8.72
experts 2.34, 2.46, 4.96
final-offer arbitration approach to
disputes 2.46
group value 8.03–8.05, 8.18, 8.42, 8.51–8.79,
8.88
homeless value 8.03
judge, role of the 2.46
maximization 8.15, 8.24–8.26, 8.61–8.62
measurement 2.37–2.46
operating value, whether there is a 2.34,
2.38–2.42
public interest 2.44–2.46
qualification value 2.43
realizable priority 8.04, 8.65, 8.67, 8.71–8.74,
8.77
reorganization process, conditions for debtors
to enter the 2.34–2.46
rescue, value allocation in 5.70, 8.65, 8.71–
8.74, 8.77, 8.88
restructuring plans, confirmation of 3.44–
3.48, 3.52–3.53
tracing 8.71–8.74
veil, piercing the corporate *see* piercing the
corporate veil
venue shopping 8.83
vicinity of insolvency, in the (twilight zone)
directors 7.31–7.37, 8.13–8.31, 8.43, 11.43
limited liability 7.03–7.04
reorganization process, conditions for debtors
to enter the 2.36
wrongful trading, directors' liability
for 7.31–7.37

voidability or nullity of transactions
applicable law 9.52
avoidance of transactions 6.03, 6.05, 6.14, 6.22, 6.56, 6.60–6.65
fraudulent transactions 6.48, 6.50

wages 11.17–11.18, 11.22
guarantee schemes 11.27–11.29, 11.33, 11.35–11.39
ILO Protection of Wages Convention 11.24–11.25, 11.36, 11.41
maritime liens 11.30
repayments 4.89
Wessels, Bob 9.04
Westbrook, Jay 8.61
Widen, Bill 8.39

workers' representatives, participation of 11.08, 11.11, 11.14
workouts *see* contractual workouts
wrongful trading, directors' liability for (United Kingdom) 4.13, 7.31–7.37
civil law jurisdictions 7.31
concept and rationale 7.31–7.34
directors, duties of 8.20
duty-shifting policy 7.31, 7.33, 7.36
floating charges 7.36
limited liability 7.31–7.37
objective factors 7.34
subjective factors 7.33–7.34
third parties, assignment of claims to 7.35
vicinity of insolvency, liability in the 7.31–7.37